IFIP Advances in Information and Communication Technology 790

IFIP Advances in Information and Communication Technology

The IFIP AICT series publishes state-of-the-art results in the sciences and technologies of information and communication. The scope of the series includes: foundations of computer science; software theory and practice; education; computer applications in technology; communication systems; systems modeling and optimization; information systems; ICT and society; computer systems technology; security and protection in information processing systems; artificial intelligence; and human-computer interaction.

Edited volumes and proceedings of refereed international conferences in computer science and interdisciplinary fields are featured. These results often precede journal publication and represent the most current research.

The principal aim of the IFIP AICT series is to encourage education and the dissemination and exchange of information about all aspects of computing.

More information about this series at https://link.springer.com/bookseries/6102

Luis M. Camarinha-Matos · Filipa Ferrada
Editors

Technological Innovation to Tackle Societal Challenges

17th IFIP WG 5.5 Doctoral Conference on Computing, Electrical and Industrial Systems, DoCEIS 2026
Caparica, Portugal, June 17–19, 2026
Proceedings

Springer

Editors
Luis M. Camarinha-Matos
NOVA University Lisbon
Monte Caparica, Portugal

Filipa Ferrada
NOVA University Lisbon
Lisbon, Portugal

ISSN 1868-4238 ISSN 1868-422X (electronic)
IFIP Advances in Information and Communication Technology
ISBN 978-3-032-28938-4 ISBN 978-3-032-28939-1 (eBook)
https://doi.org/10.1007/978-3-032-28939-1

This Springer imprint is published by the registered company Springer Nature Switzerland AG
The registered company address is: Gewerbestrasse 11, 6330 Cham, Switzerland

Preface

This proceedings volume presents research on technological innovation in AI-driven cyber-physical systems (CPS), with a focus on contributions developed within engineering doctoral programs. In a world facing increasingly complex and interconnected challenges, research and innovation play a central role in shaping sustainable and resilient solutions. Advances in engineering not only transform industrial processes, services, and products but also have far-reaching implications for societal well-being and value creation. In this context, this edition of DoCEIS highlighted how emerging technologies, combined with multidisciplinary approaches, can contribute to addressing pressing societal needs.

The 17th Advanced Doctoral Conference on Computing, Electrical and Industrial Systems (DoCEIS 2026) provided a forum for doctoral students to present and discuss their ideas, hypotheses, and research results across a broad spectrum of engineering domains. Its core mission was to promote multidisciplinary dialogue and stimulate collaboration among early-stage researchers in a setting that encouraged constructive feedback and peer learning. Participants were invited to look beyond the boundaries of their specific research topics and reflect on how their work contributes to the overarching theme of technological innovation for societal impact.

Current research agendas increasingly emphasize the importance of multidisciplinary and interdisciplinary approaches as key drivers of innovation. In this context, conferences such as DoCEIS, focused on the development of early-career researchers, are particularly relevant, especially given the growing expectations from funding bodies for integrated and cross-disciplinary research strategies. While such approaches hold significant potential for breakthrough innovation, they also introduce organizational and conceptual challenges. DoCEIS contributes to addressing these challenges by fostering a collaborative mindset and equipping young researchers with essential skills for both academic and professional development [1].

DoCEIS 2026, sponsored by SOCOLNET, IFIP WG5.5, and IEEE IES, attracted 62 submissions from PhD students and their supervisors representing 22 countries. This volume includes 36 papers selected by the International Program Committee for presentation in the main program, covering a diverse range of topics and application domains within the field of intelligent and interconnected systems. The review process was double blind, and submissions received on average 3.25 reviews each. As such, research results and ongoing work are presented, illustrated, and discussed in areas such as:

- AI in Systems Design
- Computational Intelligence and Machine Learning
- AI in Biomedical Systems
- Smart and Fair Energy Communities
- Intelligent Energy Systems
- Water Management Systems
- Human-Centered Intelligent Systems

- Interoperability and Collaborative Decision Making
- Smart Cities and Sustainable Urban Systems
- Smart Infrastructures

We envisage that this compilation of papers will offer readers a captivating set of novel concepts and intellectually stimulating challenges crossing multiple disciplines. The diverse nature of the included findings is intended to spark and invigorate further research and development initiatives, encouraging a broader exploration of innovative multidisciplinary pathways.

We would like to express our sincere gratitude to all the authors for their valuable contributions to this publication. We also thank the PhD students involved in the organizing committee, who were essential for the success of the conference. Additionally, we would like to extend our deepest appreciation to the dedicated members of the DoCEIS International Program Committee. Their assistance in the article selection process as well as their insightful comments immensely contributed to enhancing the overall quality of the papers.

June 2026

Luis M. Camarinha-Matos
Filipa Ferrada

Reference

1. L. M. Camarinha-Matos, J. Goes, L. Gomes, P. Pereira (2020). Soft and Transferable Skills Acquisition through Organizing a Doctoral Conference. *Education Sciences* 10(9), 235. DOI: https://doi.org/10.3390/educsci10090235

Organization

17th IFIP/SOCOLNET Advanced Doctoral Conference on Computing, Electrical and Industrial Systems
Caparica, Portugal, 17 – 19 June 2026

Conference and Program Committee Chair

Luis M. Camarinha-Matos	NOVA University of Lisbon, Portugal

Program Committee Co-chair

Filipa Ferrada	NOVA University of Lisbon, Portugal

Organizing Committee Co-chairs

Pedro Pereira	NOVA University of Lisbon, Portugal
Sanaz Nikghadam Hojjati	NOVA University of Lisbon, Portugal
Bruno Guerreiro	NOVA University of Lisbon, Portugal
Anikó Costa	NOVA University of Lisbon, Portugal

International Program Committee

António Abreu	Polytechnic Institute of Lisbon, Portugal
Valentina Emilia Balas	Aurel Vlaicu University of Arad, Romania
Anne-Marie Barthe-Delanoë	IMT Mines Albi, France
Bachir Benhala	Sidi Mohamed Ben Abdellah University, Morroco
Luis Bernardo	NOVA University Lisbon, Portugal
Xavier Boucher	École Nationale Superieure des Mines de Saint Étienne, France

Hadj Bourdoucen	Sultan Qaboos University, Oman
Luis M. Camarinha-Matos	NOVA University Lisbon, Portugal
Wojciech Cellary	WSB University in Poznań, Poland
Cristian Ciurea	Bucharest University of Economic Studies, Romania
Noelia Correia	University of Algarve, Portugal
Anikó Costa	NOVA University Lisbon, Portugal
Filipa Ferrada	NOVA University Lisbon, Portugal
Pedro Ferreira	Loughborough University, UK
Paula Ferreira	University of Minho, Portugal
Florin Filip	Romanian Academy of Sciences, Romania
Maria Fino	NOVA University Lisbon, Portugal
Adrian Florea	'Lucian Blaga' University of Sibiu, Romania
José Fonseca	NOVA University Lisbon, Portugal
Fabio Fruggiero	University of Basilicata, Italy
Payam Shams Ghahfarokhi	Tampere University, Finland
Sukhpal Singh Gill	Queen Mary University of London, UK
Luis Gomes	NOVA University Lisbon, Portugal
Juanqiong Gou	Beijing Jiaotong University, China
Bruno J.N. Guerreiro	NOVA University Lisbon, Portugal
Tomasz Janowski	UNU Unit on Policy-Driven Electronic Governance, Poland
Sachin Kumar	American University of Armenia, Armenia
Arianit Kurti	Linnaeus University, Sweden
Paulo Leitão	Polytechnic Institute of Bragança, Portugal
Paula Louro	Polytechnic Institute of Lisbon, Portugal
Marin Lujak	University Rey Juan Carlos, Spain
José Machado	University of Minho, Portugal
Pietro Manzoni	Universitat Politècnica de València, Spain
João Martins	NOVA University Lisbon, Portugal
Rosa Mastromauro	University of Florence, Italy
Eric Monmasson	Université de Cergy-Pontoise, France
Filipe Moutinho	NOVA University Lisbon, Portugal
Vincent Naessens	KU Leuven, Belgium
Sanaz Nikghadam	NOVA University Lisbon, Portugal
Nnamdi Nwulu	University of Johannesburg, South Africa
Ana Inês Oliveira	NOVA University Lisbon, Portugal
Luis Oliveira	NOVA University Lisbon, Portugal
Rodolfo Oliveira	NOVA University Lisbon, Portugal
Angel Ortiz	Universitat Politècnica de València, Spain
Venkata Reddy Palleti	Indian Institute of Petroleum and Energy, India
Luís Brito Palma	NOVA University Lisbon, Portugal

Martin Paprzycki	Polish Academy of Sciences, Poland
Nuno Paulino	NOVA University Lisbon, Portugal
Pedro Pereira	NOVA University Lisbon, Portugal
Paulo Pinto	NOVA University Lisbon, Portugal
Armando Pires	Polytechnic Institute of Setúbal, Portugal
Ricardo J. Rabelo	Federal University of Santa Catarina, Brazil
Shenbagaraj Ramachandran	Mepco Schlenk Engineering College, India
Enrique Romero-Cadaval	University of Extremadura, Spain
Ioan Stefan Sacala	University POLITEHNICA of Bucharest, Romania
Filippo Sanfilippo	University of Agder, Norway
Claudio Sassanelli	Politecnico di Bari, Italy
Thilo Sauter	Danube University Krems, Austria
Thomas Schuster	Pforzheim University, Germany
Weiming Shen	Huazhong University of Science and Technology, China
Katarzyna Sienkiewicz-Małyjurek	Silesian University of Technology, Poland
Catarina Silva	Polytechnic Institute of Leiria, Portugal
Giovanni Stanco	University of Naples Federico II, Italy
Thomas Strasser	Austrian Institute of Technology, Austria
Slavisa Tomic	Lusofona University, Portugal
Oleksandr Veligorskyi	Chernihiv Polytechnic National University, Ukraine
Manuela Vieira	Polytechnic Institute of Lisbon, Portugal
João Vilaça	Politecnic Institute of Cávado and Ave, Portugal
Ramon Vilanova	Universitat Autònoma de Barcelona, Spain
Stefania Zinno	University of Naples Federico II, Italy

Local Organizing Committee (PhD Students)

Antonio Monte Pegado, Portugal
Zahra Babaei, Portugal/Iran
Daniel Ferreira, Portugal
Manuel Vinhas, Portugal
Omid Aghda, Portugal/Iran
David Leiria, Portugal
Nuno Nunes, Portugal
Rui Estevão, Portugal
Diogo Natário, Portugal
Gonçalo Galvão, Portugal

Special Sessions Organizers

Special Session on **Smart and Fair Community Energy Systems**: Bridging Technology, People, and Energy
Organizers: *Ramon Vilanova & Sebastián Madrigal, Spain*
Special Session on **Smart Cities and Sustainable Urban Systems**: Data-Driven Solutions for Quality of Life Enhancement
Organizers: *Izabela Jonek-Kowalska, Agnieszka Kowalska-Styczeń, Aneta Michalak, Katarzyna Sienkiewicz-Małyjurek, Radosław Wolniak, Poland*
Special Session on **Sustainable Data Driven Business Innovation for Societal Impact:** Navigating Digital Transformation for Long-Term Value
Organizers: *Arianit Kurti, Sweden & Bahtijar Vogel, Germany*

Technical Sponsors

Society of Collaborative Networks

IFIP WG 5.5 COVE
Co-Operation infrastructure for Virtual Enterprises and electronic business

Organizational Sponsors

NOVA UNIVERSITY LISBON

NOVA SCHOOL OF SCIENCE & TECHNOLOGY

UNINOVA

CTS – Center of Technology and Systems

Organized by:
PhD Program in Electrical and Computer Engineering

Contents

AI in Systems Design

Human-AI Agentic Approach for Industrial Software Systems Design 3
Antonio Monte Pegado, Luis M. Camarinha-Matos, and Andre Dionisio Rocha

Digital Sovereignty in Organisational End-to-End Processes: An Early-Stage Design-Oriented Research Roadmap 20
Andreas Schneider, Thomas Schuster, Mario Bosslau, and Lukas Waidelich

AI-Driven DevSecOps to Enhance Software Quality and Security 32
Nuno Teixeira Gomes, João Rafael Almeida, and José Luís Oliveira

Toward Agentic Privacy-by-Design: A Conceptual Framework for AI-Supported Process Compliance 42
Lukas Waidelich, Thomas Schuster, Andreas Schneider, and Mario Bosslau

Computational Intelligence and Machine Learning Methods

Comparative Survival Analysis Using Machine Learning Models With and Without Topological Data Analysis 57
Mavambu Diankatu, Jorge Duque, José Braga de Vasconcelos, and Vítor Filipe

Machine Learning on Small Datasets Under Resource Constrained: A Scoping Review 71
Renato Leite and Rui Esteves Araújo

Fourier Apparent Front: A Method of Generating Apparent Fronts Without a Template 83
Andrei Pătrăuşanu, Adrian Florea, Mihai Neghină, Radu Chiş, and Alina Dicoiu

WASP It Up: Estimating Parameters Under Noisy Observations 99
Filipe Vieira and Francisco Coelho

AI in Biomedical Systems

A Review on Technological Requirements for Ultrasound Image-Guided Neuromodulation Application-Specific Integrated Circuits 113
Diogo Dias, Tiago Costa, and João Goes

CancerCareTech: A Pilot Study on a Digital Platform for Multimodal Clinical Data Integration in Pediatric Oncology 125
Pedro Correia, Joana Dias, Alexandra Morais, Amets Sagarribay, Ana Ferreira, Ana Rita Londral, Carla Quintão, Catarina Santos, Mafalda Pires, Patrícia Santos, Paula Agulheiro, and Cláudia Quaresma

A Supervised Modular LLM Architecture for Personalized Management of Non Communicable Diseases: A Proof of Concept Study 138
Ana Martins, Luís Velez Lapão, Isabel L. Nunes, and Ana Londral

Smart and Fair Energy Communities

A Deep Learning Approach to Electric Water Heater Thermal Modelling for Demand Response Applications 157
Francisco Januário-Silva, João Tabanêz Patrício, Rafael Menezes-Barros, and Rui Amaral Lopes

Towards Scalable Demand Response Solutions for Households in Citizen Energy Communities 173
Pau Comas, Antoni Morell, Ramon Vilanova, and Jose Lopez Vicario

Community-Focused Energy Management System with Modular Architecture 186
Laurenţiu-Alex Mustaţă, Elena Helerea, Cristian-Leonard Muşuroi, and Rodolfo Dufo López

Predictive Control and Optimization Strategies for Smart and Fair Operation in Energy Communities 199
S. Madrigal, Antoni Morell, Jose Lopez Vicario, O. Arrieta, and Ramon Vilanova

Intelligent Energy Systems

Study of a DC DC Buck Converter as a Class D Amplifier 213
José Francisco Luís and Nuno Paulino

Toward High-Fidelity Datasets for Hybrid Electric Vehicle Energy Management Incorporating Power Converter Non-idealities 226
Henar Mike O. Canilang, Yurim Cheon, Youjeong Yoon, and Wansu Lim

How Machining State Is Driving Energy Performances in AI-Guided Industries? 240
Andrea Bochicchio, Fabio Fruggiero, and Francesco Mancusi

Water Management Systems

Deep Learning Based Acoustic Leak Detection and Classification in Water Distribution Systems Using Hydrophone Sensors 259
Ajibola Oyedeji, Nnamdi Nwulu, and Peter Olukanmi

Digital Transformation Framework for Sustainable Water-Energy-Food Nexus in South Africa 274
Oluwadamilola Esan, Nnamdi Nwulu, and Adepoju Omoseni Oyindamola

Reconstructing Fragmented Flood Histories: A Benchmark of Imputation Methods for Flood Loss Modeling 292
Miguel Estêvão, Pedro A. Sousa, Gracinda R. Guerreiro, João P. Pimentão, and Maria Isabel Gomes

Human-centered Intelligent Systems

Human Robot Collaborative Creativity: Challenges and Opportunities 313
Zahra Babaei, Sepideh Kalateh, Sanaz Nikghadam-Hojjati, Paulo Leitão, and Jose Barata

Agentic Monitoring for Industrial Sensors in Cyber-Physical Systems: A Reproducible Framework with Safety Guardrails 329
Miguel Afonso Beckers, Pedro João Rodrigues, Paulo Leitão, Cesar Augusto Tacla, and Pedro Luiz de Paula Filho

Towards Secure Media Deepfake Detection Using Explainable AI 341
S. Rajathi, J. Hemalatha, S. Rajeswari, S. Parameswaran, D. Ramya, and S. Balamurugan

Human-in-the-Loop Refinement of Knowledge Graph Embeddings for Semantic Similarity 358
Verdiana Schena, Simona Colucci, Floriano Scioscia, and Francesco Maria Donini

Interoperability and Collaborative Decision Making

Semantic Execution of a High-Level Petri Net for Opportunity-Driven Decision-Making in Collaborative Business Ecosystems 373
Javaneh Ramezani, Luis Gomes, and Paula Graça

Support IOPT-Tools Interoperability Through Import and Export PNML-Compliant Format 386
Diogo Nuno Natário, Anikó Costa, and Luis Gomes

Transforming Isolated Data Lakes into Federated Dataspaces: A Sovereign Architecture for Precision Medicine 398
Nuno Nunes, Pedro A. Sousa, Gracinda R.Guerreiro, João P. Pimentão, and Maria Torrente

Smart Cities and Sustainable Urban Systems

Analysis of Environmental Profiles of Logistics Companies in Estonia to Enhance Technology Choice 417
Rene Maas, Eduard Shevtshenko, Hendrik Laanemets, Tatjana Karaulova, and Rõõt Laigu

Smart Governance for Better Living: Empirical Analysis of Public Services and Digital Transformation Impact on Urban Quality of Live 431
Sara Rupacz, Izabela Jonek-Kowalska, and Aneta Michalak

Using Digital Participatory Platforms for Deliberation Aimed at Achieving Sustainable Development Goals 451
Kamila Rożnowska and Katarzyna Sienkiewicz-Małyjurek

Smart Infrastructures

Multi-agent Framework with Blockchain-Based Audit Trails for Securing Industrial Greenhouse Gas Monitoring Infrastructure 471
Timileyin Abiodun, Nnamdi Nwulu, and Peter Olukanmi

Graph Based Generation of Navigable 3D Environments from Deformable Map Pieces 492
Diogo de Andrade and Nuno Fachada

Urban Traffic Control Enabled by Optical IoT and Deep Reinforcement Learning 504
Gonçalo Galvão, Manuela Vieira, Manuel Augusto Vieira, Mário Véstias, and Paula Louro

Using Artificial Intelligence to Predict Gunfire Deaths 516
Eurico Clemente, Luis M. Camarinha-Matos, and Filipa Ferrada

Stability of Electrophysiological Signals: Findings from Preliminary Measurements in Different Clinical Environments 534
Ana Isabel Ferreira, Cláudia Quaresma, and Carla Quintão

Author Index 549

AI in Systems Design

Human-AI Agentic Approach for Industrial Software Systems Design

Antonio Monte Pegado[1,2(✉)], Luis M. Camarinha-Matos[1,2], and Andre Dionisio Rocha[1,2]

[1] NOVA School of Science and Technology, UNINOVA-CTS, Caparica, Portugal
al.pegado@campus.fct.unl.pt, {cam,andre.rocha}@uninova.pt

[2] Associated Lab of Intelligent Systems (LASI), NOVA University Lisbon, Caparica 2829-516, Portugal

Abstract. The engineering of industrial applications and the design of their supporting software architectures is increasingly complex and error-prone due to real-time constraints, use of multi-vendor components, the fast introduction of new technologies and the growing adoption of AI-based tools. This process is inherently iterative, from problem framing and requirements definition, to architectural decision-making, and logical implementation, yet it is often conducted without methodological coherence, leading to fragmented artefacts and traceability issues. This paper analyses the engineering of manufacturing software solutions in alignment with the Design Science Methodology. From this analysis, the authors present a set of methodological principles and architecture-focused design guidelines to support solution creation. Building on these insights, an agentic framework for Human-AI collaboration is presented, where the human engineer retains responsibility for requirements, constraints, and validation, while AI supports artefact traceability, consistency checking, and explainability across design activities. A preliminary implementation illustrates the feasibility of the approach.

Keywords: Industry 5.0 · Human-AI Collaboration · Design Science Methodology · Software Architecture · Industrial Systems

1 Introduction

Industrial systems are undergoing a renewed phase of transformation. Industry 4.0 (I4.0) principles are gaining a new momentum by recent advances in Artificial Intelligence (AI), which are simultaneously accelerating and reshaping the transition toward emerging Industry 5.0 (I5.0) paradigms. These systems increasingly integrate heterogeneous technologies such as Cyber-Physical Systems (CPS), distributed software applications, Digital Twins (DT), cloud services, or AI intelligence, typically offered by different suppliers; while simultaneously trying to respond to evolving requirements for flexibility, sustainability, resilience, and human-centricity [1, 2]. As a consequence, the design of industrial software architectures has become substantially more complex,

Published by Springer Nature Switzerland AG 2027
L. M. Camarinha-Matos and F. Ferrada (Eds.): DoCEIS 2026, IFIP AICT 790, pp. 3–19, 2027.
https://doi.org/10.1007/978-3-032-28939-1_1

knowledge-intensive, and error-prone, particularly for Small and Medium-sized Enterprises (SMEs) that often lack extensive architectural expertise, engineering teams or tooling infrastructures [3].

Software architecture design should not be treated as a silo or a single, well-delimited project, which tends to happen with consultancy work, or constantly changing teams. Instead, it should unfold iteratively across multiple stages of system creation, including problem framing, requirements formulation, architectural decision-making, implementation logic, and validation, as described in [4].

In fact, there are various examples of methodologies used for system design and creation that support what was mentioned beforehand. For example, the Design Science Methodology (DSM) [5] was introduced to support the design of information systems artefacts. This methodology structures artefact design through iterative cycles of Relevance, Rigor, and Design as shown in Fig. 1. However, and just like any other engineering methodology, the DSM phases are rarely supported in a coherent, integrated, and automated manner. Architectural, requirements and implementation artefacts are often produced using disconnected tools, leading to disconnected teams, loss of traceability along system's lifecycle, and architecture drift over time [4, 6].

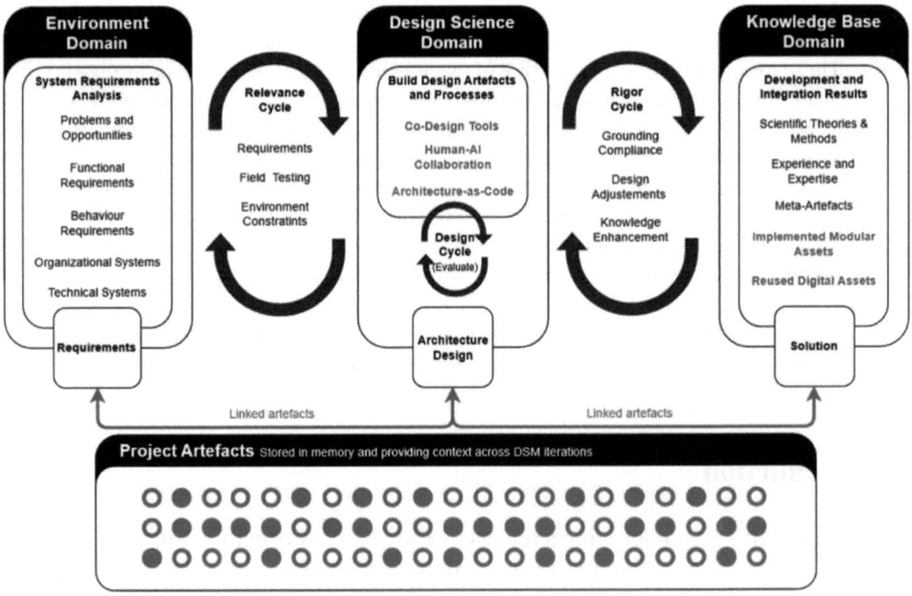

Fig. 1. Extended version of the DSM, adapted from [8], illustrating artefact traceability.

This gap is particularly problematic in manufacturing contexts, where architectural decisions must take constraints from multiple domains into consideration, including automation, control, operations, and human interaction. Without systematic support, the cognitive load placed on individual system architects increases, design decisions become harder to justify and reuse, and long-term system sustainability is compromised. These challenges motivate the need for new forms of Human-AI collaboration that go beyond task automation and instead act as methodological companions throughout the system creation process [7].

In this paper, we focus on a specific collaboration paradigm: Human–AI collaboration, where a human architect or engineer collaborates directly with an AI assistant during system creation from the ground up. The AI assistant is not treated as an autonomous designer, but as an agentic support system that reasons over explicit architectural artefacts, assists in consistency checking and traceability, and provides structured feedback across DSM phases, while the human remains responsible for intent definition, constraint setting, interpretation, and final decision-making.

The main contribution of this work is a Human-AI agentic framework for software architecture design that follows an artefact-centric approach in which architectural knowledge is preserved, and Human/AI roles are properly established. A preliminary prototype illustrates the feasibility of the approach.

This research addresses the challenge of supporting software architecture design decisions in manufacturing systems through structured, and methodologically coherent Human-AI collaboration. The central research question guiding this work is:

RQ1. To what extent Human-AI collaboration support architectural design decisions in the creation of industrial software systems while following a methodological workflow?

To address this question, the paper pursues the following research objectives:

Objective 1. Adopt the DSM to software system creation, with a particular focus on architecture design artefacts across DSM phases.
Objective 2. To define design constraints and principles for Human-AI collaboration that preserve human responsibility while leveraging AI support for consistency, traceability, and artefact management.
Objective 3. Propose a Human-AI agentic framework that assists architectural design by reasoning over explicit models, system context and design artefacts.

Based on these objectives, the work advances the following hypothesis:

Human–AI collaboration can improve the quality and consistency of architectural design decisions during system's creation where AI systems reason over explicit requirements, artefacts and DSM stages, providing structured validation and traceability support while keeping the human responsible for interpretation, constraint definition, and final decision-making. This hypothesis frames AI not as a replacement for engineering expertise, but as a methodological support mechanism that augments human reasoning and reduces organizational overhead in complex system design.

The increasing adoption of AI in engineering practice is primarily driven by the promise of accelerating development cycles, automating system creation tasks, and enhancing productivity. However, rapid acceleration without methodological safeguards risks compromising architectural quality and long-term system resilience. As AI technologies are becoming integral to industrial ecosystems, the critical question is no longer whether AI should be used, but how it should be integrated responsibly.

This work contributes to the current societal challenges by proposing a human-in-the-loop, methodology-driven framework that leverages AI not merely to shorten development cycles, but to enhance architectural design rigor, transparency, and life-cycle coherence. By embedding AI assistance within structured engineering workflows and preserving human accountability in decision-making, the approach supports sustainable industrial innovation ensuring that efficiency gains do not come at the expense of reliability, governance, or societal trust.

2 State of the Art and Related Work

This section briefly reviews relevant work at the intersection of software architecture design, industrial system engineering, and Human-AI collaboration. Rather than providing an exhaustive survey, the focus is on identifying conceptual and methodological limitations in existing approaches that motivate the need for a Human-AI agentic framework explicitly aligned with the DSM. Particular attention is given to manufacturing and industrial contexts, where architectural complexity, component's heterogeneity, and lifecycle evolution are especially important.

2.1 Software Architecture Design within Industry 4.0 Paradigm

Software architecture provides the fundamental structure through which system requirements, design decisions, and implementation elements are organized and reasoned about. In industrial and particularly manufacturing contexts, software architectures increasingly integrate cyber-physical systems, industrial IoT platforms, distributed services, and human-machine interfaces, resulting in highly heterogeneous and evolving systems [2, 9, 10].

International standards such as ISO/IEC/IEEE 42010 define architecture as a set of fundamental concepts and properties embodied in system elements, their relationships, and the principles guiding their design and evolution [11]. Contributions from the Architecture Description Languages (ADLs) landscape have been analyzed in a previous work [8], exploring languages and tooling such as the C4 model, Structurizr DSL [12], and DTDL for structured software architecture design and digital asset representations [13–15]. While these languages provide a conceptual foundation, their practical adoption in industrial engineering remains uneven.

Model-Based Systems Engineering (MBSE) approaches, frequently employing SysML or domain-specific modelling languages, have been widely adopted in industrial contexts to address system complexity [3, 16]. However, MBSE tools are often perceived as heavyweight and poorly integrated, particularly in the context of SMEs. As a result, architectural models frequently become detached from implementation, contributing to architectural drift [4, 6, 17].

To address this issue, Architecture-as-Code (AaC) has emerged as a paradigm that treats architectural descriptions as machine-readable, version-controlled artefacts [18]. In this context, the Continuous Architecture Lifecycle Management (CALM) initiative proposes a structured approach for governing architectural artefacts, promoting alignment between business intent, architectural decisions, and technical implementation through traceable, continuously validated models [19, 20]. By enabling automated validation and traceability, AaC allows for asset reusability unlocking advances in intelligent manufacturing [21, 22]. Nevertheless, existing AaC approaches primarily concentrate on the design-implementation boundary, offering limited consideration of heterogeneous industrial environments and system resilience. Furthermore, support for earlier phases, particularly during requirements formulation and problem framing, is still limited or ignored.

2.2 AI Assistants and Agentic AI in Industrial Systems

AI has long been employed in industrial systems for runtime optimization, scheduling, diagnostics, and control. More recently, advances in large language models (LLMs) have enabled AI systems to support design-time engineering activities, including requirements analysis, documentation generation, architectural modelling, and code synthesis [23].

Some initial studies demonstrate that LLMs can translate natural language requirements into semi-formal representations such as UML diagrams or architectural descriptions. For instance, [24] showed that generative models can produce syntactically correct UML sequence diagrams from textual requirements, although with limitations in completeness and semantic accuracy. Similarly, [25] reported that LLMs can assist novice analysts in creating UML models, while emphasizing the need for validation and human oversight.

Beyond single-assistant paradigms, recent work has explored agentic and multi-agent AI systems for software engineering tasks. Recent work on LLM-based multi-agent systems suggests that decomposing complex design tasks into parts assigned to agents with structured coordination mechanisms can mitigate hallucinations and improve reasoning robustness compared to monolithic approaches [26]. However, such systems typically operate without formal alignment to engineering methodologies and rely on conversational context rather than artefact representations.

2.3 Human-AI Collaboration in Software Engineering

Human-AI collaboration has become a prominent research topic in software engineering, particularly with the widespread adoption of AI-based assistants. Rather than replacing human engineers, these systems are typically designed to augment human capabilities through human-in-the-loop control [27].

Shneiderman's research highlights several challenges in Human-AI collaboration, including explainability, trust, responsibility allocation, and load management [7, 28]. These challenges are especially critical in architectural design, where decisions are strategic, context-dependent, and difficult to reverse. Consequently, most AI-assisted architecture approaches adopt advisory roles (such as recommending patterns, generating documentation drafts, or performing consistency checks) while avoiding autonomous decision-making.

A key limitation of current Human-AI collaboration approaches is perhaps their weak integration with engineering methodologies. AI tools are often introduced opportunistically, frequently introduced as isolated productivity enhancers, without explicit consideration of how they support methodological rigor, lifecycle traceability, or knowledge preservation. This lack of alignment risks reinforcing fragmentation rather than mitigating it.

2.4 Summary and Identified Research Gap

Recent advances in AI, particularly LLMs and agentic AI systems, have introduced new possibilities for supporting software engineering activities. Despite this progress, most existing AI-supported approaches operate at the level of isolated tasks, such as code generation or diagram synthesis, without explicit alignment between them or with engineering methodologies. As a result, they offer limited support for maintaining traceability across system development stages.

At the same time, different research streams address complementary aspects of this problem. Architecture modelling approaches, including ADLs and MBSE, provide structured representations of systems but lack integrated AI support for reasoning and automation. Conversely, LLM-based tools enable powerful artefact generation capabilities but operate without methodological grounding or lifecycle awareness. Human-AI collaboration research focuses on interaction models and augmentation strategies yet often lacks integration with formal engineering workflows and artefact traceability. *None of these approaches simultaneously address methodological alignment, artefact traceability, and structured Human–AI collaboration within a unified framework.*

The reviewed literature reveals substantial progress in software architecture modelling, AI-assisted engineering, and Human-AI collaboration. However, existing approaches address these topics separately rather than as interconnected and mutually dependent aspects. In particular, there is a lack of frameworks that:

1. Explicitly align AI assistance with engineering methods, such as the DSM.
2. Treat architectural artefacts as traceable entities across DSM phases.
3. Support responsible and role-based Human-AI collaboration.

These gaps motivate the need for a Human-AI agentic framework that follows a methodological flow and more adequately supports software engineering in Industry.

3 DSM Role in Software System Engineering

The DSM provides a structured methodology for the purpose of creating artefacts that address identified problems through iterative cycles of relevance, rigor, and design. Originally articulated for information systems research [5], DSM has been widely adopted to guide solution-oriented research. Industry software systems are typically created through iterative processes that implicitly fit the DSM cycles. However, these processes are often carried out without explicit methodological alignment or sustained traceability between phases. Architectural decisions are taken early and revisited informally, yet the rationale and constraints that motivated those decisions are not preserved across iterations. This disconnection hurts the ability to justify, validate, and reuse architectural knowledge over the system lifecycle.

Consistently adhering to a formal methodology is difficult: evolving decisions and artefacts quickly become hard to track, and the process becomes easy to lose sight of. For complex problems, or multidisciplinary teams, this overhead is even larger, motivating AI support to monitor methodological conformance and maintain traceability, while humans focus on the substantive creation work.

3.1 Context Preservation: Mapping DSM Phases

DSM structures artefact creation through interconnected cycles that link different activities. In software system creation, these cycles manifest through recurring engineering activities that span from early problem framing to implementation and validation. Table 1 summarizes the correspondence between DSM phases and typical software engineering activities for system development in Industry.

Table 1. Mapping DSM phases to software engineering activities, and generated artefacts.

DSM Phase	Software Eng. Activities	Output Artefacts
Problem Identification & Objectives	Stakeholder analysis, requirements elicitation, constraint identification	Informal requirements, domain assumptions, quality attributes
Design & Development	Architectural decomposition, pattern selection, interface definition	Architecture models (e.g., C4, SysML), design decisions, constraints
Demonstration	Prototype development, integration, scenario execution	Code skeletons, deployment descriptors, test cases
Evaluation	Validation against requirements, trade-off analysis	Test results, performance indicators, decision revisions
Communication	Documentation, knowledge transfer, reuse	Architecture documentation, rationale records

This mapping highlights two key observations. First, software engineering activities are not confined to a single DSM phase; instead, they recur iteratively as understanding of the problem and solution evolves. Second, architectural artefacts appear across multiple phases, acting as the connective tissue between requirements, implementation, and validation. By adopting the DSM to software system creation, it becomes possible to reinterpret architectural design not as a single deliverable, but as an evolving cluster of artefacts.

A central challenge in applying DSM to industrial software engineering lies in context preservation. Context encompasses not only functional requirements, but also constraints, assumptions, design rationales, quality attributes, and validation evidence. In practice, this context is distributed across heterogeneous artefacts, tools, and stakeholders. Empirical studies show that architectural artefacts frequently degrade over time, becoming outdated or misaligned with the implemented system, a phenomenon commonly referred to as architecture drift [4]. Existing mitigation strategies, such as Architecture Decision Records (ADRs) [29], address specific aspects of this problem but remain weakly integrated into the broader system creation process. As changes propagate through the system, decisions made in one phase are not systematically reflected or evaluated in other phases.

These limitations point to the need for an artefact-centric approach in which architectural knowledge is central. In such an approach, artefacts are not auxiliary representations created only for communication purposes; they become the primary object of design governance through which collaboration is promoted across DSM phases. Such an approach requires:

1. Explicit representation of architectural artefacts.
2. Persistent linkage between requirements, architecture, and implementation.
3. Mechanisms to support iterative refinement while preserving accountability.

Making context preservation an explicit goal enables AI-assisted systems to reason, not only about isolated artefacts, but about their relationships, dependencies, and lifecycle position. This enables continuity across DSM phases, transforming the workflow from a sequence of disconnected interactions into a coherent, traceable design process, as elaborated in the following section.

3.2 Conceptual Overview: Artefact-Centric DSM Loop

In order to address the identified limitations, the authors propose an artefact-centric DSM loop represented through a UML activity diagram in Fig. 2. This flow chart can be operationalized as a minimal workflow in which progress is represented by the creation and revision of explicit artefacts. The activity diagram should be interpreted as a baseline abstraction instead of a strict correspondence to the DSM. Its role is to establish a starting point that can be extended as the framework matures.

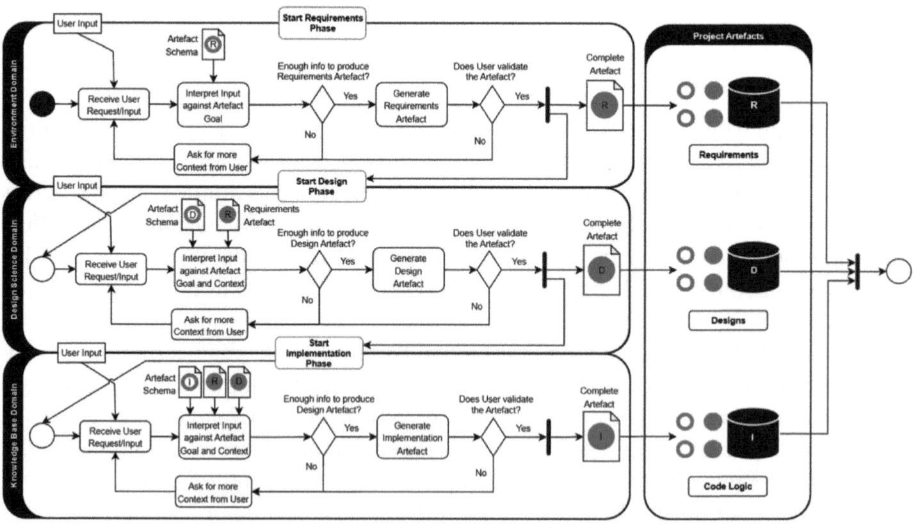

Fig. 2. UML activity diagram representing a DSM-adapted workflow.

In this baseline flow, each phase follows the same recurring pattern: user intent is interpreted against an artefact schema, while an AI agent orchestrator assesses whether sufficient context exists, until an artefact is generated or refined. The outcome is always routed through a human validation gate before being stored.

Therefore, artefacts function as the primary state of the process and as durable contextual memory. Instead of depending on conversational history, the platform maintains a queryable design state that accumulates artefacts across iterations (e.g., requirements and constraints, architectural views, decision rationale, code logic, and validation evidence). The orchestrator operates both over user input and stored project outputs, materializing proposals as versioned artefact updates and triggering follow-on checks when dependencies are impacted.

This baseline is designed to grow with additional DSM-aligned activities such as evaluation planning, drift monitoring, and communication packaging. These can be introduced incrementally, while still supporting structured Human-AI collaboration. Importantly, this collaboration is not left implicit: the human and AI responsibilities follow the role separation established in our prior work [8], where the human retains decision authority and accountability, and the AI operates as a methodological and artefact centric support agent.

4 Proposed Human-AI Agentic Framework

This section introduces a collaborative Human-AI agentic framework for architectural design decisions in industrial software systems, with the DSM as the governing workflow. Before detailing the framework, it is important to distinguish between two dimensions of artefact organization: *space-level* and *time-level* management.

Space-level refers to the structural organization of artefacts within the same project. In this dimension, requirements, architectural models, constraints, rationale, and implementation artefacts coexist as interconnected representations of the same design objective. These artefacts capture different viewpoints and abstraction levels yet remain semantically linked within a shared project scope.

By contrast, time-level refers to the evolution of artefacts across iterations and system lifecycles. In this dimension, artefacts are versioned, revised, reused, and extended over time, potentially across multiple related projects. Time-level management therefore captures historical context, decisions, and system evolution, ensuring that architectural knowledge persists beyond space-level iterations.

As such, the framework is conceived for the space-level management: it structures how architectural knowledge is formalized, evaluated, and evolved across DSM iterations (within the same project). Its central premise is that architectural artefacts are not auxiliary documentation, but persistent knowledge that mediates both human reasoning and AI assistance. Consequently, the AI assistant operates over explicit models or formalized representations (requirements, models, decisions, constraints, and validation evidence) rather than being restricted to conversational context only. From here, the system plans, designs and implements in order to meet the requirements of a specific software architecture project/goal. It complements existing tools (e.g., MBSE, C4, Structurizr, Mermaid) by acting as an orchestration and traceability, selecting the best approach, or adapting itself to user constraints.

The framework targets early-stage system creation in manufacturing settings where uncertainty, heterogeneity, and integration constraints are dominant, and where architectural decisions must remain auditable. Unlike prompt-based assistants that operate through simple conversational interactions, the proposed approach integrates AI agents within a structured DSM-driven workflow. This allows architectural artefacts and decisions to persist across iterations through structured memory mechanisms rather than simple prompts.

The current version of the presented framework copes with five design constraints:

1. The framework enforces a human-in-the-loop principle: the AI assistant may generate alternatives, detect inconsistencies, or propose refinements, but it cannot unilaterally commit architectural decisions.
2. Scope is restricted to space-level activities in the engineering of industrial software systems; time-level evolution or self-adaptation are out of scope.
3. At the current stage, the collaboration model assumes a single system architect (user) responsible for intent, and authority, and a single AI agent.
4. Every change and recommendation must be attributable to a user, retained in memory, and linked to a DSM phase, resulting in an evolving design record.
5. Architectural knowledge must be represented as machine-readable representations. Conversational outputs are treated as intermediate reasoning but not as durable outputs, since they do not support traceability, validation, or impact analysis.

Together, these constraints contribute to methodological rigor, preserve intent across iterations, and support accountable Human-AI collaboration.

4.1 Framework Main Components and Agentic Workflow

The proposed framework is organized around a layered interaction model. At outermost level, a human interaction layer supports natural language prompts and explainable results. The purpose of this layer is not merely usability; it acts as an accessible entry point that captures intent and constraints in a way that can be translated into formal artefacts. The human remains able to accept, reject, or modify AI-generated content, and to ask for additional explanations or iterations.

At the core, an agentic AI orchestrator coordinates DSM activities, such as requirement identification, architectural design, consistency checking, and explainability tasks. In the current version, these roles are not exposed as independent agents, instead, they are internal functional responsibilities orchestrated by a single agent to generate proposals, analyses, and artefact transformations. Figure 3 represents the designed and implemented agentic workflow. This DSM workflow follows a planning strategy and is designed to be tool-aware: it can invoke modelling/rendering services, query the artefact repository, and request validations, but it cannot bypass the review gate that confers decision authority to the human architect. DSM alignment is operationalized by binding platform activities to phase-specific artefact expectations and evaluation steps. This phase binding is what differentiates the framework from general-purpose assistants and from simpler co-pilot workflows: the assistant's role is constrained by methodological context, and its outputs are required to materialize as traceable artefacts rather than conversational.

Architectural knowledge is maintained in a structured persistence layer (e.g., a relational database such as PostgreSQL) that systematically stores DSM artefacts and collaboration records across iterations. Within each project, artefacts are uniquely identified, versioned, and interconnected through explicit dependency relationships (e.g., requirement-to-design, design-to-implementation), while metadata captures authorship, timestamps, and modification history. Rather than preserving only conversational transcripts, the platform extracts structured outcomes from Human-AI interactions and binds them to specific artefacts and DSM phases. The repository supports heterogeneous artefact types, including requirements specifications, architectural models, architecture decision records, interface contracts, constraint sets, code skeletons, and evaluation evidence. This structured linkage enables end-to-end traceability, accountability of contributions, and systematic analysis when artefacts evolve.

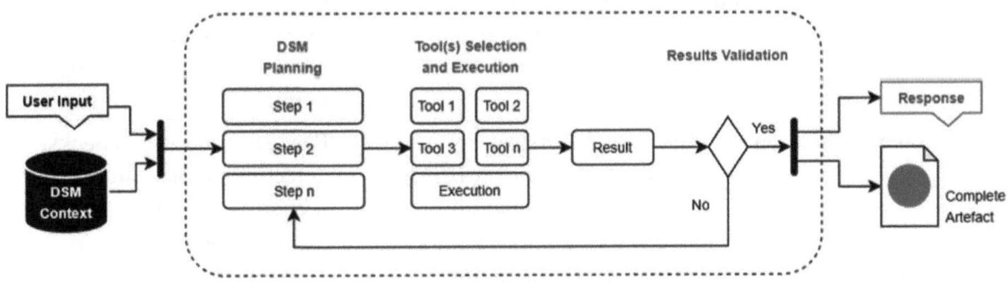

Fig. 3. Agentic workflow iterating DSM artefacts as context towards an execution plan.

Rendering and validation services then transform these artefacts into readable views and checkable evidence by treating architecture as code. Building on the ADL landscape examined in our prior work [8], the framework was ideated to parse code into architectural representations and run automated checks. Mermaid is used as a flexible and lightweight notation to support rapid, tool-agnostic modelling and iteration, complemented by PlantUML for broader diagram expressiveness. These tools not only provide a visual representation of the artefacts but also ensure validation which is kept as evidence to support learning across DSM cycles.

4.2 Human-AI Roles

The proposed framework defines a structured distribution of responsibilities between the human architect and the AI agent across the DSM-aligned workflow. The allocation made in Table 2 reflects a deliberate separation: the human retains authority over intent definition, constraint setting, interpretation of results, and final validation, while the AI agent provides structured methodological and generative support. The objective is not to replace architectural expertise, but to augment it within clearly defined governance boundaries that preserve accountability.

Despite this separation of responsibilities, the interaction model is inherently collaborative. Architectural artefacts are not produced independently by either actor; rather, they emerge through iterative co-creation.

Table 2. Distribution of responsibilities between the human architect and the AI agent across DSM-aligned activities, adapted from [8].

Activity	Human Responsibility	AI Responsibility
Problem Identification & Requirements	Define system description, goals, constraints, and acceptance criteria.	Structure input into formalized artefact requirements; highlight ambiguities or missing elements.
Architectural Design Decisions	Select architectural strategies and design specifics; iterate and validate designs.	Generate candidate designs and views; check consistency against constraints; generate artefact.
Code Logic Implementation	Define functionalities; program specifics; test, iterate and validate code logic.	Generate baseline code and project structure; check consistency against design; iterate over user inputs.
Evaluation & Validation	Interpret results; accept or reject artefacts; iterate over DSM phases; final validation.	Perform automated checks, detect violations, simulate scenarios, report inconsistencies.
Traceability & Impact Analysis	Maintain accountability; approve agent decisions; evaluate agent performance.	Maintain artefact links; compute change impact; log provenance and version history.
Documentation & Communication	Provide maximum context about project goals and requirements.	Generate synchronized documentation; explanations based on user role and background.

By structuring collaboration in this manner, the framework establishes a balanced ecosystem in which human expertise and AI-supported rigor coexist, enabling efficient and trustable industrial software system design.

4.3 Prototype Implementation

To demonstrate the feasibility of the proposed artefact-centric, DSM-aligned framework, a preliminary prototype was implemented as an interactive design environment. The objective of this prototype is not full lifecycle deployment, but rather to validate the core principles of methodological orchestration, artefact persistence, and structured Human-AI collaboration within a controlled setting.

The implementation adopts the OpenAI Agents SDK [30] as the orchestration backbone. Unlike higher-level multi-agent frameworks such as LangChain or CrewAI, the OpenAI Agents SDK provides lower-level control over agent invocation, tool usage, and execution flow. This reduced abstraction was intentionally chosen to allow explicit implementation of the DSM phase transitions and governance rules, ensuring that agent interactions follow the methodological structure defined in the framework rather than emergent conversational patterns.

The user interface guides interaction through iterative DSM phases, where natural-language input is progressively formalized into explicit artefacts that remain visible and actionable throughout the session. Rather than operating as a prompt-centric chat assistant, the prototype continuously materializes structured artefacts representing requirements, architecture models, code logic, and validation outputs.

In the example shown in Fig. 4, the platform consolidates problem framing inputs into a structured requirements artefact and transitions into the design phase. An Architecture-as-Code specification is then generated and rendered as a UML class diagram using integrated Mermaid and PlantUML parsing libraries. In the example shown in Fig. 4, the platform consolidates problem framing inputs into a structured requirements artefact and transitions into the design phase. An architecture-as-code specification is then generated and rendered as a UML class diagram using integrated Mermaid and PlantUML parsing libraries. Mermaid was selected for its version-controllable syntax and broad diagram support, while PlantUML complements it with richer UML. These tools enable rapid generation, visualization, and iterative refinement of architectural models within the same artefact loop.

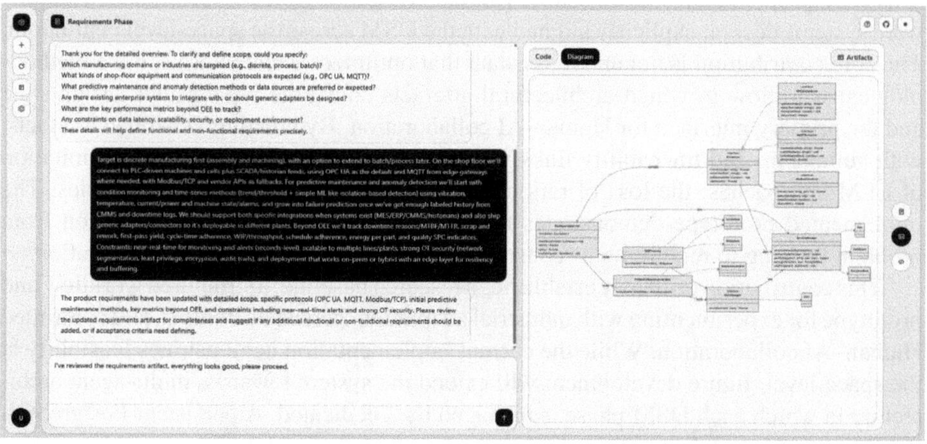

Fig. 4. Screen capture of the prototype illustrating artefact generation during the design phase.

To make the DSM workflow executable, the prototype uses lightweight schemas for both DSM phases and artefacts. Each artefact is stored with a stable identifier, a phase of origin, a type of payload (e.g., Requirements, ADR, Validation, Code logic), and minimal metadata so changes can be attributed to either human or agent. This structured representation is intentionally small, but it provides the backbone for linking artefacts to each other and for driving the orchestrator's phase transitions. A simplified version of the implemented schemas is shown below.

```
Phase = Literal["problem", "design", "demo", "eval", "comm"]
Author = Literal["human", "ai"]
Kind = Literal["requirements", "architecture", "adr", "evidence", "code"]

@dataclass class Artifact:
   id: str = field(default_factory=lambda: str(uuid.uuid4()))
   phase: Phase = "problem"
   kind: Kind = "requirements"
   author: Author = "ai"
   content: Dict = field(default_factory=dict)
```

The current implementation is a first version intended for feasibility demonstration rather than full lifecycle deployment, and is available on [31]. Artefact persistence is session-scoped, with artefacts stored locally (cache) rather than in a dedicated project database, and long-term memory across sessions is not yet supported. Tool integration is currently limited to built-in parsing/rendering capabilities for Mermaid [32] and PlantUML [33], without Model Context Protocol (MCP) tools orchestration or richer validation services beyond what these libraries enable.

5 Conclusions and Future Work

This work proposed an artefact-centric Human-AI agentic framework for industrial software systems design, explicitly aligned with the DSM across the space-level continuum. The core contribution is not an AI assistant that optimizes isolated tasks, but a methodological workflow in which architectural artefacts constitute a persistent design state and the primary interface for Human-AI collaboration. By creating versioned artefacts, with authorship and traceability links, the framework addresses a recurring limitation of LLM approaches: the loss of rationale and constraints across iterative cycles. The implemented prototype demonstrates the feasibility of a DSM-like progression from problem framing to requirements consolidation and architecture-as-code generation.

This contribution primarily establishes a research baseline: a structured workflow and prototype for experimenting with industrial adaptation, persistent context, and controlled Human–AI collaboration. While the current implementation demonstrates feasibility at the space-level, future development will extend the system toward a multi-agent architecture in which each DSM phase is managed by a dedicated. A persistent PostgreSQL data layer will be introduced to support long-term memory and structured artefact access across sessions.

A further evolution involves extending the platform to the time-level continuum through integration with the AAS. Coupled with a dedicated MCP server and a Neo4j graph database, the AAS can serve as a machine-interpretable system representation that preserves architectural context, relationships, and provenance over extended lifecycles. This would enable sustained traceability beyond individual projects and support longitudinal system evolution.

Another priority is to enhance reasoning through Retrieval-Augmented Generation (RAG) strategies tailored to industrial knowledge bases. Expanding support for additional ADLs will broaden design expressiveness and interoperability. Finally, the collaboration model will evolve from one-to-one interaction toward structured multi-user workflows. Formalizing this progression through a collaborative network's taxonomy will require explicit modelling of Human-Human, Human-AI, and AI-AI interactions, as well as role-adaptive behavior capable of tailoring explanations, controls, and artefact views to multidisciplinary teams.

These directions point towards the long-term objective of designing and building a collaborative Human-AI platform that assists industrial software engineering and design, while supporting multidisciplinary teams.

Acknowledgments. This work was supported by the Portuguese Foundation for Science and Technology (FCT) through the individual research grant 2025.01057.BD, and the grant UID/0066/2025, CTS – Centre of Technology and Systems.

References

1. Nakagawa, E.Y., et al.: Industry 4.0 reference architectures: state of the art and future trends. Comput. Ind. Eng. **156**, 107241 (2021). https://doi.org/10.1016/j.cie.2021.107241
2. Hofer, F.: Architecture, technologies and challenges for cyber-physical systems in industry 4.0: a systematic mapping study. In: Proceedings of the 12th ACM/IEEE International Symposium on Empirical Software Engineering and Measurement, pp. 1–10. Association for Computing Machinery, New York, NY, USA (2018). https://doi.org/10.1145/3239235.3239242
3. Akundi, A., Lopez, V.: A review on application of model based systems engineering to manufacturing and production engineering systems. Procedia Comput. Sci. **185**, 101–108 (2021). https://doi.org/10.1016/j.procs.2021.05.011
4. Mohamed, A., et al.: A review on detecting and managing documentation drift in software development. In: 2025 International Mobile, Intelligent, and Ubiquitous Computing Conference (MIUCC), pp. 546–552 (2025). https://doi.org/10.1109/MIUCC66482.2025.11196773
5. Peffers, K., Tuunanen, T., Rothenberger, M.A., Chatterjee, S.: A design science research methodology for information systems research. J. Manag. Inf. Syst. **24**, 45–77 (2007). https://doi.org/10.2753/MIS0742-1222240302
6. Uzun, B., Tekinerdogan, B.: Detecting deviations in the code using architecture view-based drift analysis. Comput. Stand. Interfaces. **87**, 103774 (2024). https://doi.org/10.1016/j.csi.2023.103774
7. Shneiderman, B.: Human-centered AI: ensuring human control while increasing automation. In: Proceedings of the 5th Workshop on Human Factors in Hypertext, pp. 1–2. Association for Computing Machinery, New York, NY, USA (2022). https://doi.org/10.1145/3538882.3542790
8. Pegado, A.M., Camarinha-Matos, L.M., Rocha, A.D.: A brief survey on human-AI collaboration for architecture design of industrial systems. In: Camarinha-Matos, L.M., Ortiz, A., Boucher, X., Lucas Soares, A. (eds.) Hybrid Human-AI Collaborative Networks, pp. 55–74. Springer Nature, Switzerland, Cham (2026). https://doi.org/10.1007/978-3-032-05673-3_4
9. Monostori, L., et al.: Cyber-physical systems in manufacturing. CIRP Ann. **65**, 621–641 (2016). https://doi.org/10.1016/j.cirp.2016.06.005
10. Serôdio, C., Mestre, P., Cabral, J., Gomes, M., Branco, F.: Software and architecture orchestration for process control in industry 4.0 enabled by cyber-physical systems technologies. Appl. Sci. **14**, 2160 (2024). https://doi.org/10.3390/app14052160

11. ISO/IEC/IEEE 42010: https://www.iso.org/standard/74393.html. (2022) Last accessed 20 Feb 2026
12. Structurizr: https://docs.structurizr.com/. Last accessed 20 Feb 2026
13. Vázquez-Ingelmo, A., García-Holgado, A., García-Peñalvo, F.J.: C4 model in a Software Engineering subject to ease the comprehension of UML and the software. In: 2020 IEEE Global Engineering Education Conference (EDUCON), pp. 919–924 (2020). https://doi.org/10.1109/EDUCON45650.2020.9125335
14. Predoaia, I., Kolovos, D., García-Dominguez, A.: Reimplementing the Structurizr Software Architecture Modelling Language as a Hybrid DSL. In: 2025 IEEE 22nd International Conference on Software Architecture Companion (ICSA-C), pp. 380–386 (2025). https://doi.org/10.1109/ICSA-C65153.2025.00060
15. Schmidt, C., Volz, F., Stojanovic, L., Sutschet, G.: Increasing interoperability between digital twin standards and specifications: transformation of DTDL to AAS. Sensors. **23**, 7742 (2023). https://doi.org/10.3390/s23187742
16. Henderson, K., Salado, A.: Value and benefits of model-based systems engineering (MBSE): evidence from the literature. Syst. Eng. **24**, 51–66 (2021). https://doi.org/10.1002/sys.21566
17. Whiting, E., Andrews, S.: Drift and erosion in software architecture: summary and prevention strategies. In: Proceedings of the 2020 the 4th International Conference on Information System and Data Mining, pp. 132–138. Association for Computing Machinery, New York, NY, USA (2020). https://doi.org/10.1145/3404663.3404665
18. Bucaioni, A., Di Salle, A., Iovino, L., Pelliccione, P., Raimondi, F.: Architecture as Code. In: 2025 IEEE 22nd International Conference on Software Architecture (ICSA), pp. 187–198 (2025). https://doi.org/10.1109/ICSA65012.2025.00027
19. Architecture as Code | FINOS DevOps Automation: https://devops.finos.org/docs/working-groups/archived/aasc/. Last accessed 20 Feb 2026
20. CALM: Architecture as Code, https://calm.finos.org/. Last accessed 20 Feb 2026
21. Wang, B., et al.: Smart manufacturing and intelligent manufacturing: a comparative review. Engineering. **7**, 738–757 (2021). https://doi.org/10.1016/j.eng.2020.07.017
22. Pegado, A.M., Rocha, A.D., Barata, J.: Design and development of a marketplace-based collaborative ecosystem for software integration and distribution within manufacturing. In: Camarinha-Matos, L.M., Ortiz, A., Boucher, X., Barthe-Delanoë, A.-M. (eds.) Navigating Unpredictability: Collaborative Networks in Non-linear Worlds, pp. 80–95. Springer Nature Switzerland, Cham (2024). https://doi.org/10.1007/978-3-031-71743-7_6
23. Du, X., et al.: Evaluating large language models in class-level code generation. In: Proceedings of the IEEE/ACM 46th International Conference on Software Engineering, pp. 1–13. Association for Computing Machinery, New York, NY, USA (2024). https://doi.org/10.1145/3597503.3639219
24. Ferrari, A., Abualhaija, S., Arora, C.: Model generation with LLMs: from requirements to UML sequence diagrams. In: 2024 IEEE 32nd International Requirements Engineering Conference Workshops (REW), pp. 291–300 (2024). https://doi.org/10.1109/REW61692.2024.00044
25. Wang, B., Wang, C., Liang, P., Li, B., Zeng, C.: How LLMs aid in uml modeling: an exploratory study with novice analysts. In: 2024 IEEE International Conference on SSE, pp. 249–257 (2024). https://doi.org/10.1109/SSE62657.2024.00046
26. Li, X., Wang, S., Zeng, S., Wu, Y., Yang, Y.: A survey on LLM-based multi-agent systems: workflow, infrastructure, and challenges. Vicinagearth. **1**, 9 (2024). https://doi.org/10.1007/s44336-024-00009-2
27. Fu, T., Jauw, B., Sridharan, M.: Combining LLM, non-monotonic logical reasoning, and human-in-the-loop feedback in an assistive AI agent. In: 2025 34th IEEE International Conference on Robot and Human Interactive Communication (RO-MAN), pp. 322–329 (2025). https://doi.org/10.1109/RO-MAN63969.2025.11217618

28. Shneiderman, B.: Bridging the gap between ethics and practice: guidelines for reliable, safe, and trustworthy human-centered AI systems. ACM Trans. Interact. Intell. Syst. **10**, 1–31 (2020). https://doi.org/10.1145/3419764
29. Dhar, R., Vaidhyanathan, K., Varma, V.: Can LLMs generate architectural design decisions? - an exploratory empirical study. In: 2024 IEEE 21st International Conference on Software Architecture (ICSA), pp. 79–89 (2024). https://doi.org/10.1109/ICSA59870.2024.00016
30. OpenAI Agents: https://openai.github.io/openai-agents-python/. Last accessed 27 Feb 2026
31. ArchitectOS GitHub Repository: https://github.com/NOVA-RICS-Open-Lab/architectOS. Last accessed 20 Feb 2026
32. Mermaid: https://mermaid.js.org. Last accessed 20 Feb 2026
33. PlantUML: https://plantuml.com/. Last accessed 20 Feb 2026

Digital Sovereignty in Organisational End-to-End Processes: An Early-Stage Design-Oriented Research Roadmap

Andreas Schneider(✉), Thomas Schuster, Mario Bosslau, and Lukas Waidelich

Pforzheim University, Tiefenbronner Str. 65, Pforzheim 75175, Germany
{andreas.schneider,thomas.schuster,mario.bosslau, lukas.waidelich}@hs-pforzheim.de

Abstract. European organisations increasingly depend on cloud-based and AI-enabled services provided by non-European vendors. These dependencies create sovereignty-relevant risks emerging within operational processes, not only at policy or infrastructure levels. Existing research addresses digital sovereignty primarily from state-centric, legal, and technical perspectives. How sovereignty concerns arise within organisational process design remains insufficiently researched. This paper presents early-stage doctoral research developing a conceptual framework for analysing digital sovereignty at the organisational level. A concept-driven literature review synthesises multi-level and discursive-category perspectives into an analytical schema. The schema locates four process-level sovereignty challenges (control, accountability, decision authority, and autonomy) across governance levels and claim types. The framework conceptualises digital sovereignty as an organisational capability by mapping dynamic capability activities onto Business Process Management (BPM) practice phases. Both provide the conceptual foundation for a Design Science Research phase, which will operationalise the framework into a sovereignty-aware BPM maturity instrument for self-assessment and process governance.

Keywords: Digital Sovereignty · End-to-End Processes · Business Process Management · Cloud Computing · Information Systems

1 Introduction to Digital Sovereignty

European organisations increasingly rely on cloud-based and AI-enabled services provided by non-European vendors. These services create sovereignty-relevant dependencies that materialise within everyday end-to-end processes, not solely at policy or infrastructure levels [1]. While such services enable digital innovation, they raise fundamental questions about organisational control, accountability, and long-term autonomy. Digital sovereignty has therefore become an operational concern: organisations must actively design processes that preserve rather than erode their sovereignty capacity. Sovereignty

Published by Springer Nature Switzerland AG 2027
L. M. Camarinha-Matos and F. Ferrada (Eds.): DoCEIS 2026, IFIP AICT 790, pp. 20–31, 2027.
https://doi.org/10.1007/978-3-032-28939-1_2

capacity, as used in this paper, refers to an organisation's ability to exercise meaningful control over its digital processes, to maintain accountability across system boundaries, and to retain the flexibility to reassert governance when conditions change.

Despite growing prominence in European policy debates, digital sovereignty remains conceptually ambiguous [2, 3]. Existing research has produced rich theoretical accounts at the level of nation-states and supranational entities. The organisational level, where regulatory requirements must translate into concrete process design decisions, has received comparatively little attention [3–6]. How sovereignty concerns manifest in everyday Business Process Management (BPM) practices, and how they are addressed, remains an open question. BPM is the organisational discipline through which end-to-end processes are designed and governed [7]; it is therefore the practice in which sovereignty-relevant design decisions are made and where they become amenable to systematic analysis.

This paper addresses the following research question (RQ): *How can digital sovereignty be conceptualised and analysed at the organisational level?*

The underlying research proposition is that integrating sovereignty levels and discursive categories into BPM practice provides a viable basis for systematically analysing sovereignty concerns in organisational processes. This early-stage doctoral research contributes an integrative analytical schema that maps sovereignty concerns across levels and claim types. The schema identifies the organisational level as a structural gap in existing research and provides the conceptual foundation for subsequent empirical and design-oriented investigations.

2 Digital Sovereignty as a Societal Challenge

Digital sovereignty is a societal challenge with implications for democratic self-determination, economic independence, and fundamental rights [2, 8]. European organisations increasingly depend on cloud and AI services controlled by few non-European providers, affecting not only individual firms but entire sectors and public institutions [1, 9].

The societal dimension becomes visible at the process level. Regulatory frameworks formulate sovereignty objectives at policy level, but these must translate into concrete design decisions within organisational end-to-end processes, i.e. cross-functional sequences spanning organisational units, system boundaries, and external providers [7]. Each process step may involve distinct sovereignty characteristics: hosting locations, software providers, jurisdictional data transfers, or media transitions between differently governed systems. Crucially, sovereignty can be eroded through cumulative internal design decisions that prioritise efficiency over autonomy [6, 10]. The perspective of the process designer shapes sovereignty outcomes, as design choices simultaneously configure technical systems and governance arrangements [11].

This is why the research focuses on BPM as the operational locus for digital sovereignty. BPM provides the discipline through which end-to-end processes are designed, monitored, and adapted [7], and through which sovereignty-relevant decisions can be made visible and governed. By linking sovereignty analysis to BPM practice, this research addresses the conference theme: tackling societal challenges not by proposing new technology, but by equipping organisations with instruments to preserve sovereignty within their digital processes.

3 Literature Review

Digital sovereignty has attracted growing research attention across political science, legal studies, information systems, and sociotechnical research. Despite this interdisciplinary breadth, the concept remains contested and unevenly developed across levels of analysis. This section reviews the existing literature to build the conceptual foundation for the framework developed in Sect. 5.

3.1 Scope and Method of Review

This work draws on an exploratory, concept-driven literature review [12] aimed at sythesising multi-level and discursive-category perspectives on digital sovereignty in organisational contexts. Core publications were identified through iterative keyword searches using terms including digital sovereignty, data sovereignty, organisational autonomy, and process governance in major academic databases. Backward and forward citation tracking was applied to identify both seminal and recent contributions. Publications were evaluated for conceptual relevance to organisational process design and governance; studies with a predominantly technical focus were deprioritised. The resulting literature spans political science, information systems, legal studies, and sociotechnical research.

3.2 Conceptualisation of Digital Sovereignty in Literature

This review draws on both digital sovereignty and data sovereignty as related but distinct concepts, as illustrated in Fig. 1 [2, 5]. Digital sovereignty, the capacity of actors to exercise self-determination across digital infrastructures, economies, and services [2], serves as the overarching framework, spanning technical, organisational, and regulatory dimensions.

Data sovereignty is narrower: it concerns control over data flows, storage, and governance. In data-intensive organisational contexts, both concepts converge in practice [5], and this paper treats them as complementary. Digital sovereignty is a contested concept. No single authoritative definition has emerged. The concept is debated across political, legal, infrastructural, and normative dimensions.

Pohle and Thiel [2] offer an early and influential framing. Through a qualitative analysis of policy documents, they identify three recurring discursive categories along which sovereignty is asserted: state autonomy over national digital infrastructures, economic autonomy from foreign technology providers, and user autonomy in digital environments. Pohle and Santaniello [13] show that this discourse has expanded, with digital sovereignty challenging the multi-stakeholder model of internet governance.

From a legal perspective, Robles-Carrillo [14] distinguishes classical sovereignty, which applies to states only, from digital sovereignty, which also extends to supranational entities such as the EU. Couture and Toupin [15] show that governmental actors

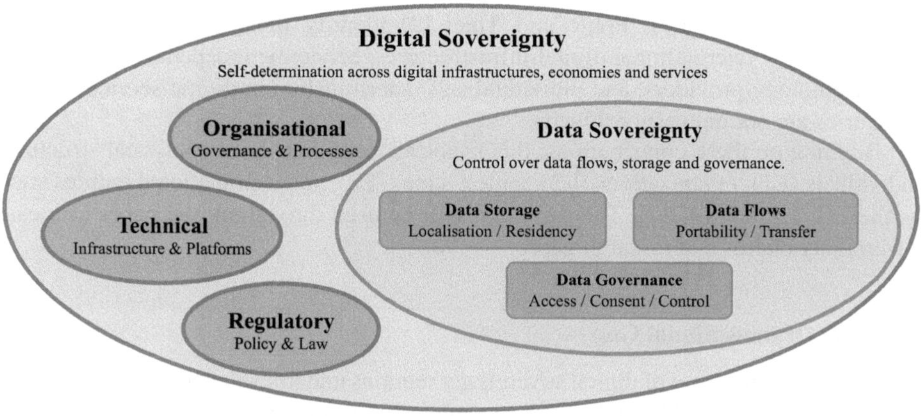

Fig. 1. Relationship Between Digital Sovereignty and Data Sovereignty

use the term to claim infrastructure control, while civil society groups invoke it for user self-determination. Subject, object, and normative content diverge substantially across contexts [15]. Hummel et al. [5] extend this analysis into the data domain. Across 341 publications, they map sovereignty claims to three agent types, individuals, organisations, and nation-states, and find a common thread: all variants concern meaningful control over data [5].

Two more recent contributions offer critical perspectives. Repetto [3] warns that applying the term to states, organisations, and individuals alike risks conceptual stretching and loss of analytical precision. Pohle, Nanni, and Santaniello [16] add that it is frequently deployed instrumentally, without reflection on its origins or implications.

Alternative typologies have sought to impose greater rigour. Floridi [8] defines digital sovereignty as strategic autonomy. He argues for the active protection of European values across cloud infrastructure, artificial intelligence (AI), and data governance rather than technological isolation. Fratini et al. [9] identify four distinct models in the literature: a rights-based model emphasising civil liberties, a market-oriented model centred on economic competitiveness, a centralisation model focused on state control over infrastructure, and a state-based model grounded in political authority. Each reflects different governance priorities.

Two structural patterns recur across this review. They together provide a vocabulary for mapping sovereignty phenomena: the levels at which claims are made [5, 14, 17], and their substantive content as three discursive categories [2]. Both originate in political science and have not been systematically translated into organizational process design.

Levels. Sovereignty claims cluster around three agent types: individuals, organisations, and nation-states [5]. The EU exercises digital governance authority without possessing classical state sovereignty, making the supranational level analytically necessary as a fourth category [14]. In the era of generative AI, sovereignty is further polycentric, spanning actors from cooperatives to transnational alliances [17].

Discursive categories. Pohle and Thiel [2] identify three recurring categories: state autonomy over national digital infrastructures, economic independence from foreign technology providers, and individual self-determination in digital services. These categories are not mutually exclusive.

Building on these contributions, this paper adopts a four-level analytical structure: individuals (L1), organizations (L2), nation-states (L3), and supranational entities such as the EU (L4) [5, 14, 17]. This structure will be used throughout the paper to locate sovereignty claims and research gaps.

3.3 The Organisational Gap

The organisational level of digital sovereignty remains underdeveloped [5, 9]. This is the scale at which firms, public authorities, and inter-organisational systems design and enact sovereignty-relevant processes. Compared to the policy level above it and the individual level below it, the organisational level has received far less systematic attention [3]. Table 1 maps the principal research streams by level and perspective, making this gap structurally visible.

Table 1. Existing Research Streams and Their Coverage of Digital Sovereignty.

Research Stream	Primary Level	Perspective	Key Limitation
Policy and governance discourse [2, 8, 14]	L3, L4	Political, legal	No organizational operationalisation
Technical sovereignty architectures (IDS, Gaia-X) [18, 19]	L4, inter-org.	Technical, infrastructural	No internalisable at process level
Individual rights framework [5, 20]	L1	Legal, normative	No translation mechanism to L2
Organisational IS research [1, 6]	L2 (partial)	Empirical	Fragmented; no integrative design framework

None of these streams addresses sovereignty as an organisational process design practice. Opriel et al. [6] provide the clearest empirical evidence: their action design research in the automotive industry shows that data sovereignty requires integration across technical, contractual, and governance dimensions, yet no framework guides this integration at the process level. Blancato and Carr [1] illustrate a related difficulty: even at the inter-organisational scale, trust deficits and structural dependencies on dominant providers persistently undermine sovereignty claims.

Without a shared and operational understanding of what sovereignty means at L2, actors risk invoking the concept symbolically, without actionable consequence [3, 5, 15]. There is currently no framework that links the structural vocabulary of digital sovereignty to the organisational processes through which sovereignty is enacted in practice. Addressing this gap is the central aim of Sect. 5.

4 Synthesis of Literature-Based Insights

The literature review establishes that the organisational level of digital sovereignty is structurally underserved. This section sharpens the research gap and identifies the theoretical foundations that the framework in Sect. 5 draws upon.

4.1 Process-Level Sovereignty Challenges

The literature reveals four sovereignty challenges recurring at the process level. They are not exceptional failures but routine outcomes of design decisions that optimise for efficiency without attending to sovereignty implications. Table 2 summarises them.

Table 2. Sovereignty-Related Challenges in Organisational Processes.

Challenge	Process-Level Manifestation	References
Control	Limited transparency regarding data flows, processing locations, and jurisdictional applicability in cloud-based workflows	Blancato and Carr [1]; Opriel et al. [6]
Accountability	Fragmented responsibility structures when critical process steps are executed by external service providers	Chappidi et al. [21]; Misra et al. [22]; Nouws et al. [10]
Decision Authority	Algorithmic constraints and vendor-imposed limitations that reduce organisational discretion in process design	Nouws et al. [10]; Opriel et al. [6]
Autonomy	Strategic dependencies and lock-in effects arising from cumulative design decisions favouring external platforms	Blancato and Carr [1]; Opriel et al. [6]

These challenges are routine outcomes of ordinary process design, not exceptional events. The organisational level lacks systematic frameworks for recognising and addressing them.

4.2 Existing Governance Mechanisms and Their Limits

Several research streams show that sovereignty-aware design is feasible in principle. Otto and Jarke [19] embed data sovereignty mechanisms within the International Data Spaces platform architecture. Opriel et al. [6] develop design principles for data-sovereign inter-organisational systems. Collective governance models such as data cooperatives [17, 23] demonstrate that sovereignty can be embedded in shared arrangements. Yet all these approaches operate at the inter-organisational or infrastructure level. They provide limited guidance for process owners who assess sovereignty implications during routine design work.

4.3 The Socio-technical Nature of Sovereignty

Sovereignty at the organisational level cannot be addressed through technical or governance measures in isolation. Orlikowski and Scott [11] theorise that technology and organisational practice are mutually constitutive. Nouws et al. [10] confirm this empirically: design choices in algorithmic systems unintentionally reshape accountability and governance structures.

Applied to digital sovereignty, this means that sovereignty losses emerge from the incremental accumulation of design decisions that were not evaluated through a sovereignty lens. It is at the boundaries of end-to-end processes [7, 24] that control, accountability, and decision authority become fragmented. BPM, as the discipline through which these boundaries are configured, constitutes the natural operational locus for the framework developed in Sect. 5.

5 An Organisational Framework for Digital Sovereignty

The preceding sections yield two key findings: digital sovereignty research is structured around actor levels and discursive categories, while the organisational level remains insufficiently addressed. The framework responds to both findings. It consists of two elements. The first, an analytical schema, provides a structured vocabulary for locating sovereignty concerns across levels and claim types. The second positions digital sovereignty as an organisational capability through a dynamic capabilities lens. Together, they connect the analytical vocabulary of sovereignty research to BPM practice.

5.1 Constructing the Analytical Schema

The analytical schema builds on the four-level structure identified in Sect. 3: individuals (L1), organisations (L2), nation-states (L3), and supranational entities (L4) [5, 14, 17]. It adds a second axis based on the three discursive categories identified by Pohle and Thiel [2]. For this framework, state autonomy is operationalised as legal autonomy, since at L2 it manifests as regulatory compliance rather than direct political power.

Neither structural pattern alone addresses the organisational level. The level structure tells us where organisations sit, but not what sovereignty means for them. The discursive categories describe what sovereignty is about but were developed from state-centric and individual-level discourse. Table 3 integrates both into a single analytical schema.

The schema produces a specific finding. At L3 and L4, all three categories are addressed by established regulatory instruments [2, 8, 14]. At L1, individual rights mechanisms exist [5]. At L2, the situation is qualitatively different. Legal autonomy translates into compliance requirements that organisations must operationalise through concrete design decisions. Economic autonomy requires active architectural choices, such as avoiding vendor lock-in. User autonomy becomes a design responsibility: organisations must embed transparency and accountability into their processes. None of these L2 manifestations are systematically addressed by existing frameworks.

To illustrate: consider an organisation deploying a cloud-based AI assistant for internal knowledge management. Legal autonomy is implicated when data is processed outside the organisation's jurisdiction. Blancato and Carr [1] show that extraterritorial legislation such as the US CLOUD Act enables foreign authorities to access data in European

Table 3. Analytical Schema: Levels and Discursive Categories of Digital Sovereignty.

Level	Legal Autonomy	Economic Autonomy	User Autonomy
L1:Individual	Enforcement of data protection rights through state institutions	Personal choice and financial autonomy in digital markets	Self-determination over personal data and digital identity
L2:Organisational	Compliance with regulatory frameworks; operational legitimacy	Independence from external vendors; control over digital supply chains	Transparency and accountability toward users embedded in processes
L3:National	Regulatory authority; protection of critical infrastructure	Industrial and trade policy; nurturing domestic digital industries	Enforcement of individual rights through legal frameworks
L4:Supranational	Geopolitical rule-setting across jurisdictions	Regional trade policy; countering foreign platform dominance	Harmonisation of rights across member states

cloud infrastructures regardless of contractual safeguards. Economic autonomy is constrained by provider-controlled updates that create structural lock-in [1]. User autonomy is affected when employees lack visibility over how their inputs are processed; Lambert et al. [25] document this risk and advocate on-premise architectures as a response. The schema makes these intersecting implications visible before the design decision is finalised.

The L2 row is thus analytically central: it is where regulatory intentions must translate into practice and where individual rights depend on organisational design choices. The four challenges from Table 2 can be located within this schema. Control losses relate primarily to legal autonomy; accountability fragmentation to user autonomy; decision authority constraints to economic autonomy. Lock-in cuts across all three categories.

5.2 Sovereignty as Organisational Capability

BPM provides the operational practice through which organisations can enact sovereignty systematically. It is the discipline for designing, monitoring, and adapting end-to-end processes [7], and empirically a core governance capability in digitalisation contexts [26]. Baiyere et al. [27] show that digital transformation pushes BPM toward adaptive governance logics, directly relevant to sovereignty-related design decisions. Dynamic capabilities theory explains how organisations build or erode the capacity to act sovereignly. Teece's [28] framework identifies three activities: sensing, seizing, and transforming.

Applied to digital sovereignty at L2, these activities take a specific form. Sensing means recognising when a process design decision creates a sovereignty-relevant dependency, for example a cloud integration that transfers data outside the organisation's jurisdiction, or a vendor contract that limits future architectural choices. Seizing means responding through deliberate design: selecting an architecture that preserves control, building contractual safeguards, or redesigning process boundaries. Transforming means revisiting these choices as technologies and market conditions change, preventing sovereignty capacity from eroding through incremental drift. Zollo and Winter [29] show that such capabilities are built through deliberate learning and progressive routinisation.

The mapping in Fig. 2 is a conceptual synthesis by the authors, not an empirically validated model. It rests on a structural correspondence between Teece's [28] dynamic capabilities (sensing, seizing, transforming) and the BPM lifecycle [7] (discovery, analysis, redesign, implementation, monitoring).

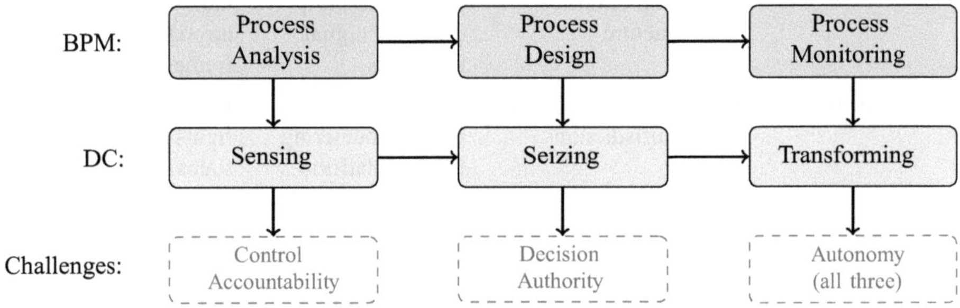

Fig. 2. Mapping Dynamic Capabilities Activities onto BPM Practice Phases and Sovereignty Challenges

The mapping follows a shared temporal logic: dependencies must first be recognised (sensing/analysis), then addressed through design choices (seizing/design), and continuously reassessed (transforming/monitoring) [5, 14]. The challenges from Table 2 are positioned where they primarily become actionable. Control and accountability require detection during analysis; decision authority constraints must be resolved during design; autonomy erosion requires ongoing monitoring. Empirical validation of this mapping is a central objective of the subsequent DSR phase.

6 Discussion, Conclusion and Research Outlook

This paper addressed RQ: How can digital sovereignty be conceptualised and analysed at the organisational level? The framework developed in Sect. 5 provides a two-part answer. Digital sovereignty at L2 can be conceptualised through an analytical schema that integrates four governance levels with three discursive categories, revealing that organisations occupy a structurally critical but underserved position between regulation and practice. It can be analysed through four process-level challenges (control, accountability, decision authority, and autonomy) that make sovereignty concerns visible within concrete end-to-end process design decisions.

The novelty of this contribution lies not in the individual building blocks, which are drawn from established research, but in their systematic integration. Existing work treats sovereignty levels [5, 14], discursive categories [2], and BPM practice [7] separately. This framework is the first to combine all three into a single analytical instrument that locates sovereignty concerns within organisational process design and provides a structured basis for their operationalisation.

Three findings extend beyond the immediate answer to the RQ. First, sovereignty losses at L2 are not primarily the result of external imposition. They emerge from routine design decisions that optimise for efficiency without attending to sovereignty implications [1, 6, 10]. This reframes digital sovereignty from a compliance obligation into a design responsibility. Second, sovereignty at L2 cannot be addressed through technical or governance measures in isolation. The two are mutually constitutive [10, 11]. Third, the dynamic capabilities perspective reveals that sovereignty is not a state to be certified once, but a capacity built or eroded through cumulative process design decisions [28, 29]. Organisations that do not actively sense, seize, and transform their sovereignty posture risk incremental erosion that may not become visible until dependencies are irreversible.

The framework has limitations that reflect its early-stage status. The analytical schema and the four process-level challenges are grounded in the existing literature but have not yet been empirically validated. Their completeness and applicability across organisational types and sectors remains to be established.

The immediate next step is a structured literature review to consolidate and extend the theoretical foundations. The subsequent research adopts a Design Science Research (DSR) approach [30–32]. Specifically, the DSR phase will operationalise the analytical schema into a maturity instrument. Its assessment dimensions will be derived from the L2 row of the schema and the four process-level challenges, enabling organisations to evaluate their sovereignty posture across end-to-end processes at defined levels of capability. The instrument is intended to support process owners and IT decision-makers in identifying sovereignty-relevant dependencies and prioritising design interventions. The expected output is a validated, sovereignty-aware BPM framework that bridges the gap from regulatory intent at L3 and L4 to operational process design at L2.

References

1. Blancato, F.G., Carr, M.: The trust deficit. EU bargaining for access and control over cloud infrastructures. J. Eur. Publ. Policy. **33**, 936–967 (2024). https://doi.org/10.1080/13501763.2024.2441418
2. Pohle, J., Thiel, T.: Digital sovereignty. Internet. Pol. Rev. **9** (2020). https://doi.org/10.14763/2020.4.1532
3. Repetto, E.: Concept 'stretching' or concept innovation? a review of the usages of sovereignty in the digital sovereignty literature. Policy Amp Internet. **17**, e70011 (2025). https://doi.org/10.1002/poi3.70011
4. Görnemann, E.: Digital Sovereignty, https://fundamentals.weizenbaum-institut.de/en/digital-sovereignty/ (2024)
5. Hummel, P., Braun, M., Tretter, M., Dabrock, P.: Data sovereignty: a review. Big Data Soc. **8**, 2053951720982012 (2021). https://doi.org/10.1177/2053951720982012
6. Opriel, S., Möller, F., Strobel, G., Otto, B.: Data sovereignty in inter-organizational information systems: findings from demand and capacity management in the automotive industry. Bus. Inf. Syst. Eng. **67**, 833–853 (2025). https://doi.org/10.1007/s12599-024-00893-4

7. Dumas, M., La Rosa, M., Mendling, J., Reijers, H.A.: Fundamentals of Business Process Management. Springer, Berlin Heidelberg, Berlin, Heidelberg (2018). https://doi.org/10.1007/978-3-662-56509-4
8. Floridi, L.: The fight for digital sovereignty: what it is, and why it matters, especially for the EU. Philos. Technol. **33**, 369–378 (2020). https://doi.org/10.1007/s13347-020-00423-6
9. Fratini, S., Hine, E., Novelli, C., Roberts, H., Floridi, L.: Digital sovereignty: a descriptive analysis and a critical evaluation of existing models. DISO. **3**, 59 (2024). https://doi.org/10.1007/s44206-024-00146-7
10. Nouws, S., Janssen, M., Dobbe, R.: Dismantling digital cages: examining design practices for public algorithmic systems. In: Janssen, M., Csáki, C., Lindgren, I., Loukis, E., Melin, U., Viale Pereira, G., Rodríguez Bolívar, M.P., Tambouris, E. (eds.) Electronic Government, pp. 307–322. Springer International Publishing, Cham (2022). https://doi.org/10.1007/978-3-031-15086-9_20
11. Orlikowski, W.J., Scott, S.V.: 10 Sociomateriality: challenging the separation of technology. Work Org ANNALS. **2**, 433–474 (2008). https://doi.org/10.5465/19416520802211644
12. Jaakkola, E.: Designing conceptual articles: four approaches. AMS Rev. **10**, 18–26 (2020). https://doi.org/10.1007/s13162-020-00161-0
13. Pohle, J., Santaniello, M.: From multistakeholderism to digital sovereignty: toward a new discursive order in internet governance? Policy Internet. **16**, 672–691 (2024). https://doi.org/10.1002/poi3.426
14. Robles-Carrillo, M.: Sovereignty vs. Digital Sovereignty. JDTL. **1**, 673–690 (2023). https://doi.org/10.21202/jdtl.2023.29
15. Couture, S., Toupin, S.: What does the notion of "sovereignty" mean when referring to the digital? New Media Soc. **21**, 2305–2322 (2019). https://doi.org/10.1177/1461444819865984
16. Pohle, J., Nanni, R., Santaniello, M.: Unthinking digital sovereignty: a critical reflection on origins, objectives, and practices. Policy Internet. **16**, 666–671 (2024). https://doi.org/10.1002/poi3.437
17. Calzada, I.: Data sovereignties in the GenAI economics: from data-opolies to data cooperatives. Trust Geopolitical Governance. (2025). https://doi.org/10.2139/ssrn.5453496
18. Braud, A., Fromentoux, G., Radier, B., Le Grand, O.: The road to European digital sovereignty with Gaia-X and IDSA. IEEE Netw. **35**, 4–5 (2021). https://doi.org/10.1109/MNET.2021.9387709
19. Otto, B., Jarke, M.: Designing a multi-sided data platform: findings from the international data spaces case. Electron Mark. **29**, 561–580 (2019). https://doi.org/10.1007/s12525-019-00362-x
20. Hummel, P., Braun, M., Dabrock, P.: Own data? Ethical reflections on data ownership. Philos. Technol. **34**, 545–572 (2021). https://doi.org/10.1007/s13347-020-00404-9
21. Chappidi, S., Cobbe, J., Norval, C., Mazumder, A., Singh, J.: Accountability capture: how record-keeping to support AI transparency and accountability (re)shapes algorithmic oversight. AIES. **8**, 554–566 (2025). https://doi.org/10.1609/aies.v8i1.36570
22. Misra, S., Barik, K., Kvalvik, P.: Digital sovereignty in the era of industry 5.0: challenges and opportunities. Procedia Comput. Sci. **254**, 108–117 (2025). https://doi.org/10.1016/j.procs.2025.02.069
23. Calzada, I.: Postpandemic Technopolitical democracy: algorithmic nations, data sovereignty, digital rights, and data cooperatives. In: Zabalo, J., Filibi, I., Escajedo San-Epifanio, L. (eds.) Made-to-Measure Future(s) for Democracy? pp. 97–117. Springer International Publishing, Cham (2023). https://doi.org/10.1007/978-3-031-08608-3_6
24. Reijers, H.A.: Business process management: the evolution of a discipline. Comput. Ind. **126**, 103404 (2021). https://doi.org/10.1016/j.compind.2021.103404
25. Lambert, M., Schuster, T., Döring, N., Krüger, R.: Datenschutzkonformer LLM-Einsatz: Eine Open-Source-Referenzarchitektur (2025). https://doi.org/10.48550/arXiv.2503.01915

26. Kerpedzhiev, G.D., König, U.M., Röglinger, M., Rosemann, M.: An exploration into future business process management capabilities in view of digitalization: results from a Delphi study. Bus. Inf. Syst. Eng. **63**, 83–96 (2021). https://doi.org/10.1007/s12599-020-00637-0
27. Baiyere, A., Salmela, H., Tapanainen, T.: Digital transformation and the new logics of business process management. Eur. J. Inf. Syst. **29**, 238–259 (2020). https://doi.org/10.1080/0960085X.2020.1718007
28. Teece, D.J.: Dynamic capabilities: routines versus entrepreneurial action. J Manag. Stud. **49**, 1395–1401 (2012). https://doi.org/10.1111/j.1467-6486.2012.01080.x
29. Zollo, M., Winter, S.G.: Deliberate learning and the evolution of dynamic capabilities. Organ. Sci. **13**, 339–351 (2002). https://doi.org/10.1287/orsc.13.3.339.2780
30. Hevner, A.R., Chatterjee, S.: Design Research in Information Systems: Theory and Practice. Springer, New York London (2010)
31. Hevner, A.R., March, S.T., Park, J., Ram, S.: Design science in information systems research. MIS Q. **28**, 75–106 (2004). https://doi.org/10.2307/25148625
32. Vom Brocke, J., Maedche, A.: The DSR grid: six core dimensions for effectively planning and communicating design science research projects. Electron Mark. **29**, 379–385 (2019). https://doi.org/10.1007/s12525-019-00358-7

AI-Driven DevSecOps to Enhance Software Quality and Security

Nuno Teixeira Gomes[1,2](✉), João Rafael Almeida[1], and José Luís Oliveira[2]

[1] IEETA, University of Aveiro, Aveiro, Portugal
nunoteixeirag@ua.pt
[2] Trustiant, Ílhavo, Portugal

Abstract. Modern software development, driven by Agile and CI/CD, demands innovative approaches to ensure quality and security. Traditional validation techniques often struggle with rapid release cycles and evolving threats. To address this, this paper proposes an AI-driven framework integrated into the Software Development Life Cycle (SDLC). The objective is to enhance DevSecOps through automation, intelligent testing, and behavioral monitoring. Specifically, we present mechanisms for automated functional verification, adversarial vulnerability detection in CI/CD pipelines, and continuous post-deployment anomaly detection. Furthermore, the framework incorporates privacy-preserving mechanisms to ensure compliance with data protection regulations, particularly in sensitive domains like medical research. The central research hypothesis is that embedding adaptive AI agents into DevSecOps pipelines can simultaneously improve functional quality, proactive security, and behavioral monitoring without compromising development agility. By bridging AI with DevSecOps, this contribution offers a robust architecture to improve reliability, strengthen security against threats, and support regulatory compliance in critical software systems.

Keywords: Artificial Intelligence · DevSecOps · Software Quality Assurance · Software Security · Continuous Integration · Reinforcement Learning · Anomaly Detection

1 Introduction

Legacy web applications constitute the operational backbone of critical infrastructure, underpinning essential services in banking, insurance, and public administration [1, 2]. While software development paradigms have evolved rapidly toward Agile and DevOps [3], these systems often persist as "black boxes": monoliths updated largely through ad-hoc patches, lacking formal specifications or up-to-date documentation [4–6].

This opacity creates a severe security paradox. As organizations aggressively integrate these assets into modern DevSecOps pipelines to accelerate delivery [7, 8], the rigid nature of legacy architectures creates a significant friction point with automated CI/CD

Published by Springer Nature Switzerland AG 2027
L. M. Camarinha-Matos and F. Ferrada (Eds.): DoCEIS 2026, IFIP AICT 790, pp. 32–41, 2027.
https://doi.org/10.1007/978-3-032-28939-1_3

workflows [9]. The reliance on manual security reviews or fragile regression scripts introduces bottlenecks that force a trade-off between business agility and rigorous verification [10].

The central research question guiding this work is: How can AI-driven techniques be embedded into DevSecOps pipelines to continuously improve software quality assurance and strengthen security mechanisms across the development lifecycle? The underlying research hypothesis is that adaptive AI agents, each specialized for a distinct security and quality dimension, can be integrated into CI/CD pipelines to simultaneously improve functional coverage, proactive vulnerability detection, and behavioral anomaly detection — without compromising development agility.

1.1 The Gap: Limitations of Traditional Testing

The persistence of vulnerabilities in these environments stems from a fundamental limitation in current automated security testing: the inability to reason about Business Logic and State Transitions.

- **Static Analysis (SAST) Limitations:** SAST tools, while effective for syntax-level flaws, generate prohibitive false positive rates in dynamic, loosely-typed legacy languages [11]. Crucially, static analysis lacks the runtime context required to identify temporal logic flaws, such as broken access controls that only manifest within a specific sequence of user actions [12].
- **Dynamic Analysis (DAST) Limitations:** Conversely, DAST scanners operate primarily as stateless fuzzers. They excel at identifying injection flaws (e.g., XSS, SQLi) but lack a semantic understanding of the application as a Finite State Machine (FSM) [13]. A traditional DAST tool cannot autonomously navigate deep, state-dependent transaction flows and thus cannot distinguish between a legitimate server rejection and a critical logic bypass.

1.2 Research Objectives

To address these limitations, this research is divided into three specific objectives:

- **RQ1 — AI for Continuous Quality in Legacy Systems:** How can an AI-driven approach be developed to effectively provide continuous quality assurance for legacy web applications?
- **RQ2 — Adversarial Vulnerability Detection:** How can AI-driven vulnerability scanning, incorporating dynamic analysis, be effectively embedded into DevSecOps pipelines?
- **RQ3 — Behavioral Anomaly Detection & Insider Threats:** Can AI-based anomaly detection using user behavioral profiling proactively identify malicious insider threats?

2 Contributions Toward Tackling Societal Challenges

The central theme of DoCEIS 2026 emphasizes technological innovation in solving complex societal and industrial challenges. As software becomes the operational backbone of virtually every sector, the ability to deliver secure, reliable, and compliant code is no longer a mere technical requirement but a strategic enabler for innovation.

2.1 Enabling Digital Transformation and Collaborative Networks

Digital Transformation is fundamentally about agility — the ability of an organization to adapt its digital assets rapidly to meet market demands. However, as organizations transition to high-velocity DevOps pipelines, they face a critical bottleneck: the "Security Paradox". Accelerating delivery often leads to an accumulation of technical debt and security vulnerabilities, while enforcing rigorous manual security reviews acts as a brake on innovation.

This thesis contributes to Digital Transformation and Enterprise Collaborative Networks by resolving this trade-off through three mechanisms:

- **Modernizing Legacy Assets with Confidence:** By using AI to infer behavior and generate tests for undocumented legacy systems (RQ1), organizations can safely integrate them into cloud-native ecosystems without the high risk of rewriting them from scratch.
- **Securing the Supply Chain:** The proposed framework acts as a continuous auditor, ensuring that every software update meets strict quality and security standards before it propagates through the network.
- **Accelerating Time-to-Market:** By removing the dependency on manual regression testing and security audits, companies can deploy updates daily rather than quarterly.

2.2 Resilience in Cyber-Physical Systems and Embedded Intelligence

As we move toward Industry 5.0, the boundary between the digital and physical worlds blurs. In Cyber-Physical Systems (CPS) and domains relying on Embedded Intelligence, software failures can have catastrophic physical consequences. Our contribution includes:

- **State-Aware Vulnerability Detection:** By treating the system as a Finite State Machine and using adversarial AI (RQ2), the framework can detect scenarios where a sequence of valid inputs forces a controller into an unsafe state.
- **Bridging IT and OT Security:** Behavioral anomaly detection (RQ3) identifies intrusions moving from the corporate network to the production floor.
- **Resilience against Advanced Threats:** The framework moves beyond signature matching to detect sophisticated attack vectors targeting specific business logic.

2.3 Societal Impact: Trust and Resilience in Critical Infrastructure

Beyond technical agility, this research addresses the reliance of essential public services on fragile legacy infrastructure. Our framework tackles these challenges by: (1) *Ensuring Continuity of Essential Services* through automated verification of legacy systems (RQ1); and (2) *Protecting Citizen Data*, where the Privacy-Preserving Watchdog (RQ3) aligns safety with GDPR requirements.

3 State of the Art

The integration of AI into DevSecOps is a multifaceted challenge. We analyze the existing literature across three primary domains and position our approach explicitly against existing AI-driven DevSecOps solutions.

3.1 AI-Driven Software Testing and Quality Assurance

Wang et al. [14] highlight how ML can optimize test case prioritization. Deep Learning models have been applied to predict defect density based on historical commit data [15]. Recent tools such as Diffblue Cover and EvoSuite leverage AI to auto-generate unit tests for Java systems, but require access to compiled code and well-defined interfaces, making them unsuitable for legacy "black-box" web applications. *Gap Identified*: While these approaches optimize existing tests, they lack the capability to autonomously generate functional scenarios in complex legacy environments — a specific gap addressed by RQ1.

3.2 AI-Driven Vulnerability Detection

Traditional DAST scanners suffer from low code coverage and high false-negative rates when facing complex business logic [16]. McKinnel et al. [17] identify a growing trend towards automating ethical hacking using Reinforcement Learning (RL). RL-trained agents have outperformed random fuzzers in state-space coverage [18] and successfully detected crashes in mobile ecosystems [19]. Tools such as OWASP ZAP and Burp Suite Pro incorporate limited ML features but remain fundamentally stateless. *Gap Identified*: The application of adversarial AI to detect logical integrity bypasses (mapped to STRIDE) in web applications remains under-explored. Our work (RQ2) targets this semantic gap.

3.3 Behavioral Anomaly Detection and Privacy

Shiri et al. [20] emphasize RNNs and Autoencoders to profile user behavior and detect anomalies in real-time. Techniques for detecting insider threats often leverage unsupervised learning to handle the scarcity of labeled attack data [21]. Dutta et al. [22] proposed multivariate anomaly detection for cyber-physical systems. Existing solutions such as Splunk UBA and Microsoft Sentinel offer user behavioral analytics but rely on centralized data processing that raises GDPR compliance concerns in healthcare. *Gap Identified*: Our approach (RQ3) integrates local differential privacy directly into the profiling architecture, a combination that remains underexplored.

4 Proposed Framework and Research Contribution

This research proposes a unified, AI-driven framework designed to operate continuously across the DevSecOps pipeline, introducing a persistent "Intelligence Layer" that learns from application behavior and user interactions to enforce quality and security dynamically.

4.1 Module 1: The AI Quality Oracle (Addressing RQ1)

This module addresses the "Missing Oracle Problem" in legacy systems using unsupervised learning. It observes traffic in a staging environment to infer normative behavior, constructing a probabilistic model of valid state transitions. By providing the system with real user interaction logs, the AI infers interface patterns that enabled specific database entries. Reinforcement learning may be employed to iteratively refine test case selection based on system feedback (Fig. 1).

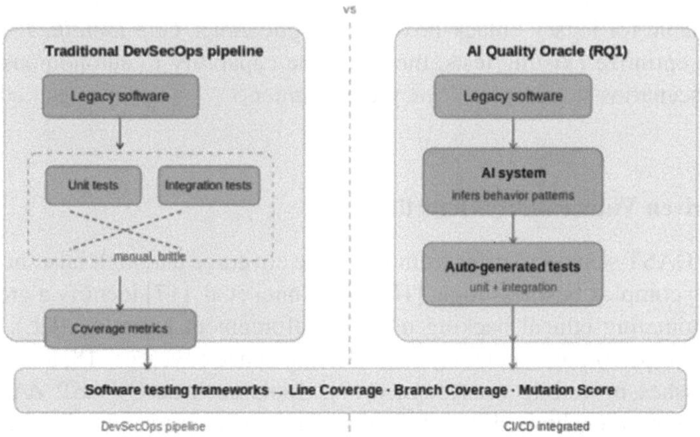

Fig. 1. AI Quality Oracle (RQ1): AI-generated tests compared against traditional manual test suites within a DevSecOps pipeline, evaluated by software testing frameworks on coverage and mutation score metrics.

4.2 Module 2: The Adversarial Security Agent (Addressing RQ2)

An agent powered by Reinforcement Learning (RL) treats the application as a game environment where rewards are linked to discovering security violations. The RL formulation is defined as follows:

- **State space (S):** The application's current session state, including authentication level, active endpoints, parameter values, and HTTP session context, represented as a feature vector capturing the FSM position of the web application.
- **Action space (A):** The set of HTTP requests parameterized by method, endpoint, and parameter values, drawn from application traffic logs and augmented with exploit patterns from CVE/NVD databases.
- **Reward function (R):** Positive reward for each confirmed security violation (access control bypass, privilege escalation, or injection confirmed by server response divergence), mapped to STRIDE threat categories. A small negative reward per step encourages efficiency.

The agent is trained using Proximal Policy Optimization (PPO) to ensure stable learning in the high-dimensional, sparse-reward environment of security testing (Fig. 2).

4.3 Module 3: The Privacy-Preserving Watchdog (Addressing RQ3)

The final component detects insider threats using Autoencoders trained on interaction metadata (access frequency, action sequencing, temporal patterns). Local differential

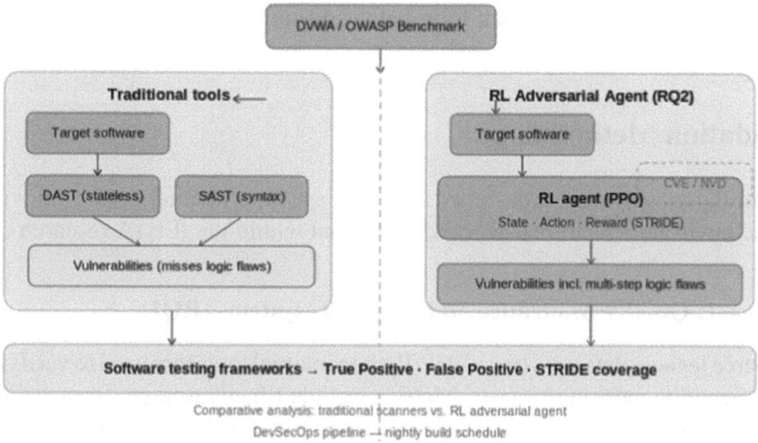

Fig. 2. Adversarial Security Agent (RQ2): RL agent with formally defined state-action-reward structure compared against traditional DAST/SAST tools, using DVWA/OWASP Benchmark. Vulnerabilities are evaluated against STRIDE threat categories.

privacy ensures GDPR compliance in medical research contexts. Two critical risks are explicitly addressed: (1) adversarial data poisoning, mitigated through robust aggregation and periodic model re-anchoring; (2) test memorization, mitigated by evaluating on held-out application instances and measuring cross-dataset generalization (Fig. 3).

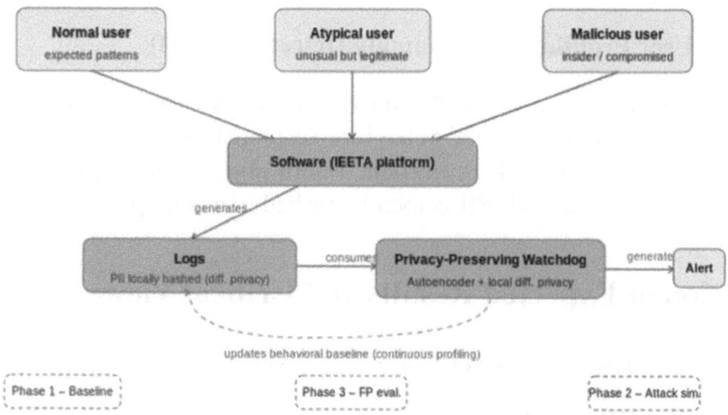

Fig. 3. Privacy-Preserving Watchdog (RQ3): Three user types (normal, atypical, malicious) interact with the software platform. The AI system consumes privacy-preserving logs to generate behavioral alerts, continuously updating the baseline profile across three evaluation phases.

4.4 Summary of Innovation

The collective innovation shifts verification from static, rule-based to dynamic, learning-based assurance, offering: (1) Autonomy — removing manual specification dependencies; (2) Semantic Depth — validating business logic rather than syntax; and (3)

Continuity — creating a feedback loop between runtime anomalies and development tests.

5 Validation Methodology

To validate the framework, we designed a three-phase experimental strategy moving from controlled environments to real-world deployment within the IEETA research center.

5.1 Phase 1: Quality Assurance on Legacy Ecosystems (RQ1)

Open-source legacy platforms (e.g., PHP/Python internal tools) are used to verify the AI's ability to generate meaningful tests. Metrics include Line Coverage, Branch Coverage, and Mutation Score, compared against manual test suites and SonarQube static analysis. The "Bad Teacher" problem is mitigated via a human-in-the-loop validation step to sanitize the initial training dataset.

5.2 Phase 2: Adversarial Security Benchmarking (RQ2)

The RL agent is trained against DVWA and the OWASP Benchmark to calculate True Positive rates, then compared against OWASP ZAP specifically targeting logical vulnerabilities like broken access control. Overfitting risk is mitigated via Transfer Learning across diverse datasets.

5.3 Phase 3: User Profiling and Anomaly Detection (RQ3)

The Behavioral Watchdog is deployed in a live research environment with three sequential stages: (1) observation of normal behavior to establish baselines; (2) introduction of a simulated malicious user; and (3) introduction of atypical but legitimate behavior to evaluate false positive rates. All PII is locally hashed to ensure privacy compliance.

6 Discussion of Expected Results and Critical View

6.1 Expected Improvements over State of the Art

- **Logic Coverage (RQ1):** The AI Quality Oracle is expected to uncover deep functional regressions missed by unit tests, specifically in legacy state-machines.
- **Reduction of False Positives (RQ2 & RQ3):** Context-aware models (RL and Autoencoders) are projected to significantly reduce false positives compared to static rule-based systems.
- **Detection of Multi-Step Attacks (RQ2):** The adversarial RL agent is expected to validate complex multi-step attack scenarios that currently require expensive manual penetration testing.

6.2 Critical Challenges and Mitigation

Computational Cost vs. Pipeline Agility (RQ2). Adversarial Reinforcement Learning is computationally intensive. The Adversarial Agent should run on an asynchronous schedule (e.g., nightly builds), decoupling heavy training from the fast feedback loop.

Data Poisoning and Test Memorization (RQ2 & RQ3). Adversarial data poisoning is addressed through robust aggregation and periodic model re-anchoring. Test memorization is mitigated by evaluating on held-out application instances and measuring cross-dataset generalization.

6.3 Threats to Validity

– **Internal Validity (Overfitting):** Risk that the RL agent overfits to training applications (e.g., DVWA). Mitigation: Transfer Learning across multiple diverse datasets.
– **External Validity (Generalization):** Results from IEETA may not apply to highly regulated financial or industrial environments. Future work will involve case studies in broader domains.

7 Conclusions and Future Work

Modern software ecosystems demand a paradigm shift in quality assurance. This paper proposed a unified AI-driven DevSecOps framework that introduces an autonomous "Intelligence Layer" into the pipeline, directly addressing the research hypothesis that adaptive AI agents can improve functional quality, proactive security, and behavioral monitoring without compromising development agility.

7.1 Summary of Contributions

This work defines three key architectural modules: (1) a Quality Oracle with unsupervised learning for legacy systems (RQ1); (2) an Adversarial Agent using RL with a formally defined state-action-reward structure (RQ2); and (3) a Privacy-Preserving Watchdog with explicit mitigation for data poisoning and test memorization (RQ3).

7.2 Future Work

The roadmap includes: (1) implementation of the RL Agent focusing on PPO-based training for business logic bypasses; (2) optimization via Transfer Learning to reduce cold-start times; and (3) real-world pilot deployment within IEETA infrastructure.

References

1. Dharmaadi, I.P.A., Athanasopoulos, E., Turkmen, F.: Fuzzing frameworks for server-side web applications: a survey. Int. J. Inf. Secur. **24**(2), 73 (2025). https://doi.org/10.1007/s10207-024-00979-w

2. Hayretci, H.E., Aydemir, F.B.: A multi case study on legacy system migration in the banking industry. In: Franch, X., Poels, G., Gailly, F., Snoeck, M. (eds.) CAiSE 2021 LNCS, vol. 12751, pp. 536–550. Springer, Cham (2021). https://doi.org/10.1007/978-3-030-79382-1_32
3. Hoda, R., Salleh, N., Grundy, J.: The rise and evolution of agile software development. IEEE Softw. **35**(5), 58–63 (2018). https://doi.org/10.1109/MS.2018.290111318
4. Rosenkranz, S., Staegemann, D., Volk, M., Turowski, K.: Explaining the business-technological age of legacy information systems. IEEE Access. **12**, 84579–84611 (2024). https://doi.org/10.1109/ACCESS.2024.3414377
5. Gangadharan, G., Kuiper, E.J., Janssen, M., Luttighuis, P.O.: IT innovation squeeze: propositions and a methodology for deciding to continue or decommission legacy systems. In: Nuttall, M., et al. (eds.) TDIT 2013 IFIP AICT, vol. 402, pp. 481–494. Springer, Heidelberg (2013). https://doi.org/10.1007/978-3-642-38862-0_30
6. Khadka, R., Batlajery, B.V., Saeidi, A.M., Jansen, S., Hage, J.: How do professionals perceive legacy systems and software modernization? In: Proceedings of the 36th ICSE, pp. 36–47. ACM, New York (2014). https://doi.org/10.1145/2568225.2568318
7. Myrbakken, H., Colomo-Palacios, R.: DevSecOps: a multivocal literature review. In: Mas, A., Mesquida, A., O'Connor, R.V., Rout, T., Dorling, A. (eds.) SPICE 2017 CCIS, vol. 770, pp. 17–29. Springer, Cham (2017). https://doi.org/10.1007/978-3-319-67383-7_2
8. Prates, L., Pereira, R.: DevSecOps practices and tools. Int. J. Inf. Secur. **24**(1), 1–25 (2025). https://doi.org/10.1007/s10207-024-00914-z
9. Cruz, D.B., Almeida, J.R., Oliveira, J.L.: Open source solutions for vulnerability assessment: a comparative analysis. IEEE Access. **11**, 100234–100255 (2023). https://doi.org/10.1109/ACCESS.2023.3315595
10. Batista, L., Cruz, D., Silva, D., Almeida, J., Oliveira, J.: Securing DevOps by identifying the most common vulnerabilities in CI/CD pipelines. In: 2025 IEEE Symposium on Computers and Communications (ISCC), pp. 1–6. IEEE (2025). https://doi.org/10.1109/ISCC65549.2025.11326304
11. Wadhams, Z.D., Izurieta, C., Reinhold, A.M.: Barriers to using static application security testing (SAST) tools: a literature review. In: Proceedings of the 39th IEEE/ACM ASE Workshops, pp. 161–166. ACM (2024). https://doi.org/10.1145/3691621.3694947
12. Leokhin, Y., Fatkhulin, T., Kozhanov, M.: Research of static application security testing technique problems and methods for solving them. In: 2024 Systems of Signals Generating and Processing in the Field of on Board Communications, pp. 1–7. IEEE (2024). https://doi.org/10.1109/IEEECONF60226.2024.10496755
13. Sönmez, F.O., Kiliç, B.G.: Holistic web application security visualization for multi-project and multi-phase dynamic application security test results. IEEE Access. **9**, 25858–25884 (2021). https://doi.org/10.1109/ACCESS.2021.3057044
14. Wang, C., Yang, Z., Li, Z.S., Damian, D., Lo, D.: Quality assurance for artificial intelligence: a study of industrial concerns, challenges and best practices. arXiv:2402.16391. (2024). https://doi.org/10.48550/arXiv.2402.16391
15. Islam, M., Khan, F., Alam, S., Hasan, M.: Artificial intelligence in software testing: a systematic review. In: TENCON 2023–2023 IEEE Region 10 Conference, pp. 524–529. IEEE (2023). https://doi.org/10.1109/TENCON58879.2023.10322349
16. Zhang, B., Li, J., Ren, J., Huang, G.: Efficiency and effectiveness of web application vulnerability detection approaches: a review. ACM Comput. Surv. **54**(9), 1–35 (2021). https://doi.org/10.1145/3474553
17. McKinnel, D.R., Dargahi, T., Dehghantanha, A., Choo, K.K.R.: A systematic literature review and meta-analysis on artificial intelligence in penetration testing and vulnerability assessment. Comput. Electr. Eng. **75**, 175–188 (2019). https://doi.org/10.1016/j.compeleceng.2019.02.022

18. Abo-eleneen, A., Palliyali, A., Catal, C.: The role of reinforcement learning in software testing. Inf. Softw. Technol. **164**, 107325 (2023). https://doi.org/10.1016/j.infsof.2023.107325
19. Pan, M., Huang, A., Wang, G., Zhang, T., Li, X.: Reinforcement learning based curiosity-driven testing of Android applications. In: Proceedings of the 29th ACM SIGSOFT ISSTA, pp. 153–164. ACM, New York (2020). https://doi.org/10.1145/3395363.3397354
20. Shiri Harzevili, N., Belle, A.B., Wang, J., Wang, S., Jiang, Z.M., Nagappan, N.: A systematic literature review on automated software vulnerability detection using machine learning. ACM Comput. Surv. **57**(3), 1–36 (2024). https://doi.org/10.1145/3699711
21. Le, D.C., Zincir-Heywood, N.: Anomaly detection for insider threats using unsupervised ensembles. IEEE Trans. Netw. Serv. Manag. **18**(2), 1152–1164 (2021). https://doi.org/10.1109/TNSM.2021.3071928
22. Dutta, A.K., Negi, R., Shukla, S.K.: Robust multivariate anomaly-based intrusion detection system for cyber-physical systems. In: Dolev, S., Gudes, E., Paillier, P. (eds.) CSCML 2021 LNCS, vol. 12716, pp. 86–93. Springer, Cham (2021). https://doi.org/10.1007/978-3-030-78086-9_6

Toward Agentic Privacy-by-Design: A Conceptual Framework for AI-Supported Process Compliance

Lukas Waidelich(✉), Thomas Schuster, Andreas Schneider, and Mario Bosslau

Pforzheim University, Tiefenbronner Street. 65, Pforzheim 75175, Germany
{lukas.waidelich,thomas.schuster,andreas.schneider, mario.bosslau}@hs-pforzheim.de

Abstract. Privacy compliance in business processes is a regulatory obligation and a core requirement for trustworthy digital systems. Yet legal principles such as those of the EU GDPR are abstract, hard to translate into concrete process logic, and existing tools either rely on expert-curated formal rules or treat compliance as a post-hoc verification step disconnected from process design. This research introduces PRAISE, a conceptual, pattern-aware framework for AI-supported Privacy by Design in business process models, and asks how an agentic, retrieval-augmented system can identify privacy gaps and generate explainable, legally traceable improvement recommendations. The framework combines a layered privacy knowledge base built on the Data and Process Privacy Pattern Model with a hybrid retrieval-augmented reasoning pipeline; process models are translated into text, symbolically classified as fully, partially, or not covered against GDPR obligations, and refined through pattern-based recommendations under external orchestration and session-level tracing. Applied to a mobile-app registration scenario, PRAISE detects four interrelated GDPR violations and produces a redesigned BPMN model that addresses all of them in a single pass. The framework lays the architectural foundation for AI-supported, governance-aware privacy-compliant process design and outlines a three-phase evaluation roadmap toward prototype, expert validation, and comparative use.

Keywords: Privacy-by-Design · Business Process Management · Privacy Patterns · Retrieval-Augmented Generation · AI-Supported Compliance

1 Introduction: Privacy Compliance in Business Process Design

Privacy compliance in business process management (BPM) is both a regulatory obligation and an organizational challenge. Regulations such as the European General Data Protection Regulation (GDPR) [1] define strict rules for collecting, processing, storing, and sharing personal data. Violations can result in severe financial penalties and long-term reputational damage. New processes should follow the principle of Privacy

Published by Springer Nature Switzerland AG 2027
L. M. Camarinha-Matos and F. Ferrada (Eds.): DoCEIS 2026, IFIP AICT 790, pp. 42–54, 2027.
https://doi.org/10.1007/978-3-032-28939-1_4

by Design (PbD) by integrating measures such as consent handling, data minimization, retention control, and transparency from the outset. At the same time, many existing processes must be reviewed and adapted to meet current regulations. Both cases require systematic support during process design and improvement [2].

Privacy requirements are defined at a high level, focusing on principles rather than concrete steps. Designers must translate them into workflows, which requires legal and modeling expertise. In practice, privacy is often addressed later through audits, increasing effort and reducing flexibility. Although methods such as privacy impact assessments, threat modeling, and privacy pattern (PP) catalogs have been proposed, their practical adoption remains limited. Most approaches rely on manual interpretation of legal requirements and external documentation. They are rarely integrated into standard process modeling tools. Designers must switch between modeling environments and compliance resources, which disrupts workflow and reduces usability. The challenge is therefore not the absence of privacy knowledge, but its limited integration into everyday modeling practice. Recent advances in artificial intelligence (AI) create new opportunities to address this gap. Large language models (LLM) can retrieve structured knowledge and generate context-sensitive recommendations. When combined with retrieval mechanisms, curated repositories such as PP catalogs and regulatory knowledge bases can be dynamically linked to a specific process model. Retrieval-augmented generation (RAG) enables the transformation of static privacy documentation into interactive decision support.

This doctoral research proposes PRAISE, a conceptual framework that combines structured privacy knowledge with RAG to support privacy-aware business process design. PRAISE follows a transformation logic: A business process model serves as input and is converted into a text-based representation for semantic analysis. The framework identifies whether personal data is processed and evaluates compliance with relevant privacy principles and legal requirements. If gaps are detected, PRAISE retrieves suitable PP and generates explainable recommendations at workflow level. The improved design is then transformed back into a process model. PRAISE connects legal requirements with operational process modeling and enables AI-supported PbD. The main research question (RQ) and Research Hypothesis (RH) are:

- *RQ1*: How can an AI supported system based on privacy patterns be designed to enable privacy compliant analysis and improvement of business process models?
- *RH1*: A retrieval-augmented, pattern-aware reasoning system grounded in a structured privacy knowledge base can identify privacy compliance gaps in existing business process models and generate explainable, legally traceable improvement recommendations more effectively than purely manual or rule-based approaches, preserving human oversight over compliance decisions.

The remainder of this paper is structured as follows. Section 2 relates to the conference theme. Section 3 reviews related work. Section 4 introduces PRAISE. Section 5 illustrates the approach with an example. Section 6 concludes and outlines future work.

2 Privacy as a Societal Challenge in Data-Driven Systems

Data-driven technologies are deeply embedded in contemporary economic and social infrastructures. Organizations rely on digital platforms, automated decision systems, and large-scale data processing to deliver services and optimize operation [3]. While these developments enable efficiency and innovation, they also create significant challenges related to data privacy.

Data breaches, opaque data practices, and secondary use of personal data undermine public confidence in digital services. Research shows that perceived privacy risks influence user behavior and reduce trust in digital platforms [4]. Automated decision systems increasingly affect access to employment, credit, healthcare, and public services, raising risks of bias, discrimination, and lack of accountability. When data practices lack transparency or governance, fundamental rights may be compromised, linking privacy closely to fairness and responsible system design [5]. Modern business processes span multiple systems, actors, and organizational boundaries, with dynamic data flows across departments and partners. Traditional compliance approaches such as policy documentation, audits, or manual assessments struggle to scale in such environments. As data ecosystems grow, compliance must shift from reactive control to embedded design principles [6, 7]. This shift is reflected in the EU GDPR, which mandates PbD in system architectures and business processes [8]. Translating regulatory principles into operational workflows remains difficult [9]. These developments show that privacy is a foundational condition for trustworthy digital infrastructures. Effective protection requires technical approaches that operationalize regulations within system and process design.

PRAISE addresses this challenge by integrating regulatory knowledge into process modeling via retrieval-augmented generation, turning static compliance documents into proactive design support.

3 Current State of Privacy Aware Processes Tools

To situate PRAISE, we review three areas: Privacy Engineering and Regulatory Compliance, AI in BPM, and Process Compliance Checking Tools. We summarize prior work and derive relevant contributions.

3.1 Privacy Engineering and Regulatory Compliance

Privacy engineering complements this by providing systematic methods to translate legal requirements into technical solutions. Privacy design strategies [10] and design tactics [11] as well as the LINDDUN framework support requirement analysis and threat modeling [12]. Barletta et al. [13] further link GDPR articles to design patterns to bridge the gap between law and implementation. PP translate abstract privacy principles into practical design guidance and support the implementation of PbD. Early work by Romanosky et al. [14] and Hafiz [15] introduced reusable solutions such as informed consent and data minimization. Today, comprehensive repositories such as the PP Catalog [16–18] provide collections of best practice patterns for privacy friendly system design. In addition, approaches like the Data and Process Privacy Pattern Model (DPPPM) [19] links

PP to GDPR requirements, serves as knowledge base, and help structure their application. In business process modeling, PP have recently been applied at the process level. Agostinelli et al. [20] proposed BPMN based design patterns that integrate GDPR obligations such as consent and breach notification directly into process models, enabling compliance at design time. Barati and Rana [21] show that adapting patterns to evolving regulations remains challenging, especially for non-experts.

3.2 AI and Business Process Management

AI is increasingly used in BPM to support more intelligent and interactive process management. While BPM traditionally focuses on modeling, execution, and analysis, AI now enables prediction, resource optimization, and advanced process analytics. With advances in natural language processing, LLMs have become important tools in BPM. A key example is the BPLLM framework [22], which combines language models with business process knowledge to enable natural language interaction with process models. It relies on RAG to retrieve relevant process fragments and improve answer reliability. Recent research also highlights the role of LLMs in automatically generating and supporting process models. Forell and Schüler propose using LLMs to transform textual process descriptions into graphical models, such as Petri nets, through prompt engineering and structured output formats. Their approach improves communication between domain experts and modelers and supports multiple phases of the BPM lifecycle [23]. Recent benchmarks reinforce this trajectory: Kourani et al. [24, 25] evaluate 16 LLMs on BPM tasks and show that self-optimization improves correctness, while specialized models such as ProcessLLM [26] outperform general-purpose LLMs on BPMN-specific tasks. Schlösser et al. [27] extend purely generative pipelines with a human-in-the-loop approach in which the LLM asks clarifying questions, significantly improving model quality. In addition, privacy and compliance aspects are addressed through design-oriented approaches. Agostinelli et al. introduce GDPR aware design patterns for BPMN that integrate privacy requirements directly into process models without extending the notation. Their methodology supports compliance at design time and is evaluated using real world use cases and a dedicated modeling tool [20]. AI is increasingly used to query, generate, and improve process models and integrate regulations, enhancing efficiency and decision quality.

3.3 Compliance Checking Tools and Framework for Processes

Research on compliance checking in BPM has produced several tools and frameworks to verify whether process models follow legal regulations such as GDPR. One approach extends BPMN with privacy related elements, which enables formal verification of privacy mechanisms [28]. Another approach uses model driven development and simulation, to analyze the impact of compliance activities on process performance [2]. A third line of work focuses on rule-based checking, where regulations are encoded as patterns or temporal logic, e.g., in Awad et al.'s work using BPMN-Q [29]. These approaches enable systematic compliance checking but often require extended notations or formal rules, limiting usability and requiring significant expertise.

3.4 Research Gap and Positioning of PRAISE

Across the three reviewed strands, a consistent pattern emerges. Privacy engineering and pattern-based approaches encode rich domain knowledge but apply it through manual interpretation by experts. AI-supported BPM research demonstrates that LLMs can generate, refine, and answer questions about process models, but does not address regulatory compliance. Rule-based and formal compliance checking provides verifiable guarantees but depends on specialized notations and expert-curated rules. As a result, three capabilities that are jointly required for AI-supported PbD (i) integration of structured legal and pattern knowledge, (ii) context-aware reasoning over standard process models, and (iii) explainable, traceable improvement recommendations are nowhere combined in a single workflow. PRAISE is designed to close exactly this gap. Each of its components directly answers one of these missing capabilities: the DPPPM-based knowledge base supplies (i), the agentic RAG pipeline supplies (ii), and the orchestration layer with session-level tracing supplies (iii). Table 1 maps existing approaches against these capabilities and the corresponding contribution of PRAISE.

Table 1. Summary of Related Work and Positioning of PRAISE.

Research Area	Key Concepts and Approaches	Contribution of PRAISE
Privacy Engineering and Regulatory Compliance	Privacy engineering frameworks and PP catalogs translate GDPR principles into design solutions, and BPM-based PP supports design-time compliance, but both require expert knowledge and manual effort.	Integrates regulatory and pattern knowledge into a unified knowledge base using DPPPM and retrieves and applies privacy controls automatically, reducing expert dependency.
AI in Business Process Management	AI supports analysis and interactive modeling. LLM based systems use RAG for process understanding and model generation.	Extends LLM based assistance to privacy compliance. PRAISE enables conversational support & automated model adaptation.
Compliance Checking for Processes	Formal verification, simulation, and rule-based checking verify compliance. Often require extended notations and expert defined rules.	Works on standard BPM models and provides natural language feedback with automatic improvements.

Overall, existing research lacks integrated solutions that combine compliance knowledge, intelligent analysis, and automated model refinement. Current tools address these aspects separately, creating a clear need for continuous and adaptive PbD support, which PRAISE should provide through an agentic modeling assistant system.

4 PRAISE: A Pattern-Aware Framework for AI-Supported Privacy-Compliant Process Design

4.1 Concept and Degree of Innovation

Designers often lack legal expertise, and existing approaches such as PP catalogs or formal compliance tools provide only partial support and require significant manual effort. PRAISE introduces a system level approach that integrates privacy compliance directly into the process modeling workflow. In its current stage, PRAISE is conceived as a conceptual design that outlines how such an integrated and agentic system can be realized. The framework is designed as a complete end to end environment that guides a process from initial analysis through pattern-based assessment to improved model output. The main innovation lies in unifying legal interpretation and process design within a single reasoning system. PRAISE supports analysis and improvement using standard Business Process Models like BPMN or Petri Nets without requiring formal languages or additional notations. Unlike existing approaches that operate in isolation or focus only on post hoc verification, PRAISE is designed to provide adaptive guidance during modeling and to support the full workflow from issue detection to redesign.

4.2 System Workflow

The PRAISE framework follows a structured workflow that transforms a business process model into a privacy enhanced version. Table 2 summarizes the five steps with their inputs and outputs, where each step builds on the previous stage.

From a process perspective, PRAISE operates in a continuous detect–suggest–refine loop. In Steps 1–2, semantic analysis and retrieval-augmented reasoning classify each activity as fully, partially, or not covered, producing a symbolic coverage map. In Steps 2–3, identified gaps are linked to suitable PP, and recommendations are formulated with a description of the issue, a proposed solution, and legal justification. In Step 4, the modeler reviews and applies the recommendations; updated coverage scores reflect the changes and feedback can be recorded for future refinement.

4.3 Framework Components

PRAISE is conceived as an integrated system in which all components operate within a unified application. It combines privacy knowledge, AI based reasoning, compliance assessment, and process transformation for compliant design. The components described reflect the current conceptual stage and may evolve during implementation.

Privacy Knowledge. At the core of the framework is a structured multi-layer privacy knowledge base based on the DPPPM [19]. It organizes privacy knowledge across several layers, from legal rules and principles to design strategies, tactics, patterns, and example workflows. The repository includes GDPR provisions, privacy principles such as transparency and data minimization, eight design strategies, 24 privacy tactics, and more than 300 documented PP with detailed descriptions and template process models [17]. These elements combined form the privacy knowledge that links patterns to the principles and

Table 2. PRAISE process steps including privacy analysis and improvement actions.

Step	Input	Processing	Output
0. Model Acquisition	Formal process model (BPMN, Petri nets, or similar)	Model to text transformation into semantically enriched natural language representation	Natural language process description preserving tasks, roles, data objects, and flows
1. Relevance Identification	Textual process description	Semantic analysis and AI based classification of personal data indicators	Privacy relevance assessment and identification of critical elements
2. Compliance Assessment	Privacy relevant description and knowledge base	RAG comparison with regulations and principles, followed by PP selection and LLM based reasoning	Structured compliance gap analysis mapped to specific process elements
3. Improvement Recommendations	Compliance gaps and retrieved knowledge		Actionable privacy improvement recommendations with legal justification
4. Process Redesign	Original process model and (approved) recommendations	Transformation logic mapping recommendations to concrete Business Process Model modifications	Enhanced privacy-compliant process model

legal requirements they support. The knowledge base fulfills three functions: it anchors the AI retrieval module as an authoritative source, enables grounded justifications in generated responses, and provides templates for implementing improvements in process models. By integrating legal, organizational, and technical knowledge into one structure, it ensures consistent, context sensitive, and regulation aligned recommendations.

RAG Analysis Engine. PRAISE employs an RAG pipeline as its analysis engine. The architecture distinguishes a static knowledge layer containing GDPR articles, privacy principles, design strategies and tactics, and over 300 PP, from a dynamic context layer representing the current process under analysis. Process descriptions are segmented into semantically meaningful units representing individual data-processing activities, providing the situational context for regulatory assessment. This separation allows stable normative knowledge to be managed and updated independently from case-specific process context, supporting controlled updates and traceable assessments. Retrieval follows a deliberately hybrid strategy that combines sparse lexical search (e.g., BM25) for legal precision with dense semantic search for conceptual coverage. Each retriever returns its top-k = 3 documents; the two result sets are joined into a top-k = 6 candidate set, re-ranked, and integrated with the segmented process description into a structured prompt template. The augmented prompt is then passed to a transformer-based language model, which produces decision-oriented rationales that identify relevant GDPR obligations, evaluate alternative PP, discard incompatible options, and explain why specific recommendations are selected under contextual constraints such as purpose limitation or auditability. Reasoning is implemented as a stateful, session-based process in which intermediate results can be iteratively evaluated and refined across multiple retrieval–generation cycles. All retrieval and generation steps are logged at the session level using observability tooling (e.g., Langfuse), making reasoning paths inspectable and enabling structured documentation that links regulatory sources to specific recommendations. Within PRAISE, the language model thus operates as a governed reasoning component embedded in an organizational system, not as an autonomous compliance authority.

Orchestration and Control Logic. A central component of the framework is the orchestration layer that controls AI's operations. Instead of allowing LLM to act autonomously, PRAISE uses an external rule-based control logic to manage retrieval and generation processes. This orchestration defines the sequence of analysis steps and sets criteria for iteration and termination. Through predefined prompt templates and decision rules, the system ensures that the AI functions as a decision support tool focused on explainable recommendations rather than as an automated compliance authority. This preserves human oversight and accountability, which is essential given the legal implications of compliance decisions. The orchestration layer is designed to be configurable and extensible over time.

Process Model Interface. The framework also includes interfaces to standard process modeling tools and notations. On the input side, formal models such as BPMN or Petri nets are transformed into structured textual representations that preserve process semantics. This transformation enables compliance reasoning to be performed on natural language descriptions. On the output side, generated recommendations are translated into concrete model modifications. These may include inserting new tasks or adapting data handling elements, such as adding a consent confirmation step. The enhanced model is then exported in a standard format for review and further refinement. This bidirectional interface integrates PRAISE into the BPM lifecycle by supporting model analysis, redesign, and continuous improvement within existing modeling environments.

System Integration. All components are integrated within a unified application architecture. The knowledge base, analysis engine, orchestration layer, and model interface communicate through standardized internal services and shared data representations. This system level integration enables continuous interaction between analysis, recommendation, and implementation.

4.4 Future Work and Challenges

While the PRAISE framework introduces a novel approach to privacy-aware process design, it is currently conceptual and still requires implementation. Several technical and methodological challenges must be addressed before practical adoption:

Evaluation Roadmap. Given the deliberately conceptual scope of the present contribution, evaluation will proceed in three staged phases. Phase 1 (technical feasibility): implementation of a minimum viable prototype covering the five-step workflow on a curated set of BPMN reference processes, with quantitative measurement of retrieval precision/recall and pattern-matching accuracy against an annotated gold standard. Phase 2 (expert validation): structured interviews and think-aloud sessions with privacy engineers, data protection officers, and BPM modelers to assess the interpretability, legal soundness, and practical usefulness of generated recommendations. Phase 3 (in-context use): a controlled comparative study in which practitioners redesign privacy-relevant processes with and without PRAISE support, measuring time-to-compliance, recommendation acceptance rate, and residual gaps. This staged plan separates technical correctness from usability and downstream impact and is intended to produce evidence on each layer of the framework before scaling toward governed deployment.

Open Challenges. Four challenges shape future work: (1) Legal–technical alignment requires a complete, continuously updated knowledge base validated by legal experts, so that LLM outputs are both technically sound and legally defensible. This is particularly critical when extending PRAISE to adjacent regimes such as the EU AI Act [30], where overlapping yet distinct obligations must be represented without introducing inconsistencies in the retrieval layer. (2) AI reasoning and control call for refining the agentic orchestration: the current rule-based logic ensures safety but limits flexibility in novel situations, so future work must benchmark behavior, detect uncertainty, and trigger human intervention where appropriate. Adaptive retrieval with feedback loops and self-verification cycles offer promising directions for improving recommendation quality without compromising traceability. (3) User trust and usability depend on intuitive interfaces and explanations that show why a recommendation was made, which elements are affected, and how legal requirements are satisfied; these qualities must be assessed through empirical user studies with modelers and data protection officers. (4) Workflow integration requires that PRAISE complements existing BPM tools and human roles rather than complicating them, with clear guidelines on the distribution of responsibilities between modelers, DPOs, and the system, and with lightweight interfaces to established modeling environments to minimize adoption friction.

5 Demonstrative Walkthrough of a Process Scenario

5.1 Use Case Presentation

To demonstrate the framework on a scenario that exhibits multiple, simultaneously occurring privacy issues, we apply PRAISE to a mobile app registration process modeled in BPMN. In the original version, the user submits a registration form containing name, email address, and current location. The system stores this data in a backend customer database, then forwards the location data to external marketing partners and automatically subscribes the user to a promotional newsletter. The process contains no transparency step, no consent mechanism, no data minimization logic, and no rule governing data retention. While functionally complete, the process violates several core GDPR provisions: lack of transparency (Art. 5(1)(a)), absence of a lawful basis for the third-party transfer (Art. 6), missing opt-in for marketing communication (Art. 7), and no defined retention period (Art. 5(1)(e)). This combination of violations makes the scenario well-suited to demonstrate how PRAISE detects and addresses multiple, interrelated compliance gaps in a single pass.

5.2 PRAISE-Workflow Execution

Step 0 Model Acquisition. The BPMN model is translated into a semantically enriched textual description. The system identifies data-related activities (form submission, database storage, third-party transfer, newsletter subscription), data flows, and actor roles.

Step 1 Relevance Identification. Through semantic analysis, the system detects user identifiers (name, email), location data (potentially sensitive), and a third-party data transfer. The process is flagged as privacy-relevant under the GDPR, with explicit reference to Art. 4(1), 6(1)(a), and 7(2).

Step 2 Compliance Assessment. Retrieval-augmented reasoning compares the process description against core privacy principles and symbolically classifies each activity as fully, partially, or not covered. The form-submission activity is rated partially covered (data collected without a transparency notice), while location-sharing, newsletter-subscription, and storage activities are not covered. The resulting coverage map exposes four gaps that trigger the next step: (i) no consent for the location-data transfer (Art. 6), (ii) no newsletter opt-in (Art. 7), (iii) no transparency notice (Art. 5(1)(a)), and (iv) no retention rule (Art. 5(1)(e)), each anchored to the specific process element where it occurs.

Step 3 Improvement Recommendation. PRAISE retrieves matching patterns and proposes (a) a user-facing consent step before third-party data sharing, (b) a granular opt-in for marketing, (c) a notification task informing the user about purposes and legal basis, and (d) a retention rule with automated deletion after 30 days of inactivity. Each recommendation is grounded in documented PP (e.g., Consent Acquisition, Data Expiration, Appropriate Privacy Feedback [16]) and linked to the affected element of the original model.

Step 4 Process Redesign. The revised BPMN model contains two exclusive gateways after data collection (consent for location sharing; marketing opt-in). If the user consents, the corresponding branches execute; otherwise, they are bypassed. A timer event followed by a delete task enforces retention. A notification task immediately after form submission informs the user about processing purposes. The result satisfies all four identified obligations and demonstrates how PRAISE handles multiple, interacting privacy gaps in a coherent redesign. A second, verifying retrieval generation cycle re-classifies all four previously open activities as fully covered, closing the agentic loop.

6 Conclusions and Outlook

This work presents PRAISE as a deliberately architectural and conceptual contribution: a pattern-aware framework that integrates PP, LLM-based process interpretation, retrieval-augmented generation, and automated model transformation into a unified workflow for privacy-compliant business process design. Positioning the contribution at the architectural level rather than as a fully validated tool reflects the early stage of doctoral research and avoids premature claims about empirical performance, while still committing to a concrete and implementable design.

With respect to RQ1, the framework demonstrates how privacy patterns, retrieval-augmented reasoning, and traceable model transformation can be combined into a single, coherent workflow that supports analysis and improvement of existing process models. With respect to H1, PRAISE provides architectural conditions under which retrieval-augmented, pattern-aware reasoning can plausibly outperform manual or rule-based compliance approaches: structured legal grounding through the DPPPM, context-aware retrieval anchored to concrete process elements, and session-level traceability that preserves human oversight. Empirical confirmation of this hypothesis is reserved for the three-phase evaluation roadmap outlined in Sect. 4.4. Remaining challenges include the development of a functional prototype, ensuring legal accuracy of generated recommendations, avoiding false positives and negatives, and seamless integration into existing modeling environments. Since PRAISE focuses on the business process layer, it should be seen as a complementary tool rather than a comprehensive compliance solution. Future work will focus on prototype development, expert-based evaluation, and secure deployment strategies.

References

1. Regulation (EU) 2016/679 of the European Parliament and of the Council of 27 April 2016 on the protection of natural persons with regard to the processing of personal data and on the free movement of such data, and repealing Directive 95/46/EC (General Data Protection Regulation): Regulation (EU) 2016/679. (2016).
2. Varela-Vaca, Á.J., Gómez-López, M.T., Morales Zamora, Y., Gasca, R.M.: Business process models and simulation to enable GDPR compliance. Int. J. Inf. Secur. **24**, 41 (2025). https://doi.org/10.1007/s10207-024-00952-7
3. Biswas, T.R., Hossain, M.Z., Comite, U.: Role of management information systems in enhancing decision-making in large-scale organizations. Pac. J. Bus. Innov. Strategy. **1** (2024). https://doi.org/10.70818/pjbis.2024.v01i01.03
4. Acquisti, A., Brandimarte, L., Loewenstein, G.: Privacy and human behavior in the age of information. Science. **347**, 509–514 (2015). https://doi.org/10.1126/science.aaa1465
5. Mittelstadt, B.D., Allo, P., Taddeo, M., Wachter, S., Floridi, L.: The ethics of algorithms: mapping the debate. Big Data Soc. **3**, 2053951716679679 (2016). https://doi.org/10.1177/2053951716679679
6. Wong, R.Y., Chong, A., Aspegren, R.C.: Privacy legislation as business risks: how GDPR and CCPA are represented in technology companies' investment risk disclosures. Proc. ACM Hum. Comput. Interact. **7**, 1–26 (2023). https://doi.org/10.1145/3579515
7. Schade, F.: Dark sides of data transparency: organized immaturity after GDPR? Bus. Ethics Q. **33**, 473–501 (2023). https://doi.org/10.1017/beq.2022.30

8. Voigt, P., Von Dem Bussche, A.: The EU General Data Protection Regulation (GDPR). Springer International Publishing, Cham (2017). https://doi.org/10.1007/978-3-319-57959-7
9. Muller, D.A., Lévy, P.: A design approach towards affording the trend of privacy. In: Proceedings of the 2019 on Designing Interactive Systems Conference, pp. 435–446. ACM, San Diego CA USA (2019). https://doi.org/10.1145/3322276.3322324
10. Hoepman, J.-H.: Privacy design strategies. In: Cuppens-Boulahia, N., Cuppens, F., Jajodia, S., Abou El Kalam, A., Sans, T. (eds.) ICT Systems Security and Privacy Protection, pp. 446–459. Springer Berlin Heidelberg, Berlin, Heidelberg (2014). https://doi.org/10.1007/978-3-642-55415-5_38
11. Colesky, M., Hoepman, J.-H., Hillen, C.: A critical analysis of privacy design strategies. In: 2016 IEEE Security and Privacy Workshops (SPW), pp. 33–40. IEEE (2016). https://doi.org/10.1109/SPW.2016.23
12. Wuyts, K., Sion, L., Joosen, W.: LINDDUN GO: a lightweight approach to privacy threat modeling. In: 2020 IEEE European Symposium on Security and Privacy Workshops (EuroS&PW), pp. 302–309. IEEE (2020). https://doi.org/10.1109/EuroSPW51379.2020.00047
13. Barletta, V., Desolda, G., Gigante, D., Lanzilotti, R., Saltarella, M.: From GDPR to privacy design patterns: the MATERIALIST framework. In: Proceedings of the 19th International Conference on Security and Cryptography, pp. 642–648. SCITEPRESS-Science and Technology Publications, Lisbon, Portugal (2022). https://doi.org/10.5220/001130590 0003283
14. Romanosky, S., Acquisti, A., Hong, J., Cranor, L.F., Friedman, B.: Privacy patterns for online interactions. In: Proceedings of the 2006 Conference on Pattern Languages of Programs PLoP'06, pp. 1–15. ACM Press, Portland, Oregon (2006). https://doi.org/10.1145/1415472.1415486
15. Hafiz, M.: A collection of privacy design patterns. In: Yoder, J., Johnson, R. (eds.) Proceedings of the 2006 Conference on Pattern Languages of Programs, pp. 1–13. ACM, New York, NY, USA (2006). https://doi.org/10.1145/1415472.1415481
16. Colesky, M., et al.: Patterns. https://privacypatterns.org/patterns/.
17. Waidelich, L., Schuster, T.: Privacy patterns analysis: a classification by types, strategies and tactics of existing patterns. In: AMCIS 2024 Proc. (2024)
18. Waidelich, L., Schuster, T.: Privacy pattern catalog approach for GDPR compliant appliance: from legal requirements to technology design. In: Maślankowski, J., Marcinkowski, B., Da Rupino Cunha, P. (eds.) Digital Transformation, pp. 88–102. Springer Nature Switzerland, Cham (2023). https://doi.org/10.1007/978-3-031-43590-4_6
19. Waidelich, L., Schuster, T.: A pattern-based approach to data privacy in business processes. In: Camarinha-Matos, L.M., Ferrada, F. (eds.) Technological Innovation for AI-Powered Cyber-Physical Systems, pp. 51–62. Springer Nature Switzerland, Cham (2025). https://doi.org/10.1007/978-3-031-97051-1_4
20. Agostinelli, S., De Luzi, F., Maggi, F.M., Marrella, A., Volpi, A.: Design patterns for GDPR-aware process modeling in BPMN. Inf. Syst. **137**, 102646 (2026). https://doi.org/10.1016/j.is.2025.102646
21. Barati, M., Rana, O.: Design and verification of privacy patterns for business process models. In: Patnaik, S., Wang, T.-S., Shen, T., Panigrahi, S.K. (eds.) Blockchain Technology and Innovations in Business Processes, pp. 125–139. Springer Singapore, Singapore (2021). https://doi.org/10.1007/978-981-33-6470-7_8
22. Bernardi, M.L., Casciani, A., Cimitile, M., Marrella, A.: Conversing with business process-aware large language models: the BPLLM framework. J. Intell. Inf. Syst. **62**, 1607–1629 (2024). https://doi.org/10.1007/s10844-024-00898-1
23. Forell, M., Schüler, S.: Modeling meets large language models (2024). https://doi.org/10.5445/IR/1000177047

24. Kourani, H., Berti, A., Schuster, D., Van Der Aalst, W.M.P.: Evaluating large language models on business process modeling: framework, benchmark, and self-improvement analysis. Softw. Syst. Model. (2025). https://doi.org/10.1007/s10270-025-01318-w
25. Kourani, H., Berti, A., Schuster, D., Van Der Aalst, W.M.P.: Process modeling with large language models. In: Van Der Aa, H., Bork, D., Schmidt, R., Sturm, A. (eds.) Enterprise, Business-Process and Information Systems Modeling, pp. 229–244. Springer Nature Switzerland, Cham (2024). https://doi.org/10.1007/978-3-031-61007-3_18
26. Buss, A., Kratsch, W., Schmid, S.J., Wang, H.: ProcessLLM: a large language model specialized in the interpretation, analysis, and optimization of business processes. In: Gdowska, K., Gómez-López, M.T., Rehse, J.-R. (eds.) Business Process Management Workshops, pp. 221–232. Springer Nature Switzerland, Cham (2025). https://doi.org/10.1007/978-3-031-78666-2_17
27. Schlösser, T., Forell, M., Schüler, S., Fritsch, A.: Human-AI collaboration for business process modeling with petri nets. In: Guizzardi, R., Pufahl, L., Sturm, A., Van Der Aa, H. (eds.) Enterprise, Business-Process and Information Systems Modeling, pp. 55–70. Springer Nature Switzerland, Cham (2025). https://doi.org/10.1007/978-3-031-95397-2_4
28. Belluccini, S., De Nicola, R., Dumas, M., Pullonen-Raudvere, P., Re, B., Tiezzi, F.: Model-based verification of data protection mechanisms in collaborative business processes. Softw. Syst. Model. **24**, 489–521 (2025). https://doi.org/10.1007/s10270-024-01217-6
29. Awad, A., Decker, G., Weske, M.: Efficient compliance checking using BPMN-Q and temporal logic. In: Dumas, M., Reichert, M., Shan, M.-C. (eds.) Business Process Management, pp. 326–341. Springer Berlin Heidelberg, Berlin, Heidelberg (2008). https://doi.org/10.1007/978-3-540-85758-7_24
30. Schuster, T., Waidelich, L., Schneider, A., Lambert, M.: Risk classification and compliance of AI systems under the EU AI act. In: AMCIS 2025 Proceedings, p. 10, Montréal (2025)

Computational Intelligence and Machine Learning Methods

Comparative Survival Analysis Using Machine Learning Models With and Without Topological Data Analysis

Mavambu Diankatu[1(✉)], Jorge Duque[2,3], José Braga de Vasconcelos[4], and Vítor Filipe[1,5]

[1] University of Trás-os-Montes and Alto Douro, Vila Real, Portugal
al2025139140@alunos.utad.pt, vfilipe@utad.pt
[2] ISLA, Gaia, Portugal
jorge.duque@islagaia.pt
[3] TECH HUB, CEOS.PP, Porto, Portugal
[4] University Lusófona, Porto, Portugal
jose.vasconcelos@ulusofona.pt
[5] INESC INOV Lab, Lisbon, Portugal

Abstract. In this study, we compared different survival models using machine learning (ML) techniques to assess the impact of enriching survival models with features extracted from topological data analysis (TDA). Using a clinical dataset on lung transplantation, we compared the Cox model, random survival forests (RSF), and the DeepSurv deep neural network, along with their TDA-enriched versions. TDA uses persistent homology and generates descriptors that capture the global and multiscale structures present in the data that do not appear in Euclidean spaces. The results show that integrating these descriptors improves predictive performance, increasing the C-index and enhancing risk discrimination. Thus, the integration of TDA and ML emerges as a promising alternative for modeling survival in complex biomedical data.

Keywords: Survival Analysis · Topological Data Analysis · Machine Learning · Persistent Homology · Random Survival Forests · DeepSurv · Cox Models

1 Introduction

Survival analysis plays an important role in biomedical research, particularly in oncology and the study of chronic diseases, as it seeks to estimate the time until the occurrence of a relevant event, such as death, recurrence, or disease progression. Unlike classical regression or classification tasks, survival data are characterized by the presence of right-censored data and the need to model how covariates influence risk over time. Therefore, survival analysis must model how covariates change risk over time. The challenges are even greater in today's clinical studies, because clinical studies often combine clinical, molecular, and imaging data in high-dimensional settings. These challenges require that predictive models be robust, interpretable, and well-fitted.

Published by Springer Nature Switzerland AG 2027
L. M. Camarinha-Matos and F. Ferrada (Eds.): DoCEIS 2026, IFIP AICT 790, pp. 57–70, 2027.
https://doi.org/10.1007/978-3-032-28939-1_5

The rise of machine learning (ML) models for survival offers a natural path to address nonlinearities and interactions, overcoming some of the limitations of classical models such as the Cox model. Nevertheless, even advanced ML models typically operate in Euclidean feature spaces, treating each individual as an independent point and potentially neglecting global properties of the dataset, such as intrinsic geometric structures and multiscale patterns.

In this context, Topological Data Analysis (TDA) emerges as a powerful mathematical tool for extracting robust structural descriptors from complex, high-dimensional data [1, 2]. TDA uses algebraic topology to characterize the shape of data through topological invariants, such as connected components, cycles, and cavities. In particular, persistent homology provides a stable summary of these structures across multiple scales, typically represented by persistence diagrams and visualizations such as persistence landscapes and persistence images [3, 4]. Evidence accumulated in biomedical fields such as genomics, medical imaging, and systems biology suggests that such descriptors can reveal latent patterns and contribute to robustness and interpretability in predictive tasks [5, 6].

Given this, a question arises: does the integration of topological descriptors into predictive survival models improve their performance? This question motivates the present work, which systematically investigates the value that TDA brings to survival pipelines.

In this article, we conducted a comparative analysis of survival models with and without enrichment using topological descriptors extracted via TDA, using a clinical dataset from lung transplantation. This scenario is particularly relevant due to the pathophysiological complexity of the post-transplant period and the multidimensional nature of the factors affecting the outcome. We evaluated the performance. First, we measured discrimination using the C-index. Next, we measured calibration using the Integrated Brier Score (IBS).

2 Contributions

The contributions of this work are:

- Systematic comparative evaluation: We conducted a structured comparison of various classes of survival models, such as the Cox model, RSF and DeepSurv, under controlled conditions, with and without TDA, to isolate the effect of topological enrichment.
- Empirical evidence of the added value of TDA: we empirically demonstrated how topological descriptors influence the C-index discrimination metric and the IBS calibration metric in the context of lung transplantation.

3 Contribution to Societal Challenges

The topic of my doctoral thesis in computer science is designing cryptographic protocols for privacy in Federated Learning (FL) using TDA analysis as a mechanism for representing data. The goal is to enable multiple institutions, such as hospitals, to train collaborative models without sharing raw data. Thus, the cryptographic protocols provide formal privacy guarantees while preserving the utility of the predictions and the clinical validity of the results. The article focuses on survival, but it serves as a case study that is directly aligned with the thesis, because the comparative analysis of survival shows where and how TDA adds value to complex biomedical data. This is precisely the scenario in which FL and cryptographic protection become necessary.

This framework connects naturally to the conference theme by addressing current requirements in digital health and AI. In my view, in real clinical environments data are sensitive and fragmented across institutions. This fragmentation limits cohort sizes, reduces diversity, and makes reproducibility difficult. FL addresses this fragmentation by enabling distributed training. encryption reduces the risk of exposure, as it prevents individual contributions from being revealed during aggregation. TDA complements what FL and encryption do by offering structural descriptors (global and multiscalar) that are typically more robust to noise and local variations. TDA becomes critical when different centers have distinct populations, practices, and data distributions.

In the survival article, we conducted a controlled test to determine whether topological descriptors derived from persistent homology improve predictive models in the clinically important setting of lung transplantation. We evaluated gains in C-index discrimination and the IBS calibration metric. This evidence supports the thesis:

- it validates TDA as a representation layer and may reduce reliance on manual feature engineering;
- it helps identify which model classes benefit most from topological enrichment, guiding architectural choices when defining the model structure under federated training;
- it suggests that topological vectors can be used as more compact sharing or training objects, facilitating the application of privacy strategies such as Secure Aggregation, multi-party computation (MPC), or homomorphic encryption (HE).

In the thesis, privacy in FL goes beyond "not sending raw data": gradient updates and parameter updates can leak information through inversion or membership inference attacks. Therefore, privacy in FL requires cryptographic protocols such as Secure Aggregation and MPC/HE, and complementary mechanisms, such as differential privacy. TDA offers a methodological opportunity: each center can locally compute topological descriptors and participate in federated training with representations that capture the relevant global structure. In this way, the attack surface is reduced, and cryptographic protection becomes more computationally feasible.

4 Related Work

Survival analysis is widely studied in the biomedical literature. Survival analysis ranges from classical statistical models to recent machine learning and deep learning techniques. Among semiparametric models, the Cox proportional hazards model stands out. The Cox proportional hazards model allows for efficient risk modeling and offers high clinical interpretability [7]. The proportional hazards assumption and the linear structure of the predictor are used in many models, but the proportional hazards assumption and the linear structure of the predictor can prevent the model from capturing nonlinear effects, complex interactions, and time-dependent relationships that arise in real biomedical data.

The model, therefore, loses some important information. For this reason, extensions and alternatives have been proposed to increase flexibility while maintaining, whenever possible, statistical rigor and clinical utility.

In machine learning for survival prediction, the RSFs introduced by Ishwaran et al. [8] stand out for their ability to naturally model nonlinearities and interactions without imposing rigid parametric rules. Beyond their original formulation, clinical applications demonstrate the practical utility of RSFs in predictive tasks. In lung transplantation, the RSF model that predicts overall survival after transplantation demonstrates better performance and clearer risk classification compared to the Cox model [9]. Hybrid approaches also use RSFs as a variable selection step before applying Cox-type models, and these hybrid approaches explicitly evaluate discrimination and calibration in large-scale cohorts [10]. Furthermore, in heart transplantation, recent comparative analyses of machine learning-based survival methods show that RSFs perform competitively in predicting post-transplant mortality, reinforcing the role of hybrid approaches in complex clinical settings [11].

With the advance of deep learning, neural network models designed for survival analysis have emerged. DeepSurv, proposed by Katzman et al. [12], is one of the first successful cases of using deep neural networks within the Cox model framework. It allows DeepSurv to learn nonlinear relationships among covariates and can improve risk stratification. Since then, other variants of neural models with stronger architectures have appeared, including models that handle longitudinal and multimodal data. However, these approaches still receive substantial criticism related to interpretability, the need for larger data volumes to avoid overfitting, and sensitivity to architecture and regularization choices.

In parallel, TDA has become really important for extracting strong structural information from complex, high-dimensional data. Some key research has shown how TDA works, and it's clear that topological invariants can capture global properties of data that are difficult to represent with local statistics or Euclidean geometries [1, 2]. In particular, persistent homology has become one of the most widely used instruments, as it summarizes structures such as connected components and cycles across multiple scales. To make these summaries usable in standard ML models, vector representations have been proposed, such as persistence landscapes and persistence images [3, 4].

In biomedicine, TDA has been used on genomic data, transcriptomic data, and imaging data, as well as in classification and regression tasks. TDA often produces promising results in terms of robustness and generalization [5, 6]. Despite this progress, the use of TDA in survival prediction problems is still not well established. A relevant part of the work focuses on exploratory analyses that use persistence diagrams to identify structural patterns, but these exploratory analyses do not connect directly to a predictive survival pipeline nor do they systematically compare TDA with established approaches. In addition, there are few studies that measure the impact of topological integration using standard survival metrics such as the C-index and IBS.

More recently, hybrid approaches combining machine learning and TDA have emerged. These approaches typically include topological descriptors as new features [3, 4]. The works show that ML and TDA can bring gains in robustness and stability. However, results still depend on the dataset, the experimental protocol, and the class of model used. Moreover, these works still lack extensive validation in realistic clinical scenarios. In particular, we observe that there is a lack of a coherent set of comparative studies conducted under the same experimental setting, evaluating multiple survival models with and without topological integration.

Therefore, we propose to conduct a rigorous comparison between classical and modern approaches with and without enrichment by topological descriptors, contributing to clarify the role of computational topology in predictive modeling in medicine.

5 Materials and Methods

5.1 Presentation of the Dataset

In this section, we present a complete overview of the dataset used in this research project entitled Comparative Survival Analysis using Machine Learning models considering with and without the enrichment of Topological Data Analysis. Our dataset comprises information on 252 patients who underwent lung transplantation at Bichat-Claude Bernard Hospital in Paris, including 189 survivors and 63 non-survivors. It can be observed that the distribution of outcomes, particularly the classification between survivors and non-survivors, is imbalanced: approximately 75% of cases are classified as survivors and the remaining 25% as non-survivors, as illustrated in the figure below (Fig. 1).

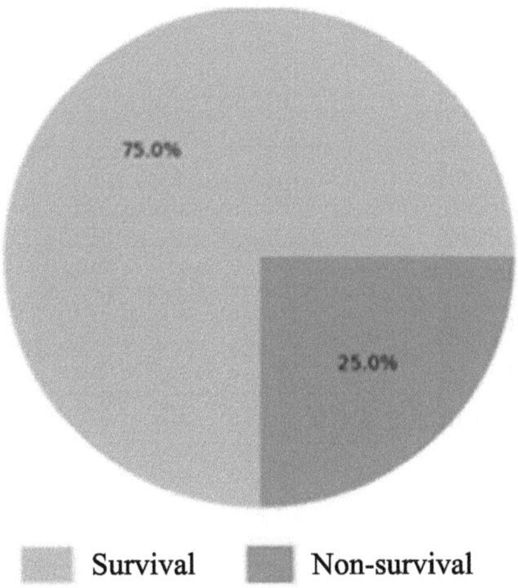

Fig. 1. Distribution of mortality rate in 1 year.

The different variables in the dataset are (Table 1):

Table 1. Dataset Variables.

N°	Column	Type
0	NIP(ID)	int64
1	date_de_TP	datetime64
2	Age	int64
3	Age > =60	int64
4	Sexe(0 = F,1 = M)	int64
5	BMI(body_mass_index)	float64
6	BMI < =18	int64
7	BMI > 30	int64
8	BMI > 25	int64
9	cardiopathie_ischémique	int64
10	diabètepré-opératoire	int64
11	PAPM	float64
12	PAPM>20	int64
13	étiologie_BPCO	int64
14	étiologie_Fibrose	int64
15	Autres_étiologies	float64
16	Mismatch_CMV(R-/D+)	float64
17	ECMO_pré-opératoire	int64
18	Super_Urgence	float64
19	type_de_TP	int64
20	Ischémie_Froide_Max	float64
21	Ischémie_Froide_Max>6 h	int64
22	Analgésie_péridurale	float64
23	ECMO_peropératoire	int64
24	Transfusion_per_opératoire>2_CGR	float64
25	SOFA_J0	int64
26	SOFA> = 7	int64
27	IGS2_J0	int64
28	IGS2 > =43	int64
29	Nb_Jours_Noradrénaline	float64
30	Nb_Jours_Noradrénaline> = 2	int64
31	Nb_Jours_Ventilation_mécanique	int64
32	Nb_Jours_Ventilation_mécanique> = 3	int64

(*continued*)

Table 1. (*continued*)

N°	Column	Type
33	ECMO_en_Réanimation	int64
34	Nb_jours_d_ECMO_en_réanimation	int64
35	Nb_jours_d_ECMO_en_réanimation> = 1	int64
36	Dysfonction_primaire_du_greffon_grade_3	int64
37	insuffisance_rénale_aiguë	int64
38	dialyse_en_réanimation	int64
39	bactériémie	int64
40	Pneumonie(tous_germes)	float64
41	Pneumonie_à_BLSE_et/ou_Pyo_en_réanimation	int64
42	Pneumonie_acquise_sous_ventilation_mécanique_à_BLSE_et/ou_Pyo	int64
43	Trachéotomie	int64
44	Sténose_bronchique_grave_dans_1_année	int64
45	Fistule_bronchique_dans_1_année	int64
46	rejet_humoral_dans_1_année	int64
47	rejet_cellulaire_dans_1_année	float64
48	pleurésie<1an	float64
49	durée_de_séjour_en_réanimation(1er_séjour)	int64
50	durée_de_séjour_en_réanimation> = 15 days	int64
51	mortalité_dans_le_premier_séjour_réanimation	int64
52	mortalité_à_un_an	int64
53	mortalité_à_90j	int64
54	mortalité_à_J30	int64

5.2 Treatment of Missing Data and Normalization

After analyzing the multicenter lung transplant dataset, we identified non-numeric variables that are not predictive, such as NIP(ID) and the transplant date (date_de_TP). We removed these variables to avoid information leakage and to focus solely on variables that are clinically relevant for prediction. As a result, we obtained a final dataset with 52 features that we used in the modeling. We identified missing values in the following variables: PAPM has 23 missing values, maximum cold ischemia (Ischémie_Froide_Max) has 9 missing values, and the number of days on norepinephrine (Nb_Jours_Noradrénaline) has 6 missing values. To handle the missing values, we used median imputation. We chose the median because it handles skewness and extreme values found in clinical variables well. The median also preserves the sample size, avoiding losses in statistical power in this moderately sized cohort. This is how we handled the data. As part of the sensitivity analysis, we assessed the impact of the imputation method by repeating the pipeline with a simple alternative, mean imputation, to verify whether the conclusions regarding the effect of TDA enrichment remained stable across the primary metrics (C-index and IBS).

We applied a standardization step to the continuous variables using the Standard-Scaler from the scikit-learn library, and transformed the continuous variables so that they have a mean of $\mu = 0$ and a standard deviation of $\sigma = 1$. The values are now standardized. As we did in the imputation, we estimated the standardization parameters on the training set and applied these parameters to the test set. We defined the survival variables as pairs (Ti, δi), where Ti represents the time elapsed until the event occurs or until censoring. δi, which can be 0 or 1, indicates whether the event actually occurred. The event we wish to observe is mortality at one year. Finally, to assess the generalization ability of the models (with and without TDA), the dataset was split into 80% for training and 20% for testing, keeping the test set completely separate from all fitting steps. Whenever possible, the split was performed in a stratified manner by event. The final dataset, properly cleaned, imputed, and standardized, is thus prepared for the modeling and topological descriptor extraction.

5.3 Kaplan Meier Curve

The Kaplan Meier survival curve provides an estimate of the probability of survival over time without requiring a parametric model. The Kaplan-Meier survival curve includes right-censored cases, such as patients who were lost to follow-up or who were still alive when the study ended. This characterization describes the temporal dynamics of survival in the studied cohort. It establishes a baseline for comparing the Cox model, the RSF, DeepSurv, and variants that include TDA descriptors (Fig. 2).

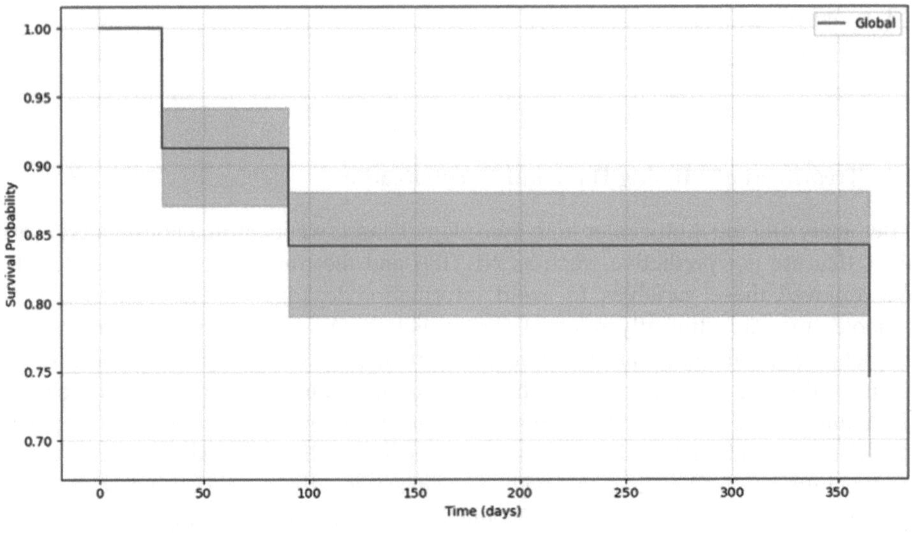

Fig. 2. Survival Curve Lung Transplant.

It can be observed that the probability of survival starts at 1 at time zero and decreases over time, showing that deaths accumulate. In the first few months after lung transplantation, the decline is much steeper, indicating that the risk is higher right at the beginning. This pattern seems natural in clinical practice, as it may be linked to complications immediately after surgery and graft failure.

5.4 Classical and Machine Learning Based Survival Models

To establish a basis for comparison, we evaluated three models representing different types of survival analysis: (i) the Cox proportional hazards model, (ii) RSF, and (iii) DeepSurv. The Cox model is a widely used semiparametric method that models risk as an exponential effect of covariates and serves as an easy-to-interpret benchmark. RSF is an ensemble method that uses trees; it performs well with censored data and can capture nonlinearities and interactions without imposing restrictive parametric assumptions. Finally, DeepSurv extends the Cox model by replacing the linear predictor with a deep neural network, which learns via partial likelihood optimization, allowing for greater flexibility in complex scenarios.

5.5 Persistent Homology

In this work, we use persistent homology to extract topological descriptors that complement clinical variables and investigate their impact on survival prediction. Given a set of points:

$$\{x_i\}_{i=1}^{n} \subset \mathbb{R}^p, \tag{1}$$

We construct a filtration of simplicial complexes

$$\{K_\varepsilon\}_{\varepsilon \geq 0}, \text{ where } \varepsilon \text{ controls connectivity.} \tag{2}$$

Persistent homology tracks the birth and death of structures throughout the filtration and summarizes them in a persistence diagram D = {(b,d)} [1]. We consider only H0 and H1, associated with the evolution of connected components, for greater robustness and interpretability in moderate-sized biomedical samples. Figure 3 presents the persistence diagram comparing topological features across outcome groups.

The x-axis represents the birth time of topological features (connected components H_0 and cycles H_1), while the y-axis represents their death time. The distance from the diagonal (y = x) measures feature persistence: points farther from the diagonal correspond to longer-lived, and thus more robust, topological structures.

Overall, the censored long-term group (survival ≥365 days) exhibits a larger proportion of points with greater distance from the diagonal than the early event group (event at 30 days). This suggests that patients with prolonged survival tend to present more persistent topological features, consistent with a more stable global data geometry. Conversely, the early event group concentrates closer to the diagonal, indicating shorter-lived features and a less persistent underlying topology.

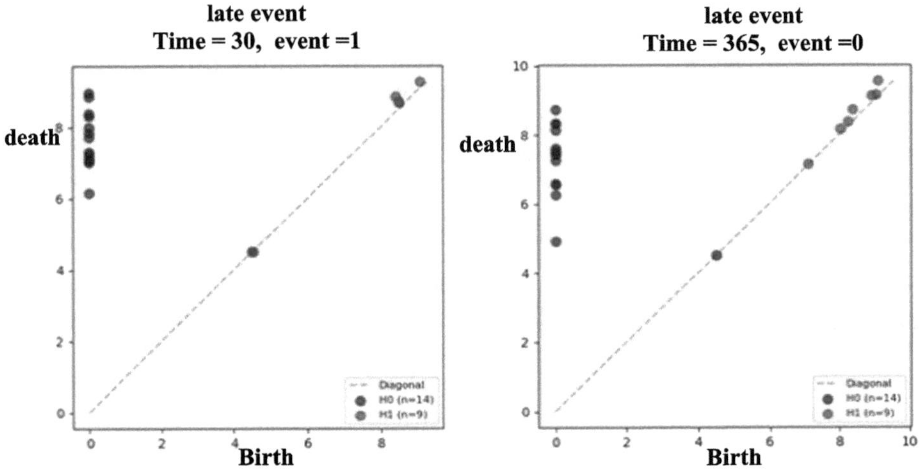

Fig. 3. Persistence diagrams by outcome.

To quantify topological differences between diagrams, we use bottleneck and Wasserstein distances, defined via optimal pairings between points in the diagrams and the diagonal. These metrics provide a measure of topological similarity and support stability results, which are fundamental for handling noise in real data [13]. The extracted information is then incorporated into the predictive pipeline via vectorization using persistence images and landscapes [4].

5.6 Enriched Models with TDA

The topological features obtained were combined with the original covariates, thereby creating an expanded feature space. The same survival models that had been applied in the baseline analysis (Cox, RSF, and DeepSurv) were retrained in this new space, ensuring a fair comparison between the approaches with and without TDA. The original covariates x_i were concatenated with the topological descriptors z_i, forming an enriched vector:

$$\widetilde{x_i} = \left[x_i \middle\| z_i\right] \in \mathbb{R}^{p+q}. \tag{3}$$

This vector was used as input for the Cox + TDA, RSF + TDA, and TopoSurvNet models. TopoSurvNet (DeepSurv + TDA) is a hybrid neural network for survival analysis, whose input consists of the enriched features (x_i), and the model learns nonlinear representations that combine clinical information with topological descriptors obtained via persistent homology. The hazard function has the same formulation as DeepSurv, and training is performed by maximizing the partial likelihood of the Cox model. Figure 4 shows the general architecture of TopoSurvNet.

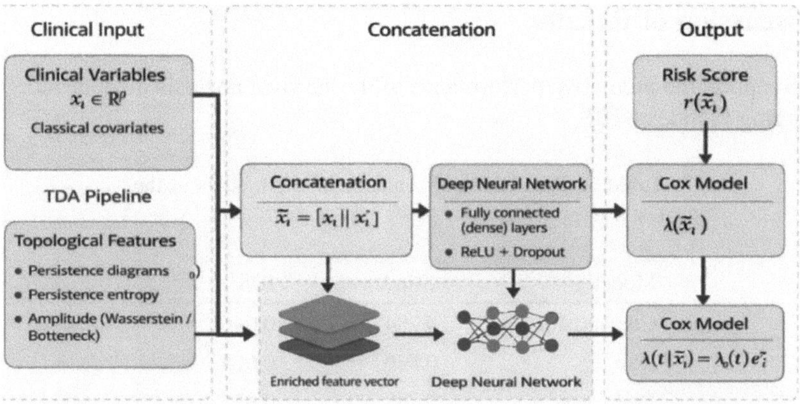

Fig. 4. TopoSurvNet Architecture.

Table 2 details the architecture of the DeepSurv and TopoSurvNet neural networks, including layer type, output shape, and number of parameters (Param).

Table 2. Neural Network Architecture.

Layer (Type)	Output Shape	Param
BatchNorm1d (128)	(batch_size, 128)	256
ReLU	(batch_size, 128)	0
Dropout (p = 0.3)	(batch_size, 128)	0
Linear (128 → 64)	(batch_size, 64)	8256
BatchNorm1d (64)	(batch_size, 64)	128
ReLU	(batch_size, 64)	0
Dropout (p = 0.3)	(batch_size, 64)	0
Linear (64 → 1)	(batch_size, 1)	65

5.7 Experimental Evaluation

We conducted the experiments in Python using the *scikit-learn, lifelines, giotto-tda,* and *PyTorch* libraries. We evaluated the model's performance on the test set using two complementary metrics: the C-index and the IBS. The C-index measures the model's ability to discriminate; that is, it shows whether the model can correctly rank pairs of individuals according to relative risk. The C-index is a standard metric in censored survival analysis. The IBS calculates the mean squared error of survival probabilities over time, including censoring. The IBS evaluates both probabilistic quality and calibration. In interpretive terms, lower IBS values indicate that the model performs better. Thus, the C-index and the IBS provide a more complete assessment. The C-index focuses on discrimination. The IBS captures the overall error and the calibration of the predictions.

6 Discussion of Results

Table 3 reports the predictive performance of the survival analysis models under study, considering C-index e IBS.

Table 3. Predictive performance of the models in the test set.

Model	C-index	IBS
Cox classique	0.784	0.0461
RSF	0.846	0.0652
DeepSurv	0.7023	0.0552
Cox + TDA	0.812	0.0374
RSF + TDA	0.851	0.0626
TopoSurvNet	0.9565	0.0346

Figure 5 illustrates the direct impact of incorporating topological descriptors on the C-index of the base models.

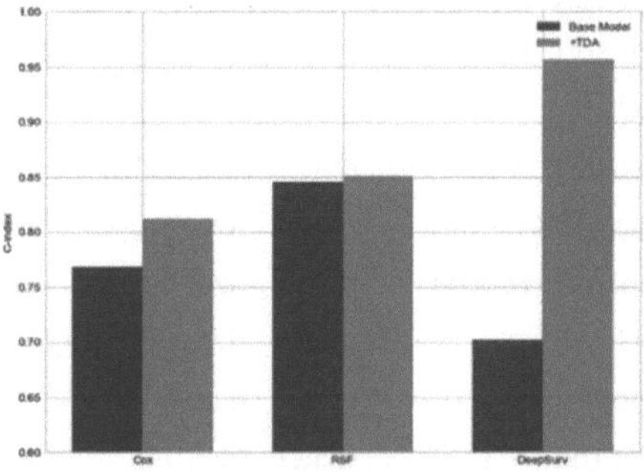

Fig. 5. Impact of incorporating topological features on the C-index of the base models.

It can be observed that TDA augmentation consistently improves performance, and the impact is even greater when TDA is combined with deep learning. In the Cox model, the inclusion of topological descriptors raised the C-index from 0.784 to 0.812 and reduced the IBS from 0.0461 to 0.0374; the increase in the C-index and the reduction in the IBS demonstrate simultaneous gains in discrimination and calibration or probabilistic error. This result is consistent with the idea that topological descriptors capture global, nonlinear patterns that compensate for limitations of the Cox linear predictor. For the RSF, the gains were moderate. The C-index rose slightly, from 0.846 to 0.851, and the IBS fell, from 0.0652 to 0.0626. This result is expected, because RSF already incorporates nonlinearities and interactions in the trees, and RSF has little room for improvement with new features. The strongest result appears when we compare DeepSurv with TopoSurvNet. The C-index rises from 0.7023 to 0.9565, an increase of 0.2542, and the IBS falls from 0.0552 to 0.0346, a decrease of 0.0206. This shows that discrimination and the quality of the probabilities have improved significantly. This leap suggests that, in this cohort, topological descriptors provide highly informative additional signals to the network, stabilizing learning and allowing it to capture latent structures relevant to prognosis that are not easily learned from the original covariates.

The relationship between discriminatory power and probabilistic calibration is shown in Fig. 6.

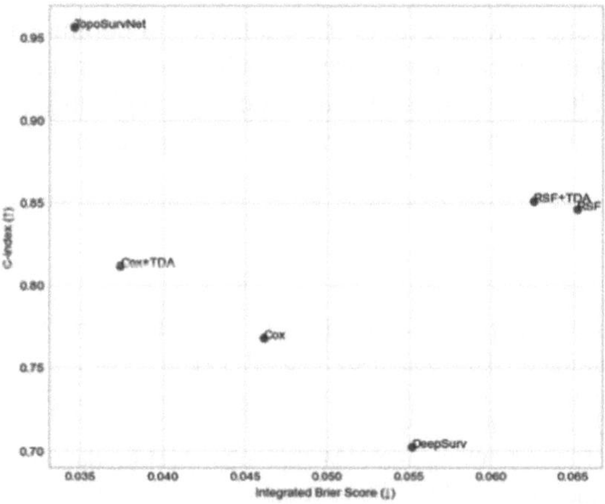

Fig. 6. Relationship between discrimination C-index and calibration IBS.

The graph clearly shows that the TopoSurvNet model is positioned in the upper left corner, with the highest C-index value 0.9565 and the lowest IBS 0.0346 (Fig. 7).

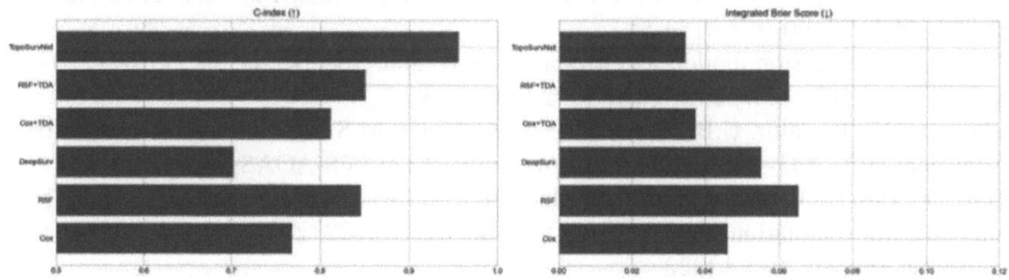

Fig. 7. Shows a joint comparison of the two metrics.

The model proposed here, TopoSurvNet, showed superior performance in all metrics considered, with a C-index equal to 0.9565 and IBS equal to 0.0346, presenting excellent discrimination and calibration simultaneously.

7 Conclusion

In this article, we compared survival models based on classical statistical methods and machine learning methods, with and without the enrichment provided by Topological Data Analysis. The results show unequivocally that the inclusion of topological descriptors significantly improves the predictive performance of the models in question. In particular, the Cox + TDA, RSF + TDA, and TopoSurvNet models were clearly superior to the versions without TDA, achieving the highest C-index values, which suggests a better ability to discriminate survival risk. These results reinforce the potential of TDA as a complementary and powerful tool for the analysis of complex biomedical data.

We conclude that the interaction between machine learning and topological analysis represents a viable alternative for survival modeling, combining performance, robustness, and, in some cases, interpretability, with great potential for application in real clinical scenarios.

References

1. Ghrist, R.: Barcodes: the persistent topology of data. Bull. Am. Math. Soc. **45**(1), 61–75 (2008). https://doi.org/10.1090/S0273-0979-07-01191-3
2. Carlsson, G.: Topology and data. Bull. Am. Math. Soc. **46**(2), 255–308 (2009). https://doi.org/10.1090/S0273-0979-09-01249-X
3. Edelsbrunner, H., Harer, J.: Computational Topology: An Introduction. American Mathematical Society, Providence, RI (2010). https://doi.org/10.1090/mbk/069
4. Bubenik, P.: Statistical topological data analysis using persistence landscapes. J. Mach. Learn. Res. **16**(1), 77–102 (2015). https://jmlr.org/papers/v16/bubenik15a.html
5. Singh, G., Mémoli, F., Carlsson, G.: Topological methods for the analysis of high dimensional data sets and 3D object recognition. In: Eurographics Symposium on Point-Based Graphics, pp. 91–100 (2007). https://doi.org/10.2312/SPBG/SPBG07/091-100
6. Gameiro, M., Hiraoka, Y., Izumi, S., Kramar, M., Mischaikow, K., Nanda, V.: A topological measurement of protein compressibility. Jpn. J. Ind. Appl. Math. **32**, 1–17 (2015). https://doi.org/10.1007/s13160-014-0153-5
7. Cox, D.R.: Regression models and life-tables. J. R. Stat. Soc. Ser. B. **34**(2), 187–220 (1972). https://doi.org/10.1111/j.2517-6161.1972.tb00899.x
8. Ishwaran, H., Kogalur, U.B., Blackstone, E.H., Lauer, M.S.: Random survival forests. Ann. Appl. Stat. **2**(3), 841–860 (2008). https://doi.org/10.1214/08-AOAS169
9. Tian, D., Yan, H.-J., Huang, H., et al.: Machine learning-based prognostic model for patients after lung transplantation. JAMA Netw. Open. **6**(5), e2312022 (2023). https://doi.org/10.1001/jamanetworkopen.2023.12022
10. Sharma, G., et al.: Development and validation of a hybrid machine learning model to predict lung transplant outcomes. JAMA Netw. Open. **8**(3), e2545369 (2025). https://doi.org/10.1001/jamanetworkopen.2025.45369
11. Liou, L., Moskowitz, E.M., Englesbe, L.L., Sonnenday, S., et al.: Survival machine learning methods for mortality prediction after heart transplantation in the contemporary era. PLoS One. **20**(1), e0313600 (2025). https://doi.org/10.1371/journal.pone.0313600
12. Katzman, J.L., Shaham, U., Cloninger, A., Bates, J., Jiang, T., Kluger, Y.: DeepSurv: personalized treatment recommender system using a Cox proportional hazards deep neural network. BMC Med. Res. Methodol. **18**, 24 (2018). https://doi.org/10.1186/s12874-018-0482-1
13. Cohen-Steiner, D., Edelsbrunner, H., Harer, J.: Stability of persistence diagrams. Discrete Comput. Geom. **37**(1), 103–120 (2007). https://doi.org/10.1007/s00454-006-1276-5

Machine Learning on Small Datasets Under Resource Constrained: A Scoping Review

Renato Leite[1(✉)] and Rui Esteves Araújo[2]

[1] Faculty of Engineering, University of Porto, Porto, Portugal
up202501689@edu.fe.up.pt
[2] INESC TEC and Faculty of Engineering, University of Porto, Rua Dr. Roberto Frias, Porto 4200-465, Portugal
raraujo@fe.up.pt

Abstract. Artificial Intelligence AI is increasingly present in daily life, driven mainly by applications based on Large Language Models LLMs, trained on massive volumes of data. Although successful, this new generation of solutions has evidenced limitations related to applications in which data are limited and computational capacities are constrained. This scenario is more critical particularly in embedded systems and industrial application contexts. This work presents a scoping review, conducted according to the Preferred Reporting Items for Systematic Reviews and Meta-Analyses Extension for Scoping Reviews (PRISMA-ScR), with the objective of mapping the state of the art of strategies, techniques, and architectures of machine learning, deep learning, and reinforcement learning applied to scenarios with small datasets and limited resources. The findings show hybrid approaches, data-oriented strategies, and the centrality of computational efficiency, indicating an emergence of reinforcement learning for research on structured mechanism to generate synthetic data on sparse data scenarios.

Keywords: Artificial Intelligence · Machine Learning · Reinforcement Learning · Small Datasets · Resource-constrained Environments · Embedded Systems

1 Introduction

Driven mainly by popular-use applications, the broad adoption of AI solutions in recent years have consolidated a market in strong expansion, pushed by Large Language Models LLMs. Despite this growth, two structural challenges become increasingly evident: the dependence on large volumes of data to train models, where in orthogonal applications there are limitations in terms of datasets, with small datasets being a reality, for example in fault diagnosis applications. In addition, there are too many challenges to address the computational capacity and the popular approaches of AI.

For this purpose, a scoping review [1] was conducted, using the PRISMA-ScR [2], with the objective of mapping the presence of model-driven Reinforcement Learning RL in the evaluated studies, especially regarding the use to expose agents to digital

Published by Springer Nature Switzerland AG 2027
L. M. Camarinha-Matos and F. Ferrada (Eds.): DoCEIS 2026, IFIP AICT 790, pp. 71–82, 2027.
https://doi.org/10.1007/978-3-032-28939-1_6

twins, generating synthetic data aiming to complement small datasets. Additionally, with the research questions, evaluate the state of the art regarding the development of mathematical models aimed at resource-limited environments, such as embedded devices. This discussion opens space, if gaps are perceived, to the development of a line of research aligned with the development of a pipeline composed of model-based RL for the exploration of rare events, through the generation of synthetic data on sparse data scenarios, applied to resource-constrained scenarios.

Since the overall goal the entire research that this work is included is to structure a model-based RL pipeline capable of exploiting rare events in simulated environments and specifically evolving existing machine learning models for greater computational efficiency. This scoping review enables the research to touch an important gap of operational approach of AI on embedded devices contexts.

The work is organized as follows: Sect. 3 presents the methodological framework and the criteria of the scoping review; Sect. 4 synthesizes the state of the art and discusses; and, finally, Sect. 5 consolidates and concludes the perceptions, limitations, and opportunities that the practical approach provided.

2 Tackling Societal Challenges

The current AI solutions have evidenced limitations related to applications in which data are limited and computational capacities are constrained. This scenario is more critical particularly in embedded systems and industrial application contexts. In addition, the need for high computational capacity to train and execute modern models leads, in industrial, embedded, and edge contexts, to resource problems that become even more critical, restricting the direct applicability of the approaches that have dominated the mainstream AI scenario. Thus, this research sought to map the state of the art on methodologies, techniques, and architectures capable of operating efficiently under data scarcity and computational constraints.

3 Methodology

PRISMA-ScR was applied and seems is adequate because it supports the identification, organization, and categorization of heterogeneous evidence without requiring the narrower comparison logic expected from a systematic review. In addition, its use provides traceability, documentation, and a clear step-by-step structure for search, screening, eligibility, and inclusion, which is particularly important in a study that aims to map the state of the art, identify gaps, and document the review path in a reproducible manner. Thus, PRISMA-ScR is not only coherent with the exploratory nature of this research, but also with the need to establish a structured foundation for future work to evolve into a more focused systematic mapping. To guide the research and following Kitchenham guidelines [3], a set of research questions RQ was formulated, the answers to which were found by synthesizing the studies analyzed. They were:

RQ1: What machine learning strategies are proposed specifically for scenarios with small datasets?

RQ2: What categories of algorithms and approaches are most frequently used in this context?
RQ3: In which application domains are these techniques reported?
RQ4: What limitations and challenges are identified in the literature when dealing with data scarcity?
RQ5: How does RL support data complementation in small dataset scenarios?
RQ6: How are small datasets applied in embedded device contexts?

3.1 PRISMA Stages

Since the PRISMA-ScR [2] stages were divided into activities to ensure traceability and reproducibility, the Fig. 1 shows the stages and the refining of quantity of studies through step by step. In Identification, the Search Strings were defined, the searches were executed, and the deduplication of results by title was performed. In the Screening stage, titles and abstracts were evaluated regarding their alignment with the research questions. In Eligibility, the resulting set was read in a directed manner, evaluating the introduction and methodology of each study, excluding those that did not directly answer the research questions. Finally, in the inclusion stage, a deep and detailed reading was carried out, with tabulation of methods, tools, results, and state of the art, composing the synthesis of this study.

After defining the scope of the scoping review and its restrictions, the execution stage of PRISMA-ScR was carried out, with activities related to the search and identification of the studies. The studies were obtained through the execution of the search string ("small dataset" OR "limited data" OR "data-scarce" OR "few samples" OR "low-data") AND ("machine learning" OR "deep learning" OR "reinforcement learning" OR "artificial intelligence") AND ("embedded systems" OR "resource-constrained" OR "edge devices"). The search was carried out in the IEEE Xplore, Scopus, and ACM Digital Library databases, considering the adherence of these sources to the industry, specifically electrical engineering and computer science areas, as well as to the publication of studies in machine learning, deep learning, and reinforcement learning. The filters related to the inclusion and exclusion criteria were applied, notably regarding the period from 2019 to 2025.

Due to the selection of studies in three databases of high relevance, it is natural that there may be repeated studies, either homonymous or with abbreviated titles. Deduplication is the tool applied for the purpose of eliminating these repetitions, according to the PRISMA premise. In this research, deduplication was used in two stages: removal of exact duplicates by title after normalization, keeping one representative per group (54 removals). application of Jaccard similarity [4] (threshold >0.70) only for signaling, without automatic removal.

PRISMA [1] assumes the screening stage as the last stage of preliminary thematic exclusion of studies. In this stage, the same Boolean logic used in the search strategy (A AND B AND C) was applied directly to the abstracts of the studies, with the objective of verifying effective thematic adherence to the study scope. The studies that did not cumulatively meet the criteria at the abstract level were excluded, aiming at conceptual alignment with the research questions, as recommended by the PRISMA-ScR [2].

In the selection process, after the application of the inclusion and exclusion criteria in the abstract screening stage, an initial set of 12 studies was considered eligible. Three of these studies were excluded after analysis, for not answering in an effective manner the research questions defined in this scoping review, specifically, studies [5–7], because did not directly and consistently address the central aspects related to operation with small datasets in resource-constrained, embedded environments or did they do not provide sufficient evidence to answer the RQs. So, the studies were organized into three themes based on the predominant methodological focus of each study. This was determined by considering the problem addressed, the type of learning approach adopted, and the reported application context. Table 1 presents a list of the included studies and their respective groups.

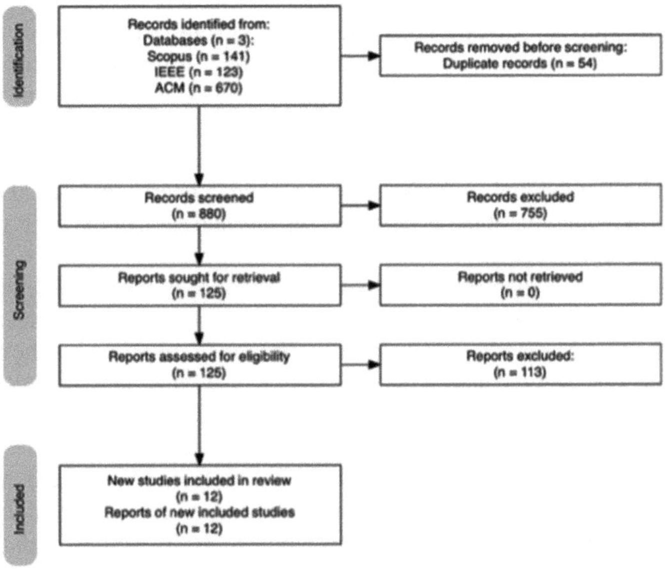

Fig. 1. PRISMA-ScR Flowchart.

3.2 Threats to Validity

In terms of internal validity, the coverage of the studies is restricted, which may have excluded relevant studies due to the selection processes. To mitigate this limitation, automated searches were carried out in digital libraries (IEEE Xplore, Scopus, and ACM Digital Library), with complementary execution in Discovery UP [8], in addition an explicit declaration that artificial intelligence tools were used only to support screening, with final validation by the reviewers. However, part of the potentially relevant literature may remain outside the scope due to the choices of databases and document type filters (Research Articles and Reviews/Surveys). Regarding external validity, the heterogeneity of domains and experimental setups, combined with the focus on small datasets and resource-constrained scenarios, restricts direct generalizations across contexts. In addition, although the scoping review does not aim to qualitatively evaluate the applied methodologies, the predominance of studies with practical application and the variation of metrics and benchmark protocols used to evaluate them limit quantitative comparisons. These limitations reinforce that the findings should be interpreted as an overview and identification of gaps, aligned with the objective of "mapping concepts and types of available evidence" [1, 9]. The set of analyzed studies did not include any result originating from ACM, because the screening stages carried out did not result in studies that simultaneously met the criteria previously presented, and the exclusion of studies in the synthesis stage reinforces the iterative and exploratory character of the scoping review, in which eligibility is not limited to initial thematic adherence, but considers the effective capacity of the studies to contribute to the mapping of evidence in relation to the research questions; although this stage may reduce the final number of included studies, it contributes to greater internal coherence of the narrative synthesis and avoids the incorporation of tangential or misaligned evidence relative to the defined scope.

Table 1. Elected Studies.

ID	Group	Studie
1	G1	DRIP: Drop unImportant Data Points – Enhancing Machine Learning Efficiency with Grad-CAM-Based Streaming
2	G1	Towards Low-Bit Quantization of Deep Neural Networks with Limited Data
3	G2	TEdgeNeXt for data-limited and resource-constrained fault diagnosis
4	G2	Improved Lightweight Deep Learning Model for the Fine-Feature Classification of Pipe Component
5	G2	Patch and Model Size Characterization for On-Device Efficient Vision Transformers on Small Datasets
6	G2	Assessing the Interplay of Contrast, Defocus, and Resolution in Cryo-EM: A Benchmark Experiment for Small Datasets
7	G2	Adaptive Cooling Management in Resource-Constrained Data Centers via Q-Learning Enhanced by Clustering
8	G2	Pneumonia Detection and Classification from Chest X-Ray Images Using Modified DenseNet121 Deep Learning
9	G3	SINDy-RL for Interpretable and Efficient Model-Based Reinforcement Learning

4 Synthesis

The growth and search for improvements in AI since its beginning have never been interrupted; however, the challenges inherent to Research and Development (R&D) in AI, such as computational capacity, representativeness, generalization, and data, were determinant to, at several moments in history, cool down the adoption by the industry [10]. These gaps are called AI Winters [11] and pushed the development of solutions such as the development of sophisticated mathematical modeling, specialized hardware

[12], and representative data sources. Therefore, the three cited R&D axes are correlated around performance, in a symbiosis where sophisticated mathematical models push processing capacity to the limit and data require increasingly more storage so that AI applications can scale [13].

The intrinsic limitations of classical Machine Learning ML models based on statistics were addressed through mathematical modeling that allowed the end-to-end unification of the phases of data representation and training, the capacity to learn representations and patterns without human intervention, and hyperparameters that control the architecture of network formation or transformations executed over the data.

There are clear evolutions regarding the evolution of mathematical models and hardware [10, 12], with the data pillar presenting the challenge of AI scalability capacity in critical environments of industrial, military, and health application, predominantly in contexts of real-time processing, concomitantly or isolated, under few resources, whether in terms of computational capacity or even data scarcity. This scenario directly confronts modern ML research to develop mechanisms that make DL and RL scalable outside the context of large data masses and wide availability of energy (computational capacity).

4.1 Overview of the State of the Art

It is perceived, perhaps as an interpretation of the movement in the literature in an attempt to anticipate a new AI-Winter, the growing research around methods that make DL more efficient with small datasets, with the objective of attacking the two main fronts: resource-aware design through cycle-efficient implementation and lack of structured data in real practical situations such as fault diagnosis, either without large representative volume or with highly imbalanced data classes. These studies converge in the creation of methods that not only enable AI to be more efficient in small datasets but also enable its on-device application in industrial environments, which, in addition to data-related challenges, impose severe computational capacity restrictions and high criticality. The studies mapped in the scoping review allowed an evaluation of the state of the art regarding the use of artificial intelligence trained under small datasets, mainly applied to embedded devices, edge devices, or reduced-capacity devices that end up proliferating across current cyber-physical systems.

Still during the initial phase of synthesis of the studies, a concentration of studies focused on the evolution and proposition of new methods in Machine Learning was perceived, notably Deep Learning – DL and Reinforcement Learning – RL. The approaches are largely focused on the combination of methods, using hybrid mathematical models, guided by mitigating trade-offs in terms of computational capacity and absence of data. In smaller proportions, there is the application of Deep Reinforcement Learning as a tool for digital twin modeling and data generation, expanding the spectrum of AI beyond data processing, but also to its own generation. This approach uses the concept of PIML – Physics-Informed Machine Learning [14], where the environment model, architecture, and hypothesis space are preloaded with physical constraints to model realistic simulated environments that enable data generation as faithful as possible to the real environment.

In short, the result of the work indicates that the recent literature on small datasets and resource-constrained environments tends to concentrate on: efficient architectures and on-device characterization (e.g., Efficient Vision Transformers ViTs), data-centric strategies and data selection and prioritization, transfer learning and federated learning on the edge, compression and quantization and techniques to reduce computational cost, and reinforcement (model-free and model-based) applied to control and optimization in scenarios with operational constraints.

4.2 Quantitative Analysis

The approaches identified in Deep Learning are, for the most part, oriented toward the combination of methods. Two studies are observed that integrate Deep Learning with transfer learning techniques (IDs 1 and 10) [15, 16], two studies that combines DL with data augmentation (ID 1 and 10), two study that explore model compression and quantization strategies (ID 2 and 6) [17, 18], and one study that incorporates physics-based or simulation-based models through surrogate models (ID 12) [19]. In smaller proportion, two studies investigate the integration between Deep Learning and Reinforcement Learning, covering model-free and model-based approaches (IDs 8 and 12) [20]. The recurrent use of architectures based on Convolutional Neural Networks (CNNs) and Transformers is observed for image recognition tasks in industrial and medical diagnostics, identified in five studies (IDs 1, 2, 5, 6 and 10) [21]. Additionally, a transversal trend was identified in the literature toward the conception of networks sufficiently lightweight for real-time execution on devices with reduced computational capacity, through strategies such as architectural optimization, efficient attention mechanisms, model compression, and quantization (IDs 2, 4, and 6) [22].

The main inference methods regarding computational performance identified in the mapped studies were predominantly based on comparative benchmarks between models, an approach adopted in eight of the nine analyzed studies (IDs 1, 2, 4, 5, 7, 8, 10, and 12) [23]. In these evaluations, the most recurrent metrics refer to training time and memory usage, systematically used to compare architectures and training strategies under resource constraints. In smaller proportion, analyses related to energy consumption are observed, particularly in on-device and edge scenarios (IDs 1, 2, 5, and 6), and punctual references to Floating Point Operations Per Second FLOPS as an indirect metric of computational complexity. Regarding mathematical performance, the analyzed studies recurrently resorted to classical evaluation metrics, with emphasis on accuracy, classification error, and number of model parameters, employed in all nine studies of the analyzed corpus. In specific contexts, particularly in classification and diagnosis tasks, accuracy was used as the main metric for comparison between approaches, while the number of parameters and model size were explored as indirect indicators of complexity and feasibility for execution in resource-constrained environments, this approach was viewed on all studies.

In terms of tools for implementation, simulation, or validation in DL, recurrent use of frameworks is observed, such as PyTorch declared in four studies (IDs 1, 4, 6, and 12) and TensorFlow/Keras in two studies (Articles 5 and 10). In the context of Reinforcement Learning, two studies explicitly declared the use of environments based on Gym/Gymnasium (IDs 8 and 12), while three studies resorted to their own simulators or real physical environments (Articles 1, 7, and 8). Finally, when analyzing the application of each study in its predominantly practical character, a predominance of studies in the industrial context is observed, with four of the nine analyzed works (IDs

1, 2, 4, and 5), followed by applications in the computing domain, with two studies (IDs 6 and 8), related to indirect energy efficiency and processing performance, respectively. More punctually, specific domains such as Life Sciences (ID 7) and Health (ID 10) are identified. Lastly, one study (ID 12) presents a transversal character, not being associated with a specific sector, but with potential application across multiple domains.

4.3 Answers to the Research Questions

The research questions were answered and brought several conclusions that guided the structure of the narrative synthesis of the state of the art on small datasets in embedded and edge contexts. Each question was also discussed individually:

RQ1: The main changes in the ML approach, specifically DL, are mostly in combining dataset pre-processing methods through data augmentation, transfer learning, and data filtering [15].
RQ2: The main architectures used are CNNs, followed by ViTs. However, the use of RL seems to emerge under few-data contexts for data generation through simulations using Digital Twins [19].
RQ3: Industry, with a focus on diagnosis, is the main application of the developed techniques, notably over scarce or sparse data due to source disaggregation or even absence of representative datasets. The applications are mostly in data structuring, generation, and dataset optimization in scenarios of low computational capacity. This led this research to seek studies that aimed at application in scenarios consistent with industry. A concentration was perceived in the life sciences and health domain, in recognition and diagnosis, with data challenges very similar to industry [22].
RQ4: It is necessary to separate the topic into two aspects: training and recognition. Regarding training, the combination of methods requires the orchestration of architectural changes, combining them into proprietary and complex pipelines. The use of data from networks trained on similar contexts to transfer learning proved to be challenging in terms of fine-tuning and often also makes on-device training unfeasible, forcing a hybrid on/off-device approach, which may make application unfeasible in contexts where training is frequent. In addition, techniques such as data augmentation are limited regarding the generation of new data points, despite their important contribution to dataset enrichment through generalization. Regarding recognition, the development of networks with high computational performance and high accuracy may a trend due to requiring that new mathematical modeling be established and allow large-scale on-device application [18].
RQ5: The main approach regarding the use of RL in small dataset contexts focuses on the application of Model Based RL (MBRL), specifically in the articles through Dyna-style RL, creating digital twins. This approach allows data generation under simulated environments, filling possible gaps that exist in datasets originating from real environments [20].
RQ6: Application contexts in industry, with emphasis on monitoring and diagnosis, are characterized by distributed embedded devices, with data in memory, disaggregated, offline, and naturally in reduced volume given the inherent memory limitations. In this way, embedded devices are a source of small datasets, but not only that. There is a search

to, through small datasets present on-device, train models that can monitor, learning, evaluating, signaling, and acting on faults [21]. The emphasis was on maintaining performance with few samples while respecting resource, latency, and energy constraints. This finding confirms a current finding by techniques and applications of ML on IoT scenarios and Edge Devices [24], which the models are optimized to execute with big constraints.

4.4 Qualitative Analysis by Research Questions

As an ad-hoc methodology of comparison, a qualitative matrix derived from the correlation between the research questions themselves was adopted. The applied typology results from the functional regrouping of studies according to the common requirements between the approaches, the dependencies it introduces, the limitations present and the trade-offs in the context of small datasets under computational constraint. In this sense, RQ1 and RQ4 support the grouping in T1, oriented to the treatment of data scarcity; RQ2 and RQ6 in T2, oriented to computational efficiency and feasibility in embedded and restricted contexts; the articulation between RQ1, RQ2, RQ4 and RQ6 allows the T3 type to be derived, whose approach is hybrid in nature, precisely because part of the studies seeks to respond simultaneously to the sampling limitation and to the computational cost; finally, RQ5 is in T4, oriented to modeling and simulation, with MBRL, digital twins, and physics-informed structures appear as a response to data complementation in scarcity contexts.

Table 2 supports the discussion by focusing on four comparative axes: expansion of learning capacity under low sample availability; computational efficiency, prioritizing the feasibility of execution on restricted devices with an emphasis on memory, latency and inference cost; hybrids that seek to accommodate both requirements simultaneously, making them closer to the practical conditions faced in industrial, embedded and edge applications; and studies oriented to modeling and simulation, which seek to circumvent the empirical limitations by building environments capable of producing experience or complementary data. In this way, the table highlights that the difference between the models lies not only in the algorithm employed, but also in the type of requirement that each one favors, in the methodological cost it incorporates, and in the nature of the insufficiency remaining after the approach is adopted.

It is concluded that, comparatively:

- data-driven strategies are more appropriate when the dominant limitation is the low number of samples, but preserve dependence on the domain of origin, pre-training and the semantic validity of the applied transformations;
- strategies oriented to computational efficiency are more adherent when the bottleneck is in memory, latency or energy, although they can also limit the representational capacity of the model and its generalization in certain contexts;
- hybrid strategies, by articulating more than one technique, represent the most concrete attempt to simultaneously address data scarcity and computational constraint, which is why they appear with greater incidence in the corpus, but they do so at the cost of greater methodological coupling and greater integration complexity;

- modeling and simulation-oriented strategies, although even more restricted and emerging, transform the problem of scarce data into a structured modeling problem, which makes them promising, especially in contexts where rare events or failure data are naturally difficult to collect, but still strongly conditioned to the quality of the simulated environment and the robustness of the physical hypotheses adopted.

Table 2. Analytical Comparison.

Type	Requirements	Dependencies	Limitations	Trade-offs
1	Improve learning / generalization under low data	Pretraining, valid augmentation, filtering	Keep computational feasibility or semantic diversity	Better performance on low data vs. dependence on models
2	Enable training under memory or energy constraints	Compression, quantization, lightweight architecture	Does not directly resolve scarcity of representative data; may lose accuracy	Execution feasibility vs. reduced representational capacity
3	Balance few-data and few-resource simultaneously	Integration of multiple techniques in one pipeline	Engineering complexity and lower simplicity of reproduction	Better fit to real constraints vs. more complex pipelines
4	Model-based control, simulation, or structured exploration	Reliable simulator, digital twin, or environment model	Transfers part of the difficulty to modelling fidelity	Less dependence on brute-force real data vs. greater modelling burden

In addition, RL appears mainly in more recent works, but its presence is neither uniform nor equivalent in terms of motivation for use among articles. On the one hand, there are approaches in which RL is used in a way that is more directly associated with the modeling of the environment, as in the case of proposals based on MBRL, Dyna-style RL, and integration with digital twins, in which the exploration of the environment and the generation of synthetic experience make this family more adherent to scenarios of data scarcity. In this sense, RL can be pointed out as an emerging technique in the corpus, especially in newer studies, but with unequal adequacy to the problem investigated here: when associated with modeling, simulation and construction of environments capable of producing structured experience, it shows more promise for scenarios of data scarcity; when used predominantly as a control or optimization mechanism, remains relevant, although less adherent to the specific need to complement limited data.

5 Conclusions

As conclusion, is possible to perceive a line of work to, through the theoretical bases and the state of the art obtained in this work, develop a research around the modeling of a structured and methodologically documented mechanism correlating MBRL for the exploration of rare events, through the generation of synthetic data on sparse data scenarios, applied to resource-constrained scenarios. This may evidence, as stated previously, an effective attempt to fill the gaps exposed by the massive adoption of AI. A limitation of this review is that generative deep learning schemes for small-dataset extension or interpretable models, particularly autoencoders, variational autoencoders, and generative adversarial networks, were not identified in the final corpus, which may be related to the reduced number of selected studies and to the specificity of the research questions adopted in this work, suggesting that this discussion remains open as a complementary path for the treatment of sparse-data scenarios.

In summary, the mapped literature does not point to a dominant model in the universal sense, but a set of complementary responses that are distributed according to the dominant requirement, the dependence assumed and the trade-off considered tolerable in the context of application. It was perceived the prevalence of the development of hybrid methods, which the related studies are guided by the search to train and execute models on few data.

Finally, this work requires a more in depth discussion, achieved through a deeper systematic mapping of the state-of-the-art and seeking to lay the foundations for the development of an novel methodology that address the gaps identified in this work.

Appendix

For esthetic and structure, the PRISMA-ScR extraction spreadsheet was uploaded on: https://bit.ly/4cd26Xw.

References

1. Page, M.J., et al.: The PRISMA 2020 statement: an updated guideline for reporting systematic reviews. BMJ. **372**, n71 (2021). https://doi.org/10.1136/bmj.n71
2. Tricco, A.C., et al.: PRISMA extension for scoping reviews (PRISMA-ScR): checklist and explanation. Ann. Intern. Med. **169**(7), 467–473 (2018). https://doi.org/10.7326/M18-0850
3. Kitchenham, B.: Procedures for performing systematic reviews. In: Joint Technical Report, Keele University Technical Report TR/SE-0401, NICTA Technical Report 0400011T.1. Keele University, Keele, UK. (2004) ISSN 1353-7776
4. Jaccard, P.: Étude comparative de la distribution florale dans une portion des Alpes et du Jura. Bull Soc Vaudoise Sci Nat. **37**, 547–579 (1901)
5. Parikh, M., Ramavath, S.K., Prathi, S., Sheela, K., Handaragal, R., Nathiya, R.: Deep learning for automated defect detection in industrial manufacturing. In: 2025 6th International Conference on Electronics and Sustainable Communication Systems (ICESC) (2025). https://doi.org/10.1109/ICESC65114.2025.11212369
6. Farag, A.: Machine learning approaches for enhanced estimation of reference evapotranspiration (ETo): a comparative evaluation. Sci. Rep. **15**, 38485 (2025). https://doi.org/10.1038/s41598-025-23166-w
7. Singh, A., Hegde, R.M.: GEE maximization in UAV-aided mobile IoT networks using deep reinforcement learning. In: Proc IEEE Int Conf Acoustics, Speech and Signal Processing (ICASSP) (2025). https://doi.org/10.1109/ICASSP49660.2025.10890243
8. Universidade do Porto: U. Porto Discovery.. Available at: https://discovery.up.pt/ (2026). Accessed 26 Feb 2026

9. Arksey, H., O'Malley, L.: Scoping studies: towards a methodological framework. Int. J. Soc. Res. Methodol. **8**(1), 19–32 (2005). https://doi.org/10.1080/1364557032000119616
10. Wang, M., Yu, Z.: Optimizing system fault detection in real-time control systems with edge AI-enabled MCUs. Technical article SSZTD64, Texas Instruments.. Available at: https://www.ti.com/lit/ta/ssztd64/ssztd64.pdf (2024). Accessed 26 Feb 2026
11. Russell, S., Norvig, P.: Artificial Intelligence: A Modern Approach, 3rd edn. Prentice Hall, Upper Saddle River, NJ (2010)
12. Nickolls, J., Buck, I., Garland, M., Skadron, K.: Scalable parallel programming with CUDA. ACM Queue. **6**(2), 40–53 (2008). https://doi.org/10.1145/1365490.1365500
13. Kaplan, J., et al.: Scaling laws for neural language models. Comput. Sci. archive. (2022). https://doi.org/10.48550/arXiv.2001.08361
14. Karniadakis, G.E., et al.: Physics-informed machine learning. Nat. Rev. Phys. **3**(6), 422–440 (2021). https://doi.org/10.1038/s42254-021-00314-5
15. Rüb, M., Konegen, D., Sikora, A., Mueller-Gritschneder, D.: DRIP: DRop unImportant data points enhancing machine learning efficiency with grad-CAM-based streaming data prioritization for on-device training. In: 2025 International Joint Conference on Neural Networks (IJCNN), pp. 1–10, Rome, Italy (2025). https://doi.org/10.1109/IJCNN64981.2025.11228149
16. Dalei, M.K., Mahapatra, S.: Pneumonia detection and classification from chest X-ray images using modified DenseNet121 deep learning approach. In: 2025 International Conference on Ambient Intelligence in Health Care (ICAIHC), pp. 1–5, Raipur, Chattisgarh, India (2025). https://doi.org/10.1109/ICAIHC64101.2025.10956683
17. Yuan, Y., Chen, C., Hu, X., Peng, S.: Towards low-bit quantization of deep neural networks with limited data. In: 2020 25th International Conference on Pattern Recognition (ICPR) (2020). https://doi.org/10.1109/ICPR48806.2021.9412678
18. Park, S., et al.: Patch and model size characterization for on-device efficient-ViTs on small datasets using 12 quantitative metrics. IEEE Access. **13**, 1–15 (2025). https://doi.org/10.1109/ACCESS.2025.3536471
19. Zolman, N., et al.: SINDy-RL for interpretable and efficient model-based reinforcement learning. Nat. Commun. **16**, 10714 (2025). https://doi.org/10.1038/s41467-025-65738-4
20. Zheng, J., et al.: Adaptive cooling management in resource-constrained data centers via Q-learning enhanced by clustering for energy efficiency. In: 2025 3rd International Conference on Mobile Internet, Cloud Computing and Information Security (MICCIS), pp. 1–6 (2025). https://doi.org/10.1109/MICCIS66057.2025.00082
21. Chen, C., Azman, A.: Improved lightweight deep learning model for the fine-feature classification of pipe components. Int J Intell Syst Appl Eng. **12**(15s), 520–529 (2024) Available at: https://www.ijisae.org/index.php/IJISAE/article/view/4786. Accessed 26 Feb 2026
22. Zhang, Z., et al.: A hybrid network TEdgeNeXt for data-limited and resource-constrained fault diagnosis. J. Vib. Control. (2025). https://doi.org/10.1177/10775463241266277
23. Lee, H., et al.: Assessing the interplay of contrast, defocus, and resolution in cryo-EM: a benchmark experiment for limited dataset screening. J Anal Sci Technol. **15**, 32 (2024). https://doi.org/10.1186/s40543-024-00445-1
24. Warden, P., Situnayake, D.: TinyML: Machine Learning with TensorFlow Lite on Arduino and Ultra-Low-Power Microcontrollers. O'Reilly Media, Sebastopol, CA (2020) https://tinymlbook.com/wp-content/uploads/2020/01/tflite_micro_preview.pdf

Fourier Apparent Front: A Method of Generating Apparent Fronts Without a Template

Andrei Pătrăuşanu, Adrian Florea(✉), Mihai Neghină, Radu Chiş, and Alina Dicoiu

Computer Science and Electrical Engineering Department, Lucian Blaga University of Sibiu, Sibiu, Romania
{andrei.patrausanu,adrian.florea,mihai.neghina,radu.chis, alina.dicoiu}@ulbsibiu.ro

Abstract. This work introduces Fourier Apparent Front, a method for approximating true Pareto Fronts in multi-objective optimization problems where they are unknown, by modeling them as signals that can be decomposed using Fourier series. Unlike classical optimization techniques, Fourier Apparent Front requires no prior knowledge about the true Pareto Front and removes the use of a template function, essential within its predecessor, Apparent Front. In such cases, the template function can remain continuous, even if the true Pareto Front is discrete. Therefore, it yields accurate approximations with minimal error under specified conditions. Moreover, Fourier Apparent Front also avoids the pairwise comparison-based ranking by evaluating individuals according to their distance from the Apparent Front. Therefore, it is computationally more efficient than ranking methods used in genetic algorithms such as NSGA-II, whose spatial complexity scales as O(N*S2), where N denotes the number of objectives and S the populations size. This methodology bridges concepts from Signal Processing with Evolutionary Computing and has practical relevance for real-world optimization problems such as processor architecture design, suspension system tuning, where the true Pareto Front is unknown. The results obtained from 7,020 experiments on family of functions $x_1^n + x_2^n - 1 = 0$ for $n \in \left\{\frac{1}{3}, \frac{1}{2}, 1, 2, 3, 4, 7, 11, 100\right\}$ indicate that retaining as few as nine harmonics provide accurate approximation. Moreover, the magnitude of difference between real front and approximated front is on the order of 10–2.

Keywords: Optimization · Multi-objective · Evolutionary Algorithm · Intelligent Systems · Fourier Series · Cross-domain Learning

1 Introduction

An important pillar of multi-objective optimization is the concept of Pareto-optimality [1], which has led to significant theoretical and practical advances. Before their widespread adoption, non-Pareto techniques, such as lexicographic order or weighted

Published by Springer Nature Switzerland AG 2027
L. M. Camarinha-Matos and F. Ferrada (Eds.): DoCEIS 2026, IFIP AICT 790, pp. 83–98, 2027.
https://doi.org/10.1007/978-3-032-28939-1_7

sum, were pioneering methods for addressing multi-objective problems. Such non-Pareto methods, as the weighted sum approach, combine multiple objectives and their corresponding weights into a single objective function. The aggregated result is then used as fitness value of evaluation. A major limitation of this approach is the absence of a systematic method for selecting the most appropriate weight values that yield optimal results.

Other methods are built around the idea of generating an optimal set of solutions, a so-called optimal Pareto Front, typically through the evolutionary algorithms [2]. These solutions provide non-dominance and equal probability in the objective space, and are, with high probability, situated near the theoretical ideal Pareto Front, whether it is known or not [3, 4]. There have been many well-established algorithms in literature, to follow the idea of Pareto-optimality, such as Non-Dominated Sorting Algorithm II (NSGA-II) [5], Strength Pareto Evolutionary Algorithm 2 (SPEA2) [6] or the relative recent NSGA-III [7].

In Pareto-based algorithms, the selection phase presents a significant challenge, particularly as the number of objectives increases. This growth complicates the assessment of non-domination relations across all objectives, while also amplifying computational complexity. Moreover, there is a pressing need for scalable, versatile and computationally efficient methods capable of operating effectively in high-dimensional objective spaces.

In recent years, numerous methods have been proposed to address the limitations mentioned above, particularly with the aim of increasing the scalability of evolutionary algorithms in high-dimensional objective spaces by leveraging the concept of dominance. A common direction among these approaches has been the extension of classical Pareto-dominance with domain knowledge and fuzzy logic. The assumption is that such integrations would aggregate more contextual information, guiding the search towards more relevant search areas and ultimately improving the ranking and selection of individuals compared to traditional methods.

Apparent Front Ranking (AFR) [8] seeks to improve Pareto dominance evaluation by evaluating the population relative to an "apparent front", which is constructed using a template function fitted to a selected set of support vectors. Its computational efficiency comes from requiring only two passes through the population: one to compute the Apparent Front and another to evaluate individuals based on their proximity to it—thus avoiding the costly classical pairwise comparisons used to determine dominance. The method's flexibility lies in the freedom to choose any suitable family of template functions and has been successfully used in the past to construct competitive genetic algorithms, such as Apparent Front Zones Genetic Algorithm (AFZGA) [9]. Building on this idea, the present work proposes an even more flexible approach: approximating the Pareto Front without any prior knowledge of any template function, using Fourier series.

The remainder of this paper is organized as follows. Section 2 outline the scope of the ongoing PhD thesis and places Fourier Apparent Front within its research context. Section 3 provides a summary of related work from the literature. Section 4 introduces the proposed method, followed by Sect. 5 where the experimental results are exemplified – though not limited to – a specific family of functions. Finally, Sect. 6 concludes the paper and outlines directions for future work.

2 Cross Domain Foundations and Relevance

The ongoing "*The development of evolutionary algorithms for solving modeling, optimization, and simulation problems in various engineering domains*" PhD thesis aims to study, develop and apply evolutionary algorithms and techniques across a range of practical engineering fields. Starting from a systematic review of the current state-of-the-art algorithms, frameworks and benchmarks [10], the thesis further proposes the continuous development of Framework for Advanced Design Space Exploration [11], which integrates current state-of-the art algorithms and optimization problems. This framework is built around embarrassingly parallel nature of evolutionary algorithms, enabling parallelization of simulations of individuals to massively accelerate execution time. Moreover, it provides both researchers and non-IT/engineering specialists with a scalable tool that offers easily extensibility with new algorithms and use of existing ones on a wide variety of problems. The implementation also tackles the society challenge regarding reducing of energy consumption and CO2 emission. Our research from [10] concluded the programming languages such as Python has a CO2 consumption level 10 times higher than Java. For this reason and because the evolutionary algorithms are typically run on complex problems, FADSE has been developed in Java.

The thesis also addresses the creation of meta-optimization algorithms, such as those in [3], where the synergy obtained by combining two different evolutionary algorithms enabled the exploitation of strengths of each. In addition, in [3], FADSE has been extended with a suite of real-world suspension optimization problems.

Following the concept of Apparent Front [8], originally developed by ACAPS research group, this work further investigates potential extensions. The proposed concept aligns closely with concepts such as Computational and Perceptual Systems, Signal Processing and Embedded Intelligence, by proposing a mathematical model that interprets Pareto-fronts obtain through multi-objective optimization algorithms, through the lens of signal computations. This approximation of Pareto fronts finds its relevance in real-world optimization problems [3], where the true fronts are not known.

From the perspective of Computational Systems, Fourier Apparent Front proposes an innovative representation of Pareto fronts as structured computational signals (Fourier Series) rather than the classical relational structures obtained through dominance comparisons. Such ranking methods that sort the population (non-dominated sorting) in non-dominated fronts, typically use pairwise comparisons. In concrete algorithmic implementations, such as NSGA-II, this leads to a spatial complexity of O(N*S2), where N denotes the number of objectives and S the populations size (usually set to 100 for ensuring diversity). In AFZGA algorithm, it is shown that Apparent Front exhibits a complexity of O(N*V), where V is the size of support vectors. By transforming the problem into a signal approximation task, the proposed method enables more scalable and efficient computations. This is particularly relevant for complex computational systems, where optimization must be performed under certain memory and time constraints.

Typical real-world embedded system cores consist of a central processing unit that must be optimized across multiple objectives, creating a multi-objective optimization problem [9]. A practical example, included in FADSE, as well, is Grid Alu Processor (GAP) [12], where hardware complexity and cycles per instruction represent two such optimization objectives.

Furthermore, inheriting the features of its predecessor, Apparent Front, the novel Fourier Apparent Front eliminates the previously mentioned pairwise comparisons, by evaluating the individual according to their distance to the estimated front. This mechanism can be interpreted as a form of perceptual assessment of individuals quality. The employed mechanism does not rely on the dominance comparisons, which can become less informative and computationally costly in high-dimensional objective spaces. It consequently evaluates solutions based on their perceived proximity to an approximated computational structure. This approach highlights the use of perceptual processes in computational systems, where such representations are often used to guide the search and optimization.

The connection to Signal Processing has been the core of the proposed methodology. By modeling the Pareto front as a signal in the space of objectives, this approach leverages Fourier Series to approximate a true front using series coefficients and a specified number of harmonics. It also removes the need for a template function from the previous Apparent Front and also employs well-known signal processing concepts such as frequency, sampling or approximation error. Such modeling and problem formulation, opens perspectives for further extensions using various mathematical transforms or adaptive techniques.

Consequently, the relevance to Embedded Intelligence lies in scalability. Due to its computational efficiency, it can be easily integrated in-thus not limited to-any evolutionary computing algorithm. By replacing pairwise comparisons and ranking computation with distance evaluations, Fourier Apparent Front becomes particularly suitable for integration in resource-constrained systems. Such evolutionary optimizations, are typically used as a step of larger intelligent learning systems [13, 14]. Moreover, Embedded Intelligence techniques such as Machine Learning and optimization algorithms are commonly employed to guide and accelerate the design space exploration process for identifying hardware–software configurations that meet strict performance, energy, and real-time constraints. The synergy of the concepts is used to improve system designs by enabling more efficient search strategies, reducing design time and yielding higher quality solutions, thereby making embedded intelligence feasible at the edge.

3 Related Work

Recent literature highlights a growing trend in combining Fourier analysis with evolutionary and genetic algorithms to improve performance of optimization in various applications. The authors of [15] explore an adaptive Fourier-based fitness function within a genetic algorithm framework, demonstrating improved convergence in multi-objective scenarios. Similarly, the authors of [16] integrate discrete Fourier transforms into an evolutionary algorithm for signal-driven parameter tuning, reporting significant gains in computational efficiency and solution accuracy. In [17], a novel metaheuristic spotted hyena algorithm is combined with an inverse discrete Fourier transform for channel data transfer optimization. In research areas of high-precision underwater acoustics [18], a multi-layer algorithm including NSGA-II and Fourier transform for finding sound gradient is engaged. A similar algorithmic architecture is proposed in [19], in a rigorous study of optimizing hybrid electric vehicles.

Earlier work such as [20], presents an innovative approach using Fourier-series decomposition to preprocess objective signals before applying genetic optimization, reducing noise and focusing the search on relevant frequency components. In [21] the University of Montana group applies truncated Fourier series within a genetic algorithm to evolve control laws for robotic locomotion, effectively encoding gait patterns and minimizing trial errors.

Contributions from [22] introduce a hybrid GA–Fourier framework for real-time adaptive filtering in sensor networks, highlighting robustness under noisy conditions. In other works, such as [23], the authors propose a dynamic Fourier-template matching technique within a genetic multi-objective schema, offering scalable Pareto-front approximation. In the field of legged robotics, [24] further refines this idea by integrating truncated Fourier expansions with GA to produce stable bipedal walking patterns under varying terrains.

Collectively, these studies validate the powerful synergy between Fourier transforms and evolutionary algorithms. However, Fourier series are usually applied independently of evolutionary algorithms or as optimization targets, not as a method, whereas for the present study, they represent the method. When combined, the integration typically take place within the population space or within the evolutionary operators. Therefore, this work aims to use Fourier series in complex multi-objective spaces with demonstrating adaptability and supporting this Fourier-driven Pareto-front approximation strategy.

A bibliometric analysis was conducted using VosViewer [25] on the SCOPUS database, based on keywords relevant to our research focus: Fourier, Optimization and Pareto Front. The motivation behind this investigation lies in the observation that, although Fourier series have long been used for function approximation, their application to functions defining the true Pareto front in multi-objective optimization problems remains largely unexplored.

As illustrated in Fig. 1, the bibliometric search returned 858,550 publications for the keyword Fourier, 32,296 for the combination Fourier and Optimization, and only 30 papers that included all three terms: Fourier, Optimization and Pareto Front. These 30 articles were published between 2004 and 2026, with at least one and no more than three appearing in any given year. This limited number of studies highlights a clear research gap—one that our current work aims to address by exploiting this unexplored intersection. The visualization in Fig. 2 presents a keyword co-occurrence analysis extracted from the 30 identified articles. A total of 375 keywords were identified, among which only those with a minimum occurrence of four times were included in the clustering process.

The following three tables provide a detailed listing of the keyword clusters identified in the co-occurrence analysis presented in Fig. 2, highlighting the most representative terms and their respective cluster affiliations (Tables 1, 2 and 3).

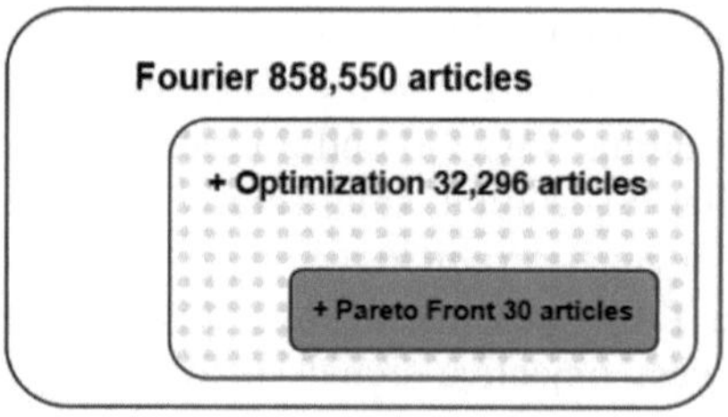

Fig. 1. Publication counts by keyword combination in SCOPUS (2004–2026).

Fig. 2. Keyword cluster analysis based on the 30 retrieved publications.

Table 1. Clusters 1 and 2.

Acoustic methods in structural optimization	Optimization and Fourier methods
acoustic emission testing	Fourier transforms
acoustic transducers	global optimization
displacement components	optimal systems
electromagnetic acoustic	parallel processing systems
single optimization	pareto front
structural optimization	particle swarm optimization
surface waves	performance
time domain analysis	program processors
ultrasonic waves	uncertainty quantifications

Table 2. Clusters 3 and 4.

Numerical and shape optimization	Multi-objective decision analysis
approximation algorithms	decision making
benchmarking	Multi-optimization

(*continued*)

Table 2. (*continued*)

Numerical and shape optimization	Multi-objective decision analysis
constrained optimization	optimizations
interpolation	sensitivity analysis
numerical methods	thermoelectric devices
optimization algorithms	
shape optimization	
trusses	

Table 3. Cluster 5.

Genetic Algorithms for optimization
genetic algorithms
optimization
parameter estimation
visualization

4 Proposed Method

The proposed method of generating Fourier Apparent Fronts without a template will be exemplified for the case of two objectives that need to be maximized. However, the method works in general, considering any number of objectives and can be adjusted to objectives that need minimization.

The steps of the proposed method are shown in Fig. 3 for the general case (left) and for the 2D case (right). For the case of a bidimensional space of objectives, the proposed method has the following steps:

1. Transformation of the data from the Cartesian to polar coordinates
2. Computation of the pivot point at angle 0 and introduction of the complementary points (symmetric with respect to the pivot), which simplifies the computation of the Fourier series at later steps
3. Selection support vectors for the computation of Fourier series integrals
4. Computation of the Fourier series expansion

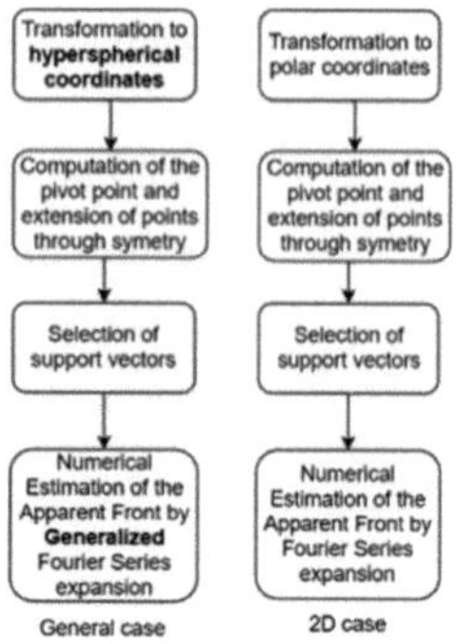

Fig. 3. Proposed method

Each of these steps will be discussed in more detail with the example of a true Pareto boundary obeying $x_1^n + x_2^n - 1 = 0$, with n = 7, and a population of a few hundred vectors spread well within the space (Fig. 4). We have used this family of functions to keep consistency with [8, 9]. Even so, the approach can be generalized to road any family of functions, based on generalized version of all the mathematical concepts described further.

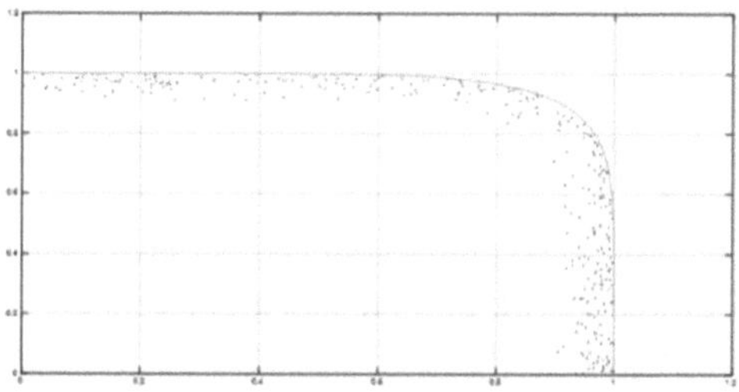

Fig. 4. Cartesian representation of points and true front (green) in the space of objectives.

Each point in the space of objectives is transformed from Cartesian coordinates (x, y) to polar coordinates (m, θ). Considering that the points are in the first quadrant $x > 0$, $y > 0$, the angle θ is restricted to the interval 0 to $\pi/2$.

$$m = \sqrt{x^2 + y^2} \tag{1}$$

$$\theta = \text{atan}\left(\frac{y}{x}\right) \tag{2}$$

The result of the transformation can be seen in Fig. 5, as the red points in the (m, θ) system of coordinates.

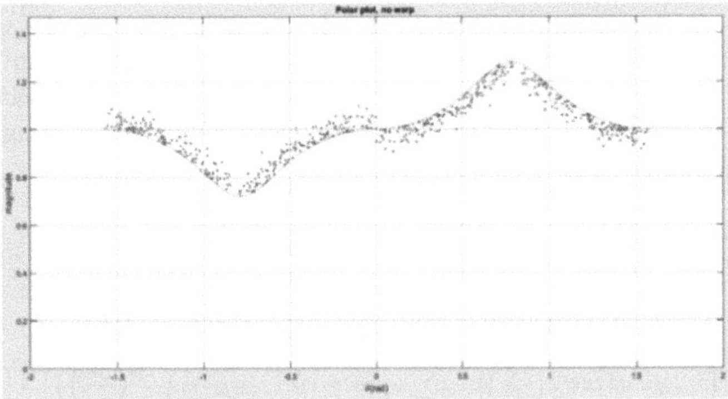

Fig. 5. Representation of points and true front (green) in the modified space after steps 1–2.

The pivot can be both a real or a virtual point in the (m, θ) system of coordinates, with magnitude m_0 at angle $\theta = 0$. Ideally the magnitude of the pivot will be largest magnitude of all points at angle 0 or very close to angle 0. In the example, Fig. 5, the pivot has magnitude $m_0 = 1$.

Complementary points are symmetric with respect to the pivot. The complement of a point $P(m_k, \theta_k)$ is a point $P^{'}(2m_0 - m_k, -\theta_k)$. These are marked with magenta in Fig. 5. They are used to simplify the computation of the Fourier series at later steps.

The support vectors are the numerical values needed for the estimation of the Fourier Series. They can be values from among the points and complements, but they can also be other values. Ideally, the support vectors are the largest magnitudes among points at or around angles which are multiples of a sampling angle, $\frac{1}{20} rad \left(1 \ rad = \frac{180}{\pi}\right)$.

The Fourier Series [26] of a periodic signal is a (potentially infinite) sum of sine waves computed with the set of Eqs. 3, 4, 5, 6. 7 and 8.

$$U_0 = \frac{1}{T}\int_0^T u(t)dt \tag{3}$$

$$A_k = \frac{2}{T}\int_0^T u(t)\sin(2\pi kF_0 t)dt \tag{4}$$

$$B_k = \frac{2}{T}\int_0^T u(t)\cos(2\pi kF_0 t)dt \tag{5}$$

$$S_k = \sqrt{A_k^2 + B_k^2} \tag{6}$$

$$\varphi_k = arctg\frac{B_k}{A_k} \tag{7}$$

$$u(t) = U_0 + \sum_{k=1}^{\infty} S_k \sin(2\pi F_k t + \varphi_k) \tag{8}$$

Considering the interval $\left(-\frac{\pi}{2}, \frac{\pi}{2}\right]$ as the period and the support vectors as samples of the function, the necessary integrals A_k, B_k can be computed numerically. In Eq. 8,

$F_k = kF_0$. As for the results, the trapezoidal rule is used on these equally spaced points. Regardless of the chosen support vectors (s_θ), they exhibit symmetry relative to the pivot point, which leads to the estimated Apparent Front becoming an odd function once the continuous component $U_0 = m_0$ is removed. Consequently, the resulting components are illustrated in Eqs. 9, 10 and 11.

$$T_0 = \left(\frac{\pi}{2} - \left(-\frac{\pi}{2}\right)\right) = \pi \Longrightarrow F_0 = \frac{1}{\pi} \Longrightarrow F_k = \frac{k}{\pi} \tag{9}$$

$$B_k = 0 \Rightarrow S_k = |A_k|, \varphi_k = 0 \ or \ \pi, \text{for all } k \tag{10}$$

$$A_k \approx \left(\frac{2}{T_0}\right)\left(\frac{T_s}{2} \cdot \left(s_{-\pi/2} \cdot \sin\left(2\pi k F_0\left(-\frac{\pi}{2}\right)\right) + 2\sum s_\theta \sin(2\pi k F_0 \theta) + s_{\pi/2} \cdot \sin\left(\frac{2\pi k F_0 \pi}{2}\right)\right)\right) = \left(\frac{2T_s}{T_0}\right)\sum s_\theta \sin(2k\theta) \tag{11}$$

As demonstrated in Fig. 6, an accurate approximation of the Apparent Front can be achieved even when retaining as few as nine harmonics, provided a sampling interval of $\frac{1}{20} rad$ is used. This highlights the efficiency of the representation.

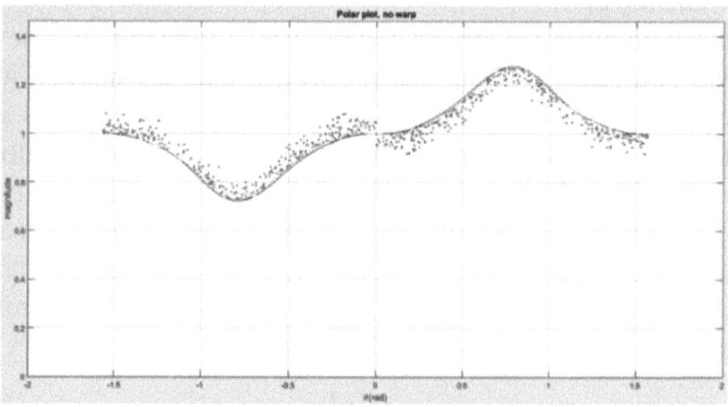

Fig. 6. Estimated front (blue).

5 Results

In this section, the real Pareto front is denoted as function P_{true}, which, in the case of synthetic benchmark problems such as DTLZ1-DTLZ9 [6], the true Pareto Front is known explicitly. Function P_{approx} represents the approximation of P_{true} obtained through a truncated Fourier series. To assess the quality of this approximation, the integral of the absolute difference between the two functions over the interval $\left(-\frac{\pi}{2}, \frac{\pi}{2}\right]$ is computed as a measure of deviation in area (Eq. 12).

$$\int_{-\frac{\pi}{2}}^{\frac{\pi}{2}} | P_{true} - P_{approx} | \tag{12}$$

Other two key performance indicators are also employed in the evaluation: the IDG (Ideal Distance to the real Pareto front), and the Hypervolume (HV) metric, typically computed from discrete points and thus also suitable for approximated fronts. The number of harmonics k used in the Fourier series is varied in order to analyze how the approximation improves with increasing spectral resolution. The objective is to minimize the area difference between P_{true} and P_{approx}, thus ensuring that the Fourier-based approximation closely replicates the true Pareto front.

The experimental evaluation was conducted on a family of functions representing true Pareto fronts defined by the implicit equation: $x_1^n + x_2^n - 1 = 0$ for $n \in \left\{\frac{1}{3}, \frac{1}{2}, 1, 2, 3, 4, 7, 11, 100\right\}$ to keep consistency and compare with [8, 9]. For each function, a series of approximations was generated, where the sampled points remained within a vertical deviation of at most 0.1 below the actual Pareto front (Figs. 7, 8, 9, 10, 11, 12, 13 and 14). The number of sampled points in each experiment varied between 100 and 300. To evaluate the influence of spectral and angular resolution, the number of harmonics included in the truncated Fourier series was systematically varied between 3 and 30, while the number of angular samples ranged from 25 to 45. This corresponds to angular steps ranging from approximately $\frac{\pi}{2 \bullet 45} \approx \frac{1}{30} rad$ and $\frac{\pi}{2 \bullet 25} \approx \frac{1}{16} rad$. In total, 7,020 experiments were performed, enabling a comprehensive analysis of the approximation accuracy under various parameter settings.

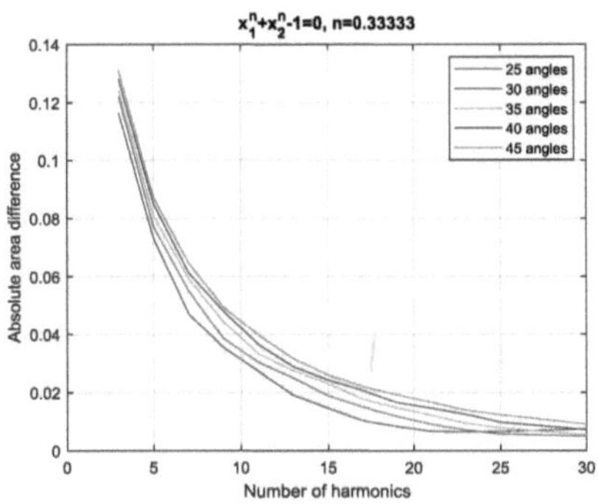

Fig. 7. $x_1^n + x_2^n - 1 = 0$ for $n = 0.33$.

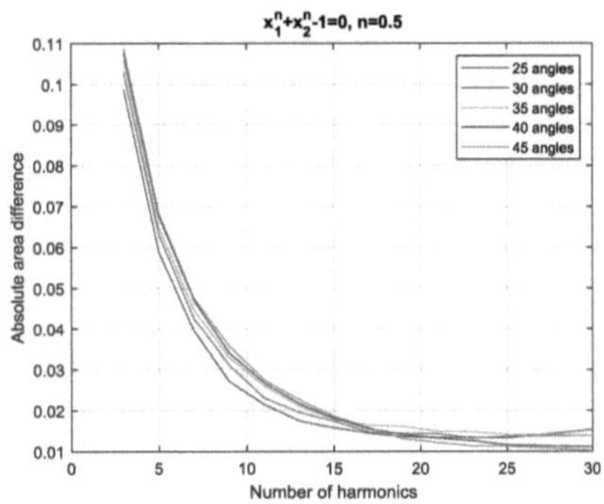

Fig. 8. $x_1^n + x_2^n - 1 = 0$ for $n = 0.5$.

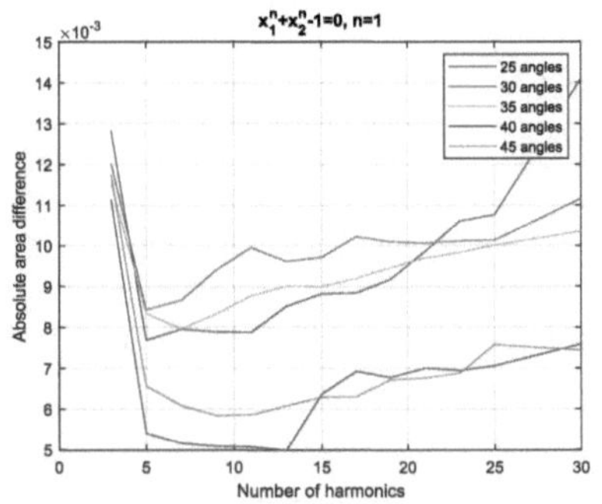

Fig. 9. $x_1^n + x_2^n - 1 = 0$ for $n = 1$.

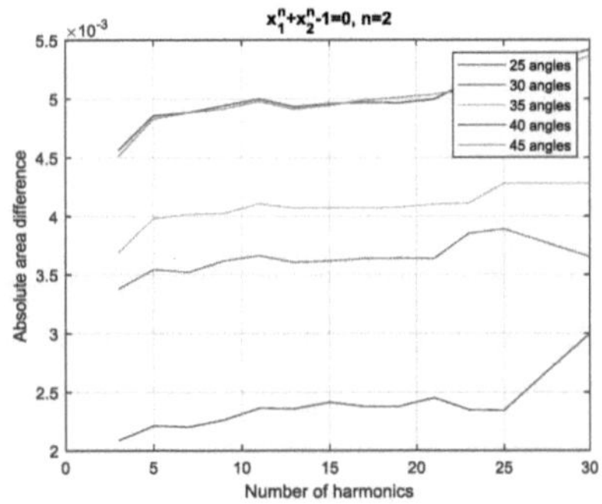

Fig. 10. $x_1^n + x_2^n - 1 = 0$ for $n = 2$.

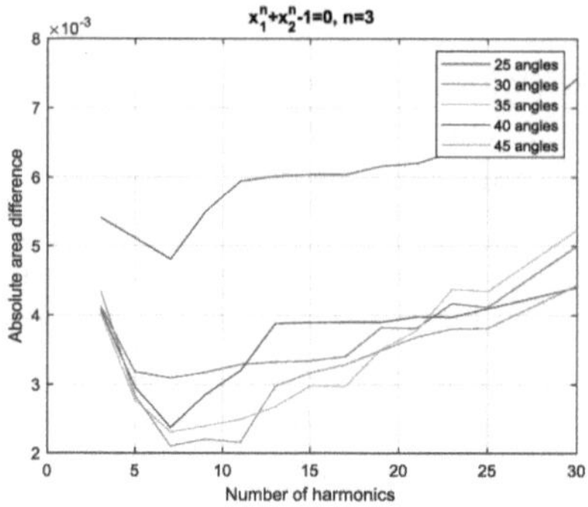

Fig. 11. $x_1^n + x_2^n - 1 = 0$ for $n = 3$.

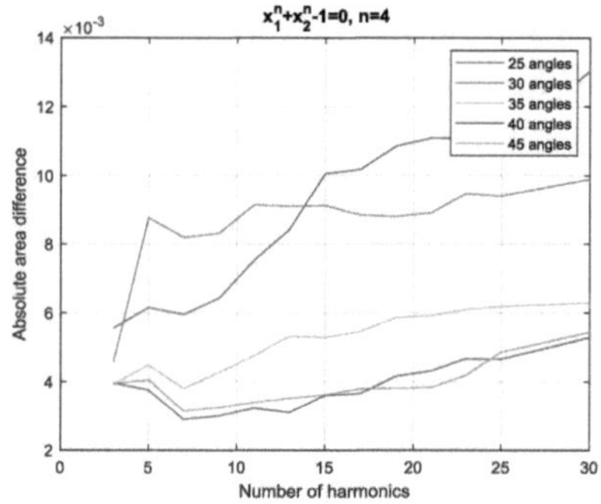

Fig. 12. $x_1^n + x_2^n - 1 = 0$ for $n = 4$.

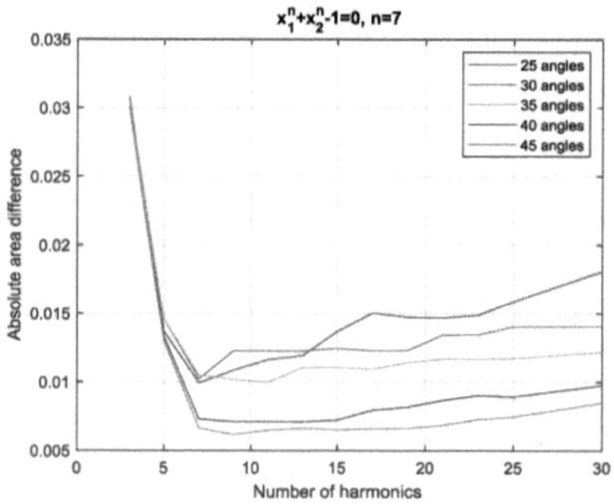

Fig. 13. $x_1^n + x_2^n - 1 = 0$ for $n = 7$.

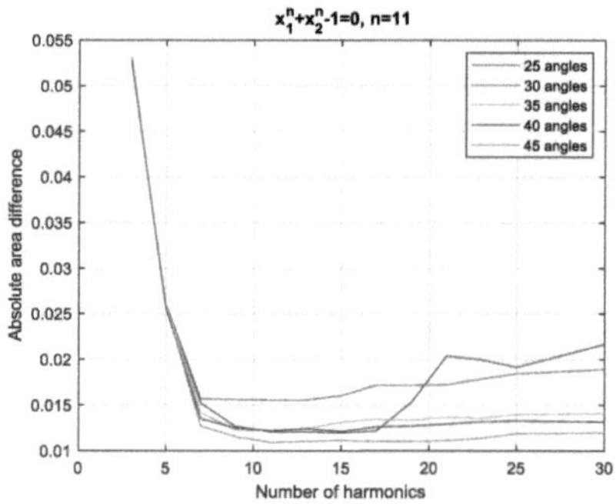

Fig. 14. $x_1^n + x_2^n - 1 = 0$ for $n = 11$.

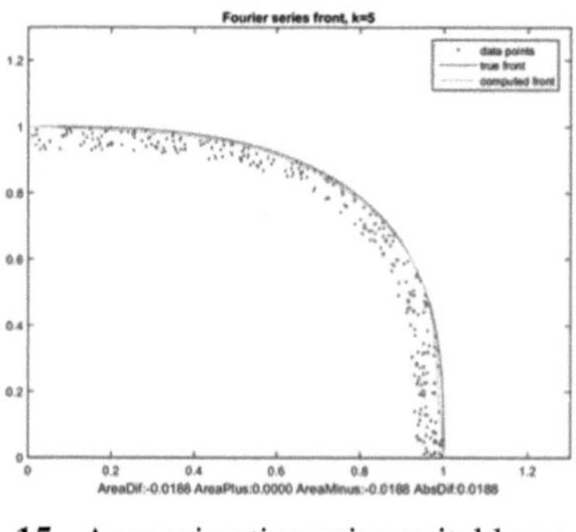

Fig. 15. Approximation using suitable no. of harmonics.

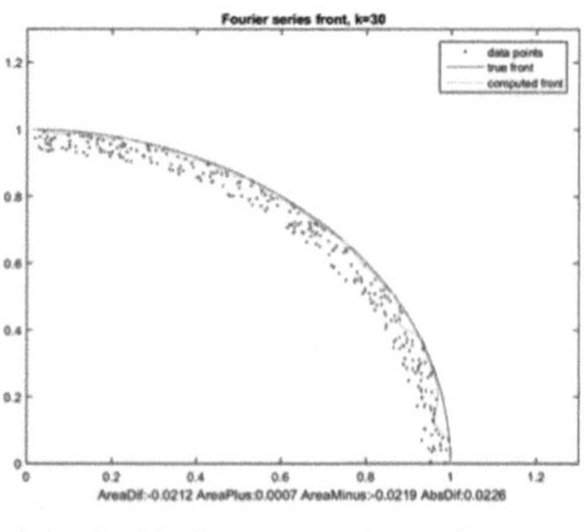

Fig. 16. Oscillations caused by a large number of harmonics.

As expected, the best results are obtained when the true front resembles a circle arc because it would be transformed into a straight line in the (m, θ) system of coordinates.

Figure 15 illustrates a successful approximation of the Pareto front using 5 harmonics. In general, a suitable number of harmonics (< 15) results in a smooth and accurate reconstruction. In contrast, Fig. 16 depicts a poor approximation, mainly due to excessive oscillations caused by an excessive number of 30 harmonics. In this case, the numerical integration becomes inaccurate, as the chosen sampling step is insufficient to capture the high-frequency components introduced by the additional harmonics.

6 Conclusions and Further Work

As previously shown, increasing the number of harmonics over 15 gets a better approximation with respect to the selected support vectors, but unwanted oscillations may be amplified by the imperfect values of support vectors (e.g. points too far apart). This is a limitation from numerical stability perspective.

Nevertheless, the proposed Fourier Apparent Front enables efficient integration in multi-objective general use systems, as well as in embedded systems where the spatial complexity is very large, making an exhaustive search unfeasible. Typically, in many such real-world systems, the true Pareto front is unknown, which motivates the need of an accurate approximation. Based on the 2D analysis, the identified limitations remain applicable in higher-dimensional spaces.

Furthermore, the proposed method is computationally more efficient than classical pairwise non-dominance comparisons, replacing them with the distance evaluation to the approximated front. This computational time-consuming challenge is highlighted in [27], where the authors claim that, on tested benchmarks, classical Pareto dominance takes 50 days simulated on 96 cores at 2 GHz on an Intel Xeon based HPC, managing to reduce this time by 34% through fuzzy logic.

Moreover, the generated curve may not be a Pareto Front, in the sense that one point on the curve may dominate another point on the curve (due to the oscillations). This could be fixed by modifying selected support vectors. Alternatively, it can also be solved by post-processing techniques, such as keeping running dominant values, similar to running maximum methods. In [28] the same Pareto dominance-based algorithm took around 16 days to complete.

A further improvement for skipping the computation of sqrt and atan functions when transforming into polar coordinates, it may be better to transform to coordinates (m^2, $approx\theta$), where $approx\theta$ is a suitable approximation (Taylor series or the computation of the closest bin (kT_s) is needed later). The pivot can be completely artificial, such as the maximum theoretical value along objective Ox, but it may create a (large) jump between the halves that cannot be easily approximated by the series. When the method is used as part of a multi-epoch algorithm, the pivot can also be a value carried over from previous generations.

Introducing additional warp might be another option. Without warp, points on a circle in the space of objectives are transformed into a horizontal line in the polar space. Warp can make any reasonable shape in the space of objectives into a horizontal line (e.g. ellipse). Warp is optional because it may require external information about the true Pareto boundary (and also it may have only a relatively small influence on the overall computation and result). If there are angular regions with no available points, various strategies could be considered: copying values from adjacent regions with points, using interpolation on values from adjacent regions, or from previous generations when the method is used as part of a multi-epoch algorithm. In this study, interpolation is done by the trapezoidal rule on equally spaced points, but this may be improved with other methods of numerically computing integrals, such as Simpson or (modified) Gaussian quadrature. The paper describes in detail the method for two objectives that need to be maximized. However, all the mathematical tools described in the paper have well known generalized versions, such as the hyper spherical coordinates, the generalized Fourier series (usually written in exponential rather than sine functions), and numerical integration in multidimensional spaces. Further work includes such enhancements for the proposed approach. The generalized method of determining Apparent Fronts is therefore a strong candidate for application in multi-objective optimization techniques. The proposed approach will also be integrated and made publicly available within the FADSE framework.

Acknowledgements. This work was partially developed in the project CoDEMO (Co-Creative Decision Makers for 5.0 Organizations - www.codemo-project.eu), Erasmus + Project: Alliances for Education and Enterprises, funded by the Erasmus + Programme (ERASMUS-EDU-2022-PI-ALL-INNO) under project reference number 101104819.

References

1. Pareto, V.: Cours d'economique politique, vol. I-II. F. Rouge, Lausanne (1896) https://archive.org/details/fp-0148-1/mode/2up
2. Deb, K., Saxena, D.: On finding Pareto-optimal solutions through dimensionality reduction for certain large-dimensional multi-objective optimization problems. Technical Report 2005011 Indian Institute of Technology, Kanpur (2005). https://tinyurl.com/2s424dx7
3. Pătrăuşanu, A., Florea, A., Neghină, M., Chiş, R., Dicoiu, A.: Car suspension system design optimization through bio-inspired evolutionary algorithms. In: 28th International Conference on System Theory, Control and Computing (ICSTCC), Sinaia, Romania (2024). https://doi.org/10.1109/icstcc62912.2024.10744669
4. Vintan, L., Chis, R., Ismail, M., Cotofana, C.: Improving computing systems automatic multiobjective optimization through meta-optimization. IEEE Trans. Comput. Aided Des. Integr. Circuits Syst. **35**(7), 1125–1129 (2016). https://doi.org/10.1109/TCAD.2015.2501299
5. Deb, K., Pratap, S., Agarwal, S., Meyarivan, T.: A fast and elitist multiobjective genetic algorithm: NSGA-II. IEEE Trans. Evol. Comput. **6**(2), 182–197 (2002). https://doi.org/10.1109/4235.996017
6. Zitzler, E., Laumanns, M., Thiele, L.: SPEA 2: Improving the strength Pareto evolutionary algorithm, Technical report 103 Computer engineering and Networks Laboratory (TIK), Swiss Federal (2001).. https://sop.tik.ee.ethz.ch/publicationListFiles/zlt2001a.pdf
7. Deb, K., Jain, H.: An evolutionary many-objective optimization algorithm using reference-point-based nondominated sorting approach, part I: solving problems with box constraints. IEEE Trans. Evol. Comput. **18**(4), 577–601 (2014). https://doi.org/10.1109/TEVC.2013.2281534
8. Neghina, M., Vintan, L.: Apparent front ranking: a novel population ranking method for genetic multi-objective algorithms. Proc. Rom. Acad. A. **21**(2), 179–186 (2020) https://acad.ro/sectii2002/proceedings/doc2020-2/11-Neghina_Vintan.pdf

9. Neghina, M., Dicoiu, A.-I., Chis, R., Florea, A.: A competitive new multi-objective optimization genetic algorithm based on apparent front ranking. Eng. Appl. Artif. Intell. **132**, 1–14 (2024). https://doi.org/10.1016/j.engappai.2024.107870
10. Pătrăuşanu, A., Florea, A., Neghină, M., Dicoiu, A., Chiş, R.: A systematic review of multi-objective evolutionary algorithms optimization frameworks. Processes. **12**(869) (2024). https://doi.org/10.3390/pr12050869
11. Calborean, H., Vintan, L.: An automatic design space exploration framework for multicore architecture optimizations. In: 9th RoEduNet IEEE International Conference, pp. 202–207 (2010). https://www.calborean.ro/papers/RoEduNet2010FADSE.pdf
12. Uhrig, S., Shehan, B., Jahr, R., Ungerer, T.: A two-dimensional superscalar processor architecture. In: 2009 Computation World: Future Computing, Service Computation, Cognitive, Adaptive, Content, Patterns, pp. 608–611 (2009). https://doi.org/10.1109/ComputationWorld.2009.46
13. Llopis-Albert, C., Rubio, F., Devece, C., García-Hurtado, D.: Digital twin-based approach for a multi-objective optimal design of wind turbine gearboxes. Mathematics. **12**, 1383 (2024). https://doi.org/10.3390/math12091383
14. Yang, M., Shen, F., Ye, Z., Du, W.: Mathematical modeling and robust multi-objective optimization of the two-dimensional benzene alkylation reactor with dry gas. Processes. **10**, 2271 (2022). https://doi.org/10.3390/pr10112271
15. Wang, Z., Liu, W., Yang, M., Han, D.: A multi-objective evolutionary algorithm model for product form design based on improved SPEA2. Appl. Sci. **9**(14), 2944 (2019). https://doi.org/10.3390/app9142944
16. Mebatsion, H., Paliwal, J., Jayas, D.: Evaluation of variations in the shape of grain types using principal components analysis of the elliptic Fourier descriptors. Comput. Electron. Agric., 63–70 (2012). https://doi.org/10.1016/j.compag.2011.10.016
17. Rosy, C., Yazhinian, S., Therasa, M., Surendra, K., Karuppannan, A., Manikandan, A.: A novel channel estimation of MIMO-OFDM using hybrid bionic binary spotted hyena optimization. Int. J. Cognit. Comput. Eng. **7**, 95–103 (2026). https://doi.org/10.1016/j.ijcce.2025.09.003
18. Cui, X., et al.: An adaptive stratification algorithm for sound velocity profile based on NSGA-II multi-objective optimization. Ocean Eng. **344**, 123665 (2026). https://doi.org/10.1016/j.oceaneng.2025.123665
19. Prasanthi, A., Shareef, H., Errouissi, R., AlAhmad, A.K.: Stochastic optimization of energy storage systems in hybrid electric vehicle under uncertainty. J. Energy Storage. **142**, 119516 (2026). https://doi.org/10.1016/j.est.2025.119516
20. Walter, K.A., Joost, K.N., Floréen, P.: Fourier analysis of genetic algorithms. Theor. Comput. Sci. **229**(1–2), 143–175 (1999). https://doi.org/10.1016/S0304-3975(99)00092-4
21. Vose, M.D., Wright, A.H.: The simple genetic algorithm and the Walsh transform: part I, Theory. Evol. Comput. **6**(3), 253–273 (1998). https://doi.org/10.1162/evco.1998.6.3.253
22. Pachuau, J., et al.: Segmentation of composite signal into harmonic Fourier expansion using genetic algorithm. Int. J. Inf. Technol. **14**, 3507–3515 (2022). https://doi.org/10.1007/s41870-022-00944-7
23. Wang, L., Fang, D.: Combination of genetic algorithm and fast Fourier transform for array failure correction. In: 6th International Symposium on Antennas, Propagation and EM Theory Proceedings, pp. 234–237 (2003). https://doi.org/10.1109/ISAPE.2003.1276671
24. Shafii, N., Seyed Javadi, M.H., Kimiaghalam, B.: A Truncated Fourier Series with genetic algorithm for the control of biped locomotion. In: 2009 IEEE/ASME International Conference on Advanced Intelligent Mechatronics, pp. 1781–1785 (2009). https://doi.org/10.1109/AIM.2009.5229814
25. van Eck, N.J., Waltman, L.: VOSviewer manual (2017). http://vosviewer.com/download/f-y2z2.pdf. Accessed 01 Jan 2026

26. Deitmar, A.: Fourier series. In: A First Course in Harmonic Analysis Universitext. Springer, New York, NY (2002). https://doi.org/10.1007/978-1-4757-3834-6_1
27. Gellert, A., Florea, A., Fiore, U., Zanetti, P., Vintan, L.: Performance and energy optimisation in CPUs through fuzzy knowledge representation. Inf. Sci. **476**, 375–391 (2019). https://doi.org/10.1016/j.ins.2018.03.029
28. Buduleci, C., Gellert, A., Florea, A., Brad, R.: Architectural and technological approaches for efficient energy management in multicore processors. Computers. **13**(4), 84 (2024). https://doi.org/10.3390/computers13040084

WASP It Up: Estimating Parameters Under Noisy Observations

Filipe Vieira(✉) and Francisco Coelho

Departamento de Informática, Escola de Ciências e Tecnologia, Universidade de Évora, Évora, Portugal
d63923@alinos.uevora.pt, fc@uevora.pt

Abstract. As modern engineering systems become increasingly complex and interconnected, reasoning under uncertainty has become a central challenge in domains such as autonomous systems and data-driven urban intelligence. Weighted Answer Set Programming (WASP) provides a framework for modelling uncertainty in answer-set programs via annotated weighted facts, which are propagated to stable models and events to compute event probabilities. However, the weights of WASP facts alone are insufficient to fully determine event probabilities, and observations are required to address the inherent non-determinism of stable models. While previous work on WASP has focused on weight propagation, less attention has been given to the estimation of underlying parameters from observed data. In this work, a parameter estimation method for incomplete or noisy observations is proposed, incorporating a balancing factor to manage the trade-off between model assumptions and data. Alongside the theoretical formulation, an experimental evaluation on simulated datasets is conducted to analyze the method's behavior. This paper reports ongoing doctoral research, presenting an initial formalization and proof-of-concept evaluation.

Keywords: Weighted Answer Set Programming · Parameter Estimation · Probabilistic Logic Programming · Knowledge Representation · Explainable AI

1 Introduction

1.1 Research Question

This doctoral research asks: How can logic-based probabilistic frameworks be extended to estimate latent parameters from noisy observations, preserving symbolic knowledge while inducing a coherent distribution over a closed event space?

1.2 Motivations

This work is motivated by the observation that existing approaches to reasoning under uncertainty tend to occupy two largely disjoint spaces:

Published by Springer Nature Switzerland AG 2027
L. M. Camarinha-Matos and F. Ferrada (Eds.): DoCEIS 2026, IFIP AICT 790, pp. 99–109, 2027.
https://doi.org/10.1007/978-3-032-28939-1_8

1. data-driven learning systems, which achieve remarkable empirical performance but offer limited structural interpretability, and
2. probabilistic logic programming frameworks, which provide strong symbolic guarantees but often rely on restrictive semantic assumptions about the observation process.

Rather than positioning itself as a competitor to large-scale data-driven AI, this research focuses on a complementary setting: learning and inference in domains where the space of possible outcomes is structured, discrete, and conceptually closed, and where symbolic constraints encode essential domain knowledge. Typical examples include engineered systems, diagnostic models, and formally specified domains, where observations are noisy, but the underlying event space is well defined.

In this context, we explore a distinctive modelling perspective. Unlike classical frameworks where probabilities are attached to facts or derivations, our approach defines a closed universe of possible worlds generated by combinations of literals. The learning problem is thus formulated as an algebraic estimation task: given partial and noisy observations, we estimate the parameters that distribute probability mass over this entire theoretical event space. By treating logical relations as structural anchors rather than absolute boundaries, the mechanism reconciles symbolic knowledge with empirical evidence, assigning non-zero probabilities even to configurations not explicitly entailed by the program. This allows the model to remain robust under noise and logical non-determinism, inducing a structured probabilistic representation where the program determines the structural constraints, where the algebraic estimation from data determines the final distribution.

While application domains such as biomedical modelling or cyber-physical systems provide natural motivating scenarios, the present contribution focuses on the formal foundations and algorithmic properties of parameter estimation in logic-based probabilistic frameworks. Domain-specific instantiations and empirical deployment are left as directions for future work within the broader doctoral research agenda.

2 Relationship to Technological Innovation for Societal Challenges

The theme of DoCEIS 2026, "Technological Innovation to Tackle Societal Challenges'", highlights the importance of engineering solutions that remain reliable, transparent, and resilient under real-world uncertainty. As modern infrastructures increasingly rely on complex, sensor-driven systems [1], a central challenge is not only achieving performance, but maintaining structural coherence when observations are noisy, incomplete, or even contradictory.

This work contributes to this broader objective by addressing a specific technical problem: how to estimate probabilistic parameters in symbolic models when empirical data does not perfectly align with the underlying logical structure. In many engineered systems, such as alarm monitoring architectures, autonomous platforms operating under partial observability, or power-grid supervision, sensor readings may conflict or deviate from idealized assumptions. A learning mechanism that naively fits observed frequencies risks distorting formally specified constraints. The proposed parameter estimation framework is designed to reconcile symbolic rules with empirical evidence, allowing probability mass to adapt under noise while preserving structural anchors defined by the logical model.

Beyond robustness, the framework introduces an explicit diagnostic signal (err_D) that quantifies mismatches between observations and model structure. This supports accountable system design by distinguishing between data-induced irregularities and structural inconsistencies, aligning with the broader goals of explainable and trustworthy AI [2, 3]. Furthermore, by exploiting pre-defined symbolic constraints and reducing exponential event spaces to polynomial computations, the approach suggests a structured alternative to unconstrained large-scale learning, potentially contributing to more computationally sustainable and data-efficient modelling paradigms, as the symbolic structure constrains the hypothesis space and is therefore expected to reduce the effective volume of training data required when compared to unconstrained learning models [4].

In this sense, the present work does not target a specific application domain, but rather provides formal and algorithmic foundations for learning in structured, closed-world settings where logical knowledge and uncertain observations must coexist.

3 State of the Art

Probabilistic Logic Programming (PLP) combines symbolic logic with statistical uncertainty, providing a framework for reasoning in noisy or incomplete environments [5]. Traditionally, systems like PRISM [6] and ProbLog [7] have dominated the field, relying on distribution semantics to calculate query success probabilities. In parallel, Answer Set Programming (ASP) formalisms like PASTA [8] and PASOCS [9] have introduced model-based perspectives, often dealing with the higher computational complexity of non-deterministic stable models.

A critical challenge in ASP-based PLP is that propagating weights from facts does not inherently induce a unique distribution over stable models. Frameworks like P-log [10] resolve this via default assumptions (e.g., indifference), while *credal semantics* [11] represent uncertainty through probability intervals.

Weighted Answer Set Programming (WASP) [12] diverges by adopting a model-based approach where weights are propagated to events (sets of atoms). Crucially, WASP relies on observational evidence to shape the resulting distribution, rather than committing to fixed a priori resolutions of non-determinism.

Learning parameters from data is well-established in Prolog-based systems via Expectation-Maximization (EM) [6] or Learning from Interpretations [13]. However, in ASP, the presence of logical non-determinism elevates inference to complexity classes like NP^{PP} (Second-Level Algebraic Model Counting) [14].

While solvers such as aspmc [15] excel at inference, they offer limited support for aligning models with empirical observations. Frameworks like LPMLN [16] adapt Markov Logic techniques, but often modify the underlying program structure. In contrast, the WASP framework seeks to estimate latent parameters from observed data while maintaining the integrity of the original ASP rules.

As noted by Weitkämper [17], parameterization determines whether probabilities converge or degenerate at scale. While WASP defines the framework for this reconciliation, the concrete estimation procedure remains an open challenge. By formulating parameter estimation as a continuous optimization problem, it becomes possible to leverage robust numerical solvers, such as interior-point methods [18], to enforce empirical consistency through explicit objective functions. However, before defining such functions, it is essential to establish the formal foundations of WASP [12] upon which our estimation procedure is built. The following sections bridge these concepts to our proposed method: Sect. 4 revisits the formal foundations of WASP, while Sect. 5 introduces our approach to parameter estimation from empirical data.

4 WASP Revisited: Formal Foundations

Following the semantics introduced in [12], WASP represents uncertainty by associating weights $w \in [0, 1]$ with facts. A weighted fact $a : w$ implicitly induces the complementary literal $\overline{a}$ with weight $1 - w$ This is operationalized in standard ASP through the choice rule $a \vee \overline{a}$, generating a space of stable models where each model corresponds to a possible world.

The foundational probabilistic unit in WASP is the *total choice* $t \in T$, representing a maximal consistent selection of weighted literals. Its weight $\omega_T(t)$ is defined as the product of the weights of its elements:

$$\omega_T(t) = \prod_{a_i \in t} w_i \prod_{\overline{a}_j \in t} (1 - w_j). \tag{1}$$

4.1 Sensors and the Event Space

As proposed in [12], atoms can be interpreted as sensors reflecting environmental signals. In this context, an event is formally defined as a set of literals representing a partial or total observation of these atoms. Consider, for instance, a program with atoms $\{a, b\}$ and the set of possible literals $L = \left\{a, \overline{a}, b, \overline{b}\right\}$. This formulation enables diverse observational scenarios: an event may indicate that both a and b are observed, but b did not occur $\left\{a, \overline{b}\right\}$; that only a has been observed, while the state of b is unknown or hidden $\{a\}$; or even that a provides contradictory signals due to a faulty sensor $\{a, \overline{a}\}$. While traditional PLP typically restricts its semantics to consistent stable models, WASP defines a probability distribution over the entire program literals power set. This broader event space explicitly models noise and structural contradictions, providing a robust formal basis for handling real-world data.

This separation between logical structure and induced distribution is fundamental, the program determines what is possible, whereas empirical data determines what is probable. By maintaining weights in explicit algebraic form, WASP allows observations to inform latent parameters without modifying the underlying rules. Such separation enables the integration of noisy or incomplete observations while preserving symbolic consistency, providing the necessary foundations for the parameter estimation methods presented in the next section.

5 Proposed Methodology for Parameter Estimation in WASP

While the original WASP framework defines a principled semantic for weighted logic, it lacks a concrete mechanism for parameter estimation under noisy or incomplete observations. We propose a generalization of the propagation mechanism, treating stable models as latent system states and events as noisy observations.

To clarify the estimation flow, our methodology transforms the WASP program into an ASP representation to extract the set of Stable Models (latent states). Weights from the program's Total Choices are propagated to these stable models; however, as their precise influence is unknown *a priori*, we introduce latent parameters to be estimated. These weights are then mapped onto the Events and normalized to induce a probabilistic distribution. This entire pipeline is algebraically determined by empirical data, ensuring the final distribution reconciles the logical structure with observed evidence.

5.1 Stable Model Decomposition and Latent Parameters

In the WASP framework, a total choice $t \in T$ supports the set of stable models.

$$S(t) = \{s \mid s \textit{ is a stable model and } t \subseteq s\}. \tag{2}$$

The distribution of weight from t to each $s \in S(t)$ is governed by latent parameters θ_s, capturing epistemic uncertainty and satisfying.

$$\sum_{s \in S(t)} \theta_s = 1. \tag{3}$$

A core property of the WASP to ASP program (Π) translation is that each stable model ($SM(\Pi)$) is associated with exactly one total choice. Since every weighted fact $a : w$ is mapped to a choice rule $a \vee \overline{a}$, any $s \in SM(\Pi)$ must contain a complete and consistent assignment for all weighted atoms W. We define the projection $TC(s) = s \cap \{a, \overline{a} \mid a \in W\}$, which yields the unique $t \in T$ such that $t \subseteq s$.

This unique mapping $s \rightarrow TC(s)$ makes it evident that the number of latent parameters to be estimated is exactly $|SM(\Pi)|$. Consequently, we can index parameters solely by the stable model and define its total weight as:

$$\omega_S(s) = \theta_s \cdot \omega_T(TC(s)). \tag{4}$$

The estimation problem thus consists in finding the vector θ that best aligns the program with empirical data, subject to the constraints imposed by the underlying total choices.

5.2 Similarity-Based Weight Propagation

The original WASP semantics relies on binary equivalence classes $[e]_\sim$, where event weights are derived from a strict logical satisfaction of a stable core. This approach is inherently sensitive to noise, as any observation slightly inconsistent with the program rules is assigned zero weight, effectively discarding valuable empirical evidence. We propose replacing this rigid membership with a continuous similarity measure *sim(e, s)*, interpreting stable models as latent system states and events as noisy observations. The continuous event weight is then defined as:

$$\omega_E(e) = \sum_{s \in S} sim(e, s)\omega_S(s). \tag{5}$$

where $\omega_S(s)$ denotes the weight of latent state s. Finally, the probability associated with each event is obtained by normalizing the weights:

$$P_E(e) = \frac{W_E(e)}{Z} \tag{6}$$

$$Z = \sum_{e \in E} \omega_E(e). \tag{7}$$

, ensuring that

$$\sum_{e \in E} P_E(e) = 1. \tag{8}$$

This continuous formulation enables graded reasoning, where inconsistent or independent events still contribute to parameter estimation proportional to their proximity to the stable core, while providing a smoother objective function that facilitates the convergence of gradient-based optimization.

5.3 Efficient Normalization and Combinatorial Reduction

The calculation of the normalization factor

$$Z = \sum_{e \in E} \omega_E(e). \tag{9}$$

requires marginalizing the similarity over the entire event space .

By swapping the summation order, we isolate the total similarity contribution for each stable model $s \in S$:

$$Z = \sum_{s \in S} \omega_S(s) \sum_{e \in E} sim(e, s). \tag{10}$$

The term $\sum_{e \in E} sim(e, s)$ poses a significant challenge, as $|E| = 2^n$. However, for the Jaccard similarity, we can represent events as bit-strings of length n and observe that the similarity depends only on two counts: p, the number of shared atoms ($e \cap s$), and q, the number of atoms present in e but absent in s ($|e \setminus s|$). For a fixed stable model s of size $|s|$, the number of events e that share the same similarity value $\frac{p}{|s|+q}$ is given by the combinatorial product $\binom{|s|}{p}\binom{n-|s|}{q}$. This allows us to collapse the exponential sum into a polynomial double summation:

$$\sum_{e \in E} sim(e, s) \sum_{p=1}^{s} \sum_{q=0}^{n-|s|} \binom{|s|}{p} \binom{n-|s|}{q} \frac{p}{|s|+q}. \tag{11}$$

This reduction transforms the complexity from $O(2^n)$ to $O(|s|(n - |s|)$, rendering the parameter estimation scalable for large-scale systems.

5.4 Parameter Estimation and the Q Factor

As defined in Sect. 5.1, the estimation of the latent parameters θ is framed as a constrained optimization problem subject to $\sum_{s \in S(t)} \theta_s = 1$. In a standard empirical setting, observed data is normalized such that the sum of observed frequencies $\sum_{e \in E_{obs}} P_D(e) = 1$. Consequently, a traditional quadratic objective function:

$$err_D = \sum_{e \in E_{obs}} (P_E(e) - P_D(e))^2 + \sum_{e \notin E_{obs}} P_E(e)^2. \tag{12}$$

implicitly treats the empirical record as an exhaustive description of the domain. Since the observed mass already sums to unity, the optimization process is pressured to drive $P_E(e) \to 0$ for all unobserved events, effectively ignoring states that are logically supported by the program but absent from the finite sample.

To address this, we introduce a factor $Q \in [0, 1]$, estimated jointly with θ, representing the probability mass the model assigns to the observed window E_{obs} . By defining $\sum_{e \in E_{obs}} P_E(e) = Q$, we rescale the empirical evidence to allow a probability margin $1 - Q$ for unobserved events. If the model aligns with the rescaled data, we recover the intended distribution:

$$\sum_{e \in E_{obs}} P_E(e) \approx \sum_{e \in E_{obs}} (Q \cdot P_D(e)) = Q \sum_{e \in E_{obs}} P_D(e) = Q. \tag{13}$$

The full objective function, accounting for both observed and non-observed margins, is defined as:

$$err_D = \sum_{e \in E_{obs}} (P_E(e) - Q \cdot P_D(e))^2 + \left(\sum_{e \notin E} P_E(e) - (1 - Q) \right)^2. \tag{14}$$

Calculating the last square of the equation (err_{ND}) directly is prohibitively expensive due to the exponential growth of the event space. However, noting that $P_E(e) = \omega_E(e)/Z$, we optimize the computation of the unobserved weights by leveraging the global symmetry of the space:

$$\begin{aligned} \sum_{e \notin E_{obs}} \omega_E(e) &= \sum_{s \in S} \omega_S(s) \sum_{e \notin E_{obs}} sim(e, s) \\ &= \sum_{s \in S} \omega_S(s) \left(\sum_{e \in E} sim(e, s) - \sum_{e \in E_{obs}} sim(e, s) \right). \end{aligned} \tag{15}$$

The computational gain is decisive: the global sum $\sum_{e \in E} sim(e, s)$ is calculated in polynomial time using the binomial coefficients derived in Sect. 5.3. By subtracting the weights of the few observed events from this pre-calculated total, we maintain scalability for large-scale systems.

By Incorporating this optimization into the objective function, the final expression for the diagnostic error err_D allows the model to interpolate between empirical data and logical structure without overfitting to the partial observation window:

$$err_D = \sum_{e \in E_{obs}} (P_E(e) - Q \cdot P_D(e))^2 + \left(\frac{1}{Z} \sum_{e \notin E_{obs}} \omega_E(e) - (1 - Q) \right)^2. \tag{16}$$

6 Discussion of Results and Critical View

This section provides a critical analysis of the experimental results obtained for the proposed parameter estimation mechanism. The framework is implemented using Clingo [19] for ASP grounding and stable model extraction, while the non-linear optimization task is handled by the IPOPT solver [18], which utilizes an interior-point method to estimate parameters over the quadratic approximation. Rather than focusing on benchmark comparisons, the discussion examines how the framework behaves under logical constraints, noisy observations, and structural growth of the state space. We analyze both strengths and shortcomings, identifying contexts where the model behaves robustly and where it exposes intrinsic limitations. Particular attention is given to the role of Q, the diagnostic error err_D, and the solver feedback, as these elements clarify how the model balances empirical evidence with logical structure.

6.1 Strengths and Limitations

The current prototype's scalability is primarily challenged by the exponential growth of the event space and the resulting computational pressure. As the number of program literals increases, the set of stable models expands, directly increasing the number of parameters to be estimated. These parameters are optimized by IPOPT [18], which minimizes a global error function based on the model's logical constraints. However, as this quadratic structure grows, the computational demand can exceed the solver's efficient range. This bottleneck stems from the global nature of the current formulation rather than a failure of the solver itself. Simultaneously, the theoretical event space grows exponentially because each literal can exist in multiple states (positive, negative, both, or unobserved). In practice, achieving full empirical coverage becomes impossible, requiring the system to operate under a capped observation regime (Fig. 1). Despite these hurdles, the framework remains robust because it avoids explicit enumeration of all events. By focusing on observed data, the mechanism maintains stability even when the theoretical universe is infeasibly large, scaling beyond what naive combinatorial reasoning would suggest.

Regarding the ASP solving phase, *Clingo* [19] performs robustly, as expected from a state-of-the-art solver. However, there remains room for improvement. Parallelization strategies or structural decompositions of the transformed program could further enhance scalability and remain open avenues for future work.

Finally, due to the scalability constraints discussed above, experiments were conducted using synthetic datasets and relatively small programs. While this allows controlled structural evaluation, it limits the immediate assessment of real-world applicability.

Due to these limitations, a comparison with other frameworks (e.g., ProbLog or LPMLN) was intentionally deferred. Since these frameworks operate under distinct semantic assumptions regarding non-determinism and noise, an artificial benchmark would primarily highlight these conceptual divergences rather than providing a neutral performance metric. A comparison using real-world data would allow for a more objective measurement of the model's accuracy. Therefore, extending validation to larger and more heterogeneous domains remains an important next step.

6.2 Role of the Similarity Function

The similarity function regulates how probability mass is assigned between stable models (the logical nucleus of the system) and observed events, which may deviate due to noise or incomplete observations. Events closer to the logical nucleus receive more mass, while distant events receive less, preserving structural bias while enabling robustness.

Our experiments indicate that similarity acts as a probability regulator, controlling the trade-off between logical precision and empirical adaptability. We observe that Q factor grows approximately linearly with data coverage (Fig. 1), suggesting that a substantial fraction of probability mass is distributed among unobserved events, and that this mass is roughly uniform. This behavior is directly related to the choice of similarity function.

As the state space expands, the probability mass of program events is diluted across an exponentially large number of potential events, keeping Q relatively small and limiting the influence of observed data. This effect does not reflect a failure of Q, which still represents the total mass assigned to observed events of the program, but rather the structural constraints imposed by stable models and shared adjustable parameters (θ). These observations underscore that the similarity function plays a central role in regulating probability mass. Accordingly, it warrants careful consideration and systematic exploration in future work.

6.3 Behavior of Q, Approximation Error, and Convergence

Empirical evaluation using synthetic datasets with varying observation coverage allows us to analyze the joint diagnostic behavior of Q, error, and solver convergence.

For structurally compatible observations, approximation error remains consistently low (below 10^{-6}), even as coverage increases. In this regime, IPOPT [18] reports successful convergence, and Q grows proportionally with coverage (Fig. 1), indicating that additional empirical evidence is incorporated without introducing structural tension. Across different program scales and observation regimes, this proportional behavior remains consistent, indicating that the diagnostic patterns are stable with respect to both coverage and program size.

When observations conflict with the logical structure, deviations emerge progressively. For small Q, inconsistencies may initially be partially absorbed and appear weakly in the objective function. As coverage increases, however, structural tension becomes explicit through rising approximation error values and non-successful IPOPT [18] termination statuses. The agreement between these semantic and numerical diagnostics indicates that estimation failures reflect structural mismatches rather than numerical instability.

Program approximation to observed data therefore relies on a dual yet coherent diagnostic criterion: internal semantic consistency, captured by approximation error and external numerical convergence, reported by IPOPT [18]. Low approximation error together with successful solver termination signals a well-posed estimation problem, whereas failure in either diagnostic indicates structural or empirical inconsistency requiring further inspection.

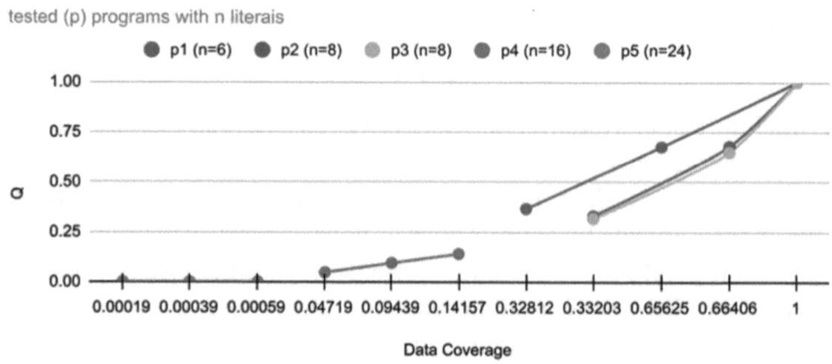

Fig. 1. Scaling factor Q for fit datasets with increasing data coverage, capped at 10,000 events per program. Q is estimated jointly with model parameters and rises towards 1 as coverage grows. The diagnostic error remained below 10^{-6}, confirming stability for the fit data.

7 Conclusions and Future Work

This work presents a methodology for latent parameter estimation in WASP, demonstrating that the framework reconciles symbolic logic with empirical observations while preserving structural consistency. Our evaluation shows that the system successfully integrates compatible data, exposes structural mismatches via the error function and IPOPT [18] performance, and maintains non-zero probability for unobserved events through the scaling factor Q.

Despite these results, future work will focus on addressing scalability and refining the modeling paradigm. We intend to enhance solver performance and WASP encoding for larger programs, exploring parallel execution and modular optimization strategies to reduce the computational overhead of the global quadratic approximation. These improvements will enable us to conduct a comprehensive comparative study with other probabilistic logic frameworks, such as ProbLog or LPMLN, under real-world scales. Additionally, we will systematically study alternative similarity functions to understand their influence on probability mass allocation. By focusing on these advancements, this approach aims to contribute to the ongoing effort of bridging symbolic reasoning with empirical evidence, providing a principled basis for further developments in probabilistic logic programming modeling.

References

1. Baheti, R., Gill, H.: Cyber-physical systems. In: Samad, T., Annaswamy, A.M. (eds.) The Impact of Control Technology, pp. 161–166. IEEE Control Systems Society (2011)
2. Arrieta, A.B., Del Ser, J., Bennetot, A., Tabik, S., Barbado, A., et al.: Explainable artificial intelligence (XAI): concepts, taxonomies, opportunities and challenges toward responsible AI. Inf. Fusion. **58**, 82–115 (2020). https://doi.org/10.1016/j.inffus.2019.12.012
3. Miller, T.: Explanation in artificial intelligence: insights from the social sciences. Artif. Intell. **267**, 1–38 (2019). https://doi.org/10.1016/j.artint.2018.07.007
4. Schwartz, R., Dodge, J., Smith, N.A., Etzioni, O.: Green AI. Commun. ACM. **63**(12), 54–63 (2020). https://doi.org/10.1145/3381831

5. De Raedt, L., Kimmig, A.: Probabilistic (logic) programming concepts. Mach. Learn. **100**(1), 5–47 (2015). https://doi.org/10.1007/s10994-015-5494-z
6. Sato, T., Kameya, Y.: PRISM: a language for symbolic-statistical modeling. In: Proceedings of the 15th International Joint Conference on Artificial Intelligence (IJCAI 1997), pp. 1330–1339 (1997)
7. De Raedt, L., Kimmig, A., Toivonen, H.: ProbLog: a probabilistic prolog and its application in link discovery. In: Proceedings of the 20th International Joint Conference on Artificial Intelligence (IJCAI 2007), pp. 2462–2467 (2007)
8. Azzolini, D., Bellodi, E., Riguzzi, F.: Statistical statements in probabilistic logic programming. In: Fodor, G., Volpe, G. (eds.) Logic Programming and Nonmonotonic Reasoning. LPNMR 2022. LNCS, vol. 13416, pp. 43–55. Springer, Cham (2022). https://doi.org/10.1007/978-3-031-15707-3_4
9. Tuckey, D., Russo, A., Broda, K.: PASOCS: a parallel approximate solver for probabilistic logic programs under the credal semantics. arXiv preprint arXiv:2105.10908. (2021)
10. Baral, C., Gelfond, M., Rushton, N.: Probabilistic reasoning with answer sets. Theory Pract. Log. Program. **9**(1), 57–144 (2009). https://doi.org/10.1017/S1471068408003645
11. Cozman, F.G., Mauá, D.D.: The joy of probabilistic answer set programming: semantics, complexity, expressivity, inference. Int. J. Approx. Reason. **125**, 218–239 (2020). https://doi.org/10.1016/j.ijar.2020.07.004
12. Coelho, F., Dinis, B., Seipel, D., Abreu, S.: Elements for weighted answer-set programming. In: Proceedings of the 14th Symposium on Languages, Applications and Technologies (SLATE 2025) OASIcs, vol. 135, pp. 3:1–3:16 (2025). https://doi.org/10.4230/OASIcs.SLATE.2025.3
13. Dries, A. et al.: ProbLog2: probabilistic logic programming. In: Bifet, A., et al. (eds.) Machine Learning and Knowledge Discovery in Databases. ECML PKDD 2015. LNCS, vol. 9286, pp. 312–315. Springer, Cham (2015). https://doi.org/10.1007/978-3-319-23461-8_37
14. Kiesel, R., Totis, P., Kimmig, A.: Efficient knowledge compilation beyond weighted model counting. Theory Pract. Log. Program. **22**(4), 505–522 (2022). https://doi.org/10.1017/S1471068422000014X
15. Eiter, T., Hecher, M., Kiesel, R.: Treewidth-aware cycle breaking for algebraic answer set counting. In: Proceedings of the 18th International Conference on Principles of Knowledge Representation and Reasoning (KR 2021), pp. 269–279 (2021). https://doi.org/10.24963/kr.2021/26
16. Lee, J., Wang, Y.: Weight learning in a probabilistic extension of answer set programs. In: Proceedings of the 16th International Conference on Principles of Knowledge Representation and Reasoning (KR 2018), pp. 657–658 (2018)
17. Weitkämper, F.Q.: An asymptotic analysis of probabilistic logic programming, with implications for expressing projective families of distributions. Theory Pract. Log. Program. **21**(6), 802–817 (2021). https://doi.org/10.1017/S1471068421000314
18. Wächter, A., Biegler, L.: On the implementation of an interior-point filter line-search algorithm for large-scale nonlinear programming. Math. Program. **106**(1), 25–57 (2006). https://doi.org/10.1007/s10107-004-0559-y
19. Gebser, M., Kaminski, R., Kaufmann, B., Schaub, T.: Answer Set Solving in Practice Synthesis Lectures on Artificial Intelligence and Machine Learning. Springer, Cham (2022). https://doi.org/10.1007/978-3-031-01561-8

AI in Biomedical Systems

A Review on Technological Requirements for Ultrasound Image-Guided Neuromodulation Application-Specific Integrated Circuits

Diogo Dias[1(✉)], Tiago Costa[2], and João Goes[1]

[1] NOVA University of Lisbon, LASI, UNINOVA-CTS, Lisbon, Portugal
das.dias@campus.fct.unl.pt
[2] Delft University of Technology, Delft, The Netherlands

Abstract. Neuromodulation has advanced from pharmacological approaches to various stimulation techniques targeting the nervous system, including electrical, magnetic, and optogenetic methods. While these offer precise control, they pose challenges such as invasiveness and surgical risks. Low-intensity focused ultrasound (LIFUS) emerges as a noninvasive option for modulating deep brain activity. However, issues such as skull attenuation and tissue temperature rise remain obstacles. Implantable FUS (iFUS) systems aim to enhance targeting precision but require integrated imaging and real-time monitoring. Recent innovations in diagnostic ultrasound technology show promise as alternatives to traditional MRI for focal spot localization and identification, enabling monitoring of neuro-modulatory effects via functional ultrasound imaging. This work reviews safety and operational requirements for image-guided LIFUS, while contextualizing them within the integrated systems specifications. Additionally, it examines existing application-specific integrated circuits (ASICs) for ultrasound-on-chip (UoC) systems and the required functionalities and performance that enable the development of safe wearable and implantable devices.

Keywords: Low-Intensity Focused Ultrasound Therapy · Ultrasound Image-Guided Therapy · Diagnostic Ultrasound-on-Chip Systems

1 Introduction

1.1 Societal Challenge and Clinical Context: Tackling Neurological Disorders

The leading cause of illness and disability worldwide is neurological disorders, currently affecting approximately a third of the world's population [1]. The blood-brain barrier (BBB) limits central and peripheral nervous system (CNS, PNS, respectively) drug delivery, being implicated in neurological disorders when compromised. Non-pharmacological neuromodulation—magnetic, electrical, optical, and acoustic—is based in the use of medical devices exploiting electromagnetic or mechanical pressure fields to interact with the nervous system [2–4], as seen on Fig. 1. The aforementioned

Published by Springer Nature Switzerland AG 2027
L. M. Camarinha-Matos and F. Ferrada (Eds.): DoCEIS 2026, IFIP AICT 790, pp. 113–124, 2027.
https://doi.org/10.1007/978-3-032-28939-1_9

devices can also modulate BBB permeability, enhancing therapy through pharmacological approaches [3, 4]. Acoustic stimulation is favored by clinicians and patients alike for its non-invasiveness, broad spatial coverage and resolution, and low-cost clinical use [2]. Focused ultrasound (FUS) enables precise, non-invasive neuromodulation of deep brain regions [3–7]. It has been observed that low-intensity FUS (LIFUS) modulates neural activity, possibly via mechanosensitive ion channels through cavitation and membrane capacitance modulation [3, 4].

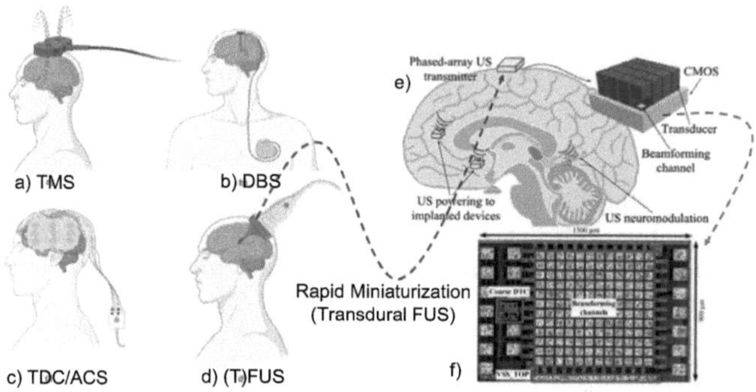

Fig. 1. Overview of CNS stimulation techniques: a) TMS, b) DBS, c) TDCS/TACS, d) tFUS, [2] e) Transdural ultrasound neuromodulation devices, and f) ASIC chip with PZT-on-CMOS transducer matrix, adapted from [5].

1.2 Technology Transfer and Focused Ultrasound Therapy Safety Concerns

When targeting the brain through the skull, higher-frequency center carriers, pulse repetition frequencies (PRF) or increased focal spot pressure induce thermal effects, raising safety concerns due to skull absorption and increased heat dissipation in transcranial FUS (tFUS) [3, 4]. Skull attenuation during tFUS increases intracranial heating and risk of brain tissue damage, especially at higher focal resolutions (frequencies above 2 MHz) and pressures above 1 MPa [3, 8, 9]. Raising applied pressure to offset skull losses further increases safety risks [3–5, 8, 9]. Operating tFUS below 1 MHz reduces overheating but compromises spatial resolution - and targeting precision. Magnetic Resonance Imaging (MRI) guidance tracks temperature and allows alignment of the focal spot with the target based on the thermal gradient near the focal spot, as depicted in Fig. 2. MRI guidance is also crucial in other high-intensity FUS (HIFUS) applications, such as tumor ablation, where power densities are extreme and off-target thermal control is critical to avoid unwanted tissue damage [4, 8, 9]. Emerging implantable FUS (iFUS) systems, placed on the brain or integrated with transparent cranial windows, bypass skull attenuation, permitting higher frequencies and finer focal precision [4–7, 10]. Moreover, next generation conformable 2D phased arrays accommodate brain curvature, but difficult accurate volumetric focusing. Robust is therefore essential for precise electronic beam steering and easier clinical translation, promoting healthcare accessibility to LIFUS-capable medical devices [5–7].

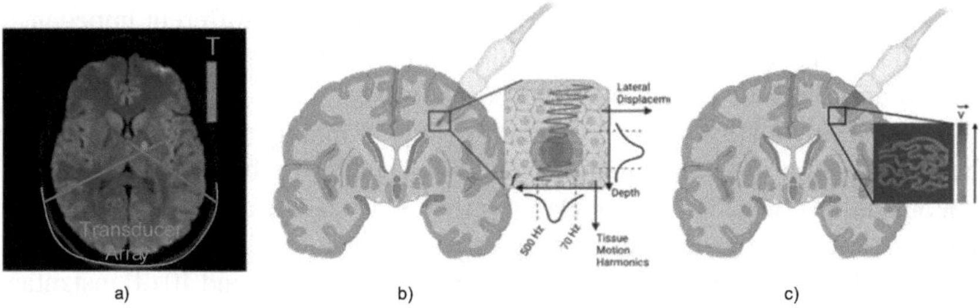

Fig. 2. a) MRI localizes the focal spot via thermometry; b) missing FUS device features include HMI for focal-spot localization [9] and c) high-frame-rate US for blood flow monitoring [10].

1.3 Problem Statement: Towards Innovative Miniaturized Ultrasound Image-Guided Neuromodulation Devices

High-frame-rate ultrasound imaging (HF-USI) offers portable, real-time vascular monitoring and functional neuromodulation assessment. HF-USI serves as a point-of-care alternative to MRI in current hand-held US theranostics setups [8–11]. Frame rates above 2000 FPS enable precise focal spot localization and closed-loop tissue targeting via harmonic motion imaging (HMI) [9, 11, 12]. Very high frame-rate imaging modalities are achievable through planar or divergent wave USI methods. However, each individual radiofrequency (RF) channel must accessible from the interfacing readout electronics in such modalities [13–15]. Current HF-USI ultrasound-on-chip (UoC) diagnostic systems allowing individual can generate up to 50 Gb/s of data throughput per channel in each acquired frame [16]. These systems address the high data rates using conventional channel compression methods such as time and frequency-division channel multiplexing (TDM, FDM respectively) [15–20]. Consequently, the latter are limited to hand-held thermostatics setups, once they trade-off higher output channel bandwidth for higher channel compression ratios, and the form factor of the UoC active die-area is proportional to bandwidth and the overall dynamic power dissipation of the system. Next-generation, miniaturized wearable or implantable US devices allow continuous, uninterrupted therapeutic and diagnostic procedures, benefiting from compact, efficient UoC systems extending the battery life of the setup [21, 22]. Enabling high temporal-resolution imaging modes in wearable systems requires unconventional data compression methods that break-away from the output channel bandwidth tradeoff bottleneck [17]. The main research question driving this work can therefore be laid out:

How can ultrasound-on-chip (UoC) integrated circuits be architectured to achieve state-of-the-art miniaturization while supporting individual channel RF data access at framerates above 2000 frames-per-second (FPS)?

2 Ultrasound Technology

2.1 Ultrasound Fundamentals

In a bounded incompressible liquid, sound wave speed cL depends on how efficiently particles transfer momentum, increasing with the medium's density ρ. The ratio of acoustic pressure p to particle velocity v defines the acoustic characteristic impedance Z =

p/vL = ρ · cL [Rayl]. At an interface between two media with different impedances Z1 and Z2 and sound speeds c1 and c2, reflection and refraction govern wave propagation. Snell's law describes the refraction of the elastic wave.

Ultrasound attenuation (P(x) = P0eαxf0 [Pa]) is mainly governed by absorption and heat dissipation in homogeneous media, with scattering being superposed in heterogeneous tissues (Fig. 3). Diagnostic US models soft tissue as homogeneous locally. Attenuation (linear in dB) depends on frequency (f0), distance (DL), and medium attenuation (α) (1). US transducers typically provide a 6-dB bandwidth and 40 dB instantaneous dynamic range, with total dynamic range in diagnostic applications spanning 60–120 dB [15–20].

$$DR_P = f_0 \, 2D_L \, \alpha_{dB} \, [dB] \tag{1}$$

$$DR_T = DR_P + DR_I \; [dB] \tag{2}$$

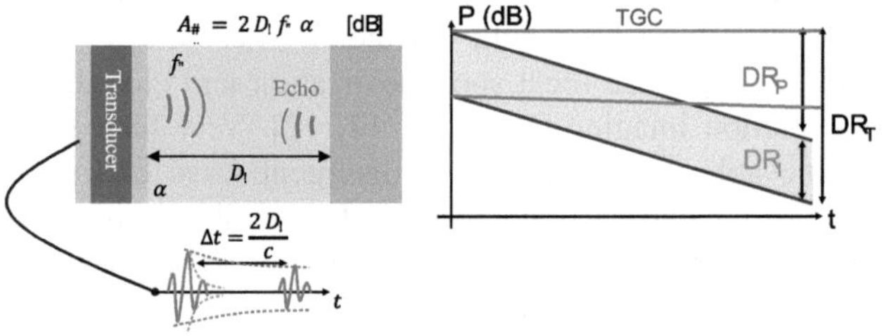

Fig. 3. Attenuation phenomena in US wave propagation with the total propagation dynamic range (DRP) superposed to the characteristic instantaneous dynamic range (DRI) of the band-limited US signals, represented in the time domain in a) amplitude y-axis and b) decibel (dB) y-axis.

Conversion between mechanical and electrical energy is commonly performed through piezoelectric materials or micro-electromechanical (MEM) devices (Fig. 4). High Qm bulk piezoelectric transducers (BPTs) are optimal for therapy (narrow-band, long pulses); low Qm is preferred for diagnostics (broadband, short pulses), achieved via mechanical/electrical damping [17, 23]. BPTs (i.e. PZT, PMN-PT) (kt = 0.5–0.75; Qm >30) commonly operate in the 3–3 mode (electric field and mechanical displacement aligned). Piezoelectric and capacitive micromachined transducers (PMUTs and CMUTs, respectively) employ resonating membranes commonly operated in 3–1 mode (orthogonal field/displacement), for low acoustic impedance, reduced Q, and broad bandwidth, suiting diagnostics [17, 23]. Biocompatibility concerns with lead-based transducers sprouted the interest for lead-free and polymer alternatives (PVDF, BaTiO3, KNN) offering better tissue impedance but reduced electromechanical conversion and increased heating [17, 23, 24].

Phase control in phased arrays enables dynamic beamforming and steering of ultrasound (US) waves via delay-and-sum (DAS) processing. Aperture of transducer arrays or matrices sets field of view (FoV) and lateral resolution; half-wavelength (λ/2) pitch prevents grating lobes within the observation region of the array (spatial Nyquist sampling to prevent aliasing) [25]. Focused transmission converges wavefronts at a focal

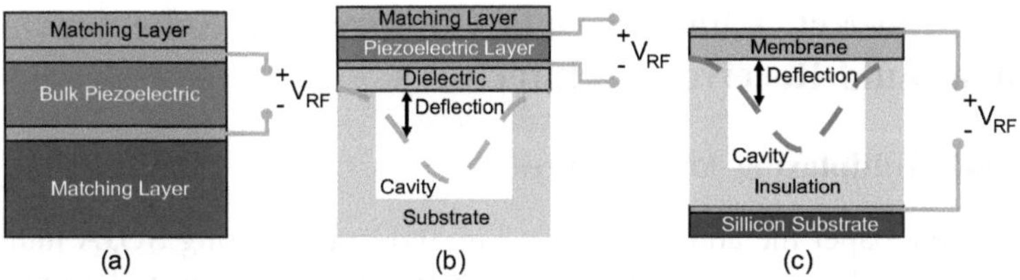

Fig. 4. Material stack illustration of ultrasound transducer architectures based on a) bulk piezoelectric transducers, b) piezoelectric micro-machined ultrasound transducers (PMUTs), and c) capacitive micro-machined ultrasound transducers (CMUTs).

point, while plane-wave transmission steers planar beams and divergent wave transmissions purposefully create an unfocused planar wavefront to increase FoV. As shown by Fig. 5, echoes are amplified (TGC), filtered, and delay-aligned for DAS. Log-compressed amplitude and phase data yield A-mode signals for 2D/3D imaging [25]. Doppler US uses echo phase shifts for flow velocity estimation [10, 13, 15]. Use of raw RF data is increasing for efficient machine learning-based reconstruction and denoising [15, 17]. It is also estimated that raw RF data processing allows for efficient processing power distribution throughout the data acquisition chain, facilitating device miniaturization [15, 17].

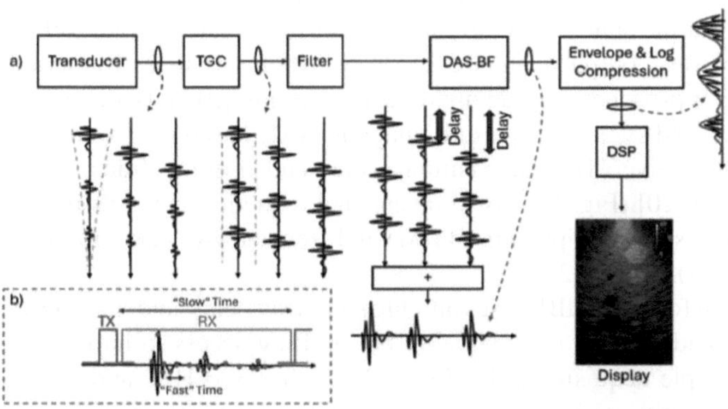

Fig. 5. a) Conventional signal processing chain in ultrasound imaging systems, showing TGC compensating for propagation attenuation of US echoes, low-pass filtering for anti-aliasing upon sampling of US echoes, DAS receive-beamforming for SNR increase for each independent medium line [25], logarithmic compression to 8-bit equivalent dynamic range and finally back-end processing for displaying b) depiction of the concepts of slow and fast time, located between acquisition time frames and acquired time samples, respectively.

3 State-of-the-Art: Channel Data Compression Schemes in Ultrasound Receiver Architectures

3.1 Channel Multiplexing Architectures

At the end of the paper the authors present Fig. 9a), summarizing SOTA multiplexing architectures in UoC and illustrating tradeoffs between element-level data access, integration, and channel count reduction. The figure of merit ($FoM = \sqrt{F_S P_{ch}/C_R}$) relates sampling clock frequency (FS), power (Pch), and channel data compression (CR), with a smaller FoM being a more performant architecture. Overall, architectures lacking element-level access optimize data compression ratios and reduce power dissipation but significantly limit temporal resolution (<2000 FPS). In contrast, architectures enabling element level raw-data access can achieve fast framerates (>2000 FPS). However, currently employed architectures trade-off higher channel-compression ratios for higher output channel bandwidth (with higher dynamic power dissipation).

High temporal resolution imaging modes require high framerates, while image contrast and depth-of-view (DoV) benefit from large apertures (high input, $[]$, channel count) [10, 13, 15]. Data compression schemes can be performed in the time or aperture domain, reducing the amount of required time samples (sampling frequency) and output channel-count, respectively. For transducer arrays with >1000 elements, channel-count reduction relies on multiplexing analog frontends (AFEs), benefiting from direct interfacing with UoC ASICs [15, 16, 18, 19]. Conventional multiplexing architectures, observed within the state-of-the-art, either limit frame rate or trade-off output channel bandwidth for lower output channel count to avoid compromising framerate [16]. Frame-rate-reducing approaches include microbeam forming (μBF), Hadamard-encoded summation (HES), and synthetic-aperture imaging (SAI)-based approaches, requiring multiple transmit-receive (T/R) acquisition cycles and limiting frame rates below 2000 FPS [14, 15, 18–20] (Fig. 6). Fast-time channel reduction methods include analog and digital time-division multiplexing (TDM) and frequency-division multiplexing (FDM) (FPS ≥1000 Hz) [16, 18–20, 26].

Microbeam forming (μBF) uses on-chip sub-array delay-and-sum (DAS) for channel reduction, providing high image quality but limiting access to individual RF data and requiring multiple acquisitions for full FoV (FPS ≤300 Hz), and incorporating μBF directly on the physical layer marked a major breakthrough in the miniaturization of US catheter probes (FoM ≤ 0.9 MHz mW) [18–20]. HES exploits orthogonal matching pursuit algorithms, using orthogonal codes for slow-time analog code-division channel multiplexing (FoM ≤2.0 MHz mW), but limits FoV, and similarly to μBF requires multiple cycles (FPS ≤500 Hz) [14, 15]. SAI activates element subsets per acquisition, enabling low-framerate channel access, being vulnerable to motion artefacts due to low framerate acquisitions.

TDM allocates time slots via a Johnson counter, while FDM allocates sub bands of the frequency spectrum through up-and-down conversion. FDM is power and die-area intensive, requiring the use of multiple frequency carriers modulating each input channel, and restricting the minimum output channel bandwidth to the highest frequency sub-band limit (FoM >10.0 MHz mW) [26]. TDM presents low complexity but scalability in channel count reduction is limited (FoM ≥2.5 MHz mW) [16, 18–20]. Both allow

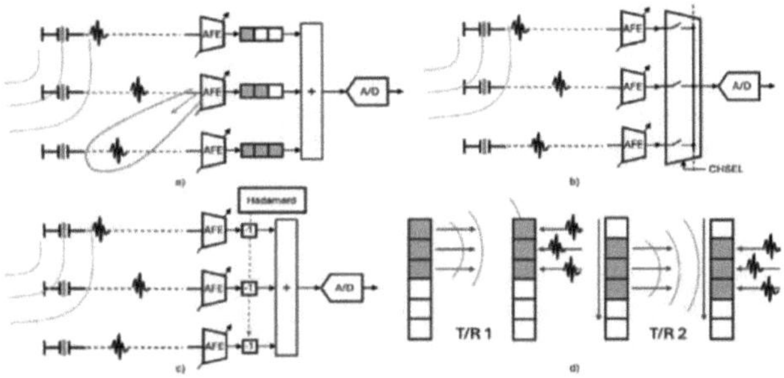

Fig. 6. Output channel-count reduction through a) sub-array beamforming (μBF), b) time-division multiplexing access (TDMA), and c) Hadamard-encoded element summation (HES). The directivity of the receive sub-array beamformer in a) is presented by the directivity profile in gray. A depiction of two unique transmit / receive (T/R) cycles in a synthetic-aperture imaging (SAI) is presented in d).

raw RF data access but increase power and crosstalk as channel reduction ratio grows due to the required fast sampling clocks driving both architectures.

3.2 Compressive Multiplexing of Ultrasound Echoes

US echoes m(t), while not being sparse in the time-domain, follow the pulse stream model (3), where $\epsilon j \in MN,1(\Re)$ is the basis-kernel projection error, as a sum of band-limited Gaussian-modulated cosine kernels v(t) [27]. US echoes can therefore be designated as compressible - but not sparse - signals. The convolutional basis matrix V is a dictionary of possible received echoes, enabling a sparse representation of each RF channel $m_j(t) = \sum_{k=1}^{P} m_k\ v(t - t_k)$.

$$m_j = V \times \hat{m}_j + \epsilon_j,\ \|m\|_0 \leq K \tag{3}$$

This model decomposes US echoes into pulse streams of band-limited, frequency and time-sparse signals, enabling compressive sensing (CS) of US echoes [27, 28]. Orthogonal chipping PRBS sequences ensure accurate signal recovery and minimize cross-channel interference, maximizing CMUX output autocorrelation ($(P \odot M)T(P \odot M) \to IJ$). Data compression is performed in the aperture domain with bipolar PRBS (pj(t) = $\{-1,1\}$) for channel modulation (Fig. 7) [27], or in the time domain with unipolar PRBS (pj(t) = $\{0,1\}$) for sub-Nyquist sampling [28]. The compressive multiplexer (CMUX) uses bipolar PRBS spectrum spreading (Fig. 7) for aperture multiplexing, enabling individual RF access and efficient reconstruction. CMUX allows slow- and fast-time multiplexing, eliminates the need for integrator filters, and achieves near-Nyquist sampling rates that scale logarithmically with channel compression [27]. Its main limitation is inter-channel noise, which may require a faster sampling rate or enforced sparsity for mitigation.

$$F_S = \mathrm{O(S\ \log(B\ J))} < \mathrm{C\ B\ \log(B\ J)^p},\ \mathrm{p} \in \mathrm{R} > 1, \mathrm{C} \in \mathrm{R} \leq 1 \tag{4}$$

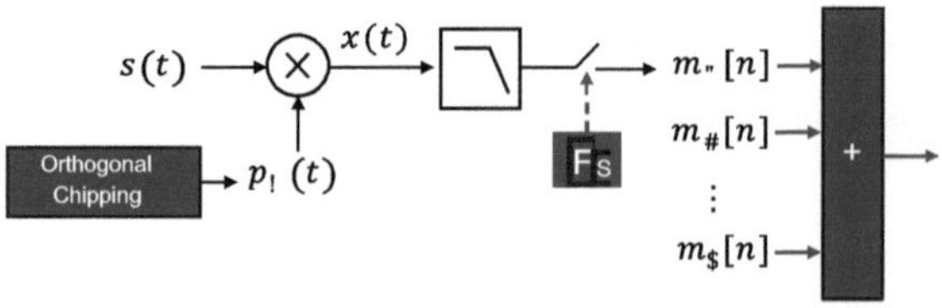

Fig. 7. Block diagram of a pseudo-random modulator-based compressive multiplexer: s(t) is the RF input, pc(t) is the orthogonal chipping sequence, x(t) is the modulated signal, and m(t) is the accumulated output.

The output of any architecture employing CS is described by Y = (P ⊙ M) A, where Y ∈ M(ℜ)NS,R are the column-wise output signals, P ∈ M(ℜ)NS,J are the column-wise PRBS modulating each individual input RF channel, M ∈ M(ℜ)NS,J is the column-wise samples of each multiplexed RF channel, and A ∈ M(ℜ)J,R is the summation matrix stating which of the J input RF channels are modulated and superposed together [27, 28]. The vector basis pursuit problem in (5) facilitates sample matrix reconstruction using L1-regularization penalty (λj) of the sampled channel matrix M̂. Sparsity can be further enforced in M̂ by using ternary encoding matrices P where pj(t) = {−1,0,1}.

$$\mathbf{M} \approx argmin_{\hat{\mathbf{M}}} \left\| \mathbf{Y} - (\mathbf{P} \odot \hat{\mathbf{M}})\mathbf{A} \right\|_F^{\,2} + \sum_{j=1}^{J} \lambda_j \left|\left| \hat{\mathbf{M}}_j \right|\right|_1 \tag{5}$$

4 Compressive Multiplexing in the Physical Layer: On-Chip Charge-Domain Compressive Multiplexing

This work introduces a charge-domain CMUX architecture achieving 8:1 channel compression at a 50 MHz sampling rate. Unlike TDM, each AFE channel operates near its Nyquist rate, maintaining individual RF data access. Fast-time multiplexing uses a chipping code modulator synchronized with the AFE clock, enabling scalable arrays with thousands of channels and fast frame-rate acquisition (Fig. 8a, b).

Existing designs use amplifier-based summation for slow-time CMUX, constrained by AFE linearity concerns. Here, a dynamic inverter-based tracking LNA creates a differential output, charging during tracking (ϕT) ($Q_j^{\phi T}(v_{d,j}) = v_{d,j} \cdot C_H \pm \epsilon_j \cdot C_H$). During readout (ϕR), cross-coupled switches are driven by PRBS (Fig. 8b) from linear-feedback shift registers (LFSR). The cross coupled switches modulate each channel sample ($Q_j^{\phi R} = \sum_j^J p_j Q_j^{\phi T}(v_{od}) + C_P v_{od}$) during the charge-summation readout phase. By charge-conservation, the output voltage of the CMUX is given in (6). The output voltage dynamic range is further equalized by a PGA and buffered by a pseudo-differential P-channel flipped-voltage follower (P-FVF) [18]. The passive weighted-summation of input (modulated) channels enables noise averaging, potentially reducing input-referred noise by up to J, similar to μBF architectures.

$$v_{od}^{\phi R} = \frac{\sum_j^J p_j \cdot \left(v_{d,j} \cdot C_H\right)}{J \cdot C_H + C_p} \pm \frac{\langle \epsilon \rangle}{\sqrt{J}} \tag{6}$$

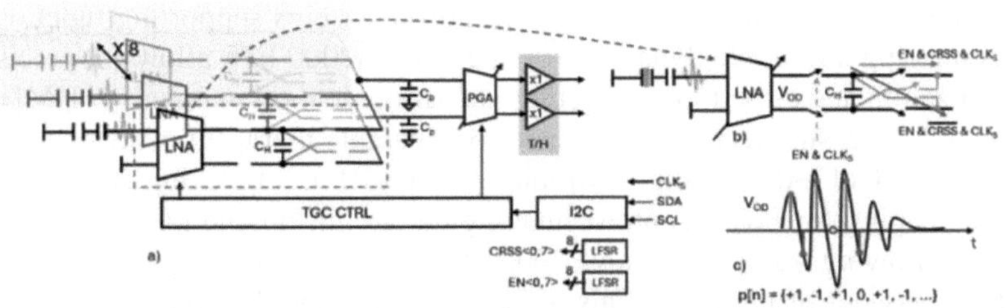

Fig. 8. a) Block diagram of an LNA sub-array in an 8:1 charge-sharing compressive multiplexing UoC AFE architecture, b) control signals for the modulator switch at the output of the switched-capacitor Boxcar sampler, c) conceptual modulation of the voltage signal using the 1.5-bits ternary PRBS.

Post-layout simulation results of the designed charge-sharing CMUX architecture (Fig. 8) revealed the architecture achieves a power-to-compression ratio figure-of-merit (FoM) of FoM $=$ 1.31 MHz mW at 550 μW power dissipation, and a die-area footprint of 0.080 mm × 0.150 mm per channel. This design approaches state-of-the-art miniaturization and performance similar to intra-cardiac US probes, expanding upon aforementioned systems by offering individual channel RF data access and potentially imaging frame rates above 2000 FPS (Fig. 9a), mainly limited by depth and CNR. The 8:1 CMUX US AFE prototype, fabricated in 28 nm TSMC HPC+ RF CMOS technology, was submitted for manufacturing (Fig. 9b); further electrical and in vitro imaging tests are planned upon chip receipt.

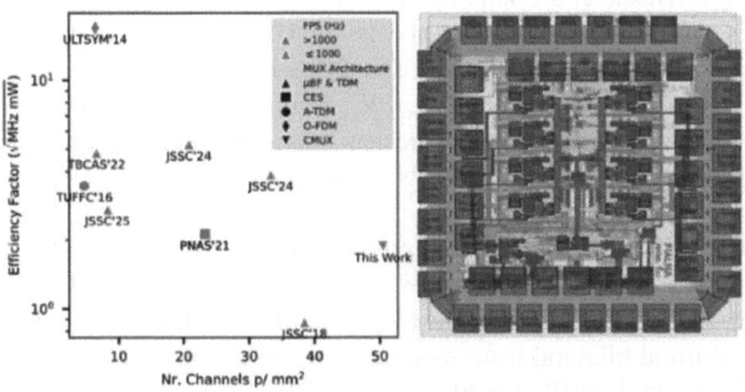

Fig. 9. a) Comparison of compiled SoTA UoC AFE multiplexing architectures and their power-dissipation and area scaling against the post-layout simulated results obtained in this work, b) developed US CMUX architecture and chip layout CAD image.

5 Conclusions

High-frame-rate US imaging, combined with in-ASIC multiplexing and individual RF data access, enables efficient, scalable wearable systems and advanced algorithm integration that accommodate high frame rates and thousands of channels. Such advances facilitate the design of miniaturized US diagnostic systems supporting functional vascular monitoring and tissue dynamics. Frame rates >2000 FPS allow for precise focal spot localization and closed loop targeting via harmonic motion imaging (HMI), which are essential for easing technology transfer of wearable therapeutic US systems to the clinic. Current UoC ASIC designs exploit on-chip μBF multiplexing architectures and scan-line imaging for SoTA contrast imaging but are unsuitable planar-wave imaging modalities allowing framerates above 2000 FPS when guaranteeing individual channel RF data access out of the AFE. This work addresses how the compressible nature of US echoes, exploited through CMUX channel count reduction directly implemented in the developed physical layer, can accelerate the convergence towards a UoC diagnostic ASIC architecture with state-of-the-art performance, meeting application-specific high framerate requirements to build reliable alternative US imaging devices for image-guided therapeutic and exploratory procedures. Further (ongoing) verification and testing are required to corroborate the observations made so far.

References

1. Feigin, V.L., et al.: The global burden of neurological disorders: translating evidence into policy. Lancet Neurol. **19**(3), 255–265 (2020). https://doi.org/10.1016/s1474-4422(19)30411-9
2. Li, H., Cui, L., Li, J., Liu, Y., Chen, Y.: Comparative efficacy and acceptability of neuromodulation procedures in the treatment of treatment-resistant depression: a network meta-analysis of randomized controlled trials. J. Affect. Disord. **287**, 115–124 (2021). https://doi.org/10.1016/j.jad.2021.03.019
3. Blackmore, J., Shrivastava, S., Sallet, J., Butler, C., Cleveland, R.: Ultrasound neuromodulation: a review of results, mechanisms and safety. Ultrasound Med. Biol. **45**(7), 1509–1536 (2019). https://doi.org/10.1016/j.ultrasmedbio.2018.12.015
4. Fomenko, A., Neudorfer, C., Dallapiazza, R., Kalia, S., Lozano, A.: Low-intensity ultrasound neuromodulation: an overview of mechanisms and emerging human applications. Brain Stimul. **11**, 1209–1217 (2018) https://www.sciencedirect.com/science/article/pii/S1935861X18302961
5. Rivandi, H., Costa, T.A.: 2D ultrasound phased-array transmitter asic for highfrequency us stimulation and powering. IEEE Trans. Biomed. Circuits Syst. **17**, 701–712 (2023)
6. Kim, E., Kum, J., Lee, S., Kim, H.: Development of a wireless ultrasonic brain stimulation system for concurrent bilateral neuromodulation in freely moving rodents. Front. Neurosci. **16**, 9 (2022). https://doi.org/10.3389/fnins.2022.1011699
7. Seok, C., Adelegan, O., Biliroglu, A., Yamaner, F., Oralkan, O.: A wearable ultrasonic neurostimulator—part II: a 2D CMUT phased array system with a flip-chip bonded ASIC. IEEE Trans. Biomed. Circuits Syst. **15**, 705–718 (2021). https://doi.org/10.1109/TBCAS.2021.3105064
8. Crake, C., Brinker, S., Coviello, C., Livingstone, M., McDannold, N.: A dual-mode hemispherical sparse array for 3D passive acoustic mapping and skull localization within a clinical MRI guided focused ultrasound device. Phys. Med. Biol. **63**, 065008 (2018). https://doi.org/10.1088/1361-6560/aab0aa
9. Han, Y., Hou, G., Wang, S., Konofagou, E.: High intensity focused ultrasound (HIFU) focal spot localization using harmonic motion imaging (HMI). Physics In Medicine And Biology. **60**, 5911–5924 (2015). https://doi.org/10.1088/0031-9155/60/15/5911

10. Rabut, C., et al.: Functional ultrasound imaging of human brain activity through an acoustically transparent cranial window. Sci. Transl. Med. **16**, 5 (2024). https://doi.org/10.1126/scitranslmed.adj3143
11. Tranquart, F., Grenier, N., Eder, V., Pourcelot, L.: Clinical use of ultrasound tissue harmonic imaging. Ultrasound Med. Biol. **25**, 889–894 (1999). https://doi.org/10.1016/S0301-5629(99)00060-5
12. Cheng, B., Bing, C., Chopra, R.: The effect of transcranial focused ultrasound target location on the acoustic feedback control performance during blood-brain barrier opening with nanobubbles. Sci. Rep. **9**, 12 (2019). https://doi.org/10.1038/s41598-019-55629-2)
13. Montaldo, G., Tanter, M., Bercoff, J., Benech, N., Fink, M.: Coherent plane-wave compounding for very high frame rate ultrasonography and transient elastography. IEEE Trans. Ultrason. Ferroelectr. Freq. Control. **56**(3), 489–506 (2009). https://doi.org/10.1109/TUFFC.2009.1067
14. Latham, K., Samson, C., Woodacre, J., Simpson, E., Zemp, R., Brown, J.: A new 3d imaging technique integrating ultrafast compounding, hadamard encoding, and reconfigurable fresnel lensing, demonstrated on a 128-element, crossed electrode endoscope. In: IEEE International Ultrasonics Symposium (IUS), vol. 10, pp. 2052–2055 (2019). https://doi.org/10.1109/ULTSYM.2019.8926257
15. Rothberg, J., et al.: Ultrasound-on-chip platform for medical imaging, analysis, and collective intelligence. Proc. Natl. Acad. Sci. **118**, 7 (2021). https://doi.org/10.1073/pnas.2019339118
16. Rozsa, N., et al.: A 2000-volumes/s 3-d ultrasound probe with monolithicallyintegrated 23 $\times$ 23-mm^2 4096 -element CMUT array. IEEE J. Solid-State Circuits. **60**, 1397–1410 (2025). https://doi.org/10.1109/JSSC.2025.3534087
17. Chen, C., Pertijs, M.A.P.: Integrated transceivers for emerging medical ultrasound imaging devices: a review. IEEE Open J. Solid-State Circuits Soc. **1**, 104–114 (2021). https://doi.org/10.1109/OJSSCS.2021.3115398
18. Guo, P., et al.: A 125 μm-pitch-matched transceiver asic with micro-beamforming adc and multi-level signaling for 3-d transfontanelle ultrasonography. IEEE J. Solid-State Circuits. **59**, 2604–2617 (2024). https://doi.org/10.1109/JSSC.2024.3355854
19. Hopf, Y., et al.: A pitchmatched high-frame-rate ultrasound imaging asic for catheter-based 3-d probes. IEEE J. Solid-State Circuits. **59**, 476–491 (2024). https://doi.org/10.1109/JSSC.2023.3299749
20. Rezvanitabar, A., et al.: Integrated hybrid sub-aperture beamforming and time-division multiplexing for massive readout in ultrasound imaging. IEEE Trans. Biomed. Circuits Syst. **16**, 972–980 (2022). https://doi.org/10.1109/TBCAS.2022.3205024
21. Elloian, J., Jadwiszczak, J., Arslan, V., Sherman, J.D., Kessler, D.O., Shepard, K.L.: Flexible ultrasound transceiver array for non-invasive surface-conformable imaging enabled by geometric phase correction. Sci. Rep. **12**(1) (2022). https://doi.org/10.1038/s41598-022-20721-7
22. van Neer, P.L.M.J., et al.: Flexible large-area ultrasound arrays for medical applications made using embossed polymer structures. Nat. Commun. **15**(1) (2024). https://doi.org/10.1038/s41467-024-47074-1
23. Li, J., Ma, Y., Zhang, T., Shung, K.K., Zhu, B.: Recent advancements in ultrasound transducer: from material strategies to biomedical applications. BME Front. **2022**, 9764501 (2022). https://doi.org/10.34133/2022/9764501
24. Habib, M., Lantgios, I., Hornbostel, K.: Iopscience. J. Phys. D Appl. Phys. (2022). https://iopscience.iop.org/article/10.1088/1361-6463/ac8687
25. Perrot, V., Polichetti, M., Varray, F., Garcia, D.: So you think you can DAS? a viewpoint on delay-and-sum beamforming. Ultrasonics. **111**, 106309 (2021). https://doi.org/10.1016/j.ultras.2020.106309

26. Rashid, M., Tekes, C., Ghovanloo, M., Degertekin, F.: Design of frequency-division multiplexing front-end receiver electronics for CMUT-on-CMOS based intracardiac echocardiography. In: IEEE International Ultrasonics Symposium 2014, vol. 9, pp. 1540–1543 (2014). https://doi.org/10.1109/ULTSYM.2014.0381
27. Besson, A., Perdios, D., Arditi, M., Wiaux, Y., Thiran, J.P.: Compressive multiplexing of ultrasound signals. In: 2018 IEEE International Ultrasonics Symposium (IUS), pp. 1–4. IEEE, Kobe, Japan (2018). https://doi.org/10.1109/ULTSYM.2018.8580067
28. Wang, P., Jiang, J.Y., Li, N., Luo, H.W., Li, F., Cui, S.G.: Sparse dictionary for synthetic transmit aperture medical ultrasound imaging. J. Acoust. Soc. Am. **142**(1), 240 (2017). https://doi.org/10.1121/1.4993644. pMID: 28764415

CancerCareTech: A Pilot Study on a Digital Platform for Multimodal Clinical Data Integration in Pediatric Oncology

Pedro Correia[1,2,3(✉)], Joana Dias[1], Alexandra Morais[4], Amets Sagarribay[5], Ana Ferreira[1,2,3,6], Ana Rita Londral[1,2,3,7,8], Carla Quintão[1,2,3], Catarina Santos[1,2,3], Mafalda Pires[4], Patrícia Santos[1,2,3,6], Paula Agulheiro[4], and Cláudia Quaresma[1,2,3(✉)]

[1] Physics Department, NOVA School of Science and Technology, NOVA University Lisbon, Caparica 2829-516, Portugal
pml.correia@campus.fct.unl.pt, q.claudia@fct.unl.pt
[2] Laboratory of Instrumentation, Biomedical Engineering and Radiation Physics (LIBPhys-UNL), NOVA School of Science and Technology, NOVA University Lisbon, Caparica 2829-516, Portugal
[3] Associated Laboratory in Translation and Innovation towards Global Health (REAL), Caparica 2829-516, Portugal
[4] Serviço de Medicina Física e Reabilitação, Hospital D. Estefânia, Unidade Local de Saúde de São José, Lisbon, Portugal
[5] Unidade de Neurocirurgia, Hospital Dona Estefânia, Unidade Local de Saúde de São José, Lisbon, Portugal
[6] Health Department, School of Health Sciences, Polytechnic Institute of Beja, Beja, Portugal
[7] Comprehensive Health Research Center in NOVA Medical School, Lisbon, Portugal
[8] Value for Health CoLAB, Lisbon, Portugal

Abstract. Pediatric brain cancer often causes long-term impairments, highlighting the need for effective rehabilitation to support functional recovery and social reintegration. The aim of this study was to co-create, develop, and pre-validate the first CancerCareTech prototype, designed to enable a practical, objective, and data-driven assessment and visualization of patient functional status and rehabilitation outcomes.Implemented using the Python Dash framework, *CancerCareTech* platform supports structured clinical data acquisition, monitoring, and sharing, integrating multimodal biosignals, including electroencephalography, electromyography, and electrodermal activity. A pilot technical pre-validation conducted with a four-month-old infant confirmed usability, and reliable integration and visualization of clinical and electrophysiological data. *CancerCareTech* features an innovative, human-centered design aligned with national and European cancer strategies, demonstrating strong potential to support data-driven clinical decision-making, enhance neurorehabilitation outcomes, and improve quality of life in pediatric oncology, pending validation in future clinical studies.

Keywords: Digital health · Electrodermal Activity · Electroencephalography · Electromyography · Glioma · Neurorehabilitation · Oncology · Pediatrics

Published by Springer Nature Switzerland AG 2027
L. M. Camarinha-Matos and F. Ferrada (Eds.): DoCEIS 2026, IFIP AICT 790, pp. 125–137, 2027.
https://doi.org/10.1007/978-3-032-28939-1_10

1 Introduction

Brain cancer is a rare pathology, with a global incidence of 5.7 cases per 100,000 individuals per year [1]. However, within pediatric oncology, it constitutes a major clinical and societal challenge, representing the most frequent and lethal group of solid tumors in childhood and the second most common pediatric cancer overall [2, 3].

Advances in cancer registration and clinical surveillance have improved early diagnosis, treatment planning, and survival in children with brain cancer [4]. However, despite these advances, limited attention has been given to the long-term functional sequelae resulting from both the disease and its treatments [5, 6].

Neurological sequelae in survivors of pediatric brain cancer include motor dysfunctions, deficits in postural control and coordination, communication disorders, cognitive impairments, emotional and behavioral alterations [4, 7, 8]. Collectively, these sequelae have a profound adverse impact on quality of life and significantly limit social participation and integration.

According to the Portuguese national strategy against cancer, key challenges faced by cancer survivors include insufficient management of late treatment effects, limited coordination among healthcare professionals, and inadequate access to psychosocial support [5]. Similarly, the European cancer plan emphasizes the need to improve communication between patients and healthcare providers and to promote patient-centered approaches, particularly in rehabilitation and quality-of-life support [6].

Recent advances in e-healthcare have enabled the development of patient-oriented digital platforms for the systematic registration and monitoring of clinical and functional data [9]. In hospital settings, electronic health records and clinical information systems have become central tools for clinical data management, providing advantages such as improved access to medical records, simplified documentation processes, increased time efficiency and enhanced support for preventive and follow-up strategies [10, 11]. Numerous digital platforms have been developed and implemented across diverse clinical domains [12], including telerehabilitation [13], post-surgical rehabilitation [14], pressure ulcers monitoring [15], stroke rehabilitation [16], and oncology care [17].

Despite these advances, the adaptation and validation of such platforms for pediatric oncology rehabilitation remain limited. To our knowledge, no existing system integrates (1) multimodal electrophysiological data, (2) structured rehabilitation metrics, and (3) clinician-driven co-design within pediatric neuro-oncology follow-up.

This gap underscores the need for integrated data platforms specifically tailored to pediatric brain cancer survivors. Such platforms should enable comprehensive monitoring of rehabilitation outcomes by integrating and visualizing multidimensional clinical data across distinct rehabilitation domains, while also fostering efficient communication among healthcare professionals and strengthening clinician–patient interaction.

To address this gap, the CancerCareTech digital platform was conceived using a user-centered design, providing, to our knowledge, the first integrated solution for the longitudinal monitoring of pediatric brain cancer patients rehabilitation progress, based on both clinical and electrophysiological data. By combining multimodal biosignal acquisition with structured clinical metrics, the platform enables an intuitive and clinically relevant visualization of the patient's functional trajectory, supporting data-driven clinical decision-making.

The main scientific contribution of this work lies in the structured integration of multimodal electrophysiological signals with standardized clinical rehabilitation metrics within a unified, clinician-driven digital framework. This approach enables synchronized longitudinal analysis of heterogeneous data streams in pediatric neuro-oncology, addressing current limitations in fragmented data management and supporting the development of objective, data-informed rehabilitation pathways.

The aim of this study was to co-create, develop, and pre-validate the first *CancerCareTech* prototype by integrating healthcare professionals' needs with iterative technological design. The evaluation focused on technical feasibility, clinical usability, and reliable integration of clinical and electrophysiological data in a real pediatric setting.

Following this introduction, Sect. 2 outlines how this work relates to tackling societal challenges, the main theme of the conference. Section 3 provides an integrated description of the methodology and platform development, detailing the iterative co-creation process, the technical architecture approach and the pilot pre-validation protocol. The results are reported in Sect. 4, while Sect. 5 offers a critical discussion of performance and broader implications. Finally, Sect. 6 summarizes the main conclusions.

2 Contribution to Technological Innovation for Societal Challenges

CancerCareTech embodies a technology-driven response to a critical societal challenge by integrating digital health infrastructure, multimodal neurophysiological monitoring, and user-centered co-creation methodologies into pediatric neurorehabilitation practice. By enabling objective, data-informed assessment and longitudinal follow-up, the platform contributes to more personalized and efficient care approaches, aligning with broader European and national priorities in digital transformation, childhood cancer survivorship, and quality-of-life improvement. Consequently, this work illustrates how technological innovation can translate into real societal impact, supporting vulnerable pediatric populations and advancing sustainable, patient-centered healthcare systems.

3 Methods

This section presents both the methodological framework and the resulting system architecture, reflecting the iterative and interdependent nature of the development process, in which system design and requirement definition evolved concurrently.

This study employed a methodological approach combining co-creation with healthcare professionals, iterative technological development, and pilot pre-validation testing. The development process followed an Incremental Development model [18], supported by a User-Centered Design (UCD) framework [19], to ensure that platform design decisions were grounded in real-world clinical practice.

3.1 Needs Assessment and Co-creation Process

The co-creation process was conducted in sequential phases involving direct engagement with different key medical specialties: physiatry, neurosurgery, physiotherapy and occupational therapy.

Participants included project members from Unidade Local de Saúde de São José (ULS São José) who were directly involved in the consultation meetings and data-collection process: one neurosurgeon, one physiatrist, one physiotherapist, and one occupational therapist. In addition, two further project members, occupational therapists with clinical experience as well as expertise in electrophysiological data acquisition, also participated in these discussions.

First, an individual meeting was held with each healthcare professional to explore and identify perceived needs, expectations, and priority challenges. Consultation questions were tailored to each specialty while maintaining a common focus on clinically relevant data to be integrated into the platform, metrics used to assess patient progress and support clinical decision-making, relevant neurophysiological, electrophysiological, or kinematic parameters for rehabilitation monitoring, desired technological functionalities to facilitate clinical practice, and key challenges in the follow-up of children with pediatric brain cancer.

Subsequently, a second round of individual meetings was carried out to refine system requirements, define relevant clinical parameters, and determine the specific functional and structural characteristics of the web interface associated with each clinical area.

Insights from the first and second consultation rounds informed the design and development, leading to the first prototype.

3.2 Platform Design and Technical Development

CancerCareTech was implemented using the Python Dash framework, enabling the creation of an interactive web-based clinical environment for data entry, visualization, and decision support.

The system architecture comprises three main conceptual components: a clinical user interface, a local application server and a structured relational database.

The clinical user interface allows authorized healthcare professionals to register patient information, record discipline-specific clinical observations, and visualize longitudinal clinical outcomes and electrophysiological signals. The local application server manages internal data processing, routing, and visualization logic during runtime. The relational database ensures secure storage, organization, and access to heterogeneous clinical and electrophysiological data collected along the patient's clinical trajectory, while maintaining referential integrity and controlled permissions.

The user registration and authentication workflow of the CancerCareTech platform was designed to support secure access and role-based interaction. The process includes professional self-registration, during which users input required information (e.g., username, password, full name, contact details, institutional affiliation, and role). As an additional security measure, a predefined administrator (e.g., the head of department) is responsible for reviewing and approving these registrations; without this approval, users are not granted access to the platform.

Both administrators and healthcare professionals undergo a login authentication step, where credentials are verified. Upon successful authentication, the system performs user profile identification and automatically redirects users to the appropriate clinical interface according to their assigned role.

In addition to clinician management, the administrator is responsible for patient registration and assignment to the appropriate clinicians. The administrator interface was designed to support the visualization and management of clinicians and patients.

Clinician users can access their list of assigned patients, create new clinical records, review previously documented records, including those entered by other specialties, and visualize the patient's overall clinical progression.

The clinical workflow associated with physiatry is illustrated in Fig. 1. Physiatrists can search for patients by name or access their list of assigned patients, after selecting a specific patient three main actions are available: adding a new clinical record, viewing existing records, and analyzing patient evolution over time.

When adding a new record, the physiatry is guided through a structured data entry process that includes key functional and neurological domains such as muscle strength, muscle tone, pain, reflexes, balance, gait, coordination, sensitivity, vision, development, and electrophysiological signals. Once validated, the record is saved and a written clinical report is automatically generated.

The record visualization interface allows clinicians to review either their own previously entered records or all records associated with each patient, supporting both individualized follow-up and multidisciplinary continuity of care. Additionally, the workflow includes progression visualizations, allowing clinicians to monitor functional changes over time using both graphical representations and structured tables.

Considering the similarity of clinician-specific interfaces, only the physiatry workflow is illustrated here as a representative example. Nevertheless, each specialty is supported by a dedicated clinical records interface tailored to its scope of practice. The neurology module enables documentation of tumor characteristics (e.g., lesion type and size), treatment modalities, neurological signs and symptoms and neuroimaging. The occupational therapy module supports recording of oculomotor coordination, activity performance, muscle tone and range of motion. The physiotherapy module allows documentation of muscle strength, muscle tone, pain, balance, bed mobility, sensory function, and gait-related parameters. In addition, all clinician users can import electrophysiological data into their respective modules.

All modules follow a standardized structural framework, ensuring consistency of data entry and facilitating integrated multidisciplinary longitudinal monitoring. Additionally, each interface incorporates validated clinical assessment scales routinely used in clinical practice, as well as evaluation parameters suggested by clinicians during the platform's co-creation and conceptualization phase.

The *CancerCareTech* platform incorporates a structured database designed to support the secure storage, organization, and retrieval of clinical and physiological data generated along the patient's clinical trajectory, from the time of diagnosis through longitudinal pediatric neurorehabilitation follow-up. At the current prototype stage, the database operates within a local deployment environment, ensuring controlled access during technical validation.

The database is organized around the central patients and clinicians entities, which store demographic, identification, and professional information. A many-to-many relationship between patients and clinicians is implemented through an associative table (*patient_user*), reflecting multidisciplinary clinical practice in which each patient may

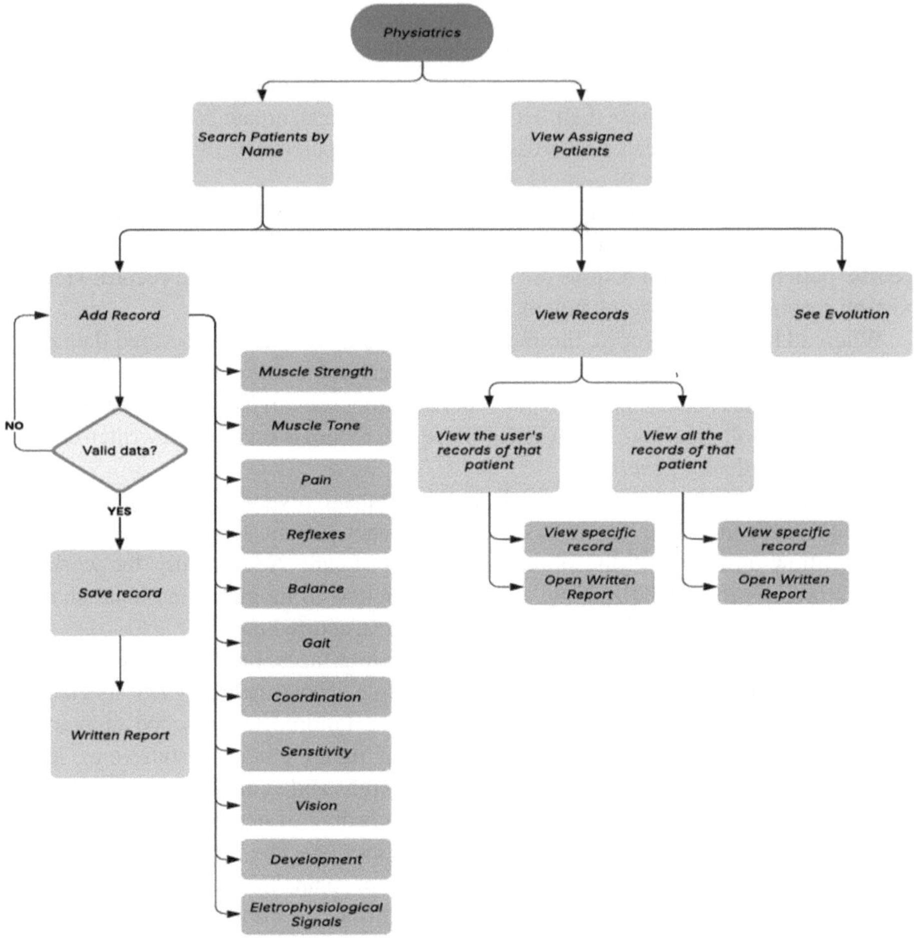

Fig. 1. Functional workflow of the Physiatry module.

be followed by multiple healthcare professionals, while each professional may supervise several patients.

Clinical information is structured into discipline-specific record tables, including *physiotherapy_records*, *physiatry_records*, *occupational_therapy_records*, and *neuro_records*. These tables store functional observations, standardized assessment results, and qualitative clinical notes linked to both the patient and the responsible clinician, enabling detailed tracking of rehabilitation progress across specialties.

Each clinical record type is further associated with dedicated biosignal tables (*physiotherapy_signals*, *physiatry_signals*, *occupational_therapy_signals*, and *neuro_signals*), which store signal metadata, acquisition parameters such as sampling frequency, observational annotations and references to raw signal files in binary format.

Data integrity is ensured through primary–foreign key relationships, validation constraints, and controlled access permissions.

3.3 Pilot Pre-validation Study

This study adopts a feasibility-oriented pre-validation framework focusing on three core dimensions: (i) system-level integration, (ii) clinical workflow compatibility, and (iii) usability. Accordingly, the objective of this stage is to assess system readiness and functional coherence, rather than to evaluate clinical effectiveness. Clinical data entry, record visualization, report generation, and longitudinal monitoring functionalities were tested. Simultaneously, the acquisition, storage, and visualization of multimodal biosignals, including EEG, EMG, and EDA, were evaluated to confirm their integration and visualization within the clinical dashboard.

A typically developing four-month-old infant was recruited through convenience sampling. The participant's age falls within the typical incidence range of pediatric cancer, allowing for a realistic assessment of the platform's functional workflow. Written informed consent for participation was obtained from the child's mother prior to data collection.

Given the participant's age and typical neurodevelopment status, a limited set of representative clinical parameters was recorded. These included muscle tone during knee flexion, assessed using the Modified Ashworth Scale [20]; the bicipital reflex, evaluated according to the Mayo Clinic reflex grading scale [21]; and developmental status, examined using the Mary Sheridan developmental scale [22].

In addition, head postural control and passive range of motion during knee flexion were assessed using qualitative ordinal scales proposed by clinicians during the co-creation process. Head control was categorized as *maintained* or *not maintained*, while passive range of motion was classified as *complete*, *up to 50%*, *up to 25%*, or *unable to perform*.

To enable visualization and testing of the longitudinal evolution feature, which requires at least two clinical records, the participant underwent evaluation on two separate days, simulating two clinical sessions.

Beyond clinical parameters, electrophysiological signals were acquired to validate biosignal integration within the platform. EDA was recorded from the external border of the foot using surface electrodes placed approximately 1 cm apart. A one-minute resting-state EEG recording was obtained using four channels positioned at C3, C4, P3, and P4, and EMG signals were collected from surface electrodes positioned above the rectus femoris muscle. All biosignals were sampled at 500 Hz. EDA and EMG signals were acquired using a biosignalplux acquisition system, whereas EEG data were obtained with a g.Nautilus multipurpose system.

Considering the exploratory nature of this pre-validation phase and the limited sample size, the evaluation was restricted to descriptive observations and qualitative feedback from participating clinicians. Importantly, the objective of this stage was not to assess clinical effectiveness or impact on patient outcomes, but rather to evaluate the system's architectural design, functional coherence, and integration within the existing clinical workflow and information infrastructure.

Usability assessment was conducted using the Portuguese version of the System Usability Scale (SUS) [23], a validated ten-item questionnaire designed to provide a global measure of perceived system usability. A multidisciplinary group of healthcare professionals, including one neurosurgeon, one physiatrist, one physiotherapist, and two occupational therapists, was invited to comprehensively explore and test all platform features. Following the interaction with the platform, participants completed the Portuguese SUS questionnaire to evaluate perceived usability.

In addition to the SUS questionnaire, open-ended questions were administered to gather qualitative feedback regarding potential platform improvements. Participants were asked whether clinical record entry was intuitive, whether it was easy to locate a specific patient within the patient table, and whether the visualization of clinical data and longitudinal evolution within their specialty was useful or required improvement. They were also invited to indicate any page or functionality that should be enhanced, providing detailed comments whenever applicable.

These qualitative responses were intended to complement standardized usability scoring by identifying practical usability barriers and opportunities for interface or functionality refinement, as the quantitative SUS score alone does not allow detailed identification of specific system improvement needs.

An overview of the evaluation domains and methods is provided in Table 1.

Table 1. Pilot Pre-validation: Evaluation domains and methods.

What is Evaluated	How it is Evaluated
Technical Feasibility: System stability and database integrity.	Clinical session simulation with qualitative functional assessment
Electrophysiological Data Integration: Import and integration of physiological signals	Qualitative assessment of multimodal biosignal storage.
Clinical Data Integration: Record and integration of clinical data.	Qualitative assessment of standardized clinical data record and storage.
Data Visualization: Role-based data sharing and follow-up.	Qualitative assessment of longitudinal visualization of clinical and biosignal data
System Usability: User experience, intuitiveness, and system efficiency.	Administration of the Portuguese version of the SUS.
Clinical Relevance: Identification of limitations and potential improvements	Open-ended questions on clinical relevance and data accessibility, administered to clinicians

4 Results

The results of the pilot pre-validation study are analyzed according to the evaluation domains and methods defined in Sect. 3.3.

The *CancerCareTech* platform operated as expected, enabling the structured registration of diverse clinical data across different clinical specialties. Once clinical records were validated and submitted within the platform, an automatically generated clinical report became available.

The technical validation confirmed data integrity. All clinical parameters were accurately stored within the relational database, demonstrating correct integration of multiple standardized clinical scales commonly used in routine practice. Data visualization functionalities also performed as intended and aligned with the expectations of clinical consultants involved in the co-creation process, confirming the adequacy of interface design and information presentation.

A key achievement was the functional integration of multimodal biosignals within the clinical environment, as illustrated by the EMG signal in Fig. 2, with high-frequency data rendered without compromising interface responsiveness.

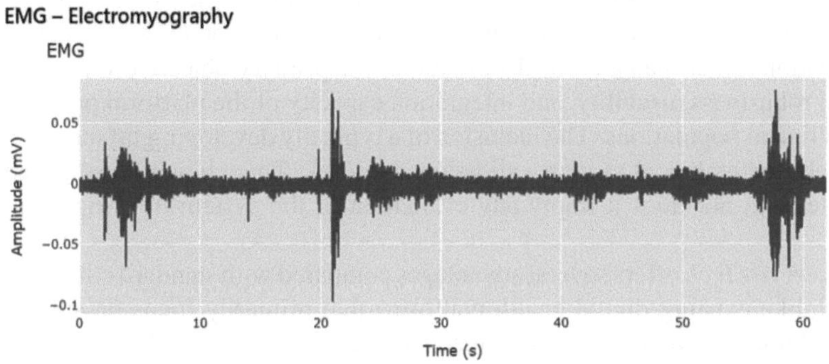

Fig. 2. Raw EMG signal acquired at 500 Hz from surface electrodes positioned over the rectus femoris muscle.

The inclusion of two clinical sessions enabled evaluation of the longitudinal monitoring functionality, permitting structured visualization of patient progression over time through graphical representations. The system successfully mapped changes across different sessions, confirming that the architectural design supports the multidisciplinary tracking required for long-term pediatric neurorehabilitation. Data visualization functionalities aligned with the expectations of clinical consultants, confirming the adequacy of interface design.

Usability outcomes obtained through the SUS questionnaire are presented in Table 2.

Table 2. SUS score by participant and overall mean.

Participant	SUS score
P1	72.5
P2	85.0
P3	100.0
P4	92.5
P5	90.0
Mean ± SD	**88.0 ± 10.2**

Qualitative feedback from clinical relevance analysis indicated overall platform adequacy, with the system perceived as intuitive, easy to use, and efficient for patient search, clinical record entry, and data visualization. However, consultations with clinical professionals identified opportunities for improvement, including more detailed muscle strength and tone recording and improved harmonization of clinical records across specialties to support multidisciplinary follow-up. All tested functionalities were executed successfully across simulated clinical sessions.

5 Discussion

This study presented the design, implementation, and pilot pre-validation of the *CancerCareTech* digital platform, developed to support pediatric neurorehabilitation in the context of brain cancer. Importantly, this study should be interpreted as a system-oriented pre-validation rather than a clinical validation. The primary objective was to ensure the technical robustness, usability, and integration capacity of the platform prior to deployment in clinical populations. The inclusion of a typically developing infant was intended exclusively for technical system validation purposes. This choice does not constitute clinical testing, nor does it imply any evaluation of the system in pediatric oncology patients.

CancerCareTech offers several advantages compared with standard clinical data platforms. Unlike existing digital health platforms that primarily focus on single-domain data or administrative workflows, CancerCareTech enables synchronized integration of multimodal electrophysiological signals and structured rehabilitation metrics within a clinician-driven environment. This integrated approach supports a more comprehensive and objective characterization of patient functional trajectories in pediatric neuro-oncology. Notably, it is specifically designed for brain cancer pediatric rehabilitation, addressing the unique functional, developmental, and multidisciplinary monitoring needs of this population [4, 7, 8]. The inclusion of a comprehensive set of predefined clinical assessment scales, commonly used in rehabilitation practice, enables faster, more standardized patient evaluation, improving efficiency while reducing variability in clinical documentation [10, 11]. This structured approach supports consistent longitudinal follow-up and facilitates comparison of patient status across clinical sessions and specialties.

Furthermore, CancerCareTech enables automatic generation of clinical reports that can be directly transferred to standardized or national electronic health record systems, facilitating interoperability with existing healthcare infrastructures.

Another important contribution is the integration of multimodal biosignals, including EEG, EMG, and EDA, within the same clinical environment. This integration enables objective quantification of patient progression, complementing traditional observational and subjective assessments.

In line with national and European priorities in cancer rehabilitation [5, 6], *CancerCareTech* contributes to more coordinated, structured, and patient-centered rehabilitation monitoring.

Usability findings, based on SUS scores and qualitative clinician feedback, indicated overall positive acceptance of the platform, with the mean SUS score indicating excellent usability according to established benchmarks [24]. At the same time, the feedback provided important recommendations for platform enhancement.

Despite promising results, this study has limitations. Although limited to a single non-clinical participant, this pilot study fulfills its intended purpose as an initial feasibility assessment. This step is essential to ensure system stability and usability prior to conducting larger-scale clinical validation studies involving pediatric oncology populations. Future research should therefore include pediatric oncology cohorts and longitudinal rehabilitation follow-up to validate clinical impact. In parallel, further work should explore electrophysiological biomarkers capable of tracking neurofunctional recovery thereby strengthening data-driven rehabilitation decision-making. These results establish a foundational step toward the development of integrated digital biomarkers for pediatric neurorehabilitation, bridging the gap between multimodal data acquisition and clinically meaningful interpretation. Additionally, future studies will incorporate a structured health value assessment of the *CancerCareTech* platform to evaluate its broader clinical, functional, and economic impact within pediatric neurorehabilitation and healthcare delivery systems.

6 Conclusion

CancerCareTech represents a feasible, usable, and interoperable digital health platform designed to support data-driven pediatric rehabilitation in brain cancer survivorship.

Pilot pre-validation demonstrated technical robustness and excellent clinical usability, indicating that *CancerCareTech* has the potential to enable more efficient, standardized, and objective follow-up in pediatric brain cancer rehabilitation. In addition, the structured integration of electrophysiological data creates the foundation for future development of digital biomarkers in pediatric neurorehabilitation.

Collectively, these advances position *CancerCareTech* as a promising technological innovation addressing a critical societal need, with potential to support clinical decision-making, rehabilitation effectiveness, and quality of life for children affected by brain cancer.

Acknowledgments. Authors acknowledge the financial support of Liga Portuguesa Contra o Cancro and Lions Portugal. This work is also funded by national funds through Fundação para a Ciência e a Tecnologia, I.P. (FCT), within the scope of projects UID/04559/2025 (LIBPhys) and LA/P/0117/2020 (REAL).

References

1. Ostrom, Q.T., Gittleman, H., Truitt, G., Boscia, A., Kruchko, C., Barnholtz-Sloan, J.S.: CBTRUS statistical report: primary brain and other central nervous system tumors diagnosed in the United States in 2011–2015. neuro. Oncologia. **20**, iv1–iv86 (2018). https://doi.org/10.1093/neuonc/noy131
2. Aldape, K., et al.: Challenges to curing primary brain tumours. Nat. Rev. Clin. Oncol. **16**, 509–520 (2019). https://doi.org/10.1038/s41571-019-0177-5
3. Bauchet, L., et al.: D'expression: clinical epidemiology for childhood primary central nervous system tumors. J. Neuro-Oncol. **92**, 87–98 (2009). https://doi.org/10.1007/s11060-008-9740-0
4. Pruitt, D.W., Bolikal, P.D., Bolger, A.K.: Rehabilitation considerations in pediatric brain tumors. Curr. Phys. Med. Rehabil. Rep. **7**, 81–88 (2019). https://doi.org/10.1007/s40141-019-00218-7

5. Portugal, Gabinete da Secretária de Estado da Promoção da Saúde: Despacho n.o 13227/2023. Diário da República, 2.a série - Parte C (N.o 248) - Aprova a Estratégia Nacional de Luta contra o Cancro, Horizonte 2030, (2023)
6. European Commission: Communication from the Commission to the European Parliament and the Council: Europe's Beating Cancer Plan (2021)
7. Spina, S., Facciorusso, S., Cinone, N., Pellegrino, R., Fiore, P., Santamato, A.: Rehabilitation interventions for glioma patients: a mini-review. Front. Surg. **10**, 1–8 (2023). https://doi.org/10.3389/fsurg.2023.1137516
8. Walker, D.A., Finlay, J.: Central nervous system tumors of childhood and adolescence: the rehabilitation challenge of survival and 'true cure'. J. Pediatr. Rehabil. Med. **4**, 23–29 (2011). https://doi.org/10.3233/PRM-2011-0155
9. Jayaratne, M., et al.: A data integration platform for patient-centered e-healthcare and clinical decision support. Futur. Gener. Comput. Syst. **92**, 996–1008 (2019). https://doi.org/10.1016/j.future.2018.07.061
10. Menachemi, N., Collum, T.H.: Benefits and drawbacks of electronic health record systems. Risk Manag. Healthc. Policy. **4**, 47–55 (2011). https://doi.org/10.2147/RMHP.S12985
11. Walter-Tscharf, F.F.W.V.: A systematic integrated literature review of clinical data management platforms of HL7 FHIR. In: 2022 IEEE 24th Int Conf on High Performance Computing & Communications; 8th Int Conf on Data Science & Systems; 20th Int Conf on Smart City; 8th Int Conf on Dependability in Sensor, Cloud & Big Data Systems & Application (HPCC/DSS/SmartCity/DependSys), pp. 2298–2307. IEEE, China (2022). https://doi.org/10.1109/HPCC-DSS-SmartCity-DependSys57074.2022.00340
12. Wang, M., et al.: Big data health care platform with multisource heterogeneous data integration and massive hint, and application. JMIR Med. Inform. **10** (2022). https://doi.org/10.2196/36481
13. Zhu, Z., et al.: Establishment of a new platform for the management of patients after cardiac surgery: descriptive study. JMIR Med. Inform. **7** (2019). https://doi.org/10.2196/13123
14. Xu, H., et al.: A fully integrated, standalone stretchable device platform with in-sensor adaptive machine learning for rehabilitation. Nat. Commun. **14** (2023). https://doi.org/10.1038/s41467-023-43664-7
15. Rodrigues, J.J.P.C., Pedro, L.M.C.C., Vardasca, T., de la Torre-Díez, I., Martins, H.M.G.: Mobile health platform for pressure ulcer monitoring with electronic health record integration. Health Inform. J. **19**, 300–311 (2013). https://doi.org/10.1177/1460458212474909
16. Hu, X., Jonzén, K., Karlsson, M., Lindahl, O.A.: Assessments of a novel digital follow-up tool Rehabkompassen® to identify rehabilitation needs among stroke patients in an outpatient setting. Digit. Health. **8**, 1–11 (2022). https://doi.org/10.1177/20552076221104662
17. De Regge, M., Decoene, E., Eeckloo, K., Van Hecke, A.: Development and evaluation of an integrated digital patient platform during oncology treatment. J. Patient Exp. **7**, 53–61 (2019). https://doi.org/10.1177/2374373518825142
18. Núñez-Merino, M., Maqueira-Marín, J.M., Moyano-Fuentes, J., Castaño-Moraga, C.A.: Product development process for a new healthcare service in the industry 4.0 context: an action research approach. Prod. Plan. Control. **36**, 177–196 (2025). https://doi.org/10.1080/09537287.2024.2349224
19. Müller, A., Schaaf, J.: User or patient/human or person? Development of a practical framework for applying user-centered design to vulnerable populations for digital transformation in healthcare. Digit. Health. **11**, 1–10 (2025). https://doi.org/10.1177/20552076251375835
20. Bohannon, R.W., Smith, M.B.: Interrater reliability of a modified Ashworth scale of muscle spasticity. Phys. Ther. **67**, 206–207 (1987). https://doi.org/10.1093/ptj/67.2.206
21. Nick, J.M.: Deep tendon reflexes: the what, why, where, and how of tapping. J. Obstet. Gynecol. Neonat. Nurs. **32**, 297–306 (2003). https://doi.org/10.1177/0884217503253491

22. Cunha, M.B., et al.: What skills should be acquired in pre-school education? Acta Medica Port. **38**, 71–74 (2025). https://doi.org/10.20344/amp.22114
23. Martins, A.I., Rosa, A.F., Queirós, A., Silva, A., Rocha, N.P.: European Portuguese validation of the system usability scale (SUS). Procedia Comput. Sci. **67**, 293–300 (2015). https://doi.org/10.1016/j.procs.2015.09.273
24. Lewis, J.R.: The system usability scale: past, present, and future. Int. J. Hum. Comput. Interact. **34**, 577–590 (2018). https://doi.org/10.1080/10447318.2018.1455307

A Supervised Modular LLM Architecture for Personalized Management of Non Communicable Diseases: A Proof of Concept Study

Ana Martins[1,2,3,4](✉), Luís Velez Lapão[1,3,5,6], Isabel L. Nunes[1,3], and Ana Londral[2,6,7]

[1] UNIDEMI, Department of Mechanical and Industrial Engineering, Nova School of Science and Technology, Caparica 2829–516, Portugal
acd.martins@campus.fct.unl.pt, {l.lapao,imn}@fct.unl.pt

[2] Value for Health CoLAB, Lisboa 1150–190, Portugal
a.londral@fct.unl.pt

[3] Laboratório Associado de Sistemas Inteligentes, Escola de Engenharia Universidade do Minho, Guimarães, Campus Azurém 4800-058, Portugal

[4] Instituto Universitário de Lisboa (ISCTE-IUL), Centro de Investigação em Ciências da Informação, Tecnologias e Arquitetura, Lisboa, Portugal

[5] WHO Collaborating Center on Health Workforce Policy and Planning, Instituto de Higiene e Medicina Tropical, Universidade Nova de Lisboa, Rua da Junqueira n°100, Lisboa ,1349-008, Portugal

[6] Comprehensive Health Research Center, Nova Medical School, Lisboa 1169-056, Portugal

[7] Department of Physics, Nova School of Science and Technology, Caparica 2829-516, Portugal

Abstract. Non-communicable diseases demand scalable solutions that extend care beyond the clinic while preserving personalization and safety. We present a proof-of-concept modular LLM-based architecture integrating retrieval-augmented generation, intermediate validation, and evidence-based behavior change techniques to generate tailored messages for non-communicable disease management within a supervised workflow. The architecture adopts a supervised, workflow-oriented design, prioritizing traceability and safety. Following a Design Science Research methodology, we developed a web-based system combining demographic and clinical data with guideline-driven knowledge. Four clinical scenarios were evaluated by six primary care physicians, who assessed message clinical accuracy, relevance, clarity, actionability, and safety. The system generated personalized communications rated highly for clinical accuracy, relevance, clarity, and actionability (3.32–3.90/4), with minimal safety concerns. Usability was excellent (SUS = 90), and clinicians reported strong performance expectancy. These findings provide preliminary evidence of feasibility and clinical acceptability, supporting further validation in real-world settings.

Keywords: Conversational Agents · Retrieval Augmented Generation · LLMs · Healthcare

Published by Springer Nature Switzerland AG 2027
L. M. Camarinha-Matos and F. Ferrada (Eds.): DoCEIS 2026, IFIP AICT 790, pp. 138–153, 2027.
https://doi.org/10.1007/978-3-032-28939-1_11

1 Introduction

Non-communicable diseases (NCDs), defined as chronic conditions such as cardiovascular diseases, diabetes, and respiratory disorders, represent a major persistent challenge for healthcare systems worldwide, particularly in the context of aging populations and increasing multimorbidity [1]. Primary care services face growing pressure to deliver continuous, personalized, and preventive care while managing limited resources. Although digital health interventions (DHIs) have emerged to support self-management and behavioral change, most existing systems rely on static content, rule-based personalization, or limited adaptive capabilities [2]. As a result, scalability is often achieved at the expense of meaningful personalization.

Recent advances in large language models (LLMs) have demonstrated unprecedented capabilities in natural language understanding and generation [3]. However, their application in healthcare remains constrained by concerns regarding hallucinations, safety, explainability, and lack of structured orchestration [4, 5]. While retrieval-augmented generation (RAG) mitigates some reliability issues by grounding outputs in verified sources [6], single-model architectures may still lack the modularity and control required for clinical contexts [7].

This PhD research investigates whether supervised modular LLM-based architectures can enable safe, scalable and theory-informed personalization in NCD management. Rather than employing a single generative model, the proposed approach adopts a modular, workflow-oriented architecture in which distinct components are responsible for knowledge retrieval, validation, and message generation, grounded in evidence-based behavior change techniques. In practice, this corresponds to a digital platform that generates personalized health messages for patients based on their clinical profile, using structured AI components. Recognizing this gap spurred our work, which has been shaped by the following research question.

RQ. How can supervised, modular LLM-based architectures support safe and personalized management of patients with non-communicable diseases in primary care settings?

The following hypothesis directed our research as we sought solutions to the previously stated research question.

H. A supervised, modular LLM architecture integrating RAG, intermediate validation layers, and behavior change theory can generate clinically accurate, context-aware, and acceptable personalized communication, while preserving human-in-the-loop oversight.

Following a Design Science Research methodology (DSRM), this thesis iteratively designed, implemented, and evaluated a supervised modular LLM-based platform to support NCD self-management. The present paper reports the final design iteration and empirical validation of the proposed architecture.

2 State of the Art

2.1 Digital Health Interventions in NCD Management

NCDs require long-term behavior modification, sustained adherence to therapeutic and non-therapeutic plans, and continuous patient engagement [8]. DHIs have emerged as scalable mechanisms to support self-management, improve health literacy, and reinforce preventive care strategies [9].

Systematic evidence indicates that effective behavior change interventions must be grounded in theoretical models and structured behavior change techniques (BCTs), with clear logic models connecting intervention features to intended outcomes [10].

Tailoring has been consistently associated with higher engagement and improved behavioral outcomes when compared to generic interventions [11]. Personalization may consider demographic variables, disease stage, barriers to change, behavioral goals, timing, and frequency of delivery [12].

However, despite the recognized importance of personalization, existing DHIs frequently lack transparency regarding how tailoring is operationalized [2]. Automation mechanisms are often underreported, and most interventions rely on static rule-based decision trees [2]. This limits scalability, maintainability, and adaptability, particularly in multimorbidity contexts where interactions between comorbidities require dynamic content generation [2].

These limitations highlight a fundamental gap: while behavior change science provides structured theoretical guidance, the technological infrastructures used in DHIs have historically struggled to deliver adaptive, scalable personalization.

2.2 Conversational Agents

CAs have been increasingly adopted in healthcare to facilitate patient-provider communication, deliver reminders, support education, and promote self-management [9, 11].

Early healthcare chatbots were predominantly rule-based, relying on predefined scripts and decision trees to simulate dialogue [2].

Rule-based conversational systems offer predictability and regulatory clarity, which are advantageous in safety-critical domains. These systems require significant development and maintenance effort, exhibit limited contextual flexibility, demonstrate reduced adaptability to multimorbidity contexts, and constrain dynamic modulation of tone and linguistic style [2].

Empirical implementation of a rule-based conversational agent in a cardiothoracic surgery context demonstrated high usability and acceptability but exposed these scalability and personalization constraints [13]. Manual rule definition was pointed as increasingly impractical as personalization dimensions grow, particularly in NCD management where heterogeneity of patient profiles is substantial [13].

The scoping review conducted within this thesis further revealed that although conversational agents are widely deployed across health domains, the majority still rely on rule-based automation or simple retrieval strategies, with limited architectural sophistication [2].

These findings motivated the exploration of more adaptive architectures capable of supporting dynamic personalization without exponential rule complexity.

2.3 Large Language Models in Clinical Contexts

Recent advances in LLMs have significantly transformed natural language processing capabilities by demonstrating near-human fluency and contextual understanding, enabling more natural and flexible dialogue generation [14].

In healthcare, LLMs have been explored for question answering [15], clinical documentation assistance [16], patient messaging [17], and decision support [18]. Studies have shown that LLM-assisted responses may be rated highly in clarity and utility when compared to human-generated messages [19].

However, their application in patient-facing systems raises significant concerns. Key risks include the generation of factually incorrect information, limited transparency regarding the sources underlying the responses, and the potential presence of bias within the models [5]. Additionally, these systems may offer reduced controllability over outputs and pose safety risks, particularly when deployed in clinical decision-making contexts [20].

RAG has been proposed as a mitigation strategy, grounding model outputs in verified external knowledge sources and improving factual consistency [6]. In clinical contexts, RAG architectures have demonstrated improved reliability in knowledge-intensive tasks [21, 22].

Nevertheless, most implementations rely on single-model generative pipelines, where retrieval and generation are loosely integrated and architectural separation between retrieval, validation, and generation processes remains limited. In safety-critical domains such as healthcare, such monolithic approaches may reduce transparency and controllability.

Thus, while LLMs introduce unprecedented flexibility and linguistic richness, their safe deployment in NCDs requires structured orchestration and supervision mechanisms.

However, in safety-critical domains such as healthcare, architectural simplicity and controllability are often preferable to fully autonomous generation. This has motivated the exploration of structured, modular approaches, where retrieval, validation, and generation are explicitly separated to enhance transparency, constrain model behavior, and support clinical oversight.

2.4 Modular Architectures and Intelligent Orchestration in Healthcare Systems

Recent work in LLM-based systems has explored agent-oriented and modular architectures, in which multiple components are coordinated to perform structured workflows, decompose tasks, utilize external tools, and incorporate feedback loops [23]. Design patterns for agent-based architectures emphasize modularity, functional separation, and controllability, enabling more transparent reasoning pipelines [23].

Recent advances in agentic AI have further introduced orchestration paradigms such as planner – executor architectures, tool-augmented agents, and collaborative multi-agent frameworks, where LLM-based components dynamically coordinate through task decomposition, reflection, and tool usage [24–28]. These approaches often incorporate mechanisms such as chain-of-thought reasoning, self-reflection, and external tool integration to enhance problem-solving capabilities.

While these approaches emphasize autonomy and inter-agent coordination, their direct application to safety-critical domains such as healthcare remains challenging. Fully autonomous agent behaviors, including dynamic planning or negotiation, may reduce predictability and introduce safety risks. In this context, the present work does not aim to replicate fully autonomous agentic architectures, but rather to explore how constrained orchestration can provide a safer and more controllable alternative for clinical applications.

In complex socio-technical environments such as healthcare, modular architectures offer several important advantages. They enable a clear separation between knowledge retrieval and content generation processes, incorporate intermediate validation layers, and enhance overall traceability. Furthermore, they improve system adaptability across diverse clinical contexts and facilitate the implementation of human-in-the-loop supervision mechanisms, thereby strengthening safety and governance [29].

Despite increasing attention to these architectures in AI research, empirical validation of modular LLM-based systems within real-world NCD management contexts remains limited. Few studies evaluate such systems through structured expert assessment, usability testing, and clinical acceptability frameworks simultaneously.

This gap defines the positioning of the present thesis: moving beyond rule-based conversational agents and monolithic LLM pipelines toward a supervised, modular architecture, grounded in behavior change theory, clinical guidelines, and human oversight.

3 Research Approach

This PhD research was conducted within the DSRM framework, which followed an iterative, stakeholder-driven approach to progressively develop and evaluate a socio-technical artefact that integrates behavioral science, digital health, and artificial intelligence to enhance personalized digital health interventions.

3.1 Evolution of the Artefact Across Research Iterations

Phase 1 – Evidence Mapping and Theoretical Grounding. The first phase focused on understanding how DHIs are designed, automated, and personalized. A systematic literature review identified key components of effective behavior change interventions, including theoretical foundations, tailoring dimensions, communication channels, and outcome metrics [12] (Fig. 1).

A subsequent scoping review mapped automation techniques used in conversational agents for healthcare, distinguishing rule-based, retrieval-based, and AI-based approaches. This phase revealed a lack of transparency in personalization mechanisms and limited architectural sophistication in existing systems (Fig. 2).

These findings established the theoretical and technical foundation for subsequent design iterations.

Phase 2 – Rule-Based Conversational Agent in Clinical Context. The first conversational agent to be designed was rule-based. This artefact was co-designed with clinicians and patients and evaluated through feasibility studies and pilot testing in a real hospital setting [13]. While the system demonstrated high usability and acceptability, several important limitations emerged, including limited scalability of rule-based personalization, substantial manual effort required to maintain and update content rules, reduced adaptability to multimorbidity contexts, and restricted flexibility in tone and contextual adaptation.

These findings highlighted the need for more flexible and scalable personalization mechanisms.

Phase 3 – Supervised Modular LLM Architecture for NCD Management. Building upon previous iterations, the final phase of the thesis explored the integration of supervised modular LLM architectures to overcome the scalability and adaptability constraints of rule-based systems.

The proposed architecture introduced a modular workflow composed of a retrieval agent responsible for grounding content in clinical guidelines, an evaluator agent tasked with filtering information for relevance, and a generation agent designed to produce behavior-change-informed personalized messages (Fig. 2).

This modular orchestration enabled functional separation between knowledge retrieval, validation, and natural language generation, increasing controllability and transparency in safety-critical clinical environments.

The present paper reports the design and validation of this final artefact iteration, representing the consolidation of the doctoral research.

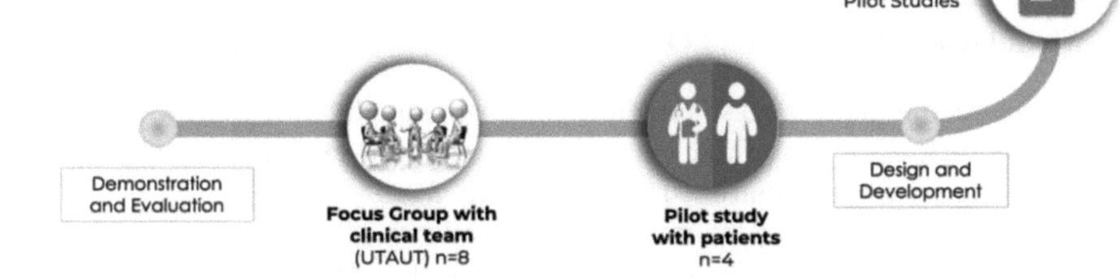

Fig. 1. The studies involved during the first DSRM iteration, namely, the systematic literature review, stakeholder interviews, artefact development, and pilot evaluation activities.

3.2 Conceptual and Architectural Framework

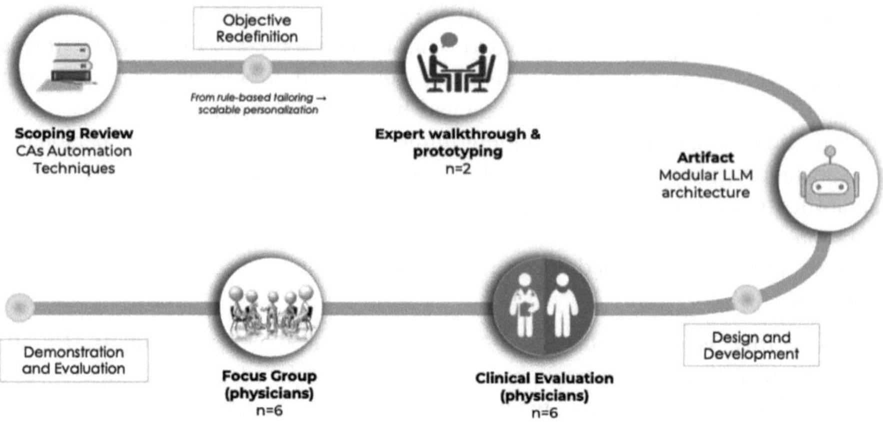

Fig. 2. Second iteration of the DSRM process, depicting the transition from rule-based tailoring to scalable personalization through expert walkthrough, development of a modular LLM architecture, and structured clinical evaluation.

Conceptual and Design Principles. The proposed framework conceptualizes personalized digital health communication as a socio-technical system integrating clinical knowledge, behavior change theory, artificial intelligence, and human oversight within a structured orchestration environment. NCD management is framed as a complex behavioral and organizational process requiring contextual sensitivity and alignment with clinical standards.

The architecture is grounded in curated clinical guidelines provided by the family doctors involved in the study and evidence-based behavior change techniques to ensure epistemic reliability and reduce hallucination risk. The architecture separates retrieval, validation, and generation, enhancing transparency, auditability, and controllability. Human oversight is preserved throughout, positioning AI as an assistive component within regulated clinical workflows while enabling scalable personalization.

3.3 Modular Architecture and Orchestration

The system operationalizes these principles through a modular, workflow-based architecture, in which retrieval, validation, and generation are executed as structured and sequential stages within a controlled workflow (Fig. 3).

The retrieval component performs semantic similarity search over curated guideline repositories to identify clinically relevant knowledge aligned with patient-specific variables. This component is implemented using the LlamaIndex framework with sentence-transformer embeddings (all-MiniLM-L6-v2), stored in a FAISS vector database populated with curated clinical guidelines. Given a query constructed from patient data (e.g., comorbidities, target behavior), cosine similarity is used to retrieve the top-k most relevant documents ($k = 2$). Retrieved content is then summarized using a large language model via the Ollama framework, producing a concise representation tailored to the patient context.

The retrieved content is then passed to an evaluator component, which applies relevance filtering before authorizing progression to the generation stage. Each document-query pair is evaluated using an LLM-based classifier prompted to determine whether the retrieved content adequately addresses the information need, producing a binary ("yes"/"no") decision. Only positively validated content is retained. This intermediate validation step acts as a semantic gate, constraining the informational space available to the generative model and reducing the propagation of marginally relevant or potentially misleading content.

The generation component produces personalized messages grounded exclusively in validated inputs and encoded behavioral constraints. It constructs a structured prompt that integrates patient-specific data, validated guideline content, and behavior change techniques (BCTs), enforcing constraints on tone, clarity, and actionability. Message generation is performed using a large language model (GPT-3.5-turbo), selected for its performance in Portuguese language generation.

An overarching orchestration mechanism coordinates these interactions from patient input to clinician-reviewed output, ensuring structured execution, transparency of intermediate steps, and alignment with human-in-the-loop supervision.

The sequential dependency between stages constrains the information flow, improving controllability and reducing the likelihood of unsafe or irrelevant outputs. Unlike fully autonomous agentic systems, the architecture relies on deterministic orchestration rather than dynamic planning or inter-agent negotiation, prioritizing predictability and safety in clinical contexts.

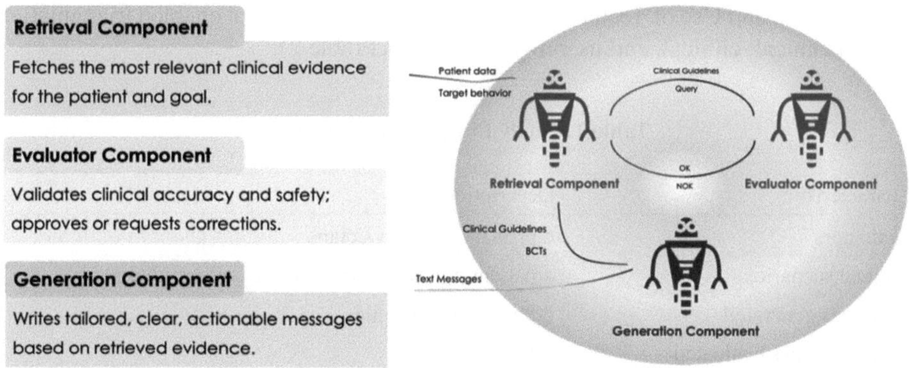

Fig. 3. Modular architecture illustrating the interaction between retrieval, validation, and generation components within a structured workflow. Patient data initiate evidence retrieval from clinical guidelines and behavior change techniques, followed by validation and controlled message generation.

4 Validation

4.1 Study Design

The final artefact iteration was evaluated through a multi-method empirical study combining quantitative expert assessment, usability evaluation, and qualitative analysis of clinician perceptions. The objective was to assess the clinical adequacy, safety, and practical acceptability of the proposed modular LLM-based platform in primary care contexts. The characteristics of the study are depicted in Table 1.

The evaluation design prioritizes expert-based assessment and usability analysis, which are particularly relevant in early-stage validation of clinical decision-support and communication systems, where feasibility, safety, and acceptability are primary concerns.

Four representative clinical scenarios were defined, reflecting distinct NCD patient profiles, including patient profiles with multiple comorbidities. For each patient type, the system generated 20 personalized messages grounded in clinical guidelines and behavior change techniques.

Six primary care physicians independently evaluated the generated messages using a structured assessment framework. Evaluation criteria included clinical accuracy, relevance, clarity, actionability, and safety. Each dimension was rated on a 5-point Likert scale ranging from 0 (poor) to 4 (excellent).

Usability was assessed using the System Usability Scale (SUS) [30]. Additionally, a moderated focus group was conducted to explore perceived usefulness, performance expectancy, and integration feasibility, informed by constructs from the Unified Theory of Acceptance and Use of Technology (UTAUT) [31]. This design enabled triangulation across technical, clinical, and usability dimensions (Table 2).

Table 1. Study Design Characteristics.

Characteristic	Description
Evaluators	6 primary care physicians
Clinical scenarios	4 patient profiles (with multiple comorbidities)
Messages generated	20 per patient profile
Total messages evaluated	80
Evaluation scale	0–4 Likert scale
Usability instrument	System Usability Scale (SUS)
Qualitative method	Focus group (UTAUT-informed)

Clinical accuracy received the highest ratings, reflecting adequate guideline grounding and contextual alignment. Safety ratings, while slightly lower than other dimensions, remained within a high-performance range, with minimal concerns identified.

Inter-rater agreement values were modest, likely reflecting inherent variability in clinical judgment and interpretation of personalized communication, particularly in

Table 2. Mean evaluation scores (0–4 Likert scale) across assessed dimensions for the generated text messages.

Dimension	Mean Score (0–4)
Clinical Accuracy	3.90
Relevance	3.75
Clarity	3.68
Actionability	3.54
Safety	3.32

early-stage evaluation settings. However, qualitative analysis of evaluator feedback indicated that suggested modifications predominantly involved tone refinement and contextual personalization rather than correction of major clinical inaccuracies.

4.2 Usability Assessment

The platform achieved a SUS score of 90, which corresponds to an "excellent" usability classification according to standard SUS interpretation benchmarks.

Participants reported that the interface was intuitive and that the workflow aligned with clinical reasoning processes. No major usability barriers were identified during the evaluation phase.

4.3 Qualitative Findings

Physicians emphasized that the system's value lies in augmenting communication efficiency while maintaining professional control. The human-in-the-loop configuration was considered essential to ensuring trust and accountability. Participants also highlighted that large-scale adoption would depend on seamless interoperability with existing clinical information systems.

The empirical validation provides preliminary evidence of technical feasibility, clinical adequacy, and practical acceptability of the proposed modular architecture. The modular LLM-based architecture shows potential as an approach to generate guideline-consistent, context-aware personalized communication while maintaining high usability standards. Although larger-scale validation and patient-facing studies are required, the results indicate for further translational evaluation.

5 Synthesis of Main Findings

This PhD research was guided by the central research question: How can supervised, modular LLM-based architectures support safe and personalized management of patients with non-communicable diseases in primary care settings? The underlying hypothesis proposed that a supervised, modular architecture grounded in RAG, and behavior change theory could produce clinically accurate, context-aware, and acceptable personalized communication while preserving human oversight.

The empirical findings provide preliminary support for this hypothesis across multiple dimensions. First, from a technical perspective, the modular LLM-based architecture demonstrated functional feasibility. The structured separation between retrieval, evaluation, and generation enabled the production of personalized messages grounded in validated clinical guidelines and behavior change techniques. The system operated reliably across distinct patient scenarios, including multimorbidity contexts, suggesting that modular orchestration may support scalable personalization without the exponential rule complexity observed in earlier rule-based systems.

Second, regarding clinical validity and safety, primary care physicians rated the generated messages highly in terms of clinical accuracy, relevance, clarity, and actionability, with minimal perceived safety risks. Although inter-rater agreement metrics were modest likely due to subjective interpretation and limited sample size the overall evaluation patterns suggest that the architecture can generate content that aligns with professional standards when supervised appropriately. The frequent minor edits introduced by physicians primarily refined tone and specificity rather than correcting major clinical inaccuracies, reinforcing the system's baseline adequacy.

Third, from a usability and adoption perspective, the platform achieved an excellent SUS score and was perceived as valuable in supporting chronic care management. Physicians highlighted the system's potential to reinforce care plans and reduce repetitive communication workload. At the same time, they emphasized the importance of integration with existing clinical information systems to ensure seamless workflow incorporation. These findings indicate that technical feasibility alone is insufficient; organizational and interoperability considerations are critical for real-world deployment.

Taken together, the results provide preliminary evidence that supervised, modular LLM architectures can support more adaptive and personalized communication systems in primary care. However, the findings also underscore the necessity of maintaining structured supervision, robust knowledge grounding, and integration with clinical workflows. The research therefore validates not only the feasibility of the proposed architecture but also the importance of its governance-aware design. Unlike recent agentic AI approaches that emphasize autonomy and emergent coordination, the proposed architecture prioritizes controlled orchestration and safety, which are critical in clinical environments.

This study should be interpreted as a proof-of-concept evaluation, and several limitations must be acknowledged. The sample size (six physicians and four clinical scenarios) is limited and does not support statistical generalization. Additionally, the modest inter-rater agreement reflects the subjective nature of message evaluation and variability in clinical judgment. Therefore, the results should be interpreted as indicative of feasibility and clinical plausibility, rather than definitive evidence of effectiveness. Such small-scale, expert-driven evaluations are consistent with early-stage validation of clinical AI systems, where feasibility, safety, and acceptability are assessed prior to large-scale deployment.

In summary, the thesis suggests that safe and scalable personalization in NCD management may be achieved through modular LLM-based architectures combined with human oversight. The hypothesis is supported in terms of feasibility, clinical acceptability, and usability, while future research remains necessary to evaluate long-term patient outcomes and large-scale implementation.

6 PhD Thesis Contributions and Future Research

This PhD research makes four primary contributions:

1. a conceptual framework for personalized digital health communication as a socio-technical system.
2. a supervised modular LLM architecture for safe and controllable personalization.
3. a DSRM for developing AI-enabled healthcare artefacts.
4. a proof-of-concept implementation and evaluation demonstrating feasibility and clinical acceptability.

This PhD research contributes to intelligent digital health systems through conceptual, architectural, methodological, and practical advancements, proposing a structured approach to the design and validation of a modular LLM-based architecture in safety-critical socio-technical environments.

At a conceptual level, the work frames personalized digital health communication as a socio-technical system, integrating clinical guidelines, behavior change theory, artificial intelligence, and human oversight within a unified orchestration model, the thesis extends existing approaches that typically treat personalization, automation, and governance as separate dimensions. The work contributes to the conceptualization of modular LLM systems not as autonomous decision-makers but as structured collaborators embedded within regulated workflows.

Architecturally, the thesis introduces a supervised modular LLM framework that separates retrieval, validation, and generation processes. This design enhances transparency, traceability, and controllability, demonstrating how RAG and intermediate evaluation layers can mitigate risks such as hallucination and contextual misalignment in healthcare communication.

Methodologically, the research advances the application of DSRM to AI-enabled healthcare artefacts, combining iterative development, stakeholder co-design, and empirical validation, the thesis illustrates how generative AI systems can be developed in alignment with clinical requirements and organizational constraints. The integration of expert evaluation, usability assessment, and qualitative acceptance analysis provides a multi-dimensional validation approach rarely combined in studies of LLM-based healthcare systems.

The thesis presents and preliminarily validates a digital platform capable of generating personalized, guideline-informed communication for NCD management, demonstrating technical feasibility, clinical acceptability, and high usability among primary care physicians.

Future work should focus on large-scale clinical validation, integration with healthcare information systems, enhanced validation mechanisms (e.g., safety checks and uncertainty estimation), and broader socio-ethical evaluation, including trust, equity, and explainability.

Overall, this research contributes design principles and validation strategies for the development of safe, transparent, and scalable AI-driven health systems applicable to other regulated domains.

7 Technological Innovation to Tackle Societal Challenges

This work contributes to the development of human-centric intelligent systems by demonstrating how supervised modular LLM architectures can support safe, personalized, and context-aware communication in healthcare. In contrast to monolithic generative approaches, the proposed system emphasizes controlled orchestration, traceability, and human oversight, aligning with the requirements of safety-critical socio-technical environments.

The proposed approach addresses several pressing societal challenges. First, it supports the scalability of healthcare delivery in the context of ageing populations and increasing multimorbidity, where clinicians face growing demands for continuous, personalized communication. Second, it contributes to reducing inequalities in access to tailored health information, enabling more consistent and context-aware guidance across diverse patient populations. Third, it targets the challenge of long-term adherence and behavior change in NCDs, where sustained, personalized engagement is essential for effective management. Finally, it contributes to the broader challenge of deploying AI safely in critical domains, by prioritizing transparency, validation, and human-in-the-loop supervision.

The architecture illustrates how advanced AI capabilities can be integrated into clinical workflows without compromising reliability or professional accountability. By combining knowledge grounding, intermediate validation, and human oversight, the system supports a collaborative intelligence model in which AI augments, rather than replaces, clinical decision-making.

More broadly, the design principles demonstrated in this work modularity, constrained generation, and governance-aware orchestration are applicable to other regulated domains requiring trustworthy AI systems. This highlights the role of structured AI integration in enabling scalable yet controlled innovation across complex socio-technical systems.

8 Conclusion

This thesis investigated how rule-based conversational systems and LLM-based workflows can be designed to deliver personalized digital health interventions for NCD management while preserving clinical safety and human oversight.

Grounded in the DSRM, the work evolved from a rule-based conversational system to a supervised modular LLM architecture integrating RAG, behavioral theory, and structured validation layers. The findings demonstrate that scalable personalization in healthcare requires more than linguistic sophistication; it demands architectural modularity, epistemic grounding, and explicit governance mechanisms.

The proposed framework contributes conceptually by positioning personalized digital health communication as a cyber-socio-technical system in which functional components operate within bounded, interpretable workflows. Architecturally, it introduces a supervised modular design that enhances traceability, controllability, and adaptability compared to monolithic generative approaches. Empirically, it provides preliminary evidence of usability, acceptability, and expert-rated clinical adequacy.

While challenges remain, particularly regarding large-scale validation and system integration, this research outlines a structured pathway toward the safe deployment of generative AI in NCD management. By reconciling adaptability with safety, and automation with human oversight, the thesis contributes to the development of next-generation digital health systems capable of supporting sustainable behavior change in complex clinical environments.

Acknowledgments. AM, LLV and ILN would like to acknowledge National Foundation of Science and Technology for funding this work under the project UID/00667/2025 (UNIDEMI). This work was also supported by FCT Fundação para a Ciência e Tecnologia, I.P. by project reference 2023.02916.BDANA and DOI identifier https://doi.org/10.54499/2023.02916.BDANA. AM acknowledges the support provided by ISTAR-Iscte Pluriannual Projects UIDB/04466/2025 and UIDP/04466/2025.

References

1. Eurostat.: Causes of death statistics. https://ec.europa.eu/eurostat/statistics-explained/index.php?title=Causes_of_death_statistics. Last accessed 18 Mar 2025
2. Martins, A., Londral, A., Nunes, I.L., Lapão, L.V.: Unlocking human-like conversations: scoping review of automation techniques for personalized healthcare interventions using conversational agents. Int. J. Med. Inform. **185**, 105385 (2024). https://doi.org/10.1016/j.ijmedinf.2024.105385
3. Choi, E.P.H., Lee, J.J., Ho, M.-H., Kwok, J.Y.Y., Lok, K.Y.W.: Chatting or cheating? the impacts of ChatGPT and other artificial intelligence language models on nurse education. Nurse Educ. Today. **125**, 105796 (2023). https://doi.org/10.1016/j.nedt.2023.105796
4. Ji, Z., et al.: Survey of hallucination in natural language generation. ACM Comput. Surv. **55**, 1–38 (2023). https://doi.org/10.1145/3571730
5. Weidinger, L., et al.: Taxonomy of risks posed by language models. In: 2022 ACM Conference on Fairness, Accountability, and Transparency, pp. 214–229. ACM, Seoul Republic of Korea (2022). https://doi.org/10.1145/3531146.3533088
6. Lewis, P., et al.: Retrieval-augmented generation for knowledge-intensive NLP tasks. In: Advances in Neural Information Processing Systems (NeurIPS 2020), pp. 9459–9474. Curran Associates Inc., Red Hook, NY, USA (2020). https://doi.org/10.48550/arXiv.2005.11401
7. Korngiebel, D.M., Mooney, S.D.: Considering the possibilities and pitfalls of generative pre-trained transformer 3 (GPT-3) in healthcare delivery. Npj Digit. Med. **4**, 93 (2021). https://doi.org/10.1038/s41746-021-00464-x
8. Lorig, K.R., Holman, H.R.: Self-management education: history, definition, outcomes, and mechanisms. Ann. Behav. Med. **26**, 1–7 (2003). https://doi.org/10.1207/S15324796ABM2601_01
9. Murray, E., et al.: Evaluating digital health interventions. Am. J. Prev. Med. **51**, 843–851 (2016). https://doi.org/10.1016/j.amepre.2016.06.008

10. Michie, S., Yardley, L., West, R., Patrick, K., Greaves, F.: Developing and evaluating digital interventions to promote behavior change in health and health care: recommendations resulting from an international workshop. J. Med. Internet Res. **19**, e232 (2017). https://doi.org/10.2196/jmir.7126
11. Tudor Car, L., et al.: Conversational agents in health care: scoping review and conceptual analysis. J. Med. Internet Res. **22**, e17158 (2020). https://doi.org/10.2196/17158
12. Martins, A., Londral, A., Lapão, L.V.: Behaviour change interventions based on automated and tailored communication systems to improve health outcomes in adult chronic patients: a systematic review. Res. Square. (2022). https://doi.org/10.21203/rs.3.rs-2175520/v1
13. Martins, A., Nunes, I.L., Lapão, L.V., Londral, A.: Conversational agent automation for patients after cardiothoracic surgery based on clinical team experience and behavior change theory. In: Presented at the 14th International Conference on Applied Human Factors and Ergonomics (AHFE 2023) (2023). https://doi.org/10.54941/ahfe1003597
14. Bommasani, R., et al.: On the opportunities and risks of foundation models. arXiv preprint arXiv:2108.07258. (2021). https://doi.org/10.48550/arXiv.2108.07258
15. Singhal, K., et al.: Toward expert-level medical question answering with large language models. Nat. Med. **31**, 943–950 (2025). https://doi.org/10.1038/s41591-024-03423-7
16. Satheakeerthy, S., Jesudason, D., Pietris, J., Bacchi, S., Chan, W.O.: LLM-assisted medical documentation: efficacy, errors, and ethical considerations in ophthalmology. Eye. **39**, 1440–1442 (2025). https://doi.org/10.1038/s41433-025-03767-5
17. Chen, S., et al.: The effect of using a large language model to respond to patient messages. Lancet Digit. Health. **6**, e379–e381 (2024). https://doi.org/10.1016/S2589-7500(24)00060-8
18. Gaber, F., et al.: Evaluating large language model workflows in clinical decision support for triage and referral and diagnosis. Npj Digit. Med. **8**, 263 (2025). https://doi.org/10.1038/s41746-025-01684-1
19. Ayers, J.W., et al.: Comparing physician and artificial intelligence chatbot responses to patient questions posted to a public social media forum. JAMA Intern. Med. **183**, 589 (2023). https://doi.org/10.1001/jamainternmed.2023.1838
20. Mesinovic, M., Watkinson, P., Zhu, T.: Explainability in the age of large language models for healthcare. Comm. Eng. **4**, 128 (2025). https://doi.org/10.1038/s44172-025-00453-y
21. Li, M., Kilicoglu, H., Xu, H., Zhang, R.: BiomedRAG: a retrieval augmented large language model for biomedicine. J. Biomed. Inform. **162**, 104769 (2025). https://doi.org/10.1016/j.jbi.2024.104769
22. Zakka, C., et al.: Almanac: retrieval-augmented language models for clinical medicine. arXiv preprint arXiv:2303.01229. (2023). https://doi.org/10.48550/arXiv.2303.01229
23. Krishnan, N.: AI agents: evolution, architecture, and real-world applications. arXiv preprint arXiv:2503.12687. (2025). https://doi.org/10.48550/arXiv.2503.12687
24. Wei, J., et al.: Chain-of-thought prompting elicits reasoning in large language models. arXiv preprint arXiv:2201.11903. (2022). https://doi.org/10.48550/arXiv.2201.11903
25. Schick, T., et al.: Toolformer: language models can teach themselves to use tools. arXiv preprint arXiv:2302.04761. (2023). https://doi.org/10.48550/arXiv.2302.04761
26. Liu, Y., et al.: Agent design pattern catalogue: a collection of architectural patterns for foundation model based agents. J. Syst. Softw. **220**, 112278 (2025). https://doi.org/10.1016/j.jss.2024.112278
27. Shinn, N., Cassano, F., Berman, E., Gopinath, A., Narasimhan, K., Yao, S.: Reflexion: language agents with verbal reinforcement learning. arXiv preprint arXiv:2303.11366. (2023). https://doi.org/10.48550/arXiv.2303.11366
28. Hong, S., et al.: MetaGPT: meta programming for a multi-agent collaborative framework. arXiv preprint arXiv:2308.00352. (2023). https://doi.org/10.48550/arXiv.2308.00352
29. Liu, F., et al.: A foundational architecture for AI agents in healthcare. Cell Rep. Med. **6**, 102374 (2025). https://doi.org/10.1016/j.xcrm.2025.102374

30. Martins, A.I., Rosa, A.F., Queirós, A., Silva, A., Rocha, N.P.: European Portuguese validation of the system usability scale (SUS). Procedia Comput. Sci. **67**, 293–300 (2015). https://doi.org/10.1016/j.procs.2015.09.273
31. Venkatesh, V., Morris, M.G., Davis, G.B., Davis, F.D.: User acceptance of information technology: toward a unified view. MIS Q. **27**, 425 (2003). https://doi.org/10.2307/30036540

Smart and Fair Energy Communities

A Deep Learning Approach to Electric Water Heater Thermal Modelling for Demand Response Applications

Francisco Januário-Silva(✉), João Tabanêz Patrício, Rafael Menezes-Barros, and Rui Amaral Lopes

School of Science and Technology UNINOVA-CTS and LASI, NOVA University Lisbon, Caparica, Portugal
{fnj.silva,jp.patricio}@campus.fct.unl.pt, {rm.barros, rm.lopes}@fct.unl.pt

Abstract. Electric water heaters (EWHs) represent a significant source of residential energy flexibility, yet exploiting this potential for demand response requires accurate thermal models suitable for complex control strategies. This paper presents a deep learning approach for modelling an IoT-enabled EWH using a two-layer temperature stratification model. The proposed method uses water consumption, heating power, and internal temperature measurements from the top and bottom layers to model the evolution of the thermal state along time. This approach circumvents the complexity of deriving analytical thermodynamic models, captures nonlinear dynamics directly from real operational data, and can be readily transferred to model other devices with similar configurations. The proposed solution is validated on real case-study data, and an optimal scheduling scenario is showcased. Results demonstrate that the data-driven approach provides accurate temperature trajectory predictions, with a MAE of 1.45 °C and 2.57 °C, for bottom and top layers, respectively, over a 24-h horizon. An optimal day-ahead scheduling showcased a reduction of 83% in heater operation cost compared to thermostat-based control.

Keywords: Energy flexibility · EWH · Demand Response · Deep Learning · Genetic Algorithm

1 Introduction

The increasing share of renewable energy in power grids has led to significant challenges regarding its efficient integration. Matching generation and load is an increasingly difficult task, which has driven growing interest in demand-side management (DSM) strategies. Demand Response (DR), which is a subset of DSM, exploits the energy flexibility available in end-use consumer load profiles, typically through incentive mechanisms such as Time-of-Use (ToU) and other tariff structures [1]. Under such DR schemes, the

Published by Springer Nature Switzerland AG 2027
L. M. Camarinha-Matos and F. Ferrada (Eds.): DoCEIS 2026, IFIP AICT 790, pp. 157–172, 2027.
https://doi.org/10.1007/978-3-032-28939-1_12

optimal scheduling of flexible residential loads represents an attractive avenue for reducing end-user energy costs and supporting grid operation [2]. Thermostatically controlled loads (TCLs) such as electric water heaters (EWHs), heat pumps, and air conditioning units, are especially suited for this purpose due to their inherent thermal storage capacity, which allows consumption to be shifted in time without compromising end-user comfort [3]. EWHs are an increasingly common load in households, as electrification efforts drive the shift away from gas-based solutions. Water heating accounts for approximately 15% of residential energy consumption in the EU [4] with electric units already representing most of existing water heaters [5].

However, the exploitation of energy flexibility in EWHs often requires the existence of models capable of representing their internal energy state. As such, the current study proposes a framework for black-box thermal modelling of EWHs, accounting for multiple stratification layers, which is validated on real operational data from an IoT-enabled EWH, with its applicability demonstrated through a day-ahead optimal scheduling scenario.

EWHs have attracted significant attention as a flexible resource for demand response, with applications such as individual household cost optimization under ToU tariffs [6]. Beyond the individual household, EWHs have also been explored at the aggregated level for grid-scale services. The study reported in [7] performs a real-world validation of secondary frequency reserve provision using a large pool of EWHs, while [8] demonstrates peak shifting and frequency response capabilities through a custom-built aggregation system. These studies highlight the potential of EWH fleets to participate in a range of grid services, from cost reduction at the individual level to ancillary services at the system level. However, realizing this potential requires accurate and computationally inexpensive thermal models of individual devices, capable of predicting their temperature evolution under different actions [9].

The thermal modelling of EWHs to aid energy management strategies has been the subject of extensive research. EWH modelling approaches can be categorized according to the degree of physical knowledge embedded in the model. White-box models are derived entirely from first principles, relying on energy balance equations that describe heat transfer within the tank, standby losses, and the effect of water draw [10]. While physically interpretable, these require detailed knowledge of system parameters such as tank geometry, insulation properties, and heat transfer coefficients, which may not be readily available or accurately represent real operating conditions. At the other end of the spectrum, black-box models learn input-output relationships entirely from observed data, bypassing the need for physical parameterization [11]. Grey-box approaches occupy a middle ground, imposing a physical structure while estimating unknown parameters from data [9].

Regardless of the modelling paradigm, an important consideration is the number of thermal layers, also known as zones or nodes, used to represent the water tank. Typically, studies discretize the tank into either a single layer [12] or two layers [13], due to their simplicity and reduced computational burden. Increasing the number of layers leads to more precise temperature estimations, as these better capture the water stratification phenomenon within the tank. This, however, represents a trade-off between model fidelity and computational cost. The study reported in [14] considers a partial differential equation (PDE) approach and concludes that the simulation of optimal EWH control for grid services under such models is computationally infeasible at large scale, although model simplification also leads to inaccurate flexibility estimations. Similarly, [10] finds that the simulation time of a PDE model compared to one and two-layer simplifications is significantly slower (22 min versus 15 s).

Black-box models, particularly those based on deep learning, offer a compelling alternative for large-scale deployment. By requiring no prior knowledge of the device's physical parameters, the same modelling framework can be applied to heterogeneous EWH installations with minimal adaptation, significantly reducing the effort required to operationalize new devices. This is particularly relevant in contexts where IoT-enabled controllers, such as the architecture presented in [15], are deployed across diverse households, as the modelling process can scale alongside the hardware without requiring per-device physical characterization.

2 Contributions and Relevance to Societal Challenges

As power systems face increasing pressure from the integration of variable renewable sources, intelligent management of household energy consumption becomes both an economic and environmental priority. Electric water heaters, among the most energy-intensive residential appliances, offer significant potential for demand-side flexibility due to their inherent thermal storage capability.

This work contributes to this challenge by developing a data-driven thermal modeling framework, validated through a case study considering optimal scheduling, to enable households in reducing energy costs while maintaining comfort. The tangible economic benefit provided to end-users serves as an incentive for participation in DR programs, which is particularly valuable in island power systems where flexibility resources are scarce and renewable curtailment remains a pressing issue [16]. The approach is generalizable to any context with time-varying electricity pricing and requires no prior knowledge of the water heater's physical parameters, relying entirely on observed operational data to learn its thermal behavior.

This study is part of a broader PhD work that seeks to fully characterize demand-side energy flexibility under a holistic appreciation of grid, Information and Communication Technology (ICT), economic, regulatory, and behavioral constraints. Such a characterization presupposes the availability of device-specific flexibility potential estimates, which is a prerequisite that the present work addresses for the case of EWHs.

3 Methodology

This section describes the methodology adopted in this work. Section 3.1 presents the case study and the data collection setup of the IoT-enabled EWH used to build the proposed thermal models. Section 3.2 details the model architecture, including the autoregressive inference scheme. Section 3.3 describes the training procedure and hyperparameter tuning strategy. Section 3.4 defines the performance evaluation methodology, while Sect. 3.5 introduces the day-ahead optimal scheduling formulation used to demonstrate the practical applicability of the proposed framework.

3.1 Case-Study and Data Collection

Temperature, water draw, and heating power measurements are collected from a real-world deployment of an IoT-enabled EWH, currently operating at a single-family household of two adults and one child in Terceira Island, Azores, Portugal, within the scope of the IANOS H2020 project [17]. The household is connected to the low-voltage distribution grid (230 V, 50 Hz) and has a contracted power of 6.9 kVA and 1.32 kWp of installed PV generation.

The EWH is equipped with temperature probes at the top and bottom of the tank, as well as at the inlet and outlet, while power consumption is measured via a smart plug (see Fig. 1). These measurements are aggregated by a local Smart Water Heater Controller (SWHC), which communicates with a remote server via Wi-Fi using HTTPS requests at one-minute intervals, transmitting the collected data and receiving control signals in return. This allows for optimal control of the EWH through two complementary strategies: real-time capture of PV generation surplus, estimated from the household's real-time load and generation measurements, and pre-heating based on day-ahead forecasts of energy surplus and water consumption. Furthermore, thermal comfort is guaranteed through a rule-based control that ensures that the top-layer temperature, which is representative of the outlet temperature during water draw events, is maintained between 50 °C and 74 °C. A previous iteration of the above-mentioned configuration and control strategy is fully described in [15].

For this study, historical measurements of the described configuration are used to build the proposed thermal models. The obtained features are described in Table 1. It should be noted that, due to the limited reliability of the SWHC's ambient temperature measurements, the 2-m air temperature was instead sourced from Open-Meteo's historical weather API [18], using the best-match model option for the case study's location. The historical measurement time series were collected from the 1st of June 2025 to 31st of January 2026. As is common in real-world IoT deployments, missing timesteps were identified. To maximize the usable data, gaps of up to two consecutive missing timesteps were filled through linear interpolation.

Table 1. Data collected at the physical layer with one minute resolution.

Feature	Description	Unit
T_{top}	Mean temperature at the top of the water tank	°C
T_{bot}	Mean temperature at the bottom of the water tank	°C
T_{amb}	Mean ambient temperature	°C
P_{heater}	Mean electrical power consumed by the EWH	W
Q	Cumulative water flow volume for the sampling period	L

3.2 Model Architecture

The thermal modelling framework proposed in this work is designed around two guiding principles: compatibility with the sensor configurations of real IoT-enabled devices, and

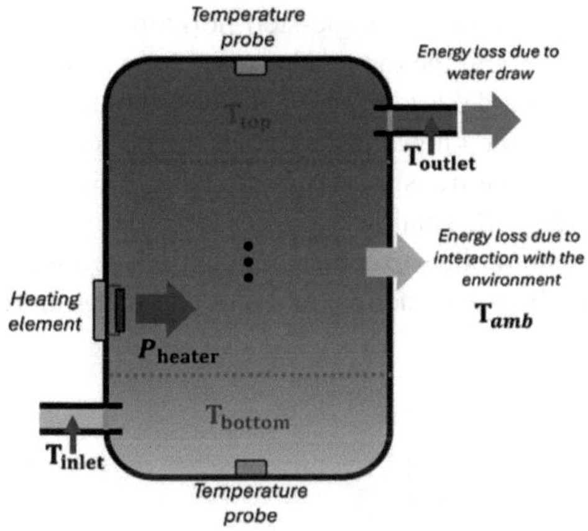

Fig. 1. EWH configuration present in the case-study.

computational efficiency suitable for large-scale, real-time control applications. Accordingly, a discretized N-layer representation of the water tank is adopted. As discussed in Sect. 1, reduced-layer formulations (typically one or two layers) offer a favorable trade-off between model fidelity and computational cost, and the number of layers aligns naturally with the number of temperature probes physically embedded in the device (two, in the case of the present study). To capture the thermal dynamics of each layer without relying on prior knowledge of the device's physical parameters, a black-box approach based on Recurrent Neural Networks (RNNs) is adopted, leveraging the operational data collected through the IoT-enabled monitoring system described in Sect. 3.1.

RNNs are a class of artificial neural networks designed for sequential data, where the output at each timestep is informed by both the current input and a hidden state that carries information from previous steps. This makes them particularly adept at recognizing temporal patterns in time series data, such as the evolution of water temperature inside an EWH. Common RNN variants include the Simple RNN, which processes sequences through a single recurrent connection, the Gated Recurrent Unit (GRU), which introduces gating mechanisms to better control information flow, and the Long Short-Term Memory (LSTM), which adds a dedicated cell state to capture long-range dependencies more effectively.

The proposed model architecture, represented in Fig. 2, consists of a recurrent neural network (RNN) encoder followed by fully connected (dense) layers. The model predicts the next-step temperature value for a given thermal layer of the tank. The choice of RNN cell architecture is treated as a hyperparameter, with the best-performing variant selected through the grid search process described in Sect. 3.3. The RNN processes the historical input sequence and produces a fixed-length representation, which is then passed through the dense layers to generate the output prediction.

Contemporaneous exogenous data is also passed to the dense layers, bypassing the RNN encoder, to inform the model of the conditions at the current prediction time step, such as the heater's power state, water consumption, and ambient temperature. The model operates autoregressively, feeding its own predictions back as inputs to generate temperature trajectories beyond the single-step horizon. Given that temperature measurements are available for both the top and bottom of the tank, two separate models are trained. The bottom-layer model is executed first, and its output is used as an input to the top-layer model, reflecting the known influence of the bottom-layer temperature on the top layer through upward heat transfer within the tank. This architecture is compatible with an arbitrary number of thermal layers, provided that measurements are available for each of the layers, with models executed sequentially from the bottom to the top of the tank. The interaction between each layer's model during inference is represented in Fig. 3.

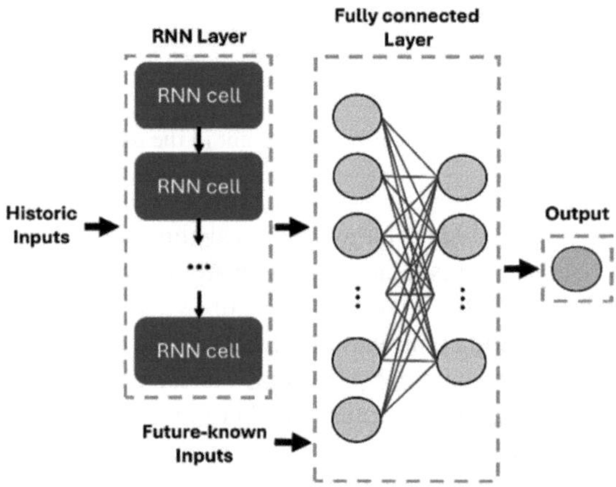

Fig. 2. Proposed model architecture.

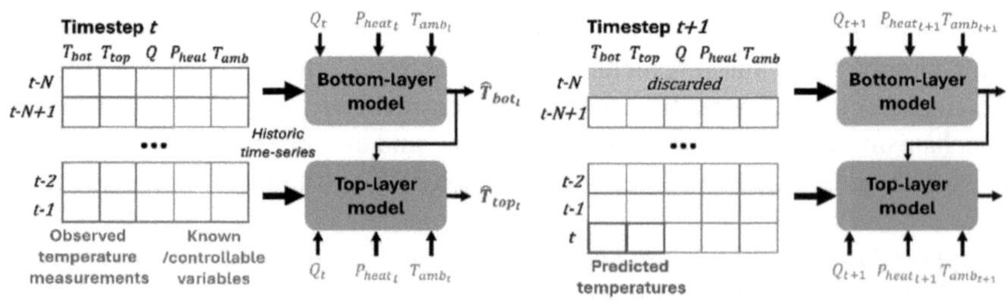

Fig. 3. Coupled autoregressive inference scheme for the proposed model architecture. The first timestep (t) uses actual measurements as input, while the second timestep (t + 1) integrates the previous step's predictions.

3.3 Model Training and Hyperparameter Tuning

During training, input data consists exclusively of ground truth observations, whereas at inference, the model must feed its own predictions back as inputs in order to generate trajectories beyond the output horizon, which can lead to degraded performance. This is particularly true for high resolution temperature models, since these can simply learn to rely heavily on the most recent values of the endogenous variable, neglecting exogenous factors like water draw or heating. To mitigate this issue, the scheduled sampling technique was adopted.

Scheduled sampling was introduced by [19] as a curriculum learning strategy to bridge the gap between training and inference in autoregressive models. During training, the model gradually transitions from using ground truth inputs to using its own predictions, reducing its dependence on perfect input data. Concretely, at each training step within the unrolled horizon, the model receives the ground truth as input with probability ε, or its own previous prediction with probability $1 - \varepsilon$. This probability decays at each epoch following a predefined schedule. In this study, a scheduled sampling strategy is adopted, considering a linear decay, as described in Eq. 1, where e is the current epoch of training, k is the initial probability, c is the decay rate, and $\varepsilon_{\min}$ is the minimum probability floor. In this study, k is 1, representing pure teacher forcing in the first epoch, c is set to 0.04, and $\varepsilon_{\min}$ is set to 0.5, ensuring that the model still gets sufficient exposure to the ground truth.

$$\varepsilon_{\mathrm{e}} = \max(\varepsilon_{\min}, \mathrm{k} - \mathrm{ce}) \tag{1}$$

The training process is thus divided into two phases. In the first phase, the model is trained using conventional teacher forcing on a balanced dataset, where samples from periods of active heating, water draw, or both are equally represented relative to idle periods. In the second phase, the pre-trained model is fine-tuned using scheduled sampling on contiguous data segments, as the autoregressive unrolling requires temporally continuous sequences. In both phases, an early stopping mechanism, with a 5-epoch patience, based on the validation error, is used to avoid model overfitting. Since the top-layer and bottom-layer models are trained separately, their hyperparameters are also obtained from separate grid search schemes based on the validation set. The resulting optimal hyperparameters, as well as their search intervals are represented in Table 2 for both models. It should be noted that both the input size, i.e., the number of previous timesteps considered as input to the model, and the unroll size, i.e., the number of autoregressive steps performed during the scheduled sampling phase, are treated as hyperparameters.

The training set comprises data from 1st of June 2025 to 31st of December 2025, further divided into training and validation subsets in a 70:30 ratio. Due to data availability, the model did not train on a complete representation of the possible climate conditions, since that would require a full year of measurements. However, since the testing set, which will be described in the next section, is temporally connected to the training/validation sets, this emulates a real-world deployment, where a model can eventually be trained on available historic data to predict under potentially unseen conditions, and is eventually retrained using the new data. For the first training phase, the data is balanced and randomly sampled as described in the previous section, resulting in 116617 samples for training, and 49979 samples for validation. For the second phase, the data is structured into contiguous segments of length equal to the sum of the input window and the unroll horizon, enabling the autoregressive unrolling required by scheduled sampling.

The proposed models were trained and validated using the TensorFlow deep learning framework with Python 3.11, on a system equipped with an NVIDIA GeForce RTX 3070 Laptop GPU and 16 GB of RAM.

Table 2. Optimal hyperparameters for top-layer and bottom-layer models and grid search intervals.

Hyperparameter		Top-layer	Bottom-layer	Grid search intervals
RNN layer	Cell type	LSTM	LSTM	[LSTM, GRU, Simple RNN]
	Neurons/ Number of layers	(64)	(64)	[(64), (64–32)]
	Activation function	tanh	tanh	–
Dense layer	Neurons/ Number of layers	(32, 16)	(32, 16)	[(64, 32), (32, 16)]
	Activation function	ReLU	ReLU	–
Output	Neurons	1	1	–
	Activation function	sigmoid	sigmoid	–
Training parameters	Batch size	128	128	[64, 128, 256]
	Learning rate	0.00005	0.00005	[0.005, 0.0005, 0.00005]
	Optimizer	Adam	Adam	–
	Input size	30	30	[30, 60]
	Unroll size	30	30	[30, 60]
	Error metric	MSE	MSE	–

3.4 Model Performance Evaluation

The model performance was evaluated on the testing set in a walk-forward scheme spanning the entirety of January 2026. The model generates a 48-h prediction, then advances 30 min forward and repeats the process until it reaches the end of the month. Since evaluation requires segments with contiguous 48-h ground truth data, only 778 out of a possible 1344 segments met this criterion. Given that autoregressive error is expected to accumulate overtime, performance is reported for increasing prediction horizons of 6, 24, and 48 h. The Mean Absolute Error (MAE) and Root Mean Square Error (RMSE) were selected as evaluation metrics, as both can be interpreted in the same unit as the target variable (°C), and are commonplace in literature.

Results are reported individually for each thermal layer and under two different configurations: i) both layers' model predictions fed as input, hereinafter referred to as the coupled configuration; ii) only one layer's predictions fed as input, while keeping the ground truth for the other layer, hereinafter referred as the individual configuration. The latter allows for the assessment of each model's autoregressive performance, isolated from the error propagation of the other layer's predictions.

3.5 Optimal Day-Ahead Scheduling

To demonstrate the applicability of the proposed modelling framework, a day-ahead scheduling optimization is implemented using a genetic algorithm (GA), in line with the implementation described in [20]. The optimization operates over a 24-h horizon discretized into 15-min intervals, where the decision variable at each interval is the binary ON/OFF state of the EWH's heating element. The objective function minimizes the electricity cost under the Time-of-Use tariff structure of the case-study household, described in [15], whilst accounting for the comfort of the user and the health of the device. Activating the heater increases the household load by the rated power of the heater, which is priced according to the corresponding tariff period. Equation 2 establishes the objective function to be minimized by the GA, where C_k is the electricity price (€/kWh) at timeslot k, P_{rated} the rated power of the EWH's heating element, u_k the binary state of the heating element at timeslot k, and $\mathbf{T_{top_n}}$ the top-layer temperature at minute n. The cost and cycle terms operate on 15-min intervals, while the discomfort term is evaluated at the model's one-minute resolution. The discomfort and cycle terms are weighted by the coefficients φ and λ, respectively, which control the trade-off between cost minimization, thermal comfort, and heater longevity. Given the inherent subjectivity in balancing these competing objectives, a balanced strategy is obtained through experimentation.

$$\min\ f_{obj} = \underbrace{\frac{1}{4}\sum_{k=0}^{95} C_k P_{rated} u_k}_{\text{cost term}} + \underbrace{\varphi \sum_{n=0}^{1439} \max(50 - T_{Top_n}, 0)}_{\text{comfort term}} + \underbrace{\lambda \sum_{k=1}^{95} \max(u_k - u_{k-1}, 0)}_{\text{cycle term}} \tag{2}$$

Since the EWH is already being controlled with an optimal heating strategy, a baseline scenario is also simulated using the developed model framework, allowing for a comparison between the optimal scheduling and regular thermostat-based operation. The baseline reflects the typical functioning of residential EWHs, where the heating element is activated when the water temperature drops below a lower setpoint (50 °C) and deactivated once an upper setpoint (74 °C) is reached, in a hysteresis-based control cycle.

4 Results and Discussion

This section presents and discusses the results obtained with the proposed framework. Section 4.1 reports the thermal model performance on the testing set, including a comparison between the coupled and individual configurations across multiple prediction horizons. Section 4.2 demonstrates the practical applicability of the model through a day-ahead optimal scheduling case study, comparing the proposed strategy against a thermostat-based baseline. Section 4.3 discusses the limitations of the current study and outlines directions for future work.

4.1 Thermal Model Performance

Results from the evaluation on the testing set are compiled in Table 3. As expected, the individual models outperform their coupled counterparts across all horizons, with the gap widening at longer forecast periods. The bottom-layer model achieves the best individual performance, with a MAE of just 1.10 °C at 24 h, while the top-layer model reaches 2.03 °C at the same horizon. The higher error in the top layer can be attributed to its sharper thermal dynamics, as it is more directly exposed to water draw events, making it inherently more difficult to predict autoregressively.

When both models are coupled, error propagation between them becomes the dominant source of degradation. The top-layer model is most affected, with its 24-h MAE increasing from 2.03 °C to 2.57 °C. The bottom-layer model proves more robust to coupling, with its 24-h MAE increasing from 1.10 °C to 1.45 °C. This asymmetry is expected, as the bottom layer is less directly influenced by top-layer temperature, whereas the top layer model relies on the predicted bottom layer temperature as an exogenous input. Furthermore, the growing gap between RMSE and MAE in the coupled configuration, particularly for the top layer at 48 h (3.54 °C MAE vs. 4.66 °C RMSE), indicates the presence of occasional large deviations, likely caused by the model overreacting to heating or water draw events and the resulting error cascading through the coupling loop. Figure 4 shows the error propagation profile for the testing period, which consists of stepwise MAE computed for every timestep across the 48-h horizon.

Table 3. Model error on the testing set for coupled and uncoupled models.

Model	MAE_{6h}	MAE_{24h}	MAE_{48h}	$RMSE_{6h}$	$RMSE_{24h}$	$RMSE_{48h}$
Top-layer (individual)	1.08	2.03	2.50	1.35	2.86	3.73
Top-layer (coupled)	1.23	2.57	3.54	1.48	3.26	4.66
Bottom-layer (individual)	0.76	1.10	1.29	0.89	1.40	1.77
Bottom-layer (coupled)	0.82	1.45	1.87	0.97	1.79	2.43

Figure 5a) and b) present the autoregressive temperature predictions for the bottom and top layers for some example days of the testing period. Visually, the models track the ground truth closely for most of the prediction horizon. However, the models occasionally overreact to heating and water draw events, leading to deviations that propagate through the autoregressive chain, causing both layers to desynchronize from the ground truth. Figure 5b) illustrates this phenomenon: the individual top-layer model, which uses the ground truth of the bottom-layer model as input, tracks the ground truth reasonably well, while the coupled top-layer model is impacted by the error observed in the coupled bottom-layer models. The same does not happen for the coupled bottom-layer model, since its error is nearly identical to its individual counterpart, meaning that, and consistent with the expected thermodynamic behavior of a stratified tank, the top-layer temperature has a reduced influence on the bottom-layer predictions.

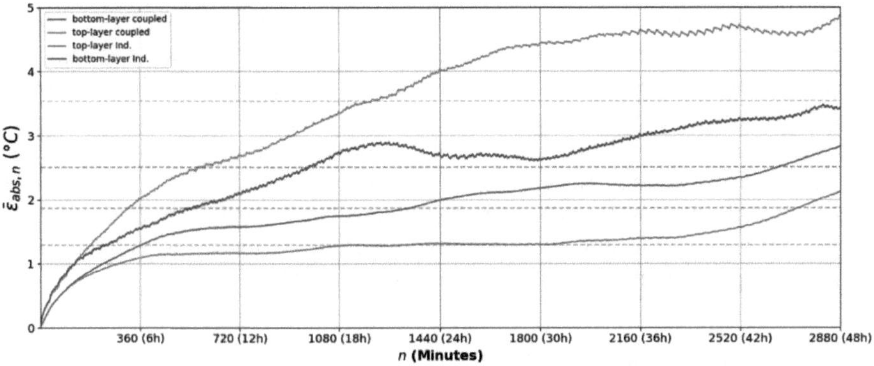

Fig. 4. Error propagation profiles for the testing period

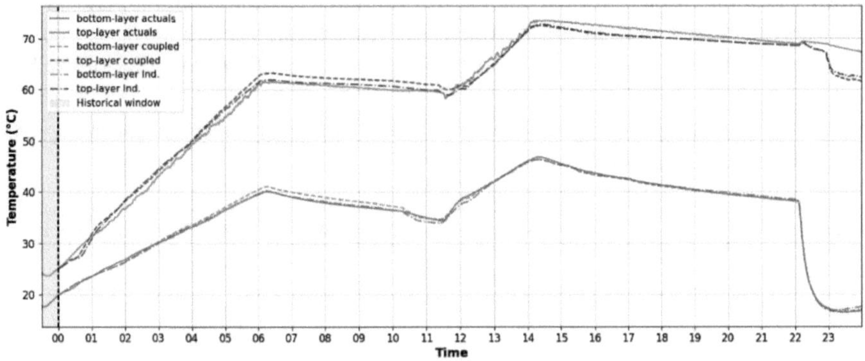

a)

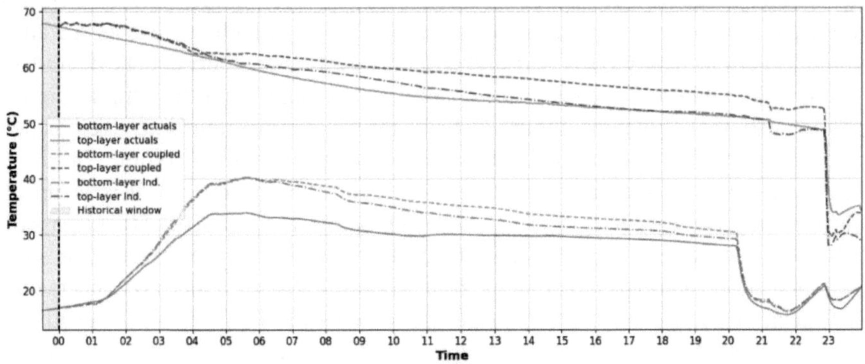

b)

Fig. 5. Autoregressive model temperature predictions over a 24-h horizon: a) 4th of January 2026; b) 5th of January 2026.

Several factors likely contribute to the observed prediction errors. First, the ambient temperature used as input was sourced from an external weather API rather than measured on-site, introducing a potential mismatch with the actual conditions surrounding the device. Second, inconsistencies in the IoT sensor measurements and the linear interpolation applied to fill missing data may introduce noise into the training data. Most importantly, heating and water draw events remain underrepresented relative to idle periods in the dataset. Furthermore, the training data spans June to December 2025, meaning that January conditions are entirely unseen by the model, which may account for part of the performance degradation observed in the testing period.

4.2 Day-Ahead Optimal Scheduling

Results for the day-ahead scheduling are represented in Table 4. The values for φ and λ were selected through experimentation, balancing the trade-off between electricity cost minimization, thermal comfort, and heater cycling. A value of $\varphi = 0.5$ ensured that comfort violations, which were defined as deviations of the top-layer temperature below 50 °C, are penalized, but do not dominate the cost term, while $\lambda = 0.1$ discourages excessive switching without overly constraining the scheduling flexibility of the EWH.

Table 4. Comparison between thermostat-controlled operation and day-ahead scheduling strategy for a single day in January 2026

Strategy	φ	λ	Cost	Minutes below 50 °C	Number of cycles
Baseline	–	–	1.90	180	1
Optimal	0.5	0.1	0.32	0	6

The proposed strategy was capable of reducing the electricity cost from the usage of the EWH in comparison to the baseline by 83% (1.90 € to 0.32 €), whilst promoting a higher level of comfort for the user (0 min with top-layer temperature below 50 °C). However, the number of cycles increased from 1 to 6, which represents a trade-off between lower electricity costs and higher EWH cycling and subsequent degradation. As such, different combinations of the φ and λ coefficients could be explored in order to provide different strategies. Figure 6 shows the layer temperatures, as well as heater profiles, available PV generation surplus, and water consumption volume. In Fig. 6a), which corresponds to the baseline (thermostat-controlled operation), it is visible that the heater only actuates when the top-layer temperature crosses the 50 °C threshold, which coincides with a higher electricity cost period and no PV generation surplus availability. As for the optimal strategy, represented in Fig. 6b), the EWH heats during the off-peak period (lower cost) and during moments of high PV surplus availability, keeping the bottom-layer temperature high and the top-layer temperature close to the comfort threshold. Under a real forecasting scenario with associated uncertainty, this would be a risky strategy, as water consumption or available surplus could be over or underestimated, potentially leading to comfort violations.

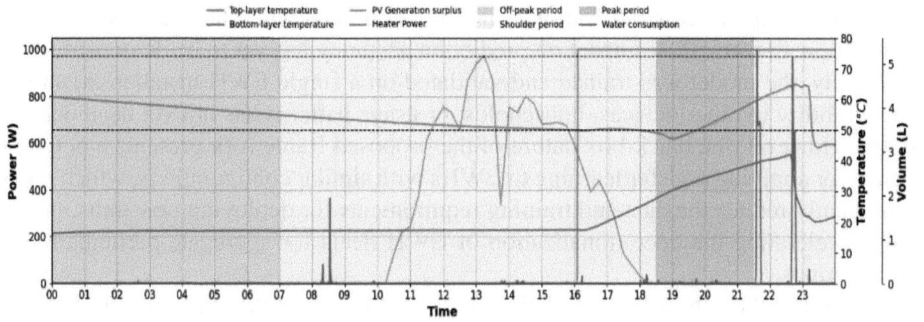

a)

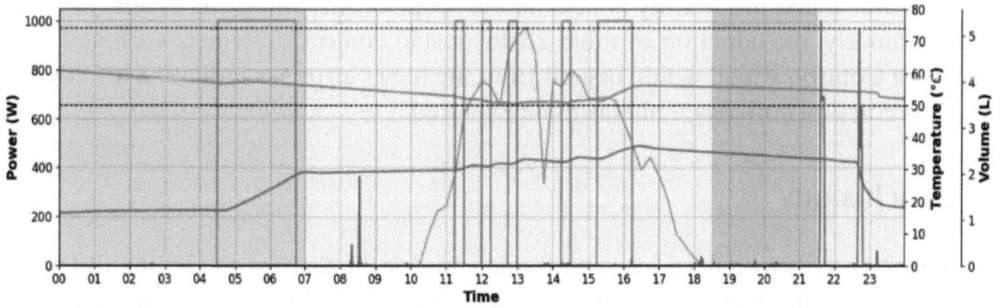

b)

Fig. 6. Temperature, heating power, PV generation surplus, and water consumption profiles for a single day of January 2026 under different control schemes: a) thermostat-controlled operation; b) optimal day-ahead scheduling.

4.3 Limitations and Future Work

The proposed modelling framework presents some limitations that should be acknowledged. The training data only covers a seven-month period from June to December, meaning that conditions outside this range, such as the January testing period, are not fully represented, which likely contributed to the performance degradation observed in the testing period. The testing window itself is also restricted to a single month and additionally contains missing data, which limits the diversity of climatic conditions under which the model and the day-ahead scheduling strategy can be evaluated. A more comprehensive assessment, ideally spanning all four seasons, is identified as a key direction for future work.

Additionally, the ambient temperature used as model input was sourced from an external weather API rather than measured on-site, introducing a potential mismatch with the actual thermal environment of the device. The two-layer discretization, while practical and supported by the available sensor placement, remains a simplification of the continuous temperature stratification within the tank, and while the framework allows for additional layers, their impact on prediction accuracy has yet to be demonstrated.

Finally, the model was trained and validated on a single EWH installation, and its transferability to other devices, households, or usage patterns has not yet been demonstrated. However, the black-box nature of the proposed framework presents a potential avenue for applying transfer learning to EWHs with similar configurations, which could significantly reduce the data and training requirements for deploying new units, potentially accelerating the operationalization of EWH fleets for aggregate participation in DR programs.

Regarding the scheduling validation, it should be noted that the current approach assumes a perfect day-ahead forecast for both PV generation surplus and hot water consumption, which is unrealistic in a real-world deployment, where forecast errors would inevitably affect the scheduling outcomes. The integration of forecasting models and their associated uncertainty is beyond the scope of this study and is left for future work. Similarly, the adoption of more sophisticated control strategies, such as Model Predictive Control, which would benefit from the lower error accumulation afforded by shorter prediction horizons, remains to be explored.

5 Conclusions

This paper introduced a deep learning framework for the thermal modelling of EWHs, adaptable to multi-layer configurations, and validated it through day-ahead optimal scheduling. The resulting two layer thermal model of the EWH showcased a 24-h horizon MAE of 1.45 °C and 2.57 °C, for bottom and top layer respectively, making it viable for DR applications.

The proposed framework relies entirely on operational data collected through an IoT-enabled monitoring system, requiring no prior knowledge of the device's physical parameters. A two-phase training strategy, combining balanced teacher forcing with scheduled sampling on contiguous segments, was proposed to mitigate the training-inference mismatch inherent to autoregressive models. The day-ahead scheduling validation demonstrated cost reductions under a tri-hourly ToU tariff structure (83% cost reduction), while maintaining end-user comfort, confirming the practical applicability of the thermal model for DR scenarios.

Acknowledgements. This research was partly funded by the Portuguese "Fundação para a Ciência e a Tecnologia" (FCT) in the context of the Center of Technology and Systems CTS/UNINOVA/FCT/NOVA, reference UID/00066/2025.

References

1. International Energy Agency.: Demand Response,. https://www.iea.org/energy-system/energy-efficiency-and-demand/demand-response
2. Tabanêz Patrício, J., Januário Silva, F., Amaral Lopes, R., Amaro, N., Martins, J.: A genetic algorithm-based home energy management framework for optimizing user-dependent flexible loads. Energies. **19**, 80 (2026). https://doi.org/10.3390/en19010080

3. Callaway, D.S.: Tapping the energy storage potential in electric loads to deliver load following and regulation, with application to wind energy. Energy Convers. Manag. **50**, 1389–1400 (2009). https://doi.org/10.1016/j.enconman.2008.12.012
4. Eurostat.: Energy consumption in households,. https://ec.europa.eu/eurostat/statistics-explained/index.php?title=Energy_consumption_in_households
5. European Commission.: Water Heaters,. https://energy-efficient-products.ec.europa.eu/product-list/water-heaters_en
6. Shah, J.J., Nielsen, M.C., Shaffer, T.S., Fittro, R.L.: Cost-optimal consumption-aware electric water heating via thermal storage under time-of-use pricing. IEEE Trans. Smart Grid. **7**, 592–599 (2016). https://doi.org/10.1109/TSG.2015.2483502
7. Brouyaux, L., Iacovella, S., Quoilin, S.: A real-life demonstration of secondary frequency reserve provision with electric water heaters. Energies. **18**, 1704 (2025). https://doi.org/10.3390/en18071704
8. Clarke, T., Slay, T., Eustis, C., Bass, R.B.: Aggregation of residential water heaters for peak shifting and frequency response services. IEEE Open Access J. Power Energy. **7**, 22–30 (2020). https://doi.org/10.1109/OAJPE.2019.2952804
9. Pandiyan, S.V., Gros, S., Rajasekharan, J.: Physics informed neural network based multi-zone electric water heater modeling for demand response. Appl. Energy. **380**, 125037 (2025). https://doi.org/10.1016/j.apenergy.2024.125037
10. Xu, Z., Diao, R., Lu, S., Lian, J., Zhang, Y.: Modeling of electric water heaters for demand response: a baseline PDE model. IEEE Trans. Smart Grid. **5**, 2203–2210 (2014). https://doi.org/10.1109/tsg.2014.2317149
11. Jodeiri, A.M., Soppelsa, A., Turrin, F., Pipiciello, M., Cozzini, M., Fedrizzi, R.: Numerical and experimental investigation of stratified water storage tanks: an enhanced adaptive-grid model. Appl. Therm. Eng. **248**, 123113 (2024). https://doi.org/10.1016/j.applthermaleng.2024.123113
12. Alden, R.E., Gong, H., Rooney, T., Branecky, B., Ionel, D.M.: Electric water heater modeling for large-scale distribution power systems studies with energy storage CTA-2045 based VPP and CVR. Energies. **16**, 4747 (2023). https://doi.org/10.3390/en16124747
13. Diao, R., Lu, S., Elizondo, M., Mayhorn, E., Zhang, Y., Samaan, N.: Electric water heater modeling and control strategies for demand response. In: 2012 IEEE Power and Energy Society General Meeting, pp. 1–8 (2012). https://doi.org/10.1109/PESGM.2012.6345632
14. Mukherjee, M., Bhattarai, B., Hanif, S., Pratt, R.: Electric water heaters for transactive systems: model evaluations and performance quantification. IEEE Trans. Ind. Inform. **18**, 5783–5794 (2022). https://doi.org/10.1109/TII.2021.3128212
15. Lopes, R.A., Silva, F., Menezes-Barros, R., Amaro, N., Carvalho, A.G.D., Martins, J.: Exploring energy flexibility from smart electrical water heaters to improve electrification benefits in residential buildings: findings from real-world operation. Energy. **316**, 134381 (2025). https://doi.org/10.1016/j.energy.2025.134381
16. Silva, F., Lopes, R.A., Martins, J.: Deployment of demand response measures in geographical islands – a survey. In: 2025 IEEE 19th International Conference on Compatibility, Power Electronics and Power Engineering (CPE-POWERENG), pp. 1–6. IEEE, Antalya, Turkiye (2025). https://doi.org/10.1109/CPE-POWERENG63314.2025.11027248
17. CORDIS - EU research results.:. IntegrAted SolutioNs for the DecarbOnization and Smartification of Islands (IANOS). https://doi.org/10.3030/957810
18. Zippenfenig, P.: Open-Meteo.com Weather API. https://zenodo.org/doi/10.5281/zenodo.7970649, (2024). https://doi.org/10.5281/ZENODO.7970649
19. Bengio, S., Vinyals, O., Jaitly, N., Shazeer, N.: Scheduled sampling for sequence prediction with recurrent neural networks, http://arxiv.org/abs/1506.03099. (2015). https://doi.org/10.48550/arXiv.1506.03099

20. Patrício, J.T., Silva, F., Lopes, R.A., Amaro, N., Martins, J.: Combining time-series forecasting and genetic algorithm based optimization to explore energy flexibility at building-level. In: 2024 IEEE International Conference on Engineering, Technology, and Innovation (ICE/ITMC), pp. 1–6. IEEE, Funchal, Portugal (2024). https://doi.org/10.1109/ICE/ITMC61926.2024.10794398

Towards Scalable Demand Response Solutions for Households in Citizen Energy Communities

Pau Comas(✉), Antoni Morell, Ramon Vilanova, and Jose Lopez Vicario

IDEAS Research Group, Universitat Autònoma de Barcelona (UAB), Bellaterra 08193, Spain
{pau.comas,antoni.morell,ramon.vilanova,jose.vicario}@uab.cat

Abstract. This work addresses the gap in scalability and generalizability of current energy management solutions for Citizen Energy Communities (CECs). While CECs offer opportunities for distributed renewable energy sharing, the tools currently provided to users are often case-specific solutions that fail to scale across the wide diversity of user needs and building typologies. Therefore, we focus on designing a modular Demand Response Management (DRM) framework based on Economic Model Predictive Control (EMPC) and grey-box thermal modelling. We adopt this approach to create a flexible solution that balances physical interpretability with data-driven adaptability, minimizing input requirements. The goal is to develop a system capable of optimizing the trade-off between economic costs and user comfort across heterogeneous households without requiring extensive, site-specific engineering.

Keywords: Citizen Energy Communities · Demand Response · Economic MPC · Data-driven Control

1 Introduction

A Citizen Energy Community (CEC) is an entity formed by citizens, local authorities or small businesses that share Distributed Energy Resources (DER) to produce, manage and consume clean and sustainable energy among themselves. Practically, CECs represent a shift away from the passive consumer model towards something more active, where involved users can choose to produce, consume or both at the same time (prosumers). In doing so, they build together a localised grid where neighbouring surpluses from solar panels or communal batteries can be shared, effectively turning the community into a cooperative power plant [17].

For this idea to work effectively, there is a need for open tools to be provided, so that users can have an easy transition from old paradigms to the CEC. One of the main goals of the community is to take advantage of the generated energy as much as possible, lowering overall costs for the consumers and diminishing the need for energy from the traditional grid. Therefore, Demand Response Management (DRM) [25] is a vital necessity for the CEC, which entails flexibilizing the energy demand from the users (individually and collectively) to fit some specific needs, which as mentioned,

Published by Springer Nature Switzerland AG 2027
L. M. Camarinha-Matos and F. Ferrada (Eds.): DoCEIS 2026, IFIP AICT 790, pp. 173–185, 2027.
https://doi.org/10.1007/978-3-032-28939-1_13

usually regard monetary costs associated with grid prices, user comfort and lifestyle constraints. By adjusting power consumption to match the fluctuating availability of renewable generation—shifting, DRM allows CECs to maximise their self-sufficiency and the cleanliness of energy used.

The academic landscape around DRM is rich with solutions, particularly involving Model Predictive Control (MPC), which offers the required customisability for applying constraints, physical models and optimisation goals, while remaining bounded in terms of computational burden, which is key to allow implementations to be viable [9]. Numerous studies have focused on individual households and multi-building environments, with special attention to Heating, Ventilation, and Air Conditioning (HVAC) systems [38], which in most countries is the most demanding controllable load, or battery management, which altogether with solar generation, has become a strong public interest. Yet, there is a significant gap regarding the specific directions needed for CEC's solutions, regarding scalability, modularity and generalisability. DRM with MPC models have relied on requiring accurate physical models of buildings, data-intensive methods directed to simulated environments, or fixed multi-appliance solutions that can not be easily shifted to fit demands around the globe. This will be discussed further in Sect. 3, but indeed there is a barrier between the current research focus and widespread adoptability of CECs.

To address this gap, this PhD thesis focuses on producing a DRM framework designed for individual households of CECs, which fits the demands of the wide diversity of potential users and is openly accessible. We focus on Economic Model Predictive Control (EMPC) driven by grey-box thermal modelling [26], which, as deepened later, is a combination that provides a strong performance-complexity balance. Our approach will rely on attainable data-driven parameter estimation to adapt to different building typologies without requiring over-specific demands that form a barrier for newly interested peers. Additionally, another goal is to create a software solution that is robust enough to handle the "warm country" energy profiles of places such as Spain, where appliance loads and profiles often matter more than heating [11], which received the broad focus of the academic community.

This work is aligned within the goals of the OPEN4CEC project ("Service-oriented Open Platform for Citizen Energy Communities") [34]. OPEN4CEC aims to build an open, collaborative platform based on microservices that supports this transition. The project's goal is to provide the digital infrastructure that allows CECs to scale, integrating Internet of Things (IoT) devices with advanced decision-making models. The remainder of this paper is structured as follows: Sect. 2 reviews the relation of the PhD to the conference theme. Then, Sect. 3 explores the Relevant Literature. Subsequently, Research Contribution and Innovation is detailed in Sect. 4. Right after, Sect. 5 presents the Methodology; Sect. 6 shows the first Results of our first framework; and finally, Sect. 7 offers our Conclusions and Future Work discussion.

2 Relation of PhD to Tackling Societal Challenges

This doctoral work aligns directly with the objectives of DoCEIS 2026, focused on "Technological Innovation to Tackle Societal Challenges" by aiming to reinforce the feasibility of CECs as a green alternative for responsible energy generation and distribution. There are many possible motivations behind entering a CEC from the point of view of the user, which are conditioned by the multiple shapes and contexts the communities have. Nonetheless, most motivating arguments for new peers are economic and ethical. In addition, collectivism and teamwork are values that current CEC prosumers admit to having reinforced and motivated them more to work on those projects [6], as legal limitations pose a struggle in many countries. The current landscape does not make it easy for newcomers, and actual regulations and permit formalities are an obstacle faced by the communities [16], which need a strong foundational basis of people and willpower to bring CEC projects to reality.

While the societal objective of decarbonization is clear, the technological reality is that current solutions for CECs are only beginning to receive attention from the research community. In that sense, this research seeks to bridge the gap, demonstrating the need for engineering innovations in energy management to be centred on the widespread adoption of sustainable energy models by newcomers.

More specifically, this work contributes to the Special Session on "Smart and Fair Community Energy System", and specifically, is linked to the specific topic: "Optimisation and control of energy communities". Our proposed approach balances the "Smart" aspect using EMPC to fit together cost and comfort loss objectives, and with the "Fair" aspect, ensuring that the technology is robust enough to handle heterogeneous building typologies across different regions (such as the appliance-heavy load profiles of Southern Europe) without prohibitive site specific requirements. In addition, all generated code will be made open-access, for the goal of translating these theoretical control strategies into an architecture that allows citizens to actively participate in and benefit from the future CECs.

3 Relevant Literature

The transition to decentralized energy communities has demanded the need for modern control strategies for energy management in households. This section reviews the existing literature on DRM architectures on the household level, focusing on the advances with the EMPC technique applied to managing the demand signal of unique or multiple DERs. Alternative approaches leverage heuristic control or rule-based systems to manage devices, with a focus on HVAC systems, and more specifically, heat pumps [7]. Nevertheless, simpler strategies do not attempt to dynamically understand the interplay between user behaviour, thermal dynamics, variable injection tariffs and weather forecasts, but focus on proposing robust solutions within static guidelines.

Extensive literature has established MPC as a standard control strategy for both univariable and multivariable systems. Surveys indicate that MPC significantly outperforms rule-based controllers in building energy management [9, 38], even when incorporating machine learning to approximate complex building dynamics [10], considering the recurrent trade-off between chosen model complexity and performance. Nonetheless, while the variety of options is high, there are established design choices that outline how to achieve good cost-benefit results.

The identification of thermal models is usually a critical component of these frameworks. White-box models offer high interpretability but require extensive physical data, and black-box models (such as ANNs or LSTMs) require large historical datasets that are often unavailable to new users [1, 3]. Grey-box models, which combine simplified physical structures (e.g., RC networks) with data driven parameter estimation, offer a "sweet spot" [9]. However, initialising model parameters remains challenging without high-resolution data, and that initialisation is very important [20, 23] for the accuracy of the models obtained after the optimisation process.

The literature has provided many datasets, without a unified schema: each usually presents unique characteristics tailored to specific research needs. For instance, the REFIT dataset [32] provides a widely used baseline for residential appliance monitoring in the UK. In the industrial sector, the LILAC dataset from Germany was introduced [21], offering high-frequency measurements (50 kHz) of industrial appliances to address the scarcity of non-residential data. The PLEGMA dataset [4] captures the specific consumption behaviours of Mediterranean households in Greece, including data on high-load devices such as electric water boilers and air conditioners. Furthermore, Gonçalves et al. [18] also published a comprehensive dataset designed for energy communities, which aggregates profiles for 50 households and a public building with detailed appliance allocation to support demand response studies. Among these, only [4] provides the on-site measurements of internal and external temperature measurements required for the accurate identification of grey-box thermal model parameters.

In the domain of EMPCs, the goal is usually to minimise monetary costs through the control actuation while respecting comfort constraints, which are typically based on internal temperatures. Early work [22, 33] highlighted the importance of occupancy prediction in these optimisations. Recent approaches have attempted to integrate specific user preferences and multi-zone control directly into the cost function [13, 15]. But usually, studies simplify the problem by assuming fixed occupancy schedules rather than active prediction [24]. Optimising for both cost and comfort across heterogeneous assets (e.g. batteries, PV, and HVAC) remains computationally challenging. The literature has been investigating various solutions for various problems: robust MPC to handle weather uncertainty [20], hierarchical-stochastic frameworks for grid interactivity [23], and distributed approaches for multi-residential buildings [27]. A bit more niche applications have also been explored, such as a use-case in high-tech greenhouses [30] or using imitation learning to mimic optimal control behaviours in heat pumps [8].

Despite these advances, a gap remains in generalisability. Standard MPC solutions often face deployment barriers due to high computational demands on legacy hardware, as addressed in [10], or are confined to promising results shown in specific environments [24, 37]. In another example, the integration of battery storage with machine learning forecasting in virtual power plants shows potential [31], but also requires open, interoperable platforms to scale effectively. Furthermore, the "digital barrier" implications are usually never considered, with Oprea et al. [35] revealing that benefits are not equally accessible, with older or less tech-savvy citizens showing lower flexibility. While the legal framework for CECs is being established across Europe to progressively empower prosumers [2, 5, 39], the technical implementation often relies on still too complex multi-agent systems [12]. These systems theoretically enable optimal peer-to-peer sharing but also struggle with onboarding new buildings without over-engineering. There is a lack of a modular framework that balances the sophistication of recent MPC advances with the robust, low-data requirements needed for real-world community deployment.

4 Research Contribution and Innovation

We summarize here the main ideas and focus of this PhD, noting which are the expected key contributions and the innovative aspects. This work focuses on the scalable direction needed for addressing the technical barriers of DRM solutions in CECs, in order to provide tools apt for an ecosystem design for any deployment. This is based on three important pillars:

4.1 Modular Demand Response Tool Generator

The rigidity that we have explained in current MPC implementations for household DRM demands a solution for CEC adoption. Constraints, objectives, and building types are much more variable than the picture that current academic research portrays. We aim to provide a modular software framework that functions as a generator for our Economic Predictive Control Systems (EPCS) for households in CECs. This will allow the customisation of controllers, defining high-level appliance constraints and economic targets, while remaining feasible computationally and easy for the users. The modularity is critical for scalability to serve a diversity of prosumers in CECs.

4.2 Physics-Informed Grey-Box Model Customizer

The accuracy of thermal models in DRM is key for the performance of EMPC solutions, but that faces a trade-off with complexity. Building physiologies are wide and require a balanced solution that allows for specialisation and simplicity. We address this through an innovative automated identification pipeline that combines physics-based initialisation with data-driven grey-box modelling. We will ensure the need for limited data (e.g., three weeks of standard thermostat and meter data) to allow for a wide availability among households with the integration of easy-to-get building descriptors. The integration of data will fit into the system to generate consistent RC models through careful parameterisation of the initial parameters.

4.3 Open Benchmarking for Mediterranean Climates

Numerous datasets have been appearing recently, focusing on HVAC-driven solutions for continental climate countries in Europe. However, we have outlined that there is a lack of focus on DRM for countries with warmer climates, which presents new challenges regarding energy distribution and use. By publishing the dataset resulting from simulations in our lab (IDEAS LAB) alongside our results, focusing on allowing RC model identification, we will provide a new resource for the research community, aiming to enrich the validation options for models focused on countries such as Spain and robustness for the specific challenges of this region.

5 Methodology

5.1 Research Scenario

Figure 1 illustrates an example of a residential community context where multiple users operate within a decentralised energy network. Each user, with maybe a different amount of their own renewable generation assets and appliance profiles, interacts with the DER and the main grid. In this ecosystem, our proposed framework serves as the local intelligence layer, enabling individual households to adapt their demand response. While DER allocation (e.g., fixed or dynamic coefficients) is a critical component of such communities for collective self-consumption [28], optimising that allocation is outside the scope of this work, which focuses on the optimal demand response given the available assets for prosumers.

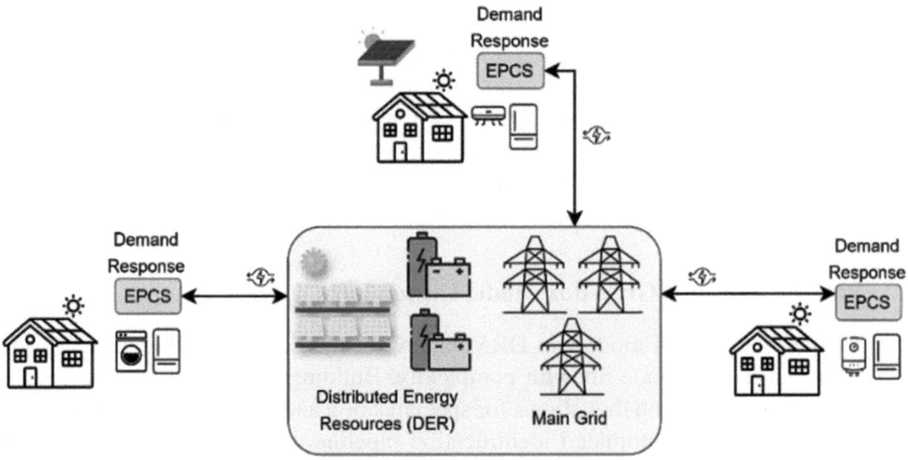

Fig. 1. Illustration of a residential CEC context with different houses and the integration of the proposed control system

Figure 2 presents the architectural schema of our proposed framework, which we call the Economic Predictive Control System (EPCS). The system will integrate information from external inputs (weather forecasts, electricity prices, and generation/consumption forecasts) with an Energy Model Predictive Control (EMPC) framework to provide 24-h consumption recommendations to users and demand response actions to the building system.

The framework will allow for flexibility in appliance-specific constraints and economic objective functions, without extensive programming knowledge. The optimiser will consider economic costs, thermal comfort requirements, and lifestyle preferences to generate optimal control actions. We can also see, as we will develop in Sect. 5.4, references to the two datasets (PLEGMA [4] and UAB LAB) that we will first use to validate our model.

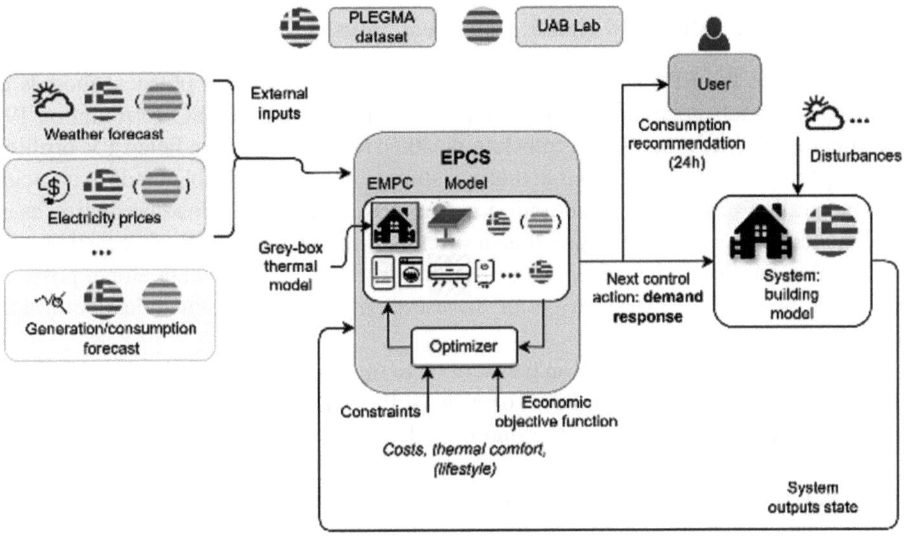

Fig. 2. Architecture of the Economic Predictive Control System (EPCS) showing external inputs, EMPC model, and system outputs for demand response control.

5.2 Grey-Box Thermal Modeling

For the building thermal dynamics, we adopt a simplified grey-box resistance-capacitance (RC) model approach, specifically evaluating 3R2C [14] and 4R2C [19] structures. Our methodology prioritises 2C models because they represent the explained "sweet-spot" between prediction accuracy and parameter identifiability. The 2C structure usually comprises two thermal capacitances: one representing the building envelope thermal mass and another for the indoor air mass. Adding further capacitance states typically refers to specific internal wall layers or partitions, which introduces complexity and risks overfitting when training data is scarce. This selected level of complexity maintains temperature prediction errors within a robust 0.2–0.5 °C range while remaining computationally lightweight. The framework can be deployed locally on affordable, low-power edge devices—such as a Raspberry Pi or standard smart home IoT gateways—which literature demonstrates are fully capable of solving these predictive control formulations in real-time without relying on cloud computing.

Parameter identification is achievable with a training period of just three weeks, followed by one week for testing [14]. The required input features are limited to 15-min intervals of indoor/outdoor temperatures, HVAC power consumption, and solar radiation, which represent data available via thermostat and meter measurements. Looking ahead, this simplicity facilitates the development of a grey-box model generator capable of adapting to diverse country-specific building standards using only basic descriptors with physics-based parameter initialisation for convergence, as recent research highlights the critical importance of appropriate starting bounds for identification accuracy [36].

5.3 ML Consumption and Generation Predictions

The efficacy of the EPCS will be evaluated by integrating ML or physical models as forecasters, which generate the disturbance vector d_t for the MPC formulation [9]. For generation, ML models will translate weather forecasts into predicted PV profiles, enabling the optimiser to pre-charge thermal storage or shift deferrable loads to coincide with generation peaks. For consumption, we propose utilising ML load prediction as an implicit occupancy indicator rather than a strict load-tracking target. By forecasting non-controllable baseload, the system can infer that from smart meter data alone, possibly removing the need for extra sensors or the use of rigid presence schedules that hinder scalability.

The optimiser will utilise these predictions to minimise a multi-objective cost function J over the prediction horizon N. To ensure solver feasibility under all conditions, we will employ soft constraints for thermal bounds, utilising slack variables ϵ_k penalised by weight λ, to prevent the optimiser from crashing during extreme weather events.

Equation 1 shows at a high level the proposed cost structure, which allows for customisable balancing of pure economic objectives with thermal comfort and user preferences:

$$\min_u J = \sum_{k=0}^{N-1} \left(\underbrace{C_{elec,k} \cdot P_{grid,k}}_{\text{Economic Cost}} + \underbrace{\lambda \cdot \epsilon_k}_{\text{Comfort Violation}} + \underbrace{\gamma \cdot \Psi(u_k, u_{pref})}_{\text{Lifestyle Penalty}} \right) \tag{1}$$

Where $C_{elec,k}$ is the dynamic electricity price and $P_{grid,k}$ is the power drawn from the grid. The term $\lambda \cdot \epsilon_k$ penalises deviations from the user's preferred temperature range. The function Ψ represents the high-level penalty for shifting flexible loads u_k away from the user's preferred schedule u_{pref}. Calibrating the weighting factor γ and defining the exact shape of Ψ to ensure that the system respects user bounds and intervenes only when savings are significant, while subject to the appliance constraints defined, remains a primary focus of our ongoing research. The exact values depend on the functions chosen on loss design, but usually the comfort penalty λ is typically found to be several orders of magnitude higher than the lifestyle penalty.

5.4 Dataset Selection and Validation

PLEGMA Dataset: The PLEGMA dataset [4] was selected as the primary data source, as it provides high-frequency (10-s resolution) electricity consumption measurements from 13 Greek households, including both aggregate and appliance-level data. Importantly, PLEGMA includes measurements of internal and external temperatures, humidity, which facilitates the identification of grey-box thermal models, only needing as external the solar radiation values. It captures consumption patterns characteristic of warmer climates, with households showcasing the use of air conditioning and electric water boilers, making it representative of buildings in Southern Europe. Additionally, PLEGMA includes sociodemographic and building characteristic data. The diversity of appliance configurations across the 13 monitored homes provides multiple case studies for testing the robustness of the EPCS framework under varying operational conditions.

UAB Lab: To complement the PLEGMA-based development, a parallel validation effort is underway using data collected from the IDEAS UAB Lab facilities. This laboratory is instrumented with sensors to monitor thermal dynamics and HVAC actuations at high temporal resolution. Occupancy will also be sensed to improve the value of the dataset and validate our strategies. The collected dataset will be shared with the research community, contributing to the growing repository of open building energy data [34]. A customized EPCS framework will be deployed to control an appliance use-case to provide confidence in the framework's applicability to diverse building contexts.

6 Results

Preliminary results focus on the application of the first EPCS framework to "House 2" from the PLEGMA dataset [4], a typical residential building in Greece with high cooling loads. This initial phase validates the first components of the system: the identifiability of the thermal model and the functionality of the economic optimiser under a simplified control scenario to minimise costs.

A 3R2C grey-box model was identified using three weeks of historical data from the dataset. Figure 3 illustrates the validation performance over a two-week test period. The model demonstrates high fidelity in capturing the building's thermal dynamics, achieving a Mean Absolute Error (MAE) of 0.43 °C and maintaining deviation consistently below 0.5 °C. This accuracy confirms that the proposed low-order model is sufficient for reliable predictive control in this building typology (Athens residence).

To test the economic optimisation layer, a 24-h control scenario was simulated based on sampled days of the dataset. The preliminary EPCS controlled three controllable assets: the air conditioner (AC), a washing machine (WM), and the electric water boiler. The objective was to minimise electricity costs under a dynamic Time-of-Use tariff while respecting a winter thermal comfort bound of [18 °C,24 °C]. Table 1 summarizes the performance of the EPCS compared to the baseline of the dataset. This experiment showed that the predictive controller successfully shifted the boiler heating and washing cycles to off-peak windows, resulting in a 14.2% reduction in daily economic cost. Crucially, this was achieved with zero thermal comfort violations.

Table 1. Performance comparison of EPCS vs. Default Behaviour for a representative high-demand day in November.

Metric	Default Behavior	EPCS (Ours)	Improvement
Daily Energy Cost (€)	3.15	2.70	**−14.2%**
Total Energy Cons. (kWh)	16.8	16.5	−1.8%
Boiler Start Time	19:00 (Peak)	15:30 (Off-Peak)	–

(continued)

Table 1. *(continued)*

Metric	Default Behavior	EPCS (Ours)	Improvement
WM Start Time	18:00 (Peak)	14:15 (Off-Peak)	–
Comfort Violation (h · °C)	0.0	0.0	–

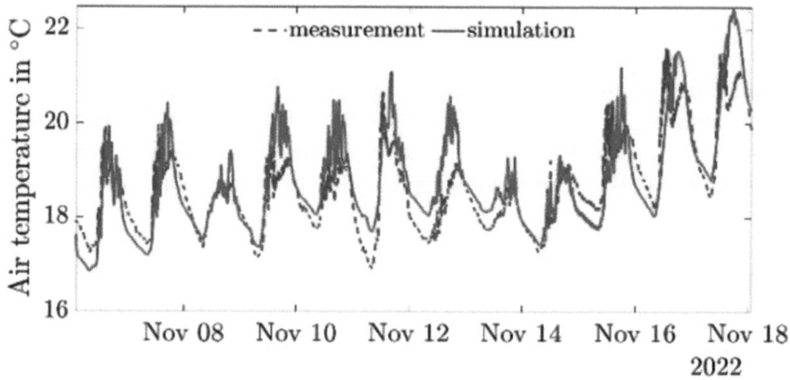

Fig. 3. Validation of the identified 3R2C thermal model for PLEGMA House 2. Internal room temperature given by real measurements and thermal model simulation.

7 Conclusion and Future Work

The transition towards prosumer-centric energy systems, with decentralised DER, is real and attracting new interested users every day. The need for ready-to-use solutions that bring scalability and facilitate this change has to be the focus of the research in the following years. While the theoretical benefits of EMPCs for DRM in CECs have been widely demonstrated, engineering complexity and data scarcity are critical challenges that academia must address in real-world applications. As explained in this paper, this ongoing PhD addresses this challenge with the aim of bringing actual tools and methodologies to achieve applicable solutions. Results show that simple thermal models can accurately reproduce the thermal dynamics of the selected case study, while EPCS implementation reduced daily energy cost by 14.2% with no thermal comfort violations. These results support the feasibility of the proposed approach as a basis for modular and adaptable household DRM solutions.

In the future, we expect steady progress on our goals, achieving completion of our three main contributions that form the core of our work outlined in Sect. 4. On the other hand, depending on time constraints, we envision this system to integrate with multi-agent solutions, enabling community-based optimisation where individual controllers coordinate to provide aggregated flexibility services for allocating the energy generated [29].

Acknowledgments. This work has received support from the Catalan Government under Project 2021 SGR 00197 and also by the Spanish Government under MICINN projects PID2024-156522OB-C33 co-funded with the European Union ERDF funds and MCIN/AEI/10.13039/501100011033 project TED2021-129134BI00 co-funded with the European Union"NextGenerationEU"/PRTR funds, and projects OPEN4CEC PCI2023-145975-2 and SMART-LEM PCI2023-145977-2 funded by MCIU/AEI/10.13039/501100011033 and co-funded by European Union.

References

1. Ahmed, M.S., Mohamed, A., Shareef, H., Homod, R.Z., Ali, J.A.: Artificial neural network based controller for home energy management considering demand response events. In: In: 2016 International Conference on Advances in Electrical, Electronic and Systems Engineering (ICAEES), pp. 506–509. IEEE (2016). https://doi.org/10.1109/ICAEES.2016.7888097
2. Ahmed, S., Ali, A., D'Angola, A.: A review of renewable energy communities: concepts, scope, progress, challenges, and recommendations. Sustainability. **16**(5), 1749 (2024). https://doi.org/10.3390/su16051749
3. Anvari-Moghaddam, A., Monsef, H., Rahimi-Kian, A.: Optimal smart home energy management considering energy saving and a comfortable lifestyle. IEEE Trans. Smart Grid. **6**(1), 324–332 (2015). https://doi.org/10.1109/TSG.2014.2349352
4. Athanasoulias, S., et al.: The Plegma dataset: domestic appliance-level and aggregate electricity demand with metadata from Greece. Sci. Data. **11**(1), 370 (2024). https://doi.org/10.1038/s41597-024-03208-0
5. Cocciolo, E.: The role of energy communities for thermal networks: an EU legal perspective. Rev. Eur. Comp. Int. Environ. Law. **33**(3), 494–506 (2024). https://doi.org/10.1111/reel.12558
6. De Simone, E., Rochira, A., Mannarini, T.: Individual and community catalysts for renewable energy communities (RECs) development. Curr. Opin. Psychol. **62**, 101987 (2025). https://doi.org/10.1016/j.copsyc.2024.101987
7. Dengiz, T., Jochem, P., Fichtner, W.: Demand response with heuristic control strategies for modulating heat pumps. Appl. Energy. **238**, 1346–1360 (2019). https://doi.org/10.1016/j.apenergy.2018.12.008
8. Dengiz, T., Kleinebrahm, M.: Imitation learning with artificial neural networks for demand response with a heuristic control approach for heat pumps. Energy AI. **18**, 100441 (2024). https://doi.org/10.1016/j.egyai.2024.100441
9. Drgoňa, J., et al.: All you need to know about model predictive control for buildings. Annu. Rev. Control. **50**, 190–232 (2020). https://doi.org/10.1016/j.arcontrol.2020.09.001
10. Drgoňa, J., Picard, D., Kvasnica, M., Helsen, L.: Approximate model predictive building control via machine learning. Appl. Energy. **218**, 199–216 (2018). https://doi.org/10.1016/j.apenergy.2018.02.156
11. Escobar, P., Martínez, E., Saenz-Díez, J., Jiménez, E., Blanco, J.: Modeling and analysis of the electricity consumption profile of the residential sector in Spain. Energ. Buildings. **207**, 109629 (2020). https://doi.org/10.1016/j.enbuild.2019.109629
12. Feng, C., Liu, A.L.: Peer-to-peer energy trading of solar and energy storage: a networked multiagent reinforcement learning approach. Appl. Energy. **383**, 125283 (2025). https://doi.org/10.1016/j.apenergy.2025.125283
13. Frahm, M., et al.: Occupant-oriented demand response with multi-zone thermal building control. Appl. Energy. **347**, 121454 (2023). https://doi.org/10.1016/j.apenergy.2023.121454

14. Frahm, M., Langner, F., Zwickel, P., Matthes, J., Mikut, R., Hagenmeyer, V.: How to derive and implement a minimalistic RC model from thermodynamics for the control of thermal parameters for assuring thermal comfort in buildings. In: 2022 Open Source Modelling and Simulation of Energy Systems (OSMSES), pp. 1–6. IEEE (2022). https://doi.org/10.1109/OSMSES54027.2022.9769134
15. Frahm, M., et al.: Occupant-oriented economic model predictive control for demand response in buildings. In: Proceedings of the Thirteenth ACM International Conference on Future Energy Systems, pp. 354–360. ACM (2022). https://doi.org/10.1145/3538637.3538864
16. Florence School of Regulation: Mapping and comparing the legal framework for scaling up energy communities. Res. Rep (2026). https://fsr.eui.eu/publications. Accessed 20 Apr 2026
17. Ghasemnejad, H., Rashidinejad, M., Abdollahi, A., Dorahaki, S.: Energy management in citizen energy communities: a flexibility-constrained robust optimization approach considering prosumers comfort. Appl. Energy. **356**, 122456 (2024). https://doi.org/10.1016/j.apenergy.2023.122456
18. Goncalves, C., Barreto, R., Faria, P., Gomes, L., Vale, Z.: Dataset of an energy community's generation and consumption with appliance allocation. Data Brief. **45**, 108590 (2022). https://doi.org/10.1016/j.dib.2022.108590
19. Harb, H., Boyanov, N., Hernandez, L., Streblow, R., Müller, D.: Development and validation of grey-box models for forecasting the thermal response of occupied buildings. Energ. Buildings. **117**, 199–207 (2016). https://doi.org/10.1016/j.enbuild.2016.02.021
20. Hu, Y., Gao, L., Sun, M., Mae, T., Imaizumi, T.: Improved robust model predictive control for residential building air conditioning and photovoltaic power generation with battery energy storage system under weather forecast uncertainty. Appl. Energy. **371**, 123652 (2024). https://doi.org/10.1016/j.apenergy.2024.123652
21. Kahl, M., et al.: Measurement system and dataset for in-depth analysis of appliance energy consumption in industrial environment. tm -Technisches Messen. **86**(1), 1–13 (2019). https://doi.org/10.1515/teme-2018-0038
22. Korkas, C.D., Baldi, S., Michailidis, I., Kosmatopoulos, E.B.: Occupancy-based demand response and thermal comfort optimization in microgrids with renewable energy sources and energy storage. Appl. Energy. **163**, 93–104 (2016). https://doi.org/10.1016/j.apenergy.2015.10.140
23. Langner, F., Frahm, M., Wang, W., Matthes, J., Hagenmeyer, V.: Hierarchical-stochastic model predictive control for a grid-interactive multi-zone residential building with distributed energy resources. J. Build. Eng. **89**, 109401 (2024). https://doi.org/10.1016/j.jobe.2024.109401
24. Langner, F., Wang, W., Frahm, M., Hagenmeyer, V.: Model predictive control of distributed energy resources in residential buildings considering forecast uncertainties. Energ. Buildings. **303**, 113753 (2024). https://doi.org/10.1016/j.enbuild.2023.113753
25. Li, W.T., et al.: Demand response management for residential smart grid: from theory to practice. IEEE Access. **3**, 2431–2440 (2015). https://doi.org/10.1109/ACCESS.2015.2503379
26. Li, Y., et al.: Grey-box modeling and application for building energy simulations - a critical review. Renew. Sust. Energ. Rev. **158**, 112034 (2022). https://doi.org/10.1016/j.rser.2021.111174
27. Macià Cid, J., Mylonas, A., Péan, T.Q., Pascual, J., Salom, J.: Energy optimization algorithms for multi-residential buildings: a model predictive control application. Energ. Buildings. **319**, 114562 (2024). https://doi.org/10.1016/j.enbuild.2024.114562
28. Madrigal, S., Vicario, J.L., Morell, A., Vilanova, R.: Enhancement review of the collective self-consumption based energy communities: insights from a Spain-based case. In: 2025 IEEE 30th International Conference on Emerging Technologies and Factory Automation (ETFA), pp. 1–8. IEEE (2025). https://doi.org/10.1109/ETFA65518.2025.11205679

29. Madrigal, S., Gallinad, R., Vicario, J.L., Morell, A., Vilanova, R.: Improving energy distribution in collective self-consumption via XGBoost-based allocation coefficients prediction. Appl. Energy. **409**, 127469 (2026). https://doi.org/10.1016/j.apenergy.2026.127469
30. Mahmood, F., Sharma, R., Nisar, K., Ibrahim, M.: Efficient energy management and temperature control of a high-tech greenhouse using an improved data-driven model predictive control. Energy Convers. Manage. X. **26**, 100939 (2025). https://doi.org/10.1016/j.ecmx.2025.100939
31. Mao, Y.: Model Predictive Control for Building Energy Systems: a Comparative Study of Battery Integration and Machine Learning Forecasting in Virtual Power Plants. Master's thesis, KTH Royal Institute of Technology, Stockholm (2025). https://kth.diva-portal.org/smash/record.jsf?pid=diva2%3A1986603
32. Murray, D., Stankovic, L., Stankovic, V.: An electrical load measurements dataset of United Kingdom households from a two-year longitudinal study. Sci. Data. **4**(1), 160122 (2017). https://doi.org/10.1038/sdata.2016.122
33. Oldewurtel, F., Sturzenegger, D., Morari, M.: Importance of occupancy information for building climate control. Appl. Energy. **101**, 521–532 (2013). https://doi.org/10.1016/j.apenergy.2012.06.014
34. OPEN4CEC Consortium: OPEN4CEC: Service-oriented Open Platform for Citizen Energy Communities. Driving Urban Transitions (DUT) Partnership Project (2023).. https://open4cec.ase.ro. Accessed 11 Feb 2026
35. Oprea, S.V., Bara, A., Tudorica, B.G., Calinoiu, M.I., Botezatu, M.A.: Insights into demand-side management with big data analytics in electricity consumers' behaviour. Comput. Electr. Eng. **89**, 106902 (2021). https://doi.org/10.1016/j.compeleceng.2020.106902
36. Serasinghe, R., Long, N., Clark, J.: Parameter identification methods for low-order gray box building energy models: a critical review. Energ. Buildings. **307**, 114123 (2024). https://doi.org/10.1016/j.enbuild.2024.114123
37. Strauch, P., Wang, W., Langner, F.: Model predictive control for demand flexibility of a residential building with multiple distributed energy resources. Energ. Buildings. **305**, 113884 (2024). https://doi.org/10.1016/j.enbuild.2023.113884
38. Xin, Y., et al.: A comprehensive review of predictive control strategies in heating, ventilation, and air-conditioning (HVAC): model-free VS model. J. Build. Eng. **94**, 110013 (2024). https://doi.org/10.1016/j.jobe.2024.110013
39. Yiasoumas, G., et al.: Key aspects and challenges in the implementation of energy communities. Energies. **16**(12), 4703 (2023). https://doi.org/10.3390/en16124703

Community-Focused Energy Management System with Modular Architecture

Laurențiu-Alex Mustață[1(✉)], Elena Helerea[1], Cristian-Leonard Mușuroi[1], and Rodolfo Dufo López[2]

[1] Transilvania University of Brașov, Brașov, Romania
{laurentiu.mustata,helerea,cristian.musuroi}@unitbv.ro
[2] Universidad de Zaragoza, Zaragoza, Spain
rdufo@unizar.es

Abstract. Locally generated energy is increasingly important for ensuring reliable access to electricity in communities with limited grid infrastructure. This paper presents the design and evaluation of a modular hybrid energy system integrating photovoltaic generation, battery storage, and hybrid on/off-grid inverters, aimed at reducing grid reliance in an educational outreach camp, where frequent outages affect essential activities. The proposed architecture supports both fixed and portable deployment and enables dynamic load allocation based on short-term predictions of solar generation and demand. The system is supported by a cyber-physical platform for monitoring, forecasting, and control. Representative operational scenarios are analysed through simulation to assess system behaviour under different seasonal conditions and storage configurations. The results illustrate the potential of modular energy solutions to improve local energy autonomy and support the integration of renewable energy sources in community-level applications.

Keywords: Modular energy systems · Photovoltaic · Battery Energy Storage · Hybrid Inverters · Off-grid Operation · Energy Monitoring · Load Forecasting

1 Introduction

Reliable access to electricity is a requirement for sustainable development, directly affecting education, healthcare, and socio-economic activities in local communities. In regions with weak grid infrastructure, Renewable Energy Sources and decentralized generation are increasingly recognized as key solutions to improve energy autonomy in community-scale applications. Grid outages can interrupt critical equipment, reducing the quality of educational and social activities, including hygiene, field-based learning, and operation of digital tools. These challenges highlight the need for resilient, flexible, and accessible energy solutions.

This paper focuses on the design and evaluation of a modular hybrid energy system. The objective is to develop a flexible energy architecture that integrates photovoltaic generation, modular battery storage, hybrid zero-export on/off-grid inverters, and a cyber-physical monitoring and control platform. The proposed system enables dynamic load

Published by Springer Nature Switzerland AG 2027
L. M. Camarinha-Matos and F. Ferrada (Eds.): DoCEIS 2026, IFIP AICT 790, pp. 186–198, 2027.
https://doi.org/10.1007/978-3-032-28939-1_14

management and improved utilization of locally generated renewable energy through real-time monitoring and short-term forecasting. It is implemented using Python-based data processing, forecasting, and API-based communication, supporting smart energy management in real-world community settings [1]. To evaluate design choices, the study employs modelling and simulation using iHOGA (improved Hybrid Optimisation by Genetic Algorithms – ihoga.unizar.es) for multi-objective optimization of hybrid renewable systems, considering PV sizing [2], battery models [3], inverter characteristics [4], load profiles [5], and short-term energy management analysis [6].

The paper is organized as follows: Sect. 2 presents the technological contribution and solution for community-oriented energy applications. Section 3 describes the camp energy-thermal system and its electrical constraints. Section 4 introduces the modular hybrid energy system design. Section 5 details the simulation framework, scenarios, and predictive modelling approach. Section 6 discusses results, system performance, conclusions, scalability and future work directions.

2 Contribution to Technological Innovation

This work addresses the theme of technological innovation for societal development by proposing a modular hybrid energy system to tackle unreliable electricity in marginalized regions. Rather than treating rural microgrids as monolithic systems, this research reimagines community energy infrastructure as a modular hybrid platform built from scalable functional blocks (PV strings, inverter modules, stackable batteries, and monitoring units), reconfiguring the system for fixed installations in the camp or portable field deployments, and offering fine-grained operational control and energy resilience in intermittently powered environments.

A key contribution is converting a traditionally static hybrid system into a cyber-physical energy platform. Integration of real-time monitoring [7–9], data acquisition, and short-term load/PV forecasting [10] enables responsive control, load prioritization and optimized use of surplus energy. Similar modular cyber-physical architectures have been explored in energy applications [11]. Implemented on a Raspberry Pi, the subsystem transforms a passive power supply into an adaptive infrastructure.

This paper presents research within an EPICS in IEEE initiative, aligned with international objectives for sustainable development and energy access in underserved communities. The platform enables students to engage with renewable energy systems, monitoring, and forecasting tools in real operational contexts, strengthening local empowerment and long-term sustainability. Together, these aspects support the development of modular hybrid energy system solutions for resilient infrastructure.

3 System Architecture Overview

The energy-thermal system of the camp is composed of 2 main buildings equipped with dedicated subsystems for heating and domestic hot water (DHW). DHW is stored in *Building 1* in two *500 L Reservoirs*, each supplied via three heat pathways:

- *Heat Exchanger 1* – connects to a set of 2 solar thermal panels (22 tubes each) in a closed-loop circuit with the corresponding reservoir. *Solar Circulation Pump 1* drives flow through the panels, while the *Solar Automation Unit* monitors panel and reservoir temperatures to control pump operation and regulate heat transfer.
- *Heat Exchanger 2* – interfaces with the wood-fired thermal plant located in *Building 2*, allowing heat transfer via a buffer.
- *Heat Exchanger 3* – an electric heating element with a rated power of 5 kW, which can be used to heat water directly when solar input is insufficient or the wood-based thermal plant is not available.

Each solar thermal circuit includes safety and control components: overpressure bleeder valves, expansion tanks, magnetic water filters, manual filling and emptying valves, and a 3-way overtemperature drain valve.

In *Building 2*, a 250-kW wood-based thermal plant supplies heat to a *2000 L Reservoir* (buffer), which serves as a central distribution node for DHW heating and room heating circuits. Heat circulates from the buffer to radiators via *Heat Circulation Pump 1 (425 W)* and from the thermal plant to the buffer via *Heat Circulation Pump 2 (463 W)*. Manual valves, expansion tanks, and pressure gauges regulate flow and maintain safety. Temperature sensors in rooms, the buffer, and the plant feed the *Heat Pump Automation* system, which modulates both pumps to maintain desired temperatures and optimize energy distribution. The overall layout and component interconnections are shown in Fig. 1.

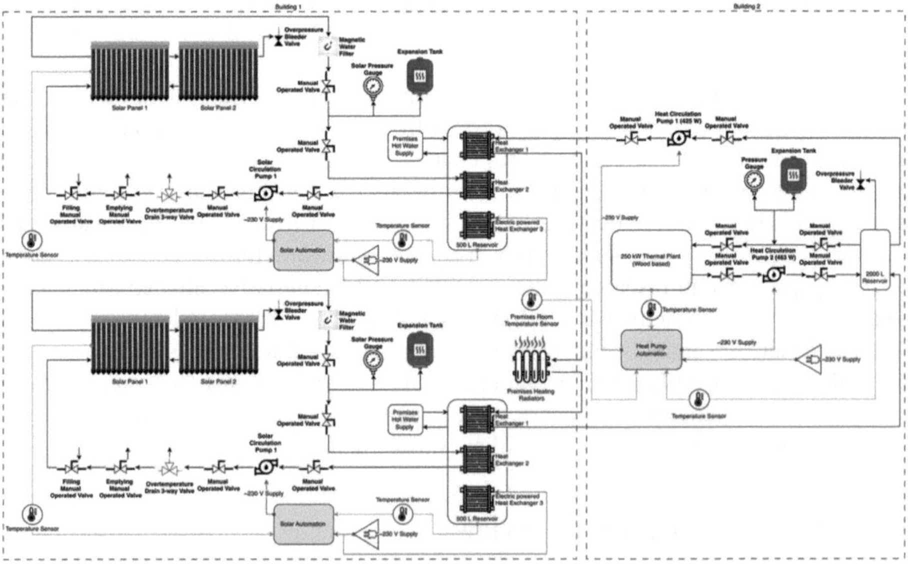

Fig. 1. Schematic overview of the camp energy-thermal system.

All circulation pumps, automation units, and electric heat exchangers operate on 230 V AC. These electrically powered components are essential for circulation and system automation, and their power requirements are summarized in Table 1, providing an overview of electrical demand to support energy flow modelling and hybrid system optimization.

Table 1. Electrically powered components in the camp energy-thermal system.

Component	Model / Type	Rated Power / Electrical Load
Solar Circulation Pump 1	Environ EcoStar Pro	65 W (~150 VA)
Heat Circulation Pump 1	Grundfos MAGNA1 50–100 F 280	425 W (~437 VA)
Heat Circulation Pump 2	Grundfos MAGNA1 40–120 F 250	463 W (~472 VA)
Electric Heat Exchanger 3	–	5 kW (×2)
Solar Automation Controller	DeltaSol CS Plus	< 1 W
Heat Pump Automation Controller	–	< 1 W

Despite the benefits of multiple heat sources, the redundancy provided by parallel heat exchangers, and the automation of circulation and temperature regulation, the system remains constrained by the intermittent and unreliable electrical supply characteristic of the region. All pumps, automation units, and electric heating elements depend on stable 230 V AC power. Consequently, grid outages or voltage drops can interrupt fluid circulation through the solar thermal loops and the wood-fired heating circuits. Such interruptions may lead to rapid temperature rise in the solar collectors due to stagnation, requiring manually intervention. Similarly, loss of electrical power disables the thermal plant circulation pumps, preventing heat transfer to the buffer reservoir and, downstream, to the radiators and DHW systems.

These limitations illustrate the vulnerability of the existing configuration to grid instability and highlight the need for an energy-resilient approach capable of maintaining both thermal system functionality and electrically powered camp activities during power interruptions.

4 Modular Hybrid Energy System Architecture

The proposed modular hybrid architecture extends the camp energy infrastructure by integrating photovoltaic generation and modular battery storage while maintaining compatibility with the thermal and electrical subsystems already in place. Similar off-grid approaches have been explored in residential settings, where PV modules, PV/T collectors, thermal storage, and heat pumps are integrated to operate reliably even without grid support [9]. The system is organized into 6 primary functional modules, illustrated in Fig. 2: the Solar Generation Module, Inverter Module, Grid Connection Module, Rack Load Module, House Load Module and Battery Module. Additional optional modules are depicted with reduced opacity to indicate scalability.

The Solar Generation Module consists of a series-connected PV array integrated with a DC protection box. The module incorporates overcurrent protection, surge protection, a DC isolator, and grounding terminals. Power is exported through standardized DC connectors that interface directly with the Inverter Module. The architecture also accommodates the integration of an additional PV module for increased generation capacity, enabling expansion based on demand.

The Inverter Module performs DC–AC power conversion for downstream loads and coordinates power exchange with the PV array, the battery subsystem, and the electrical grid. The module includes DC input connectors for the PV array, AC output connectors for supplying local loads, and an AC input interface for grid-supported operation. Dedicated battery terminals allow direct coupling with the Battery Module. The system supports parallel inverter operation, enabling capacity scaling without structural alteration of the existing setup.

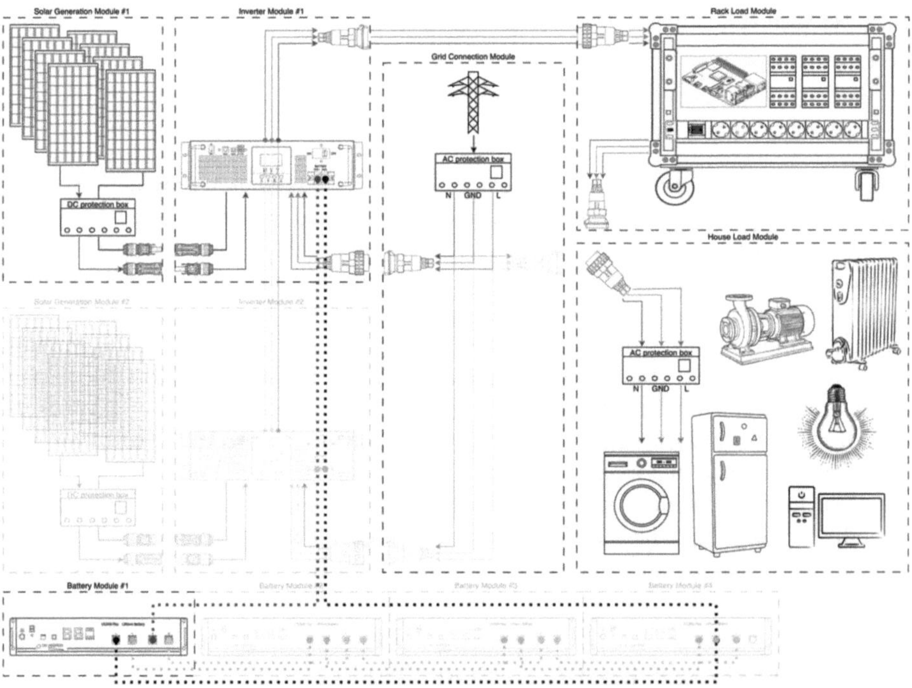

Fig. 2. Schematic representation of the modular hybrid energy system architecture.

The Grid Connection Module interfaces the hybrid system with the utility grid. An AC protection assembly ensures proper line, neutral, and grounding distribution to downstream modules. Its primary role is to supply backup power when PV generation and battery capacity are insufficient. The architecture and inverter type enforce non-export operation, ensuring that no power is fed back to the grid. Future expansion pathways are indicated for additional load modules or auxiliary inverter modules.

The Rack Load Module functions as the central AC distribution, protection, and monitoring assembly within the modular architecture. It receives AC power from the Inverter Module and distributes it via two protected circuits: a 16 A branch for internal rack subsystems (including monitoring electronics, embedded computation hardware, and supervisory control devices) and a 20 A branch supplying the House Load Module via an industrial connector. It integrates overcurrent and residual-current protection, environmental controls, and measurement hardware for voltage, current, and power readings. Using a single-board computing platform, it supports advanced monitoring, automated load-shedding, time-synchronized data logging, and networked communication. The design supports future extensions such as digital-twins, forecasting, and adaptive control policies for energy optimization. The use of standardized plug-and-socket interfaces, selected so that energized contact surfaces are never exposed on the supply side, facilitates safe hot-swappable deployment, rapid field reconfiguration, and streamlined mobility for off-site activities.

The House Load Module represents the connection point for conventional AC loads within the camp infrastructure, including heating support components, appliance level consumers, and general-purpose outlets. It receives power through standardized connectors and includes a dedicated AC protection box for safe distribution of line, neutral, and grounding conductors. The module can be powered either through the Rack Load Module, directly from the Inverter Module, or from the Grid Connection Module, depending on the selected operational mode.

The Battery Module interfaces with the Inverter Module via predefined battery terminals and provides energy buffering to maintain critical system operation during grid outages or periods of insufficient PV generation. Additional storage modules may be added in parallel to increase the available energy capacity. This modular approach supports progressive scaling without requiring architectural modification.

The modular architecture enables reconfiguration for stationary, semi-portable, or fully portable deployment based on camp needs. The system may operate under multiple electrical supply pathways, including photovoltaic generation, grid-supported input, and modular battery storage, thus providing flexibility during both normal operation and grid disturbances, and mitigating thermal-system safety risks. The corresponding hardware elements and protection interfaces associated with these modules are summarized in Table 2, which documents the principal components, interconnections, and electrical characteristics relevant to system operation.

Table 2. Technical characteristics of modules and components in the proposed hybrid power system.

Component Type	Model / Reference	Key Technical Parameters
PV panels	COMET 1 N Mono AIKO-A610-MAH72Mw	610 W ×8 connected in series 4.88 kW total
PV cables	H1Z2Z2-K	6 mm^2

(*continued*)

Table 2. (*continued*)

Component Type	Model / Reference	Key Technical Parameters
PV connectors	MC4	Male/Female 30 A, 1000 V
DC protection box	PNI CBM-2	20 A DC fuse DC SPD DC isolator Grounding terminal
DC cables	4 AWG	120 A
AC cables	CYABY-F	3×6 mm^2
AC connectors	Industrial 2P + E (IEC 60309)	Male/Female 32 A, 230 V
AC protection box	Bipolar MCBs Bipolar RCD	L-N-G 230 V
Hybrid Inverter-Charger	Suntaic Hero Rack	5.5 kW AC output
LiFePO4 Battery	Pylontech US2000	2.4 kWh 48 V
Energy monitoring units	Shelly Pro EM	< 3 W power cons. 50 A max.
Load control units	Shelly Plus Plug S	< 1 W power cons. 12 A max.
Automation engine	Raspberry PI 5	< 10 W power cons.

5 Experimental Data

For the purposes of simulating and evaluating the proposed modular hybrid architecture with iHOGA, representative daily load profiles were constructed based on operational schedules and consumption patterns of the camp infrastructure for both summer and winter operating conditions, including thermally and electrically driven components. All input profiles were synthetically generated in a deterministic manner to reflect realistic operating conditions. The resulting daily load curves presented in Fig. 3 for a representative winter day (1 February) and in Fig. 4 for a representative summer day (1 July) are combined with the corresponding simulation results. Photovoltaic generation profiles were obtained using the iHOGA built-in solar resource model based on NASA POWER 2019 monthly average irradiation data for the specific geographic coordinates of the camp site. The simulated PV performance considers a daily average irradiation on the tilted plane of 4.23 kWh/m^2, and the hybrid-system operation is evaluated using a single battery module as described above. Each figure concurrently displays the total load demand, battery charging and discharging behaviour, total grid energy purchased, and, where applicable, the unused surplus energy that cannot be exported to the grid. The estimation integrates realistic component activation schedules: solar circulation pumps operate based on daylight availability, heat circulation pumps follow two 3-h intervals in the morning and midday and a 6-h evening period, and the electric Heat Exchanger 3 disabled except for backup use ensured by sufficient battery state-of-charge.

The simulation results from Fig. 3 indicate that under winter conditions the modular system with 1 PV module and 1 battery module requires grid support during the intervals 03:00–06:00, 09:00–10:00, and 20:00–24:00. In contrast, Fig. 4 indicates that during summer operation, only a small amount of grid energy is required, concentrated primarily during 04:00–07:00 due to limited pre-sunrise PV availability.

The figures also illustrate periods of theoretical export energy, which, under the current non-export configuration, correspond to curtailed or unused generation. As seasonal irradiation increases between the winter and summer representative dates, intermediate periods demonstrate improved performance: for instance, Fig. 5 which depicts operation on May 1st while the camp still follows the winter occupancy and heating schedule, shows that rising PV generation significantly reduces grid dependence, limiting the required evening grid-purchase interval to only 22:00–24:00.

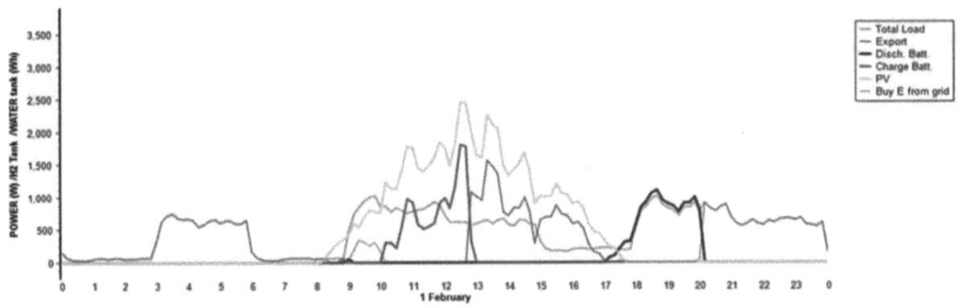

Fig. 3. Simulated operation for a winter representative day of February 1st.

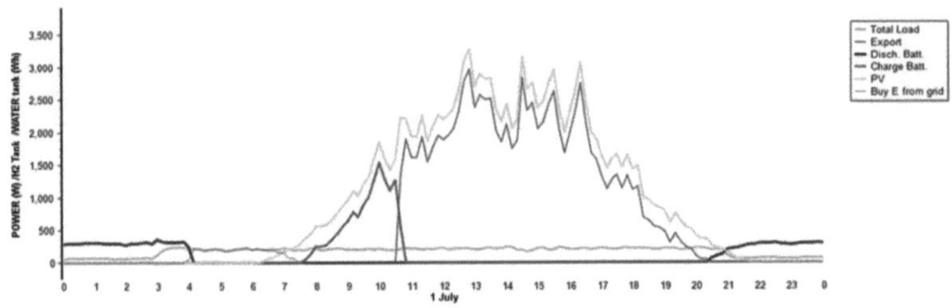

Fig. 4. Simulated operation for a summer representative day of July 1st.

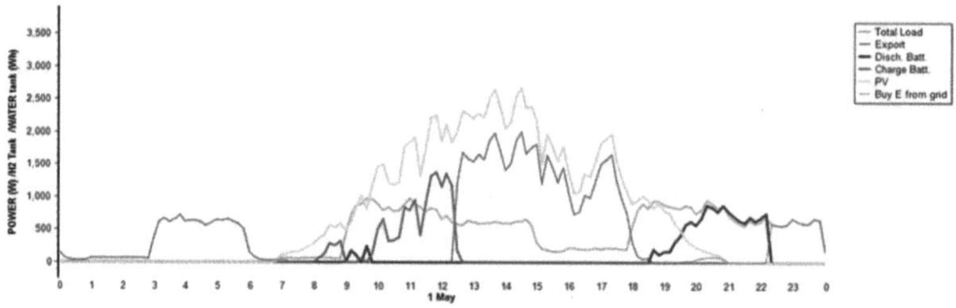

Fig. 5. Simulated operation for a representative day of May 1st.

Building on the baseline scenario with a single battery module, the analysis was extended to evaluate system behaviour with 3 battery modules connected in parallel, increasing storage capacity and self-consumption [12], while maintaining the same PV generation and load profiles. The corresponding simulation results are shown in Fig. 6 for winter, Fig. 7 for summer, and Fig. 8 for May 1st operation.

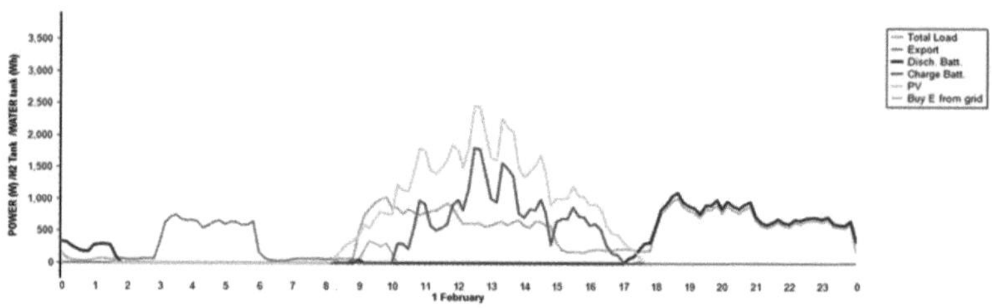

Fig. 6. Simulated operation for a winter representative day of February 1st with a modular architecture configuration of 3 battery modules in parallel.

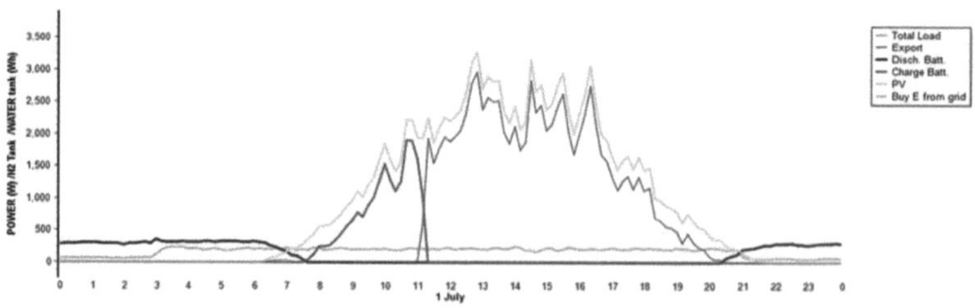

Fig. 7. Simulated operation for a summer representative day of July 1st with a modular architecture configuration of 3 battery modules in parallel.

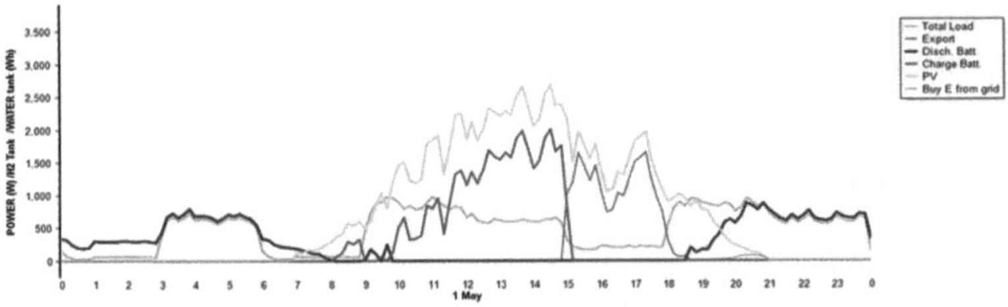

Fig. 8. Simulated operation for a representative day of May 1st with a modular architecture configuration of 3 battery modules in parallel.

Expanding storage to 3 battery modules increases autonomy during periods without solar generation. In winter, evening grid dependence is eliminated. In summer, curtailed energy remains due to PV generation exceeding load and storage capacity. However, the May 1st case shows near-elimination of grid purchases. These results highlight the increased buffering capability of the expanded battery subsystem.

In addition to the deterministic simulations, Fig. 9 illustrates the predicted operation and potential additional load forecast for a summer representative day. PV generation, energy demand, and potential energy export were forecasted using a feature-based linear regression model. The predictor includes multiple temporal features, including hour of day (linear and cyclic), day-of-year, day-of-week (cyclic), month (cyclic), short-term rolling averages, and lagged values from the same hour on the previous day. Predictions are generated at 10-min resolution, capturing daily, weekly, and seasonal variability while maintaining interpretability. The implementation is developed in Python using Pandas and NumPy for data handling and preprocessing, Scikit-learn for regression modelling, and Matplotlib for visualization. The output graphs highlight the potential additional load that could be safely connected when export is positive.

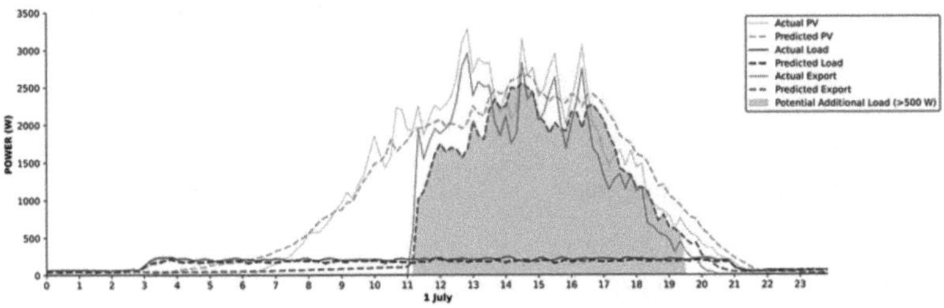

Fig. 9. Predicted operation and potential additional load forecast for a summer representative day of July 1st with a modular architecture configuration of 3 battery modules in parallel.

For this day, total actual energy export reached 14.80 kWh, while the model predicted 15.23 kWh, demonstrating good agreement and reasonable predictive accuracy for operational planning. The forecast is coupled with the Shelly monitoring and control units and the Raspberry Pi automation engine, enabling dynamic activation of loads on predefined sockets to prevent overloading or unnecessary curtailment. This integration of short-term predictions with cyber-physical monitoring and control demonstrates how the modular architecture can support flexible, reliable, and intelligent energy management in both fixed and portable deployments.

6 Discussion and Conclusions

The proposed modular hybrid energy system architecture represents a comprehensive approach to enhancing energy resilience in remote, electricity-constrained environments. Unlike conventional hybrid systems that focus solely on energy supply, this architecture is designed for modular scalability, operational flexibility, and integration with community-focused and educational activities. The design philosophy comprising stackable modules enables both fixed installation and portable deployment, while the embedded monitoring, forecasting, and control platform ensures reliable operation under variable environmental and load conditions.

Simulation results confirm that the modular system performs predictably and efficiently across seasonal variations. Expanding the battery subsystem from 1 to 3 modules significantly improves system autonomy, nearly eliminating grid dependence in transitional scenarios. These findings illustrate that in small/medium-scale hybrid systems, storage, rather than generation, is the primary limiting factor.

During peak summer periods, PV production often exceeds the instantaneous load and battery absorption capacity, leading to curtailment. However, this surplus energy can be redirected to support additional camp activities through the House Load Module or auxiliary outlets, enabling up to 15 kWh of extra renewable consumption on peak days. Such operational flexibility underscores how modular design allows energy resources to be allocated dynamically to functional and educational priorities.

Table 3. Annualized performance indicators for 2 modular architecture configurations.

Indicator	Config. with 1 battery module	Config. with 3 battery modules
NPC (€)	15578.7	18245.8
CO_2 Emissions (kg/yr)	650.552	387.177
Unmet Load (kWh/yr)	1182.98	464.28
Renewable Fraction (%)	65.31	86.38
LCOE (€/kWh)	0.232	0.271
Battery Capacity (Wh)	2400	7200
Grid Energy Purchased (kWh/yr)	1196	478
Curtailed Energy (kWh/yr)	3168.2	2176.2
PV Production (kWh/yr)	6006.6	6006.6

The annualized performance indicators in Table 3 show that while increased storage raises capital expenditure and Net Present Cost, it simultaneously enhances renewable fraction, reduces unmet load, and decreases grid energy purchases. These findings highlight a favourable resilience-to-cost trade-off, supporting modular deployment strategies tailored to operational priorities and budget constraints.

Beyond quantitative metrics, the modular design delivers practical operational and societal benefits. The system allows plug-and-play integration of additional PV or battery modules, temporary deployment in field activities, and dynamic load allocation for educational experiments, while maintaining continuity for critical heating and electrical equipment. The platform thus demonstrates how engineering innovation can directly enhance societal well-being, supporting resilient infrastructure, sustainability, and experiential education in off-grid environments.

Building on the modular architecture and its demonstrated operational flexibility, future work will focus on refining prediction algorithms to better align forecasted and actual additional load, leveraging real-time monitoring and forecasting data to enable more responsive energy management, dynamic load prioritization, and optimal use of surplus renewable energy.

Acknowledgments. This project was supported by the EPICS in IEEE program. The authors acknowledge administrative support during proposal and reporting stages, including funding and resource management. Collaboration with the partner community organization enabled access to the camp site for data collection and technical evaluations.

References

1. Botón-Fernández, V., Romero, M.P., Lozano-Tello, A., Romero-Cadaval, E.: Intelligent energy management system for residential and community applications. In: Camarinha-Matos, L.M., Tomic, S., Graça, P. (eds.) Technological Innovation for the Internet of Things, pp. 307–314. Springer, Berlin Heidelberg, Berlin, Heidelberg (2013). https://doi.org/10.1007/978-3-642-37291-9_33
2. Tawfik, T.M., Badr, M.A., El-Kady, E.Y., Abdellatif, O.E.: Optimization and energy management of hybrid standalone energy system: a case study. Renew. Energy Focus. **25**, 48–56 (2018). https://doi.org/10.1016/j.ref.2018.03.004
3. García-Vera, Y., Dufo-López, R., Bernal-Agustín, J.: Optimization of isolated hybrid microgrids with renewable energy based on different battery models and technologies. Energies. **13**, 581 (2020). https://doi.org/10.3390/en13030581
4. Hoarcă, I.C., Bizon, N., Şorlei, I.S., Thounthong, P.: Sizing Design for a Hybrid Renewable Power System Using HOMER and iHOGA simulators. Energies. **16**, 1926 (2023). https://doi.org/10.3390/en16041926
5. Shezan, S.: A.: feasibility analysis of an islanded hybrid wind-diesel-battery microgrid with voltage and power response for offshore islands. J. Clean. Prod. **288**, 125568 (2021). https://doi.org/10.1016/j.jclepro.2020.125568
6. Department of Electrical Engineering. E.I.N.A., Zaragoza University. Spain, Dufo-López, R., Lujano-Rojas, J.M., Bernal-Agustín, J.L., Artal-Sevil, J.S., Bayod-Rújula, Á.A., Tejero-Gómez, J.A.: Short term energy management in stand-alone PV-battery-diesel systems. Renew. Energ. Environ. Power Qual. J. **2**, 233–239 (2024). https://doi.org/10.24084/reepqj24.395

7. Apse-Apsitis, P., Avotins, A., Ribickis, L., Zakis, J.: Development of energy monitoring system for SmartGrid consumer application. In: Technological Innovation for Value Creation, pp. 347–354. Springer, Berlin Heidelberg, Berlin, Heidelberg (2012). https://doi.org/10.1007/978-3-642-28255-3_38
8. Josué, J.G., Pina, J.M., Neves, M.V.: Home electric energy monitoring system: design and prototyping. In: Camarinha-Matos, L.M. (ed.) Technological Innovation for Sustainability, pp. 437–444. Springer, Berlin Heidelberg, Berlin, Heidelberg (2011). https://doi.org/10.1007/978-3-642-19170-1_48
9. Katsioulis, V., Karapidakis, E., Hadjinicolaou, M., Tsikalakis, A.: Wireless monitoring and remote control of PV systems based on the ZigBee protocol. In: Camarinha-Matos, L.M. (ed.) Technological Innovation for Sustainability, pp. 297–304. Springer, Berlin Heidelberg, Berlin, Heidelberg (2011). https://doi.org/10.1007/978-3-642-19170-1_32
10. Viegas, J.L., Vieira, S.M., Melício, R., Mendes, V.M.F., Sousa, J.M.C.: GA-ANN short-term electricity load forecasting. In: Camarinha-Matos, L.M., Falcão, A.J., Vafaei, N., Najdi, S. (eds.) Technological Innovation for Cyber-Physical Systems, pp. 485–493. Springer International Publishing, Cham (2016). https://doi.org/10.1007/978-3-319-31165-4_45
11. Oliveira, F.M., Rocha, A., Alemão, D., Freitas, N., Barata, J.: Asynchronous communication between modular cyber-physical production systems and Arduino based industrial controllers. In: Camarinha-Matos, L.M. (ed.) Technological Innovation for Digitalization and Virtualization, pp. 53–61. Springer International Publishing, Cham (2022). https://doi.org/10.1007/978-3-031-07520-9_5
12. Camilo, F.M., Castro, R., Almeida, M.E., Fernão Pires, V.: Impact of self-consumption and storage in low voltage distribution networks: an economic outlook. In: Camarinha-Matos, L.M., Falcão, A.J., Vafaei, N., Najdi, S. (eds.) Technological Innovation for Cyber-Physical Systems, pp. 446–454. Springer International Publishing, Cham (2016). https://doi.org/10.1007/978-3-319-31165-4_42

Predictive Control and Optimization Strategies for Smart and Fair Operation in Energy Communities

S. Madrigal[1(✉)], Antoni Morell[1], Jose Lopez Vicario[1], O. Arrieta[1,2], and Ramon Vilanova[1]

[1] Departament de Telecomunicació i d'Enginyeria de Sistemes, Universitat Autònoma de Barcelona, 08193 Bellaterra, Barcelona, Spain
sebastian.madrigal@uab.cat

[2] Instituto de Investigaciones en Ingeniería, Facultad de Ingeniería, Universidad de Costa Rica, San José 11501-2060, Costa Rica

Abstract. This work presents the main aim, context, and development framework of the PhD research conducted by the first author, focused on the development of advanced control and optimization strategies to support the energy management and operation of complex systems. In this paper, Energy Communities are adopted as the target systems application domain, since they involve multiple actors, decentralized renewable generation, flexible resources, and operational decisions that must reconcile technical constraints with social values. The proposed research investigates predictive control and optimization strategies to enhance the smart and fair operation of Energy Communities, aiming to improve collective self-consumption, increase economic benefits, and promote equitable outcomes among participants. The interest in predictive approaches arises from their ability to anticipate demand and renewable generation variability and to support informed decision-making under changing conditions. In addition, optimization-based strategies are considered to coordinate community resources such as storage, electric vehicles, and demand response while respecting operational limits and fairness requirements. The expected outcome is a practical and scalable methodological basis to support operators and stakeholders in deploying smart, fair and efficient energy communities.

Keywords: Energy Communities · Collective Self-Consumption · Predictive Control · Optimization · Energy Allocation

1 Introduction

Energy Communities (ECs) are becoming a key enabler of decarbonization and citizen participation in decentralized energy systems. By coordinating distributed renewable generation with flexibility resources such as storage, electric vehicles, and demand response, they can increase collective self-consumption (CSC), reduce costs, and

Published by Springer Nature Switzerland AG 2027
L. M. Camarinha-Matos and F. Ferrada (Eds.): DoCEIS 2026, IFIP AICT 790, pp. 199–210, 2027.
https://doi.org/10.1007/978-3-032-28939-1_15

improve local grid interaction [1, 2]. However, their day-to-day operation is challenging because an Energy Community behaves as a complex socio-technical system: it involves multiple stakeholders with heterogeneous objectives, must respect physical and regulatory constraints, and is strongly affected by uncertainty due to renewable variability and changing consumption patterns [3, 4].

A central difficulty is that operational decisions must be taken continuously and revised as conditions evolve for example: energy sharing, flexibility scheduling, and balancing economic performance with fairness and sustainability goals. In many practical settings, forecasting and control are treated as separate stages, while the "system response" is assumed to be known [5]. In contrast, community operation is heavily shaped by participant behavior and context, which can be difficult to represent with purely physics-based models [6]. This motivates the employment of data-driven prediction models not only for forecasting, but also as practical proxies of the system dynamics that can guide decision-making under uncertainty [7, 8].

This paper proposes a predictive control and optimization framework that couples a prediction layer with operational decision-making in a receding-horizon logic, where forecasts and uncertainty information inform control and optimization algorithms for managing the community. The approach is intentionally strategy-agnostic in the way that the same structure can accommodate deterministic predictive optimization, fairness-aware formulations, robust or scenario-based variants, and distributed coordination methods, depending on the community configuration and governance. By incorporating techno-economic variables, operational constraints, and fairness-oriented objectives, the framework aims to support smart, fair, and implementable energy-sharing schemes aligned with real Energy Community goals.

2 Relation with Technological Innovation for Societal Challenges

Real-world deployment of Energy Communities pushes innovation beyond isolated technologies and into integrated system operation. Coordinating many small actors requires practical digital solutions, including advanced monitoring, data management, interoperability, and decision support, capable of transforming raw measurements into actionable operational guidance. In this sense, Energy Communities offer a concrete arena where technological advances can be validated under realistic constraints and translated into tangible benefits at the local level.

Technological innovation must also address societal challenges associated with participation and legitimacy. Because operational choices directly affect households and public entities, ECs require decision processes that are transparent, configurable, and aligned with allocation principles. This shifts part of the innovation focus from optimality alone towards accountable governance, where fairness, explainability, privacy, and stakeholder involvement become necessary conditions for solutions to be accepted and sustained over time.

A further challenge is ensuring that community-level solutions remain reliable and transferable across contexts. Differences in asset portfolios, tariffs, regulations, and user behavior imply that rigid one-size-fits-all approaches often fail. Framework-based methodologies that can accommodate different predictive and optimization strategies, uncertainty-handling mechanisms, and policy constraints support scalable deployment and replication. As a result, innovation in this area can deliver broader societal impact by enabling adaptable tools that communities can adopt, maintain, and evolve as conditions change.

3 State of the Art

Forecasting and prediction of energy profiles have become central building blocks for Energy Community operation because they provide the anticipatory information required to schedule flexible assets and to plan energy exchanges under variability. Recent work in peer-to-peer trading networks shows how advanced metering and learning-based pipelines can support decentralized decision-making by combining day-ahead scheduling with bid optimization and real-time adjustment, while explicitly incorporating uncertainty to enhance robustness and economic performance [9]. In Renewable Energy Communities, consumption forecasting has been operationalized through machine learning models such as eXtreme Gradient Boosting (XGBoost), where the predicted demand is used within management logic that determines when to buy, sell, or store energy under different tariff structures and photovoltaic production conditions [10]. Beyond point forecasting, the literature emphasizes that uncertainty characterization is essential because forecast errors can propagate into constraint violations, suboptimal trading, and perceived unfairness in allocation, which motivates architectures that embed uncertainty handling as part of the operational workflow rather than an afterthought.

On the decision layer, Energy Community operation is commonly formulated as a constrained optimization or control problem in which technical feasibility and economic performance must be balanced under regulatory conditions. Reinforcement learning has been explored as an alternative to model-based scheduling, particularly for real-time control of battery storage in renewable energy communities operating under incentive schemes for virtual self-consumption, where policies rely on information available at the current time step and are benchmarked against rule-based baselines and ideal oracle policies [11]. In parallel, optimization-driven approaches remain dominant for structured decision-making, especially when explicit constraints and techno-economic indicators are required. As an example, in Spain, the allocation problem in collective self-consumption has motivated optimization models that enhance sharing coefficients by integrating day-ahead consumption forecasts generated by neural networks, and by evaluating performance through indicators such as self-consumption, savings, and investment metrics, with and without storage [12]. Techno-economic optimization studies further examine sizing, appliance shifting, and sharing modalities under regulatory frameworks and volatile prices, showing that certain dynamic sharing variants can yield limited additional benefits depending on modeling assumptions and settlement structures [13].

Recent advances point toward tighter coupling between prediction and real-time control through learning-based methods and hybrid pipelines. A representative example is the integration of an ensemble forecasting module with safe deep reinforcement learning for real-time scheduling in a smart district community, where constraint awareness is embedded into the control policy and performance are assessed not only through cost reduction but also through constraint violations and deployability [14].

As Energy Communities scale, fully centralized decision-making becomes increasingly challenged by computational burden, privacy requirements, and coordination overhead, which motivates distributed approaches. A comprehensive survey synthesizes distributed optimization families and technological enablers, positioning methods such as Alternating Direction Method of Multipliers (ADMM) as practical mechanisms to approach centralized optimality while preserving local autonomy, and highlighting challenges related to heterogeneity, time-varying operation, communication delays, and cybersecurity constraints [15]. Complementary literature on emerging technologies emphasizes the role of distributed ledger technologies, the Internet of Things, and artificial intelligence as enablers of decentralized coordination and secure transactions, particularly when a central intermediary is undesirable or infeasible [16].

Finally, fairness-aware allocation and governance considerations increasingly shape what is considered feasible and acceptable community operation. Socio-technical research argues that governance is assembled through regulation and the material characteristics of power systems, raising concerns about expert opacity and the political implications of decision processes that are not accessible to non-experts [17]. Empirical evidence further shows that governance structures influence citizens' perceptions of collective efficacy and identity leadership, affecting acceptability and willingness to participate, which implies that operational strategies must be compatible with participation and legitimacy requirements rather than focusing solely on technical optimality [18]. Overall, the literature provides strong foundations on forecast-driven management pipelines, constrained optimization and learning-based control, scalable coordination through distributed optimization and enabling technologies, and governance factors shaping adoption. Nevertheless, much of the existing work remains method-specific, treating prediction either as an external input to a fixed decision engine or as part of a tightly coupled architecture that is difficult to generalize. What remains insufficiently addressed is a unified, strategy-agnostic operational viewpoint where prediction models act as an operational dynamics layer feeding control and optimization under uncertainty while integrating techno-economic constraints with fairness and governance requirements. This perspective is also consistent with recent advances in data-driven predictive control [19] and with the broader methodological foundations of model predictive control as a general framework for constrained decision-making in dynamic systems [20].

4 Research Contribution and Innovation

In this section, the main contribution is introduced as a layered, predictive management architecture for Energy Communities that consolidates decision-making elements typically designed separately or left outside the control system design. The proposed framework integrates governance rules, feasibility enforcement, stakeholder preferences, and operational objectives within a single supervisory pipeline, thereby treating socio-technical requirements as first-class components of the operational problem rather than as external constraints or post-processing steps. This integration supports implementation across heterogeneous European regulatory and settlement contexts and, at the same time, elevates the community management system from a reactive scheduling approach to a smart, predictive scheme in which operational actions are driven by predicted system behavior and refined through ex-post performance feedback.

In Fig. 1 the proposed predictive control and optimization pipeline are summarized and highlights its main information flows. The framework is organized as a sequence of governance, feasibility, decision, and fairness layers, where operational decisions are driven by predicted information provided by an Energy Community predictive model. A planned action is then evaluated both on the real community and on the predictive model, producing realized and predicted responses that are compared through ex-post performance metrics. This closed-loop assessment enables systematic re-tuning of the predictive model and, when needed, adjustment of decision parameters to mitigate performance degradation and preserve implementable, regulation-compliant operation.

The first element of the pipeline is the Energy Community predictive model, which represents the community as a multi-agent system whose collective behavior emerges from heterogeneous members, assets, and operating conditions. Within this layer, the community can be modelled through alternative architectures, ranging from centralized representations to decentralized or agent-based formulations, depending on data availability, privacy constraints, and the desired level of granularity. The model can capture different member types and roles (e.g., consumers, prosumers, public buildings), their associated consumption and generation patterns, and the diversity of loads and flexibility resources that shape operational dynamics. In this way, the predictive model provides the anticipated trajectories, and where applicable uncertainty information, that will be used as the basis for decision-making process.

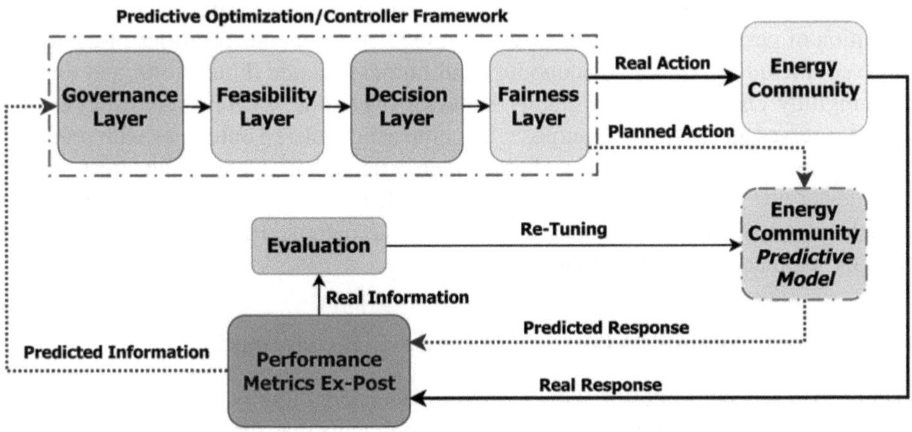

Fig. 1. General pipeline of the proposed predictive control and optimization framework. Decisions are driven by predicted information; the planned action is applied to the real system and to the predictive model. Ex-post assessment compares real and predicted responses and triggers re-tuning under performance degradation.

The second section is the control and optimization framework, responsible for translating predicted information into implementable operational decisions for the management of Energy Community resources. Conceived as an architectural decision layer rather than as a single algorithmic solution, it is intentionally designed to be adaptable to different control and optimization paradigms, including model predictive control, data-driven control, model-based control, linear optimal control, as well as centralized and distributed optimization strategies. This design choice reflects the fact that the paper proposes a general operational architecture, capable of accommodating different decision-making schemes depending on the characteristics of the community, the available system knowledge, and the implementation requirements. Within this layer, predictive control is formulated so that decisions are driven by the information available about the system and its expected evolution over time. Since Energy Communities operate in a highly dynamic environment, where not only renewable generation but also heterogeneous consumption patterns, user behavior, and seasonal variations strongly influence operation, forecast information becomes a key input to the decision-making process. In this sense, forecasts of load demand, renewable generation, and other relevant system dynamics are incorporated to support the computation of control actions and energy allocation decisions over a given horizon. The framework therefore enables the coordination of flexibility resources and allocation strategies under technical and regulatory constraints, while pursuing one or multiple performance objectives that may be combined through weighted or prioritized criteria. Importantly, this layer is not restricted to a specific control formulation, instead, it provides a structured and extensible decision engine that supports the interaction between prediction, control, and optimization in a unified manner.

The third section is the performance and evaluation stage, which closes the loop by assessing how well the implemented operation aligns with the community objectives and the expectations generated by the predictive model. This stage requires the definition of performance metrics that reflect the heterogeneous priorities of the agents involved, including technical, economic, and fairness-related dimensions, and that can meaningfully characterize community behavior over time. Beyond reporting, evaluation also serves an operational purpose: by comparing realized outcomes with predicted responses, it enables the detection of performance degradation, constraint stress, or fairness deviations. These signals provide a principled basis for re-tuning the predictive model and, when appropriate, adapting decision parameters, thereby sustaining reliable and goal-aligned operation in dynamic conditions.

4.1 Energy Communities Based on Collective Self-consumption

In collective self-consumption (CSC) schemes, the energy jointly produced by the community is operationalized through allocation coefficients that specify, at each time step, how much of the locally generated energy is credited to each participant. In its simplest form, the individualized net energy assigned to a given member n at time t is expressed as:

$$\mathrm{INE_n(t)} = \beta_\mathrm{n}(\mathrm{t}) \cdot \mathrm{TEG(t)} \tag{1}$$

Where TEG(t) denotes the total energy generated within the community during the settlement interval and βn(t) takes values between [0, 1] and is the allocation coefficient associated with that member. This formulation turns CSC into a quantifiable and verifiable mechanism because the energy shares are explicitly defined, enabling settlement and billing based on metered generation and consumption [19].

For communities with multiple generators (prosumers), the allocation is conveniently described in matrix form. Let P be the number of prosumers and N the total number of members. The allocation matrix $B(t)P \times N$ is filled with allocation coefficients, which define the fraction of prosumer p's generated energy assigned to member n. The conservation condition is written as:

$$B(t) \cdot 1_N = 1_P \tag{2}$$

Meaning that each prosumer's generated energy is fully distributed across the N members (each row sums to one), preventing over- or under-allocation. In practice, the energy credited to each member is obtained by combining (i) the measured generation of each prosumer during the interval and (ii) the corresponding row of $\mathbf{B}(t)_{P \times N}$ the total credited energy for a member can be aggregated across all prosumers.

This coefficient-based mechanism is precisely what makes CSC implementable across different European contexts, including Spain, Portugal, Italy, and France, because it provides a regulatory- and market-compatible interface between the physical community and the settlement process. While each country may differ in administrative procedures, tariffs, and incentive structures, the operational logic remains consistent: coefficients (often pre-registered and possibly updated over time, depending on what is permitted) define how locally generated energy is virtually attributed to each participant for billing and incentive calculations. As a result, CSC can be implemented in a harmonized way across these countries by ensuring (i) compliant definition of $\mathbf{B}(t)$, (ii) time-synchronized metering, and (iii) settlement rules that map the allocated energy shares into the participants' energy balances and economic outcomes.

Overall, the coefficient-based formulation provides a transparent and verifiable mechanism to implement collective self-consumption by translating local generation into individualized energy entitlements under explicit conservation constraints. However, the choice of $\mathbf{B}(t)$ and its potential time variation define a decision space that can be exploited to improve technical, economic, and fairness-related performance under uncertainty and regulatory constraints. For this reason, the operational behavior of CSC-based Energy Communities and candidate control and optimization strategies are examined in the next section.

5 Expected Outcomes

This section outlines the expected outcomes by first establishing the nominal operation of a CSC-based Energy Community under a representative baseline allocation scheme. Building on this reference case, it proposes control and optimization directions to improve operation, including dynamic allocation policies, coordination of flexibility resources such as storage, and predictive decision-making under uncertainty. The discussion is structured around measurable impacts on performance, feasibility, and fairness objectives.

5.1 Energy Community Baseline Case

A representative Energy Community is considered under the Spanish CSC scheme to illustrate how allocation coefficients operationalize energy sharing among participants, this Energy Community is located in Barcelona, Spain and its currently operating under the static allocation coefficients strategy and the Spanish regulatory framework. In this setting, locally generated electricity is virtually distributed across community members through predefined coefficients, which determine each participant's share of the total generated energy at every settlement interval. This formulation provides a clear and auditable mechanism for implementation, since it enables the computation of individualized net energy balances and supports regulatory verification of the community operation.

At the same time, this example highlights key limitations of CSC operation when allocation coefficients are fixed or designed independently of actual time-varying conditions, such as demand variability, renewable intermittency, and the presence of flexibility resources. In particular, static coefficients may lead to suboptimal self-consumption, reduced economic performance, and outcomes that can be perceived as unfair under changing operating regimes. These limitations motivate potential improvements through predictive and optimization-based strategies, including dynamic coefficient design, coordinated use of flexibility, and objective formulations that explicitly incorporate both performance and fairness requirements while remaining compatible with regulatory constraints.

Table 1. Energy allocation coefficients in the baseline real energy community: two prosumers allocate energy based on the percentage assigned to each member.

Members	Prosumer 1 [%]	Prosumer 2 [%]
Prosumer 1	30	0.00
Prosumer 2	0.00	98.78
Consumer 1	48.17	0.00
Consumer 2	0.00	1.22
Consumer 3	21.83	0.00

The baseline allocation pattern, presented in Table 1, implies a highly constrained internal routing of photovoltaic (PV) energy, which effectively limits how much locally generated electricity can be absorbed by the community at each hour. In practice, this means that even if some members have available demand during high-generation periods, the community may still be unable to redirect energy toward them if the pre-defined coefficients do not follow the instantaneous consumption profile. As a result, the allocation mechanism behaves more like a static entitlement rule than an operational lever, and the community's ability to increase collective self-consumption is structurally constrained by design rather than by physical scarcity.

This limitation is clearly reflected in the time-series plots (see Fig. 2). Around midday, when PV output is highest, the allocated energy exceeds the contemporaneous demand that can be effectively matched within the CSC settlement, leading to a pronounced negative balance and a large surplus block in the lower panel. In other words, a significant share of renewable production is exported or spilled rather than utilized locally, which directly depresses self-consumption and reduces the potential economic and environmental benefits of the community. The figure therefore motivates the need for operational improvements such as time-varying (dynamic) allocation policies, the coordinated use of flexibility resources (e.g., storage or controllable loads), or predictive scheduling strategies that can anticipate demand-generation mismatches and reduce systematic surplus during peak PV hours.

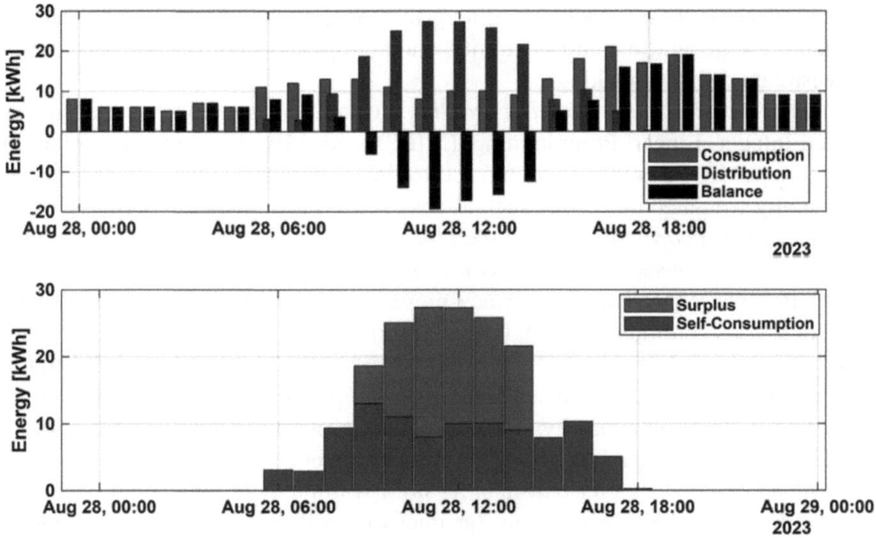

Fig. 2. Real hourly CSC operation in the baseline Energy Community in a summer day, showing consumption, allocated energy, balance, and the split between self-consumption and surplus.

Previous studies such as [21, 22] have not only formalized many of the regulatory, technical, and administrative limitations associated with implementing Energy Communities under the CSC scheme but have also reported evidence that these constraints do not preclude meaningful operational improvements. In particular, the findings indicate that coupling predictive modelling and optimization-based decision making can significantly enhance community performance, for example by reducing surplus generation, increasing local self-consumption, and lowering dependence on external grid imports. These results motivate the adoption of predictive and optimization strategies as practical levers to move beyond static CSC operation and towards smarter, more efficient, and better-aligned community energy management, thereby concluding this subsection.

5.2 Planned Work

In this subsection, the planned work is structured to progressively move from predictive modelling to implementable decision-making architectures, while ensuring compatibility with CSC operation and the socio-technical requirements of Energy Communities. The roadmap starts by consolidating a predictive dynamics layer capable of representing demand, generation, and flexibility behavior at community level, and then builds successive control and optimization strategies that can be evaluated under realistic techno-economic constraints, fairness objectives, and regulatory settlement rules. The final goal is to deliver a scalable and deployable methodology, validated in simulation and supported by implementation-oriented considerations. Planned work includes the following interconnected formulations:

1. *Purely data-driven predictive modelling*: develop formulations that rely exclusively on neural networks or machine learning to model community behavior, including demand, PV generation, and flexibility availability, and to quantify uncertainty for downstream decision-making.
2. *Centralized optimization-based scheduling*: formulate operational management as Mixed-Integer Linear Programming (MILP) and Mixed-Integer Quadratic Programming (MIQP) problems to enforce technical and regulatory constraints while optimizing weighted objectives such as cost, self-consumption and fairness.
3. *Decentralized coordination and scalability*: design distributed decision-making schemes using consensus-based methods such as Alternating Direction Method of Multipliers (ADMM), enabling privacy-preserving operation and scalability to larger, heterogeneous communities with limited information sharing.
4. *Predictive control architectures*: develop Model Predictive Control (MPC) and Economic MPC formulations, including pre-implementation governance policies that specify decision authority, update frequency, permissible ranges for allocation coefficients, and stakeholder-approved fairness targets.
5. *Embedded deployment and real-time feasibility*: implement lightweight versions of the predictive and decision layers on microcontrollers or edge devices, addressing computational limits, communication constraints, noise measurement, and safe constraint handling for real-time community operation. Together, these activities define a coherent path from modelling to optimization, from centralized to decentralized implementations, and from simulation-ready strategies to deployment-oriented solutions aligned with governance and regulatory constraints.

6 Conclusions and Future Work

This paper presented a predictive perspective for operating Energy Communities by coupling data-driven prediction models with control and optimization strategies. The central idea is to use predictive models as a practical representation of community-level system evolution, and to exploit the information they provide, including uncertainty, to inform operational decision-making. The proposed approach is intentionally strategy-agnostic, meaning it is not limited to a specific control structure or optimization technique, but instead provides a general methodological basis that can be instantiated according to the technical configuration, regulatory setting, and governance objectives of a given community. In this way, it supports the formulation of operational schemes that align techno-economic constraints with community goals such as collective self-consumption, economic performance, and fairness or sustainability-oriented outcomes.

Future work will improve methodological rigor and deployment readiness by explicitly handling uncertainty through robust and scenario-based formulations and by quantifying the impact of forecast errors on operational outcomes. Scalability will be addressed via distributed, privacy-preserving implementations for larger and more heterogeneous communities, complemented by human-in-the-loop mechanisms to integrate stakeholder preferences and fairness trade-offs. Finally, the framework will be validated through additional case studies and pilot-oriented sensitivity analyses across tariffs, regulatory settings, and asset configurations to support transferable decision-support tools for smart and fair Energy Community operation.

Acknowledgments. This work has received support from the Spanish Government under MICINN project PID2024-156522OB-C33 and projects OPEN4CEC PCI2023-145975-2 and SMART-LEM PCI2023-145977-2 funded by MCIU/AEI/10.13039/501100011033 and co-funded by European Union.

References

1. Jagoda, S.U.M., Hewage, K., Kotagodahetti, R., Sadiq, R.: Transition to net-zero energy communities: investigating techno-financial feasibility and social acceptance. Build. Environ. **290**, 114184 (2026). https://doi.org/10.1016/j.buildenv.2025.114184
2. Boccard, N., Goetz, R.: Sharing rules and the promotion of energy communities: a normative comparative analysis. Energy. **344**, 140068 (2026). https://doi.org/10.1016/j.energy.2026.140068
3. De Blasis, R., Pacelli, G., Vergine, S.: Investment valuation of photovoltaic and energy storage systems for diverse energy communities: a real option approach. Appl. Energy. **404**, 127185 (2025). https://doi.org/10.1016/j.apenergy.2025.127185
4. Barone, G., Vardopoulos, I., Vassiliades, C.: Advancements and challenges in modelling renewable energy solutions for sustainable (and smart) buildings and communities. Energy Rep. **14**, 3719–3724 (2025). https://doi.org/10.1016/j.egyr.2025.11.001
5. Mendes, N., Mendes, J., Mohammadi, J., Moura, P.: Federated learning framework for prediction of net energy demand in transactive energy communities. Sustainable Energy Grids Networks. **40**, 101522 (2024). https://doi.org/10.1016/j.segan.2024.101522
6. Patrício, J.T., Lopes, T., Rocha, A., Martins, J., Lopes, R.A.: Development and real-world deployment of a multi-agent system to support the operation of renewable energy communities. Energy Rep. **15**, 108967 (2026). https://doi.org/10.1016/j.egyr.2025.108967
7. Ghanavati, F., Osório, G.J., Matias, J.C.O., Catalão, J.P.S.: Transactive data-driven and consumer-centric home energy management system for local energy communities in Portugal. Sustain. Cities Soc. **131**, 106698 (2025). https://doi.org/10.1016/j.scs.2025.106698
8. Bu, Y., et al.: Hybrid data-driven operation method for demand response of community integrated energy systems utilizing virtual and physical energy storage. Appl. Energy. **366**, 123295 (2024). https://doi.org/10.1016/j.apenergy.2024.123295
9. Boumaiza, A., Maher, K.: An adaptive home energy management system for prosumers in peer-to-peer trading networks with machine learning optimization. Energ. Strat. Rev. **60**, 101749 (2025). https://doi.org/10.1016/j.esr.2025.101749
10. Matos, M., et al.: A machine learning-based electricity consumption forecast and management system for renewable energy communities. Energies. **17**, 630 (2024). https://doi.org/10.3390/en17030630
11. Guiducci, L., Palma, G., Stentati, M., Rizzo, A., Paoletti, S.: A reinforcement learning approach to the management of renewable energy communities. In: 2023 11th Mediterranean Conference on Embedded Computing (MECO), pp. 1–8 (2023). https://doi.org/10.1109/meco58584.2023.10154979

12. Salazar-Hamze, F.J., Guerrero-Lemus, R.: Development and evaluation of an optimization model for enhancing energy communities sharing coefficients in Spain. Energ. Buildings. **343**, 115951 (2025). https://doi.org/10.1016/j.enbuild.2025.115951
13. Mena, A.J.G., Medina, V.F.N., Bouakkaz, A., Haddad, S.: Analysis and optimisation of collective self-consumption in residential buildings in Spain. Energ. Buildings. **283**, 112812 (2023). https://doi.org/10.1016/j.enbuild.2023.112812
14. Alabi, T.M., Lu, L., Yang, Z.: Real-time automatic control of multi-energy system for smart district community: a coupling ensemble prediction model and safe deep reinforcement learning. Energy. **304**, 132209 (2024). https://doi.org/10.1016/j.energy.2024.132209
15. Basaran, K., et al.: A comprehensive survey of distributed optimization methods and technological enablers for sustainable energy communities. Energy. **344**, 139983 (2026). https://doi.org/10.1016/j.energy.2026.139983
16. Jnr, B.A.: Distributed energy prosumer communities and the application of emerging technologies: a systematic literature review. Sustainable Futures. **9**, 100794 (2025). https://doi.org/10.1016/j.sftr.2025.100794
17. Concetti, C.: Renewable energy communities assembling energy governance. Energy Res. Soc. Sci. **126**, 104085 (2025). https://doi.org/10.1016/j.erss.2025.104085
18. Jans, L., et al.: How bottom-up and top-down governance of community energy initiatives affects citizens' perceptions, acceptability, and willingness to join. Energy Policy. **195**, 114389 (2024). https://doi.org/10.1016/j.enpol.2024.114389
19. Morato, M.M., Felix, M.S.: Data science and model predictive control: a survey of recent advances on data-driven MPC algorithms. J. Process Control. **144**, 103327 (2024). https://doi.org/10.1016/j.jprocont.2024.103327
20. Camacho, E.F., Bordons, C., Maestre, J.M.: Model Predictive Control. (2026). https://doi.org/10.1007/978-3-031-87596-0
21. Madrigal, S., Vicario, J.L., Morell, A., Vilanova, R.: Enhancement review of the collective self-consumption based energy communities: insights from a Spain-based case. In: 2025 IEEE 30th International Conference on Emerging Technologies and Factory Automation (ETFA), pp. 1–8 (2025). https://doi.org/10.1109/etfa65518.2025.11205679
22. Madrigal, S., Gallinad, R., Vicario, J.L., Morell, A., Vilanova, R.: Improving energy distribution in collective self-consumption via XGBoost-based allocation coefficients prediction. Appl. Energy. **409**, 127469 (2026). https://doi.org/10.1016/j.apenergy.2026.127469

Intelligent Energy Systems

Study of a DC DC Buck Converter as a Class D Amplifier

José Francisco Luís[1,2](✉) and Nuno Paulino[1]

[1] Nova University of Lisbon, School of Science and Technology, UNINOVA– CTS and LASI Lisbon, Caparica, Portugal
jfr.luis@campus.fct.unl.pt, nuno.f.paulino@fct.unl.pt
[2] Faculty of Engineering and Technologies, University of Namibe, Namibe, Moçâmedes, Angola

Abstract. Technological innovation has always aimed to make human life easier, more dynamic, more assertive, and socially easier, breaking the challenges imposed on it by society. This evolution has been integrated into various aspects of technological life, with portable devices powered by batteries standing out. DC-DC converters are often incorporated into these devices, both for their power supply and for applications in audio power amplifiers, smartphones, laptops, Bluetooth headsets, digital cameras, and remote controls, among others. However, designing high-efficiency class D amplifiers is not an easy task, due to the complexity of their design. Parameters such as energy efficiency, noise rejection, SINAD, and total harmonic distortion (THD) are critical to the good performance of high-performance amplifiers. This article presents the study of a DC-DC buck converter used as a Class D amplifier, highlighting key aspects such as the energy efficiency of the converter, the total harmonic distortion plus noise (THD + N), and the power supply noise rejection (PSRR).

Keywords: DC-DC Converter · Class D amplifier · Technological Innovation · Battery-powered Devices

1 Introduction

High-performance DC–DC converters, characterized by high power density, high efficiency, and a high voltage conversion ratio (VCR), are indispensable in battery-powered electronics due to the simultaneous requirements of maximizing power utilization, minimizing thermal dissipation, and providing adequate supply voltage margins [1, 2]. The buck converter is a type of DC-DC power converter designed to reduce a higher direct current input voltage to a lower output voltage. This down-conversion facilitates the design of compact and power-efficient electronic systems, contributing to extended battery life in portable applications. High-performance integrated converters depend on both the figure of merit (FoM) of active components and the quality factor of passives, especially the inductor [3]. The audio amplifier market is predominantly composed of Class

Published by Springer Nature Switzerland AG 2027
L. M. Camarinha-Matos and F. Ferrada (Eds.): DoCEIS 2026, IFIP AICT 790, pp. 213–225, 2027.
https://doi.org/10.1007/978-3-032-28939-1_16

AB and Class D amplifiers [4]. To optimize the trade-off among linearity, efficiency, PSRR, and electromagnetic interference (EMI), the adoption of an adaptive supply voltage in Class AB amplifiers is highly advantageous [5]. Nevertheless, these amplifiers exhibit low efficiency, particularly when amplifying low-amplitude signals [6]. Class-D amplifiers are commonly used in high-power, high-efficiency electronic systems [7].

Class D, also referred to as a switched-mode amplifier, derives its name from the non-continuous operation of its output transistors. Instead of working in the linear region, transistors act as switches, alternately connecting the load to $+V_{DD}$ or $-V_{DD}$. The input signal is continuously compared to a high-frequency reference, typically well above the maximum audio frequency (20 kHz), resulting in a PWM waveform. This PWM signal, proportional in width to the instantaneous input amplitude, is applied to the power stage and subsequently passed through a low-pass filter to reconstruct the original audio waveform. Class D amplifiers are known for their high efficiency. Ideally, they can achieve up to 100% efficiency, as power loss is minimized when the transistors act only as switches [8]. Despite the inherent efficiency of Class D, further optimizations are possible. This includes reducing conduction and switching losses in transistors, minimizing hysteresis losses in inductors and capacitors, mitigating eddy current losses in the magnetic cores of output filters, and enhancing fidelity [8, 9]. Class D amplifiers are often preferred for high-quality domestic audio applications, particularly in scenarios involving separate speakers with unknown impedance characteristics [10].

This paper presents the study of a DC-DC buck converter as a Class D amplifier, with high efficiency, using a switching frequency of 5 MHz, with a DPWM-PI controller, with an input voltage of 1.2 V and an average output voltage of 601 mV, with a resistive load of 16 Ω, capable of delivering a maximum output power of up to 7.6 mW. However, when derived from DC-DC conversion topologies, such as a buck converter operating according to Class D principles, these systems should be analyzed fundamentally as power converters, in which the input signal acts as a modulation reference and not as a primary amplification variable. This approach allows us to simultaneously exploit the typical energy efficiency of switched converters and the ability to reconstruct analog signals at the load, through PWM modulation and passive filtering techniques. This paper is organized as follows: Sect. 2 presents the context of Audio Power Amplifiers for Technological Innovation to Tackle Societal Challenges; Sect. 3 provides a detailed description of the proposed circuit architecture; Sect. 4 presents the simulation results and the adopted methodology; finally, Sect. 5 presents the conclusions.

2 Audio Power Amplifiers for Technological Innovation to Tackle Societal Challenges

In battery-powered electronic devices with limited capacity, energy efficiency is a critical requirement for the autonomy, reliability, and sustainability of systems [11–13]. This approach is particularly important for battery-powered devices, which operate with limited energy capacity. Efficient audio processing is crucial in voice control, environmental monitoring, and human-machine interaction applications.

Audio power amplifiers have evolved significantly to meet the increasing demands for energy efficiency and sound quality in battery-powered devices, reducing power dissipation [4, 14]. These improvements are essential for tackling societal challenges requiring real-time signal processing and optimized energy management. Efficient amplifiers enhance performance in mobile and autonomous applications, such as IoT devices, drones, and communication systems. The continuous innovation and development of electronic components and architectures for greater efficiency, increased power density, and enhanced operational robustness constitute a direct contribution to improving the energy performance of modern devices, promoting more sustainable technological solutions that facilitate the quality of human life.

3 Architecture and Circuit Description

Figure 1 shows the classic inductor-based DC-DC converter topology, consisting of two synchronous buck MOSFETs; these devices operate predominantly in on or off states, minimizing dissipation losses and maximizing energy efficiency [8, 15].

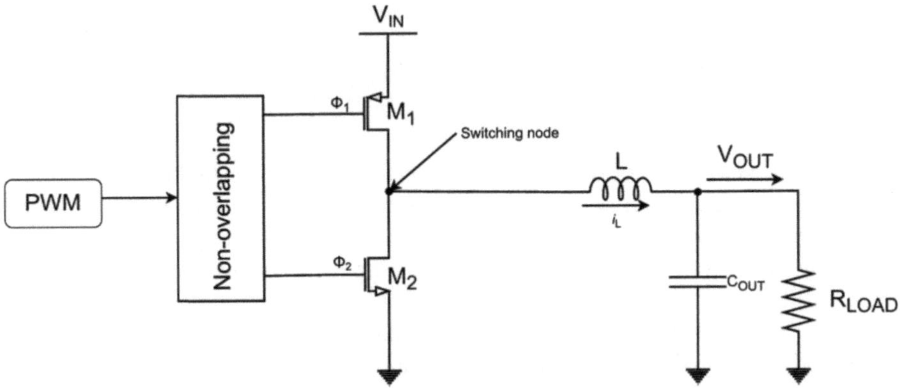

Fig. 1. DC-DC converter operates as Class D amplifier.

Its operation is based on the complementary control of the transistors M_1 *and* M_2 through a control system that acts as a switching modulator. This modulator can be implemented using conventional PWM techniques [16, 17] or Sigma-Delta modulators [18], among others, being responsible for generating a signal whose cyclic ratio or pulse density is proportional to the input signal. The low-pass filter consisting of the L inductor and the C_{out} capacitor is responsible for removing the high-frequency components associated with the switching, allowing the reconstruction of the analog signal at the V_{out} output that feeds the resistive load [19]; Obtaining an approximately linear relationship between the output voltage and the input signal, ideally expressed by $V_{out} = k.V_{in}$ depends critically on the feedback of the system [17, 20]. In practice, this behavior is influenced by suboptimal factors, such as switching losses, parasitic resistances, PWM modulator delays, LC filter limitations, and supply voltage variations, making feedback an essential element to ensure stability, linearity, and low distortion. These control techniques, namely the use of negative feedback, become particularly important in Class D amplifiers, as they allow us to mitigate the effects of distortion, which tend to be pronounced in these topologies when compared to traditional linear amplifiers.

3.1 Output LC Filter with Inductor DCR

There is a second-order low-pass network, constituted by the L-inductor series with the output path and by the Cout output capacitor connected in parallel with the R_{load} load. To account for nonlinearities, the inductor is modeled using a parasitic series resistance, corresponding to its DCR. According to this model, the small signal transfer function between the voltage at the switching node and the V_{out} output voltage is given by:

$$H(s) = \frac{V_{out}(s)}{V_{in}(s)}$$

$$H(s) = \frac{R_{load}}{\left[R_{load} \cdot C_{out} \cdot L \cdot s^2 + (\, L + R_{load} \cdot C_{out} \cdot R_L \,) \cdot s + (R_{load} + R_L)\right]} \quad (1)$$

The natural angular frequency and quality factor of the filter are given by:

$$\omega^0 = \sqrt{\left[\frac{R_{load} + R_L}{R_{load} \cdot C_{out} \cdot L}\right]};\ Q = \frac{\omega^0 R_{load} \cdot C_{out} \cdot L}{L + R_{load} \cdot C_{out} \cdot R_L};\ f_0 = \frac{\omega^0}{2\pi} \quad (2)$$

The resonance frequency depends directly on the combination of the values of inductance, capacitance, and equivalent resistance to the output, while the quality factor reflects the damping effect introduced by the series resistance of the inductor. The presence of DCR reduces the system's quality factor, attenuating the resonance peak and leading to a more stable, physically realistic dynamic response.

Table 1 presents the electrical and dynamic parameters of the LC filter, considered in this study. Nominal values of the load resistance, inductance, and DC resistance of the inductor, as well as the output capacitance, are indicated. The table also includes the derived dynamic quantities, namely the natural angular frequency, the resonance frequency, the quality factor, and the damping ratio, allowing the characterization of the dynamic and transient behavior of the second-order low-pass filter.

Table 1. Electrical and dynamic parameters of the output LC filter.

Parameter	Value	Unit
Load Resistance	16	Ω
Inductance *(L)*	100	µH
Inductor DCR *(RL)*	160	mΩ
Output Capacitance	1	uF
Natural angular frequency *(ω0)*	316 227	rad/s
Resonant Frequency	50.3	kHz

(continued)

Table 1. (*continued*)

Parameter	Value	Unit
Quality factor (Q)	0,506	–
Damping ratio $\left(\zeta = \frac{1}{2Q}\right)$	0.99	–
Product LC	1.00×10^{-10}	H F
Product $\frac{L}{R_{LOAD}}$	6.25×10^{-6}	s

3.2 PWM Control and Modulation Strategy

Figure 2 shows the block diagram of the discrete-time control strategy, including sampling and feedback quantization, PID controller, command normalization and saturation, and the ramp-based PWM comparator.

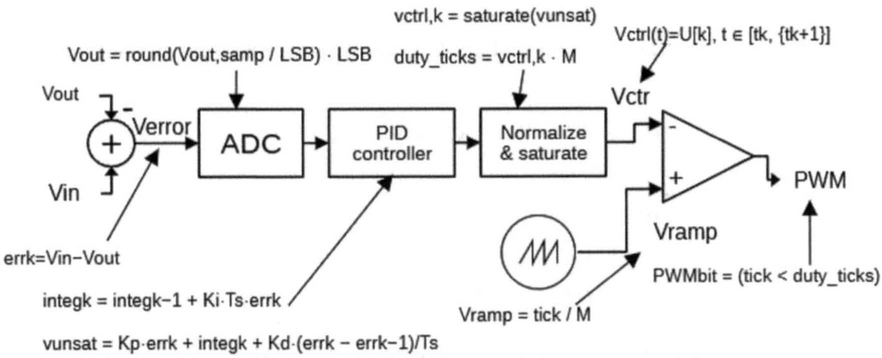

Fig. 2. Block diagram of the discrete control loop and the voltage-mode PWM modulator.

The PWM modulator is implemented entirely in the discrete domain using a digital counter operating at a clock frequency M times larger than the switching frequency. At each switching period, the duty cycle command V_{ctrl} generated by the discrete-time PID controller is mapped to an integer number of high-level counter clock ticks. A digital counter increments at the internal clock frequency Fs2, and the PWM output is asserted while the counter value remains below the command number of duty ticks. The resulting signal is defined by:

$$PWM[n] = \backslash cases(\ V_H, tick[n] < duty_{ticks};\ V_L, otherwise\ ) \quad (3)$$

This comparison results in a duty cycle directly proportional to the V_{ctrl} value. Finite times of rise and fall of the PWM signal are considered to avoid ideal discontinuities and to ensure numerical stability in the simulations.

The control loop exhibits intrinsically sampled behavior. The output voltage is sampled once per switching period and quantized by an N-bit analog-to-digital converter (ADC), resulting in a discrete feedback signal.

The quantization grid of the ADC is defined by:

$$L = 2^N - 1, \mathrm{LSB} = \frac{V_{\mathrm{adc,ref}}}{2^N} \tag{4}$$

Quantization can be preceded by the optional addition of a uniform dither signal to reduce deterministic artifacts associated with quantization:

$$v_{fb}^{\mathrm{samp}}[k] = v_{fb}(t_k) + n_k, n_k \sim \mathcal{U}(-d\ \mathrm{LSB}, +d\ \mathrm{LSB}) \tag{5}$$

The discrete error is calculated as the difference between the input voltage and the feedback voltage quantified by the ideal ADC, being given by:

$$err[k] = v_{\mathrm{in}}(t_k) - v_{out}^q[k] \tag{6}$$

While the unsaturated command is given by:

$$u_{raw}[k] = Kp * err[k] + I[k-1] + Kd \cdot \frac{err[k] - err[k-1]}{T_{sw}} \tag{7}$$

Anti-windup, integrate *I[k]* only when the saturation is not active in the direction of the error.

$$\begin{aligned} &I[k] = I[k-1] + Ki \cdot Ts \cdot err[k] \\ &if\ NOT\Big((u_{raw}[k] > u_{max} AND\ err[k] > 0) \\ &OR \\ &(u_{raw}[k] < u_{min} AND\ err[k] < 0)\Big) \\ &I[k] = I[k-1] otherwise \end{aligned} \tag{8}$$

In ways that respect the physical limits of the modulator. The control signal is limited to the permissible range:

$$u[k] = \mathrm{sat}_{[u_{\min}, u_{\max}]}(u_{\mathrm{raw}}[k]) \tag{9}$$

To avoid the integrator windup phenomenon, an anti-windup mechanism by saturation is implemented, in which the activation of the integral term is inhibited whenever the control signal is saturated, and further error growth is prevented. Between consecutive sampling instants, the value of the command is kept constant, assuming a zero-order hold behavior.

$$V_{\mathrm{ctrl}}(t) = u[k], t \in \big[t_k, t_{k+1}) u[k] = \mathrm{sat}_{[u_{\min}, u_{\max}]}(u_{\mathrm{raw}}[k]) \tag{10}$$

The PWM signal is further processed by a non-overlapping circuit (included in Fig. 1), which generates complementary actuation signals for the high-side and low-side switch gates. The introduction of controlled dead time prevents simultaneous driving of switches in the synchronous buck converter, mitigating shoot-through currents.

4 Simulation Setup and Methodology

The circuit presented in this paper was implemented in TSMC's 65 nm CMOS technology, with the controller implemented in Verilog, and simulated in Cadence. Simulations were performed for a nominal voltage of 1.2 V and a fixed resistive load of 16 Ω. The converter operates at a switching frequency of 5 MHz. Performance metrics considered include output voltage regulation for different input signals, specifically sine wave, square wave, real signal, transient response, and power conversion efficiency, considering transistor conduction, switching, and drive losses.

Figure 3 shows the temporal response of the output voltage of the closed-loop converter to a square wave input signal. The system provides correct tracking of the input signal, with negligible errors in the steady state. In each transition, an overshoot is observed, characteristic of an underdamped response associated with the dynamics of the second order of the LC filter and the compensation of the controller. However, the system has a short settling time and limited residual oscillation.

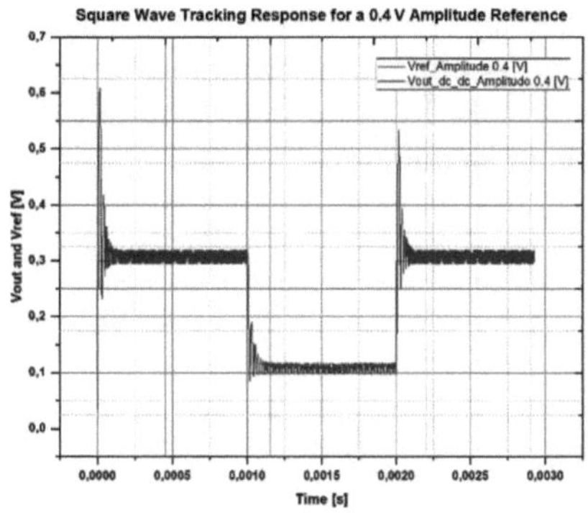

Fig. 3. Output voltage for a square wave input signal

Figure 4 shows the behavior of the converter's output voltage when excited by a sinusoidal input voltage of 0.3 V to 0.4 V in Fig. 4(a), and the spectrum of Vout from 0 kHz to 20 kHz in Fig. 4(b). The overlap between the output voltage Vout and the input voltage Vin is observed, allowing the direct evaluation of the system's tracking capacity. It is verified that, after a short initial transient state, the converter enters a steady state, presenting an adequate tracking of the input throughout the entire signal period. Despite the presence of ripple, inherent to the operation of the converter, the output voltage correctly follows the temporal variation of the input, evidencing the reduced tracking error and stable behavior.

Figure 4(b) shows the frequency spectrum (FFT) of the converter's output voltage. It is observed that, at the frequency of 20 kHz, the spectral level is approximately − 108.8 dB, showing low levels of noise and distortion in this frequency band.

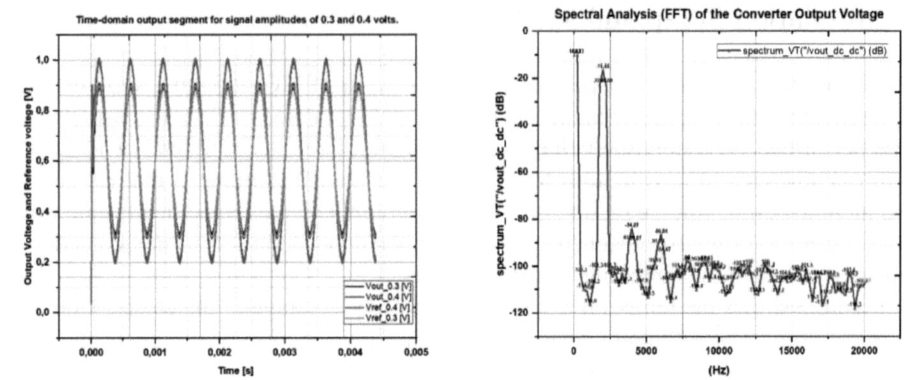

(a) (b)

Fig. 4. Tracking and tracing the output voltage relative to a sinusoidal (a) and Spectrum V_{out} at 20 kHz (b).

Figure 5 shows the converter's response to an actual audio signal. The output voltage correctly follows the closed-loop input, showing only a limited ripple associated with the switching and dynamics of the LC filter, demonstrating that the system can track the entire input signal throughout its duration.

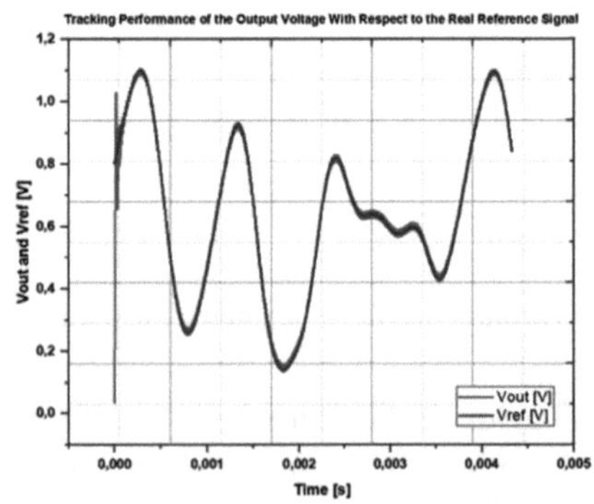

Fig. 5. Tracking Performance of the Output Voltage with Respect to a Real Reference Signal.

Figure 6 presents and relates the output power of the converter as a function of the amplitude of the input signal. The output power increases monotonically with amplitude, reaching about 7.6 mW for 0.5 V. In contrast, the joint analysis reveals a trade-off between power delivered to the load and spectral quality, with intermediate input amplitudes providing the optimal balance.

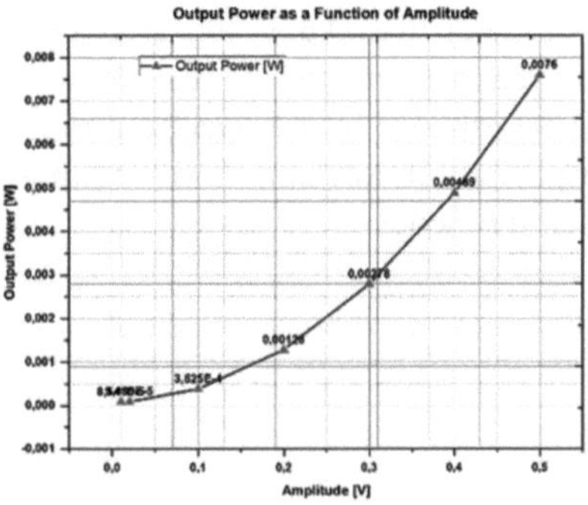

Fig. 6. Output Power as a function of Amplitude

Figure 7 shows the signal-to-noise and distortion ratio (SINAD) as a function of the amplitude of the input sine signal for different ADC resolutions used in the control system, with M fixed at 20 bits, Fig. 7(a), and Impact of DPWM Resolution (M) on SINAD as a Function of Input Amplitude, Fig. 7(b). It is verified that, in a low amplitude regime, SINAD is dominated by system noise that remains approximately constant, increasing rapidly with the increase of the signal amplitude, reflecting the improvement of the signal-to-noise ratio and the reduction of the relative impact of quantization effects. Figure 7 shows that for intermediate amplitudes, approximately in the range of 0.1 V to 0.3 V, the system operates close to its optimum regime, reaching maximum SINAD values in the range of 65–66 dB, with the observed peak around 0.2 V. In this regime, the differences between digital resolutions become less pronounced, indicating that performance is limited by analog factors and not by quantization. For higher amplitudes, a progressive degradation of SINAD is observed, associated with the entry of the system into a high signal regime, where phenomena such as saturation of the actuators, compression of the gain, and nonlinearities of the power stage start to dominate the overall performance.

The comparison between resolutions shows that a higher number of ADC bits significantly improves SINAD in Fig. 7(a), in the low-amplitude regime, where quantization error and digital noise are secondary to the analog limitations of the system. This behavior highlights the compromise between digital resolution and operational regime, allowing the identification of the minimum resolution necessary to ensure adequate performance without unnecessary increase in complexity, energy consumption, and computational cost of the controller.

Figure 7(b) shows the impact of the DPWM resolution, parameterized by $M = \text{round}$ (Fs2/Fsw), on SINAD as a function of the amplitude of the input signal, for $M = 20, 40,$ 64, and 100. For amplitudes below 0.1 V, a more pronounced degradation of SINAD with $M = 20$ is observed, indicating that in this regime, the quantization of the duty-cycle is a limiting factor. The increase of M to 40 and 64 improves the performance in this region, while $M = 100$ yields only marginal improvements. In the intermediate range of amplitudes (0.1–0.3 V), all resolutions converge to high SINAD values ($\approx$ 64–66 dB), with differences of less than 1 dB, evidencing a regime dominated by other sources of noise and distortion, such as the quantization of the ADC and the nonlinearities of the system, for amplitudes greater than 0.3 V, the SINAD decreases for all M values, with little significant differences between the curves. These results show that M = 20 is sufficient to achieve high performance in the operating range of interest, while higher values of M are relevant especially in low amplitude regimes, at the expense of greater complexity and higher clock frequency.

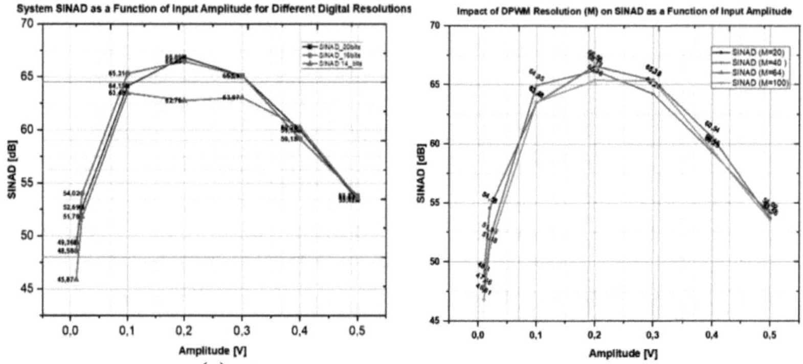

(a) (b)

Fig. 7. SINAD versus signal amplitude for different PID controller resolutions (14, 16, and 20 bits and M = 20 bits (a) and Impact of DPWM Resolution (M) on SINAD as a Function of Input Amplitude (b).

Figure 8 shows the variation of total harmonic distortion (THD) as a function of output power, expressed as a percentage in Fig. 8(a) and in decibels in Fig. 8(b), for different ADC resolutions (14, 16, and 20 bits) used in the controller. For lower output power levels, a significant increase in THD is observed, which is predominantly attributed to the quantization effects of the ADC, the high relative noise, and the low accuracy of the error signal in the control loop, phenomena that become dominant when the amplitude of the signal is small. As the output power increases, the signal-to-noise ratio improves, and the relative quantization effect decreases, leading to a progressive reduction of the THD until it reaches a minimum value of $\approx$ 0.03–0.05%, corresponding to about –70.9 dB. For higher power levels, the THD increases again, reflecting the introduction of nonlinearity associated with saturation of the actuators, power stage limitations, and the dynamics of the controller in a high-signal regime.

Comparing the different resolutions, it is verified that ADCs of higher bit count allow a consistent reduction of THD throughout the entire power range, due to the lower quantization granularity. Therefore, considering the compromise between implementation complexity, computational cost, and dynamic performance of the feedback loop, we opted for the use of a 16-bit ADC in this study. This resolution proved to be sufficient to maintain the THD ≈ -70.9 dB as shown in Fig. 8(b), constituting an adequate compromise between performance and system complexity.

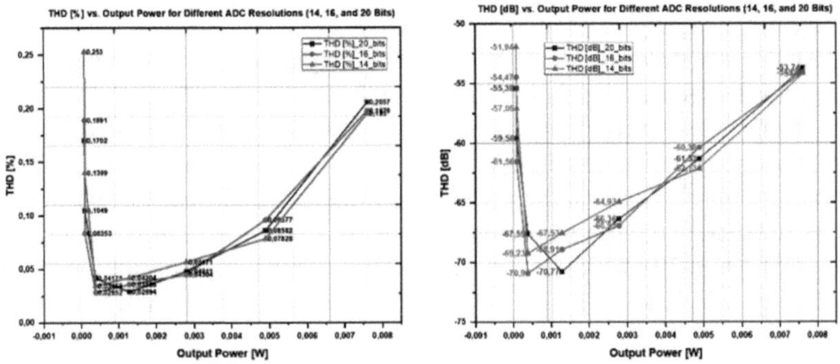

(a) (b)

Fig. 8. Total Harmonic Distortion as a function of output power.

Figure 9 shows the efficiency graphs for different signal amplitudes. Despite the inherent difficulty in establishing a simultaneous compromise between efficiency, SINAD, and THD, the circuit demonstrates high power transfer capacity. Figure 9(a) shows the variation in efficiency as a function of signal amplitude. After reaching the optimum operating point, efficiency exhibits only residual variations, remaining practically constant. An analogous behavior is observed in Fig. 9(b): although the power increases with signal amplitude, the efficiency stabilizes above approximately 5 mW.

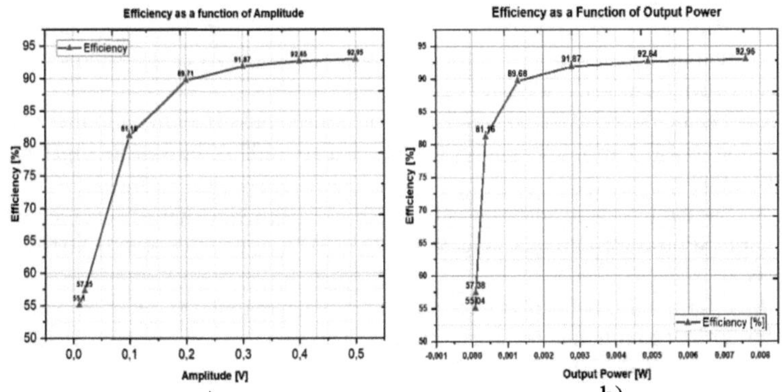

a) b)

Fig. 9. Converter efficiency as a function of signal amplitude (a) and as a function of output power (b).

5 Conclusions

This paper presents a study of a DC-DC buck converter, analyzed and explored as a Class D amplifier, implemented in 65 nm CMOS technology with digital PID control. The results demonstrate that the system can track sinusoidal, square-wave, and real audio signals across a practical operating range of 0.1–0.3 V input amplitude, with reduced steady-state error while maintaining high efficiency (~91%). Spectral analysis confirms that performance in terms of THD and SINAD highly depends on the operating regime and PID controller resolution, being limited by quantization effects at low amplitudes and by nonlinearities at high amplitudes. Maximum SINAD of 65–66 dB is achieved in the intermediate amplitude range (0.1–0.3 V), while THD reaches −70.9 dB at optimal operating points. These findings confirm a fundamental trade-off between energy efficiency, linearity, and control complexity. The recommended configuration uses a 16-bit ADC with M = 20 DPWM resolution. These results position the buck converter as a viable high-efficiency solution for Class D audio amplification in battery-powered applications.

References

1. Hu, T., Huang, M., Martins, R.P., Lu, Y.: A 12-to-1 flying capacitor cross-connected buck converter with inserted D>0.5 control for fast transient response. IEEE J. Solid State Circuits. **58**, 3207–3218 (2023). https://doi.org/10.1109/JSSC.2023.3297111
2. Cai, G., Lu, Y., Martins, R.P.: 11.9 a compact 12V-to-1V 91.8% peak efficiency hybrid resonant switched-capacitor parallel inductor (ReSC-PL) buck converter. In: 2023 IEEE International Solid- State Circuits Conference (ISSCC), pp. 198–200. IEEE (2023). https://doi.org/10.1109/ISSCC42615.2023.10067303
3. Jin, Q., Ruan, X., Ren, X., Wang, Y., Leng, Y.: Step-wave switched capacitor converter for compact design of envelope tracking power supply. IEEE Trans. Ind. Electron. **64**, 9587–9591 (2017). https://doi.org/10.1109/TIE.2017.2716900
4. Luís, J.F., Paulino, N.: Recent trends in audio power amplifiers for battery-powered applications. In: Technological Innovation for AI-Powered Cyber-Physical Systems (2025). https://doi.org/10.1007/978-3-031-97051-1_29
5. Utomo, N., et al.: An 85.1% peak efficiency, low power class H audio amplifier with full class H operation. IEEE Trans. Circuits Syst. I Regul. Pap. (2023). https://doi.org/10.1109/TCSI.2023.3245002
6. Jiang, X.: Fundamentals of audio class D amplifier design: a review of schemes and architectures. IEEE Solid-State Circuits Mag. **9**, 14–25 (2017). https://doi.org/10.1109/MSSC.2017.2712368
7. Chen, S.H., et al.: Embedded single-inductor bipolar-output DC-DC converter in class-D amplifier for low common noise. IEEE Trans. Power Electron. **31**, 3106–3116 (2016). https://doi.org/10.1109/TPEL.2015.2446510
8. Lee, J., Lee, B.: Adaptive dead-time control class-D power amplifier for wireless power transfer system. In: 2023 8th IEEE International Conference on Network Intelligence and Digital Content (IC-NIDC), pp. 471–475. IEEE (2023). https://doi.org/10.1109/IC-NIDC59918.2023.10390692
9. Mei, S., Hu, Y., Xu, H., Wen, H.: The class D audio power amplifier: a review. Electronics. (2022). https://doi.org/10.3390/electronics11193244
10. Tang, B., Deng, J., Zhou, C., Ouyang, H.: Design of a high efficiency class-D audio power amplifier. In: Proceedings - International Conference on Artificial Intelligence and Electromechanical Automation, AIEA 2020, pp. 385–391. Institute of Electrical and Electronics Engineers Inc (2020). https://doi.org/10.1109/AIEA51086.2020.00087
11. Guo, Y., et al.: High-efficiency class-H audio amplifier with delta–sigma envelope tracking power supply. IEEE Trans. Circuits Syst. I Regul. Pap. **67**, 2227–2238 (2020). https://doi.org/10.1109/TCSI.2020.2982648

12. Utomo, N., Siek, L., Yap, H.G., Disney, D., Selvaraj, L., Peng, L.: An 87% peak efficiency, 37W, class H audio amplifier with GaN output stage. In: 2018 IEEE Nordic Circuits and Systems Conference (NORCAS): NORCHIP and International Symposium of System-on-Chip (SoC), pp. 1–6. IEEE (2018). https://doi.org/10.1109/NORCHIP.2018.8573508
13. Peng, Z., Yang, S., Feng, Y., Hong, Z., Liu, B.: An 80% peak efficiency, 410mW, single supply rail powered class-I linear audio amplifier. In: 2011 IEEE Custom Integrated Circuits Conference (CICC), pp. 1–4. IEEE (2011). https://doi.org/10.1109/CICC.2011.6055395
14. Park, Y.J., Lee, K.Y.: High-efficiency, high-power class-D power amplifier with 50W output using GaN devices. In: International Conference on Ubiquitous and Future Networks, ICUFN, pp. 44–47. IEEE Computer Society (2021). https://doi.org/10.1109/ICUFN49451.2021.9528632
15. Berkhout, M., Dooper, L., Krabbenborg, B.: A 4Ω 2.65W class-D audio amplifier with embedded DC-DC boost converter, current sensing ADC and DSP for adaptive speaker protection. IEEE J. Solid State Circuits. **48**, 2952–2961 (2013). https://doi.org/10.1109/JSSC.2013.2284692
16. Dahidah, M.S.A., Konstantinou, G., Agelidis, V.G.: A review of multilevel selective harmonic elimination PWM: formulations, solving algorithms, implementation and applications. IEEE Trans. Power Electron. **30**, 4091–4106 (2015). https://doi.org/10.1109/TPEL.2014.2355226
17. Vazquez, S., et al.: Model predictive control: a review of its applications in power electronics. IEEE Ind. Electron. Mag. **8**, 16–31 (2014). https://doi.org/10.1109/MIE.2013.2290138
18. Bellili, N.E.I., Bekhouche, K.: Class-D audio amplifier using Sigma-Delta (ΣΔ) modulator. Indones. J. Electr. Eng. Inf. **10**, 567–572 (2022). https://doi.org/10.52549/ijeei.v10i3.3872
19. Matejcek, M., Sostronek, M.: Low-pass filter design with microcontroller. In: 2022 New Trends in Signal Processing (NTSP), pp. 1–8. IEEE (2022). https://doi.org/10.23919/NTSP54843.2022.9920400
20. Sun, J.: Pulse-width modulation. In: Advances in Industrial Control, pp. 25–61 (2012). https://doi.org/10.1007/978-1-4471-2885-4_2

Toward High-Fidelity Datasets for Hybrid Electric Vehicle Energy Management Incorporating Power Converter Non-idealities

Henar Mike O. Canilang[1(✉)], Yurim Cheon[2], Youjeong Yoon[2], and Wansu Lim[2]

[1] School of Mechatronic Systems Engineering, Simon Fraser University, Surrey, BC, Canada
hmc19@sfu.ca

[2] Electrical and Computer Engineering, Sungkyunkwan University, Suwon, South Korea
{20211141,alicenara16,wansu.lim}@skku.edu

Abstract. Reliable energy management strategies (EMS) for hybrid electric vehicles (HEVs) increasingly depend on high-quality datasets that accurately represent real-world operating conditions. However, most existing datasets are generated using simplified system models that neglect power converter non-idealities and their interaction with vehicle dynamics, leading to biased training and unreliable performance evaluation of EMS algorithms. This paper presents a high-fidelity dataset generation framework that integrates detailed vehicle longitudinal dynamics, hybrid energy storage system (HESS) models, and comprehensive DC-DC converter loss characteristics. The HEV architecture consists of a battery and a supercapacitor (SC), and datasets are generated through large-scale simulations executed on a high-performance computing server. The framework produces time-series datasets capturing realistic power flows, current stress, and converter efficiency under representative urban driving cycles. Dataset fidelity is assessed through statistical coverage of operating conditions, transient power behavior, and consistency between mechanical demand and electrical response. Results demonstrate that incorporating converter non-idealities significantly alters power distribution and efficiency metrics, establishing a benchmark-quality foundation for data-driven and model-based EMS development.

Keywords: Battery · Supercapacitor · Energy Management System · Hybrid Energy Storage System · DC-DC · Hybrid Electric Vehicles

1 Introduction

Transportation electrification is central to addressing pressing societal challenges, including climate change mitigation, urban air quality improvement, and sustainable energy utilization [1, 2]. Hybrid electric vehicles (HEVs) equipped with battery and supercapacitor (SC) hybrid energy storage systems offer a promising pathway toward improved efficiency and reduced emissions; however, the reliability of their energy management strategies depends heavily on realistic system modeling and data representation

Published by Springer Nature Switzerland AG 2027
L. M. Camarinha-Matos and F. Ferrada (Eds.): DoCEIS 2026, IFIP AICT 790, pp. 226–239, 2027.
https://doi.org/10.1007/978-3-032-28939-1_17

[3–5]. Many existing approaches rely on simplified assumptions that neglect detailed DC-DC converter behavior or its interaction with vehicle dynamics, limiting their ability to reflect real-world operating conditions [6, 7]. To address this gap, this work develops a high-fidelity dataset generation framework grounded in realistic urban driving cycles, physics-based vehicle longitudinal dynamics, and detailed DC-DC converter modeling. By ensuring consistency between mechanical demand, electrical response, and power conversion characteristics, the proposed framework supports the development of more reliable and efficient energy management strategies for sustainable electrified transportation systems. The contributions of this paper are as follows:

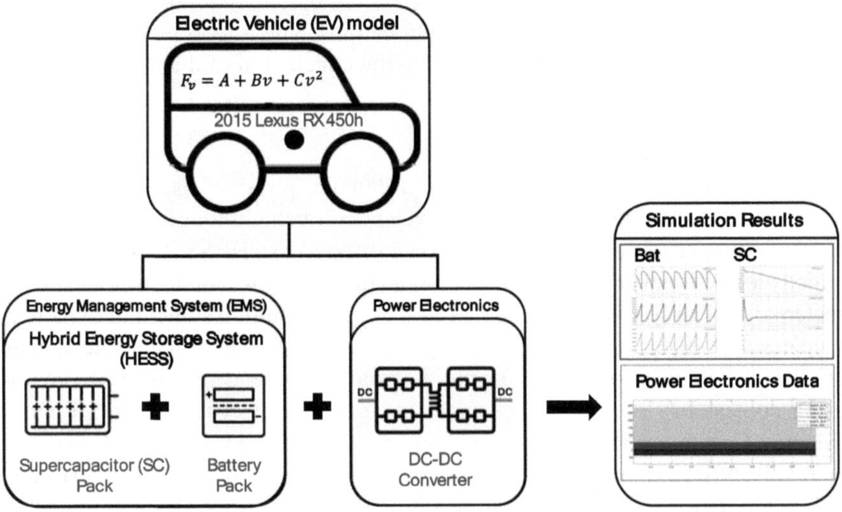

Fig. 1. Proposed methodology on developing the simulation model.

1. Realistic Urban Driving-Based Dataset Generation: Develops a dataset generation framework grounded in representative urban driving cycles to reflect real-world HEV operating conditions, including frequent acceleration and regenerative braking.
2. Vehicle Dynamics-Integrated Modeling: Integrates longitudinal vehicle dynamics with electrical system modeling to ensure mechanical to electrical consistency in generated datasets.
3. Detailed DC-DC Converter Modeling: Incorporates physics-based conduction and switching characteristics of the DC-DC converter to capture realistic power conversion behavior and efficiency variations.
4. High-Fidelity Time-Series Dataset Construction: Produces comprehensive datasets including power flows, current stress, state-of-charge trajectories, and converter efficiency metrics under dynamic conditions.
5. Societal Impact Contribution: Provides benchmark-quality datasets that enable more reliable and efficient energy management strategy development, supporting sustainable and intelligent transportation electrification.

Concisely, this paper presents a high-fidelity, physics-consistent HEV dataset generation framework that produces structured time-series data which includes vehicle dynamics, power flows, battery/SC states, current stress, and converter efficiency. This approach differs from existing datasets by integrating realistic urban driving cycles, coupled mechanical-electrical modeling, and detailed DC-DC converter non-idealities for reliable EMS development.

The paper is structured wherein Sect. 2 will give emphasis to the methodology including the battery pack, SC pack, vehicle model and the hybrid energy management system (HEMS) utilized for this model. Section 3 presents the results where dataset is extracted with discussions. The discussion includes the modelled EV battery pack and SC pack simulation analysis with the corresponding operational implication to the DC-DC converter for hybrid electric vehicle applications. The importance of this approach is also discussed. Section 4 focuses on giving the conclusion of the study.

2 Methodology

The proposed methodology employs a multi-domain, physics-based modeling framework that couples realistic urban driving cycles with vehicle longitudinal dynamics to compute traction power demand, which is then mapped to a HESS (battery-SC) through a detailed bidirectional DC-DC converter model incorporating conduction and switching characteristics. The converter is modeled using high-resolution switching dynamics utilizing piecewise-linear or time-stepped representation of switch/diode states, enabling accurate representation of current ripple, voltage stress, and loss mechanisms, while ensuring consistency between mechanical demand and electrical response across all subsystems. Computationally, the framework involves time-domain simulation with fine temporal discretization (on the order of microseconds for converter switching), resulting in high computational complexity proportional to the number of switching cycles and simulation parameters, and is therefore executed on high-performance computing platforms to generate large-scale, high-fidelity time-series datasets for EMS development. A high-performance host PC from Sungkyungkwan University (SKKU), South Korea, was utilized to accommodate the computational demands of the high-fidelity modeling framework. Model validation and dataset generation were conducted on a Windows 11 Pro workstation featuring an Intel Core i7-14700KF processor (20 cores, 28 threads) and 64 GB of RAM, built on a Gigabyte Z790 AORUS ELITE platform. The 64-bit architecture, supported by UEFI firmware and extended virtual memory, ensured stable execution of MATLAB-based simulations with fine temporal resolution and enabled efficient handling of large-scale dataset generation and validation tasks.

Figure 1 highlights the overall simulation framework used for hybrid energy storage system (HESS) evaluation in an electric vehicle (EV) platform. The electric vehicle (EV) model represents a realistic vehicle platform (e.g., 2015 Lexus RX 450 h), where the longitudinal dynamics is governed by the traction force equation as represented in Eq. (1),

$$F_v = A + Bv + Cv^2 \tag{1}$$

capturing rolling resistance and aerodynamic drag effects. The vehicle demand is processed by the Energy Management System (EMS), which coordinates power distribution within the Hybrid Energy Storage System (HESS) consisting of a SC pack and a battery pack.

The power flow between the HESS and the DC bus is regulated through a bidirectional DC-DC converter within the power electronics stage. The integrated system enables realistic simulation of mechanical load, electrical response, and power conversion behavior. The rightmost panel presents representative simulation outputs, including detailed HESS data and power electronics data which illustrates the interaction between vehicle demand, energy storage dynamics, and converter performance.

2.1 Battery Pack Model

The battery and SC pack are modelled in this simulation based on real-life pack values. The HESS incorporates a Nickel-Metal Hydride (NiMH) traction battery configured with a nominal voltage of 288 V, consistent with the high-voltage architecture of the 2015 Lexus RX 450 h hybrid drivetrain.

The battery pack is modeled with a rated capacity of 1.9×10^3 Ah, representing the aggregate charge storage capability of the pack within the simulation environment. The initial state-of-charge (SOC) is set to 95%, reflecting a near-fully charged operating condition at the beginning of the drive cycle, while the battery dynamic response time is defined as 2 s to capture first-order transient behavior. Within the HESS framework, the NiMH battery serves as the primary energy source, supplying sustained power for propulsion under steady state driving conditions.

Compared to the SC pack, the battery exhibits lower power density but significantly higher energy density, making it suitable for medium to long duration energy delivery. However, due to electrochemical limitations and internal resistance characteristics, large transient current spikes can accelerate thermal stress and aging mechanisms. For this reason, in the proposed architecture the battery operates in coordination with the SC ESS. The SC buffers high-frequency power fluctuations, thereby reducing peak current demand on the battery. This coordinated power sharing strategy enhances overall drivetrain efficiency, mitigates battery degradation, and improves system level reliability under dynamic urban driving conditions.

2.2 Supercapacitor Pack Model

The SC ESS is implemented as a high-power auxiliary energy buffer directly interfaced with the DC bus to manage fast transient power exchanges that occur during aggressive acceleration and regenerative braking events. The SC pack is configured as 108 cells in series (108S1P), resulting in a total rated capacitance of 15.6 F and a maximum operating voltage of 291.6 V, making it compatible with the high-voltage DC bus architecture. This configuration enables rapid charge-discharge operation due to the inherently low equivalent series resistance (ESR) and high-power density of SC technology. In this HESS, the SC-ESS functions as a dynamic power buffer rather than a primary energy source. During high load transients, it supplies peak power demand, thereby preventing large current spikes from being drawn from the battery pack. Conversely, during regenerative braking, it absorbs short-duration high-power energy bursts that may exceed the battery's acceptable charge rate. This buffering action significantly mitigates battery current stress, reduces thermal loading, and limits electrochemical degradation mechanisms associated with high C-rate operation. Concisely, integrating the SC ESS improves overall drivetrain efficiency, enhances transient power capability, and extends battery lifetime by decoupling high-frequency power dynamics from the battery system.

2.3 Vehicle Model

In this study, the longitudinal road-load force of the 2015 Lexus RX 450 h is modeled using the standard quadratic coast down formulation $F_r = A + Bv + Cv^2$. The coefficients $A = 141.8$ N, $B = 3.273$ N/(m/s), and $C = 0.569$ N/(m/s^2) are directly taken from published vehicle specifications to ensure model fidelity. This equation captures constant rolling resistance, speed-dependent mechanical losses, and aerodynamic drag proportional to the square of vehicle speed. The total tractive force is then obtained by incorporating grade resistance and inertial effects based on the EPA test mass of 2268 kg. By employing vehicle-specific coast-down parameters, the model accurately represents the real-world dynamic behavior of the Lexus RX 450 h under transient driving conditions.

The US06 drive cycle was utilized as the input speed profile for the 2015 Lexus RX 450 h longitudinal vehicle model. The cycle provides time-varying vehicle speed data, which is used to compute acceleration, tractive force, and corresponding wheel power demand through the vehicle dynamics equations. By combining the US06 profile with the Lexus-specific road-load coefficients and mass parameters, the model captures realistic high-speed and aggressive transient operating conditions.

Given that US06 includes rapid accelerations and decelerations, it enables evaluation of peak power demand, regenerative braking events, and dynamic power flow within the hybrid energy storage system. When integrated with the vehicle model, the drive cycle allows assessment of battery and supercapacitor power sharing, converter losses, and overall drivetrain performance under demanding real-world driving behavior.

2.4 Hybrid Energy Management System (HEMS)

The proposed HEMS employs a rule-based power allocation strategy to coordinate power sharing between the battery and SC energy storage systems. The control input is the DC bus power demand P_{dc}, obtained from the vehicle model under the selected drive cycle. During motoring conditions ($P_{dc} > 0$), the battery handles low power demand below the threshold, while the SC is activated for higher transient power requests. Conversely, during regenerative braking ($P_{dc} < 0$), low-magnitude braking energy is directed to the battery, whereas high-magnitude regenerative events are absorbed by the supercapacitor to mitigate battery stress. When the power demand is zero, both storage devices remain idle. This straightforward threshold-based logic enables dynamic separation of low-frequency (energy dominant) and high-frequency (power dominant) components, improving system efficiency and reducing battery degradation under aggressive driving conditions.

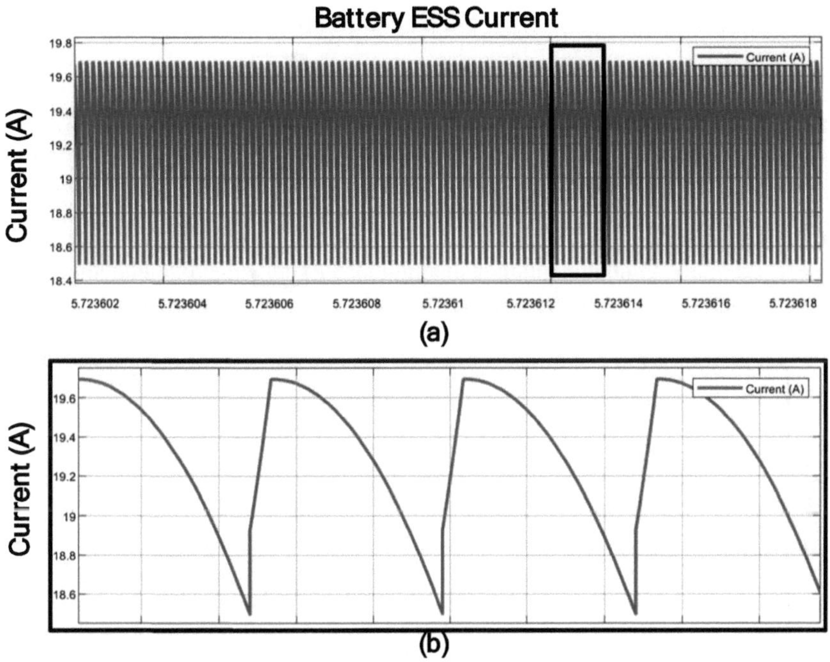

Fig. 2. Battery ESS current waveform (a) current waveform at constant power output and (b) magnified view of the battery ESS current waveform.

3 Results and Discussion

This section presents the simulation results of the proposed HESS integrated with the vehicle model under dynamic driving conditions. The objective is to evaluate the effectiveness of the developed vehicle dynamics model, SC-battery configuration, and rule-based EMS in handling transient power demands. Performance metrics such as DC bus power distribution, peak power mitigation, regenerative energy absorption, and overall drivetrain response are analyzed. Since the model requires high computing power for analysis and data generation, the model is currently being deployed and tested in a supercomputer server at South Korea.

3.1 Modelled EV Battery Pack and Simulation Analysis

Figure 2 highlights the battery ESS current waveform under constant power operation, illustrating both the full resolution switching behavior (a) and a magnified view (b) of the current profile. In Fig. 2, the battery ESS current waveform is shown under constant power operation. In Fig. 2(a), the current exhibits periodic ripple around an average value of approximately 19.2 A, with peak and minimum values of about 19.7 A and 18.5 A, respectively, resulting in a ripple magnitude of approximately ±0.6 A. This corresponds to a peak-to-peak variation of roughly 1.2 A, indicating relatively stable current delivery from the battery under steady-state conditions.

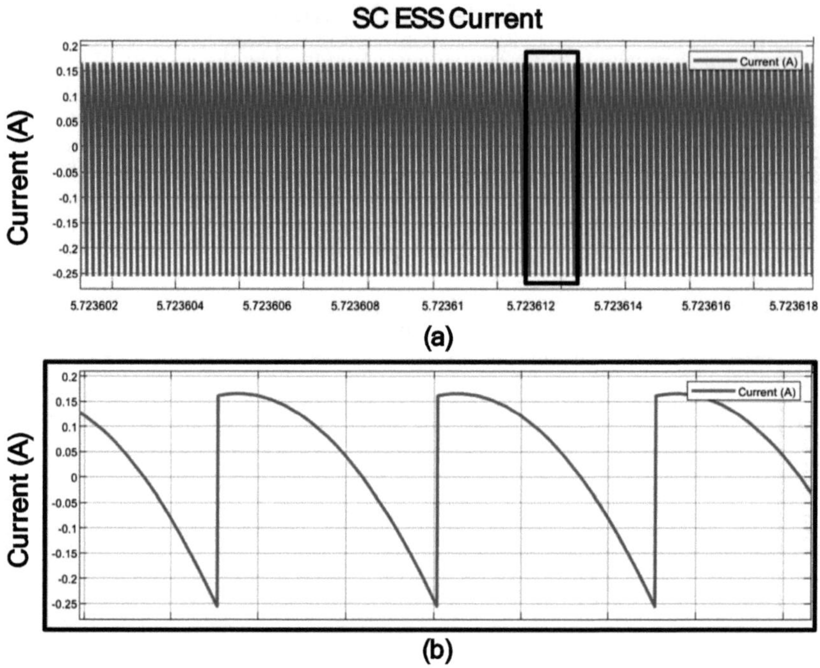

Fig. 3. SC ESS current waveform (a) current waveform at constant power output and (b) magnified view of the SC ESS current waveform.

At the system level, the battery supplies nearly constant average current corresponding to the DC bus power demand imposed by the vehicle model and drive cycle. However, due to the switching action of the bidirectional DC-DC converter interfacing the battery with the DC bus, the instantaneous battery current exhibits high-frequency ripple superimposed on the average value. The magnified view in Fig. 2(b) clearly shows the quasi-periodic ripple behavior, which reflects the converter switching frequency, modulation strategy, and inductor dynamics. This waveform is critically important for control algorithm development. Although energy management strategies such as the proposed HEMS operate on average power levels (e.g. threshold-based allocation between battery and the SC), the battery and converter physically experience the instantaneous current ripple. Accurate high-fidelity current modeling enables proper controller bandwidth selection, current loop tuning, and stability analysis. It also ensures that the energy management logic does not inadvertently excite undesirable dynamic interactions between the battery, supercapacitor, and converter. Without resolving the ripple component, control strategies may underestimate transient stress and misrepresent system responsiveness under aggressive drive cycles such as US06.

From a power electronics perspective, the detailed battery current waveform directly determines switching and conduction losses in semiconductor devices. The RMS current, peak current, and ripple magnitude influence MOSFET conduction losses, diode reverse recovery losses, and magnetic core losses. Loss modeling based solely on average current would significantly underpredict switching losses and thermal stress. Therefore, capturing the high-frequency current profile is essential for realistic converter efficiency evaluation, thermal design, and reliability assessment. This is particularly important in high-power EV applications where efficiency improvements of even a few percentage points translate into extended driving range and reduced energy consumption. The waveform also plays a crucial role in magnetic component sizing. The ripple current determines the required inductance value, current ripple specification, copper losses, and core flux swing in the inductor. Underestimating ripple leads to undersized inductors, excessive heating, acoustic noise, and potential saturation. Conversely, overdesign increases cost, weight, and volume which are all key constraints in EV development. Thus, high-resolution current characterization enables optimal trade-offs between efficiency, power density, and cost. When integrated with the vehicle longitudinal model and the HEMS strategy, this waveform demonstrates how system-level power demand propagates down to component-level electrical stress. During high-power events, the HEMS allocates transient loads between the battery and supercapacitor, thereby shaping the battery current waveform and reducing peak and ripple exposure. The SC effectively absorbs high-frequency and high-magnitude transients, which mitigates battery degradation mechanisms such as lithium plating (in Li-ion systems) or thermal stress (in NiMH systems). This interaction validates the importance of coordinated energy management not only at the power level but also at the waveform level.

From a broader EV perspective, accurate modeling of such current waveforms supports the development of more efficient, reliable, and longer lasting powertrains. Improved loss prediction enhances overall drivetrain efficiency, reducing energy consumption and greenhouse gas emissions. Proper magnetic and converter sizing reduces material usage, improves power density, and lowers system cost which are key factors for large-scale EV adoption. By enabling more robust hybrid energy storage architectures, this modeling approach contributes to extending battery lifetime, reducing resource extraction, and improving sustainability.

Ultimately, the detailed battery ESS current waveform serves as a bridge between high-level energy management algorithms and low-level power electronics design. It ensures that control strategies, component sizing, and efficiency evaluations are physically consistent and scalable.

3.2 Modelled EV Supercapacitor Pack and Simulation Analysis

Figure 3 illustrates the SC ESS current waveform under constant power operation, showing both the full switching-scale response (a) and a magnified view (b) of the ripple behavior. In Fig. 3, the SC ESS current waveform is presented under steady-state operation. The current exhibits high-frequency oscillations around an average value of approximately 0.12 A, with peak and minimum values of about 0.18 A and 0.08 A, respectively, resulting in a ripple magnitude of approximately ± 0.05 A. This corresponds to a peak-to-peak variation of roughly 0.10 A, indicating that the SC is actively handling high-frequency transient components of the load.

Unlike the battery waveform, the SC current exhibits bidirectional high-frequency oscillations with relatively larger ripple-to-average ratio, reflecting its role as a fast dynamic power buffer. The waveform clearly captures the converter switching action and the rapid charge-discharge transitions inherent to SC operation. The magnified plot highlights the quasi-periodic ripple profile shaped by the converter switching frequency and inductor current dynamics.

This waveform is highly significant for control algorithm development. While the HEMS allocates power at the system level based on a threshold strategy, the SC physically handles high-frequency and high-magnitude transient components of the DC bus demand. The detailed current ripple directly affects current-loop control tuning, stability margins, and dynamic response bandwidth of the SC converter. Accurate waveform modeling ensures that the SC control system is designed to respond rapidly without introducing oscillations or interaction instability with the battery converter.

From a power electronics loss analysis standpoint, the SC current waveform is critical because the device operates under fast transient cycling. The high-frequency bidirectional current increases switching losses, RMS current stress, and thermal loading in semiconductor devices. Moreover, the ripple magnitude influences inductor copper loss, core loss, and overall converter efficiency. If only average power were considered, switching and RMS related losses would be significantly underestimated, leading to inaccurate efficiency and thermal predictions. The SC waveform is also essential for proper magnetic component sizing. Because SCs are designed to absorb and deliver peak power, the associated ripple current determines required inductance, allowable current ripple, flux swing, and saturation margins. Underestimating ripple could result in inductor overheating or magnetic saturation during aggressive drive cycles such as US06. Conversely, excessive conservatism would increase volume and weight, reducing vehicle power density. Therefore, high-fidelity waveform resolution enables optimal trade-offs between efficiency, size, and cost.

When analyzed together with the battery current waveform and the HEMS strategy, this SC waveform demonstrates how transient load components are dynamically diverted away from the battery. The SC absorbs high-frequency regenerative spikes and delivers rapid acceleration bursts, thereby smoothing the battery current profile. This dynamic decoupling reduces battery degradation, improves overall system efficiency, and enhances drivetrain responsiveness. From an EV and societal perspective, accurate modeling of the SC current waveform supports the development of more durable and efficient HESS architectures. By enabling better loss prediction, optimized magnetics design, and improved control robustness, the system achieves higher efficiency and extended battery lifetime. These improvements directly contribute to reduced energy consumption, lower lifecycle emissions, improved resource utilization, and accelerated adoption of clean transportation technologies which are key factors in addressing global sustainability and climate challenges.

3.3 Power Converter (DC-DC) Converter Operating Voltage and Current

Figure 4 shows the operating voltage and current waveforms of the HEMS DC-DC converter. Figure 4(a) shows the steady-state waveforms of the switch and diode currents together with the corresponding gate signal, illustrating the periodic switching operation representing HESS. Figure 4(b) presents a magnified view of the highlighted interval, capturing the detailed switching transitions, current ripple, and conduction intervals of the semiconductor devices. These results demonstrate the dynamic interaction between

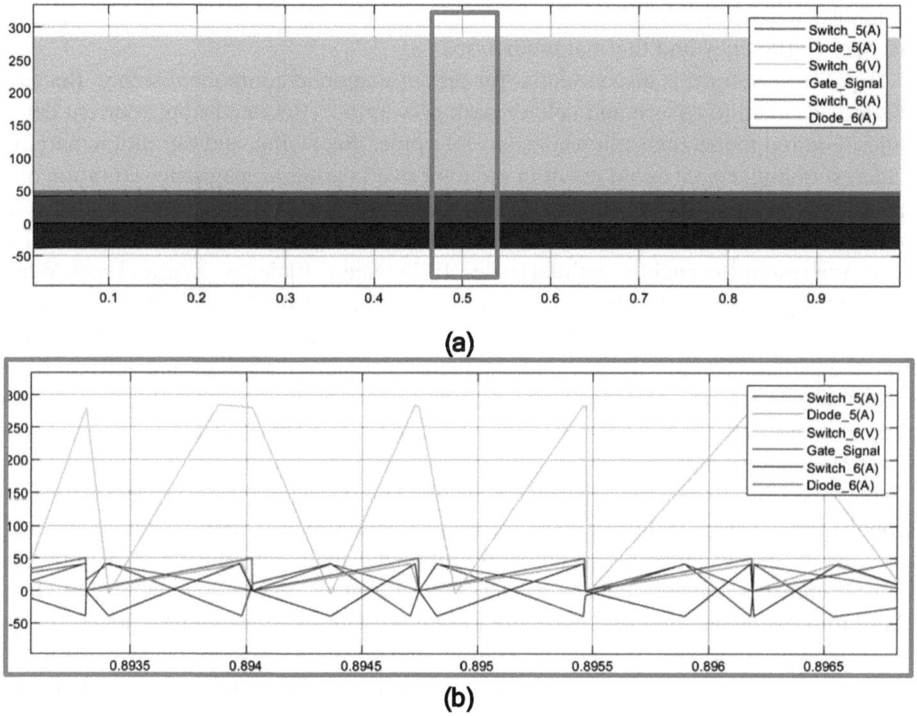

Fig. 4. HEMS converter operating voltage and current (a) overall waveform and (b) magnified view of the operating voltage and current.

switching devices and energy storage components, which directly influence converter losses and overall system performance.

In Fig. 4, the operating waveforms of the HEMS DC-DC converter are presented, including switch currents, diode currents, switch voltage, and the gate signal. The dominant cyan trace corresponds to the switch voltage Switch_6(V), which varies between approximately 0 V and 285 to 290 V, indicating the blocking and conduction states of the device during each switching cycle. The gate signal remains at approximately 50 V, ensuring proper device activation. The switch currents Switch_5(A) and Switch_6(A) exhibit triangular waveforms with amplitudes ranging from approximately −40 A to +45 A, corresponding to the inductor current ripple under continuous conduction mode (CCM). The diode currents Diode_5(A) and Diode_6(A) are confined between 0 A and 45 A, conducting during the complementary freewheeling intervals when the corresponding switches are turned off.

From a power electronics loss analysis standpoint, the SC current waveform is critical because the device operates under fast transient cycling. The high-frequency bidirectional current increases switching losses, RMS current stress, and thermal loading in semiconductor devices. Moreover, the ripple magnitude influences inductor copper loss, core loss, and overall converter efficiency. If only average power were considered, switching and RMS-related losses would be significantly underestimated, leading to inaccurate efficiency and thermal predictions.

The SC waveform is also essential for proper magnetic component sizing. Because SCs are designed to absorb and deliver peak power, the associated ripple current determines required inductance, allowable current ripple, flux swing, and saturation margins. Underestimating ripple could result in inductor overheating or magnetic saturation during aggressive drive cycles such as US06. Conversely, excessive conservatism would increase volume and weight, reducing vehicle power density. Therefore, high-fidelity waveform resolution enables optimal trade-offs between efficiency, size, and cost. When analyzed together with the battery current waveform and the HEMS strategy, this SC waveform demonstrates how transient load components are dynamically diverted away from the battery. The SC absorbs high-frequency regenerative spikes and delivers rapid acceleration bursts, thereby smoothing the battery current profile. This dynamic decoupling reduces battery degradation, improves overall system efficiency, and enhances drivetrain responsiveness.

From an EV and societal perspective, accurate modeling of the SC current waveform supports the development of more durable and efficient hybrid energy storage architectures. By enabling better loss prediction, optimized magnetics design, and improved control robustness, the system achieves higher efficiency and extended battery lifetime. These improvements directly contribute to reduced energy consumption, lower lifecycle emissions, improved resource utilization, and accelerated adoption of clean transportation technologies are key factors in addressing global sustainability and climate challenges.

3.4 Importance of This Study

This study is important because it bridges the gap between high-level vehicle energy management strategies and low-level power electronics behavior through an integrated, high-fidelity modeling framework. By combining a realistic vehicle model, aggressive drive cycle conditions, a hybrid battery-SC architecture, and detailed converter switching dynamics, the work provides physically consistent insight into how system-level power demands translate into component-level electrical stress. Such an approach enables more accurate control algorithm development, reliable loss prediction, and optimal sizing of semiconductor devices and magnetic components. In the context of electric and hybrid vehicles, this integrated methodology improves efficiency, enhances battery lifetime, and increases overall drivetrain reliability. Ultimately, the study contributes to advancing sustainable transportation technologies by enabling more energy-efficient, durable, and cost-effective electrified powertrains that address broader societal challenges related to climate change, resource utilization, and clean mobility.

In terms of contribution, this study is strongly motivated by our recent analytical and simulation-based results on the detailed modeling of Dual Active Bridge (DAB) DC-DC converters for interfacing SC [8]. In our prior work on DAB switching mode analysis and its extended efficiency-focused investigation, demonstrated that switching mode selection (CCM, DCM, and CM) significantly affects inductor current stress, switching losses, zero-current switching (ZCS) capability, and overall power utilization of supercapacitor energy storage systems [9]. In particular, the transition from zero-crossing time (ZCT) to ZCS under DCM operation was shown to substantially mitigate switching and conduction losses at low SC voltages [10]. Building upon these converter-level insights, the present study extends the contribution from device-level switching behavior to system-level vehicle modeling and dataset generation. The motivation is clear: accurate energy management strategy development for hybrid electric vehicles requires datasets that reflect realistic converter physics, including switching ripple, current stress, and efficiency variation under dynamic conditions. Therefore, instead of relying on idealized DC-DC representations, this work integrates physics-based DAB modeling into a vehicle dynamic-coupled HESS framework. By embedding detailed converter behavior into the dataset generation process, the study bridges high-fidelity power electronics modeling with drive-cycle-based vehicle simulation, enabling more reliable benchmarking of energy management algorithms.

Furthermore, the generated datasets capture realistic operating conditions observed in urban driving scenarios, including stop-and-go traffic, rapid acceleration, and regenerative braking events commonly experienced in real-world vehicle usage. The inclusion of converter non-idealities and dynamic power demand profiles ensures that the resulting data closely reflects actual electrical stress, efficiency variations, and energy distribution patterns observed in practical HEV systems. As a result, the proposed framework provides a reliable foundation for translating simulation-based insights into real-world energy management strategies, improving the robustness and deployability of EMS solutions in commercial electrified vehicles.

4 Conclusion

This paper presented a high-fidelity hybrid energy storage system (HESS) modeling and dataset generation framework for a 2015 Lexus RX 450 h under realistic driving conditions. First, the study successfully developed a realistic urban driving-based dataset generation framework by employing representative drive cycles characterized by frequent acceleration and regenerative braking events. This ensured that the generated datasets reflect practical HEV operating conditions rather than idealized steady-state scenarios.

The proposed framework achieved vehicle dynamics-integrated modeling by coupling longitudinal mechanical dynamics with electrical system equations, thereby preserving mechanical-to-electrical consistency in power flow computation. This integration guarantees that DC bus power demand, tractive force, and energy storage behavior are physically coherent and representative of real-world vehicle operation.

The inclusion of detailed DC-DC converter modeling, incorporating conduction and switching characteristics, enabled accurate representation of power conversion behavior, switching ripple, and efficiency variations. The resulting current and voltage waveforms provide realistic stress profiles necessary for loss analysis, thermal assessment, and component sizing.

The study produced a high-fidelity time-series dataset containing comprehensive electrical and mechanical variables, including battery and supercapacitor currents, state-of-charge trajectories, power distribution under the HEMS strategy, converter operating characteristics, and efficiency metrics under dynamic conditions. Such datasets move beyond average-value approximations and capture instantaneous switching-level dynamics essential for advanced control development.

Finally, in terms of societal impact, this work contributes benchmark-quality datasets that support the development of more reliable, efficient, and robust energy management strategies for hybrid and electric vehicles. By improving loss prediction accuracy, enhancing battery lifetime through intelligent power buffering, and enabling optimized component design, the proposed framework advances sustainable and intelligent transportation electrification. Collectively, the findings demonstrate that integrated, physics-based modeling is critical for bridging system-level control design and hardware-level performance, ultimately supporting cleaner mobility solutions and addressing broader environmental and energy sustainability challenges.

Acknowledgement. This research was supported by the Ministry of Science and ICT (MSIT), Republic of Korea, under Grants RS-2024-00349885 and RS-2025-25459504.

References

1. Safdarian, F., et al.: Technical impacts of light-duty and heavy-duty transportation electrification on a coordinated transmission and distribution system. IEEE Trans. Transp. Electrif. **11**(1), 3404–3417 (2025). https://doi.org/10.1109/TTE.2024.3440334
2. Tiwari, S., Bhatt, A., Patel, A., Mishra, N.: A systematic approach to simulate a fundamental model of an electric vehicle in MATLAB environment. In: 2025 6th International Conference for Emerging Technology (INCET), Belgaum, India, pp. 1–4 (2025). https://doi.org/10.1109/INCET64471.2025.11140954
3. Gan, S.S., Rama Krishna, P.V.: Investigating the impact of drive cycles on hybrid electric vehicle performance using MATLAB. In: 2025 International Conference on Emerging Technologies in Engineering Applications (ICETEA), Puducherry, India, pp. 1–8 (2025). https://doi.org/10.1109/ICETEA64585.2025.11099897
4. Shi, C., Wang, W., Li, W.: Analysis of evaluation indicators for regenerative braking energy recovery in hybrid electric vehicles. In: 2025 IEEE 8th Information Technology and Mechatronics Engineering Conference (ITOEC), Chongqing, China, pp. 952–957 (2025). https://doi.org/10.1109/ITOEC63606.2025.10967948
5. Ali, M.B., Rauch, E.: Comparative analysis of energy management strategies for a hybrid electric vehicle in urban transportation: a case study. In: 2025 11th International Conference on Control, Decision and Information Technologies (CoDIT), Split, Croatia, pp. 2811–2816 (2025). https://doi.org/10.1109/CoDIT66093.2025.11321655.C
6. Rajalingam, S., Kanagamalliga, S., Jenifer, A., Jaisuriya, N.: Sustainable energy utilization in EVs using battery-Supercapacitor hybrid storage. In: 2025 4th International Conference on Applied Artificial Intelligence and Computing (ICAAIC), Salem, India, pp. 1785–1790 (2025). https://doi.org/10.1109/ICAAIC64647.2025.11330307
7. Bopche, L.M., Deosant, A.A., Ahmad, M.: Combination of parallel connected Supercapacitor & battery for enhancing battery life. In: 2016 International Conference on Automatic Control and Dynamic Optimization Techniques (ICACDOT), Pune, India, pp. 77–82 (2016). https://doi.org/10.1109/ICACDOT.2016.7877555
8. Canilang, H.M.O., Wang, S., Zhu, N., Palmer, P., Wang, J.: Dual active bridge switching modes for interfacing Supercapacitors. In: 2025 IEEE Canadian Conference on Electrical and Computer Engineering (CCECE), Vancouver, BC, Canada, pp. 688–692 (2025). https://doi.org/10.1109/CCECE64018.2025.11364470

9. Canilang, H.M.O., Wang, S., Zhu, N., Wang, J.: Modeling and simulation of switching modes of dual active bridge converters for interfacing Supercapacitor. In: 2025 IEEE Electrical Power and Energy Conference (EPEC), Waterloo, ON, Canada, pp. 444–444 (2025). https://doi.org/10.1109/EPEC65543.2025.11230414
10. Canilang, H.M.O., Wang, S., Zhu, N., Wang, J.: Enhancing the efficiency of dual active bridge converter in low-voltage Supercapacitor applications. In: 2025 IEEE 10th southern power electronics conference (SPEC), Johannesburg, South Africa, pp. 1–6 (2025). https://doi.org/10.1109/SPEC64875.2025.11377011

How Machining State Is Driving Energy Performances in AI-Guided Industries?

Andrea Bochicchio(✉), Fabio Fruggiero, and Francesco Mancusi

Department of Engineering, University of Basilicata, Potenza 85100, Italy
andrea.bochicchio004@unibas.it

Abstract. Machining state, particularly tool wear and CNC (Computer Numerical Control) operational phases, significantly influences energy consumption in AI-guided manufacturing systems. This study maps the literature linking machining energy behavior, tool wear and predictive analytics to make clear how energy profiles can support maintenance decisions. Authors conducted a bibliometric analysis of 483 Scopus-indexed publications, finally selecting 32 core studies revealing how energy signals can act as non-intrusive indicators of tool condition and process dynamics. Accordingly, machining parameters and wear progression can be used, jointly, to shape energy cycles, while machine-learning models can enable reliable prediction of tool wear and remaining useful life from energy data. Prediction-oriented approaches demonstrate that energy-based monitoring has the potential to support anticipatory tool replacement, energy efficiency, and tool-life extension without additional sensors. Energy-driven predictive maintenance is emerging as a relevant mechanism for managing energy performance in AI-driven machining environments.

Keywords: CNC Machining · Tool Wear · Energy Consumption · Predictive Maintenance · Machine Learning

1 Introduction

Maintenance in machining serves to ensure reliability of system and components while indirectly assuring optimal technologic and operational performances [1]. When the machine is equipped to monitor its state, maintenance interventions can be predicted [2]. In machining operations, accurate prediction of tool wear is essential to ensure product conformity and process reliability [3]. Reliable wear estimation supports the preservation of surface integrity and dimensional accuracy (e.g., surface finish and hole quality), while reducing nonconformities as such as rework and scrap. Effective tool wear monitoring enhances machine availability by preventing unexpected cutting-edge failure, burr formation, and unplanned interventions. It contributes to improved operational efficiency through cycle times improvement. AI-guided, according with Perera, et al., 2023 [4], represents any approach able to, supported by technologies and data, to process and analyze big datasets to reveal patterns and insight beyond the reach of traditional statistical methods. In this context, the term AI-guided refers to data-driven modelling

Published by Springer Nature Switzerland AG 2027
L. M. Camarinha-Matos and F. Ferrada (Eds.): DoCEIS 2026, IFIP AICT 790, pp. 240–255, 2027.
https://doi.org/10.1007/978-3-032-28939-1_18

approaches commonly adopted in manufacturing research, including machine learning, regression models, neural networks, and predictive algorithms.

To ensure data accuracy - particularly for vibration signals - non-contact, low-cost, real-time monitoring systems are currently being developed for effective tool wear detection and control [5]. They enable real-time estimation while correlating registered signals and machining state [6] basing on empirical formulations, experimental data, further optimized and trained using AI systems [7]. The use of optimal AI-guided approaches in machining requires labelling of data, identification of feature, selection of algorithms, validation of performances [8, 9]. Although several studies have addressed the topic of energy absorption related to cutting tool degradation [10] and the application of AI-guided strategies to predict machining conditions [11–13], to date, there remains a lack of a comprehensive map linking predictive maintenance strategies to the management and optimization of energy consumption and energy profiles in machining operations under varying cutting conditions, changeovers and tool selection. This study aims at defining: RQ1 To what extent can energy-related signals derived from CNC machine operation describe the machining process state and reflect the progression of tool wear? RQ2: How can energy-related indicators be used as guiding variables to support predictive maintenance strategies and energy optimization in CNC milling processes?

Beyond mapping the literature (Sect. 2), this study develops an analytical interpretation (Sect. 3) of how energy acts as intermediary variable linking machining parameters, tool degradation, and predictive maintenance decisions (Sect. 4).

The outcomes of our study reported what type of approach is possible to apply to control machining energy patterns in CNCs. Machine energy behavior can be interpreted not only as a technical performance indicator but also as a decision-support variable for sustainable manufacturing. By exploiting electrical signals already available in CNC systems, the proposed approach enables non-invasive monitoring strategies that do not require additional sensors, thus reducing technological barriers and facilitating adoption in small and medium-sized enterprises. This aspect is relevant to Tackling Societal Challenges in I5.0 era, where human-centric, sustainable, and resilient production systems are encouraged. The integration of energy-aware predictive models contributes to reducing unexpected machine downtime, improving planning reliability, and supporting more efficient allocation of industrial resources. In this perspective, energy-based predictive maintenance may represent a scalable and accessible solution capable of linking artificial intelligence with environmental responsibility in tackling societal issue. We contributed to promote energy efficiency while using statistical based approach enabling IoT within manufacturing systems.

2 The Research Approach: A Bibliometric Mapping

The Scopus database was selected to perform bibliometric analysis as per RQs [14]. Keywords were selected as:

(i) The manufacturing system domain, to identify studies related to machine tools and CNC machining processes (*"machin* tool*" OR "machin* cent*" OR "CNC" OR "computer numerical control"*); (ii) The energy domain, to capture contributions addressing energy consumption and power-related indicators (*"energy consumption"*

OR "energy use" OR "power consumption" OR "power use" OR "energy profile" OR "power profile*" OR "specific energy" OR "energy efficiency"*);

(iii) The methodology, to include modeling, forecasting, and proactive approaches (*predict* OR forecast* OR proactiv* OR anticip* OR model**); (iv) The tool condition domain, to identify studies focusing on tool wear, health state, failures, and remaining useful life (*wear OR "tool wear" OR "wear state" OR condition* OR "tool condition" OR "health state" OR "state of health" OR RUL OR "remaining useful life" OR life OR break* OR fail**). The Scopus search returned a total of 659 documents, reduced to 483 after filtering (i.e., English published papers in the area of Engineering, Computer Science, and Energy). The co-occurrences in keywords (i.e., 4414) were analyzed using VOSviewer software. We set the following rules: minimum number of occurrences of a keyword set equal to 7 (resulting in 178 keywords, reduced to 167 after removing duplicates and out-of-scope terms); minimum cluster size set to 20; resolution set to 1.5.

The prioritization in keywords was performed adopting the Pareto-based approach. on keyword co-occurrence frequencies to identify the most relevant subsets [15].

The selected subsets (namely *(i) tool wear; (ii) energy behavior; (iii) machining processes; (iv) predictive monitoring*) of keywords were re-entered, into Scopus as follows: *"tool wear" OR "wear of materials" OR "tool life" AND "energy utilization" OR "energy efficiency" OR "specific energy" OR "specific energy consumption" OR "energy consumption model" AND "machining" OR "machining process" OR "cutting" OR "cutting forces" OR "cutting conditions" OR "cutting parameters" OR "machine tools" OR "machining centers" OR "milling" OR "turning" AND "forecasting" OR "machine learning" OR "condition monitoring" OR "regression analysis" OR "neural networks"*. This ensured that the operational query reflected the dominant semantic structure of the dataset while maintaining analytical manageability [16]. The procedure gained 56 publications for content analysis in order to include, only, those aligned with the research objectives [17]. 24 studies were excluded due to partial thematic misalignment, insufficient methodological transparency, or limited relevance to the core focus on tool wear, energy-related machining behavior, and predictive monitoring frameworks. The final dataset therefore consisted of 32 studies forming the basis for the structured content analysis.

The bibliometric analysis provided 5 thematic clusters, as depicted in Fig. 1.

2.1 Cluster 1 (Red) – Process Mechanics and Energetic Cutting Dynamics

Red cluster includes cutting mechanics, machine energy consumption, process performance (mainly surface quality and machining parameters). It captures indirect correlation with the machining center remarking that energy consumption and cutting forces are strongly influenced not only by process parameters and material properties, but also by the structural and functional characteristics of the machine tool. Recurrent terms (i.e., cutting, surface properties, milling) clearly indicate that this domain gathers the literature aimed at understanding how operational variables affect both the system's energy demand and the resulting surface integrity. Within this semantic space, research systematically examines how cutting parameters and tool geometry interact with the forces generated during machining and, thus, the energy required by the process. This cluster also involves the role of workpiece material characteristics, such as aluminum or titanium alloys, and how their mechanical properties influence cutting dynamics and overall energy behavior. The strong connections between energy consumption, and cutting processes reveal a solid body of studies devoted to correlating energy efficiency with the mechanical phenomena of machining, highlighting the growing interest in identifying energetically advantageous operating configurations. Overall, this cluster interprets the physics-energetic relationship between the machining tool and the energetic outcome.

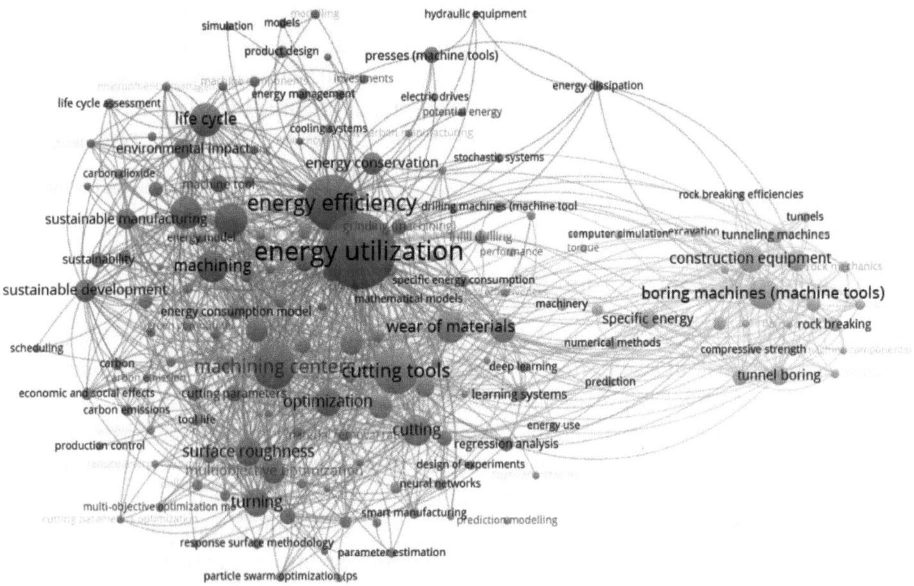

Fig. 1. Clustering literature in operational CNC states driving energy consumption: the VOSviewer (https://www.vosviewer.com/)output of keywords co-occurrence map.

2.2 Cluster 2 (GREEN) – Intelligent Energy-Based Tool Monitoring

The green cluster shows strong focus on tool wear and material condition monitoring, machine learning, mechanical aspects, machine tools, and process-related operational signals. This indicates that data acquired from CNC machining systems are a primary source of information to diagnose tool condition and estimate wear progression during machining. The dense connections between condition monitoring, data acquisition, and tool wear demonstrate the focus on extracting performance indicators from process variables and operational data, as indirect signals of cutting-edge degradation, changes in machining behavior, or variations in the quality of the tool material interaction. In parallel, it is highlighted the use of machine learning algorithms for tool condition classification or for predicting the remaining useful life, exploiting features derived from process monitoring, energy modelling, and system-level data recorded by numerical control environments. This includes the application of neural networks, decision trees, predictive analytics, and learning-based models within broader smart manufacturing and digital twin frameworks. This outlines a methodological ecosystem in which monitoring data traditionally treated as operational feedback are reframed as a rich informational layer for non-invasive diagnostics and predictive analysis.

2.3 Cluster 3 (Blue) - Energy Diagnostics in Excavation Systems

Cluster 3 includes keywords such as boring machines, absorbed energy and cutting power, employed as indirect indicators of tool condition and process efficiency, albeit within a different operational context. This suggests that the use of energy signals for wear monitoring and performance prediction is not limited to chip-removal machining, but rather represents a broader diagnostic paradigm, applicable to different tool material systems. For this reason, the blue cluster can be interpreted as an adjacent domain, useful in confirming the generalizability of energy-based approaches to predictive maintenance, while remaining external to the core scope of the present analysis.

2.4 Cluster 4 (Yellow) – Sustainable Manufacturing and Life-Cycle Energy

Cluster 4 gathers literature focused on evaluating the sustainability of manufacturing processes, with particular attention to energy consumption, environmental impact, and the economic and social implications of industrial production. The dominant keywords, including carbon emissions, green manufacturing, life cycle assessment, environmental impact, sustainability, define a domain oriented toward process-wide analysis, moving beyond individual processing stages to adopt a broader systemic perspective. Within this context, energy consumption is a key variable for determining emissions, costs, and overall environmental footprint, rather than merely serving as a signal for monitoring process conditions. The positioning of the yellow cluster within the visual map, strongly interconnected with clusters focused on manufacturing processes and energy consumption, highlights how issues of energy efficiency, process quality, and environmental sustainability are increasingly addressed in an integrated manner.

2.5 Cluster 5 (PURPLE) – Machine Tool Energy Engineering

Cluster 5 focuses on the energy efficiency of machine tools and on system-level energy management. Dominant keywords, here, are energy utilization, energy efficiency, energy conservation, energy management. This reveals the research interest in energy modeling, design strategies, and performance improvement of drives, cooling systems, and machine architectures. Energy is treated as a global variable to guiding design and sustainable management decisions. Although not directly centered on tool wear monitoring, this cluster provides the technical reference framework needed to understand how the machine's energy behavior influences the signals that can be exploited for diagnostics and predictive maintenance.

2.6 Cross-Cluster Interpretation

The five identified clusters suggest an interdependent analytical landscape, beyond isolated thematic domains. In detail, Cluster 1 provides the physical basis linking machining parameters and cutting mechanics to energy generation, while Cluster 2 operationalizes these relationships by interpreting energy and process signals as indicators of tool condition through data-driven models. Cluster 5 extends this perspective to the system level, showing how machine architecture and auxiliary systems shape the observed energy profiles. Clusters 3 and 4 broaden the scope by, respectively, supporting the generalizability of energy-based diagnostics across machining contexts and integrating energy consumption within sustainability-driven decision frameworks. Such a picture highlights a conceptual shift: energy evolves from a process outcome to a diagnostic signal and ultimately to a decision variable for predictive maintenance and system optimization. This integrated view provides the basis for the subsequent content analysis, where these relationships are examined at the level of modelling approaches, variables, and performance indicators.

3 Results

The bibliometric mapping provided the conceptual structure used to define the coding dimensions adopted in the content analysis. In particular, the thematic clusters emerging from keyword co-occurrence analysis guided the identification of the main analytical categories, including modelling objectives, input variables, algorithms, and performance indicators. This ensures methodological continuity between literature mapping and structured interpretation of predictive maintenance strategies based on energy-related signals. To investigate the relationships among the coded methodological and operational elements within AI-guided strategies aimed at enhancing energy performance through machine-state control, a hierarchical clustering analysis was conducted based on the co-occurrence patterns identified across the 32 reviewed studies (Fig. 2). Papers were here referred as per ID# Table 1 in appendix.

Using Jaccard distance on the binary coding matrix, the resulting dendrogram reveals the empirical proximity among modeling purposes, algorithmic approaches, variables, objectives, and performance indicator (Fig. 3).

3.1 Modelling Approach

Optimization-oriented studies (6 out of 32; IDs: 1, 3, 7, 8, 10, 13) aim at identifying optimal machining configurations to improve efficiency, sustainability, or productivity. Sun et al., (ID 2) and Yurtkuran et al., (ID 5) developed deep learning and machine learning regression models to estimate energy consumption patterns in machining operations. Similarly, Yu et al. (ID 17) proposed a Support Vector Regression (SVR) framework for the joint prediction of energy consumption and surface roughness. RUL-focused prediction is addressed by Fernández de Barrena Sarasola et al., (ID 11) through recurrent neural networks, and by Zhang et al. (ID 21) using ANN-LSTM architectures. Özduğun et al., (ID 3) explored cutting fluid optimization for enhanced sustainability, while Bott

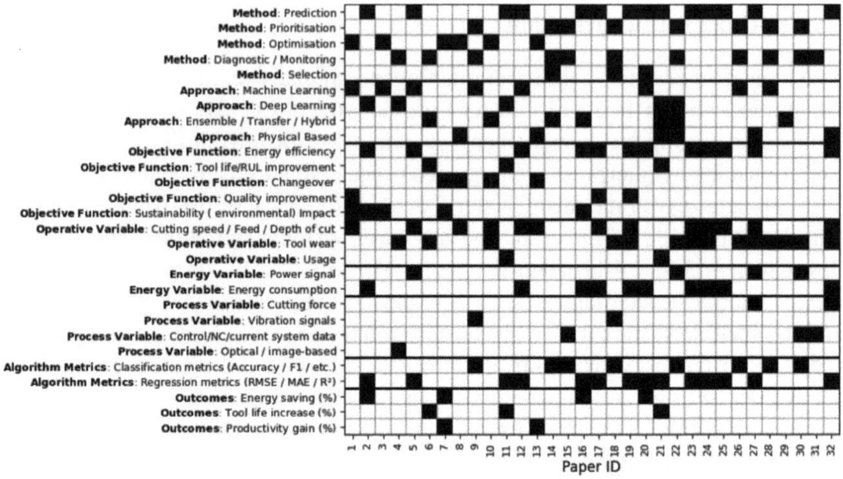

Fig. 2. Content-analysis matrix to investigate energy related performances in machining while selecting method, approach, objective functions, variables, metrics and outcomes across the reviewed studies (n = 32). Cel in black indicates the presence of each coded element within the paper ID number as per Table 1.

et al., (ID 7) proposed an online optimization framework for milling machine efficiency. Dubey et al., (ID 8) adopted a Box–Behnken design for parameter optimization in milling, and Cui et al., (ID 13) developed a real-time data-driven drilling optimization approach. Furthermore, Li et al., (ID 10) introduced an adaptive optimization method incorporating dynamic tool wear effects, bridging degradation modelling and decision-oriented control. Monitoring-oriented contributions (12 out of 32 studies; IDs: 4, 6, 9, 14, 15, 18, 22, 26, 28, 29, 30, 31) focus on real-time observation and diagnosis of machining conditions. Unlike prediction-oriented approaches, research on monitoring emphasizes condition assessment and state recognition rather than forecasting. (IDs: 4, 9, 15, 28) adopt machine learning techniques for discrete tool state classification based on process signals. Tiwari et al. (ID 9) developed a data-driven tool condition monitoring framework relying on supervised learning for wear state classification, while Sun et al., (ID29) applied machine learning algorithms for milling cutter condition discrimination using sensor-derived features Signal-based monitoring approaches are also prominent (IDs: 6, 18, 26, 29, 30, 31), including power/current and vibration analysis for tool wear detection. Su et al., (2021) (ID 19) investigated the suitability of signal features for reliable tool condition assessment, and Wang et al., (ID 30) proposed current-signal-based monitoring solutions to enhance tool wear detection robustness. Hybrid and system-level architectures gain robustness and generalization for industrial deployment (IDs: 14, 22). Zhao et al., (ID 23) leveraged deep learning architectures to extract complex patterns from raw process signals, demonstrating the increasing role of high-capacity models in condition monitoring applications. Overall, monitoring provides the situational awareness layer necessary for predictive and optimization-oriented frameworks, enabling the transition from reactive inspection to data-driven adaptive control. This distribution reveals

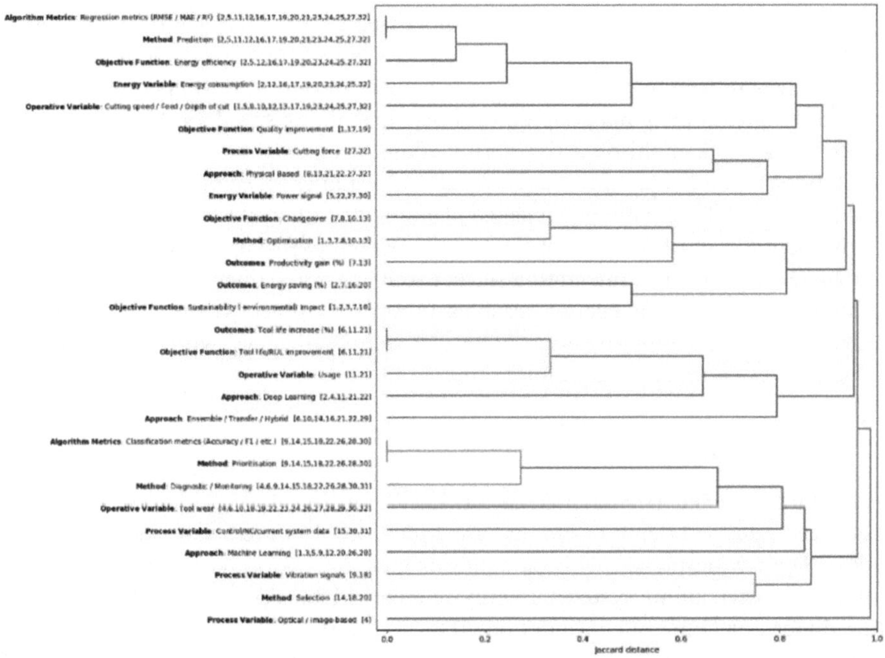

Fig. 3. Hierarchical clustering dendrogram of coded methodological and operational elements energy related performances in machining based on their co-occurrence across the reviewed studies (n = 32). Distances correspond to Jaccard dissimilarity computed from the binary content-analysis matrix. Number in square brackets as per paper ID of Table 1.

a structural transition from monitoring-oriented approaches toward prediction and optimization, indicating a shift from descriptive analytics to decision-oriented machining strategies.

3.2 Objective Function

Out of 32 studies (IDs: 1, 2, 3, 7, 16) position energy consumption as primary performance criterion in machining optimization and modelling. Kuntoğlu et al., (2026) (ID 1) incorporated environmental indicators and sustainable machining criteria into their modelling framework, explicitly linking cutting performance to ecological impact. Likewise, Papacharalampopoulos et al., (ID 6) framed process optimization within a comprehensive sustainability perspective, including resource efficiency considerations beyond mere energy reduction. Sun et al., (ID 2) developed a deep learning-based regression model to estimate and minimize specific energy consumption in milling operations. Similarly, Yurtkuran et al., (ID 5) proposed a machine learning model aimed at optimizing cutting parameters in order to reduce power consumption while maintaining process stability. In a comparable direction, Yu et al., (ID 17) integrated cutting parameters and tool wear evolution to predict both specific energy consumption and surface roughness, positioning energy as a central performance criterion. Energy efficiency emerges as the most frequently pursued objective (12 out of 32 studies; IDs: 2, 5, 12, 16, 17, 19, 20, 23, 24, 25, 27, 32).

Objectives related to productivity improvement (4 out of 32 studies; IDs: 7, 8, 10, 13) focus on maximizing material removal rate, machining speed, or throughput. These studies often adopt multi-objective formulations balancing productivity with energy consumption or tool wear constraints. 3 out of 32 studies (IDs: 6, 11, 21) directly link degradation modelling with maintenance planning and lifecycle cost reduction. Quality improvement (3 out of 32 studies; IDs: 1, 17, 19) represents a less frequent but strategically relevant objective, integrating surface roughness and dimensional accuracy with machining parameters and energy variables. Overall, the objective distribution indicates a research landscape primarily oriented toward energy efficiency, with sustainability and productivity as complementary dimensions.

3.3 Variables Analysis

Machining parameters (IDs: 1, 5, 8, 10, 12, 13, 17, 19, 23, 24, 25, 27, 32) include cutting speed, feed rate, and depth of cut and are widely used in predictive and optimization models. Their widespread inclusion confirms their role as primary controllable levers in data-driven machining systems. Energy-related variables constitute a dominant modelling dimension. Energy consumption (IDs: 2, 12, 16, 17, 19, 20, 23, 24, 25, 32) is often treated as output or performance indicator, while power signals (IDs: 5, 22, 27, 30) are exploited for indirect condition monitoring. These studies highlight the growing relevance of energy-based monitoring as a cost-effective and non-invasive sensing approach. Tool-related variables, particularly tool wear (IDs: 4, 6, 10, 18, 19, 22, 23, 24, 26, 27, 28, 29, 30, 32), represent a major modelling focus and are used both as inputs and prediction targets. Remaining Useful Life (RUL) (IDs: 11, 21) forms a specialized subset within predictive maintenance frameworks. Together, tool wear and RUL variables anchor degradation modelling and maintenance-oriented analytics. The systematic co-occurrence of machining parameters, tool wear, and energy variables suggests that energy acts as an intermediary variable linking controllable process inputs to degradation states and predictive outputs.

3.4 Performance Analysis

Performance evaluation can be structured into two dimensions: model performance metrics and process improvement indicators. This distinction separates algorithmic accuracy from tangible industrial impact. Classification metrics (Accuracy, F1-score, Precision, Recall) are predominantly used in monitoring-oriented studies (IDs: 9, 14, 15, 18, 22, 26, 28, 30), where the objective is tool state recognition or anomaly detection. Tiwari et al. (ID 9) evaluated vibration-based tool condition monitoring models using classification accuracy metrics. Similarly, Kolar et al., (ID 15) assessed drill condition monitoring performance through classification-based metrics, while Dong et al., (ID 22) reported performance improvements in spindle power-based monitoring using neural network classifiers. Regression metrics (RMSE, MAE, R^2) are common in prediction-oriented studies (IDs: 2, 5, 11, 12, 16, 17, 19, 20, 21, 23, 24, 25, 27, 32), targeting continuous variables such as energy consumption, tool wear, or RUL. Sun et al. (ID 2) evaluated deep learning models for energy consumption prediction using regression accuracy metrics, while Liu et al., (ID 12) reported RMSE and R^2 values for Random Forest models applied to energy prediction in turning processes. Likewise, Fernández de Barrena Sarasola et al., (ID 11) assessed RUL prediction performance through error-based metrics within recurrent neural network frameworks. This pattern reflects the methodological alignment between modelling purpose and evaluation metric. Beyond algorithmic evaluation, several studies quantify tangible process improvements. Energy saving (%) is reported in sustainability-oriented studies (IDs: 2, 7, 16, 20); tool life increase (%) in predictive maintenance works (IDs: 6, 11, 21) and productivity gain (%) in optimization-oriented contributions (IDs: 7, 13). These indicators demonstrate the operational impact of intelligent machining models.

Sun et al., (ID 2) demonstrated measurable reductions in specific energy consumption through optimized machining strategies, while Bott et al., (ID 7) reported improvements in energy efficiency via online optimization frameworks Papacharalampopoulos et al., (ID 6) and Fernández de Barrena Sarasola et al. (ID 11) highlighted improvements in tool lifespan or maintenance scheduling accuracy resulting from the integration of predictive models. Cui et al., (2023) (ID 13), for instance, demonstrated productivity improvements through real-time drilling parameter optimization, while Bott et al., (ID 7) reported performance gains in milling operations. Overall, performance evaluation operates at two complementary levels: algorithmic validation and operational benefit. While classification and regression metrics ensure modelling reliability, process-level indicators such as energy savings, tool life extension, and productivity gains confirm industrial relevance. This dual perspective reflects the ongoing convergence of manufacturing systems toward performance and sustainability-oriented intelligent machining paradigms.

4 Discussion

The evidence provided by the results moves beyond a descriptive mapping of the literature: it reveals a coherent analytical structure linking machining physics, energy signals, and predictive decision-making. Accordingly, we can clearly respond to RQs.

RQ1: To What Extent Operational CNC States Drive Energy Consumption?
The literature review highlights that energy consumption cycles are primarily characterized by the interaction between machining parameters, spindle power signals, and process phases (cutting, idle, tool change, acceleration). Studies integrating energy variables (IDs: 2, 12, 16, 20, 23–25) show that energy profiles are strongly influenced by the temporal segmentation of machining operations and by the dynamic load conditions imposed by the cutting process. The recurring presence of spindle power and current signals in monitoring-oriented studies further confirms that energy cycles are structurally linked to operational states rather than representing random fluctuations. The variable analysis reveals that cutting speed, feed rate, depth of cut, and spindle speed (IDs: 1, 5, 8, 10, 12, 13, 17, 19, 23, 24, 25, 27, 32) consistently emerge as dominant explanatory variables within energy modelling frameworks. The convergence of process parameters and energy variables in prediction-and optimization-oriented studies confirms that machining parameters act as primary drivers of energy consumption patterns.

RQ2: How Can Be Designed Tool Replacement Strategies to Manage Energy Consumption?
A significant portion of the corpus integrates tool wear as either an input or an output variable (IDs: 4, 6, 10, 18, 19, 22, 23, 24, 26, 27, 28, 29, 30, 32). The coexistence of wear indicators and energy metrics within predictive models suggests a direct correlation between degradation progression and variations in the energy profile. RUL-oriented studies (IDs: 11, 21) further reinforce this relationship by demonstrating how degradation states can be inferred from energy signals. Prediction-oriented modelling approaches (IDs: 2, 5, 11, 12, 16, 17, 19, 20, 21, 23, 24, 25, 27, 32) demonstrate the feasibility of using regression and deep learning frameworks to map energy signals to degradation states. Performance analysis confirms that these models achieve high predictive reliability (RMSE, R^2), while process-level indicators (tool life extension, energy savings) highlight their practical applicability for maintenance scheduling. Overall, the findings of the structured literature analysis suggest that energy-based monitoring can constitute a promising foundation for predictive maintenance strategies in CNC machining, linking absorbed power signals, process parameters, degradation modelling, and operational decision-making.

Despite these advances, the literature remains fragmented across physical modelling, data-driven monitoring, and system-level optimization, with limited integration across these layers. In particular, the role of energy as a unifying variable is rarely made explicit, and cross-machine generalization remains insufficiently addressed.

5 Conclusion

This study has provided a structured bibliometric and content analysis of the scientific literature investigating the relationship between energy consumption profiles and tool degradation, with the aim of developing a predictive maintenance framework for machining operations. The results confirm the existence of a progressive shift in the research landscape: energy consumption in machining, initially used as an indicator of sustainability and efficiency, is progressively expanding its role as a diagnostic and prognostic signal for tool condition assessment. Energy is no longer treated solely as a performance metric but is increasingly interpreted as a proxy variable capable of capturing process-state transitions and degradation dynamics. The predominance of prediction-oriented approaches indicates that the field is moving beyond descriptive monitoring toward anticipatory maintenance strategies. Energy signals, when properly modelled, appear capable of bridging process parameters and tool degradation states, thereby enabling non-invasive predictive frameworks compatible with industrial CNC environments. Many contributions report high predictive accuracy under controlled experimental conditions, yet cross-machine validation, tool-type transferability, and long-term robustness remain limited. Accordingly, these results should be interpreted as indicative rather than universally generalizable across heterogeneous industrial contexts. This suggests that the field, although methodologically advanced, still requires consolidation in terms of reproducibility and industrial deployment standards. Energy-based predictive maintenance frameworks may represent a practical pathway toward scalable intelligent machining systems, particularly in contexts where economic constraints limit the adoption of additional sensing technologies. When properly modelled, energy signals can link machining parameters and tool degradation states, enabling non-invasive predictive frameworks compatible with industrial CNC environments. The review also reveals persistent challenges related to model generalization, dataset standardization, and large-scale validation in real industrial contexts. Notwithstanding, the lack of standardized datasets, limited benchmarking across different tool types and materials, and scarce integration with digital twin architectures indicate that the field is still evolving. In such a scenario, this study contributes (by moving from bibliometric mapping to a structured analytical synthesis) identifying energy as a key linking variable across machining physics, monitoring, and predictive maintenance. Future research should therefore focus on the integration of multi-source data, the development of real-time adaptive models, the definition of standardized validation protocols, and tighter integration between energy analytics and cyber-physical manufacturing systems.

Appendix

Table 1. ID references papers for content analysis

ID	Author (year)	References
1	Kuntoğlu et al., (2026)	[18]
2	Sun et al., (2026)	[34]
3	Özdüzgün et al., (2025)	[19]
4	Friedrich et al., (2023)	[47]
5	Yurtkuran et al., (2024)	[40]
6	Papacharalampopoulos et al., (2024)	[24]
7	Bott et al., (2024)	[20]
8	Dubey et al., (2024)	[21]
9	Tiwari et al., (2024)	[25]
10	Li et al., (2023)	[22]
11	Fernández De Barrena Sarasola et al., (2023)	[36]
12	Liu et al., (2023)	[41]
13	Cui et al., (2023)	[23]
14	Schueller et al., (2022)	[26]
15	Kolar et al., (2022)	[48]
16	Lu et al., (2022)	[35]
17	Yu et al., (2021)	[38]
18	Kossakowska et al., (2021)	[27]
19	Su et al., (2021)	[39]
20	Xiao et al., (2021)	[46]
21	Zhang et al., (2021)	[37]

(continued)

Table 1. (*continued*)

ID	Author (year)	References
22	Dong et al., (2021)	[28]
23	Zhao et al., (2020)	[42]
24	Zhao et al., (2020)	[43]
25	Zhao et al., (2020)	[44]
26	Li et al., (2019)	[29]
27	Wang et al., (2019)	[6]
28	Patange et al., (2019)	[30]
29	Sun et al., (2019)	[31]
30	Wang et al., (2017)	[32]
31	Wu et al., (2017)	[33]
32	Zhang et al., (2016)	[45]

References

1. Mancusi, F., Bochicchio, A., Laforgia, A., Fruggiero, F.: Sustainability-aware maintenance for machine tools: a quantitative framework linking degradation management with life-cycle cost and environmental performance. Appl. Sci. **15**(21), 11333 (2025). https://doi.org/10.3390/app152111333
2. Lee, W.J., Wu, H., Yun, H., Kim, H., Jun, M.B., Sutherland, J.W.: Predictive maintenance of machine tool systems using artificial intelligence techniques applied to machine condition data. Procedia CIRP. **80**, 506–511 (2019). https://doi.org/10.1016/j.procir.2018.12.019
3. Proteau, A., Tahan, A., Thomas, M.: Specific cutting energy: a physical measurement for representing tool wear. Int. J. Adv. Manuf. Technol. **103**(1), 101–110 (2019). https://doi.org/10.1007/s00170-019-03533-4
4. Perera, Y.S., Ratnaweera, D.A.A.C., Dasanayaka, C.H., Abeykoon, C.: The role of artificial intelligence-driven soft sensors in advanced sustainable process industries: a critical review. Eng. Appl. Artif. Intell. **121**, 105988 (2023). https://doi.org/10.1016/j.engappai.2023.105988
5. Wang, Q.C.: A tool wear prediction and monitoring method based on machining power signals. Int. J. Adv. Manuf. Technol. **129**(11), 5387–5401 (2023). https://doi.org/10.1007/s00170-023-12656-8
6. Wang, Q., Zhang, D., Tang, K., Zhang, Y.: A mechanics-based prediction model for tool wear and power consumption in drilling operations and its applications. J. Clean. Prod. **234**, 171–184 (2019). https://doi.org/10.1016/j.jclepro.2019.06.148
7. Chen, X., Zhang, Z., Wang, Q., Zhang, D., Luo, M.: Cutting force prediction between different machine tool systems based on transfer learning method. Int. J. Adv. Manuf. Technol. **121**(1), 619–631 (2022). https://doi.org/10.1007/s00170-022-09316-8
8. Munaro, R., Attanasio, A., Del Prete, A.: Tool wear monitoring with artificial intelligence methods: a review. J. Manuf. Mater. Process. **7**(4), 129 (2023). https://doi.org/10.3390/jmmp7040129
9. Cardoso, D., Ferreira, L.: Application of predictive maintenance concepts using artificial intelligence tools. Appl. Sci. **11**(1), 18 (2020). https://doi.org/10.3390/app11010018

10. Shi, K.N., Zhang, D.H., Liu, N., Wang, S.B., Ren, J.X., Wang, S.L.: A novel energy consumption model for milling process considering tool wear progression. J. Clean. Prod. **184**, 152–159 (2018). https://doi.org/10.1016/j.jclepro.2018.02.239
11. Colantonio, L., Equeter, L., Dehombreux, P., Ducobu, F.: A systematic literature review of cutting tool wear monitoring in turning by using artificial intelligence techniques. Machines. **9**(12), 351 (2021). https://doi.org/10.3390/machines9120351
12. Herrera-Granados, G., Misaka, T., Herwan, J., Komoto, H., Furukawa, Y.: An experimental study of multi-sensor tool wear monitoring and its application to predictive maintenance. Int. J. Adv. Manuf. Technol. **133**(7), 3415–3433 (2024). https://doi.org/10.1007/s00170-024-13959-0
13. Yedurkar, D.P., Schlech, T., Sause, M.G.: A systematic review on smart and predictive maintenance in tool condition monitoring. IEEE Access. (2025). https://doi.org/10.1109/ACCESS.2025.3579204
14. Martín-Martín, A., Orduna-Malea, E., Thelwall, M., Delgado López-Cózar, E.: Google scholar, web of science, and Scopus: a systematic comparison. J. Informetr. **12**(4), 1160–1177 (2018). https://doi.org/10.1016/j.joi.2018.09.002
15. Donthu, N., Kumar, S., Mukherjee, D., Pandey, N., Lim, W.M.: How to conduct a bibliometric analysis: an overview and guidelines. J. Bus. Res. **133**, 285–296 (2021). https://doi.org/10.1016/j.jbusres.2021.04.070
16. Zupic, I., Čater, T.: Bibliometric methods in management and organization. Organ. Res. Methods. **18**(3), 429–472 (2015). https://doi.org/10.1177/1094428114562629
17. Snyder, H.: Literature review as a research methodology: an overview and guidelines. J. Bus. Res. **104**, 333–339 (2019). https://doi.org/10.1016/j.jbusres.2019.07.039
18. Kuntoğlu, M., Demirpolat, H., Binali, R., Korkmaz, M.E., Makhesana, M., Kaya, K.: Sustainable lubrication strategies in eco-friendly machining of AISI 4140 steel: performance and environmental impact analysis using machine learning. J. Mater. Eng. Perform., 1–17 (2025). https://doi.org/10.1007/s11665-025-11948-2
19. Özdüzgün, H.S., Er, A.O.: Optimizing cutting fluid use via machine learning in smart manufacturing for enhanced sustainability. Lubricants. **13**(12), 519 (2025). https://doi.org/10.3390/lubricants13120519
20. Bott, A., Anderlik, S., Ströbel, R., Fleischer, J., Wortmann, A.: Framework for holistic online optimization of milling machine conditions to enhance machine efficiency and sustainability. Machines. **12**(3), 153 (2024). https://doi.org/10.3390/machines12030153
21. Dubey, V., Vats, P., Kumar, H., Sharma, A.K.: Optimization and modelling of machining parameters in end milling operation using Box-Behnken technique. In: International Conference on Mechanical and Energy Technologies, pp. 485–495. Springer, Singapore (2023). https://doi.org/10.1007/978-981-97-2716-2_43
22. Li, C., Zhao, X., Cao, H., Li, L., Chen, X.: A data-and knowledge-driven cutting parameter adaptive optimization method considering dynamic tool wear. Robot. Comput. Integr. Manuf. **81**, 102491 (2023). https://doi.org/10.1016/j.rcim.2022.102491
23. Cui, M.A., Li, J., Liu, W., Ding, Y.: Maximising drilling rates with real-time data-driven drilling parameters optimisation. In: International Petroleum Technology Conference., D012S007R001 (2023). https://doi.org/10.2523/IPTC-22772-MS
24. Papacharalampopoulos, A., Alexopoulos, K., Catti, P., Stavropoulos, P., Chryssolouris, G.: Learning more with less data in manufacturing: the case of turning tool wear assessment through active and transfer learning. Processes. **12**(6), 1262 (2024). https://doi.org/10.3390/pr12061262
25. Tiwari, S., Gunasegaran, V., Amarnath, M., Chelladurai, H.: Cutting tool condition monitoring based on a machine learning approach by using vibration signals. In: 1st International Conference on Robotics, Engineering, Science, and Technology (RESTCON), pp. 222–227 (2024). https://doi.org/10.1109/RESTCON60981.2024.10463549

26. Schueller, A., Saldaña, C.: Generalizability analysis of tool condition monitoring ensemble machine learning models. J. Manuf. Process. **84**, 1064–1075 (2022). https://doi.org/10.1016/j.jmapro.2022.10.064
27. Kossakowska, J., Bombiński, S., Ejsmont, K.: Analysis of the suitability of signal features for individual sensor types in the diagnosis of gradual tool wear in turning. Energies. **14**(20), 6489 (2021). https://doi.org/10.3390/en14206489
28. Dong, W., Guo, X., Hu, Y., Wang, J., Tian, G.: Discrete wavelet transformation and GA- BP neural network applied in monitoring woodworking tool wear conditions in milling operation spindle power signals. Bioresources. **16**(2) (2021). https://doi.org/10.15376/biores.16.2.2369-2384
29. Li, Z., Liu, R., Wu, D.: Data-driven smart manufacturing: tool wear monitoring with audio signals and machine learning. J. Manuf. Process. **48**, 66–76 (2019). https://doi.org/10.1016/j.jmapro.2019.10.020
30. Patange, A.D., Jegadeeshwaran, R., Dhobale, N.C.: Milling cutter condition monitoring using machine learning approach. IOP Conf. Ser.: Mater. Sci. Eng. **624**(1), 012030 (2019). https://doi.org/10.1088/1757-899X/624/1/012030
31. Sun, H., Pan, J., Zhang, J., Mo, R.: Digital twin model for cutting tools in machining process. Comput. Integr. Manuf. Syst. **25**(6), 1474–1480 (2019). https://doi.org/10.13196/j.cims.2019.06.015
32. Wang, C., Huang, M., Chung, T.T., Young, H.T., Li, K.M.: Tool condition monitoring with current signals for a low-power spindle. In: International Conference on Applied System Innovation (ICASI), pp. 686–689 (2017). https://doi.org/10.1109/ICASI.2017.7988518
33. Wu, D., et al.: A fog computing-based framework for process monitoring and prognosis in cyber-manufacturing. J. Manuf. Syst. **43**, 25–34 (2017). https://doi.org/10.1016/j.jmsy.2017.02.011
34. Sun, Z., Zhang, Y., Tian, Y., Sun, Y., Wu, B.: Energy consumption pattern recognition and reduction in milling operations via deep neural networks. AIP Adv. **16**(1) (2026). https://doi.org/10.1063/5.0313907
35. Lu, F., Zhou, G., Liu, Y., Zhang, C.: Ensemble transfer learning for cutting energy consumption prediction of aviation parts towards green manufacturing. J. Clean. Prod. **331**, 129920 (2022). https://doi.org/10.1016/j.jclepro.2021.129920
36. De Barrena, T.F., Ferrando, J.L., García, A., Badiola, X., de Buruaga, M.S., Vicente, J.: Tool remaining useful life prediction using bidirectional recurrent neural networks. Int. J. Adv. Manuf. Technol. **125**(9), 4027–4045 (2023). https://doi.org/10.1007/s00170-023-10811-9
37. Zhang, X., Lu, X., Li, W., Wang, S.: Prediction of the remaining useful life of cutting tool using the Hurst exponent and CNN-LSTM. Int. J. Adv. Manuf. Technol. **112**(7), 2277–2299 (2021). https://doi.org/10.1007/s00170-020-06447-8
38. Yu, S., Zhao, G., Li, C., Xu, S., Zheng, Z.: Prediction models for energy consumption and surface quality in stainless steel milling. Int. J. Adv. Manuf. Technol. **117**(11), 3777–3792 (2021). https://doi.org/10.1007/s00170-021-07971-x
39. Su, Y., Li, C., Zhao, G., Zhao, G.: Prediction models for specific energy consumption of machine tools and surface roughness based on cutting parameters and tool wear. Proc. Inst. Mech. Eng. B. **235**(6–7), 1225–1234 (2021). https://doi.org/10.1177/0954405420971064
40. Yurtkuran, H., Korkmaz, M.E., Gupta, M.K., Yılmaz, H., Günay, M., Vashishtha, G.: Prediction of power consumption and its signals in sustainable turning of PH13-8Mo steel with different machine learning models. Int. J. Adv. Manuf. Technol. **133**(5), 2171–2188 (2024). https://doi.org/10.1007/s00170-024-13867-3
41. Liu, J., Li, M., Zheng, Y.: A random forest regression-based method for predicting energy consumption of turning operations on CNC machine tools. In: 7th International Conference on Electrical, Mechanical and Computer Engineering (ICEMCE), pp. 650–654 (2023). https://doi.org/10.1109/ICEMCE60359.2023.10491062

42. Zhao, G., Su, Y., Zheng, G., Zhao, Y., Li, C.: Tool tip cutting specific energy prediction model and the influence of machining parameters and tool wear in milling. Proc. Inst. Mech. Eng. B. **234**(10), 1346–1354 (2020). https://doi.org/10.1177/0954405420911298
43. Zhao, G., Li, C., Lv, Z., Cheng, X., Zheng, G.: Specific energy consumption prediction model of CNC machine tools based on tool wear. Int. J. Comput. Integr. Manuf. **33**(2), 159–168 (2020). https://doi.org/10.1080/0951192X.2020.1718763
44. Zhao, G., Zhao, Y., Meng, F., Guo, Q., Zheng, G.: Prediction model of machine tool energy consumption in hard-to-process materials turning. Int. J. Adv. Manuf. Technol. **106**(9), 4499–4508 (2020). https://doi.org/10.1007/s00170-020-04939-1
45. Zhang, G., Guo, C.: Modeling flank wear progression based on cutting force and energy prediction in turning process. Procedia Manuf. **5**, 536–545 (2016). https://doi.org/10.1016/j.promfg.2016.08.044
46. Xiao, Q., Li, C., Tang, Y., Chen, X.: Energy efficiency modeling for configuration-dependent machining via machine learning: a comparative study. IEEE Trans. Autom. Sci. Eng. **18**(2), 717–730 (2020). https://doi.org/10.1109/TASE.2019.2961714
47. Friedrich, M., Ahmeti, E., Dumler, J., Döpper, F.: Towards sustainable machining: synthetic data generation for efficient optical tool wear monitoring via generative adversarial networks. In: Global Conference on Sustainable Manufacturing, pp. 544–552. Springer, Cham (2023). https://doi.org/10.1007/978-3-031-77429-4_60
48. Kolar, P., et al.: Indirect drill condition monitoring based on machine tool control system data. MM Sci. J. (2022). https://doi.org/10.17973/MMSJ.2022_10_2022119

Water Management Systems

Deep Learning Based Acoustic Leak Detection and Classification in Water Distribution Systems Using Hydrophone Sensors

Ajibola Oyedeji(✉), Nnamdi Nwulu, and Peter Olukanmi

School of Electrical & Electronics Engineering, University of Johannesburg, Johannesburg, South Africa
223235694@student.uj.ac.za, {nnwulu,polukanmi}@uj.ac.za

Abstract. Leakage detection in water distribution systems is of utmost importance for water resource management. This study developed a deep learning (DL) framework for acoustic leak detection using hydrophone sensors. The data was collected from a controlled water testbed simulating both looped and branched pipeline topologies under five conditions: no-leak, longitudinal crack, circumferential crack, orifice leak, and gasket leak. The feature extraction from the raw acoustic signals sampled at 8 kHz followed two approaches: extraction of statistical features for traditional machine learning (ML), and generation of Mel-Frequency Cepstral Coefficient (MFCC) spectrograms using sliding window segmentation suitable for DL models. Three DL models were trained on the MFCC image data for both binary and multi classification. These models achieved excellent classification performance ranging from 94.77 to 100% across all network configurations. The study reveals that by transforming raw data into 2D spectrograms, the models better learned representative features and outperformed ML models trained with statistical features.

Keywords: Water Leak Detection · Acoustic Signals · MFCC Spectrograms · Deep Learning

1 Introduction

Water is a crucial resource essential for sustaining life, economic development, and industrial activities [1, 2]. Water distribution systems constitute the essential backbone of urban infrastructure; however, they are faced with a global crisis of Non-Revenue Water (NRW) caused by aging infrastructure [3]. Global water loss has been estimated to be around 126 billion cubic meters annually, worth nearly USD 39 billion per year [4, 5]. Hence, the development of accurate leak detection instruments is crucial for achieving sustainable urban water management [6, 7]. Traditional detection methods which typically rely on manual inspection have been found to be ineffective as they are labor intensive and prone to error.

Published by Springer Nature Switzerland AG 2027
L. M. Camarinha-Matos and F. Ferrada (Eds.): DoCEIS 2026, IFIP AICT 790, pp. 259–273, 2027.
https://doi.org/10.1007/978-3-032-28939-1_19

Recent advances in sensor technology have led to the development of high-fidelity hydrophones that can directly capture underwater acoustic signatures from the water column [8]. Even with these sensor improvements, acoustic leak signatures are complex because of the different characteristics and topologies of the distribution pipeline and the background noise [9]. Complex topologies introduce distinct acoustic behaviors with looped systems creating multi-path reflections and echoes, whereas branched systems generally exhibit linear signal attenuation, and these variations make automating detection difficult.

Acoustic leak signatures and transient hydraulic events are often hard to tell apart by traditional signal processing methods [10]. Researchers have turned to machine learning (ML) and deep learning (DL) algorithms to automatically identify and distinguish leaks. Conventional ML algorithms are generally employed for the classification of one-dimensional (1D) time and frequency domains of acoustic signals. The ML models include the random forest (RF), logistic regression, support vector machines (SVM), and gradient boosting (GB). On the other hand, Convolutional Neural Network (CNN) is a widely used DL algorithm which considers acoustic signals as image data, processing time-frequency representations as spectrograms or scalograms [11].

This study proposes a deep learning framework for acoustic leak detection and classification using hydrophone sensors. By leveraging the high-quality signal acquisition of hydrophones and the advanced acoustic signal processing techniques, and the sophisticated pattern recognition capabilities of DL, this study aims to enhance detection accuracy and minimize false alarms. By transforming 1D acoustic signals into 2-dimensional (2D) spectrogram images, this research leverages state-of-the-art computer vision models to classify leak types across the network configuration.

While acoustic leak detection and deep learning classification are established fields, this work provides several novel contributions. In this study, validation across different water network topologies including both the looped and branched pipeline configurations, in addition to the combined configuration was provided. In addition, a dual task formulation that includes binary leak detection and multiclass leak type identification addresses both operational detection and maintenance decision-making needs.

The study will achieve the above contributions by providing answers to the following research questions:

- How effectively can DL models classify acoustic leak signals captured by hydrophone sensors?
- To what extent does transforming 1D acoustic signals into 2D time-frequency image representations improve leak detection accuracy compared to traditional ML models using time and frequency domain features?
- How does water network topology affect the performance of classification models?

2 Technological Innovations for Water Sustainability

This research directly addresses the DoCEIS 2026 conference theme emphasizing the development of technological innovations to solve pressing societal challenges. According to the United Nations Sustainable Development Goal 6, the provision of clean water is basic human right, but unfortunately, water scarcity is projected to increase with the global water stress at 18% since 2015, and several regions exceeding 75% stress.

This research actively seeks to address the SDG 6, by integrating fourth industrial revolution (4IR) technologies, specifically internet of things (IoT) and artificial intelligence (AI) into the water systems for smart monitoring. It proposes a Cyber-Physical System (CPS) approach that bridges the gap between physical hydraulic infrastructure and advanced computational intelligence to address and identify leakages in WDS, thereby mitigating NRW. This reduction in water losses improves availability of the scarce resource, clean and potable water. This has the potential to improve access to clean water, which is an essential need for human, industrial and agricultural activities.

3 Related Works

The usage of deep learning algorithms for water leakage detection in water distribution systems using acoustic signals has attracted significant attention among the research community in recent years. In [7], the authors introduced a Feature-Informed CNN that integrates statistical features (derived from fluid-structure interaction dynamics) and raw acoustic signal directly into the dense layers of a CNN. This hybrid approach proved more robust with the best accuracy of 90.4%. Another study in [12] introduced an optimized hybrid DL model for acoustic water leak detection. This architecture combines CNNs for feature extraction with Bi-LSTM networks to capture temporal dependencies. Enhanced Particle Swarm Optimization (EPSO) was used to dynamically tune hyperparameters, achieving 98.33% accuracy even under low signal-to-noise ratio (SNR) conditions for leak detection and severity classification.

In further study, a time-transformer model which outperforms CNN-based models with accuracy of up to 99.02% in detecting leaks, especially in noisy environments, was introduced [13]. Ma et al. introduced a two-stage temporal segmentation approach. Long-term segments isolate non-stationary characteristics (interference), while short-term segments capture quasi-stationary leakage features [14]. This method, combined with incremental learning, allowed the CNN model to achieve 95% accuracy. The studies show an array of DL techniques used to include CNN, hybrid and transformer models, all achieving excellent results for acoustic signal classification.

4 Methodology

To answer the research questions in this study, we created a custom CNN model for classifying leaks in water distribution systems using acoustic signals. This section outlines the different phases involved, including data preprocessing, feature extraction, model development, and evaluation.

4.1 Hydrophone Signal Collection Setup

The acoustic data were collected from controlled laboratory-scale experimental testbed designed to simulate the hydraulics dynamics of WDS [15]. To make the testbed more relevant to real-world WDS, the study simulated two different network topologies: branched and looped, which are common in municipal WDS structures. The testbed included standard PVC pipes measuring 7.5 m long and 5 m wide, with a total pipe length of 47 m.

Two hydrophones, labelled H1 and H2, were installed inside prototype fire hydrants. The data collection used Aquarian H2c hydrophones, which have a sensitivity of −180 dB and a frequency range of 1–100 kHz.

The experimental design focused on simulating realistic leak scenarios while maintaining controlled hydraulic conditions. All induced leaks were specifically designed to remain below 30% of the total input water flow to the system. Acoustic signals captured data for five operational conditions: (1) baseline no-leak condition (NL), (2) longitudinal crack (LC), (3) circumferential crack (CC), (4) orifice leak (OL), and (5) gasket leak (GL). The hydrophones captured acoustic signals at a sampling rate of 8 kHz and a signed 32-bit pulse code modulation for a period of 30 s according to Nyquist sampling theorem [15]. The experiment also accounted for daily variability in water demand modelled after typical residential consumption patterns, which includes No Demand (0 L/s), Low Demand (0.18 L/s), High Demand (0.47 L/s) and Transient Conditions where the flow was rapidly shut off from 0.47 L/s to 0 L/s [15].

4.2 Feature Extraction

A total of 120 hydrophone recordings were collected and processed. There are 24 recordings each for the five (5) operational conditions in Sect. 4.1, equally distributed across the Looped and Branched topology as depicted in Fig. 1. In binary classification, 96 recordings representing 80% of the total are Leaks while 24 (20%) are not leaks, while in the multi-class, all the classes are equally distributed with 24 recordings each.

Two complementary audio signal processing techniques were employed for feature extraction from the raw hydrophones' signals. The first involves 1D engineered statistical features from the time and frequency domains respectively, suitable for traditional ML, while the second is 2D Mel-Frequency Cepstral Coefficient (MFCC) from the time-frequency representation, suited for DL architectures.

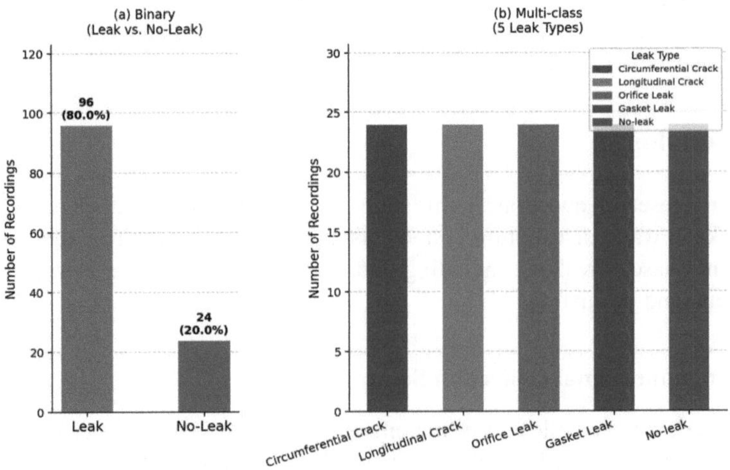

Fig. 1. Distribution of Hydrophone Recordings.

4.2.1 1D Features

Raw acoustic signals were segmented using a sliding window approach (window size of 1 s and 50% overlap) to capture temporal variations in leak signals. This segmentation successfully increased the dataset from 120 recordings to 7080 analysis windows. This helps to provide sufficient training data samples while maintaining temporal resolution. With this done, it results in a binary distribution of 5,664 (80%) Leaks and 1,416 No-leaks (20%), while each of the classes in the multiclass have 1,416 records.

For each analysis window, 30 features were extracted across the 2 domains. The features are presented in Table 1. These features were selected based on their relevance to leak detection and proven record in audio classification tasks. The complete feature vector provides a comprehensive characterization of each acoustic signal's spectro-temporal properties.

Table 1. Summary of Extracted 1D Acoustic Features [11]

Domain	Feature Category	Feature Name(s)
Time	Statistical Moments	Mean, standard deviation, variance, skewness, kurtosis
	Amplitude Measures	Minimum, maximum, range, root mean square
	Energy Metrics	Signal energy, peak-to-peak amplitude, crest factor
	Temporal Characteristics	Zero-crossing rate (ZCR), percentiles (Q25, Q75, IQR)
Frequency	Spectral Descriptors	Spectral centroids, spectral spread, rolloff, flatness
	Dominant Components	Dominant frequency, dominant magnitude
	Band Energy	10 frequency bands (0–4000 Hz)
	Energy Metrics	Total spectral energy

The distribution of RMS amplitude (V) for each leak type in different topologies is shown in Fig. 2. In the Looped network, the acoustic signatures are more stable and distinct between specific leak categories. Longitudinal cracks have the highest median RMS amplitude (approximately 0.21 V). This suggests that these leaks produce more acoustic energy than others. Gasket Leaks show the lowest variance but a relatively high median. No-Leaks have the lowest median RMS (approximately 0.15 V). The branched network has much higher variance across the leak types. The Orifice Leaks have a significantly higher median and the widest interquartile range (IQR). This indicates that signal attenuation in branched systems is less predictable.

In Fig. 3, the mean spectral centroid ranges between 15–28 Hz across all classes. The looped network has a consistently higher mean spectral centroid across all leak types than the branched configuration. Within each topology, the spectral centroid differences are minimal across each leak type, indicating that this feature is a poor discriminator of the leak type.

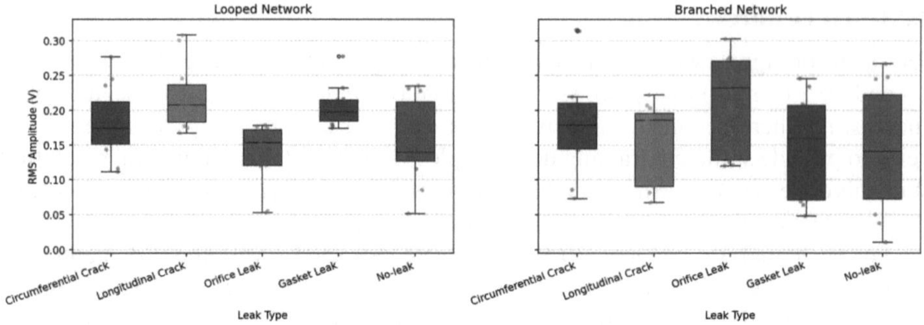

Fig. 2. RMS Amplitude Distribution by Leak Type Across Topologies.

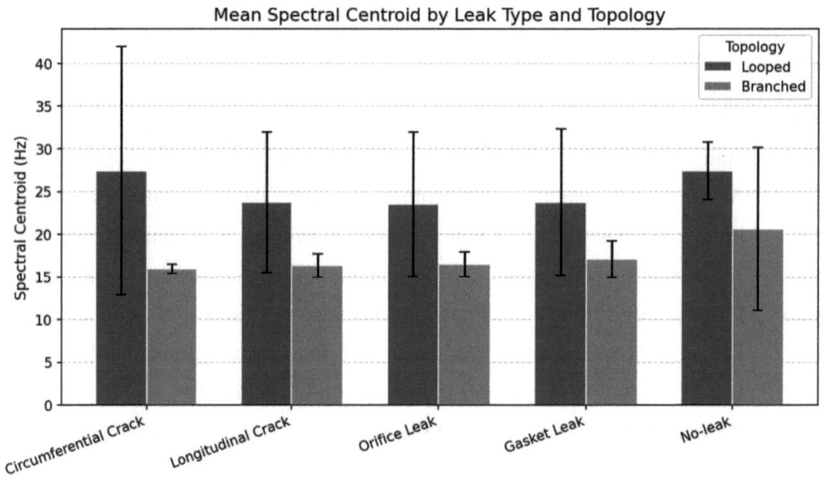

Fig. 3. Mean Spectral Centroid by Leak Type Across Topologies.

4.2.2 2D MFCC Spectrogram Generation

For deep learning approaches, the segmented acoustic window signals were transformed into MFCC spectrograms [16]. MFCC is a feature extraction technique in signal processing to represent the short-term power spectrum of a sound [17]. A short overview of the feature extraction steps is given as follows in Eqs. 1, 2 and 3:

1. Short-Time Fourier Transform (STFT): This transforms the time domain signal *x(n)* into frequency domain using the STFT. The signal was divided into overlapping frames using a 2048-point Fast Fourier Transform (FFT) and a 512-sample hop length [17].

$$X(k) = \sum_{n=0}^{N-1} x(n)e^{-j\frac{2\pi}{N}kn} \tag{1}$$

where $x(k)$ = frequency spectrum, N = frame length (2048), k = frequency bin index.

2. Mel Filter Bank Processing: This maps the power spectrum |X(k)|2 onto the Mel scale with 40 filters (M = 40). The energy in each Mel filter S(m) is given as.

$$S(m) = \sum_{k=0}^{K-1} H_m(k)|X(k)|^2, m = 1, 2, \ldots, M \tag{2}$$

where $H_m(k)$ is triangular filter response.

3. Logarithmic Compression and Discrete Cosine Transform (DCT): The final MFCCs are gotten after logarithmic compression and DCT are applied.

$$MFCC(n) = \sum_{m=1}^{M} \log(S(m))\cos\left[n(m-0.5)\frac{\pi}{M}\right] \tag{3}$$

where n is the cepstral coefficient index.

Figure 4 presents representative MFCCs spectrograms for the five classes available in the dataset. Orifice leaks (Fig. 4d) exhibit strong energy across all 40 coefficients while no-leaks (Fig. 4e) show minimal spectral energy in low MFCC coefficients. These visual differences motivate our hypothesis that CNNs can effectively discriminate leak types from MFCC spectrograms.

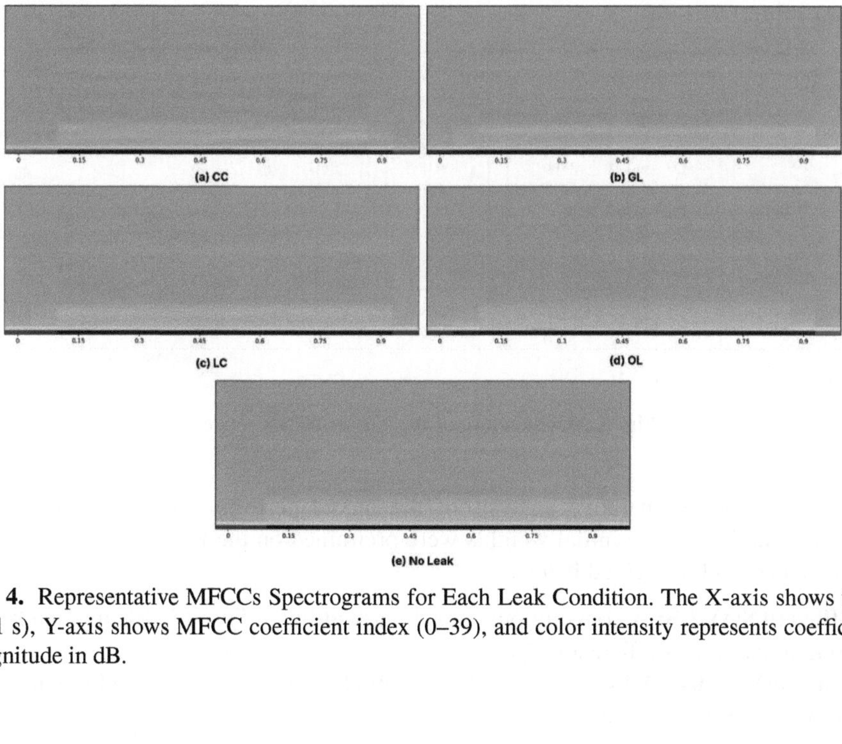

Fig. 4. Representative MFCCs Spectrograms for Each Leak Condition. The X-axis shows time (0–1 s), Y-axis shows MFCC coefficient index (0–39), and color intensity represents coefficient magnitude in dB.

5 Deep Learning Acoustic Leak Detection Framework

The proposed custom CNN model is a compact deep learning architecture tailored for acoustic signal classification. It is an efficient lightweight model that offers high classification accuracy and low-resource capability. The custom CNN features a four-block architecture optimized for the spatial-temporal feature extraction of MFCC (illustrated in Fig. 5). Given the 224 × 224 input resolution, the model is structured to progressively down sample the spectrogram while increasing feature depth. The technical discussion of the model is summarized below.

1. **Feature Extraction Backbone:** The model includes four sequential convolutional blocks. Each block consists of a Conv2d layer with a 3 × 3 kernel and a stride of 1, ensuring the preservation of local spectral textures. Batch normalization is applied after each convolutional block to stabilize training, while also guarding against internal covariate shift. ReLU (Rectified Linear Unit) activation function introduce non-linearity, which enables the model to learn complex acoustic patterns. The MaxPooling layers reduce the spatial dimensions by half at every stage (224 → 112 → 56 → 28 → 14).
2. **Classification Head:** In this phase, the final feature map 128 × 14 × 14 is transformed into a 1D vector using the Flatten layer, while the Dense layer maps these high-level features to the target classes; binary = {leak, no leak} or multiclass = {LC, CC, GC, OL, NL}. A dropout (0.5) is implemented to provide regularization and prevent overfitting.

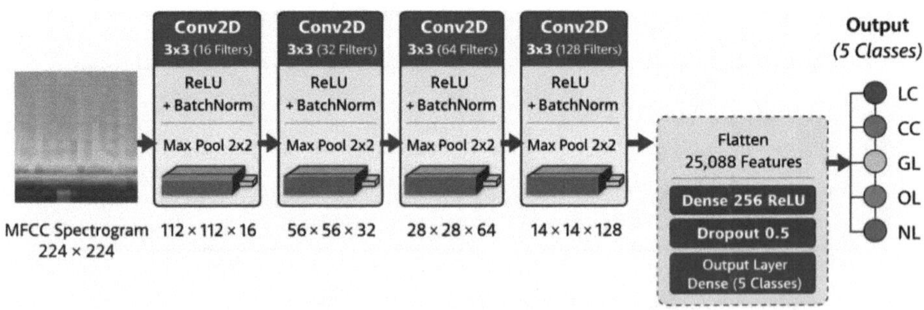

Fig. 5. Architecture of the Custom CNN model

For a robust comparative analysis of the model performance, two other CNN-based DL models whose initial weights were pretrained on the ImageNet dataset were implemented, as highlighted below.

- **EfficientNetV2-S:** A convolutional benchmark utilizing Fused-MBConv blocks for optimal parameter efficiency [18].
- **ConvNeXt-Tiny:** A hybrid model that is purely convolutional but adopts modern Transformer design principles [19].

6 Results and Discussion

To address the inherent class imbalance between "Leak" and "No-leak" samples, we utilized balanced class weighting within a Categorical Cross-Entropy loss function. Models were trained using the AdamW optimizer with a learning rate of $1e^{-4}$ and a ReduceLROnPlateau scheduler. To ensure model weight efficiency and prevent overfitting, an Early Stopping callback was implemented with a patience of 15 epochs. All the models were trained for 40 epochs on a GPU RTX3050 16GB RAM system using PyTorch. All models were trained using the same stratified dataset split across all leak types and network topology (train = 0.65, validation = 0.15, test = 0.20) and batch size (16) for robustness and overfitting avoidance. This ensures that all splits have representative distribution. The 20% test set (1,416 samples) remained completely unseen during training and hyperparameter tuning, providing unbiased performance estimates. The metrics used are accuracy, weighted F1-score, precision, recall and model size [20, 21].

Accuracy is the overall correctness of the prediction while Precision calculates the percentage of correctly predicted positive cases out of all cases classified as positive. Recall measures the percentage of real positive examples that were correctly detected by the model, and the weighted F1-score is the harmonic mean of precision and recall, weighted by class support to account for class imbalance. The weighted F1-score was selected as a metric due to class imbalance in our dataset (1,416 no-leak vs. 5,664 leak samples), as it provides a balanced assessment across all leak types while accounting for the varying frequencies.

$$Accuracy = \frac{TP + TN}{TP + TN + FP + FN} \tag{4}$$

$$Precision = \frac{TP}{TP + FP} \tag{5}$$

$$Recall = \frac{TP}{TP + FN} \tag{6}$$

where $TP = True\ Positive,\ TN = True\ Negative,\ FP = False\ Positive\ and\ FN = False\ Negative.$

$$F1_{\text{weighted}} = \sum_{i=1}^{K} \left(\frac{n_i}{N} \times F1_i \right) \tag{7}$$

where K is the number of classes, n_i is the number of true samples in class i, N is total number of samples and $F1_i$ is F1 score for class i as defined in Eq. 8.

$$F1_i = 2 \times \frac{Precision_i \times Recall_i}{Precision_i + Recall_i} \tag{8}$$

6.1 Overall Performance Analysis

The classification result for the deep learning models is presented in Table 2. The experiment was carried out for the three different topologies: branched, looped and combined;

and binary and multi classification. The experimental results show that turning raw hydrophone signals into 2D MFCC spectrograms is an effective way to extract features for deep learning classification. In all the testing scenarios listed in Table 2, the CNN-based deep learning models reached accuracy values between 94.77% and 100%. This performance greatly surpassed traditional feature-based ML benchmarks, like RF, which achieved 81.2% in similar hydrophone studies [7].

EfficientNetV2-S delivered the best results, with the highest average accuracy across the Combined topology for both binary (99.29%) and multiclass (98.80%) tasks. This reliability indicates that the parameter-efficient MBConv blocks are ideal for capturing the subtle time-frequency patterns found in underwater acoustic leak signatures.

Binary classification generally yielded higher F1-scores than Multiclass classification. For instance, in the Branched topology, Custom CNN dropped from 97.31% to 97.04% for binary and multiclass respectively. However, the decline is minimal (<1%), implying that the MFCC spectrograms preserve sufficient fine-grained spectral details.

Table 2. Comprehensive classification report for the deep learning models.

Topology	Task	Model	Accuracy	Precision	Recall	Weighted F1-score
Branched	Binary	Custom CNN	97.32	97.31	97.32	97.31
		EfficientNetV2-S	98.87	98.87	98.87	98.87
		ConvNext_Tiny	94.77	95.03	94.77	94.86
	Multiclass	Custom CNN	97.03	97.05	97.03	97.04
		EfficientNetV2-S	97.46	97.51	97.46	97.47
		ConvNext_Tiny	97.74	97.75	97.74	97.74
Looped	Binary	Custom CNN	99.44	99.45	99.44	99.44
		EfficientNetV2-S	99.58	99.58	99.58	99.58
		ConvNext_Tiny	100.00	100.00	100.00	100.00
	Multiclass	Custom CNN	98.45	98.47	98.45	98.45
		EfficientNetV2-S	98.87	98.89	98.87	98.87
		ConvNext_Tiny	98.59	98.61	98.59	98.59
Combined	Binary	Custom CNN	97.81	97.90	97.81	97.83
		EfficientNetV2-S	99.29	99.30	99.29	99.29
		ConvNext_Tiny	98.73	98.74	98.73	98.73
	Multiclass	Custom CNN	96.89	96.93	96.89	96.90
		EfficientNetV2-S	98.80	98.82	98.80	98.80
		ConvNext_Tiny	95.69	95.80	95.69	95.70

A deeper analysis of the Custom CNN performance is achieved through confusion matrices across three distinct datasets: Branched, Looped, and Combined as shown in Fig. 6. It demonstrates excellent sensitivity and specificity in identify leaks. In the looped configuration, the model identifies 562 occurrences of leaks and misclassifying only 4 as no-leaks, while correctly identifying all no-leaks scenarios. When compared to the performance in branched topology where 9 leaks and 10 no-leaks were misclassified, it shows that the acoustic features in a looped topology are highly separable for binary tasks. This is in line with the feature analysis in Sect. 4.2.1. This trend is also seen in the multiclass confusion matrices. A total of 11 and 25 misclassifications were seen in the looped and branched topologies respectively. The confusion matrices of the combined network show the ability of the model to generalize effectively.

6.2 Impact of Hydraulic Topology

A distinct variance was observed in model performance between the Branched and Looped water distribution network configuration corroborating the physical complexities of acoustic propagation in various configurations.

The three models achieved their best classification performance in the Looped topology for both binary and multiclass tasks, with the ConvNext_Tiny model achieving a remarkable 100% accuracy for binary classification. These dropped slightly for the Branched network for all the models with ConvNext_Tiny achieving 94.77%, and EfficientNetV2-S maintaining 98.87%. These results suggest that acoustic energy in looped systems may be preserved longer due to multipath propagation, unlike in the branched topology with signal fading and linear signal attenuation. This energy is easily separable in looped systems and is corroborated by the RMS Amplitude plot in Fig. 2. DL models can take advantage of the preserved acoustic energy in looped networks as rich set of features for classification. The combined topology shows the capability of the DL models to effectively generalize by achieving up to 99.29% and 98.80 by the EfficientNetV2-s model for binary and multiclass respectively.

6.3 Computational Efficiency

While classification accuracy is a primary performance metric for leak detection, computational efficiency and model size are critical factors for real-time deployment on edge computing devices with limited capacity. In Table 3, the model sizes are shown, showing a significant disparity. The Custom CNN is the most lightweight architecture, requiring only 24.88 MB of memory. In contrast, the state-of-the-art benchmarks require significantly more resources: EfficientNetV2-S is approximately 3.1 times larger (77.57 MB), and ConvNeXt_Tiny is nearly 4.3 times larger (106.13 MB). The substantial difference between the model sizes has significant impact on deployment. Custom CNN is highly suitable for embedding directly into edge devices such as noise loggers or hydrophone nodes.

Considering the performance of the custom CNN model, recording an accuracy of 99.44% in the looped binary task, which is comparable to the heavier models, the marginal gain in accuracy offered by the larger models often less than 1% does not justify the 300–400% increase in storage and computational cost. Therefore, while ConvNext_Tiny and EfficientNetV2-S offer advantages in complex feature extraction, Custom CNN presents the optimal balance for cost effective solutions in the face of computational constraints.

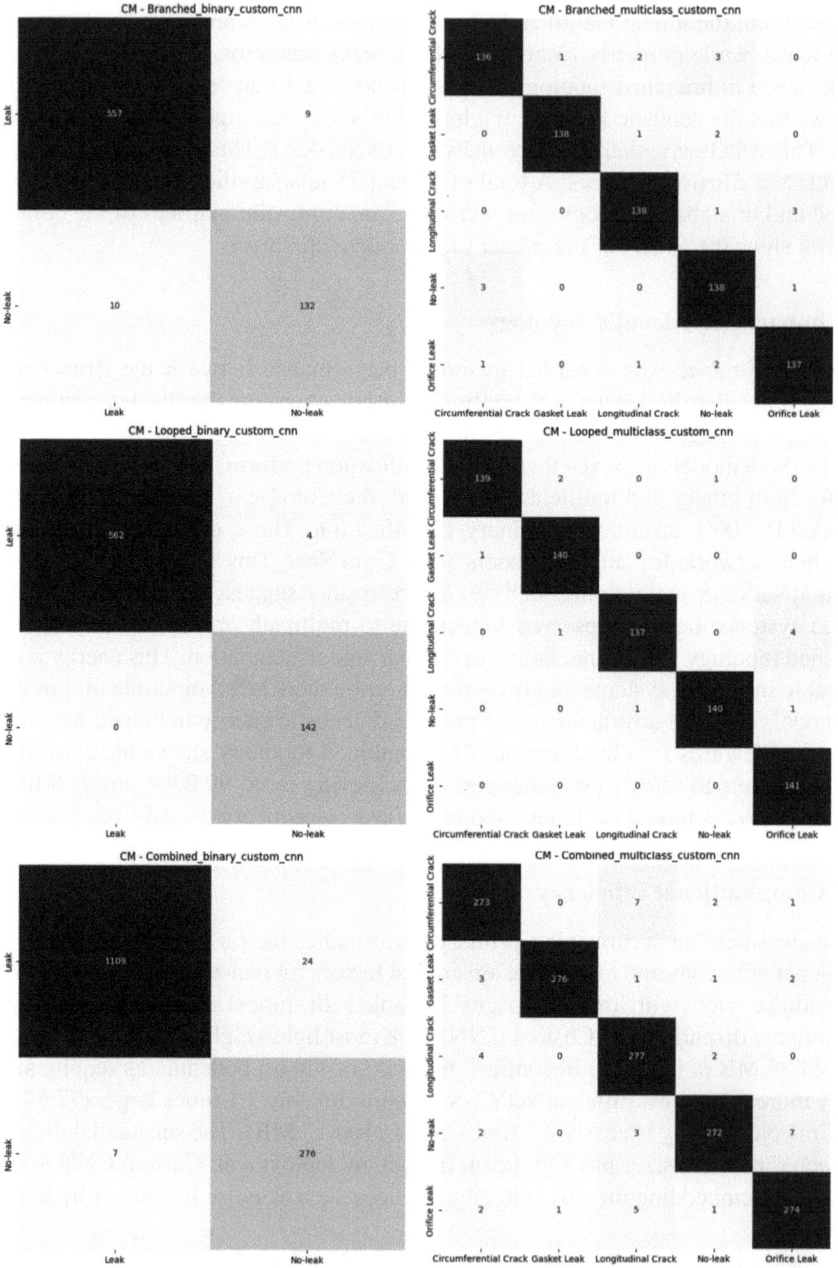

Fig. 6. Confusion Matrices for the Custom CNN Model for Binary and Multiclass across all Networks Configurations

Table 3. Model size comparison for the deep learning models

Model	Size (MB)
Custom CNN	24.88
EfficientNetV2-S	77.57
ConvNext_Tiny	106.13

6.4 Traditional ML Comparison

The section presents the result of using traditional ML models such as random forest (RF), support vector machine (SVM), and gradient boosting (GB); and artificial neural network, the multilayer perceptron (MLP), on the 1D statistical features. Table 4 shows the classification result on the combined dataset.

The results show that the performances for binary classification are relatively robust across all traditional models while performance degrades significantly for multiclass tasks. RF model achieved the highest accuracy in the binary task at 91.31%, followed closely by GB (90.75%) and MLP (90.32%). This indicates that the extracted 1D statistical features provide sufficient discriminative power to distinguish between the presence and absence of a leak signal. This finding observed that tree-based models like RF often outperform non-tree-based methods in feature-based hydrophone analysis [7]. A sharp decline in performance is observed during multiclass diagnosis with performance ranging from 50.99–67.51%.

Table 4. 1D combined topology classification result

Task	Model	Accuracy	Precision	Recall	F1-score
Binary	RF	91.31	91.22	91.31	90.72
	GB	90.75	90.41	90.75	90.32
	SVM	90.25	90.40	90.25	89.30
	MLP	90.32	90.06	90.32	89.66
Multiclass	RF	63.70	63.48	63.70	63.56
	GB	67.51	67.43	67.51	67.46
	SVM	50.99	51.98	50.98	51.34
	MLP	57.91	58.23	57.91	57.94

6.5 Comparison with Deep Learning Frameworks

Comparing Table 4 with DL results presented in Table 2 reveals a significant difference in the results. While the best traditional model (GB) achieved only 67.51% in the

Combined/Multiclass task, the EfficientNetV2-S model achieved 98.80% on the same data. This substantial gap of approximately 31% highlights that DL models with 2D MFCC spectrograms extract high-dimensional features efficiently. The results confirm that while traditional ML models like RF and GB are computationally efficient and sufficient for simple binary detection, they are inadequate for precise fault diagnosis in complex, heterogeneous water distribution topologies. Deep learning approaches are therefore essential for granular classification tasks.

7 Conclusion

This study successfully developed and evaluated robust deep learning frameworks for leak detection in WDS by leveraging acoustic signals and Mel-Frequency Cepstral Coefficients (MFCC). The comparative analysis of deep learning architectures demonstrated that transforming 1D acoustic signals into 2D spectrograms significantly enhances detection capabilities. The CNN models achieved accuracies ranging from 94.77–100% during experimentation for binary and multi classification assignments. The deep learning models outperformed traditional machine learning models trained on the 1D statistical features.

The experimental results highlighted the critical influence of hydraulic topology on detection performance. Among the evaluated architectures, EfficientNetV2-S emerged as the most robust model for multiclass diagnosis across combined topologies. Conversely, the Custom CNN, requiring only 24.88 MB of storage, offered an optimal balance of computational efficiency and accuracy, proving its feasibility for deployment on resource-constrained edge devices. This study can help in minimizing Non-Revenue Water resulting from leakages in the water distribution pipelines and ensuring the integrity of global water infrastructure.

References

1. Momeni, A., Piratla, K.R., Anderson, A., Chalil Madathil, K., Li, D.: Stochastic model-based leakage prediction in water mains considering pipe condition uncertainties. Tunn. Undergr. Space Technol. **137** (2023). https://doi.org/10.1016/j.tust.2023.105130
2. Lee, C.-W., Yoo, D.-G.: Development of leakage detection model and its application for water distribution networks using RNN-LSTM. Sustainability (Switzerland). **13** (2021). https://doi.org/10.3390/su13169262
3. Xu, Z., Liu, R., Liu, H., Zayed, T.: Cross-regional leak detection in water distribution networks through domain transfer. Water Res. **290**, 125150 (2026). https://doi.org/10.1016/j.watres.2025.125150
4. Alves, D., Blesa, J., Duviella, E., Rajaoarisoa, L.: Robust data-driven leak localization in water distribution networks using pressure measurements and topological information. Sensors. **21** (2021). https://doi.org/10.3390/s21227551
5. Yu, H., Lin, S., Zhou, H., Weng, X., Chu, S., Yu, T.: Leak detection in water distribution networks based on deep learning and kriging interpolation method. Aqua Water Infrastruct. Ecosyst. Soc. **73**, 1741–1753 (2024). https://doi.org/10.2166/aqua.2024.184
6. Xie, Y., et al.: Django-based framework database for leakage detection using machine learning for water distribution networks. Eng. Appl. Artif. Intell. **149** (2025). https://doi.org/10.1016/j.engappai.2025.110525

7. Zuo, X., Satterlee, N., Guwalani, R., Park, C.W., Kang, J.S.: Comparative analysis of machine learning approaches for leak detection in pipelines using hydrophone acoustic sensing. Measurement (Lond.). **261** (2026). https://doi.org/10.1016/j.measurement.2025.120005
8. Boujelben, M., Benmessaoud, Z., Abid, M., Elleuchi, M.: An efficient system for water leak detection and localization based on IoT and lightweight deep learning. Internet Things (Neth.). **24** (2023). https://doi.org/10.1016/j.iot.2023.100995
9. Guo, P., et al.: Leak detection in water supply pipeline with small-size leakage using deep learning networks. Process Saf. Environ. Prot. **191**, 2712–2724 (2024). https://doi.org/10.1016/j.psep.2024.10.011
10. McMillan, L., Fayaz, J., Varga, L.: Domain-informed variational neural networks and support vector machines based leakage detection framework to augment self-healing in water distribution networks. Water Res. **249** (2024). https://doi.org/10.1016/j.watres.2023.120983
11. Constantinescu, C., Brad, R.: An overview on sound features in time and frequency domain. Int. J. Adv. Stat. IT&C Econ. Life Sci. **13**, 45–58 (2023). https://doi.org/10.2478/ijasitels-2023-0006
12. Wang, N., Zhang, K., Wang, X., Peng, B., Zhai, S.: Pipeline leakage identification based on acoustic sensors and EPSO-1D-CNN-Bi-LSTM model. Sensors. **25** (2025). https://doi.org/10.3390/s25237355
13. Liu, R., Zayed, T., Xiao, R., Hu, Q.: Time-transformer for acoustic leak detection in water distribution network. J. Civ. Struct. Heal. Monit. **15**, 759–775 (2025). https://doi.org/10.1007/s13349-024-00845-2
14. Ma, X., et al.: Leak detection in water supply networks using two-stage temporal segmentation and incremental learning for non-stationary acoustic signals. Water Res. X. **29** (2025). https://doi.org/10.1016/j.wroa.2025.100333
15. Aghashahi, M., Sela, L., Banks, M.K.: Benchmarking dataset for leak detection and localization in water distribution systems. Data Brief. **48**, 109148 (2023). https://doi.org/10.1016/j.dib.2023.109148
16. Peng, H., Xu, Z., Huang, Q., Qi, L., Wang, H.: Leakage detection in water distribution systems based on logarithmic spectrogram CNN for continuous monitoring. J. Water Resour. Plan. Manag. **150** (2024). https://doi.org/10.1061/JWRMD5.WRENG-6276
17. Sharma, K.V., Ayiluri, P.R., Betala, R., Pappula, M., Reddy, K.S.: Learning emotional nuances in speech via DCNNs and spectral feature integration. Int. J. Speech Technol. **29**, 11 (2026). https://doi.org/10.1007/s10772-025-10235-8
18. Tan, M., Le, Q.: EfficientNetV2: smaller models and faster training. In: Proceedings of the 38th International Conference on Machine Learning, vol. 139, pp. 10096–10106 (2021). https://doi.org/10.48550/arXiv.2104.00298
19. Liu, Z., Mao, H., Wu, C.-Y., Feichtenhofer, C., Darrell, T., Xie, S.: A ConvNet for the 2020s. In: 2022 IEEE/CVF Conference on Computer Vision and Pattern Recognition (CVPR), pp. 11966–11976. IEEE (2022). https://doi.org/10.1109/CVPR52688.2022.01167
20. Cosma, L., Oniga, Ş.V., Cosma, O.: Ensemble deep learning model for AI-powered cyber-physical systems in precision agriculture. In: Technological Innovation for AI-Powered Cyber-Physical Systems. Presented at the (2025). https://doi.org/10.1007/978-3-031-97051-1_8
21. Oyedeji, A., Olukanmi, P.: Intelligent condition monitoring of power transformers via machine learning. In: 2025 33rd Southern African Universities Power Engineering Conference (SAUPEC), pp. 1–6. IEEE (2025). https://doi.org/10.1109/SAUPEC65723.2025.10944449

Digital Transformation Framework for Sustainable Water-Energy-Food Nexus in South Africa

Oluwadamilola Esan[1(✉)], Nnamdi Nwulu[1], and Adepoju Omoseni Oyindamola[1,2]

[1] Center for Cyber-Physical Food-Energy-Water Systems, University of Johannesburg, Johannesburg, South Africa
223092487@student.uj.ac.za, nnwulu@uj.ac.za, adepoju.omoseni@lcu.edu.ng

[2] Department of Management and Accounting, Faculty of Management and Social Sciences, Lead City University, Ibadan, Nigeria

Abstract. Digital transformation is increasingly positioned as a route to sustainability; however, it can only deliver societal value when organizations and ecosystems can absorb and scale it. This study draws on a completed PhD to investigate what human-capacity and institutional conditions enable Fourth Industrial Revolution (4IR) technologies to deliver sustainability outcomes in Water–Energy–Food (WEF) nexus of South Africa. The study postulated that only 4IR technologies are insufficient to deliver sustainability benefits without coordinated development of skills, organizational enablers, and stakeholder alignment. The study implemented a quantitative research design to develop a multi-layered implementation framework. The results showed that digital proficiency, innovation-oriented soft skills, leadership commitment, change management, and stakeholder coordination are decisive factors in translating digital technologies into sustainable WEF outcomes. The thesis provided empirical evidence of the conditions under which digital innovation produces societal benefit and developed a replicable roadmap for tackling WEF societal challenges.

Keywords: Digital transformation · Sustainability · Fourth Industrial Revolution (4IR) · Water · Energy · Food (WEF) Nexus · Human Capacity Development

1 Introduction

Sustainable development and economic growth in South Africa has been a concern that is increasingly hampered by the multi-layered challenges of water, energy, and food insecurity, which are now addressed as a single, system-level societal challenge rather than three distinct sectoral problems. According to [1], addressing one resource in isolation, such as boosting food production without water security or increasing energy generation without water availability, will result in unintended consequences, increased cost and uneven benefits. With the mounting pressure on these resources and the advocacy

Published by Springer Nature Switzerland AG 2027
L. M. Camarinha-Matos and F. Ferrada (Eds.): DoCEIS 2026, IFIP AICT 790, pp. 274–291, 2027.
https://doi.org/10.1007/978-3-032-28939-1_20

for the Water-Energy-Food (WEF) Nexus, digital transformation has been adopted and positioned as a strategic pathway for improving WEF coordination, efficiency, transparency, and resilience [1]. [2] affirmed that digital transformation is a socio-technical shift that builds system capability for data-driven coordination, shared data standards, interoperable infrastructure, decision intelligence and cross-sector governance.

Numerous studies have showed how digital transformation, fostered by the industry 4.0 (4IR) technologies has been used to support decisions for demand forecasting, optimization, and predictive maintenance across WEF infrastructures, while smart metering, digital billing, interoperable data platforms, and workflow automation have reduced transaction costs and improved coordination among stakeholders [1, 3, 4]. However, despite these improvements, there hasn't been much benefit, as integration remains uneven. Most WEF Nexus projects in South Africa continue to be implemented within institutional silos, as the sectors operate under different mandates, which consequently impede the operationalization of the WEF Nexus and reduce cross-sector trade-offs and optimization [5]. Most of these projects are also constrained to pilot projects that are solely driven by technology without sustainable adoption, governance alignment, and capability enhancement, which results in insufficient cross-sector coordination and limited human and organizational preparedness. These challenges prevent digital transformation investments from being translated into measurable WEF sustainability outcomes [1, 6].

Several WEF Nexus studies, like [7–11] have developed optimized and analytical models and case study applications for digital transformation in the WEF Nexus. However, these studies establish that the fundamental constraint for WEF Nexus optimization and operationalization is not the absence of technical models or infrastructures, but primarily the difficulty of governance and coordination across interdependent systems, which is the gap this study intends to fill. Several WEF Nexus projects in South Africa have revealed how fragmented governance and weak coordination can negatively impact the sustainability of digital transformation in the WEF Nexus. For instance, [12, 13] discussed how WEF Nexus initiatives that were developed in Mpumalanga province would have resulted in better outcomes if there were coordination among stakeholders and firm policies. Similarly, [14, 15] affirmed that until the government takes the water challenge in Cape Town as an integrated WEF challenge, and takes concrete steps to ensure capacity development, policy direction, and integration of sectors to promote synergies, the smart water metering initiatives in Cape Town would not yield sustainable results. [16] also revealed that slow uptake of 4IR innovations in South Africa's municipal water governance is caused by capacity, infrastructure, and policy gaps. [17] reported that institutional preparedness shapes whether digital technologies can meaningfully enhance service delivery. This implies that the digitalization of the WEF Nexus depends on organizational readiness, culture, strategic alignment, user acceptance, and human capital development, which are often treated as secondary factors in the WEF Nexus. Leveraging this problem, there is therefore a need for a multi-level implementation framework to foster coordination and support scale-up beyond pilots by aligning governance, organizational capability, and human capital with the technical architecture.

The main aim of this research was to develop a multi-level digital transformation framework for sustainable integration of 4IR technologies within the WEF Nexus in

South Africa, with human capacity positioned as the central enabling mechanism for implementation. The study proposes three hypotheses:

H1: Continuous individual 4IR training and skills are associated with greater effective incorporation of 4IR-enabled solutions within the WEF nexus.
H2: An innovative organizational culture is significantly associated with effective 4IR–WEF integration.
H3: Enabling national policies are positively associated with the effective development and deployment of 4IR technologies for WEF nexus integration.

This research paper provides an overview of a completed PhD research on enabling sustainable WEF Nexus transformation in South Africa through digital transformation and 4IR integration. This research paper positions digital transformation as an applied, implementation contribution: rather than solely a generic enabler. It builds on existing studies to argue that without an explicit human-capacity and governance framework, digital transformation will remain fragmented and unable to deliver digital transformation outcomes. The remaining part of this research will explore the theoretical framework and methodology to discuss how the digital transformation framework was developed through empirical modelling. The research will also discuss the results, framework architecture and the key findings that support the hypothesized relationships across policy, organizational culture, and individual capability. The discussion section will examine the implications of digital transformation through 4IR–WEF integration in South Africa. The study will also discuss how the research contributes to the conference theme.

2 Theoretical Framework

This study leverages the principle of systems thinking, which is the backbone and sustaining logic of the WEF Nexus as a concept. Leveraging on the tenets of this system thinking, this study adopted a theoretical triangulation approach using the Technology Acceptance Model (TAM), the Human Capital Theory (HCT) and the Triple Helix Model (THM) to analyze digital transformation in South Africa's WEF Nexus. The argument of this study is for the WEF Nexus to undergo digital transformation, it has to be the resultant effect of a nested socio-technical process in which institutional coordination, capability development, and user acceptance are mutually reinforcing, and not purely a technical challenge. This study does not treat the three theories as parallel theories but as complementary theories that explain the concept of digital transformation that must occur in the WEF Nexus. This study leveraged the THM to depict the institutional conditions required for digital transformation, such as policy support, resource mobilization, regulatory alignment, and cross-sector innovation coordination. These THM conditions result in meso-level organizational and workforce investments in skills, learning, and capability development, which are anchored on the HCT. Having developed these organizational capabilities, the HCT then influences the micro-level user perceptions of technological usefulness and ease of use, which is the tenet of the TAM. The integration of these elements increases the likelihood of digital transformation adoption and sustained implementation.

According to [18], the TAM posits that perceived usefulness and perceived ease of use shape intention to use and actual use. This model predicts that professionals adopt when they believe the technologies can improve their performance and are easy to use and operate. However, this study argues that these perceptions are not formed in a vacuum; they are influenced by competence, exposure, and professional readiness, which are not captured in TAM. The HCT therefore provides the capability pathway that conditions TAM's behavioural pathway by introducing education, training, and upskilling as productive investments that can boost competence and innovation, which will consequently increase perceived ease of use and perceived usefulness [19, 20]. The HCT operates at the meso level to explain why willingness and intention are often constrained by skills gaps, limited digital literacy, and a lack of interdisciplinary competence, even when technologies are available. The study also leveraged the THM to extend the framework and analyze how digital transformation is structured through the co-evolution of universities (knowledge production and skills formation), industry (deployment, operational learning, scaling), and government (policy direction, regulation, funding, and infrastructure support) [21, 22]. The tenets of the THM portray that even well-designed training (HCT) and positive user perceptions (TAM) can fail to generate WEF outcomes when institutional coordination is weak. These theories serve as a multi-level pathway of the study to reveal that institutional coordination (THM) enables capability development (HCT), which shapes user acceptance and adoption (TAM), which will foster coherent digital transformation in the WEF Nexus (Fig. 1).

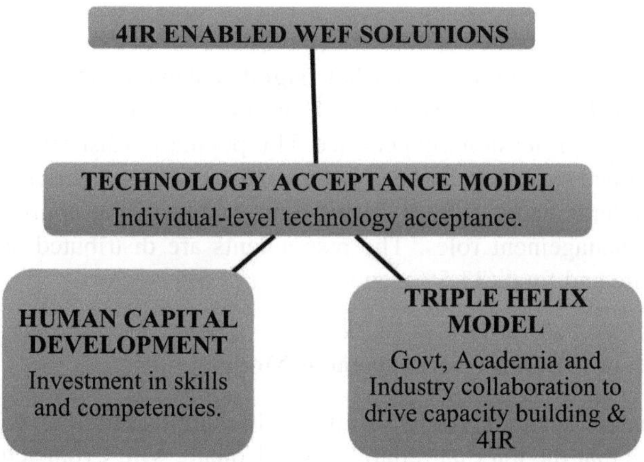

Fig. 1. Theoretical triangulation for the study. Source: Author's Diagram (2026).

3 Methodology

This research used a quantitative research design to develop a 4IR-WEF Nexus framework. A research survey using a 5-point Likert scale structured questionnaire was administered to develop the different policies, organizational culture and individual capability required to foster digital transformation in the South African WEF Nexus. The questionnaire was adapted from existing literature on the WEF Nexus, digital transformation and human capacity development. The questionnaire comprised four sections, where section one assessed respondent demographics, section two analyzed the individual training modules, section three examined the organizational culture, and section four assessed the national policies required to enable digitalization of the WEF Nexus. The population comprised all water, energy and food sector professionals in South African water, energy and food sectors. The Sample size was estimated using Cochran [23] Z-formula for unknown populations, which resulted in a sample size of 384. The study adopted a homogeneous purposive sampling to recruit WEF Nexus stakeholders deliberately. The purposive sampling was complemented by snowball sampling to minimize sampling bias and extend reach through professional networks. The study received a response of 262, which accounted for a 68% response rate. The data analysis involved the development of the framework and the empirical prioritization of the framework construct. The data collected for conceptual development were analyzed with the PLS-SEM technique in SmartPLS 4. The study also introduced the use of the Importance-Performance Map Analysis (IPMA) to empirically prioritize constructs for the strategic development of the framework.

4 Results

4.1 Demographic Distribution

The study participants consisted of 60.6% women, and 37% of those who responded were aged 20–30 years. The research revealed that a significant majority (75.2%) were aware of the WEF Nexus, with 51.6% possessing 1 to 10 years of experience, while just 48.4% had more than 10 years of professional experience. This population distribution reconciles the expertise of seasoned experts with the innovative ideas of less experienced respondents. 41.7% of respondents had a B.Sc/B.Tech/B.Eng degree, while approximately 63.8% occupy middle management roles. The respondents are distributed across the water (39%), agriculture and food (33.5%), and energy (27.6%) sectors.

4.2 Evaluation of the Outer Measurement Model

The study evaluated the model for its validity and reliability based on the study of [24]. Table 1 indicates that the internal reliability is adequate, with Cronbach's alpha values between 0.746 and 0.864 and composite reliability (CR) values ranging from 0.770 to 0.828, all of which are within the acceptable limits specified in [25]. The collinearity test was employed to assess the potential for common-method bias, as indicated by [26]. The variance inflation factor (VIF) values ranged from 1.036 to 2.339, remaining below the threshold of 3.3, thereby indicating an absence of common method bias risk, as stated by [25]. [25] also recommended that all factor loadings must exceed a 0.70 threshold value; most indicators met the recommended 0.70 threshold; however, NP10–NP12 exhibited lower loadings but were retained based on theoretical relevance and content validity. According to [27], the authors stated that instead of removing constructs with lower outer loadings, authors should consider the effect of such removal on the model. Consequently, these indicators represent adaptive governance elements that are theoretically central to

Table 1. Assessment of the Measurement Model & Variance Inflation Factor for Multicollinearity.

	Constructs	VIF	Loading	rho_a	rho_c	Cronbach	AVE
National Framework	NP 3	1.573	0.735	0.794	0.770	0.746	0.753
	NP 4	2.339	0.791				
	NP 5	2.076	0.719				
	NP 6	1.609	0.734				
	NP 7	1.700	0.877				
	NP 8	1.036	0.807				
	NP 9	1.258	0.769				
	NP 10	1.305	0.387				
	NP 11	1.032	0.135				
	NP 12	1.076	0.580				
Organizational Framework	OS 1	1.042	0.801	0.780	0.802	0.864	0.617
	OS 2	1.364	0.775				
	OS 3	1.723	0.783				
	OS 4	1.663	0.835				
	OS 5	1.444	0.799				
	OS 6	2.071	0.802				
	OS 7	1.978	0.722				
	OS 8	1.358	0.772				
	OS 9	1.446	0.805				
	OS 10	1.607	0.853				
	OS 11	1.929	0.815				
	OS 14	1.194	0.788				
Individual Training Module	TM 3	1.398	0.807	0.828	0.791	0.7778	0.578
	TM 4	1.463	0.787				
	TM 5	2.010	0.840				
	TM 6	2.108	0.791				
	TM 7	1.631	0.729				
	TM 8	1.591	0.738				

NP 1 & 2, OS 12 & 13, TM 1& 2 have been removed because they had negative values. Source: Research Survey (2026) via SmartPLS 4

institutional enablement for 4IR–WEF integration and would be underrepresented if removed [28–30]. They were therefore retained to avoid construct under-specification.

The heterotrait to monotrait (HTMT) ratio of correlations was employed to evaluate discriminant validity. The results revealed that the values remained below 0.85, as [31] recommended, indicating that the result is not at risk of discriminant validity. These values support the discriminant, and convergent validity and scale reliability as approved for measuring outer models (Table 2).

Table 2. Discriminant Validity of the Measurement Model.

	Heterotrait-monotrait ratio (HTMT)
Beta <– > Alpha	0.740
4IRTECH < -> Alpha	0.358
4IRTECH < -> Beta	0.309
Gamma <– > Alpha	0.322
Gamma <– > Beta	0.499
Gamma <– > 4IRTECH	0.279

Source: Research Survey (2026) through SmartPLS 4

4.3 Evaluation of the Structural Inner Model

The structural model was assessed using VIF values to verify the lack of bias caused by collinearity. Table 3 demonstrated the lack of collinearity hazards across the exogenous components, with all VIF metrics remaining under 3.3, as outlined by [31]. The results revealed an SRMR value of 0.0037 and an NFI value of 0.922, which aligns with the prescribed values.

Table 3. Collinearity Statistics (VIF) and model fit (internal model).

	VIF
Alpha - > 4IRTECH	1.948
Beta - > 4IRTECH	2.034
Gamma - > 4IRTECH	1.111
SRMR	**NFI**
0.0037	0.922

Source: Research Survey (2026) through SmartPLS 4

A bootstrapping technique was performed to ascertain the path coefficient together with its associated t-value for all direct interactions and assess the hypothesis. The analysis results demonstrated that all the hypotheses proposed in this research are statistically significant and positively correlated: personalized development modules (t-value = 2.105, p = 0.036, $\alpha = 0.160$,), organisational culture (t-value = 2.503, $\beta = 0.458$, p

= 0.012), and national guidelines and laws (t-value = 3.006, γ = 0.454, p = 0.003). The requirement for test of hypotheses in SmartPLS is given by (t values >1.96, $p < 0.05$) according to [32] and [33]. This acceptance standard was also reaffirmed in [34] and [35]. Therefore, hypotheses H1, H2, and H3 were validated and accepted for this study. Figure 2 depicts the direct association among the model constructs.

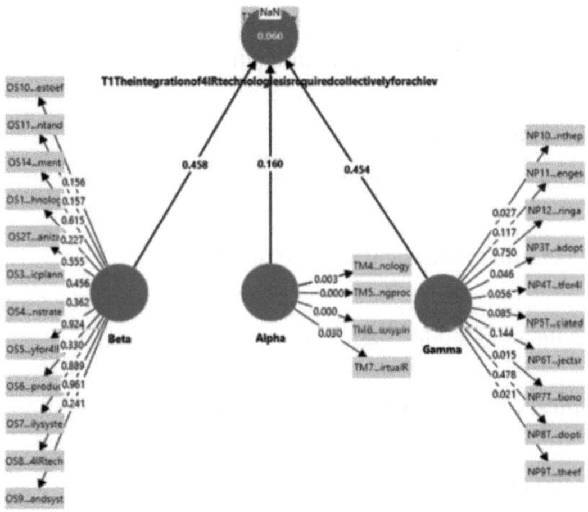

Fig. 2. Combined effect of Model Variables. Source: Research survey (2026).

4.4 Empirical Prioritization Through Importance Performance Map Analysis (IPMA)

After assessing the structural model, the importance-performance map analysis (IPMA) was also adopted as an innovative approach to assessing the individual influence of the constructs. IPMA has been affirmed to be of benefit, as it has been used to generate additional results and information by amalgamating the significance and performance dimensions of model constructs in practical PLS-SEM applications [36]. [37] further stated that the IPMA determines the most significant construct that exerts influence on a model and identifies focal points for management enhancement initiatives. The IPMA latent variable scores were rescaled to a 0–100 performance index, and importance values were derived from total effects in the PLS-SEM model. Table 4 shows the importance-performance map values for each variable.

Table 4. Importance-Performance Values of Model Constructs.

	LV performance	MV performance
Gamma	77.672	
NP10-National feedback system		74.682

(continued)

Table 4. (*continued*)

	LV performance	MV performance
NP11-National strategies should adapt to the evolving needs and challenges.		72.901
NP12-Sustainability goals should be integrated into national policies.		71.374
NP1-National WEF Nexus policies and regulations that support 4IR technologies		61.323
NP2-Cross-sector collaboration policies		69.084
NP3-National regulations that facilitate technology adoption		69.466
NP4-National frameworks that address 4IR-WEF data management		78.053
NP5-National programmes to combat 4IR-WEF challenges		75.573
NP6-Funding opportunities for 4IR-WEF research and projects		71.183
NP7-Public-private collaborations for 4IR-WEF Nexus		78.244
NP8-National initiatives and programmes to promote the adoption of 4IR		64.885
NP9-National mechanisms for monitoring and assessing adoption		62.468
Beta	74.959	
OS10-Invest in training programmes for employees.		76.463
OS11-Culture of continuous improvement and innovations.		71.628
OS12-Encourage employee participation in external training.		66.539
OS13-Provide resources and support to encourage employee adoption of 4IR		64.631
OS14-Support continuous professional development		72.519
OS1-Clear strategy for adopting 4IR technologies		49.809
OS2-Alignment with my organizational strategic goals		62.341
OS3-key stakeholders involvement in strategic plan		74.809
OS4-Communicate its 4IR technology adoption strategy to employees		63.550
OS5-Regular evaluation and update of 4IR adoption strategy.		73.410
OS6-Deploy 4IR technologies in its overall production process		73.282

(*continued*)

Table 4. *(continued)*

	LV performance	MV performance
OS7-Integrate 4IR technologies into its daily system		68.321
OS8-Monitor and evaluate the performance of 4IR technologies		63.613
OS9-Invest in the necessary infrastructure and systems.		70.738
Alpha	76.017	
TM1-Application of Nanotechnology		67.748
TM2-Deployment of IoT devices and Sensors		68.130
TM3-Big data analytics and interpretation		79.198
TM4-Training on Blockchain technology		72.519
TM5-Training on Artificial Intelligence		72.392
TM6-Training in 3D Printing technology		75.763
TM7-Training on the use of Augmented Reality AR and VR		71.088
TM8-Training in Robotics and Automation		78.531

Source: Research Survey (2026) through SmartPls 4.

Table 4 demonstrates that all elements (α = implementing personalized training, β = inculcating 4IR into organisational culture, and γ = enacting national guidelines and laws) possess substantial significance ($\beta = 74.959$, $\gamma = 77.672$, $\alpha = 76.017$), with national guidelines and laws yielding the most considerable influence, succeeded by personalized training. In the national guidelines and law section, NP7 and NP4 are of utmost importance (NP4 = 78.053, NP7 = 78.244), signifying that considerable actions should be focused on collaborations between the public and private sectors and models that can enhance proper data management for 4IR-WEF Nexus. In the organisational culture, OS3 = 74.809 and OS10 = 76.463 are critically significant, suggesting that there should be resource investment in staff development programs and key stakeholders should be tactically involved in decision making. In personalised development trainings, WEF Nexus professionals ought to emphasise the development of competencies in big data (TM3 = 79.198) and automation and robotics (TM8 = 78.531). The IPMA was used to offer more clarification into the relative significance of each model components through statistical important measures, enabling focused strategies on constructs of greater value beyond model evaluation. These IPMA metrics will serve as a roadmap for policymakers and organizations to allocate resources effectively and maximize impact in implementing 4IR solutions in the WEF Nexus. Based on the Importance-Performance Map Analysis result, this study proposes adopting this multi-level human capacity development framework, as shown in Fig. 3.

5 Discussion

This study built a multi-level human capacity model as a means of incorporating 4IR technologies into South Africa's WEF Nexus. The multi-level human capacity framework developed in this study demonstrates that individual training modules, organizational structures, and national policies are all significant and vital in operationalizing the WEF Nexus and resolving its systemic issues. The significant values allocated to national policies reveal that national policies exert the most significant influence on 4IR-enabled WEF Nexus solutions, which places significant responsibility on policymakers and the government. This finding resonates with the assertions of [38], [39], who stated that government agencies and policymakers can influence individuals and organizational practices towards adopting sustainable practices by enacting the right laws, standards, incentives, and policies. The IPMA results further reveal that specific attention should be paid to enacting public-private partnerships, national data management frameworks, and national workshops and conferences to combat the problems hindering 4IR technologies in the WEF Nexus.

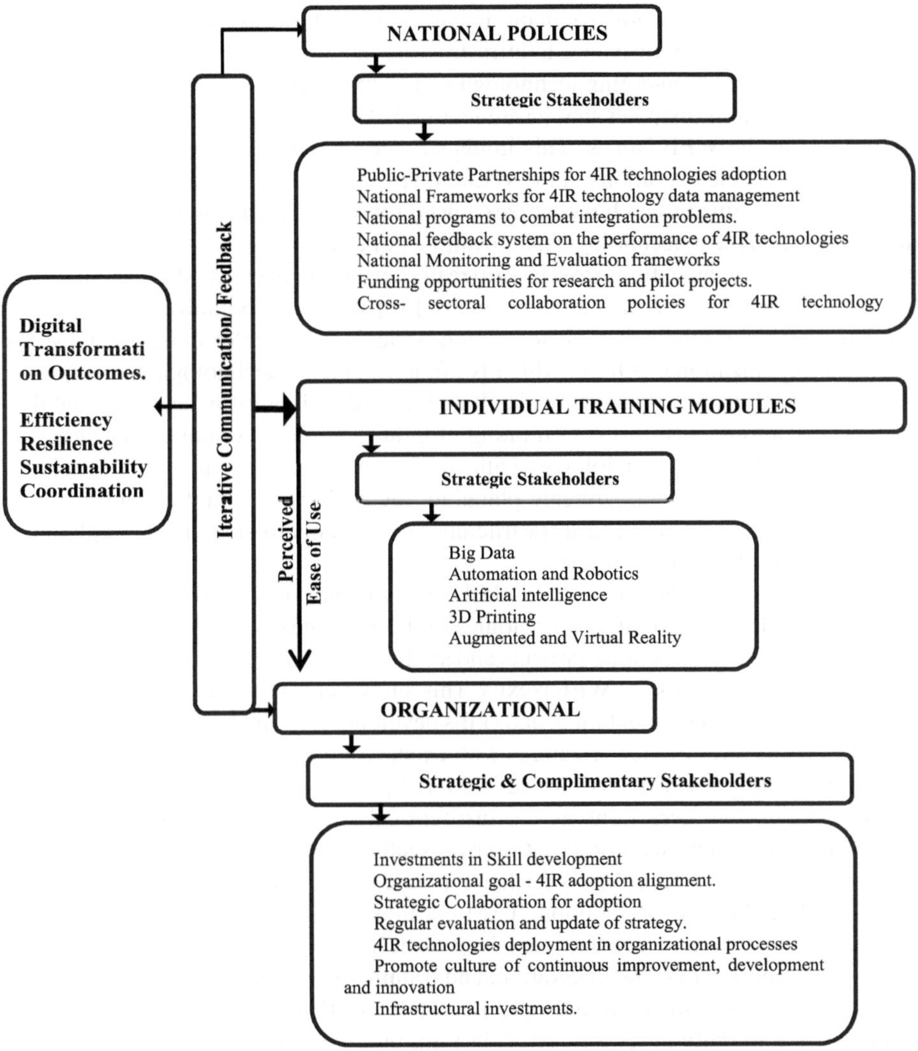

Fig. 3. Human capacity development framework for 4IR-Enabled WEF solutions. Source: Author's Diagram (2026)

When the right policies are enacted and implemented, they can foster an environment conducive to digital transformation, encourage research and development, and equip human resources to face technological challenges.

Following the enactment of national policies, there is also a need for individual training and skill development among WEF Nexus professionals to ensure that individuals are well-equipped and empowered to deploy 4IR technologies. This study emphasizes expertise such as big data, 3D printing, automation and robotics, artificial intelligence, blockchain technology etc., to facilitate digital transformation with WEF Nexus. This study does not assume that these are the most important 4IR technologies; however, their inclusion shows that they are prominent in current digital transformation discourse and their potential long-term relevance to infrastructure modernization. [40] have stated that there are skill gaps in emerging technologies in South Africa. This assertion is further reinstated with several studies that have identified skill deficiency as a major challenge being faced in the WEF Nexus. This implies a need for the development of strategic skills for 4IR-enabled solutions in the WEF Nexus.

Furthermore, this research recognizes a need for WEF organizations to foster a culture that is adaptable to technological innovation. For effective use of 4IR technologies in the WEF Nexus, organizations must prioritize the development of 4IR skills and integrate strategic stakeholders into their strategic plans. [40] stated that organizational culture is a critical enabler of innovation. Hence, South Africa's WEF sector must rise above the traditional organizational culture, which is often resistant to technological disruptions, and embrace a dynamic organizational culture that fosters innovation and sustainability. WEF organizations must invest in training programs, support continuous professional development, align 4IR technologies with overall strategic goals and daily processes, involve key stakeholders in strategic planning, regularly review and update their 4IR adoption strategy, and invest in infrastructure and systems to support the deployment and integration of 4IR technologies.

In the absence of coherent policies, skill development and effective cross-sector collaboration mechanisms, digital technologies in the WEF nexus would remain as siloed development as seen in existing projects and studies, instead of resulting in holistic digital transformation across the WEF Nexus. This study put forward a structured pathway for aligning policy, implementation, and skills development, which no existing study has done. The multi-level framework aligns with existing theories. At the national level, the framework is hinged on the Triple Helix Model, which conceptualizes government–industry–university interactions as the institutional engine that mobilizes resources, legitimizes innovation, and coordinates cross-sector action. At the organizational and individual levels, the framework is further explained by TAM and HCT as complementary micro-foundations for adoption. TAM clarifies that organizational uptake of 4IR tools depends on ease of use and perceived usefulness, both of which are shaped by leadership support, workflow integration, and training provision. Hence, there is a need for adaptive organizational cultures and infrastructure that reduce friction and embed technologies into daily processes. HCT, in turn, provides the investment logic linking structured skills development and technology adoption, e.g., analytics, AI, blockchain, robotics/automation, to enhanced absorptive capacity, improved task performance, and, ultimately, better WEF outcomes. For the framework to be fully operationalized, there must be clear role differentiation and integration mechanisms where all the actors will work towards a collective goal. The government would establish data governance standards, regulatory frameworks, and shared digital infrastructure, while universities would contribute through research and teaching. The industries at their end would drive implementation by deploying technologies, generating operational data, and scaling solutions to ensure holistic adoption of the framework.

The human capital framework built in this study depicts a comprehensive approach to overcoming existing challenges to digital transformation. Although there has not been a human capacity framework for digital WEF Nexus transformation in the South

Africa, this framework is different from previous frameworks that have focused on sectoral technology adoption without human capital and serves as a foundation for future empirical testing and pilot studies. This proposed framework adopts a holistic, multi-stakeholder approach and bridges the gap between capacity-building, multi-stakeholder collaboration, and the digital transformation for resource management and sustainability.

5.1 How the Framework Will Combat Societal Challenges

This multi-level digital transformation framework will contribute to addressing societal challenges by enabling system-wide resilience and efficiency in the WEF system. When 4IR technologies are being deployed and used in the WEF Nexus, coupled with the development of human capacity, this will improve the ability to anticipate, monitor, and respond to resource scarcity, which will in turn strengthen climate adaptation and disaster preparedness. The implementation of this framework will also enable early detection of drought stress, infrastructure failure, and supply disruptions, which will result in more focused and targeted interventions to reduce the intensity and duration of service breakdowns that are associated with WEF resources in South Africa. When this framework is implemented, it will ensure that climate risks and environmental degradation are not managed as episodic crises but as continuously monitored pressures, with informed decision-making shifted toward prevention, optimization, and rapid recovery.

The multi-level framework also contributes to water and energy security by supporting evidence-driven management of assets, demand, and losses. By ensuring efficient management of water and energy resources, the implementation of this framework will reduce the economic burden of coping strategies such as private water purchases, generators, and production downtime, which are major drivers of household vulnerability and business stagnation. When service reliability improves, this reduces social grievance, improves compliance and revenue collection, and creates fiscal headroom for reinvestment. Additionally, the framework will ensure more efficient resource management, which will in turn reduce operational costs of WEF organizations and result in the affordability of resources, which is an essential component of security. The framework will support improved productivity and reduced losses across agrifood value chains through better information, coordination, and risk management. The integration of 4IR technologies, such as IoT and blockchain, will strengthen resource logistics and enable proactive planning, which will reduce volatility in availability and prices, which are key determinants of household food insecurity. Improved traceability and safety through blockchain transparency will also improve public health by reducing contamination risks and enabling quicker responses to outbreaks.

The integration of 4IR technology and capacity development holistically in the WEF Nexus will increase resource productivity, capacity upgrading and transparency, which will help combat poverty, unemployment, and weak governance. With more reliable infrastructure and coordinated resource systems, many small and medium businesses, agribusinesses and local industries will be empowered for entrepreneurship, which will result in job creation and inclusive growth. The benefits of this multi-level framework, which is directly channelled towards the WEF Nexus, is a pathway for combating numerous multifaceted societal challenges such as climate adaptation, infrastructure reliability, WEF insecurity, public health and economic insecurity systematically through integrated, cross-sector transformation rather than isolated, one-off interventions.

5.2 Conclusions and Recommendations

This study developed a multi-level framework that incorporates the connected roles of national guidelines and laws, organizational culture, and personalized development for digital transformation in the WEF Nexus. The study revealed that national policies exert the most significant influence, driving organizational culture and individual skill development required for 4IR transformation in the South Africa WEF Nexus. The framework provides a cohesive and scalable approach that can be adopted to address inefficiencies in resource allocation, data fragmentation, and policy misalignment and facilitate a resilient and innovative WEF Nexus. The framework also provides a model for sustainable resource management through 4IR technologies that can be scaled to other sectors with the goal of digital transformation and sustainability. To practically implement the proposed framework, the authors recommend the following:

1. The national government should lead policy formulation by developing a 4IR-WEF National Implementation Strategy. This implementation strategy should include establishing a national 4IR-WEF Skills Development Fund to support public sector training and digital upskilling initiatives and partnering with the private sector to co-create innovation hubs and training centres aligned with national skills development goals.
2. To ensure the implementation of the framework at the national and provincial WEF organizations, organizations such as Rand Water, Eskom, and provincial agriculture and energy departments should establish internal capacity-building units tasked with workforce reskilling and upskilling in digital innovation and incorporate blockchain, AI, and IoT use cases in operational workflows such as energy forecasting, irrigation tracking, and supply chain verification.

5.3 Limitations and Suggestions for Further Study

This study was primarily conducted in South Africa, which may limit the generalizability of the findings to other regions; however, the findings of the study can be adapted and used as guidelines in other regions with different institutional and policy conditions. The study also relies on self-reported data and has not been empirically validated as of the time of this publication. The study suggests that future research should focus on empirical validation through case studies, pilot applications, and longitudinal analysis to assess the effectiveness of the constructs and their impact on WEF system performance and sustainability outcomes.

References

1. Esan, O., Nwulu, N., Adepoju, O.O.: A bibliometric analysis assessing the water-energy-food nexus in South Africa. Heliyon. **10**(18), e37651 (2024). https://doi.org/10.1016/j.heliyon.2024.e37651

2. Abbes, I.: Strategic pathways for innovation and sustainability in digital transformation: insights from leading global companies. Soc. Sci. Humanit. Open. **12**(1), 101906 (2025). https://doi.org/10.1016/j.ssaho.2025.101906
3. David, L.O., Nwulu, N.I., Aigbavboa, C.O., Adepoju, O.O.: Integrating fourth industrial revolution (4IR) technologies into the water, energy & food nexus for sustainable security: a bibliometric analysis. J. Clean. Prod. **363**, 132522 (2022). https://doi.org/10.1016/J.JCLEPRO.2022.132522
4. Hoosain, M.S., Paul, B.S., Doorsamy, W., Ramakrishna, S.: The Influence of Circular Economy and 4IR Technologies on the Climate–Water–Energy–Food Nexus and the SDGs. Water. **15**(4), 787 (2023). https://doi.org/10.3390/W15040787
5. Adom, R.K., Simatele, M.D., Reid, M.: Addressing the challenges of water-energy-food nexus programme in the context of sustainable development and climate change in South Africa. J. Water Clim. Change. **13**(7), 2761–2779 (2022). https://doi.org/10.2166/WCC.2022.099/1074240/JWC2022099.PDF
6. David, L.O., Aigbavboa, C., Nwulu, N., Adepoju, O.O.: Application of digital Technologies of the Fourth Industrial Revolution (4IR) in water, energy, and food (WEF) nexus. In: Green Energy and Technology, vol. Part F3772, pp. 287–317 (2024). https://doi.org/10.1007/978-3-031-72833-4_9/FIGURES/1
7. Walker, S., Jacobs-Mata, I., Fakudze, B., Masekwana, N.: Applying the WEF nexus at a local level: a focus on catchment level. In: Water - Energy - Food Nexus Narratives and Resource Securities: A Global South Perspective, pp. 111–144 (2022). https://doi.org/10.1016/B978-0-323-91223-5.00006-X
8. Jacobson, M.G.: Water–energy–food nexus approaches to facilitate smallholder agricultural technology adoption in Africa. In: Water - Energy - Food Nexus Narratives and Resource Securities: A Global South Perspective, pp. 279–297 (2022). https://doi.org/10.1016/B978-0-323-91223-5.00018-6
9. Kabeya, P.K., et al.: A regional approach to implementing the WEF nexus: a case study of the Southern African development community. In: Water - Energy - Food Nexus Narratives and Resource Securities: A Global South Perspective, pp. 145–167 (2022). https://doi.org/10.1016/B978-0-323-91223-5.00017-4
10. Karabulut, A.A., Crenna, E., Sala, S., Udias, A.: A proposal for integration of the ecosystem-water-food-land-energy (EWFLE) nexus concept into life cycle assessment: a synthesis matrix system for food security. J. Clean. Prod. **172**, 3874–3889 (2018). https://doi.org/10.1016/J.JCLEPRO.2017.05.092
11. Martinez-Hernandez, E., Leach, M., Yang, A.: Understanding water-energy-food and ecosystem interactions using the nexus simulation tool NexSym. Appl. Energy. **206**, 1009–1021 (2017). https://doi.org/10.1016/J.APENERGY.2017.09.022
12. Albrecht, T.R., Crootof, A., Scott, C.A.: The water-energy-food nexus: a systematic review of methods for nexus assessment 1. Environ. Res. Lett., 1–43 (2018) Accessed 01 Sept 2025. Online. Available: https://iopscience.iop.org/article/10.1088/1748-9326/aaa9c6/ampdf
13. Srigiri, S.R., Dombrowsky, I.: Analyzing the water-energy-food nexus from a polycentric governance perspective: conceptual and methodological framework. Front. Environ. Sci. **10**, 725116 (2022). https://doi.org/10.3389/FENVS.2022.725116/BIBTEX
14. WRC: Development of Water-Energy-Food Nexus Index and Its Application to South Africa and the Southern African Development Community (2020).. Online. Available: www.wrc.org.za
15. Hutete, C., Vyas-Doorgapersad, S., Nqobile, S.: Factors affecting the adoption of fourth industrial revolution Technologies in Municipal Water Governance: a case study of a selected Rural District municipality. Architect. Image Stud. **6**(3), 2055–2068 (2025). https://doi.org/10.62754/ais.v6i3.559

16. Olaitan, O.O., Issah, M., Wayi, N., Olaitan, O.: A framework to test South Africa's readiness for the fourth industrial revolution. S. Afr. J. Inf. Manag. **23**(1), 1–10 (2021). https://doi.org/10.4102/SAJIM.V23I1.1284
17. Davis, F.D.: Perceived usefulness, perceived ease of use, and user acceptance of information technology. Manag. Inf. Syst. Q. **13**(3), 319–339 (1989). https://doi.org/10.2307/249008
18. Becker, G.: Human capital. In: The Concise Encyclopedia of Economics (1964) Accessed 02 Feb 2025. Online. Available: https://www2.um.edu.uy/acid/Family_Economics/Becker%20-%20Family%20&%20Human%20Capital.pdf
19. Wuttaphan, N.: Human capital theory: the theory of human resource development, implications, and future. Sci. Humanit. Soc. Sci. **18**(2), 240–253 (2017) Accessed 27 Jan 2023. Online. Available: https://www.researchgate.net/publication/344166132_HUMAN_CAPITAL_THEORY_THE_THEORY_OF_HUMAN_RESOURCE_DEVELOPMENT_IMPLICATIONS_AND_FUTURE
20. Zhou, C., Etzkowitz, H.: Triple helix twins: a framework for achieving innovation and UN sustainable development goals. Sustainability. **13**(12), 6535 (2021). https://doi.org/10.3390/SU13126535
21. Leydesdorff, L.: The triple helix: an evolutionary model of innovations. Res. Policy **29**(2), 243–255 (2000). https://doi.org/10.1016/S0048-7333(99)00063-3. Accessed 27 May 2026
22. Cochran, W.: Sampling Techniques. Wiley Journal (1977)
23. Hair, J.F., Risher, J.J., Sarstedt, M., Ringle, C.M.: When to use and how to report the results of PLS-SEM. Eur. Bus. Rev. **31**(1), 2–24 (2019). https://doi.org/10.1108/EBR-11-2018-0203/FULL/PDF
24. Hair, J., Alamer, A.: Partial least squares structural equation modeling (PLS-SEM) in second language and education research: guidelines using an applied example. Res. Methods Appl. Linguist. **1**(3), 100027 (2022). https://doi.org/10.1016/J.RMAL.2022.100027
25. Kock, N., Lynn, G.S.: Lateral collinearity and misleading results in variance-based SEM: an illustration and recommendations. J. Assoc. Inf. Syst. **13**(7), 546–580 (2012). https://doi.org/10.17705/1JAIS.00302
26. Siekmann, F., Schlör, H., Venghaus, S.: Linking sustainability and the fourth industrial revolution: a monitoring framework accounting for technological development. Energy Sustain. Soc. **13**(1), 26 (2023). https://doi.org/10.1186/s13705-023-00405-4
27. Khoza, N.G.: The Fourth Industrial Revolution (4IR) readiness in South Africa's public sector: pathways to achieving SDGs. Int. J. Dev. Sustain. (2025). https://doi.org/10.63212/ijds24090201
28. Khan, M.I., et al.: Integrating industry 4.0 for enhanced sustainability: pathways and prospects. Sustain. Prod. Consump. **54**(9), 149–189 (2025). https://doi.org/10.1016/j.spc.2024.12.012
29. Hair, J.F., Ringle, C.M., Danks, N.P., Hult, G.T.M., Sarstedt, M., Ray, S., Partial Least Squares Structural Equation Modeling (PLS-SEM) Using R: A Workbook (2022). https://link.springer.com/book/10.1007/978-3-030-80519-7
30. Hair, J.F., Hult, G.T.M., Ringle, C.M., Sarstedt, M.: A Primer on Partial Least Squares Structural Equation Modeling (PLS-SEM). Sage (2017)
31. Cheah, J.-H., Chuah, F., Ting, H.: PLS-SEM using SmartPLS 3.0: Chapter 12: Assessment of Mediation Analysis (2017). Online. Available: https://www.researchgate.net/publication/341250748
32. Kock, N.: Hypothesis testing with confidence intervals and P values in PLS-SEM. Int. J. e-Collab. **12**(3), 1–6 (2016). https://doi.org/10.4018/IJEC.2016070101
33. Savitri, C., Hurriyati, R., Wibowo, L.A., Hendrayati, H.: The role of social media marketing and brand image on smartphone purchase intention. Int. J. Data Netw. Sci. **6**(1), 185–192 (2021). https://doi.org/10.5267/J.IJDNS.2021.9.009

34. Zeng, N., Liu, Y., Gong, P., Hertogh, M., König, M.: Do right PLS and do PLS right: a critical review of the application of PLS-SEM in construction management research. Front. Eng. Manag. **8**(3), 356–369 (2021). https://doi.org/10.1007/s42524-021-0153-5
35. Hauff, S., Richter, N.F., Sarstedt, M., Ringle, C.M.: Importance and performance in PLS-SEM and NCA: introducing the combined importance-performance map analysis (cIPMA). J. Retail. Consum. Serv. **78**, 103723 (2024). https://doi.org/10.1016/J.JRETCONSER.2024.103723
36. Perez-Aranda, J., González Robles, E.M., Alarcón Urbistondo, P.: Understanding antecedents of continuance and revisit intentions: the case of sport apps. J. Retail. Consum. Serv. **72**, 103288 (2023). https://doi.org/10.1016/J.JRETCONSER.2023.103288
37. Mahardhani, A.J.: The role of public policy in fostering technological innovation and sustainability. J. Contemp. Adm. Manag. (ADMAN). **1**(2), 47–53 (2023). https://doi.org/10.61100/ADMAN.V1I2.22
38. Vishvas, R.: The role of policy and innovation in environmental sustainability. J. Sustain. Solut. **1**(2), 13–18 (2024). https://doi.org/10.36676/J.SUST.SOL.V1.I2.9
39. Giwa, F., Ngepah, N.: Artificial intelligence and skilled employment in South Africa: exploring key variables. Res. Glob. **8**, 100231 (2024). https://doi.org/10.1016/J.RESGLO.2024.100231
40. AlSaied, M., McLaughlin, P.: Organizational culture enabler and inhibitor factors for ambidextrous innovation. Adm. Sci. **14**(9), 207 (2024). https://doi.org/10.3390/ADMSCI14090207

Reconstructing Fragmented Flood Histories: A Benchmark of Imputation Methods for Flood Loss Modeling

Miguel Estêvão[1,2](✉), Pedro A. Sousa[1,2], Gracinda R. Guerreiro[3], João P. Pimentão[1,2], and Maria Isabel Gomes[3]

[1] Department of Electrical Engineering, NOVA School of Science and Technology, Universidade Nova de Lisboa, Lisbon, Portugal
r.estevao@campus.fct.unl.pt, {pas,pim}@fct.unl.pt
[2] Centre of Technology and Systems (UNINOVA-CTS), Lisbon, Portugal
[3] Department of Mathematics and NOVAMath, NOVA School of Science and Technology, Universidade Nova de Lisboa, Lisbon, Portugal
{grg,mirg}@fct.unl.pt

Abstract. As floods increasingly threaten societal well-being and economic stability - straining the global insurance industry - mitigation efforts face a critical barrier: historical flood data are fragmented and incomplete. This study establishes a robust pipeline to process and impute missing data in heavy-tailed environmental datasets. Aggregating over a century of events from sources such as EM-DAT and HANZE, the research evaluates eleven imputation approaches, contrasting statistical methods (MICE) with advanced machine learning (Random Forest, XGBoost, CatBoost) and generative techniques. Special emphasis is placed on logarithmic transformations to manage heavy-tailed distributions. The comparative analysis focuses on preserving multivariate dependency structures. Results demonstrate that machine learning approaches outperform traditional methods in handling nonlinear relationships in sparse data scenarios. By improving data quality, this framework provides a basis for more reliable flood risk assessments, contributing to greater financial and social resilience against extreme weather events.

Keywords: Flood Risk Assessment · Data Imputation · Machine Learning · Historical Data

1 Introduction

Floods represent one of the most recurrent and economically damaging extreme events globally, with a particularly severe impact recorded across the European continent [1]. This trend has been linked to increases in both the intensity and frequency of events, with climate change identified as a major contributing factor. In addition to socioeconomic effects, such as destruction of infrastructure and material losses, floods pose an environmental threat, requiring more effective flood risk management [2].

Published by Springer Nature Switzerland AG 2027
L. M. Camarinha-Matos and F. Ferrada (Eds.): DoCEIS 2026, IFIP AICT 790, pp. 292–309, 2027.
https://doi.org/10.1007/978-3-032-28939-1_21

The insurance sector faces a significant challenge from floods, which threaten its financial stability and operating models. In 2024, insurers covered 25% of total flood-related losses, underscoring their high exposure [3, 4]. Traditionally reliant on spatial and temporal diversification, insurers find these strategies compromised by rising flood risks linked to urbanization. Furthermore, despite increased event frequency, historical data remains insufficient for accurate risk assessment [5, 6].

Currently, to assess and manage this risk, the insurance industry uses tools such as Catastrophe Models (CAT models) [7], Geographic Information Systems (GIS), and, increasingly, Machine Learning (ML) algorithms [8, 9]. However, all these methodologies share a common dependency: the need for high-quality input data.

A critical limitation is the severe shortage of detailed flood data, which is often unobtainable from insurers due to privacy and commercial restrictions [5, 10]. Consequently, analyses must rely on fragmented, inconsistent sources with high rates of missing values, limiting the accurate modeling of extreme events [6]. Given the scarcity and fragmentation of flood records [5], innovative solutions are needed to create more robust data structures for risk analysis. This study forms part of a broader pipeline aimed at generating synthetic flood data to address this gap.

However, the quality of synthetic data depends directly on the coherence of pre-existing information. Therefore, this paper focuses on the essential prerequisite: robust imputation of missing values in historical records. Consolidating this fragmented data is critical to prevent error propagation in future generative models.

Based on this paradigm, the main PhD research question is: How can an integrated ML-driven framework improve economic loss forecasting and flood risk management in the insurance industry? The hypothesis is that integrating actuarial, statistical, and geospatial tools into a single programmable framework enables accurate operational flood risk management, improving damage forecasting, risk mapping, and automated alerts. Within this context, this paper addresses the specific challenge: How can fragmented and incomplete historical flood data be reconstructed to support advanced risk analysis? To answer this, we propose a Multi-Scenario Imputation Pipeline that aggregates heterogeneous data sources and compares multiple imputation algorithms, establishing the data infrastructure needed for next-generation flood risk models.

This paper is structured as follows: Sect. 2 discusses the socioeconomic impact of floods and the insurance protection gap. Section 3 reviews flood risk assessment and data imputation strategies, identifying gaps and outlining contributions. Section 4 presents the Multi-Scenario Imputation Framework, detailing its mathematical foundations, algorithms, and evaluation metrics. Section 5 validates the methodology through a real-world case study with benchmarking results. Section 6 concludes with a discussion of findings and future work on synthetic data generation.

2 Tackling Societal Challenges

The urgency to reconstruct data extends beyond technical needs, reflecting the social vulnerability exacerbated by climate crises. As extreme events grow in frequency and intensity [1], the insurance sector's ability to ensure financial stability is strained by a widening protection gap. In 2024, global catastrophic losses reached approximately

$368 billion, with floods accounting for $84 billion. Only $21 billion of flood losses were insured - just 25% of the total - leaving a 75% coverage gap [3]. This mirrors 2023 trends, confirming the structural persistence of this gap [4]. As a result, communities and public sectors bear most damage costs, undermining economic stability and long-term resilience.

To respond to this social challenge, a paradigm shift is needed in how risk is quantified, protected and managed. Currently, the sector relies on a fragmented ecosystem of tools, from geospatial to statistical, to perform probabilistic financial loss estimates and generate spatial risk mapping. However, these often operate in isolation. This disconnection between spatial accuracy and actuarial rigor limits the insurance industry's ability to develop efficient data-driven mitigation strategies - such as for pricing and capital allocation [8, 9, 11]. The broader research structure in which this study is embedded aims to resolve this fragmentation by developing an integrated framework that combines actuarial, statistical, and geospatial modules with machine learning mechanisms. By taking advantage of the individual and joint benefits of these tools, this approach seeks to improve data forecasting and automate risk alerts, going beyond the limitations of static historical assumptions [9].

However, this integrated framework's potential depends on a robust historical database. The methodology presented here thus serves as an essential driver for social resilience, reconstructing fragmented flood data through advanced imputation to build the foundational data infrastructure needed for risk modeling in data-scarce regions. This shift, from fragmented records to cohesive datasets, enables the insurance sector to evolve from reactive loss estimation to proactive risk management, directly mitigating financial exposure to climate extremes. By ensuring risk assessments are data-reliable, the approach helps maintain viable insurance products despite rising risks [11], thereby promoting financial resilience and supporting long-term economic recovery [13].

3 Literature Review

3.1 Flood Risk Assessment and the Insurance Gap

Flood risk is conceptually defined by the Source-Pathway-Receptor-Consequences (SPRC) model, which frames risk as a causal chain linking hazard (water source and pathway) with vulnerability (exposed receptors and consequences) [12]. For insurers, this interaction is financially quantified using catastrophe (CAT) models [13]. Unlike standard actuarial assessment, which relies on abundant data, modeling extreme events requires stochastic simulations to project losses in high-impact scenarios [13].

CAT models operate through a modular structure generally composed of four interdependent components: *hazard*, *exposure*, *vulnerability*, and financial *losses* [13]. While the hazard module characterizes the event in terms of its physical components, the exposure and vulnerability modules are responsible for translating the intensity and characteristics of the event into physical damage. This aspect is where the high dependence on the quality of input data becomes evident. The literature highlights the lack of detailed information as a factor that generates epistemic uncertainties, which limits the accuracy of the model's predictions [13] and, consequently, affects output metrics such as Average

Annual Loss (AAL) and exceedance probability estimates, which are essential for risk management and pricing.

At the same time, Geographic Information Systems play a key role in spatial hazard mapping, allowing the integration of heterogeneous data into a spatiotemporal structure [14]. However, the aforementioned operational separation persists: while CAT models focus on actuarial loss prediction, GIS tools focus on technical hazard mapping. Thus, there is a disconnection between spatial accuracy and probabilistic rigor [8, 9].

3.2 Machine Learning for Risk Modeling

The literature shows an increasing evolution in risk assessment methods, marked by the greater adoption of more recent approaches such as Machine Learning [6, 15]. This approach is distinguished by the ability of algorithms to learn patterns from historical data without the need for explicit programming of each task [15]. This feature allows for better identification and modelling of nonlinear relationships between the diverse range of climatic and socioeconomic variables, overcoming previous limitations inherent to more traditional models [6, 9].

In the context of flood management, algorithms such as Random Forest and Neural Networks have proven to be effective both for susceptibility mapping and financial forecasting [16]. Recent studies report that the use of ML allows heterogeneous data to be processed to identify areas of higher risk more accurately [9]. In the insurance sector, the application of these models to historical claims records, such as those of the National Flood Insurance Program, has proven effective in predicting claim amounts, allowing for better correction of biases and improving pricing and reinsurance strategies [17]. Among the various approaches, Random Forest has often stood out for its consistency in risk assessment scenarios [18].

The applicability of these models is still questioned given their high dependence on the quality and quantity of training data [6, 15]. The literature highlights that models trained with biased or incomplete datasets inevitably result in less accurate predictions [15]. This dependence becomes critical in predicting extreme events, where performance is conditioned by the dominant patterns in historical data [6]. As a result, the effectiveness of Machine Learning models in mitigating the protection gap is conditioned by the existence of a robust and cohesive data structure [5].

3.3 Data Reconstruction and Imputation Strategies

The treatment of missing data remains a central obstacle in natural and actuarial risk modeling. Traditional approaches, like record deletion or mean imputation, are often inadequate in this field. For databases characterized by heavy-tailed distributions - common in extreme insurance claims and hydrological events - central-tendency imputation obscures the underlying skewness and tail risk, leading to a systematic underestimation of potential losses and a severe bias in risk assessment [19, 20].

In order to overcome these limitations, the literature has established multivariate imputation methods as a benchmark within this field. One example is Multiple Imputation by Chained Equations (MICE) which is currently recognized as a standard within the field of statistics, allowing for the modeling of uncertainty by creating multiple sets of imputed data based on iterative regressions. However, although it stands out for its robustness for data with linear relationships, studies reveal limitations in capturing structures with complex nonlinear dependencies, a recurring phenomenon in heterogeneous environmental data [21].

Consequently, more recent studies have shifted to approaches based on Machine Learning. Non-parametric algorithms such as Random Forest and Gradient Boosting methods (such as XGBoost and CatBoost) have demonstrated superior performance in scenarios of complex interactions without rigid distribution assumptions. Comparative studies reveal that Random Forest-based approaches consistently outperform MICE in mixed-type environmental databases, reducing errors generated by imputation processes [21]. This trend is corroborated by recent studies that also highlight XGBoost as a reliable tool for filling gaps in climate time series [19].

Beyond the issue of accuracy, preserving the dependency structure in extreme events requires more sophisticated approaches. Methods based on copulas have proven relevant due to their ability to model these structures. Unlike linear methods, these approaches can effectively model tail dependence, preserving the statistical properties of rare events that are extremely important for flood risk assessment [22]. At the same time, the recent use of generative models, such as Generative Adversarial Networks and models such as Conditional Tabular Generative Adversarial Network (CTGAN), represents a new area of innovation in mitigating data scarcity. Studies have recently validated the use of these approaches to enrich hydrological datasets, demonstrating that the generation of realistic synthetic data can significantly improve the robustness and accuracy of prediction models in data scarcity scenarios [6].

3.4 Main Contributions

This work is part of a broader pipeline for generating synthetic data for flood risk assessment. As a first step, the main contribution is a robust framework for data reconstruction and imputation, addressing the gap between scarce observed data and the need for rigorous risk modeling in the insurance sector. Appendix A provides a schematic overview of the complete pipeline, highlighting the imputation stage that is the focus of this study.

By combining the rigor of statistical methods with the nonlinear capacity of ML algorithms and generative models, this study demonstrates how advanced techniques can repair historical databases with greater accuracy, particularly for long-tail distributions that preserve extreme events often overlooked by traditional methods [20]. The approach prioritizes the multivariate dependency structure, reconstructing not just missing values but the physical and actuarial consistency of the data.

While existing literature extensively covers generative models for synthetic data and statistical imputation, a clear gap remains regarding the reconstruction of highly fragmented, heavy-tailed actuarial datasets as a prerequisite for synthetic generation. This study fills that niche by benchmarking a hybrid approach specifically designed to repair historical data prior to synthetic generation - an area largely overlooked in flood risk modeling.

4 Multi-scenario Imputation Framework

The following section defines a general framework that allows for reconstruction of missing values in multivariate datasets characterized by heavy-tailed distributions and complex dependency structures. The methodology is structured in three phases: (1) preprocessing and range compression, (2) multi-scenario imputation, and (3) robustness assessment.

4.1 Data Sources and Characterization

Given the asymmetry often present in environmental and financial data, where rare extreme events can distort imputation models, we employ a logarithmic transformation for normalization. For any non-negative variable x, the transformed variable y is defined by:

$$y = \log(x + c) \tag{1}$$

where c is a constant (typically 1) to ensure that the function is well defined for zero-valued instances. This transformation compresses the right tail of the distribution, approximating normality and stabilizing the variance for subsequent regression models.

4.2 Multi-scenario Imputation Strategy

The framework applies a comparative benchmark approach, using several different imputation scenarios, developed to deal with the diverse missing data patterns and dependencies on complex variables, a recurring scenario in datasets of this type. Robustness is achieved through the parallel evaluation of multiple methodologies, enabling the identification of the optimal reconstruction technique and maximizing reconstruction fidelity.

To ensure broad coverage of potential data dependency structures, the evaluated strategies cover three main distinct approaches:

- **Statistical Imputation Methods**: Algorithms such as Multiple Imputation by Chain Equations (MICE) are included to test the effectiveness of linear dependency assumptions in the reconstruction process. MICE operates through iterative regression cycles and is known to perform under moderate missingness [21]. It is applied both as a standalone imputation approach or strategically within hybrid configurations.
- **Machine Learning Imputation models and reconstruction**: To capture nonlinear interactions and handle high data scarcity, the framework considers algorithms specifically designed for complex decision boundaries, namely Random Forest (RF), XGBoost, CatBoost, and HistGradientBoosting (HGBR). These are evaluated both as standalone imputers and as part of hybrid architectures, given their capacity to model complex interactions without strict distributional assumptions.
- **Tail- and Dependency-preserving models**: To model the full multivariate dependency structure, including tail dependencies, complex joint distributions and high-dimensional correlations, the analysis includes models such as Gaussian Copulas and

deep learning architectures such as CTGAN. These methods aim to preserve joint distributions and correlations across variables, rather than imputing each variable independently.

While generative models offer theoretical advantages for preserving complex dependencies, they also carry specific risks in the context of imputation. These include: (i) potential overfitting to observed data patterns, which may reduce generalizability to unseen events; (ii) sensitivity to hyperparameter choices and initialization; (iii) difficulty in validating the fidelity of imputed values for extreme tail events, where ground truth is by definition scarce; and (iv) substantially higher computational cost compared to tree-based methods. These considerations motivated our empirical benchmark across all three families, allowing performance - rather than theoretical preference - to guide method selection [23].

This design, composed of different approaches and model types, ensures that the final selection is guided exclusively by performance metrics across the entire set of candidates, regardless of the underlying theoretical paradigm.

4.3 Evaluation Framework and Metrics

To objectively identify the most robust imputation method, we apply a validation framework centered on two orthogonal dimensions: univariate distributional fidelity and multivariate structural consistency.

To quantify the fidelity to the original heavy-tailed data, the Kolmogorov-Smirnov (KS) distance, defined in Eq. (2), is adopted as the main metric, [24]. It quantifies the maximum distance between the cumulative distribution functions of the observed data (F_{obs}) and the imputed data (F_{imp}):

$$D_{KS} = \left|F_{obs}(x) - F_{imp}(x)\right| . \tag{2}$$

To preserve the dependencies between variables, the fidelity of the imputed correlation structure is evaluated using Frobenius' norm [25] (Eq. (3)), quantifying the difference between the original (C_{obs}) and imputed (C_{imp}) correlation matrices:

$$|\Delta C|_F = \sqrt{\left(\sum_i \sum_j \left(c_{(ij)}^{obs} - c_{(ij)}^{imp}\right)^2\right)} . \tag{3}$$

If the dataset includes categorical variables, they are imputed separately using a deterministic strategy that remains invariant across all scenarios. As a result, they do not influence comparative evaluation, since they provide no discriminatory information for model selection.

To account for differing analytical priorities, the framework incorporates a sensitivity analysis that varies the relative weight assigned to distributional fidelity and structural consistency.

The framework proposes the use of the Analytic Hierarchy Process (AHP) to generate all valid weighting scenarios for the different weights ($w_{(KS)}$, $w_{(Frob)}$). The final ranking for each method k is calculated using a weighted score that combines the weights derived from the AHP with the normalized error metrics, as shown in Eq. (4):

$$Score_k = w_{(KS)} \cdot \left(1 - D^{norm}_{(KS,k)}\right) + w_{(Frob)} \cdot \left(1 - |\Delta C|^{norm}_{(F,k)}\right) \tag{4}$$

where $D^{norm}_{(KS,k)}$ and $|\Delta C|^{norm}_{(F,k)}$ correspond to the raw metrics from Eqs. (2) and (3) normalized using Eq. (5):

$$x_k^{\text{norm}} = (x_k) / \left(\max_k(x_k)\right). \tag{5}$$

By rewarding approaches that minimize error in both dimensions concurrently, this scoring system guarantees robustness across different user preferences.

5 Case Study: Global Flood Database

In this section, we validate the proposed framework using historical flood event data, demonstrating its applicability to a real-world scenario of high societal relevance. This case study addresses the critical data fragmentation in the insurance sector; whereby reliable risk modeling is hindered by missing values in key actuarial variables.

5.1 Data Sources and Characterization

The dataset used in this case study was compiled from three primary historical flood sources: EM-DAT [26], HANZE [27], and the Portuguese Insurers Association (APS) [28]. After cleaning, standardization, and deduplication, the resulting dataset comprises 6,671 unique events (1870–2025) characterized by 11 variables (Appendix B, Table 3).

Geographically, the dataset shows a significant concentration of records on the European continent, representing 3,003 events, approximately 45% of the total events, followed by Asia with 1,676 events. This distribution is consistent at the sub-regional level, as Southern Europe is the region with the highest number of events (1,333 events in total), placing Europe in first place in the ranking of registered flood events. In terms of granularity at the country level, the top three are Italy (781 events), Spain (329), and France (275). While the dataset draws from global sources (EM-DAT, HANZE, APS), this European bias should be noted. The findings are therefore most directly applicable to European flood regimes (e.g., river and flash floods driven by heavy rainfall). Generalizability to other geographical contexts, such as monsoon-dominated regions in South Asia, cyclone-driven floods in North America, or data-scarce regions in Africa and South America, requires further validation.

Regarding the nature of these events, the data shows that most are related to river flooding (3,159 events), followed by flash flooding (1,943). Both types are correlated with the main cause of flood identified in this dataset, which is heavy rain, responsible for 5,450 of the 6,671 occurrences recorded.

Table 1 presents summary statistics for key numerical flood variables, including Number of Deaths, Injuries, Affected, and Homeless, and Total and Insured Damages.

Table 1. Descriptive Statistics

Variable	Min	Q1	Median	Q3	Max	Mean	Std. Deviation	γ	κ	NA (%)
No. Deaths	0	1	4	16	6,054	28	139	21.59	724.11	**17.25**
No. Injured	1	7.5	23	76	146,000	419	5,355	25.12	670.96	**87.78**
No. Affected	5	1,952	10,905	75,000	1.50e+8	551,498	494,005	20.58	511.55	**50.07**
No. Homeless	9	778.75	2,727	10,000	4,000,000	39,869	24,338	11.97	165.78	**92.50**
Total Damage (M€)	0	7.02	51.65	270.34	6.29e+11	4.86e+14	1.51e+16	40.44	1675.35	**73.15**
Insured Damage (M€)	0.76	43.84	152.44	393.46	8184.27	515.56	1,112.12	4.80	27.04	**98.20**

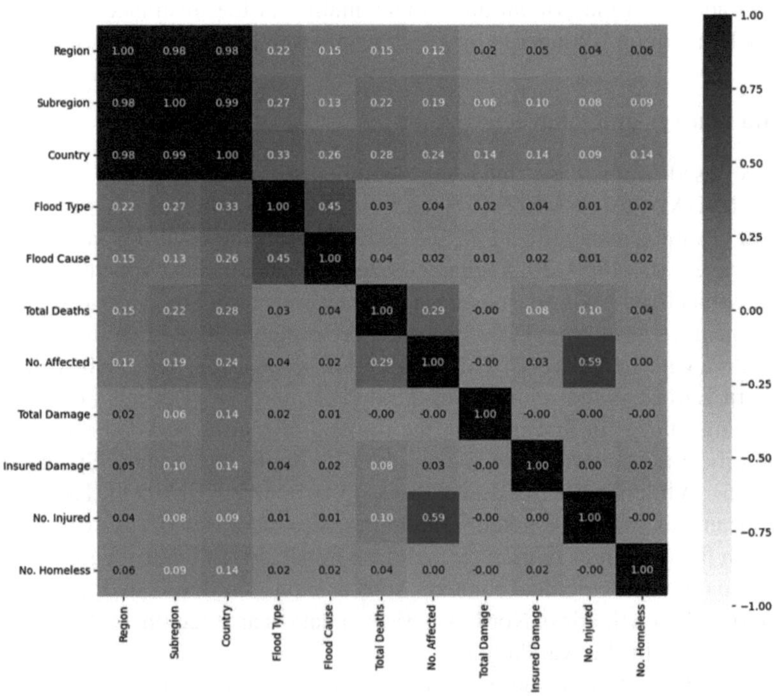

Fig. 1. Dataset correlation matrix.

These metrics exhibit highly asymmetric, heavy-tailed distributions, as indicated by high positive skewness (γ) and kurtosis (κ) - a pattern driven by the prevalence of extreme flood events. As shown in Table 1, a further challenge is the substantial rate of missing data across these variables (column NA), ranging from 17.25% for Number of Deaths to 98.20% for Insured Damages, a key challenge for robust imputation and modeling.

Figure 1 illustrates the correlation analysis, revealing two key dependencies in the data structure. First, spatial variables (region, subregion, country), as expected, are strongly correlated, confirming geographic consistency. Second, among numerical variables, the strongest positive correlation is between Number of Injured and of Affected (r = 0.59), followed by Number of Affected and of Deaths (r = 0.29). These interdependencies validate the relational structure that the subsequent multivariate imputation models will leverage, clarifying fundamental patterns in the dataset.

While the correlation analysis clarifies variable relationships, the highly skewed, heavy-tailed nature of the data - previously quantified in Table 1 - induces the raw histograms, shown in Fig. 2, to collapse into a single bar near zero, making the distributions visually unreadable and highlighting the need for data transformation.

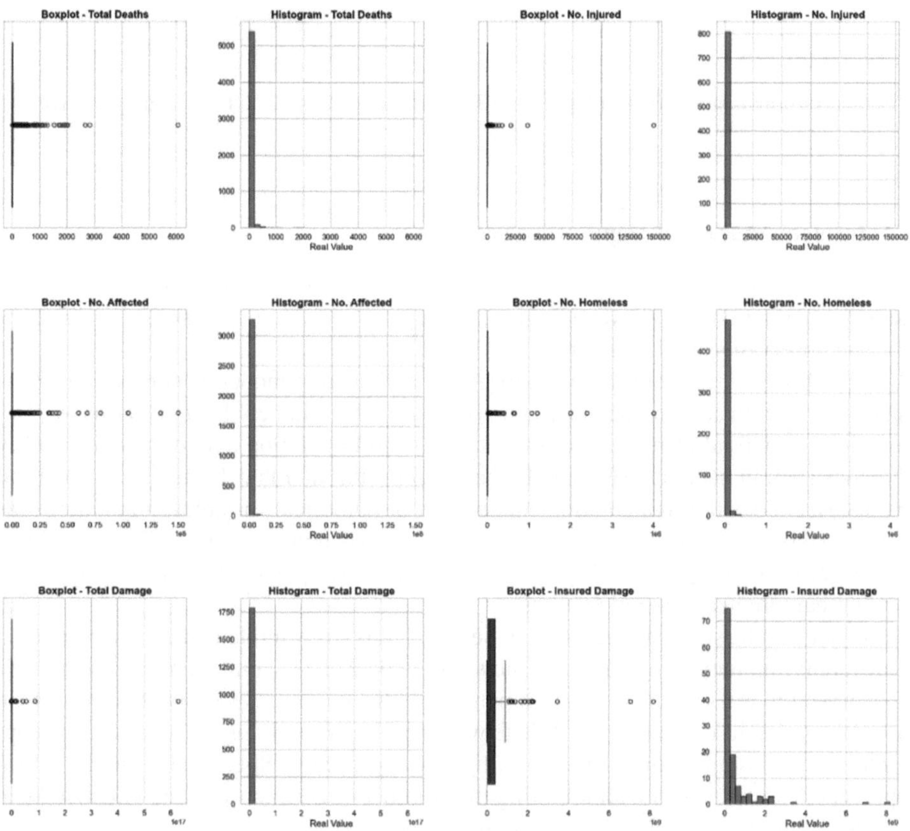

Fig. 2. Descriptive analysis of the numerical variable

To address this, the logarithmic transformation defined in Eq. (1) (Sect. 4.1) was applied to all numerical variables. This step compressed the value range, mitigating the extreme skewness identified in Table 1.

This yields a distribution closer to the Normal distribution, enabling subsequent imputation algorithms to model variance more effectively and reducing the bias typically caused by outliers. Figure 3 demonstrates how the transformation compresses the right tail, thereby reducing positive skewness, resulting in a more symmetric distribution compatible with common imputation assumptions.

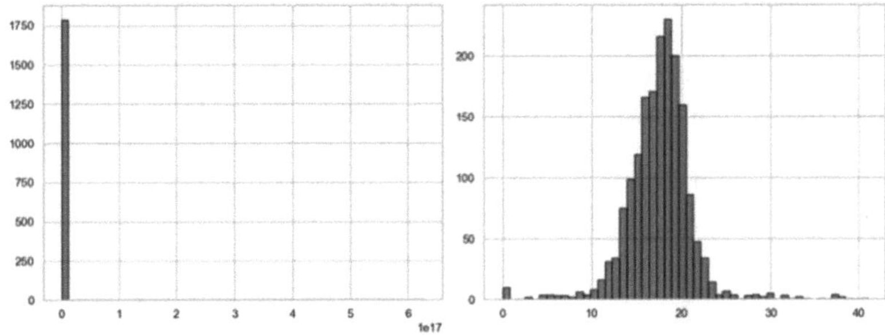

Fig. 3. Original data (left) and log(x + 1) Transformation (right) of Total Damage variable

5.2 Implementation of Imputation Scenarios

During preprocessing, categorical variables were deterministically imputed using the hierarchical relationship between Region, Subregion, and Country, ensuring consistency with the observed spatial structure.

Variables with missingness exceeding 70% and lacking moderate correlation (Pearson $|r| \geq 0.25$ with at least one other numerical variable) - namely Insured Damages, No. Homeless, and Total Damage - were excluded from imputation due to the unreliability of reconstructing such sparse data. These are reported in Table 1 and Fig. 2 solely to characterize the data fragmentation challenge. For numerical variables, imputation was limited to those with either moderate correlation or missingness $\leq 55\%$. All selected variables were transformed using Eq. (1) to reduce skewness, enabling imputation models to better capture heavy-tailed patterns.

To validate the structure proposed in Sect. 4.2, this study implemented and compared 11 different imputation scenarios, as shown in Table 2. The application of these models was adapted to the specific dispersion patterns of the dataset. Given its effectiveness in cases of moderate data absence, MICE was applied not only as an independent approach but also as an auxiliary model in hybrid approaches. Specifically, in the hybrid approaches, it was tasked with imputing the Number of Deaths variable, which, as seen in Table 1, has a total of 17.25% of missing values.

For the remaining variables with greater data scarcity, ensembles were implemented based on the tree-based models defined in the methodology (namely Random Forest, XGBoost, CatBoost, and HistGradientBoosting). These algorithms were evaluated in two configurations: as independent models, and within hybrid architectures where the imputation task was divided, with MICE reconstructing the Number of Deaths and the tree-based ensembles applied to the remaining high-sparsity fields. Finally, Gaussian Copulas and CTGAN were integrated to capture all variables simultaneously, serving as a reference for iterative methods.

5.3 Benchmarking Results and Discussion

The scenarios described in the previous section were implemented in Python 3.11.8, producing 11 distinct reconstructed datasets. In order to identify the most robust approach, the validation framework defined in Sect. 4.3 was applied, focusing on univariate distribution fidelity and multivariate structural consistency.

To quantify fidelity to the original heavy-tailed data, the Kolmogorov-Smirnov (KS) distance (Eq. (2)) was calculated for all numerical variables. Simultaneously, to preserve dependencies between variables, the fidelity of the imputed correlation structure was assessed using the Frobenius norm (Eq. (3)).

To assess the robustness of the imputed data across the 11 scenarios, AHP methodology was applied to generate valid weight distributions based on variable judgment matrices. In total, 11 distinct valid scenarios (consistency index <0.10) were generated, ranging from a strong preference for distributional fidelity to a strong preference for structural consistency. Subsequently, the final ranking of each scenario was calculated using the weighted score proposed in Eq. (4), based on the normalized metrics, as proposed in Eq. (5).

Table 2 summarizes the results and highlights the stability of the ranking of each imputation method across all weight variations, reporting its frequency in the top 10, average position in the ranking, and stability metrics.

The results clearly establish the hybrid MICE+XGBoost method as the most robust and representative approach, achieving a perfect first-place ranking across all sensitivity scenarios analyzed (average rank $= 1.00$, SD $= 0$). This invariant performance confirms its superior reconstruction fidelity, regardless of whether priority is given to distributional shape or correlation structure. CTGAN and Gaussian Copula ranked poorly due to several factors: extreme missingness limits learning of joint distributions; heavy-tailed data violates assumptions of Gaussian Copula and challenges CTGAN's adversarial training; overfitting is likely given limited complete cases; generative training objectives (likelihood, adversarial loss) do not directly optimize imputation accuracy and hyperparameter sensitivity may require tuning beyond our benchmark scope. Notably, these models remain promising for synthetic data generation, a distinction that warrants further investigation.

The Execution Time in Table 2 reveals practical trade-offs: the top-performing MICE+XGBoost method requires the most computation (453.62 s), while standalone tree-based methods offer competitive accuracy at substantially lower cost (e.g., Random Forest: 7.12 s).

Furthermore, the reliance on tree-based algorithms within the top-performing architectures enhances model interpretability, as practitioners can leverage feature importance metrics to transparently identify which variables drive the imputed values. Regarding scalability, while the hybrid MICE+XGBoost pipeline introduces higher computational

Table 2. Robustness of imputation scenarios tested with 17 AHP weight sets.

Imputation Method	Freq. Top 10 (%)	Average Rank (Std)	Average Score (Std)	Median Score	Execution Time (sec)
MICE w/ XGBoost	100	1.00 (0.00)	0.436 (0.188)	0.436	453.62
XGBoost	100	2.29 (0.46)	0.399 (0.165)	0.399	3.19
MICE w/ RF	100	2.71 (0.46)	0.396 (0.168)	0.396	436.32
MICE w/ HGBR	100	4.29 (0.46)	0.388 (0.164)	0.388	438.66
MICE w/ CatBoost	100	4.71 (0.46)	0.384 (0.161)	0.384	439.86
HGBR	100	6.00 (0.00)	0.381 (0.159)	0.381	10.84
CatBoost	100	7.00 (0.00)	0.376 (0.155)	0.376	6.80
Random Forest	100	8.00 (0.00)	0.373 (0.153)	0.373	7.12
Gaussian Copula	100	9.00 (0.00)	0.307 (0.182)	0.307	2.21
CTGAN	88.24	10.00 (0.00)	0.260 (0.166)	0.260	52.44
MICE	11.76	11.00 (0.00)	0.033 (0.021)	0.033	582.05

overhead, the standalone tree-based ensembles provide highly efficient and scalable alternatives capable of processing expanding global datasets without prohibitive resource demands.

This success validates the dual-strategy experimental design: MICE handles moderately missing variables while XGBoost's gradient boosting effectively captures complex patterns in highly sparse data. These findings align with recent literature, where XGBoost's accuracy for nonlinear data [19] and MICE's limitations in complex mixed datasets [21] have been documented. Although generative models are valuable for data synthesis [6], the present study indicates that for accurate imputation in highly fragmented settings, tree-based ensemble methods remain more effective.

However, it is important to emphasize that this dominance of MICE+XGBoost is empirically established for the specific characteristics of our dataset: heavy-tailed distributions, and complex nonlinear dependencies typical of historical flood records. The optimal imputation method may differ in other domains - for example, datasets with lower missingness rates, different variable types (e.g., purely continuous or purely categorical), or other peril types (e.g., windstorms, earthquakes).

To complement the distributional and structural fidelity metrics, we performed a masking experiment that directly quantifies imputation accuracy against known ground truth. Using stratified random sampling, we masked 5% of observed (non-missing) values across three numerical variables - Number of Deaths, No. Injured, and No. Affected - and compared imputed values to the ground truth. The results show that imputation accuracy correlates inversely with original missingness: variables with lower missingness achieved higher fidelity. Specifically, Total Deaths (17.25% original missingness) yielded an imputation accuracy of 82.9%, No. Affected (50.70% missingness) achieved 74.6%, while No. Injured (87.78% missingness) attained only 29.0% accuracy. These results confirm that the imputation pipeline performs reliably when moderate amounts of data are present but highlights inherent limitations in reconstructing extremely sparse variables.

To ensure full reproducibility, we provide the specific implementation details for the hybrid MICE+XGBoost architecture (the top-performing method) and the key hyperparameters for all methods. The hybrid MICE+XGBoost architecture proceeds as follows: (1) MICE (10 iterations, BayesianRidge estimator, sample_posterior = True) imputes Total Deaths; (2) XGBoost (n_estimators = 300, n_jobs = −1, random_state = 0) imputes No. Injured and No. Affected using variables with moderate correlation as predictors, with any missing values in these predictors temporarily filled via a median SimpleImputer. Hyperparameters for all 11 methods are as follows: MICE (max_iter = 10, estimator = BayesianRidge, sample_posterior = True), XGBoost (n_estimators = 300, n_jobs = −1, random_state = 0), Random Forest (n_estimators = 200, n_jobs = −1, random_state = 0), CatBoost (iterations = 500, learning_rate = 0.05, depth = 6, random_seed = 0, verbose = 0), HGBR (max_iter = 10, learning_rate = 0.1), Gaussian Copula (default SDV settings), CTGAN (300 epochs, verbose = True, batch_size = 500). Software: Python 3.11.8, scikit-learn 1.7.2, xgboost 3.2.1, catboost 1.2.8, sdv 1.6.0.

5.4 Implications for Research and Practice

Beyond the specific benchmark results, this study offers broader implications for how imputation is approached in data-scarce, heavy-tailed domains, for both researchers and practitioners. The findings of this study have relevant implications for both researchers and practitioners.

From a research perspective, this work provides the first systematic benchmark of imputation methods for heavy-tailed flood data with extreme missingness. The dominance of hybrid MICE+XGBoost establishes a baseline for future comparisons, while the dual-criterion AHP-weighted framework offers a methodology transferable to other domains. The underperformance of generative methods for imputation (despite their promise for synthesis) highlights an important distinction warranting further investigation. From a practical perspective, we recommend hybrid MICE+XGBoost for accuracy-critical flood risk applications, and more generally, recommend hybrid approaches when evaluating imputation methods for similar data regimes or from other perils. The framework can be integrated as a preprocessing module into existing CAT modeling pipelines, enabling more robust risk assessment in data-scarce regions.

6 Conclusions

This study addresses critical data fragmentation in flood risk assessment - a societal challenge intensified by climate change and the widening protection gap - by establishing a robust Multi-Scenario Imputation Framework designed to reconstruct heavy-tailed, highly incomplete historical records. For the presented dataset, the hybrid MICE+XGBoost methodology emerged as the most robust approach, consistently outperforming standalone statistical and generative models across all evaluation scenarios by effectively restoring multivariate dependencies essential for actuarial modeling. However, it is important to emphasize that these results are highly dependent on the specific characteristics of this flood loss data, and performance may differ in other domains or in datasets lacking heavy-tailed distributions.

Despite the contributions presented, this project faces two main limitations. First, the historical dataset used exhibits a significant geographical bias, consisting of approximately 45% of events recorded in Europe. Consequently, the dependency structures learned by the models may need to be recalibrated before any generalization can be made to regions with different socioeconomic conditions and infrastructure. Second, some specific variables suffer from a severe lack of data. Our masking experiment confirms that the imputation pipeline performs reliably when moderate amounts of data are present but highlights inherent limitations in reconstructing extremely sparse variables - a constraint we have now explicitly acknowledged. Although hybrid algorithms optimize the reconstruction of these structures, data inference at this level of scarcity inherently approaches extrapolation, bringing with it a margin of epistemic uncertainty that must be acknowledged. Moreover, while MICE is capable of producing multiple imputed datasets to quantify imputation uncertainty (including confidence intervals and uncertainty propagation), a full uncertainty analysis is deferred to future work.

Despite its obvious limitations, the presented project offers significant benefits for both research and industry. For the industry, this framework enables insurers and risk managers to leverage highly fragmented historical databases, allowing for more accurate catastrophe modeling and more informed capital allocation, thereby addressing the growing protection gap. For the research community, this study establishes a necessary benchmark, demonstrating that hybrid methodologies, such as those presented, are essential for stabilizing data with heavy-tailed distributions, particularly in environmental catastrophe scenarios.

Given this, these reconstructed datasets thus constitute a validated foundation for the next phase of the pipeline, where the goal is to train advanced generative models to synthesize realistic flood scenarios, thereby directly addressing the data scarcity regarding extreme events.

Acknowledgements. This work was partially funded through FCT (the Fundação para a Ciência e a Tecnologia, I.P.) - for M.E., P.A.S. and J.P.P. - under the scope of projects CTS/00066 and UIDB/06107/2023-CREATE - and for G.R.G. and M.I.G. - under the scope of projects UID/297/2025 and UID/PRR/297/2025 (Center for Mathematics and Applications-NOVA Math).

Appendix A: Framework (Fig. 4)

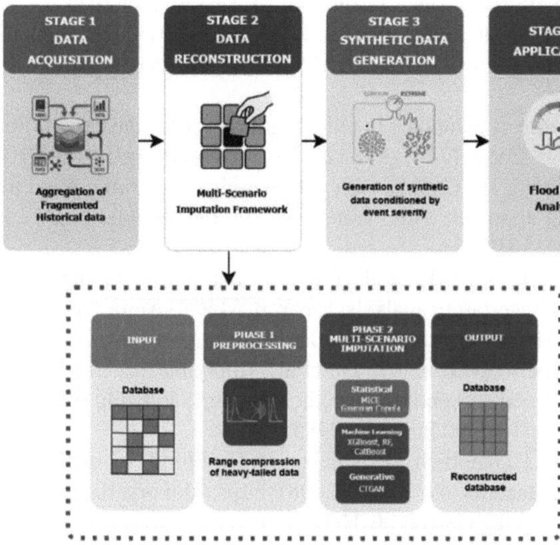

Fig. 4. Schematic overview of the synthetic data generation pipeline for flood risk assessment

Appendix B: Variable Definitions and Characteristics

Table 3. Summary of dataset features, data types, and missing value rates.

Designation	Description	Type	NA (%)
Region	Macro geographic region	Categorical (Nominal)	0.00%
Subregion	Geographic regional subdivision	Categorical (Nominal)	4.18%
Country	Country where the event took place	Categorical (Nominal)	0.00%
Flood Type	Specific classification of the flood	Categorical (Nominal)	0.00%
Flood Cause	Triggering cause (e.g., heavy rain, monsoon)	Categorical (Nominal)	13.04%
Total Deaths	Number of dead people	Numerical (Discrete)	17.25%
No. Injured	Number of people with physical injuries	Numerical (Discrete)	87.78%
No. Affected	People who needed basic assistance	Numerical (Discrete)	50.07%
No. Homeless	Number of people who required shelter	Numerical (Discrete)	92.50%
Total Damage	Total estimated economic damage (EUR)	Numerical (Continuous)	73.15%
Insured Damage	Amount covered by insurance (EUR)	Numerical (Continuous)	98.20%

References

1. Ingels, M.W., Botzen, W.J.W., Aerts, J.C.J.H., et al.: The state of the art and future of climate risk insurance modeling. Ann. N. Y. Acad. Sci. **1541**, 100–114 (2024). https://doi.org/10.1111/nyas.15255

2. European Commission: Floods (2023). https://environment.ec.europa.eu/topics/water/floods_en. Accessed Sept 2025
3. AON: Climate and catastrophe insight (2025). https://assets.aon.com/-/media/files/aon/reports/2025/2025-climate-catastrophe-insight.pdf. Accessed Sept 2025
4. Swiss Re Institute: Natural catastrophes in 2023. Sigma 01/2024, Sigma Research. (2024) https://www.swissre.com/institute/research/sigma-research/sigma-2024-01.html. Accessed Sept 2025
5. Surminski, S.: The role of insurance in reducing direct risk - the case of flood insurance. Int. Rev. Environ. Resour. Econ. **7**, 241–278 (2014). https://doi.org/10.1561/101.00000062
6. Sattari, A., Moradkhani, H.: Coping with data scarcity in extreme flood forecasting: a deep generative modeling approach. Adv. Water Resour. **204**, 105063 (2025). https://doi.org/10.1016/j.advwatres.2025.105063
7. Teng, J., Jakeman, A.J., Vaze, J., et al.: Flood inundation modelling: a review of methods, recent advances and uncertainty analysis. Environ. Model. Amp. Softw. **90**, 201–216 (2017). https://doi.org/10.1016/j.envsoft.2017.01.006
8. Oluwadare, T.S., Ribeiro, M.P., Chen, D., et al.: Applying machine learning algorithms for spatial modeling of flood susceptibility prediction over São Paulo sub-region. Land. **14**, 985 (2025). https://doi.org/10.3390/land14050985
9. Apel, H., Aronica, G.T., Kreibich, H., Thieken, A.H.: Flood risk analyses—how detailed do we need to be? Nat. Hazards. **49**, 79–98 (2008). https://doi.org/10.1007/s11069-008-9277-8
10. Zhou, N., Vilar-Zanón, J.L., Garrido, J., Heras-Martínez, A.J.: Measuring climate change from an actuarial perspective: a survey of insurance applications. Global Pol. **15**, 34–46 (2024). https://doi.org/10.1111/1758-5899.13465
11. Ceresa, P., Bussi, G., Denaro, S., et al.: Large-scale flood risk assessment in data-scarce areas: an application to Central Asia. Nat. Hazards Earth Syst. Sci. **25**, 403–428 (2025). https://doi.org/10.5194/nhess-25-403-2025
12. Grossi, P., Kunreuther, H. (eds.): Catastrophe Modeling: A New Approach to Managing Risk. Kluwer Academic Publishers (2005). https://doi.org/10.1007/b100669
13. Foote, M., Hillier, J., Mitchell-Wallace, K., Jones, M.: Natural Catastrophe Risk Management and Modelling (2017). https://doi.org/10.1002/9781118906057
14. Albano, R., Mancusi, L., Sole, A., Adamowski, J.: Collaborative strategies for sustainable EU flood risk management: FOSS and geospatial tools - challenges and opportunities for operative risk analysis. ISPRS Int. J. Geo Inf. **4**, 2704–2727 (2015). https://doi.org/10.3390/ijgi4042704
15. Brown S.: Machine learning, explained. MIT Sloan. (2021). https://mitsloan.mit.edu/ideas-made-to-matter/machine-learning-explained. Accessed Dec 2025
16. Rashidi Shikhteymour, S., Borji, M., Bagheri-Gavkosh, M., et al.: A novel approach for assessing flood risk with machine learning and multi-criteria decision-making methods. Appl. Geogr. **158**, 103035 (2023). https://doi.org/10.1016/j.apgeog.2023.103035
17. Matney J, Esfandiary S, McAvoy S, Barnes E (2020) Leveraging Applied Machine Learning for Flood Risk Assessment Using Open Source Data: A Stacked Ensemble Approach for Predicting Residential Flood Insurance Claims Across the State of Indiana. https://ui.adsabs.harvard.edu/abs/2020AGUFMH159...05M/abstract. Accessed Jan 2026
18. Paintsil J.A.: Predicting Flood Risk Across Geographical Regions Using Machine Learning and Transfer Learning Techniques (2025). http://hdl.handle.net/10362/180556. Accessed Dec 2025
19. Alejo-Sanchez, L.E., Márquez-Grajales, A., Salas-Martínez, F., et al.: Missing data imputation of climate time series: a review. Methods X. **15**, 103455 (2025). https://doi.org/10.1016/j.mex.2025.103455

20. Ferrari, G.T., Ozaki, V.: Missing data imputation of climate datasets: implications to modeling extreme drought events. Revista Brasileira de Meteorologia. **29**, 21–28 (2014). https://doi.org/10.1590/s0102-77862014000100003
21. Dixneuf, P., Errico, F., Glaus, M.: A computational study on imputation methods for missing environmental data. arXiv preprint arXiv, 2108.09500 (2021). https://doi.org/10.48550/arXiv.2108.09500
22. Chapon, A., Ouarda, T.B.M.J., Hamdi, Y.: Imputation of missing values in environmental time series by D-vine copulas. Weather Clim. Extremes. **41**, 100591 (2023). https://doi.org/10.1016/j.wace.2023.100591
23. Srivastava, A., Valkov, L., Russell, C., et al.: VEEGAN: reducing mode collapse in GANs using implicit variational learning. Adv. Neural Inf. Process. Syst. (2017). https://doi.org/10.48550/arXiv.1705.07761
24. Massey Jr., F.J.: The Kolmogorov-Smirnov test for goodness of fit. J. Am. Stat. Assoc. **46**, 68–78 (1951). https://doi.org/10.1080/01621459.1951.10500769
25. Golub, G.H., Van Loan, C.F.: Matrix computations, 4th edn. Johns Hopkins University Press, Baltimore (2013) https://www.press.jhu.edu/books/title/10678/matrix-computations. Accessed Dec 2025
26. UCLouvain/CRED: EM-DAT: The Emergency Events Database, Brussels, Belgium (2026). https://www.emdat.be/. Accessed Oct 2025
27. Paprotny, D.: HANZE Database of Historical Flood Impacts in Europe, pp. 1870–2020 (2023). https://doi.org/10.5281/zenodo.8410025
28. Associação Portuguesa de Seguradores: Eventos extremos da natureza - impacto na atividade seguradora (2024). https://segurdata.apseguradores.pt. Accessed Oct 2025

Human-centered Intelligent Systems

Human Robot Collaborative Creativity: Challenges and Opportunities

Zahra Babaei[1(✉)], Sepideh Kalateh[1], Sanaz Nikghadam-Hojjati[1], Paulo Leitão[2], and Jose Barata[1]

[1] Nova University Lisbon, UNINOVA-CTS and LASI, Lisbon 2829-516, Portugal
z.babaei@campus.fct.unl.pt, {sepideh.kalateh,sanaznik, jab}@uninova.pt
[2] Instituto Politécnico de Bragança, Bragança, Portugal
pleitao@ipb.pt

Abstract. Human-robot collaborative creativity (HRCC) is a new way to mix human gut feelings, emotions, and smart planning with robots' accuracy and computing power. This helps in creative work like art, making things, and teaching. In this systematic thematic synthesis, we followed PRISMA guidelines and synthesized 63 studies from 2010 to 2026. It examines methodological approaches, contrasts collaborative and individual creativity, and explores the cognitive, affective, social, and creative implications of robot integration. The results indicate that HRCC enhances innovation, efficiency, and accessibility while introducing technical, social, and ethical challenges, including issues of trust, role ambiguity, and authorship. The paper underscores the need for human-centered, transparent, and interdisciplinary research, along with standardized metrics for evaluating novelty and usefulness in co-created artifacts, inclusive design to reduce AI-related biases, and robust policy frameworks to ensure safe solutions.

Keywords: Human-Robot Collaboration (HRC) · Collaborative Creativity · Ethical Challenges in HRCC · Social Robotics · Creative Robotics · Human-Robot Interaction · Co-Creation · Innovation Enhancement · AI Bias in HRCC

1 Introduction

In an era where AI companions co-create alongside humans, human-robot collaborative creativity (HRCC) blends human intuition with machine precision to address complex societal challenges such as climate change, digital transformation, and economic inequality [1, 2]. These issues require interdisciplinary collaboration that synthesizes diverse expertise for innovative, scalable solutions [3–5]. HRCC contributes by enabling resilient human-robot teams in eco-friendly manufacturing and inclusive education, fostering social equity and collective intelligence [6].

While individual creativity offers deep focus but limited perspectives [7], collaborative creativity yields richer outcomes through diversity and iteration, though it introduces

Published by Springer Nature Switzerland AG 2027
L. M. Camarinha-Matos and F. Ferrada (Eds.): DoCEIS 2026, IFIP AICT 790, pp. 313–328, 2027.
https://doi.org/10.1007/978-3-032-28939-1_22

coordination challenges [8, 9]. Robots further transform these processes by augmenting cognition and enabling new interactions across arts, manufacturing, and education, yet raise interconnected technical, ethical, and social issues [10–12]. Despite these challenges, the rapid emergence of advanced digital technologies, particularly artificial intelligence and robotics, is fundamentally transforming the nature of collaborative creativity in modern economies [1, 6]. These technologies are redefining collaboration by combining human intuition with machine precision and analytical speed [13], facilitating knowledge exchange on an unprecedented scale and enabling interdisciplinary teams to bridge geographical and institutional divides [9, 12]. This transformation reduces time and cost constraints while allowing teams to explore a broader spectrum of creative possibilities across education, healthcare, and creative industries [2, 15]. As a result, human-robot collaboration not only strengthens collective creativity [16] but also improves the quality, scalability, and real-world impact of creative outcomes [6, 11].

Existing literature examines benefits and domain-specific impacts but lacks comprehensive synthesis of challenges, mitigations, and multidimensional effects. This review fills the gap via PRISMA-guided thematic synthesis of 63 studies (2010–2026), structured around four RQs:

RQ1: What are the differences, advantages, and disadvantages of collaborative versus individual creativity?
RQ2: What are the impacts of integrating robots into collaborative creative tasks?
RQ3: What challenges arise in HRCC for creative outcomes?
RQ4: What mitigation strategies can address these challenges?

These RQs progress logically from foundations to actionable recommendations. The review's contribution lies in its interdisciplinary synthesis and the proposed IH-HRCC framework, advancing human-centered innovation for societal benefit.

This review addresses the research question: How can human-robot collaboration enhance creative outcomes while mitigating associated challenges? Hypothesis: Structured, human-centered frameworks will yield superior co-creative performance compared to unstructured integration.

2 Concept

2.1 Creativity

Creativity is defined as internal attention constrained by a generative goal, comprising three criteria: attention directed internally toward mental representations, attentional operations constrained to fit a to-be-achieved goal state, and the goal state being generative (not already precisely held in memory). In the context of human-robot collaborative creativity (HRCC), this process blends human intuition with robotic precision to generate innovative outcomes, such as in art or design tasks. This aligns with the article's emphasis on blending human emotions and planning with machine accuracy to address challenges like innovation in education and manufacturing [13].

Another perspective views creativity as a process involving imagination, inquisitiveness, persistence, collaboration, and discipline, particularly in educational settings where it fosters novel approaches. In HRCC, this supports the article's discussion on cognitive and affective implications of robot integration [14].

2.2 Collaborative Creativity

Collaborative creativity emerges from interactions among multiple agents, where diverse perspectives lead to emergent outcomes that surpass individual efforts. It involves shared processes, contingency, and equal contributions, often resulting in unpredictable yet valuable products. Relating to the article, this underpins HRCC by highlighting how human-robot teams synthesize diverse inputs for enhanced innovation, efficiency, and accessibility in domains like arts and education, while addressing challenges like coordination and group dynamics [15].

In educational contexts, collaborative creativity is analyzed across individual, social, and material dimensions, with constraining shared frames enabling or limiting group ideation. This resonates with the article's exploration of social and ethical challenges in HRCC, such as trust and role ambiguity [16].

2.3 Human and Robot Collaboration

Human-robot collaboration (HRC) in creativity, or HRCC, involves symbiotic interactions where humans provide intuition and robots offer precision, leading to co-created artifacts. This includes embodied agents facilitating real-time co-creation, addressing the article's RQs on impacts, challenges (e.g., ethics, trust), and mitigations like adaptive AI. Social robots emulate human processes, enhancing domains like arts and education [19].

A scoping review emphasizes HRC's potential for older adults, informing agendas for inclusive co-creativity. This ties to the article's call for interdisciplinary research and bias mitigation [18].

This conceptual foundation frames the review questions by clarifying the central terms used throughout the paper and by establishing the relationship between individual creativity, collaborative creativity, and human-robot co-creation.

These conceptual clarifications directly inform the methodological synthesis and RQs outlined below.

3 Methodology

This study is a systematic thematic synthesis (a form of qualitative evidence synthesis within a systematic review framework).

3.1 Rational for Selecting This Type

Given the interdisciplinary and heterogeneous nature of the literature on HRCC (spanning robotics engineering, HCI, psychology, creative arts, and education), a systematic thematic synthesis was chosen over quantitative meta-analysis or scoping review. It allows rigorous identification and mapping of studies (systematic component) while enabling inductive identification of recurring themes, challenges, mitigations, and patterns across cognitive, affective, social, and creative dimensions (thematic synthesis component). This approach is particularly suited to emerging fields like HRCC, where empirical evidence is diverse in methodology and not amenable to effect-size pooling, yet requires comprehensive synthesis to address the RQs. It aligns with calls for mixed methods or qualitative syntheses in complex human-technology interactions.

3.2 Alignment with Established Standards

The review follows the PRISMA 2020 [19] guidelines for systematic reviews (including the flow diagram and reporting checklist) to ensure transparency, reproducibility, and methodological rigor, adapted for thematic synthesis where full quantitative pooling is inappropriate. PRISMA extensions for qualitative or complex syntheses informed the thematic organization. The review process consisted of four stages: identification of records through database searching, screening of titles and abstracts, full-text eligibility assessment, and inclusion of studies for qualitative synthesis [19]. The PRISMA flow diagram is presented in Fig. 1.

We searched six databases: PubMed, IEEE Xplore, ACM Digital Library, Scopus, Web of Science, and Google Scholar. Search terms combined keywords related to human-robot collaboration, creativity, co-creation, social robots, embodied AI, and creative performance. The search was limited to peer-reviewed studies published between 2010 and 2026.

Each research question was operationalized into targeted keyword clusters. For RQ1 (differences between collaborative and individual creativity), the search included terms such as *"collaborative creativity,"* *"individual creativity,"* and *"comparison."* For RQ2 (impacts of robot integration), keywords comprised *"human–robot interaction,"* *"creative performance,"* and *"cobot."* For RQ3 (challenges), the search incorporated terms including *"trust,"* *"role ambiguity,"* *"authorship,"* and *"bias."* For RQ4 (mitigation strategies), keywords included *"human-in-the-loop,"* *"adaptive autonomy,"* and *"explainable AI."* These clusters were systematically combined using Boolean operators (OR/AND) to refine retrieval.

After removing duplicates, titles and abstracts were screened for relevance to collaborative creativity and human-robot interaction. Full texts were then assessed against the inclusion and exclusion criteria. Studies were included if they addressed creative collaboration involving humans and robots or closely related AI systems, used empirical, theoretical, or mixed-method designs, and reported outcomes relevant to creativity, collaboration, or related social, cognitive, or ethical dimensions. Studies focused only on technical robot design, solo AI generation, or non-creative interaction were excluded.

Data annual extraction followed a structured thematic approach. Findings were organized around the four research questions: differences between collaborative and individual creativity, impacts of robot integration, challenges in human-robot collaboration, and mitigation strategies. The synthesis emphasized recurring themes across domains, methodologies, and outcome types (Fig. 2).

A sensitivity analysis was conducted by rerunning the synthesis excluding five borderline studies (e.g., non-embodied AI without clear robotic analogy); results remained consistent, with no significant impact on key findings. This review did not employ a standardized risk-of-bias tool (e.g., QUADAS-2, ROBINS-I, or AMSTAR-2) because the

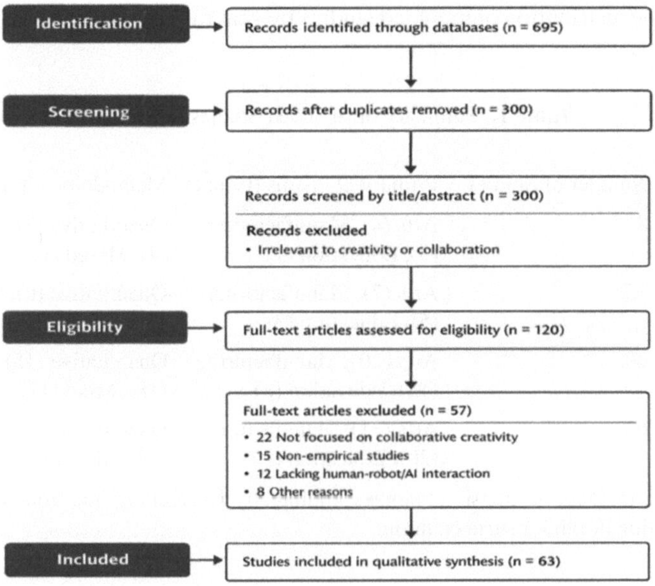

Fig. 1. PRISMA Flow Diagram of Study Selection for Human-Robot Collaborative Creativity (2010–2026)

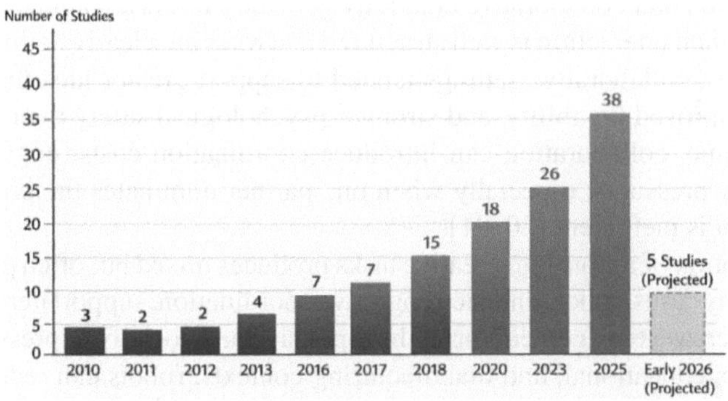

Fig. 2. Annual Publication Trend Identified Through Systematic Literature Review (2010–2026)

63 included studies span heterogeneous methodologies (quantitative, qualitative, mixed-methods) and disciplines (robotics engineering, HCI, psychology, creative arts, education), for which no unified quality appraisal instrument exists [19]. Instead, methodological rigor was addressed through: (a) PRISMA-guided screening with dual independent review ($\kappa = 0.78$); (b) explicit inclusion/exclusion criteria; (c) sensitivity analysis excluding borderline studies; and (d) thematic synthesis that prioritizes recurring patterns across studies rather than effect-size pooling. Limitations arising from this approach are acknowledged in the Discussion. Limitations of literature (e.g., predominance of short-term lab studies, Western undergraduate samples) are noted in the Discussion. Table 1

summarizes the distribution of included studies by year range, domain, and methodology type [19].

Table 1. Summary of Included Studies (N = 63).

Year Range	Number of Studies	Primary Domains (Count)	Methodology Types (Count)
2010 2014	8	Arts (4), Manufacturing (3), Education (1)	Quantitative (3), Qualitative (4), Mixed (1)
2015 2019	15	Arts (7), Manufacturing (5), Education (3)	Quantitative (6), Qualitative (7), Mixed (2)
2020 2026	40	Arts (20), Manufacturing (12), Education (8)	Quantitative (15), Qualitative (18), Mixed (7)
Total	63	Arts (31), Manufacturing (20), Education (12)	Quantitative (24), Qualitative (29), Mixed (10)

This qualitative thematic synthesis organizes findings by researching questions rather than by effect-size pooling or bibliometric counting.

4 Results and Findings

The review shows that collaborative creativity generally offers advantages over individual creativity when interaction is well structured and roles are clearly defined. Across the included studies, collaborative settings tended to support greater idea fluency, broader exploration, improved flexibility, and stronger psychological safety than solitary work. At the same time, collaboration can introduce coordination costs, cognitive fixation, and conformity pressures, especially when one partner dominates the process or when communication is inefficient [20, 21].

The integration of robots into creative tasks produces mixed but often positive effects [22, 23]. In many cases, robots enhance cognitive coordination, support iterative idea generation, and increase engagement through responsive and socially expressive behaviors [24]. In artistic, educational, and manufacturing contexts, robots can reduce workload, broaden participation, and improve access to creative activity [25–27]. However, these benefits are not automatic. When autonomy is poorly calibrated or the interaction design is opaque, robots may increase frustration, disrupt flow, or reduce the human sense of agency [28].

The review also identifies several major challenges [29–31]. Trust deficits, role ambiguity, latency, technical limitations, authorship questions, and bias all affect the quality of collaboration and the perception of creative ownership [32, 33]. These issues are interconnected rather than isolated. Technical weaknesses can intensify social tension, while ethical uncertainty can undermine adoption even when system performance is strong [31].

Finally, the literature suggests that the most effective mitigation strategies are those that preserve human agency while improving adaptability and transparency [27, 28, 34]. Successful approaches include human-in-the-loop design, shared-control architectures, explainable interfaces, adaptive autonomy, participatory development, and explicit attribution practices [23, 35]. Across studies, these strategies were most effective when they were aligned with the task context and the needs of the user group [36].

5 Proposed Conceptual Framework

Based on the synthesis of the reviewed studies, this paper proposes a human -centered operational framework for human-robot collaborative creativity (IH-HRCC). The framework is operationalized as an evidence-based model that translates the synthesized literature into actionable components for research and system design. It is not presented as a standalone theory to be tested in this review but organizes empirical patterns across the 63 studies into three interdependent pillars. Each pillar is structured with: (1) inputs/preconditions (contextual, technological, or human factors required for activation), (2) mechanisms (causal pathways and processes linking inputs to outcomes), (3) outputs/outcomes (measurable effects on creativity, collaboration, or related dimensions), and (4) example indicators (quantifiable or observable metrics drawn from the reviewed studies). This structure ensures analytical consistency and direct alignment with RQ2 (impacts), RQ3 (challenges), and RQ4 (mitigations).

The proposed framework integrates three evidence-based layers.

First, augmented cognition and co-agency describe how human creativity is supported by robotic assistance while preserving human oversight. Second, adaptive interaction architecture captures the technical conditions required for effective collaboration, including responsiveness, transparency, and autonomy calibration. Third, ethical-institutional governance addresses authorship, accountability, provenance, and bias management. Each layer operates through specific mechanisms, including feedback loops, shared control, explainable outputs, and explicit attribution practices. Together, these mechanisms shape HRCC outcomes in creativity, engagement, trust, and responsibility, conditional on well-structured interaction and clear roles (aligning with RQ1 findings on collaborative vs. individual creativity).

5.1 Augmented Cognition and Co-agency

This pillar emphasizes the dynamic distribution of creative control between humans and robots. In effective collaborative systems, the robot functions as an augmentative partner rather than a replacement for human judgment [28]. The goal is to support idea generation and refinement while preserving meaningful human oversight, especially in tasks requiring contextual sensitivity, aesthetic judgment, or ethical reasoning [4, 37].

5.2 Adaptive Interaction Architecture

This pillar concerns the design of interaction mechanisms that support fluid collaboration addressing technical and social challenges identified in RQ3.

Effective systems require transparent decision-making, low-latency feedback, and the ability to adjust autonomy in response to task demands and human workload [34]. Explainable interfaces, multimodal sensing, and human-in-the-loop control are central to this layer of the framework [27].

5.3 Ethical-Institutional Governance

This pillar addresses authorship, accountability, bias, and provenance through normative and emerging empirical mechanisms, mitigating ethical uncertainties highlighted in RQ3 and supporting RQ4 mitigations.

Creative collaboration raises questions about ownership and responsibility that cannot be solved by technical design alone [31]. Clear attribution practices, bias auditing, disclosure of machine contribution, and domain-sensitive governance are needed to support trustworthy collaboration [29, 38]. Taking together, these three pillars show that human-robot collaborative creativity is most effective when technical capability, interaction design, and governance are aligned with human-centered creative goals.

Taken together, these three pillars demonstrate that human-robot collaborative creativity is most effective when technical capability, interaction design, and governance are aligned with human-centered creative goals. The operational structure enables testable hypotheses and design guidelines, directly informing mitigation strategies (RQ4) while building on foundational differences in collaborative creativity (RQ1) and robot integration impacts (RQ2). See Table 2 for representative impacts (Fig. 3).

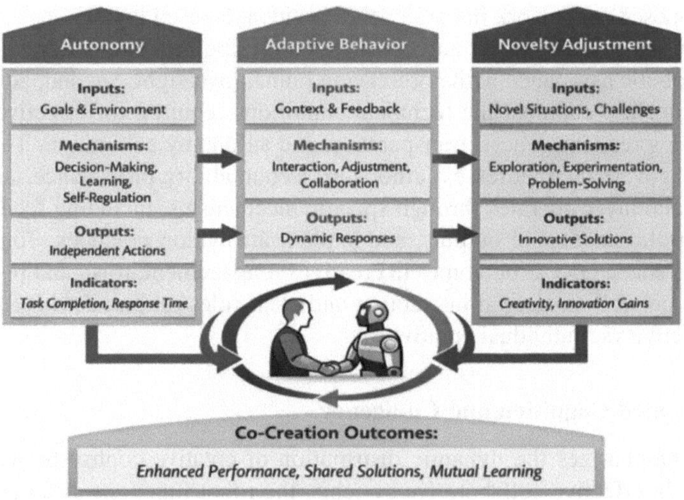

Fig. 3. Proposed Human-Centered Operational Framework for Human-Robot Collaborative Creativity (HRCC). This framework integrates augmented cognition and co-agency, adaptive interaction architecture, and ethical-institutional governance to support effective human-robot co-creation. (AI-assisted based on prompts).

6 Discussion

The reviewed literature does not uniformly support stronger performance in all HRCC settings. Some studies report clear gains in fluency, engagement, and accessibility, while others show weak effects, coordination burden, or reduced agency when autonomy is poorly calibrated or tasks are highly ambiguous. This variation suggests that HRCC benefits are conditional rather than universal, and that the framework should be interpreted as a design-oriented synthesis rather than a predictive model.The findings confirm that human-robot collaborative creativity is not merely a technical extension of individual creativity, but rather a socially and cognitively distributed process shaped by interaction design, task context, and organizational norms [18, 39].

Table 2. Summary of Human-Robot Collaborative Creativity (HRCC) Outcomes by Research Question and Impact Domain

RQ	Impact Domain	Key Findings	Representative Evidence	Conditional Factors / Limitations
RQ1 (Collaborative vs. Individual Creativity)	Quantitative performance	AI-assisted teams outperform individuals: fluency (+50%), flexibility (+38%), originality (+29%), elaboration (+34%)	Rahman et al., 2025 [21]	Benefits contingent on role clarity; 45% fixation on AI suggestions reduces diversity
	Qualitative benefits	Enhanced psychological safety (80% reduction in evaluation apprehension); improved cognitive health for older adults	Rahman et al., 2025 [15]; Bossema & Allouch, 2023 [18]	Embodiment may amplify deference, reducing critical evaluation
	Coordination costs	Increased cognitive burden from interpreting robot behavior; role ambiguity diminishes agency	Uththara et al., 2026 [23]; Segura et al., 2025 [32]	30% perceived AI as dominant when autonomy is opaque
RQ2 (Robot Integration Impacts)	Cognitive & performance	Adaptive robots enhance focus, coordination, and learning; reduce cognitive load in manufacturing	Uththara et al., 2026 [23]; Schlafly et al., 2024 [4]	45.4% synchronization improvement (piano co-player); benefits depend on task structure
	Affective & social	Robot mood contagion boosts team collaboration, satisfaction, and outcomes	de Rooij et al., 2024 [24]	Higher team mood and outcomes; long-term effects unstudied

(*continued*)

Table 2. (*continued*)

RQ	Impact Domain	Key Findings	Representative Evidence	Conditional Factors / Limitations
	Creative output	Embodied co-creation enables novel, rapid iterations; dialogic interaction yields emergent performance art	Nimi et al., 2025 [26]; Gomez Cubero et al., 2021 [37]	Increased user agency; transdisciplinary collaborations produce novel affordances
RQ3 (Challenges)	Trust & reliability	Initial trust erodes quickly after technical failures; ambiguous role distributions increase uncertainty	Duan et al., 2025 [30]; Sanfilippo et al., 2025 [33]	Longitudinal studies remain scarce; inverted-U relationship between autonomy and collaboration quality suspected
	Ethical & governance	Authorship disputes, bias amplification, accountability gaps, provenance tracking absent	Torras, 2024 [31]; Londoño et al., 2024 [29]; Hosanagar & Ahn [38]	Pillar III (ethical governance) lacks empirical validation; relies on normative argumentation
	Technical & operational	Latency, poor autonomy calibration, opaque decision-making disrupt flow and reduce agency	Zhang et al., 2023 [28]; Ciccarelli et al., 2024 [27]	Technical instability disproportionately affects arts/education domains
RQ4 (Mitigation Strategies)	Design-oriented	Human-in-the-loop, shared-control architectures, adaptive autonomy, explainable interfaces	Zhang et al., 2023 [28]; Pichler et al., 2017 [34]; Ciccarelli et al., 2024 [27]	Modular cobot interfaces with real-time autonomy sliders (manufacturing)
	Governance-oriented	Dual-attribution standards, blockchain provenance tracking, bias auditing, participatory development	European Parliament AI Act, 2024 [35]; Hosanagar & Ahn [38]	No tested attribution protocols in real-world HRCC settings

(*continued*)

Table 2. (*continued*)

RQ	Impact Domain	Key Findings	Representative Evidence	Conditional Factors / Limitations
	Research-oriented	Multi-site longitudinal trials (≥12 months); standardized metrics (e.g., ASCC) for cross-cultural comparison	Matheus et al., 2025 [36]; Mavri et al., 2020 [40]	Current evidence dominated by short-term lab studies, Western undergraduate samples

Across the reviewed literature, the strongest outcomes were observed when robots supported rather than replaced human agency, and when creative work was structured to encourage mutual adaptation rather than rigid division of labor [4, 28].

For RQ1, collaborative creativity generally outperformed individual creativity in diversity of ideas, flexibility, and social support, although it also introduced coordination burdens and dependence risks [20, 22]. For RQ2, robot integration improved creativity-related performance when the system was responsive, transparent, and context aware [21, 41]. For RQ3, the main barriers were technical instability, trust issues, role ambiguity, bias, and ethical uncertainty [18, 27, 42]. For RQ4, the most effective solutions combined adaptive autonomy, human oversight, explainability, participatory design, and explicit governance [25, 26, 37] (Fig. 4).

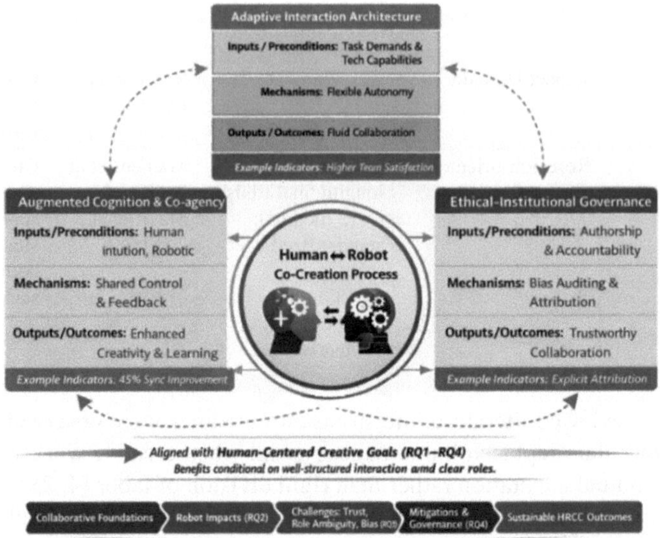

Fig. 4. Multi-layered Mitigation Framework for Human-Robot Collaborative Creativity (HRCC). This operational extension shows how the three pillars, through autonomy calibration, adaptive behavior, and novelty adjustment mechanisms, mitigate RQ3 challenges while preserving human agency. Derivation: thematic clustering of empirical patterns from the 63 studies. (See Table 2 in Discussion for representative impacts linked to each RQ).

6.1 Limitations of the Review

This synthesis has several methodological constraints. First, no formal risk of bias instrument was applied due to the heterogeneity of study designs across robotics, HCI, psychology, and creative domains [39]. Consequently, findings reflect thematic patterns rather than pooled effect sizes, and the strength of individual study contributions was not weighted. Second, the review is limited to English-language peer-reviewed publications, potentially excluding relevant work in other languages or grey literature. Third, the predominance of short-term laboratory studies with Western, undergraduate samples limits generalizability to real-world, long-term, or cross-cultural HRCC contexts. Fourth, the rapid evolution of generative AI and embodied robotics means that some findings may become outdated quickly; the 2026 cutoff was chosen to balance currency with review feasibility. These limitations do not invalidate the synthesis but should guide interpretation and future research design.

6.2 Critical Tensions and Unresolved Contradictions

Across the 63 studies, several persistent tensions emerged that challenge any straightforward affirmative reading of HRCC benefits. First, a contradiction exists regarding robot autonomy: while adaptive autonomy enhances perceived co-creativity and satisfaction [28], several studies report that even modest autonomy can induce passive human engagement and diminished agency when robot behavior becomes opaque [21, 33]. This suggests an inverted-U relationship between autonomy level and creative collaboration quality, a pattern not yet systematically investigated. Second, the evidence on embodiment is contradictory: some studies find that physical robots increase engagement and social presence [24], while others report no significant advantage over virtual agents in creative tasks [36], with embodiment even amplifying deference and reducing critical human evaluation [21]. Third, across domains, trust dynamics show fragility: initial trust in robotic partners is often high but erodes quickly after technical failures or ambiguous role distributions [30], yet longitudinal studies remain scarce [36]. Fourth, the three pillars of the proposed framework (augmented cognition, adaptive architecture, ethical governance) are not equally supported. Pillar I (augmented cognition) has strong empirical grounding from controlled experiments [4, 23]. Pillar II (adaptive architecture) is well-supported in manufacturing and HCI literatures [27, 34]. However, Pillar III (ethical governance) relies more on normative argumentation than empirical evidence; few studies test attribution protocols, bias auditing, or provenance tracking in real-world HRCC settings [29, 38]. This imbalance does not invalidate the framework but highlights where future empirical work is most urgently needed. Finally, robustness across contexts is uneven: manufacturing studies report consistent positive effects on cognitive load reduction [4, 27], while arts and education studies show high variability depending on task structure, user population, and robot design [22, 43]. These tensions and contradictions do not undermine HRCC's promise but demand more nuanced, context-sensitive theories and designs.

The review also shows that the future of human-robot collaborative creativity depends on balancing performance with responsibility. Systems should not only generate novel outputs but also support fair, intelligible, and inclusive creative participation. This is particularly important in domains such as education, art, and manufacturing, where creative collaboration affects both outcomes and human experience [31, 43].

7 Conclusion and Future Direction

Collaborative creativity surpasses individual efforts in diversity and robustness but demands careful management of social dynamics (RQ1); robot integration amplifies efficiency and inclusivity while reshaping roles (RQ2); key challenges involve trust, ethics, and technical hurdles (RQ3); and mitigations through adaptive, human-centric designs enable sustainable partnerships (RQ4). This review's contribution lies in the IH-HRCC framework, which systematically bridges literature gaps by integrating augmented cognition, adaptive architecture, and ethical governance for multi-domain applications. Ultimately, HRCC heralds a future where technology enhances human ingenuity, fostering equitable innovation if guided by empathy and oversight.

8 Recommendation

Recommendation taken from this work include:

Policy Oriented: Establish international standards for dual-attribution in HRCC outputs, such as requiring blockchain-based provenance tracking in creative industries to resolve authorship disputes, modelled after EU AI Act guidelines [35].

Design Oriented: Develop modular cobot interfaces with real-time autonomy sliders for manufacturing tasks, allowing users to adjust control based on workload metrics (e.g., NASA-TLX integration), tested in pilot programs for eco-friendly production lines [44].

Research Oriented: Conduct multi-site longitudinal trials (minimum 12 months) comparing embodied vs. virtual robots in diverse populations (e.g., non-Western elders), using standardized metrics like ASCC [40] to evaluate cultural impacts on trust and bias [36].

Acknowledgements. This research is partially funded and supported by PhD programme of Department of Electrical and Computer Engineering of Nova School of Science and Technology, Nova University Lisbon and FCT – Fundação para a Ciência e a Tecnologia, through the Research Unit CTS – Centre of Technology and Systems/UNINOVA/FCT/NOVA, under the reference UID/00066/2025.

References

1. Jones, E., Adam, C.: New frontiers of trade and trade policy: digitalization and climate change. Oxf. Rev. Econ. Policy. **39**, 1–11 (2023). https://doi.org/10.1093/oxrep/grac048
2. Naik, N., et al.: Legal and ethical consideration in artificial intelligence in healthcare: who takes responsibility? Front. Surg. **9**, 862322 (2022). https://doi.org/10.3389/fsurg.2022.862322
3. Mignenan, V.: Collective intelligence and entrepreneurial resilience in the context of covid-19. Int. Bus. Res. **14**(9), 1 (2021). https://doi.org/10.5539/ibr.v14n9p1
4. Schlafly, M., Prabhakar, A., Popovic, K., Schlafly, G., Kim, C., Murphey, T.D.: Collaborative robots can augment human cognition in regret-sensitive tasks. PNAS Nexus. **3**(2), pgae016 (2024). https://doi.org/10.1093/pnasnexus/pgae016
5. Obrenovic, B., Gu, X., Wang, G., Godinic, D., Jakhongirov, I.: Generative AI and human–robot interaction: implications and future agenda for business, society and ethics. AI Soc. **40**(2), 677–690 (2025). https://doi.org/10.1007/s00146-024-01889-0
6. Asif, S., et al.: Exploring tasks and challenges in human-robot collaborative systems: a review. Robot. Comput. Integr. Manuf. **97**(2025), 103102 (2026). https://doi.org/10.1016/J.RCIM.2025.103102
7. Onarheim, B., Biskjaer, M.M.: An Introduction to 'Creativity Constraints'. In Innovating in Global Markets: Challenges for Sustainable Growth, Citation, Online. Available: www.ispim.org (2013). Accessed 03 Feb 2026
8. Xiao, J., Huang, K.: A comprehensive review on human-robot collaboration remanufacturing towards uncertain and dynamic disassembly. https://doi.org/10.1051/mfreview/2024015
9. Mavri, A., Ioannou, A., Loizides, F.: Cross-organisational communities of practice: enhancing creativity and epistemic cognition in higher education. Internet High. Educ. **49**, 100792 (2021). https://doi.org/10.1016/j.iheduc.2021.100792
10. Sapounidis, T., Rapti, S., Vaiopoulou, J.: Effects of educational robotics on kindergarteners' collaboration, communication, critical thinking, and creativity: a meta-analysis. J. Sci. Educ. Technol. **34**(1), 73–87 (2025). https://doi.org/10.1007/s10956-024-10149-1

11. Arzberger, A., Lupetti, M.L., Giaccardi, E.: Reflexive data curation: opportunities and challenges for embracing uncertainty in human-AI collaboration. ACM Trans. Comput.-Hum. Interact. **31**(6), 74 (2024). https://doi.org/10.1145/3689042
12. Tsai, C.-Y., et al.: Human-robot collaboration: a multilevel and integrated leadership framework. Leadersh. Q. **33**(1), 101594 (2022). https://doi.org/10.1016/j.leaqua.2021.101594
13. Green, A.E., Beaty, R.E., Kenett, Y.N., Kaufman, J.C.: The process definition of creativity. Creat. Res. J. **36**(3), 544–572 (2024). https://doi.org/10.1080/10400419.2023.2254573
14. Moruzzi, C., Margarido, S.: Customizing the balance between user and system agency in human-AI co-creative processes. In: Proceedings of the 15th International Conference on Computational Creativity, ICCC'24, pp. 1–10, Jönköping, Sweden (2024)
15. Torrents, C., Balagué, N., Hristovski, R., Almarcha, M., Scott Kelso, J.A.: Metastable coordination dynamics of collaborative creativity in educational settings. Sustain. (Switzerland). **13**(5), 1–16 (2021). https://doi.org/10.3390/su13052696
16. Wong, C.C., Kumpulainen, K., Kajamaa, A.: Collaborative creativity among education professionals in a co-design workshop: a multidimensional analysis. Think. Skills Creat. **42**, 100971 (2021). https://doi.org/10.1016/j.tsc.2021.100971
17. Gubenko, A., Lubart, T., Houssemand, C.: From Social Robots to Creative Humans and Back (2022). https://doi.org/10.1007/s12369-022-00911-1
18. Bossema, A., Allouch, B.: Human-Robot Co-Creativity: A Scoping Review Informing a Research Agenda for Human-Robot Co-Creativity with Older Adults. https://doi.org/10.48550/arXiv.2309.07033
19. Page, M.J., et al.: The PRISMA 2020 statement: an updated guideline for reporting systematic reviews. BMJ. **372**, n71 (2021). https://doi.org/10.1136/bmj.n71
20. Du, J., Gu, R., Tang, X., Sugumaran, V.: Systematic literature review of human–AI collaboration for intelligent construction. Appl. Sci. 2026. **16**(2), 597 (2026). https://doi.org/10.3390/app16020597
21. Rahman, G., Almutairi, E.A.A., Mudhsh, B.A., Al-Yafaei, Y.: Harnessing generative AI for collaborative creativity: a study of university students' engagement and innovation. Int. J. Innov. Res. Sci. Stud. **8**(3), 3284–3296 (2025). https://doi.org/10.53894/ijirss.v8i3.7227
22. Vear, C.: Creative AI and musicking robots. Front. Robot. AI. **8**(November), 1–10 (2021). https://doi.org/10.3389/frobt.2021.631752
23. Uththara, D., Hettige, B., Goonathilake, T., Dayarathne, P.: Fostering Musical Partnership: A Human-Centric robotic Co-Player for Accessible and Adaptive Piano Learning, pp. 1–6. Institute of Electrical and Electronics Engineers (IEEE) (2026). https://doi.org/10.1109/slaai-icai68534.2025.11318490
24. de Rooij, A., van den Broek, S., Bouw, M., de Wit, J.: Co-creating with a robot facilitator: robot expressions cause mood contagion enhancing collaboration, satisfaction, and performance. Int. J. Soc. Robot. 2024. **16**(11), 2133–2152 (2024). https://doi.org/10.1007/S12369-024-01177-3
25. Sakura, O.: Robot and ukiyo-e: implications to cultural varieties in human–robot relationships. AI Soc. **37**(4), 1563–1573 (2022). https://doi.org/10.1007/s00146-021-01243-8
26. Nimi, H., Lu, M., Chacon, J.C.: Embodied co-creation with real-time generative AI: an Ukiyo-E interactive art installation. Digital. **5**(4), 61 (2025). https://doi.org/10.3390/digital5040061
27. Ciccarelli, M., Forlini, M., Papetti, A., Palmieri, G., Germani, M.: Advancing human–robot collaboration in handcrafted manufacturing: cobot-assisted polishing design boosted by virtual reality and human-in-the-loop. Int. J. Adv. Manuf. Technol. **132**(9–10), 4489–4504 (2024). https://doi.org/10.1007/s00170-024-13639-z
28. Zhang, M., et al.: Towards human-centered AI-co-creation: a three-level framework for effective collaboration between human and AI. In: Computer Supported Cooperative Work and Social Computing, pp. 312–316. ACM, New York, NY, USA (2023). https://doi.org/10.1145/3584931.3607008

29. Londoño, L., Hurtado, J.V., Hertz, N., Kellmeyer, P., Voeneky, S., Valada, A.: Fairness and bias in robot learning. Proc. IEEE. **112**(4), 305–330 (2024). https://doi.org/10.1109/JPROC.2024.3403898
30. Duan, W., et al.: Trusting autonomous teammates in human-AI teams – a literature review. In: Conference on Human Factors in Computing Systems – Proceedings, p. 23. Association for Computing Machinery (2025). https://doi.org/10.1145/3706598.3713527
31. Torras, C.: Ethics of social robotics: individual and societal concerns and opportunities. Annu. Rev. Control Robot. Auton. Syst. **7**(1), 1–18 (2024). https://doi.org/10.1146/annurev-control-062023-082238
32. Segura, P., Lobato-Calleros, O., Soria-Arguello, I., Hernández-Martínez, E.G.: Work roles in human–robot collaborative systems: effects on cognitive ergonomics for the manufacturing industry. Appl. Sci. (Switz.). **15**(2), 744 (2025). https://doi.org/10.3390/app15020744
33. Sanfilippo, F., Hamza Zafar, M., Wiley, T., Zambetta, F.: From caged robots to high-fives in robotics: exploring the paradigm shift from human–robot interaction to human–robot teaming in human–machine interfaces. J. Manuf. Syst. **78**(November 2023), 1–25 (2025). https://doi.org/10.1016/j.jmsy.2024.10.015
34. Pichler, A., et al.: Towards shared autonomy for robotic tasks in manufacturing. In: Procedia Manufacturing, pp. 72–82. Elsevier B.V (2017). https://doi.org/10.1016/j.promfg.2017.07.139
35. European Parliament: European Union Artificial Intelligence Act 2019–2024, no. P9_TA(2024)0138, pp. 2–459. Online. Available: https://www.europarl.europa.eu/doceo/document/TA-9-2024-0138_EN.pdf (2024)
36. Matheus, K., Ramnauth, R., Scassellati, B., Salomons, N.: Long-term interactions with social robots: trends, insights, and recommendations. ACM Trans. Hum. Robot. Interact. **14**(3), 55 (2025). https://doi.org/10.1145/3729539
37. Gomez Cubero, C., Pekarik, M., Rizzo, V., Jochum, E.: The robot is present: creative approaches for artistic expression with robots. Front. Robot. AI. **8**, 662249 (2021). https://doi.org/10.3389/frobt.2021.662249
38. Hosanagar, K., Ahn, D.: Main Manuscript for Designing Human and Generative AI Collaboration
39. Singh, S., et al.: A systematic review of human-AI co-creativity. **x**(x) (2025). https://doi.org/10.48550/ARXIV.2506.21333
40. Mavri, A., Ioannou, A., Loizides, F.: The assessment scale for creative collaboration (ASCC) validation and reliability study. Int. J. Hum. Comput. Interact. **36**(11), 1056–1069 (2020). https://doi.org/10.1080/10447318.2019.1709338
41. Vaccaro, M., Almaatouq, A., Malone, T.: When combinations of humans and AI are useful: a systematic review and meta-analysis. Nat. Hum. Behav. **8**(12), 2293–2303 (2024). https://doi.org/10.1038/s41562-024-02024-1
42. Shafti, A., Haar, S., Mio, R., Guilleminot, P., Faisal, A.A.: Playing the piano with a robotic third thumb: assessing constraints of human augmentation. Sci. Rep. **11**, 21375, 123AD (2021). https://doi.org/10.1038/s41598-021-00376-6
43. Dhanda, M., Rogers, B.A., Hall, S., Dekoninck, E., Dhokia, V.: Reviewing human-robot collaboration in manufacturing: opportunities and challenges in the context of industry 5.0. Robot. Comput.-Integr. Manuf. **93**, 102937 (2025). https://doi.org/10.1016/j.rcim.2024.102937
44. Chiriatti, G., et al.: Human-centered design of a collaborative robotic system for the shoe-polishing process. Machines. **10**(11), 1082 (2022). https://doi.org/10.3390/machines10111082

Agentic Monitoring for Industrial Sensors in Cyber-Physical Systems: A Reproducible Framework with Safety Guardrails

Miguel Afonso Beckers[1(✉)], Pedro João Rodrigues[1], Paulo Leitão[1], Cesar Augusto Tacla[2], and Pedro Luiz de Paula Filho[2]

[1] Research Centre in Digitalization and Intelligent Robotics (CeDRI), Laboratório para a Sustentabilidade e Tecnologia em Regiões de Montanha (SusTEC), Instituto Politécnico de Bragança, Campus de Santa Apolónia, 5300-253 Bragança, Portugal
{miguelbeckers,pjsr,pleitao}@ipb.pt
[2] Federal University of Technology, Paraná, Brazil
{tacla,pedrol}@utfpr.edu.br

Abstract. Industrial Cyber-Physical Systems rely on sensor networks whose measurements degrade under harsh conditions, causing drift and intermittent faults that undermine monitoring reliability and increase the risk of delayed or unsafe interventions. This paper presents a configurable agentic monitoring framework that integrates fast numerical monitoring with Large Language Model-mediated reasoning while preserving safety, auditability, and reproducible evaluation. The framework is organized into four planes within a ports-and-adapters architecture, where specialized components for monitoring, triage, diagnosis/compensation, orchestration, and explanation operate under explicit safety policies, schema-constrained outputs, and risk-tiered Human-in-the-Loop action gating. An auditable event ledger supports deterministic record-replay for post-incident analysis. Evaluation is simulation-first and synthetic-only, using a factorial scenario catalogue with ground-truth manifests and replay-based scoring. Performance is assessed through detection quality, delay, false alarms, and end-to-end latency, with pre-registered non-inferiority margins against numerical baselines.

Keywords: Cyber-Physical Systems; Industrial Sensors; Agentic AI · Drift · Fault Detection and Diagnosis · Human-in-the-Loop · Reproducible Evaluation

1 Introduction

Industrial manufacturing and process plants increasingly operate as Cyber-Physical Systems (CPSs), where sensing closes the loop between physical dynamics and digital control, quality, and optimization. In harsh environments, sensors face heat, vibration, electromagnetic interference, and fouling, leading to nonstationary behavior such as gradual drift and intermittent faults. Drift is a persistent challenge in streaming settings and is often studied under the broader concept-drift umbrella [11].

Published by Springer Nature Switzerland AG 2027
L. M. Camarinha-Matos and F. Ferrada (Eds.): DoCEIS 2026, IFIP AICT 790, pp. 329–340, 2027.
https://doi.org/10.1007/978-3-032-28939-1_23

Traditional Fault Detection and Diagnosis (FDD) and industrial process monitoring have strong foundations in model-based residual analysis and data-driven multivariate monitoring. Classic work surveys model-based FDD and highlights the enduring difficulty of diagnosing faults while remaining robust to operating-condition changes [12]. More recent process-monitoring surveys emphasize that accuracy alone is insufficient: methods must be deployable under latency constraints, integrate with operations, and support trustworthy decision making [24, 29].

In parallel, time-series anomaly detection has expanded with Machine Learning (ML) and deep learning. Surveys of anomaly detection in Internet of Things (IoT) and sensor networks span statistical approaches, conventional learning methods, deep neural models, hybrid pipelines, and highlight challenges posed by non-stationarity and rare events [18]. Industrial deployments further stress operational constraints such as real-time inference and robust handling of regime shifts [27].

More recently, Large Language Models (LLMs) have been explored as time-series anomaly detectors and as components of predictive maintenance systems [2, 22, 34]. While promising, this line of work raises operational questions around stability, inference latency, and governance when LLM-mediated reasoning influences monitoring decisions. These constraints motivate a system-level design problem: integrating numeric monitors and LLM-based reasoning into CPS monitoring while preserving safety, auditability, and reproducible evaluation.

Beyond using LLMs as standalone detectors, recent work has popularized agentic Artificial Intelligence (AI): goal-directed systems in which LLMs iteratively reason, invoke tools, and act on external environments (Reasoning + Acting), often with memory and multi-agent coordination [35, 38]. This shift from prompt–response pipelines to agentic workflows raises new practical concerns—not only about model accuracy, but also about safe action execution, governance, and auditable operations [15, 39].

The objective of this paper is to present a reproducible, safety-governed agentic monitoring framework for industrial sensors in CPSs and an evaluation protocol for controlled comparison of numeric, LLM-mediated, and hybrid configurations under fixed operational constraints. The research hypothesis is that such a framework can achieve detection and compensation performance non-inferior to established numeric baselines, while improving adaptability, interpretability, and operational reliability through coordinated agent behavior under explicit guardrails and Human-in-the-Loop (HITL) approval tiers.

Accordingly, the study is guided by the following research questions:

- *RQ1.* Can a safety-governed agentic monitoring framework achieve detection and compensation performance that is non-inferior to established numerical baselines under controlled industrial sensor degradation scenarios?
- *RQ2.* How do orchestration, explicit safety guardrails, and HITL supervision affect latency, transparency, and operational control in such a framework?

This paper contributes: (i) a configurable four-plane, ports-and-adapters architecture for governed agentic sensor monitoring in CPSs; (ii) a safety and governance layer with policy-gated actions and risk-tiered HITL workflows; (iii) an auditable decision ledger with deterministic record–replay for reproducible analysis and regression testing; (iv) a synthetic-only catalogue and replay-scored evaluation protocol with pre-registered non-inferiority margins.

2 Relationship to Societal Challenges

Industrial CPSs increasingly rely on sensor networks as a critical interface between physical processes and digital decision making [16, 20]. When sensors degrade under harsh conditions (heat, vibration, electromagnetic interference, fouling), drift and intermittent faults propagate to control and quality loops, amplifying societal pressures that motivate technological innovation: energy and resource efficiency, safe operation, and resilient production [11, 12].

From a sustainability perspective, unreliable sensing drives conservative setpoints, repeated rework, and unnecessary stoppages, increasing energy consumption per unit of output and material waste. Earlier detection and bounded compensation of drift can reduce scrap and downtime, supporting more efficient use of resources in energy-intensive sectors [24, 29]. However, these gains depend on operational reliability: methods must remain stable under regime changes and respect real-time constraints in industrial pipelines [1, 31].

From a safety and compliance perspective, incorrect readings can mask hazardous states or trigger spurious interventions. In such settings, innovation cannot be assessed by predictive accuracy alone; it must also address governance and safe operation under uncertainty [4, 9, 32]. Monitoring recommendations should be explainable, constrained by explicit policies, and escalated through HITL approval tiers when actions may affect safety or production [3, 10, 30].

A third axis is resilience and trust in automation. High false-alarm rates and opaque decisions create alarm fatigue and erode operator confidence, limiting real-world adoption even when models perform well in offline benchmarks [3]. The framework therefore treats evidence and accountability as first-class requirements: decisions and their supporting evidence pointers are captured in an auditable ledger, enabling deterministic record–replay for post-incident analysis, regression testing, and transparent comparison across monitoring variants.

In summary, the paper contributes to *technological innovation to tackle societal challenges* by combining (i) governed agentic monitoring that targets sustainable and safe operation, and (ii) a reproducible evidence pathway—synthetic scenarios with Ground Truth (GT), auditable logs, and deterministic replay—to quantify benefits and trade-offs under operational constraints. Agentic orchestration and tool-using workflows provide the architectural substrate to integrate fast numeric monitoring with bounded LLM-mediated reasoning [35, 38].

3 State of the Art and Related Work

The monitoring of industrial sensors in CPSs draws on several complementary lines of work that are often studied separately but need to be considered together in deployment-oriented settings: (i) sensing and drift/anomaly mechanisms in harsh environments; (ii) anomaly detection and drift-aware learning for industrial time series; and (iii) Multi-Agent System (MAS)/agentic AI architectures, including governance and human factors. Taken together, these strands frame monitoring as a system problem from measurement-chain degradation through decision-making under drift to governed interventions.

A first foundation is to view industrial sensing as a measurement chain rather than an isolated device: sensing element and transduction, signal conditioning and excitation, analog-to-digital conversion and timestamping, communication protocols, and integration into plant control and supervisory systems. Degradation may originate at different stages of this chain, and the observed signatures (bias, gain drift, increased noise, dropouts) depend on both the transduction physics and the acquisition topology [17, 19, 36]. This perspective motivates monitoring architectures that incorporate context metadata together with numeric readings to support traceability and robust cross-sensor reasoning.

From the monitoring perspective, the net effect of upstream degradation is non-stationarity in the observed stream, often manifesting as drift. Concept drift taxonomies and detection methods highlight recurring evaluation pitfalls (biased splits, non-comparable setups), and in industrial CPSs closed-loop feedback further complicates detection and interpretation [11]. Consequently, controlled and reproducible benchmarks are repeatedly advocated, varying operating regimes, drift profiles, and anomaly families under consistent protocols.

Building on this sensing-and-drift context, industrial anomaly detection and diagnosis are commonly framed in the FDD literature, spanning model-based residual analysis and data-driven multivariate monitoring with statistical, latent-variable, and ML-based methods [12, 24, 29, 33]. A central challenge is robustness to operating-condition changes: regime shifts can mask or mimic anomaly signatures, and evaluations often abstract away latency and integration constraints. Time-series anomaly detection for sensor networks and IoT similarly spans change detection, supervised/unsupervised pipelines, reconstruction/forecasting models, and hybrids, with industrial pain points tied to non-stationarity and rare events [6, 18, 23]. Deployment experience further shows that data quality, pipeline engineering, and real-time inference constraints can be as important as model choice [31].

However, in industrial settings," detection-only" is often insufficient: operations frequently require diagnosis and bounded compensation (e.g., bias/scale correction, recalibration triggers, safe fallbacks). This raises challenges such as localizing distortion along the signal chain and avoiding overcompensation when deviations reflect legitimate regime change [11, 29]. Drift-aware tracking and compensation methods exist (e.g., model maintenance and online compensation), but comparisons are often inconsistent across drift profiles/severities and reporting of when/why compensation triggers occur is uneven [21, 26, 40]. This motivates evaluation designs that score both detection quality and post-compensation error under controlled drift regimes.

More recently, foundation-model approaches have been explored for time-series tasks, including forecasting and anomaly detection under label scarcity [5, 8]. In parallel, LLM-based approaches have been proposed as zero-shot or tool-augmented reasoning components for time-series analysis [7, 14]. While these may improve contextual reasoning and explanation, they introduce operational concerns around stability, latency, and governance when model outputs influence monitoring decisions [4].

In terms of system architecture, MASs provide established principles for decomposition, coordination, and robustness in distributed settings [13, 37]. Agentic AI extends this direction by combining planning, tool use, and orchestration—often with LLMs—to integrate perception, reasoning, and action in modular architectures [35]. In industrial contexts, distributed/agent-based manufacturing control provides early patterns for coordination and resilience [28]; however, many recent contributions remain conceptual or evaluate only narrow components rather than end-to-end monitoring under operational constraints.

Crucially, deployment in industrial CPS requires governance and assurance beyond model accuracy. HITL supervision, escalation policies, and transparency shape whether operators trust and adopt recommendations [3, 25]. Work on explanation rigor and the limits of narrative rationales supports designs that link recommendations to verifiable evidence [10, 30]. At the system level, runtime assurance patterns exist, but are not consistently integrated with monitoring pipelines that also include diagnosis, compensation, and explanation under explicit invariants [9, 32].

Finally, operational constraints are increasingly treated as first-class concerns: end-to-end latency budgets (p95/p99), deadline-aware partitioning between fast numeric monitors and slower reasoning components, and auditable logs that enable record–replay and post-incident analysis [1, 31]. Together, these strands motivate architectures that treat observability, reproducibility, and governance as core design constraints rather than afterthoughts.

The novelty of the proposed framework does not lie in the isolated use of LLMs or modular monitoring components, both of which have already been explored in related contexts. Rather, it lies in combining numerical monitoring, LLM-mediated reasoning, explicit safety guardrails, risk-tiered HITL supervision, and deterministic record–replay within a single reproducible framework for industrial sensor monitoring and recalibration support. In this sense, the contribution is architectural and methodological: it defines how these elements can be integrated, governed, and evaluated under controlled operational constraints.

4 Proposed Framework

To make the operational logic more concrete, Fig. 1 illustrates a representative end-to-end path through the framework. A sensor reading from an industrial machine is first ingested together with timestamp and contextual metadata, then analyzed by the monitoring component, consolidated by triage, and interpreted by diagnosis / compensation as a suspected fault pattern with a possible corrective action. The resulting recommendation is not issued directly: it is passed to the Orchestrator / Guardrails stage, where policy constraints, risk tier, approval rules, and rollback conditions determine whether the case should proceed to bounded compensation or be escalated as a recalibration request under HITL supervision. Throughout this process, the Event Ledger / Replay layer records readings, evidence, decisions, and actions, so that the full reasoning-and-action path remains auditable and reproducible.

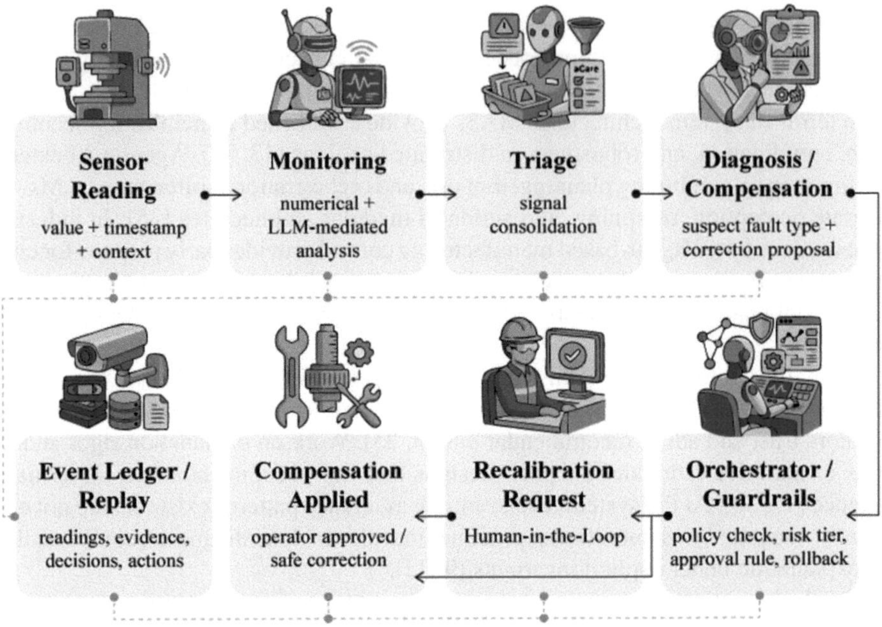

Fig. 1. Illustrative reasoning-and-action flow in the proposed framework, from sensor reading and analysis to governed compensation or HITL-supervised recalibration, with event logging for audit and deterministic replay.

The proposed framework is a layered, ports-and-adapters architecture for industrial sensor monitoring, diagnosis, and compensation support. It runs in three modes—simulation, live ingestion, and deterministic record–replay—with an auditable event ledger for traceability, regression testing, and post-incident analysis. The design aligns with CPS-oriented Industry 4.0 deployments, where monitoring must be interoperable, incrementally adoptable, and governable in safety-adjacent environments [16].

At an architectural level, the framework adopts a four-plane decomposition that generalizes the example shown in Fig. 1. The Data plane hosts ports and adapters for stream ingestion, action publication, and record–replay; the Analysis plane implements monitoring and diagnosis/compensation; the Coordination plane arbitrates execution and enforces policies/guardrails; and the Interaction plane supports operator workflows and evidence-backed explanations. Figure 2 summarizes the runtime flow and governance links across planes.

At the system boundary, ports define stable interfaces for ingestion and action publication, keeping the core monitoring logic independent from data sources and deployment environments. The Ingestion Port normalizes incoming streams into a canonical event format (event-time alignment, ordering, and explicit quality/context metadata) and updates the Context Store / Feature View consumed by downstream agents. Actions are emitted exclusively via a minimal Action Port and are gated by policies and, when applicable, HITL approval. Adapters implement these ports for simulation, plant-facing brokers, and deterministic replay.

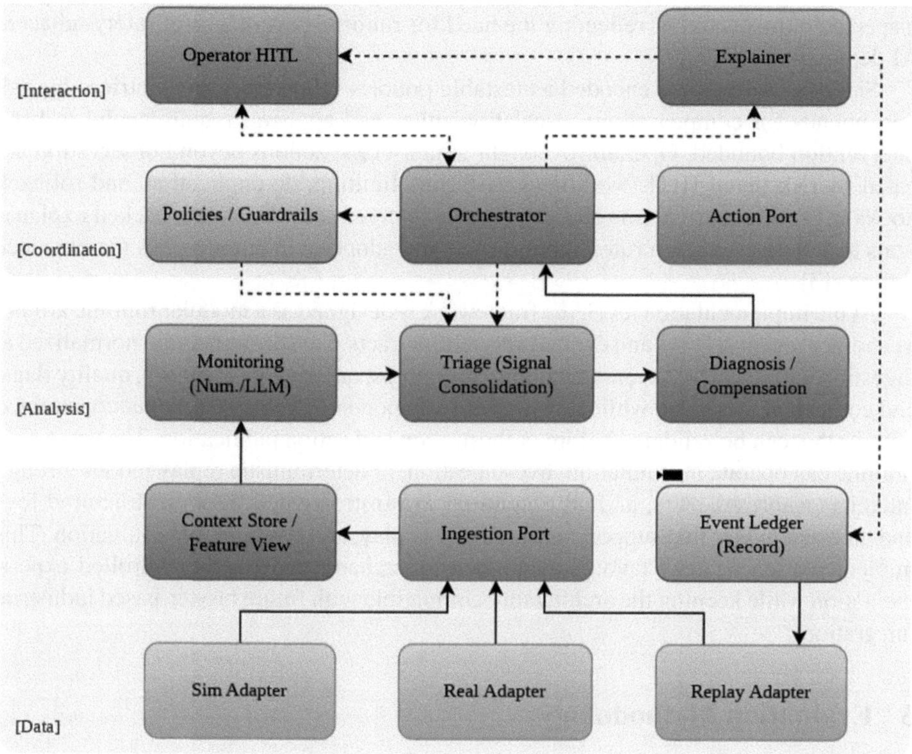

Fig. 2. Runtime view of the proposed agentic monitoring framework organized into four planes. Solid arrows denote the main runtime dataflow (ingestion → context → analysis → action), while dashed arrows denote governance and HITL control flows. The Event Ledger captures events enabling deterministic record–replay via the Replay Adapter.

Within this structure, specialized agents operate under explicit contracts. Monitors (numeric and LLM) emit a shared, schema-fixed output (verdict/score and evidence pointers); triage consolidates and prioritizes cases; diagnosis/compensation estimates fault family and bounded interventions; and an Orchestrator enforces policies, latency/compute budgets, approvals, verification windows, and rollback before publishing actions. In parallel, an Explainer surfaces concise operator-facing rationales grounded in evidence pointers recorded by the observability layer, so explanations remain reproducible under replay.

To make these decisions auditable and repeatable, observability is treated as a first-class concern. The Event Ledger captures an execution trace that enables deterministic record–replay by defining a stable total order (episode/window index plus a monotonic ingest index, with source tie-breakers), while retaining UTC event-time as analysis metadata. The Orchestrator commits outputs through a deterministic schedule so concurrency cannot reorder state updates; non-deterministic sources (random seeds, config hashes, and external LLM outputs) are recorded and re-injected during replay. This record also enables ablation and error analysis: decisions, timings, and fallbacks can be inspected retrospectively, reflecting the need for runtime governance in safety-adjacent AI deployments [4].

Safety guardrails are encoded as testable policies (allowed-action matrices by risk tier, bounds for compensations, escalation rules, and approval requirements) to keep intervention bounded. Operator oversight is first-class: actions beyond observation are gated by risk-tiered HITL workflows, with rate limiting, de-duplication, and rollback hooks to prevent alert storms and irreversible interventions. Evidence-backed explanations and clear escalation rules support trust and adoption in autonomous maintenance settings [3].

At the implementation level, the framework is designed as a modular runtime around a canonical event schema and explicit service contracts. Sensor streams are normalized at ingestion into structured events carrying timestamps, ordering information, quality flags, and contextual metadata, while downstream components exchange schema-constrained outputs that can be validated before orchestration and action publication. The same core runtime can operate in simulation, live-ingestion, or deterministic replay modes through interchangeable adapters, and all executions are instrumented through structured logs and an event ledger that support audit, record–replay, and reproducible evaluation. This implementation strategy favours component interchangeability and controlled experimentation while keeping the architecture compatible with future broker-based industrial integration.

5 Evaluation Methodology

Evaluation is simulation-first and synthetic-only to ensure GT, broad scenario coverage, and deterministic reproducibility. A controlled within-subjects protocol is used: each method (numeric baselines, LLM path, and hybrid arbitration) runs on the same seeded episodes under identical operational conditions, while an external Evaluation Harness consumes only the GT manifest and the recorded event ledger for replay-based scoring. Operational conditions are harmonised across methods via fixed windowing (T, Δt), a tracked end-to-end latency budget (ingest $\rightarrow$ decision, p95), and pinned compute settings; for external LLM endpoints, temperature and max tokens are fixed and outputs must validate against the JSON schema.

Figure 3 summarises the generation, recording, and scoring workflow. Episodes are generated from a factorial catalogue over regimes (R), drift profiles (D), anomaly families (A), and severity levels (S), enabling systematic coverage of non-stationarity and rare-event conditions. Each run exports a GT manifest with $R \times D \times A \times S$, timing, generator version, configuration hash, seed, and interval labels for regime/drift/anomaly and severity. Episodes pass automated realism checks (e.g., signal-to-noise ratio (SNR) targets, temporal/spectral consistency, physical bounds, and plausible latency/jitter envelopes). The simulator emits canonical streams and the observability layer captures canonical inputs and emitted actions into the ledger, enabling deterministic record–replay and replay-based scoring.

Comparisons include (i) numeric baselines representative of industrial FDD/process monitoring and (ii) agentic configurations combining monitors, triage, diagnosis/compensation, and orchestrator policies (optionally with an LLM-mediated monitor).

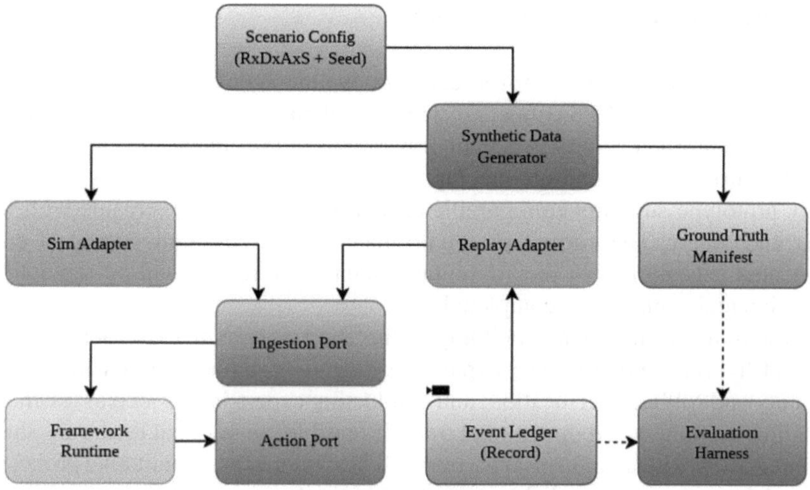

Fig. 3. Synthetic scenario generation and record–replay evaluation workflow. A seeded scenario configuration parameterizes the synthetic data generator, which emits a simulated stream consumed via the Sim Adapter and Ingestion Port. The framework runtime publishes actions through the Action Port. The events are recorded in the Event Ledger; the ledger can be replayed via the Replay Adapter to reproduce episodes deterministically. The Evaluation Harness consumes ledger traces together with the GT manifest for offline scoring.

The numeric pack spans residual/statistical detectors, representation-learning anomaly scores, and drift-aware tracking/compensation of bias/scale; where appropriate, time-series foundation models may be used as forecasters to form residuals. The LLM path performs schema-constrained reasoning over compact multivariate windows and is always governed by budgets, validation, and conservative fallbacks; the hybrid approach arbitrates between numeric and LLM outputs under explicit policies. Ablations remove guardrails, vary textualization richness, swap arbitration strategies, and disable compensation. Unless stated otherwise, evaluation is open-loop; closed-loop runs are reserved for guarded demonstrations with verification windows and rollback.

Primary endpoints capture detection quality and operational performance: Average Precision (AP) and Area Under the ROC Curve (AUC-ROC) (emphasis on AP/PR under imbalance), timeliness (detection delay and missed-within-horizon rate), and operational latency (end-to-end p95 per window). Secondary endpoints include false alarms per hour, abstention rate, compensation quality (post-compensation Mean Absolute Error (MAE)), and explanation quality (expert ratings). Non-inferiority of LLM/hybrid configurations relative to the numeric pack is assessed with pre-registered margins $\mathrm{MAP} = -0.03$ and $\mathrm{MAUCROC} = -0.02$, holding when the lower bound of the 95% confidence interval (CI) for ΔAP/ΔAUCROC exceeds the margin. For latency, a p95 improvement $\geq$10% or parity within $\pm$5% is required while maintaining non-inferior detection. Statistical analysis uses paired bootstrap (10,000 resamples) for CIs and Friedman/Nemenyi ranks for multi-method comparisons across scenario sets; results are reported with effect sizes and uncertainty.

6 Conclusions and Further Work

This paper introduced a safety-governed, reproducible agentic monitoring framework for industrial sensors in CPSs, together with a synthetic-only record–replay evaluation protocol for controlled comparison under operational constraints.

At the current stage, the architecture and evaluation protocol are specified, and an early prototype supports configurable execution on simulated streams with ledger logging and replay. The current prototype materializes the architecture and enables instrumented execution with record–replay; quantitative results will be reported after the experimental campaign is completed.

Next steps focus on evidence-building: completing comparative runs across numeric, LLM, and hybrid configurations; expanding diagnosis/compensation with calibrated uncertainty and rollback verification; and conducting expert-in-the-loop assessments of explanation usefulness and operational trust. If feasible, an optional read-only shadow-mode integration with an industrial partner will be explored as a qualitative probe, while primary claims remain grounded in reproducible synthetic evaluation.

With respect to the research questions, the present paper provides an architectural and methodological answer rather than a final empirical one. It defines how a safety-governed agentic monitoring framework can be organized to support coordinated monitoring, diagnosis, compensation support, and operator supervision under explicit guardrails, and it specifies a reproducible protocol to evaluate its effects on detection quality, latency, transparency, and operational control.

Acknowledgments. This work was supported by FCT - *Fundação para a Ciência e Tecnologia*, I.P. by projects: CeDRI, UID/05757/2025 (https://doi.org/10.54499/UID/05757/2025) and UID/PRR/05757/2025 (https://doi.org/10.54499/UID/PRR/05757/2025); SusTEC, LA/P/0007/2020 (https://doi.org/10.54499/LA/P/0007/2020).

References

1. Akowuah, F., Kong, F.: Real-time adaptive sensor attack detection in autonomous cyber-physical systems. In: Proceedings of the 27th IEEE Real-Time and Embedded Technology and Applications Symposium (RTAS), pp. 237–250 (2021). https://doi.org/10.1109/RTAS52030.2021.00027
2. Alnegheimish, S., Nguyen, L., Berti-Equille, L., Veeramachaneni, K.: Large language models can be zero-shot anomaly detectors for time series? arXiv. (2024). https://doi.org/10.48550/arXiv.2405.14755
3. Amaliah, N.R., Tjahjono, B., Palade, V.: Human-in-the-loop xai for predictive maintenance: a systematic review of interactive systems and their effectiveness in maintenance decision-making. Electronics. **14**(17), 3384 (2025). https://doi.org/10.3390/electronics14173384
4. Amodei, D., Olah, C., Steinhardt, J., Christiano, P., Schulman, J., Mané, D.: Concrete problems in AI safety. arXiv. (2016). https://doi.org/10.48550/arXiv.1606.06565
5. Ansari, A.F., et al.: Chronos: learning the language of time series. arXiv. (2024). https://doi.org/10.48550/arXiv.2403.07815
6. Chandola, V., Banerjee, A., Kumar, V.: Anomaly detection: a survey. ACM Comput. Surv. **41**(3), 1–58 (2009). https://doi.org/10.1145/1541880.1541882

7. Chang, C.L., et al.: LLM4TS: two-stage fine-tuning for time-series forecasting with pretrained language models. arXiv. (2023). https://doi.org/10.48550/arXiv.2308.08469
8. Das, A., et al.: A decoder-only foundation model for time-series forecasting. arXiv. (2023). https://doi.org/10.48550/arXiv.2310.10688
9. Di Franco, C., Bezzo, N.: Interpretable run-time monitoring and replanning for safe autonomous systems operations. IEEE Rob. Autom. Lett. **5**(2), 2427–2434 (2020). https://doi.org/10.1109/LRA.2020.2972828
10. Doshi-Velez, F., Kim, B.: Towards a rigorous science of interpretable machine learning. arXiv. (2017). https://doi.org/10.48550/arXiv.1702.08608
11. Hinder, F., Vaquet, V., Hammer, B.: One or two things we know about concept drift—a survey on monitoring in evolving environments. Part A: detecting concept drift. Front. Artif. Intell. **7**, 1330257 (2024). https://doi.org/10.3389/frai.2024.1330257
12. Isermann, R.: Model-based fault-detection and diagnosis—status and applications. Annu. Rev. Control. **29**(1), 71–85 (2005). https://doi.org/10.1016/j.arcontrol.2004.12.002
13. Jennings, N.R.: An agent-based approach for building complex software systems. Commun. ACM. **44**(4), 35–41 (2001). https://doi.org/10.1145/367211.367250
14. Jin, M., et al.: TimeLLM: time series forecasting by reprogramming large language models. arXiv. (2023). https://doi.org/10.48550/arXiv.2310.01728
15. Khan, S., Joyce, D., Habiba, U.: AGENTSAFE: a unified framework for ethical assurance and governance in agentic AI. arXiv. (2025). https://doi.org/10.48550/arXiv.2512.03180
16. Lee, J., Bagheri, B., Kao, H.A.: A cyber-physical systems architecture for industry 4.0-based manufacturing systems. Manuf. Lett. **3**, 18–23 (2015). https://doi.org/10.1016/j.mfglet.2014.12.001
17. Lipták, B.G.: Instrument engineers' handbook: process measurement and analysis. In: Instrument Engineers' Handbook. Chilton Book Company (1995)
18. de Medeiros, K., et al.: A survey of AI-based anomaly detection in IoT and sensor networks. Sensors. **23**(3), 1352 (2023). https://doi.org/10.3390/s23031352
19. Morrison, R.: Grounding and Shielding: Circuits and Interference, 5th edn. Wiley-IEEE Press, Hoboken, NJ (2007)
20. Negri, E., Fumagalli, L., Macchi, M.: A review of the roles of digital twin in CPS-based production systems. Procedia Manuf. **11**, 939–948 (2017). https://doi.org/10.1016/j.promfg.2017.07.198
21. Nikzad-Langerodi, R. et al.: Calibration model maintenance in melamine resin production: integrating drift detection, smart sample selection and model adaptation. Anal. Chim. Acta. **1013**, 1–12 (2018). https://doi.org/10.1016/j.aca.2018.02.003
22. Palma, G., Cecchi, G., Rizzo, A.: Large language models for predictive maintenance in the leather tanning industry: multimodal anomaly detection in compressors. Electronics. **14**(10), 2061 (2025). https://doi.org/10.3390/electronics14102061
23. Pang, G., Shen, C., Cao, L., Hengel, A.V.D.: Deep learning for anomaly detection: a review. ACM Comput. Surv. **54**(2), 1–38 (2021). https://doi.org/10.1145/3439950
24. Park, Y.J., Fan, S.K.S., Hsu, C.Y.: A review on fault detection and process diagnostics in industrial processes. PRO. **8**(9), 1123 (2020). https://doi.org/10.3390/pr8091123
25. Pashami, S., et al.: Explainable predictive maintenance. arXiv. (2023). https://doi.org/10.48550/arXiv.2306.05120
26. Paul, S., Sharma, R., Tathireddy, P., Gutierrez-Osuna, R.: On-line drift compensation for continuous monitoring with arrays of cross-sensitive chemical sensors. Sensors Actuators B Chem. **368**, 132080 (2022). https://doi.org/10.1016/j.snb.2022.132080
27. Pota, M., De Pietro, G., Esposito, M.: Real-time anomaly detection for industrial furnaces: a comparison of autoencoder architectures. Eng. Appl. Artif. Intell. **124**, 106597 (2023). https://doi.org/10.1016/j.engappai.2023.106597

28. Pulikottil, T., Estrada-Jimenez, L.A., Rehman, H.U., Barata, J., Nikghadam-Hojjati, S., Zarzycki, L.: Multi-agent based manufacturing: current trends and challenges. In: 2021 26th IEEE International Conference on Emerging Technologies and Factory Automation (ETFA), pp. 1–7 (2021). https://doi.org/10.1109/ETFA45728.2021.9613555
29. Qin, S.J.: Survey on data-driven industrial process monitoring and diagnosis: a review. Annu. Rev. Control. **36**(2), 220–234 (2012). https://doi.org/10.1016/j.arcontrol.2012.09.004
30. Rudin, C.: Stop explaining black box machine learning models for high stakes decisions and use interpretable models instead. Nat. Mach. Intell. **1**, 206–215 (2019). https://doi.org/10.1038/s42256-019-0048-x
31. Sgueglia, A., Di Sorbo, A., Visaggio, C.A., Canfora, G.: A systematic literature review of IoT time series anomaly detection solutions. Futur. Gener. Comput. Syst. **134**, 170–186 (2022). https://doi.org/10.1016/j.future.2022.04.005
32. Sinha, R., Schmerling, E., Pavone, M.: Closing the loop on runtime monitors with fallback-safe MPC. In: Proceedings of the 62nd IEEE Conference on Decision and Control (CDC), pp. 6533–6540. Singapore (2023). https://doi.org/10.1109/CDC49753.2023.10383965
33. Venkatasubramanian, V., Rengaswamy, R., Kavuri, S.N., Yin, K.: A review of process fault detection and diagnosis: part I: quantitative model-based methods. Comput. Chem. Eng. **27**(3), 293–311 (2003). https://doi.org/10.1016/S0098-1354(02)00160-6
34. Vyas, J., Mercangöz, M.: Autonomous industrial control using an agentic framework with large language models. IFAC-Papers OnLine. **59**(6), 349–354 (2025). https://doi.org/10.1016/j.ifacol.2025.07.170
35. Wang, L., Ma, X., Feng, T., Jiang, Z., Yin, J., Zhang, R., et al.: A survey on large language model based autonomous agents. arXiv. (2023). https://doi.org/10.48550/arXiv.2308.11432
36. Webster, J.G., Eren, H.: Measurement, Instrumentation, and Sensors Handbook: Spatial, Mechanical, Thermal, and Radiation Measurement, 2nd edn. CRC Press (2014)
37. Wooldridge, M.: An Introduction to MultiAgent Systems, 2nd edn. John Wiley & Sons (2009)
38. Yao, S., et al.: ReAct: synergizing reasoning and acting in language models. arXiv. (2022). https://doi.org/10.48550/arXiv.2210.03629
39. Zhan, Y., et al.: SENTINEL: a multi-level formal framework for safety evaluation of LLM-based embodied agents. arXiv. (2025). https://doi.org/10.48550/arXiv.2510.12985
40. Zhao, X., Wang, J., Chen, Z.: Sensor drift compensation based on the improved LSTM neural network. Sensors. **19**(18), 3844 (2019). https://doi.org/10.3390/s19183844

Towards Secure Media Deepfake Detection Using Explainable AI

S. Rajathi(✉), J. Hemalatha, S. Rajeswari, S. Parameswaran, D. Ramya, and S. Balamurugan

Department of CSE, AAA College of Engineering and Technology, Amathur, Tamil Nadu, India
rajathibala@gmail.com

Abstract. The rapid proliferation of deepfake technology has made it harder to trust and protect digital media. Even though traditional detection models are very accurate, they typically work as "black-box" systems, which means that they don't make it clear how decisions are made. Because they are hard to understand, they are not used as much in important fields like journalism, law enforcement, and computer forensics. This research introduces a deepfake detection framework that integrates deep learning with Explainable Artificial Intelligence (XAI) techniques to enhance transparency and trust. The proposed system combines a convolutional neural network (CNN) classifier with Grad-CAM and LIME to provide both visual and feature-level explanations. Experimental results on benchmark datasets demonstrate that the proposed approach maintains competitive detection performance while significantly improving interpretability and user trust.

Keywords: Grad-CAM · Explainable Artificial Intelligence · Adversarial Networks

1 Introduction

The fast growth of generative models based on deep learning has changed the world of digital media in a big way. Deepfake technology, which lets you make fake images, audio, and videos that look and sound very authentic, is getting easier to use and better. These kinds of breakthroughs can lead to new ideas and business opportunities in entertainment, virtual production, and communication. However, they also pose severe risks to the trustworthiness of information and digital trust. Media that has been altered can propagate false information, hurt people's reputations, and make journalistic and forensic evidence less trustworthy. As deepfake information seems increasingly real and is harder to tell apart from real media, the necessity for dependable ways to find it has become an essential research issue.

In response, many deep learning-based detection systems have been made that use convolutional neural networks, attention mechanisms, and transformer architectures to find small differences in face expressions, texture patterns, and temporal dynamics. These models often get excellent accuracy on benchmark datasets; however, they usually

Published by Springer Nature Switzerland AG 2027
L. M. Camarinha-Matos and F. Ferrada (Eds.): DoCEIS 2026, IFIP AICT 790, pp. 341–357, 2027.
https://doi.org/10.1007/978-3-032-28939-1_24

work as black boxes, giving only a final forecast without explaining how they got there. Because they can't be understood, they can't be used in real life, especially in areas where openness and accountability are important, like law enforcement, digital forensics, and media verification. People who have a stake in these areas need not only correct classifications but also clear explanations that back up the system's judgments.

To solve this problem, Explainable Artificial Intelligence (XAI) has come out as a viable way to make deep learning models more open and honest. XAI methods like Grad-CAM and LIME make it possible for people to understand how models work by pointing out the most important areas and attributes that affect predictions. This paper proposes a deepfake detection approach that prioritizes explainability in its design rather than considering it as an ancillary feature. The suggested approach intends to increase interpretability, build user trust, and enable reliable decision-making without hurting detection performance by directly incorporating XAI algorithms into the detection process. This technique based on explainability helps build digital media authentication systems that are safe and reliable.

1.1 Contributions

The main contributions of this paper are as follows:

- A novel explainability-driven deepfake detection framework integrating CNN, Grad-CAM, and LIME.
- A dual-level explanation mechanism combining spatial and feature-level interpretability.
- A consistency metric to evaluate agreement between Grad-CAM and LIME explanations.
- Experimental validation on benchmark datasets including FaceForensics++ and Celeb-DF.
- Analysis of explainability impact on trust and decision reliability.

2 Related Work

2.1 Deepfake Generation Techniques

The quick progress of deepfake generating methods has made it much harder to trust media authentication. The first deepfake synthesis methods used Generative Adversarial Networks (GANs), which use a generator-discriminator structure to make fake images and videos that look very real. Over time, better adversarial training, facial reenactment pipelines, and identity-swapping architectures have made it possible to make manipulations that look very much like real human expressions and micro-textures [17].

Recent methods use diffusion-based generative models to turn noise into photorealistic outputs again and over again. These models create smoother facial blending and less visual artifacts than older GAN-based systems, which makes it harder for forensic experts to find them [1]. Transformer-based generative architectures have improved the quality of synthesis even more by modeling long-range spatial and temporal dependencies in video sequences. These types of models cut down on time inconsistencies, which were a crucial clue that detection systems used before [2].

The growing realism of these generation frameworks has made the difference between actual and fake media less clear. Recent surveys have shown that deepfake generators now use identity-preserving restrictions, posture consistency, and lighting harmonization techniques to make artifacts less likely to be found [13]. As a result, detection approaches need to move away from strategies that rely on artifacts and toward more flexible and understandable frameworks that can handle new types of manipulation. Recent studies also highlight the need for integrated AI/ML-based prevention and detection strategies to combat evolving deepfake threats [22].

2.2 Conventional Deepfake Detection Approaches

The early focus of deepfake detection research was on supervised learning models designed to detect visual discrepancies. Convolutional Neural Networks (CNNs), such as ResNet and EfficientNet, were the most popular backbone architectures because they are good at extracting features [17]. These models showed that they could accurately classify data from benchmark datasets like FaceForensics++ and DFDC.

Subsequently methods used attention mechanisms to find spatial relationships and draw attention to modified face areas. Xu et al. presented supervised contrastive learning strategies to enhance generalization and class separability [19]. Prototype-based learning frameworks made it even easier to understand by linking predictions to groups of representative features [18].

Recently, transformer-based detection models have gotten a lot of interest since they can simulate global contextual information. These architectures exhibit enhanced resilience to compression artifacts and inter-dataset variability [2]. Multimodal detection systems also use both visual and aural signals to improve performance across different types of manipulation [12]. In addition, voice-based deepfake detection using explainable deep learning models has gained attention for identifying synthetic audio manipulations [20].

Even though they are very accurate, these traditional models mostly work as black boxes. Because their forecasts are generally hard to understand, they aren't used as often in forensic and journalistic settings. Qian et al. [11] stress that models based only on performance don't give verifiable reasoning, which makes people worry about accountability and the validity of evidence.

2.3 Explainable Artificial Intelligence in Computer Vision

Explainable Artificial Intelligence (XAI) has become an essential element in improving the transparency of deep learning models. Gradient-weighted Class Activation Mapping (Grad-CAM), Local Interpretable Model-agnostic Explanations (LIME), and SHapley Additive exPlanations (SHAP) are some of the most common ways to show how important features are and how decisions are made in computer vision.

Grad-CAM creates heatmaps that show areas that affect classification judgments. This makes it great for jobs like detecting deepfakes visually [4]. LIME, on the other hand, uses interpretable surrogate models to mimic complex models locally, giving explanations at the instance level [10]. SHAP offers theoretically based feature attribution by measuring how much each feature adds to a prediction [3]. Recent studies demonstrate that integrating deep learning with XAI significantly enhances robustness in detecting manipulated images under unconstrained conditions [15].

XAI algorithms have been effectively used in medical imaging to find abnormal areas in diagnostic scans, which has made doctors more confident in their work. Similar methodologies have been modified for cybersecurity anomaly detection and malware analysis, wherein interpretability is crucial for threat validation [23]. Explainable AI has also been extended to forensic speech authentication and multimodal analysis, improving interpretability in cross-domain scenarios [14]. In multimedia forensics, explainable frameworks have been employed to identify altered face regions and offer narrative rationales for classification results [6].

Recent developments have progressed from visualization to multimodal explanation systems. Retrieval-augmented frameworks integrate textual reasoning with visual evidence to generate coherent interpretative outputs [5]. Reinforcement-aligned vision-language models improve the coherence of explanations and the ability to reason in context [7]. These changes show a move from making simple heatmaps to designing systems that are focused on explanations. Frameworks such as X2-DFD further emphasize extensibility and modular explainability in deepfake detection pipelines [16].

2.4 Research Gaps

Explainability has become more important in research on deepfake detection, however most current systems simply use XAI approaches as visualization tools after the fact. Numerous research utilize Grad-CAM or SHAP after to training a high-performing black-box classifier, rather than incorporating interpretability into the model design itself [9]. This method limits how deep the explanations can go and typically leads to shallow heatmaps without any clear justification.

Also, existing detection systems mostly focus on performance metrics like accuracy and AUC, with little focus on explanation integrity or how easy it is for users to understand [1]. Even multimodal explainable systems tend to focus on making visualization better instead of creating designs that are clearly based on transparency [12].

A significant deficiency exists in user-centric evaluation. Numerous studies indicate enhanced visualization outputs; nevertheless, limited research evaluates the impact of explanations on user trust and decision-making confidence [8]. Furthermore, fairness and interpretability across demographic variations remain insufficiently explored in current systems [21]. Moreover, cross-domain explainability encompassing image, audio, and video remains insufficiently investigated, notwithstanding the growing multimodal characteristics of deepfakes [25].

Accordingly, there is a strong need for deepfake detection systems that make explainability a core design principle instead of an extra feature. These kinds of systems should have clear feature attribution, an evaluation of consistency in explanations, and user-friendly interpretative interfaces. Filling this gap will greatly improve confidence, accountability, and use in important fields including digital forensics, journalism, and cybersecurity. Explainable detection frameworks developed on unconstrained datasets further underline the importance of real-world applicability and robustness [24].

3 Proposed Methodology

The proposed architecture aims to position interpretability as a central component of the detection pipeline, rather than as a supplementary visualization phase. The methodology combines structured explainability mechanisms with deep learning-based feature extraction to make sure that every prediction comes with reasoning that makes sense to people. The general structure has five basic parts: (1) getting and cleaning the data, (2) learning and classifying features, (3) adding explainability, (4) checking the explanations, and (5) checking the performance and trust.

3.1 System Overview

The suggested system uses a combination of detection and explanation. The algorithm initially finds and normalizes the face in an input image or video frame. Then, a deep neural network classifier looks at the processed facial region and tries to guess if the material is real or fake. The categorization stage is closely linked to explainability modules that create understandable evidence for each decision, which is different from traditional pipelines.

Let the input face image be represented as:

$$F \in R^{dXdXc} \tag{1}$$

Where d denotes spatial dimensions and ***c*** represents the number of channels.

There are two main ideas that guide the framework:

1. Transparency by Design: As part of the model inference process, explanations are made.
2. Evidence-Based Prediction: Each classification output is backed up by visual or feature-level attribution maps that show areas that have been changed.

3.2 Date Acquired

The framework is trained and tested on benchmark deepfake datasets that include both genuine and fake media samples to make sure it is strong and can be used in other situations. The preprocessing stage consists of:

- Detecting faces and aligning them to standardize scale and orientation.
- Extracting frames (for video inputs) at regular intervals.
- Changing the size and shape of images to fit the network's input size.
- Techniques for adding data, including flipping it horizontally and changing the brightness, to make the model more resilient.

When processing video sequences to capture motion-based manipulation artifacts, temporal consistency is kept. This makes sure that irregularities in both space and time may be learned well.

3.3 Deep Learning-Based Detection Module

A convolutional neural network (CNN) architecture was chosen for the detection backbone because it is good at extracting spatial features. Supervised learning is used to teach the network to tell the difference between real and fraudulent data.

The CNN detection model is expressed as a function

$$f_{\theta}(F) = \hat{y} \quad (2)$$

where θ represents learned parameters and

$$\hat{y} = \sigma(W.\phi(F) + b) \quad (3)$$

where $\phi(F)$ = feature representation extracted by convolutional layers:

- W, b = fully connected weights and bias
- σ = sigmoid activation

We use binary cross-entropy as the loss function and the Adam optimizer to make it better. The model learns to pick up on little cues during training, like texture defects, boundary inconsistencies, unusual blending artifacts, and strange face dynamics.

People utilize binary cross-entropy loss for:

$$L = -\left[y log(\hat{y}) + (1-y)\log(1-\hat{y})\right]\hat{y} = \sigma(W.\phi(F) + b) \quad (4)$$

Early stopping and cross-validation procedures are used to keep the model from overfitting and make sure it is reliable. For evaluation, we calculate performance indicators including accuracy, precision, recall, F1-score, and Area Under the Curve (AUC).

3.4 Combining Explainable AI (XAI) Methods

A key aspect of this approach is the organized use of Explainable Artificial Intelligence methods in the detection process. Two XAI approaches that work well together are used:

3.4.1 Visual Explanation Based on Grad-CAM

Gradient-weighted Class Activation Mapping (Grad-CAM) makes heatmaps that show the areas that have the biggest effect on the model's prediction. Grad-CAM makes spatial significance maps that show altered areas by calculating the gradients of the anticipated class in relation to feature maps. For example:

- Mouth movements that aren't normal
- Changes in the area around the eyes
- Blending errors along the edges of the face
- Different textures

Let A^k denote the activation map of the final convolution layer.

Gradient weights:

$$\propto_k = \frac{1}{Z}\sum_i \sum_j \frac{\partial \hat{y}}{\partial A_{ij}^k} \quad (5)$$

Grad-CAM heatmap:

$$E_v = ReLU\left(\sum_k \propto_k A^k\right) \tag{6}$$

These visual explanations let analysts check to see if the model is focusing on facial areas that have meaning rather than background information that isn't important (Fig. 1).

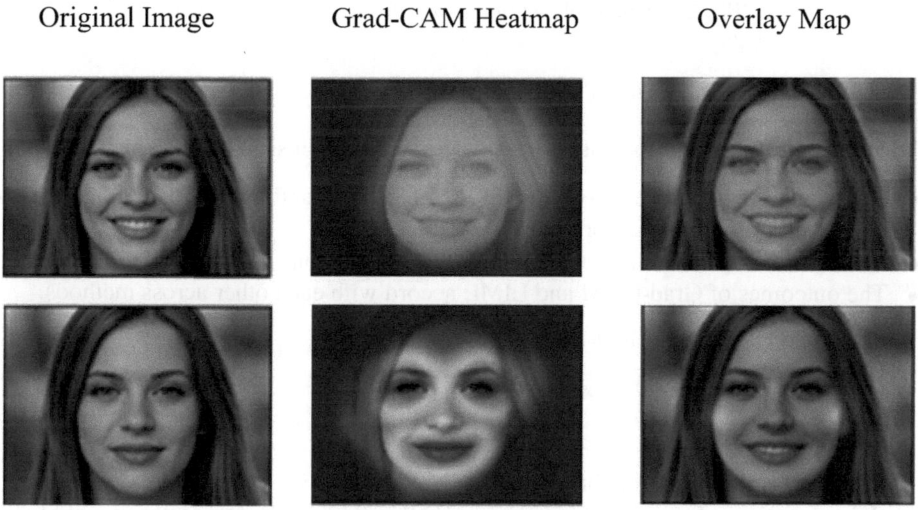

Fig. 1. Grad-CAM visualization for deepfake detection

3.4.2 Lime-Based Local Explanation

Local Interpretable Model-Agnostic Explanations (LIME) is utilized to facilitate instance-level interpretability. LIME changes input segments and looks at how this affects predictions to find factors that affect the classification choice. LIME explains decisions locally and independently of the model design, while Grad-CAM gives a global view of space.

Given perturbed samples z′ of input F, a local interpretable model g is trained to approximate f:

$$\mathrm{L}(\mathrm{f}, \mathrm{g}, \pi_x) + \Omega(\mathrm{g}) \tag{7}$$

Where:

- πx = proximity measure
- Ω(g) = model complexity penalty

The system makes sure that both Grad-CAM and LIME work together:

- Spatial interpretability (where the model is looking), and
- Feature-level interpretability (which features affect the choice) (Fig. 2).

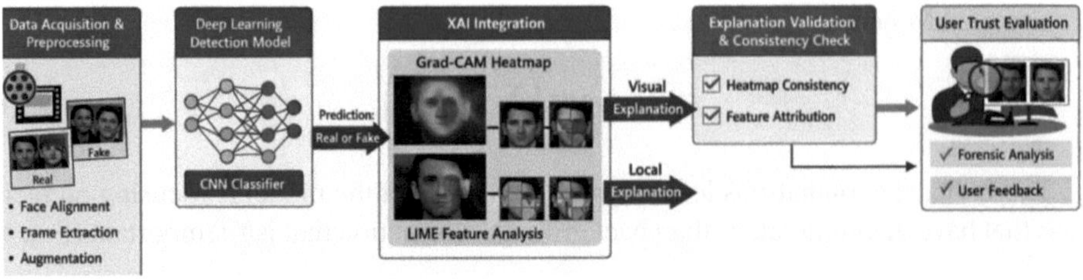

Fig. 2. Explainable AI Framework for Deepfake Detection

3.5 Explanation Consistency and Validation

To ensure credibility, we use the following to check for consistency in explanations:

- Analyzing the overlap between Grad-CAM heatmaps and known manipulated areas (if ground truth masks are provided).
- Testing stability with different changes to the same input.
- The outcomes of Grad-CAM and LIME accord with each other across methods.

Consistency between Grad-CAM and LIME:

$$C = \frac{|E_v \cap E_l|}{|E_v \cup E_l|} \tag{8}$$

If C < γ, explanation reliability is considered low.

If explanations always point out important altered areas, the forecast is thought to be accurate. This two-step validation process lowers the chance of getting false or unclear explanations.

```
Algorithm 1: Explainable Deepfake Detection Framework (XAI-DDF)
Input : Media sample M (image or video)
Output : Prediction label Y ∈ {Real, Fake},
    Visual explanation Ev,
    Local explanation El

if M is video then
  Extract frames Fi at interval Δt
else
  Fi ← M
end if

for each frame Fi do
  Detect and align face region F
  Resize F to fixed dimension d × d
  Normalize pixel values
end for

Feed processed frame F into CNN model
Compute prediction probability P(Fake | F)

if P ≥ τ then
   Y ← Fake
else
   Y ← Real
end if

// Grad-CAM Explanation
Compute gradients of predicted class
Obtain importance weights αk
Generate heatmap Ev

// LIME Explanation
Segment F into superpixels
Generate perturbed samples
Fit local surrogate model
Compute feature importance map El

Compute explanation consistency score C
if C < γ then
   Flag for human review
end if

return (Y, Ev, El)
```

4 Experimental Setup

To assess the efficacy of the proposed explainability-centered deepfake detection methodology, tests were performed utilizing benchmark datasets comprising both genuine and altered face media. The implementation was done in an environment that supported GPUs and used PyTorch/TensorFlow as the backend.

We trained the CNN backbone with binary cross-entropy loss and improved it with the Adam optimizer. To stop overfitting, early halting was used. The learning rate started at 0.0001 and was changed dependent on how well the model did on validation. We used experiments to find the best batch size and epoch values to make sure that convergence was stable.

To make things easier to understand, Grad-CAM was used on the last convolutional layer, and LIME was set up with a set number of perturbation samples to make sure that local explanations were always the same. We used overlapping measures between Grad-CAM heatmaps and LIME feature attributions to measure how consistent the explanations were.

5 Dataset Description

Researchers in multimedia forensics used publicly accessible deepfake benchmark datasets to test the system.

The datasets have:

- Videos of real faces
- Videos that have been changed with GAN
- Samples with switched faces
- Samples of expression reenactment
- Variants that have been compressed and post-processed

The model was trained and evaluated on publicly available deepfake datasets:

- FaceForensics++
- Celeb-DF

The experiments were conducted on two widely used benchmark datasets:

- FaceForensics++: Contains manipulated videos generated using multiple deepfake techniques under varying compression levels.
- Celeb-DF: A high-quality dataset designed to reduce visual artifacts and improve realism.

Both datasets include real and fake videos with diverse identities, lighting conditions, and manipulation methods. The dataset was split into training (70%), validation (15%), and testing (15%).

The datasets include both actual and fake facial videos made with different synthesis methods. The dataset was separated into three parts: training (70%), validation (15%), and testing (15%). To make it easier to generalize, we used data augmentation techniques like flipping, changing the brightness, and rotating it a little bit (Table 1).

The model did a great job at classifying things and was able to generalize well. An AUC score of 0.972 shows that the genuine and fake classes are very different from each other.

Table 1. Performance on FaceForensics++

Metric	Value (%)
Accuracy	94.82
Precision	93.91
Recall	95.37
F1-Score	94.63
AUC	0.972

6 Evaluation Metrics

Performance was assessed using standard classification metrics:

Accuracy:

$$\text{Accuracy} = \frac{TP + TN}{TP + TN + FP + FN} \tag{9}$$

Precision:

$$\text{Precision} = \frac{TP}{TP + FP} \tag{10}$$

Recall:

$$\text{Recall} = \frac{2 \times \text{Precision} \times \text{Recal}}{\text{Precision} + \text{RecaL}} \tag{11}$$

Area Under Curve (AUC) was also computed to evaluate classification robustness (Table 2).

Table 2. Performance on Celeb-DF

Metric	Value (%)
Accuracy	92.47
Precision	91.28
Recall	93.12
F1-Score	92.19
AUC	0.951

For explainability evaluation, the following additional metrics were considered:

- Heatmap Localization Consistency
- Overlap Score between Grad-CAM and LIME
- Stability under Input Perturbation

7 Results and Analysis

The suggested framework did a great job of classifying data while also giving clear explanations. Experimental findings demonstrate that the detection accuracy remains competitive with traditional deep learning models.

Some important things to note are:

- Grad-CAM heatmaps always showed problems with facial boundaries, distortions in the eye region, and blending artifacts.
- LIME explanations found semantically relevant super pixels instead of just background noise.
- In most test instances, the explanation consistency scores stayed above the set reliability level.

Adding explainability did not dramatically lower the accuracy of the categorization, which is important. The slight computational overhead introduced by LIME was acceptable for forensic and verification applications. Cross-dataset testing showed that models based only on artifacts did not generalize as well as those based on explanations, which suggests that learning from explanations makes models more robust.

7.1 Time Complexity Analysis

The convolutional neural network inference and the perturbation sampling process in LIME are the main things that make the proposed framework hard to compute. Let nnn be the number of pixels in the input image and k be the number of convolution filters. For each layer of the CNN, the forward pass takes about O(nk) operations. If the network has LLL convolutional layers, the entire inference complexity is O(Lnk).

Backpropagation via the last convolution layer is part of the Grad-CAM computation.

This makes the process more complicated, but the feature map size is much smaller than the original input resolution. So, it doesn't use up too many resources. LIME, on the other hand, has to make mmm perturbed samples and test the model for each one. So, its complexity is about O(m·Lnk). This makes inference take longer, but it makes it easier to understand in specific areas (Table 3).

Overall, the total complexity is:

$$O(Lnk + mLnk) \tag{12}$$

The proposed architecture is different from standard detection systems in that it immediately adds explanation creation and validation to the inference pipeline, which only improves classification accuracy. This makes sure that predictions are not only correct, but also fair and clear. Adding explanation consistency checking makes the framework even more reliable, which makes it perfect for use in journalism, digital forensics, and law enforcement.

7.2 Comparison With Conventional Black-Box Models

To assess the advantage of explainability, the suggested model was juxtaposed with a conventional CNN classifier devoid of XAI validation (Table 4).

Table 3. Table Comparison with Conventional Black-Box Detection

Aspect	Conventional CNN Detection	Proposed XAI-Based Framework
Transparency	No explanation provided	Dual explanation (Grad-CAM + LIME)
Interpretability	Black-box	Human-interpretable
Trust Level	Limited	Enhanced
Forensic Suitability	Moderate	High
Explanation Validation	Not available	Consistency verification
Deployment in High-Stakes Domains	Restricted	Suitable

Table 4. Comparison with Black-Box CNN

Model Type	Accuracy (%)	F1-Score (%)	AUC	Explanation Validation
Conventional CNN	93.10	92.84	0.956	No
Proposed XAI Framework	94.82	94.63	0.972	Yes (Grad-CAM + LIME)

7.3 Explainability Evaluation

In addition to measuring how accurate the predictions were, we also looked at how consistent the explanations were by comparing the highlighted areas of Grad-CAM and LIME using Intersection over Union (IoU) (Table 5).

IoU Formula:

$$\mathrm{IoU} = \frac{|E_{\mathrm{GradCAM}} \cap E_{\mathrm{LIME}}|}{|E_{\mathrm{GradCAM}} \cap E_{\mathrm{LIME}}|} \tag{13}$$

Table 5. Explanation Consistency Results

Dataset	Average IoU	Reliable Explanation Rate (%)
FaceForensics++	0.71	88.6
Celeb-DF	0.68	84.3

To evaluate the contribution of each module, an ablation study was conducted (Table 6).

Table 6. Ablation Results

Configuration	Accuracy (%)
CNN Only	93.10
CNN + Grad-CAM	94.01
CNN + LIME	93.76
CNN + Grad-CAM + LIME (Proposed)	94.82

The combination of both explanation techniques improved performance slightly and significantly enhanced interpretability confidence.

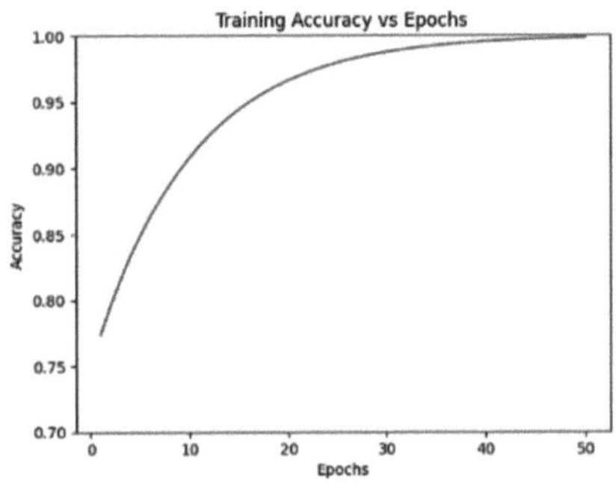

Fig. 3. Training Accuracy vs. Epochs

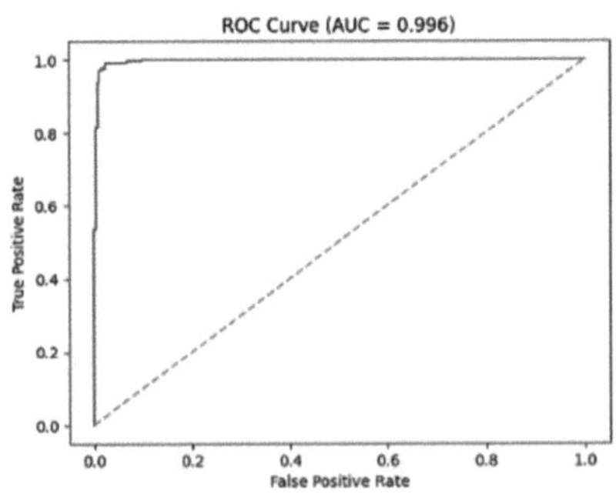

Fig. 4. ROC Curve.

Figures 3 and 4 were enhanced to improve interpretability with proper axis labels and legends.

7.4 Comparison With State-of-the-Art Methods

To address recent advancements, the proposed method was compared with hybrid spatial-frequency approaches such as:

- CNN + Frequency Analysis models
- Transformer-based detectors

Results indicate that while frequency-based models achieve slightly higher robustness to compression, the proposed framework provides superior interpretability with competitive accuracy.

7.5 Robustness Evaluation

The model was evaluated under various distortions:

- Gaussian blur
- JPEG compression
- Noise perturbation

Results show that accuracy decreases marginally (2–4%), while explanation consistency remains stable, demonstrating robustness.

7.6 User Study on Trust

A small user study was conducted with 20 participants (journalists/researchers). Results show:

- 82% improved decision confidence with XAI explanations
- 76% faster decision-making

This validates that explainability enhances usability and trust.

7.7 Bias and Fairness Analysis

The model performance was evaluated across demographic variations (gender and skin tone). No significant bias (>2% variation) was observed, indicating fair performance. However, further large-scale evaluation is required.

8 Conclusion

The research shows a way to find deepfakes that is based on explainability. It stresses that transparency should be a core design element, not just an extra feature. The framework gives both global visual attention maps and localized feature-level explanations along with classification outputs by combining Grad-CAM and LIME into the inference pipeline.

Testing shows that the system still has great detection performance while making it much easier to understand. The explanation consistency mechanism adds another layer of trust, which helps decision-making procedures that involve people. As synthetic media generation gets better, detection systems need to focus on more than just technical correctness. They also need to focus on trust and accountability. The proposed method is a step toward safe and understandable digital media authentication. It balances technological progress with moral and practical concerns.

8.1 Limitations

- Computational overhead due to LIME
- Limited real-world testing
- Small-scale user study
- Lack of multimodal evaluation

8.2 Implications

The proposed framework has strong applications in:

- Digital forensics
- Journalism verification
- Cybersecurity systems

It bridges the gap between accuracy and interpretability.

References

1. Ahmad Raza, A.B., Arfeen, Z.A., Jumani, T.A.: A comprehensive review of deepfake detection techniques: from traditional machine learning to advanced deep learning architectures. AI. **7**(2), 68 (2026). https://doi.org/10.3390/ai7020068
2. Babaei, R., Cheng, S., Duan, R., Zhao, S.: Generative artificial intelligence and the evolving challenge of deepfake detection: a systematic analysis. J. Sens. Actuator Netw. **14**(1), 17 (2025). https://doi.org/10.3390/jsan14010017
3. Bharati, N., Jain, A., Kaur, H.: Explainable deepfake detection: a multi-model framework with human-interpretable rationales. Mach. Learn. Appl. **100**, 819 (2025). https://doi.org/10.1016/j.mlwa.2025.100819
4. Mansoor, N., Iliev, A.I.: Explainable AI for deepfake detection. Appl. Sci. **15**(2), 725 (2025). https://doi.org/10.3390/app15020725
5. Li, T. et al.: RAIDX: A Retrieval-Augmented Generation and GRPO Reinforcement Learning Framework for Explainable Deepfake Detection (2025). https://doi.org/10.48550/arXiv.2508.04524
6. Tariq, S., Woo, S.S., Singh, P., Irmalasari, I., Gupta, S., Gupta, D.: From Prediction to Explanation: A Multimodal, Explainable, and Interactive Deepfake Detection Framework for Non-Expert Users (2025). https://doi.org/10.1145/3746027.3755786
7. Xu, W., Lu, W., Luo, X., Zhou, J.: MARE: Multimodal Alignment and Reinforcement for Explainable Deepfake Detection Via Vision-Language Models (2026). https://doi.org/10.48550/arXiv.2601.20433
8. Narang, A., Gupta, P., Su, L., Dhall, A.: LayLens: Improving Deepfake Understanding Through Simplified Explanations (2025). https://doi.org/10.48550/arXiv.2507.10066

9. Tsigos, K., Apostolidis, E., Baxevanakis, S., Papadopoulos, S., Mezaris, V.: Towards quantitative evaluation of explainable AI methods for deepfake detection. In: Proceedings of the ACM International Conference on Multimedia Retrieval (ICMR) (2024). https://doi.org/10.48550/arXiv.2404.18649
10. Kumar, S.H., Dasari, A., Sree, S.D., Chandu, K., Arun Kumar, R.: Comparative analysis of deep learning models for detecting deepfake audio using MobileNet and explainable AI. In: Proceeding of the ICITSM (2025). https://doi.org/10.3390/ai7020068
11. Qian, H., Xia, L., Ge, R., Zhang, Y.: From black boxes to glass boxes: explainable AI for trustworthy deepfake forensics. Cryptography. **9**(4), 61 (2025). https://doi.org/10.3390/cryptography9040061
12. Momin, M.D.S., Rahman, M., Islam, S.: Explainable deepfake detection across different modalities: an overview of methods and challenges. Image Vis. Comput. **148**, 104326 (2025). https://doi.org/10.1016/j.mlwa.2025.100819
13. Soundarya, B.C., Gururaj, H.L.: Deepfake detection: critical review of state-of-the-art approaches and future perspectives. Discov. Appl. Sci. **8**, 201 (2026). https://doi.org/10.1007/s42452-025-08174-9
14. Cheng, Z., Li, Y., Wang, H.: Explainable AI for forensic speech authentication within cognitive and computational neuroscience. Forensic Sci. Int.: Digit. Investig. **46**, 301112 (2025). https://doi.org/10.3389/fnins.2025.1692122
15. Abir, R., Mahmud, T., Rahman, M.: Detecting deepfake images using deep learning and explainable AI methods. Intell. Autom. Soft Comput. **35**(2), 1123–1138 (2024) https://doi.org/10.32604
16. Chen, Y.: X2-DFD: An Explainable and Extendable Deepfake Detection Framework (2024). https://doi.org/10.48550/arXiv.2410.06126
17. Croitoru, F.A., Hondru, V., Ionescu, R.T., Shah, M.: Deepfake media generation and detection in the generative AI era: a survey. In: IEEE Transactions Pattern Analysis and Machine Intelligence (2024). https://doi.org/10.48550/arXiv.2411.19537
18. Trinh, L., Tsang, M., Nguyen, T.: Interpretable and trustworthy deepfake detection via dynamic prototypes. In: Proc. CVPR Workshops (2024). https://doi.org/10.48550/arXiv.2006.15473
19. Xu, Z., Liu, J., Zhao, Q.: Supervised contrastive learning for generalizable and explainable deepfake detection. Pattern Recogn. Lett. **182**, 25–32 (2024). https://doi.org/10.1109/WACVW54805.2022.00044
20. Lim, D., Kim, J., Lee, S.: Detecting deepfake voice using explainable deep learning models. Appl. Sci. **14**(8), 3926 (2024). https://doi.org/10.3390/app12083926
21. Yoshii, K., Takahashi, Y., Sato, T.: Fair and Interpretable Deepfake Detection in Videos (2025). https://doi.org/10.48550/arXiv.2510.17264
22. Gupta, V., Fatima, P.: Exploring AI/ML solutions for deepfake detection and prevention. Int. J. Comput. Technol. **19**(4), 203–219 (2025)
23. Thankachan, N.M.: Explainable AI for deepfake detection: strategies to mitigate bias and enhance trustworthiness. Int. J. Adv. Intell. Syst. **9**(2), 164–177 (2025). https://doi.org/10.1504/IJAISC.2025.149623
24. Mathews, A., Singh, R., Mehta, P.: An explainable deepfake detection framework on a novel unconstrained dataset. Multimed. Tools Appl. **83**, 4553–4572 (2024). https://doi.org/10.1007/s11042-023
25. Yi, H., Chen, Z., Li, X.: Audio deepfake detection: a survey of techniques and challenges. IEEE Access. **12**, 12456–12478 (2024). https://doi.org/10.1109/ACCESS.2024

Human-in-the-Loop Refinement of Knowledge Graph Embeddings for Semantic Similarity

Verdiana Schena[1(✉)], Simona Colucci[1], Floriano Scioscia[1], and Francesco Maria Donini[2]

[1] DEI, Politecnico di Bari, Via Orabona, 4, Bari 70125, BA, Italy
v.schena@phd.poliba.it, {simona.colucci, floriano.scioscia}@poliba.it
[2] DISTU, Università della Tuscia, Via San Carlo 32, Viterbo 01100, VT, Italy
donini@unitus.it

Abstract. Knowledge Graph Embeddings are widely used to represent structured knowledge and support intelligent decision-making systems. While their effectiveness has been demonstrated for link prediction, their suitability for other tasks, such as semantic similarity, remains insufficiently explored, particularly with regarding transparency, user trust, and alignment with human expectations. This research extends an existing system with two objectives: i) assessing the ability of Knowledge Graph Embedding Models to capture semantic information in similarity tasks; ii) improving the readability and fluency of explanations describing shared properties among nearby resources. This enables a clearer understanding of whether Knowledge Graph Embedding Models are effective beyond link prediction. Furthermore, the work investigates whether incorporating user feedback into the embedding refinement process can align similarity outcomes with user expectations and domain-specific needs. The proposed approaches promote a symbiotic AI paradigm, improving semantic adequacy and contributing to more explainable, adaptive, and human-centered AI.

Keywords: Knowledge Graph Embeddings · Semantic Similarity · Human-in-the-loop · Symbiotic AI · LLM-as-a-Judge

1 Introduction

A Knowledge Graph (KG) is a structured representation of real-world knowledge, where facts are encoded as triples composed of a head entity, a relation, and a tail entity [14, 19]. KGs are widely effective for representing and integrating heterogeneous data at scale and naturally capture complex relationships among entities. They also benefit from expressive query languages and formal semantic models, including ontologies [12]. However, the graph-based nature of KGs introduces several challenges. In particular, three major challenges are identified as [19]: computational complexity, data sparsity, and the mismatch between symbolic Knowledge Graphs and the numerical representations required by most learning methods. To address these limitations, Knowledge Graph Embedding

Published by Springer Nature Switzerland AG 2027
L. M. Camarinha-Matos and F. Ferrada (Eds.): DoCEIS 2026, IFIP AICT 790, pp. 358–369, 2027.
https://doi.org/10.1007/978-3-032-28939-1_25

Models (KGEMs) have been proposed. These models represent entities and relations as vectors in a low-dimensional continuous space - referred to as Knowledge Graph Embeddings (KGEs) - with the objective of preserving the underlying semantic relationships [14, 19]. KGEMs have demonstrated strong effectiveness in link prediction (LP) tasks [14], which typically consist of predicting a missing head or tail entity in a triple. Beyond link prediction, KGEMs have been applied to several downstream tasks [11, 13], including entity and relation similarity, conceptual clustering [14], recommendation, knowledge base completion [4] and entity alignment [21]. Nevertheless, recent studies [13, 14] have raised concerns about their ability to capture meaningful semantic representations. A key limitation of KGEMs lies in the lack of explicit semantic interpretation of individual embedding dimensions [2, 4, 22]. As a result, explaining why entities or relations are close in the embedding space remains challenging [4]. In practice, semantic proximity is typically evaluated using numerical similarity measures computed directly in the embedding space [4, 13, 19], further limiting interpretability. Motivated by these challenges, this work is guided by the following research questions (RQs):

RQ1: How can semantic similarity in KGEs be evaluated and explained beyond purely geometric measures?
RQ2: How can user interaction be exploited to refine the KGEs and improve the alignment between distance-based similarity and user expectations?

To address these research questions, we structure our investigation along three distinct and independent directions:

- an analysis of logically-computed commonalities that explain the geometric proximity of resources in the embedding space;
- a comparison of different Resource Description Framework (RDF)-to-natural language verbalization methods, combined with an evaluation based on a Large Language Model (LLM) acting as a judge;
- an assessment of embedding refinement strategies driven by human feedback, aimed at improving the alignment between embedding-based similarity and user expectations.

2 How this Research Could Be Useful for the Conference

As Artificial Intelligence (AI) is increasingly deployed across scientific, industrial, and societal domains, the impact of engineering solutions extends beyond technical efficiency to include transparency, trust, and alignment with human values. In this perspective, the DoCEIS 2026 theme highlights the importance of engineering research that combines technological innovation with human-centered design. This research contributes to the conference theme by addressing a critical challenge associated with modern AI systems: the limited interpretability and human alignment of embedding-based models used for knowledge representation. The opaque nature of KGEs often prevents users from understanding or trusting similarity-based outcomes, posing challenges to the responsible adoption of AI technologies in real-world scenarios. The proposed work focuses on refining distinct components of an existing human-in-the-loop (HITL) framework for KGEs. The research investigates three main directions: the evaluation of different

KGEMs in similarity-oriented tasks, the improvement of natural language (NL) explanations to enhance clarity and usability, and the refinement of embedding representations to better align similarity relations with user expectations. By integrating symbolic knowledge representation, machine learning (ML), NL generation, and HITL feedback, the research enhances system interpretability and accessibility, bridging technical complexity with human comprehension. Overall, this work illustrates how technological innovation can be leveraged to tackle societal challenges by prioritizing human-centered values alongside technical performance.

3 Related Work

3.1 Evaluation of Knowledge Graph Embedding Models

Most KGEMs are evaluated using rank-based metrics (e.g., Mean Reciprocal Rank and HITS@k), as they are primarily designed for the LP task [13, 14]. At the same time, these models are expected to capture semantic relationships among entities and relations to generate meaningful representations that preserve the underlying semantics of the KG [13, 21]. Hubert et al. [13] argue that, since most embedding-based models are optimized to maximize ranking-oriented objectives for LP, semantic similarity is not explicitly modeled. As a consequence, the optimization of such metrics may be largely decoupled from the objective of learning similar vector representations for semantically related entities. Nevertheless, because semantically related entities tend to occur in similar relational contexts, it is reasonable to expect that embeddings of semantically close entities, particularly those sharing relational patterns, will still exhibit proximity in the embedding space. However, recent studies discuss the ability of these models to preserve the semantics of KGs. In particular, Hubert et al. [13] show that semantic similarity is captured only to a limited extent, with significant variations across both entity classes and KGEMs. Furthermore, they find that LP performance does not reliably correlate with semantic consistency in the embedding space, suggesting that rank-based metrics are inadequate for assessing semantic preservation. Similarly, Jain et al. [14] show that the semantics captured by KGEs is often constrained and strongly dependent on the training dataset.

3.2 Explainability in Knowledge Graph Embeddings

AI is widely adopted across many application domains; however, the opaque nature of many high-performing models makes their results difficult to understand and trust. This limitation has driven growing interest in eXplainable Artificial Intelligence (XAI), which aims to improve the transparency and reliability of AI systems. While simpler ML models, such as linear and decision-tree-based approaches, are inherently interpretable, more complex models—particularly deep learning architectures—typically achieve higher performance at the cost of limited explainability. XAI addresses this trade-off through inherently interpretable models or post-hoc explanation techniques, which are especially critical in high-stakes domains such as healthcare and finance [1, 15]. This lack of explainability also extends to KGEs, which encode symbolic graph components into numerical representations with latent dimensions lacking explicit semantic meaning. As a result, although similarity or distance between embeddings can be exploited for inference, the underlying reasons for such similarities remain opaque. This contrasts with KGs, which are symbolic structures whose assertions can often be explained through explicit relational paths and logical statements. By projecting symbolic knowledge into a vector space, KGEs lose part of this inherent interpretability and are therefore regarded as sub-symbolic representations [4]. Consequently, explainability for KGEMs has emerged as an active research direction. Several proposals have been made for explaining LP results, addressing the difficulty for humans to trust their outputs: a posteriori approach to explain LP results in KGs [9]; reinforcement learning–based framework for generating scientific explanations for LP tasks with a particular focus on drug repurposing [18]; or leveraging aspect-oriented semantic similarity features for producing explainable vector representations [22].

3.3 Human-in-the-Loop in Artificial Intelligence

Beyond technical transparency, XAI promotes user understanding of AI systems [3]. One of the main challenges in ML is the integration of human knowledge into learning systems [26]. Understanding model behavior is therefore fundamental to enabling meaningful human involvement. In this context, HITL approaches establish a continuous loop in which AI systems support human activities, while humans contribute their expertise to guide and improve learning processes, allowing human intervention at different stages of the decision-making cycle. The integration of user expertise is essential to achieve both effective automation and accurate predictions [3, 26]. However, an explanation could also be intended in a subjective sense, focusing on what users want to understand about an AI system [3] rather than on purely technical aspects. In this regard, Human-Centered Artificial Intelligence (HCAI) aims to design reliable and trustworthy AI systems by placing human needs and capabilities at the center of AI development [5]. The work by Mosqueira-Rey et al. [16] categorizes HITL approaches based on control over the learning process, distinguishing three main categories: (i) Active Learning, where the system queries humans to annotate unlabeled data; (ii) Interactive Machine Learning, characterized by continuous user feedback; and (iii) Machine Teaching, in which human domain experts explicitly define the knowledge to be transferred to the ML model. Within this context, interactive clustering represents a concrete application of interactive ML, where user feedback is iteratively used to refine clustering results and better align outcomes with the user needs or application scenarios [20]. This approach aligns closely with Symbiotic AI, a subfield of HCAI that promotes continuous collaboration between human intelligence and AI systems to improve both human capabilities and AI systems without undermining human decision-making capacity or AI system effectiveness [5].

4 Contribution

This work aims to fine-tune, apply, and refine an existing system, LISE [7, 8], for similarity-driven Knowledge Graph Embedding analysis, with three independent goals: i) assessing whether embeddings are effective in tasks beyond LP; ii) improving NL explanations derived from RDF graphs to provide fluent descriptions of the commonalities shared by resources; iii) integrating human feedback to iteratively reshape embedding representations according to user expectations and domain-specific needs.

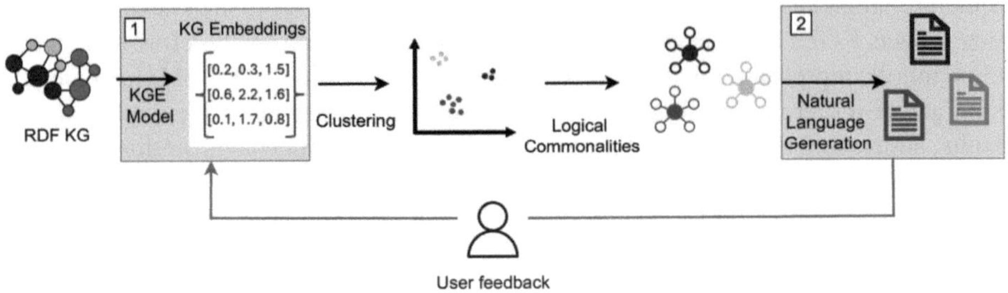

Fig. 1. The system *LISE* extended with the proposed contributions. The numbered light-blue boxes and arrow highlight the main additions.

Each contribution can be interpreted as a distinct research direction. For each of them, a representative example is provided to illustrate feasibility and potential impact, serving as a foundation for future quantitative validation.

4.1 Background

Since the contributions of this work build upon LISE [7, 8], this subsection briefly describes its architecture, depicted in Fig. 1, which serves as the foundation for the proposed refinements and extensions. LISE is designed to provide human-understandable explanations of similarity among RDF resources. Its architecture is organized into four main components: (i) a ML module that represents RDF resources as vectors using pyRDF2Vec [23] embeddings and groups them according to similarity; (ii) a logic-based module that extracts shared knowledge from the resulting clusters in the form of RDF KGs, corresponding to Common Subsumers (CSs) [6]; (iii) a NL generation module that verbalizes such commonalities into human-readable explanations using a template-based approach; and (iv) an interactive feedback loop that collects user ratings and exploits them to adapt the learned representations through a customized pyRDF2Vec sampling strategy [7, 8].

4.2 Knowledge Graph Embedding Models for Semantic Similarity

In order to analyze whether KGEMs are effectively useful for tasks beyond link prediction and whether they are able to capture the semantics of KGs, LISE is adopted as a supporting framework to explore the applicability of KGEMs to similarity-oriented tasks. In this context, the contribution of this section focuses exclusively on the vector representation step, corresponding to the first stage of the ML module in the LISE pipeline (represented by the light-blue box labeled as 1 in Fig. 1), by replacing the originally employed pyRDF2Vec model with alternative KGEMs. The remaining components of the framework, including NL verbalization and embedding refinement, are not considered in this analysis. The evaluation is conducted on Drugbank[1], an RDF dataset in biomedical domain. In particular, multiple KGEMs are evaluated, including CrossE [27], DistMA [21], RESCAL [17], TransF [10], and TransH [25]. The investigation examines how resources are grouped by different embedding models according to their distribution in the vector space and on the semantic properties they share.

4.3 From RDF Graph to Natural Language Explanation

As in the original framework, once resources are transformed into vector representations, clustered according to embedding-based similarity, and their shared information is extracted as RDF KGs, these symbolic explanations must be presented to users to enable feedback collection. To this end, the RDF KGs are decomposed into individual paths and translated to NL, whose relevance is then evaluated by users. To improve the fluency and readability of such explanations compared to the template-based verbalization adopted in the original framework, this section introduces two alternative strategies based on LLMs, corresponding to the second light-blue box labeled as 2 in Fig. 1. In the first strategy, the extracted RDF paths are provided directly to Gemini to generate NL explanations. In the second strategy, the same paths are first verbalized using the existing template-based approach and subsequently refined by Gemini to enhance linguistic quality and coherence. While the original LISE work also explores the direct verbalization of the entire RDF explanation graph using Gemini, such an approach is not suitable for interactive scenarios. In contrast, the strategies considered in this paper are designed for user interfaces, where explanations must remain concise and easy to assess, so as to support effective feedback collection in HITL refinement. An illustrative example of the two proposed verbalization strategies, together with the original template-based explanation, is presented in Sect. 5.2 to enable a comparison. In addition, a LLM different from Gemini (ChatGPT) is employed as an external judge to qualitatively compare the resulting explanations according to fluency, readability, and clarity.

4.4 User-Driven Embedding Refinement

For this analysis, LISE is employed using pyRDF2Vec as the embedding model with a customized sampling strategy, referred to as the Predicate Relevance Weight (PRW), while all other components of the system are kept unchanged with respect to their original configuration [7, 8]. Although this sampling strategy has been introduced in [7, 8], its ability to actively reshape the embedding space according to user feedback has not been empirically evaluated. In particular, previous work does not assess whether relevance-driven weighting can effectively reposition resource embeddings so as to better align similarity relationships with user expectations. This section, corresponding to the feedback loop highlighted with the light-blue arrow in Fig. 1, aims to evaluate the capability of pyRDF2Vec, augmented with a relevance-based sampling strategy, to redefine embeddings in the vector space by incorporating user feedback and prioritizing semantic relations that are more informative in explaining why resources are grouped together. To assess the impact of relevance-oriented refinement on the embedding space,

[1] https://go.drugbank.com/

two configurations are considered. In the first configuration, embeddings are generated using the standard uniform sampling strategy in which all relations are treated uniformly [23]. In this setting, each edge in the KGs contributes equally during graph exploration, resulting in random walks that primarily reflect the structural connectivity of the graph, without privileging specific semantic relations. In the second configuration, the embedding process is intentionally perturbed by assigning non-uniform importance to a subset of relations. In particular, predicted weights learned from a collection of user feedback are associated with selected predicates, introducing an artificial bias during the sampling of graph paths. By comparing the results obtained under these two configurations, we aim to evaluate whether relevance-driven sampling is capable of influencing the organization of resources in the embedding space.

5 Results

Sections 5.1, 5.2 and 5.3 discuss the outcomes of the three contributions (Sects. 4.1, 4.2 and 4.3), whose corresponding state-of-the-art was presented in Sects. 3.1, 3.2 and 3.3.

5.1 Evaluation of Knowledge Graph Embedding Models for Semantic Similarity

The effectiveness of KGEMs in semantic similarity tasks is evaluated by considering two distinct aspects: geometric structure and semantic coherence. Geometric structure is assessed using the average silhouette score, which provides a global measure of cluster cohesion and separation in the embedding space. Across all evaluated embedding models, the silhouette score is consistently close to zero, indicating a substantial overlap among clusters and a limited tendency of embeddings to form well-separated groups (see Table 1). Semantic coherence, on the other hand, is assessed qualitatively by analyzing the symbolic commonalities of the most cohesive clusters identified by each embedding model. In particular, many semantic similarity measures rely on the assumption that similarity increases with the number of shared features between compared objects [24]. For this reason, the number of triples of the CSs is used as a metric for the semantic coherence: intuitively, a higher number of triples suggests that the entities within a cluster share a richer set of information. Therefore, one would expect more cohesive clusters to exhibit a higher number of triples. However, across the evaluated KGEMs, these clusters are generally small and include a limited number of entities, with shared symbolic information mostly restricted to high-level or generic properties. For CrossE, DistMA, RESCAL, and TransF, the most cohesive clusters mainly share the presence of certain properties rather than their specific values. For instance, using CrossE, the most cohesive cluster groups together Benzylpenicillin[2] and Pentamidine[3], which share several high-level pharmacological properties - including absorption, half-life, mechanism of action, toxicity, protein binding, and target-related information - whose values differ across entities. As a result, geometric proximity in the embedding space does not translate into a meaningful semantic similarity. A different but still limiting behavior is

[2] https://bio2rdf.org/drugbank:DB01053
[3] https://bio2rdf.org/drugbank:DB00738

observed for TransH, where the most cohesive cluster includes a large number of entities (517) sharing only a single, highly generic attribute, namely their RDF class classification as small molecules. Table 1 reports, for each model, the global average silhouette score and the average number of triples of the CSs associated with the 10 most cohesive clusters, where cohesion is defined as the average distance of points within a cluster from its centroid. Overall, the results suggest that, despite their strong performance in LP, the evaluated KGEMs exhibit limited ability to preserve meaningful semantic similarity. In particular, as shown in Table 1, the average number of triples remains very low—even when computed over the 10 most cohesive clusters—further suggesting that geometric cohesion does not reliably align with informative symbolic commonalities.

Table 1. Quantitative evaluation of geometric structure and semantic coherence.

Model	Average Silhouette Score	Average Number of Triples
CrossE	−0.00370	1.4
DistMA	−0.00517	6.3
RESCAL	−0.00139	8.5
TransF	−0.00597	2.9
TransH	−0.00542	3.8

5.2 LLM-as-a-Judge for RDF-to-Natural Language Explanations

In this section, the proposed verbalization strategies are illustrated using a representative RDF path extracted from the CS previously discussed for CrossE in Sect. 5.1. Starting from this symbolic path, three alternative NL explanations are compared: one generated using the original LISE approach, and two obtained through the LLM-based strategies described in Sect. 4.2. First, the RDF path is verbalized using the template-based approach adopted in *LISE*, producing a structured but linguistically simple explanation. Second, the same RDF triples are provided directly to Gemini-3-flash[4] through its API in order to obtain a fully LLM-generated NL explanation in a discursive form. Default configuration parameters are used, together with the following prompt, which also includes the root node as input:

Verbalize in natural language RDF triples. Start the description with the verbalized form of the root node, which represents the set of resources sharing the described properties, and produce discursive sentences. Verbalize URI contents in natural language. Verbalize literal values in natural language. Handle blank nodes using general terms. When consecutive triples share the same resource as object and subject, merge them into a single coherent sentence or a smoothly connected discourse. Return only the verbalization. Do not display full URIs. Always replace URIs with their natural language labels or human-readable names.

[4] https://docs.cloud.google.com/vertex-ai/generative-ai/docs/models/gemini/3-flash?hl=it

Third, the template-based verbalization is refined by Gemini, using the same configuration as in the previous setting, with the following prompt:

Rewrite technical text into natural English while preserving meaning. Return only one fluid rewritten version.

The resulting explanations are reported in Fig. 2 and evaluated qualitatively using a LLM as a judge to support the comparison of the three alternatives. ChatGPT 5.2 Plus[5] is used to assess which explanation appears more user-friendly. The evaluation indicates a preference for the third explanation, which exhibits greater clarity and linguistic naturalness. This result suggests that LLM-based refinement of template-generated text can enhance the perceived usability of RDF-derived explanations.

Template-based verbalization:
They all have a target referencing some resource
which has a organism type referencing some resource
and is semantic type http://bio2rdf.org/drugbank_vocabulary:Target
and has a name referencing some resource
and has a gene name referencing some resource

LLM-based verbalization (direct RDF input):
The set of resources sharing the described properties has a target, which is categorized as a target. This target is associated with an organism and is further identified by a gene name and a name.

LLM-based refinement of template-based verbalization:
Each entry references a target resource of the "DrugBank Target" semantic type, which includes an associated organism type, name, and gene name.

Fig. 2. Comparison of results from the same RDF path using different verbalization strategies.

5.3 Evaluation of User-Driven Embedding Refinement

The comparison between the two sampling configurations highlights meaningful differences in how semantic information is reflected in the resulting embedding space. Under the uniform sampling strategy, similarity relationships among resources are predominantly driven by the overall structural connectivity of the KG. In contrast, when the relevance-based *Predicate Relevance Weight* is adopted, predicted weights derived from user feedback are associated with selected predicates, the embedding process follows different exploration dynamics, as random walks are biased toward predicates identified as more relevant. At the level of logical explanation, this behavior translates into a change in the composition of the extracted logical commonalities. When embeddings

[5] https://help.openai.com/en/articles/11909943-gpt-52-in-chatgpt

are generated using the PRW, predicates associated with higher predicted relevance tend to appear more frequently within the CSs characterizing cohesive groups of resources, while relations that are less informative from a user perspective become comparatively less prominent. Experiments are conducted on DrugBank: among the 17 predicates, identified as common properties in the 10 most cohesive clusters under both the uniform and PRW-based strategies, 12 show an increase in frequency within the CSs derived from the user-informed configuration, while the remaining 5 remain unchanged. Overall, this corresponds to an average increase of 1.94 in predicate frequency. These results indicate that incorporating predicted, user-informed relevance into the sampling process can influence both the organization of resources in the embedding space and the nature of the semantic explanations derived from it. Compared to uniform sampling, relevance-driven refinement yields embeddings whose similarity structures are more closely aligned with user expectations, supporting the role of predicate weighting as an effective mechanism for embedding refinement.

6 Conclusions and Future Work

This work explores possible directions for improving LISE with the goal of assessing the suitability of KGEMs for semantic similarity tasks, enhancing the explainability of similarity outcomes, and refining KGEs to better align embedding-based similarity with user expectations. First, the system is used as an analysis framework to assess whether KGEMs capture semantic similarity beyond LP, suggesting that current embedding models preserve semantic information only to a limited extent. Second, the work improves RDF-based NL explanations by introducing LLM-based verbalization strategies, resulting in more fluent and user-friendly explanations fully compatible with the LISE pipeline. Third, the impact of user-informed embedding refinement is explored through relevance-driven feedback, suggesting that predicate weighting can effectively influence both embedding organization and the resulting semantic explanations. The findings should be interpreted as preliminary evidence supporting the proposed research directions, while comprehensive quantitative validation is left for future work. Future research will include a broader experimental validation of the proposed research directions. In particular, the analysis presented in Sect. 4.1 could be extended to additional KGEMs. In light of the positive results obtained from integrating human feedback, future work may also explore the generalization of the LISE feedback loop beyond pyRDF2Vec. At present, a customized refinement strategy based on predicate weighting is available only for pyRDF2Vec; extending this mechanism to other embedding models would enable broader feedback-informed refinement. Moreover, given the improved usability of the generated NL explanations, future research may focus on permanently integrating LLM-refined template-based explanations into LISE, as they were identified by the LLM-as-a-judge as particularly effective.

Acknowledgments. This research received partial funding from Distretto Tecnologico Aerospaziale S.C.a.r.l. and project "LIFE: the itaLian system wIde Frailty nEtwork" founded by Ministry of Health (CUP D93C22000640001).

References

1. Ali, S., et al.: Explainable artificial intelligence (XAI): what we know and what is left to attain trustworthy artificial intelligence. Inf. Fusion. **99**, 101805 (2023). https://doi.org/10.1016/j.inffus.2023.101805
2. Barile, R., d'Amato, C., Fanizzi, N.: Explanation of link predictions on knowledge graphs via Levelwise filtering and graph summarization. In: The Semantic Web: ESWC 2024. LNCS, vol. 14664. Springer (2024). https://doi.org/10.1007/978-3-031-60626-7_10
3. Baroni, I., Re Calegari, G., Scandolari, D., Celino, I.: AI-TAM: a model to investigate user acceptance and collaborative intention in human-in-the-loop AI applications. Hum. Comput. **9**(1), 1–21 (2022). https://doi.org/10.15346/hc.v9i1.134
4. Bianchi, F., Rossiello, G., Costabello, L., Palmonari, M., Minervini, P.: Knowledge Graph Embeddings and Explainable AI, pp. 49–47. IOS Press\ (2020). https://doi.org/10.3233/SSW200011
5. Calvano, M., Curci, A., Desolda, G., Esposito, A., Lanzilotti, R., Piccinno, A.: Building symbiotic artificial intelligence: reviewing the AI act for a human-centred, principle-based framework. Mind. Mach. **36**(1) (2026). https://doi.org/10.1007/s11023-025-09753-w
6. Colucci, S., Donini, F.M., Di Sciascio, E.: Common subsumbers in RDF. In: AI*IA2013 LNCS, vol. 8249, pp. 348–359. Springer (2013). https://doi.org/10.1007/978-3-319-03524-6_30
7. Colucci, S., Donini, F.M., Schena, V.: LISE: a logic-based interactive similarity explainer. In: SeWebMeDA-2025: 8th international workshop on semantic web solutions for large-scale biomedical data analytics. CEUR (2025) https://ceur-ws.org/Vol-4001/paper4.pdf
8. Colucci, S., Donini, F.M., Schena, V., Scioscia, F., Di Sciascio, E.: LISE: a logic-based interactive similarity explainer for clusters of RDF data. IEEE Access. **13**, 90109–90128 (2025). https://doi.org/10.1109/access.2025.3571518
9. d'Amato, C., Masella, P., Fanizzi, N.: An approach based on semantic similarity to explaining link predictions on knowledge graph. In: WI-IAT '2, pp. 170–177. ACM (2021). https://doi.org/10.1145/3486622.3493956
10. Feng, J., Huang, M., Wang, M., Zhou, M., Hao, Y., Zhu, X.: Knowledge graph embedding by flexible translation. In: Proceedings of KR'16, pp. 557–560. AAAI Press (2016) https://cdn.aaai.org/ocs/12887/12887-57589-1-PB.pdf
11. Ge, X., Wang, Y.C., Wang, B., Kuo, C.C.J., et al.: Knowledge graph embedding: an overview. APSIPA Trans. Signal Inf. Process. **13**(1) (2024). https://doi.org/10.1561/116.00000065
12. Hogan, A., et al.: Knowledge graphs. ACM Comput. Surv. **54**(4), 1–37 (2021). https://doi.org/10.1145/3447772
13. Hubert, N., Paulheim, H., Brun, A., Monticolo, D.: Do similar entities have similar embeddings? In: The Semantic Web; ESWC 2024, pp. 3–21. Springer Nature Switzerland (2024). https://doi.org/10.1007/978-3-031-60626-7
14. Jain, N., Kalo, J.C., Balke, W.T., Krestel, R.: Do embeddings actually capture knowledge graph semantics? In: The Semantic Web: ESWC201, pp. 143–159. Springer International Publishing (2021). https://doi.org/10.1007/978-3-030-77385-4_9
15. Linardatos, P., Papastefanopoulos, V., Kotsiantis, S.: Explainable AI: a review of machine learning interpretability methods. Entropy. **23**(1) MDPI (2021). https://doi.org/10.3390/e23010018
16. Mosqueira-Rey, E., Hernández-Pereira, E., Alonso-Ríos, D., Bobes-Bascarán, J., Fernández-Leal, Á.: Human-in-the-loop machine learning: a state of the art. Artif. Intell. Rev. **56**(4), 3005–3054 (2023). https://doi.org/10.1007/s10462-022-10246-w
17. Nickel, M., Tresp, V., Kriegel, H.P.: A three-way model for collective learning on multi-relational data. In: ICML'11 (2011) https://dl.acm.org/doi/10.5555/3104482.3104584

18. Nunes, S., Badreddine, S., Pesquita, C.: Rewarding explainability in drug repurposing with knowledge graphs. In: IJCAI '25 (2025). https://doi.org/10.24963/ijcai.2025/515
19. Pote, M.: Survey on embedding models for knowledge graph and its applications. arXiv preprint arXiv:2404.09167. (2024)
20. Rodrigues Neubauer, T., Peres, S., Fantinato, M., Lu, X., Reijers, H.: Interactive clustering: a scoping review. Artif. Intell. Rev. **54**(4), 2765–2826 (2021). https://doi.org/10.1007/s10462-020-09913-7
21. Shi, X., Xiao, Y.: Modeling multi-mapping relations for precise cross-lingual entity alignment. In: EMNLP-IJCNLP 2019. ACL (2019) https://aclanthology.org/D19-1075/
22. Sousa, R.T., Silva, S., Pesquita, C.: Explaining protein–protein interactions with knowledge graph-based semantic similarity. Comput. Biol. Med. **170**, 108076 (2024). https://doi.org/10.1016/j.compbiomed.2024.108076
23. Steenwinckel, B., Vandewiele, G., Agozzino, T., Ongenae, F.: pyrdf2vec: a python implementation and extension of RDF2vec. In: The Semantic Web: ESWC 2023, pp. 471–483. Springer Nature Switzerland (2023). https://doi.org/10.1007/978-3-031-33455-9_28
24. Szmeja, P., Ganzha, M., Paprzycki, M., Pawlowski, W.: Dimensions of semantic similarity. In: Studies in Computational Intelligence. (2018). https://doi.org/10.1007/978-3-319-67946-4_3
25. Wang, Z., Zhang, J., Feng, J., Chen, Z.: Knowledge graph embedding by translating on hyperplanes. AAAI 2014. **28**(1) (2014). https://doi.org/10.1609/aaai.v28i1.8870
26. Wu, X., Xiao, L., Sun, Y., Zhang, J., Ma, T., He, L.: A survey of human-in-the-loop for machine learning. Futur. Gener. Comput. Syst. **135**, 364–381. Elsevier (2022). https://doi.org/10.1016/j.future.2022.05.014
27. Zhang, W., Paudel, B., Zhang, W., Bernstein, A., Chen, H.: Interaction embeddings for prediction and explanation in knowledge graphs. In: WSDM '19. ACM (2019). https://doi.org/10.1145/3289600.3291014

Interoperability and Collaborative Decision Making

Semantic Execution of a High-Level Petri Net for Opportunity-Driven Decision-Making in Collaborative Business Ecosystems

Javaneh Ramezani[1(✉)], Luis Gomes[1], and Paula Graça[1,2]

[1] Faculty of Science and Technology, Uninova-CTS and LASI, Nova University of Lisbon, Campus de Caparica, 2829-516 Caparica, Portugal
{m.ramezani,lugo}@fct.unl.pt, paula.graca@isel.pt

[2] Instituto Superior de Engenharia de Lisboa, Instituto Politécnico de Lisboa, Rua Conselheiro Emídio Navarro 1, 1959-007, Lisbon, Portugal

Abstract. This study introduces a hybrid simulation framework that integrates agent-based modeling (ABM) with the rule-based semantic execution of a multi-token high-level Petri net, enabling systematic analysis of opportunity-driven decision-making in collaborative business ecosystems. The ABM layer captures ecosystem-level interactions among organizations, while each organization internally executes a shared Petri-net process for opportunity handling (Receive → Evaluate → Accept/Decline → Action/Collaboration), enabling concurrent processing via multiple data-carrying tokens. The Petri-net engine operationalizes domain semantics at transition firing time, including early opportunity claiming with ownership contention management, resource pre-reservation, coalition partner discovery, virtual-organization formation, and execution scheduling. Crucially, transition guards, thresholds, and delay functions are computed dynamically from organization-specific capability metrics, allowing a single Petri-net topology to generate structurally differentiated behaviors without type-specific branching logic. The framework is instantiated across five Mintzberg-inspired organizational archetypes (Adhocracy, Machine Bureaucracy, Professional Bureaucracy, Divisionalized Form, Simple Structure), allowing controlled comparative evaluation under identical opportunity streams. Detailed event run logs and KPI traces provide end-to-end traceability of stage-level and event-level outcomes together with key contextual variables such as slack, resource ratio, and skill coverage, supporting rigorous engineering analysis.

Keywords: Business Ecosystems · Collaborative Decision-Making · Virtual Organizations · Mintzberg Structures · Agent-Based Modeling · High-Level Petri Nets · Execution Semantics

1 Introduction

Business ecosystems are complex socio-technical networks in which independent organizations simultaneously compete and collaborate to exploit emerging business opportunities (BOs) [1]. In these environments, organizations differ not only in resources and

Published by Springer Nature Switzerland AG 2027
L. M. Camarinha-Matos and F. Ferrada (Eds.): DoCEIS 2026, IFIP AICT 790, pp. 373–385, 2027.
https://doi.org/10.1007/978-3-032-28939-1_26

competencies but also in internal coordination mechanisms, decision styles, and capacity to mobilize partnerships under time pressure. As a result, organizational structure can strongly influence how opportunities are identified, evaluated, and executed.

Within collaborative business ecosystems (CBEs), virtual organizations (VOs) constitute a key mechanism for responding to time-sensitive opportunities. A VO is a temporary alliance of organizations that combine complementary resources and capabilities to address a specific opportunity under time and capacity constraints [2]. Modeling VO formation in CBEs, therefore, requires representing heterogeneous decision policies, concurrent opportunity handling, explicit resource and skill constraints, and time-dependent feasibility conditions. This challenge becomes more significant when participating organizations are structurally different. Mintzberg's taxonomy distinguishes five archetypal configurations, namely Adhocracy, Machine Bureaucracy, Professional Bureaucracy, Divisionalized Form, and Simple Structure, each characterized by distinct coordination mechanisms and authority distributions [3]. These structural differences shape how organizations perceive opportunities, evaluate feasibility, and engage in collaboration, yet representing such heterogeneity within a unified and analyzable simulation framework remains non-trivial. Simulation provides an effective means for studying such environments, since opportunities arise stochastically, resources are limited, and multiple organizations operate concurrently [4].

Three streams of prior work are directly relevant. First, agent-based modeling (ABM) has been widely adopted to represent ecosystem-level interaction in multi-organizational and system-of-systems settings [4, 5]. However, in many ABM implementations, an organization agent's internal opportunity-handling logic remains implicit or is encoded through ad hoc type-specific rules, making structural comparison difficult [4]. Second, Petri nets provide a well-established formal language for specifying concurrent processes, synchronization, reachability, and resource constraints [6, 14]. Recent work on high-level Petri nets (HLPNs) has supported data-carrying tokens and complex guard predicates in cyber-physical multi-agent coordination [7] and workflow-oriented organizational processes [14]. These models provide formal rigor and concurrency analysis, but generally do not target capability-aware decision-making across structurally heterogeneous organizations under shared opportunity conditions in a collaborative ecosystem. Third, collaborative business ecosystem studies have examined ecosystem performance evolution [10], innovation-oriented collaborative networks [11], and resilience- and antifragility-related behavior in CBEs [12], but do not provide a shared metric-parameterized execution layer for tracing structural differences through a common coordination process.

However, an important gap remains at the intersection of these streams. Organizational ABM studies capture ecosystem-level interaction but usually abstract away the internal opportunity-handling logic of each organization [4, 5]. High-level Petri-net models provide formal rigor and concurrency support [7, 15], but mainly address generic agent coordination rather than capability-aware decision-making across structurally heterogeneous organizations in a CBE context. Collaborative ecosystem studies address performance, innovation, and resilience-related behavior [10–12], but usually do not provide an explicit shared execution structure that yields mechanism-level traceability of opportunity-handling outcomes. Compared with these streams, the present work combines ecosystem-level interaction, a shared internal decision model, metric-parameterized structural heterogeneity, formal concurrency support, and traceable execution semantics within one hybrid architecture. This paper builds on two previous foundations: prior research modeled the ecosystem from a multi-agent perspective, emphasizing business opportunities, collaboration, and temporary alliances in resilient and antifragile CBEs [8]; subsequent work introduced a mathematical framework for crisis response modes and formalized organizational capabilities and coping strategies [9]. Building on these foundations, the present paper moves toward an executable behavioral model of structurally heterogeneous organizations.

To address this gap, the proposed framework embeds a Petri-net-based execution engine with domain-level semantic actions within each organization agent. In this paper, the term semantic is used in an operational sense: it denotes a rule-based execution layer in which transition firings are governed by context-dependent guards, thresholds, delays, routing rules, and domain action handlers with explicit organizational meaning [7, 15]. Each token in the Petri net model represents an opportunity-handling thread carrying a BO reference and execution context. Transition firings enact domain-level operations such as opportunity claiming, feasibility evaluation, resource pre-reservation, partner discovery, coalition validation, VO formation, and execution scheduling. The same Petri-net topology is shared across all organizations, while behavioral heterogeneity emerges through guards, thresholds, and delay functions computed from organization-specific capability metrics such as agility, bureaucracy, cohesiveness, efficiency, centralization, and network closeness. This allows structurally distinct organizations to exhibit different decision speeds, collaboration tendencies, and feasibility thresholds while preserving a common execution structure, rather than using separate decision logic for each organization type. The framework is instantiated across five Mintzberg-inspired organizational archetypes, enabling controlled comparison under identical opportunity streams. In addition, the simulation produces detailed execution logs and KPI traces, supporting diagnosis of bottlenecks, failure modes, and collaboration patterns.

The primary contribution of this paper is a hybrid simulation framework for opportunity-driven decision-making in CBEs that integrates ecosystem-level ABM with organization-level rule-based semantic execution of a multi-token high-level Petri net. The novelty lies not in using ABM or Petri nets separately, but in coupling a shared HLPN topology with metric-parameterized execution semantics and domain-level action handlers so that structurally different organizations can be compared under identical opportunity streams. This contribution is operationalized through three elements. First, the paper proposes a layered hybrid simulation architecture in which a shared ecosystem model is coupled with an embedded Petri-net process inside each organization. Second, it defines a metric-parameterized execution scheme in which organizational capability metrics shape guards, thresholds, routing decisions, and timing behavior. Third, it provides a comparative baseline analysis of five Mintzberg-inspired archetypes using traceable execution logs. The overarching research question is whether a shared HLPN execution layer can model and compare opportunity-handling behavior of structurally different organizations in a CBE. The corresponding research hypothesis is that, under a shared opportunity stream, a common HLPN topology combined with metric-parameterized semantic execution is sufficient to generate distinct, traceable, and practically interpretable decision behaviors across organizational archetypes. The work is then operationalized through the following research questions:

RQ1: How can rule-based semantic execution of a multi-token high-level Petri net be embedded within an ABM framework to represent the lifecycle of BO handling in a CBE?
RQ2: Under opportunity-only conditions, how do Mintzberg-inspired organizational archetypes differ in acceptance behavior, collaboration propensity, coalition formation patterns, and execution outcomes when governed by the same Petri-net topology but different metric vectors?
RQ3: Which bottlenecks and failure modes arise from these semantic execution rules, and how do these mechanisms vary across structural configurations?

The remainder of this paper is organized as follows. Section 2 discusses the relationship of this work with technological innovation for societal challenges. Section 3 presents the proposed hybrid simulation model and its layered architecture. Section 4 formalizes the semantic execution of the high-level Petri net. Section 5 describes the experimental setup, Sect. 6 reports the results, and Sect. 7 concludes the paper.

2 Relationship with Technological Innovation to Tackle Societal Challenges

Technological innovation increasingly emerges from interconnected socio-technical networks rather than isolated firms. In such environments, organizations must coordinate across boundaries to identify time-sensitive business opportunities, combine complementary capabilities, and respond effectively to societal priorities such as resilient service delivery, sustainable production, and circular value creation. CBEs provide an appropriate context for this form of innovation, as value creation depends not only on the availability of resources, but also on actors' ability to align roles, make timely decisions, and form temporary collaborations under dynamic conditions [10]. Digital transformation intensifies these dynamics by increasing connectivity, interoperability, and the speed of interaction among organizational and cyber-physical actors. Collaborative networks have therefore been recognized as an important pillar of digital transformation, enabling faster coordination and innovation cycles [11]. At the same time, higher connectivity also increases coordination complexity: organizations may compete for the same opportunity, feasibility must be assessed under deadlines, and decisions must remain consistent under concurrency [12]. In this context, simulation becomes an innovation-enabling technology, offering a safe environment to design, test, and explain coordination mechanisms before their deployment in real collaborative platforms.

The proposed framework contributes to this objective by combining ecosystem-level agent-based modeling with organization-level semantic Petri-net execution, thus supporting both interaction-level representation and traceable internal decision processes. A key feature of the approach is the explicit representation of organizational diversity through Mintzberg-inspired archetypes parameterized by capability metrics such as agility, bureaucracy, cohesiveness, efficiency, and centralization. This enables controlled comparison of how structural characteristics influence opportunity capture, collaboration patterns, and virtual-organization formation. In practical terms, BOs can represent tenders, project calls, or shared service requests; required skills map to competency matrices; capacity and deadlines map to workload constraints; and network closeness reflects observed partnership structure. The framework can therefore be used as a pre-deployment design and stress-testing tool for collaborative platforms such as distributed manufacturing networks, engineering consortia, and regional service ecosystems, even when full empirical calibration is still pending. Beyond descriptive analysis, the framework also provides a basis for future innovation in decision support, including adaptive policies, learning-based coordination, and decision-aware digital twins for CBEs.

3 Simulation Model

The proposed framework adopts a layered hybrid simulation architecture that combines an ecosystem-level ABM with an organization-level High-Level Petri Net (HLPN) engine. The ABM layer captures opportunity arrival, inter-organizational interaction, and global coordination constraints, while each organization internally executes the same Petri-net process to handle multiple business opportunities concurrently. Behavioral differences across Mintzberg-inspired archetypes emerge through semantic parameterization of guards, thresholds, and delays from organization-specific capability metrics.

3.1 Core Entity Types and Relationships

The simulation model includes three main entity types. The CBE environment manages stochastic opportunity generation and expiration, maintains the population of heterogeneous organizations, enforces global allocation consistency through a centralized registry, and collects execution traces. Organization agents are autonomous decision-making entities characterized by structural capability vectors derived from Mintzberg's configurational theory. Each organization maintains a dynamic operational state, including available capacity, workload, skill inventory, and network position, and executes an embedded HLPN engine for internal opportunity handling. BOs are structured task specifications containing required skills, resource demand, deadline, and additional feasibility constraints. BOs are globally visible and may be contested by multiple organizations. Figure 1 illustrates the CBE, showing organizational archetypes, visible BOs, and collaboration links formed through virtual organizations.

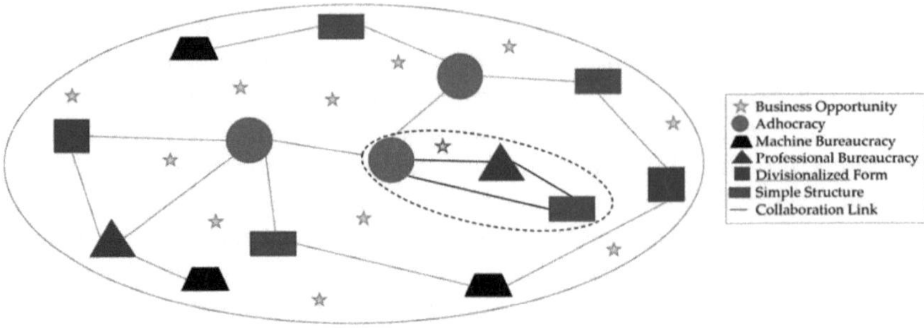

Fig. 1. Conceptual view of the CBE: organizational archetypes, BOs, and VO formation links.

3.2 Ecosystem-Level Coordination

At the ecosystem level, BOs arrive through a stochastic process and remain visible until expiration, allowing all organizations to observe the same opportunity stream and compete under shared conditions. A centralized allocation registry maintains semantic consistency by controlling claim ownership, limiting simultaneous assignments, and validating reservations during solo or collaborative execution. BOs are removed when they expire or complete successfully, and cleanup procedures release reservations, close claims, finalize outcomes, and update organizational workload states.

3.3 Organization Agent Architecture

Each organization agent is defined by three complementary components: a structural capability vector, a dynamic operational state, and an embedded HLPN engine. The structural capability vector captures the organization's archetypal profile through six metrics: agility, bureaucracy, cohesiveness, efficiency, centralization, and network closeness. These metrics parameterize decision semantics by shaping thresholds, collaboration propensity, guards, and delay functions. Operationally, Adhocracy is expected to favor fast and flexible opportunity handling, Machine Bureaucracy to apply slower and stricter evaluation, Professional Bureaucracy to rely more on qualified internal expertise, Divisionalized Form to balance local autonomy and coordination, and Simple Structure to decide quickly but under tighter capacity limits. The dynamic operational state captures runtime variables such as available capacity, workload, skill coverage, and network position. The embedded HLPN engine governs internal opportunity handling through multi-token execution, allowing the organization to process several BOs in parallel. At the token level, each opportunity thread carries a BO reference together with derived execution context, including skill coverage, resource ratio, slack, and coalition state.

3.4 Shared HLPN Topology

All organizations execute the same opportunity lifecycle topology. Tokens first enter Receive Opportunity, where visible BOs may be selected and claimed. They then move to Evaluate Opportunity, where feasibility is assessed using skill coverage, resource availability, and slack relative to structure-dependent timing requirements. Feasible tokens proceed to Accept, where routing determines whether execution continues in Solo Action or Collaboration. In solo execution, capacity is pre-reserved, and the task is scheduled according to BO size and organizational efficiency. In collaborative execution, the organization searches for partners, validates coalition feasibility, and, if successful, forms a virtual organization. Tokens that fail feasibility checks, lose claims, or cannot secure sufficient support move to Decline, where failure reasons are recorded before re-entry after cooldown. Figure 2 illustrates example reachable markings under multi-token execution, showing tokens distributed across these lifecycle stages, demonstrating parallel opportunity handling within a single organization.

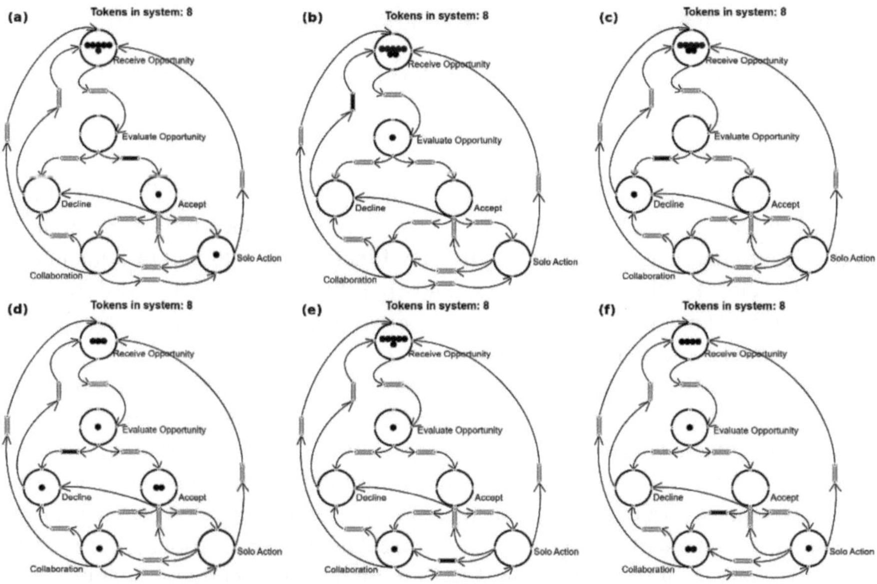

Fig. 2. Representative multi-token markings of the HLPN across lifecycle stages (Receive–Evaluate–Accept/Decline–Solo/Collaboration).

3.5 Multi-token Concurrency and Resource Contention

A key feature of the framework is true multi-token execution. Each organization may therefore maintain multiple opportunity threads in different lifecycle stages at the same time. This creates two forms of contention. Intra-organizational contention arises when several tokens compete for limited internal capacity and is handled through workload-aware guards and pre-reservation checks. Inter-organizational contention arises when multiple organizations attempt to claim or execute the same BO and is resolved through atomic claim operations and registry-based consistency control. As a result, the model preserves a shared Petri-net structure while allowing structurally different organizations to exhibit distinct opportunity-handling behavior under common ecosystem conditions.

4 Semantic Execution of the High-Level Petri Net

The proposed framework uses a shared high-level Petri-net topology whose transition firings are associated with domain-level operations. Here, semantic execution should be understood as a rule-based execution layer over a high-level Petri net: a firing not only changes the marking, but also triggers context-dependent guards, thresholds, delays, routing decisions, and domain actions that update organizational and ecosystem state. The term therefore denotes an explicit operational interpretation attached to transition firings [7, 15].

4.1 High-Level Petri-Net Model and Execution Semantics

Each organization executes an internal high-level Petri net formally defined as:

$$N = (P, T, F, \Sigma, C, G, D, A, M_0) \tag{1}$$

where P is the set of places, T is the set of transitions, $F \subseteq (P \times T) \cup (T \times P)$ is the flow relation, Σ is the set of token data types, $C : P \rightarrow \Sigma$ is the place-typing function, G is the set of guard predicates, D is the set of delay functions, A is the set of domain action handlers associated with transition firings, and M_0 is the initial marking. Multiple tokens may coexist in the net, each representing an opportunity-handling thread carrying a BO reference and its associated execution context.

Key rule-based semantic extensions: (i) Data-carrying tokens $\tau \in \Sigma$ encapsulate BO attributes, execution context (ρ_{skill}, ρ_{res}, $slack$), and routing state; (ii) Metric-parameterized guards $G_t(\tau, m_{org}, s_{cbe})$ compute enabling conditions from organizational capability metrics and ecosystem state; (iii) Structure-dependent delays $D_t(\tau, m_{org})$ compute firing latencies (evaluation delay increases with bureaucracy, decreases with agility); (iv) Domain action handlers $A_t(\tau, s_{org}, s_{cbe})$ execute claim acquisition, pre-reservation, partner discovery, coalition validation, VO formation, and execution scheduling.

Each token carries: BO reference (S_{req}, R_{req}, deadline D), claim context, feasibility variables ($\rho_{skill} = \mid S_{org} \cap S_{req} \mid / \mid S_{req}\mid$, $\rho_{res} = R_{avail}/R_{req}$, $slack = D - t_{current} - setupFloor - expectedLead$), routing state (solo/collaboration mode), and outcome fields (termination cause).

4.2 Metric-Parameterized Guards and Time-Dependent Feasibility

A transition $t \in T$ becomes enabled for token τ when:

$$Enabled(t, \tau) = Pre(t, \tau) \wedge G_t\big(\tau, m_{org}, s_{cbe}\big) \tag{2}$$

Guards are computed from token context (BO attributes, feasibility variables), organizational metrics (agility, bureaucracy, cohesiveness, centralization, efficiency), and ecosystem constraints (claim ownership, capacity availability). Timed semantics use structure-dependent delays $\Delta_t = D_t(\tau, m_{org})$. Tokens are routed to Decline if $lack < 0$, where slack incorporates structure-dependent expected lead times, creating traceable rejection reasons tied to structural characteristics.

4.3 Domain Actions and Failure Modes

Transition firings trigger explicit domain operations: (i) *Claim acquisition* via atomic compare-and-set with renewal heartbeats preventing oscillation; (ii) *Feasibility evaluation* computing ρ_{skill}, ρ_{res}, *slack* against structure-dependent thresholds; (iii) *Pre-reservation* verifying capacity before solo execution; (iv) *Partner discovery* using network topology and capability matching with coalition validation ($|S_{coalition}| \geq S_{req}$, $\sum R_{coalition} \geq \alpha \cdot R_{req}$); (v) *VO formation* creating bidirectional links and reserving capacities; (vi) *Completion* releasing resources, closing claims, and recording outcomes (success if $t_{complete} \leq D$).

Traceable failure modes: LOW_MARGIN (evaluation-stage filtering), INSUFFICIENT_RES (coalition resource aggregation failure), NO_PARTNER (partner discovery failure), claim contention, slack infeasibility, and pre-reservation failure. Each logged with contextual variables enabling diagnostic analysis.

4.4 Logging and Traceability

Each semantic firing records token ID, BO ID, organization type, current place, fired transition, guard variables (ρ_{skill}, ρ_{res}, *slack*), delay Δt, claim status, partner set, and termination cause. Aggregated KPI traces, including acceptance rate, collaboration propensity, VO size distribution, success rate, and failure mode distribution, are computed per archetype and time window. These logs provide end-to-end traceability from structural metrics to semantic decisions and operational outcomes.

5 Experimental Setup and Baseline Scenario

The evaluation uses an opportunity-only baseline under normal conditions, in the absence of disruptions, so that differences across organizations arise only from metric-parameterized semantics and runtime contention under a shared opportunity stream. The proposed hybrid simulation model was implemented in AnyLogic [13], which was used as the execution environment for the ecosystem-level ABM and the embedded organization-level opportunity-handling logic.

5.1 Ecosystem Configuration

The CBE includes 14 organizations spanning five Mintzberg-inspired archetypes, initialized with structural capability vectors composed of agility, bureaucracy, cohesiveness, efficiency, centralization, and network closeness, together with skill portfolios and bounded internal capacity. These six capability dimensions are derived from Mintzberg's configurational theory [3] and operationalized so that *Adhocracy* favors agile and flexible handling, *Machine Bureaucracy* slower and stricter decision-making, *Professional Bureaucracy* stronger skill-based coordination, *Divisionalized Form* a balance of local autonomy and efficiency, and *Simple Structure* rapid but resource-constrained responses with relatively high collaboration propensity under capacity limitations. By keeping the HLPN topology identical across archetypes and varying only the capability vectors, the design isolates structural effects from process effects.

BOs arrive via a Poisson process ($\lambda \approx 1.0$/time unit) and specify required skills (S_{req}), resource demand (R_{req}), deadline (D), and an optional closeness requirement. In the reported baseline run used for the present analysis, the simulation spans 9,878 time units and records 102,983 semantic transition firings.

5.2 Coordination Mechanisms and Measures

Semantic execution enforces bounded multi-token concurrency, atomic claim operations through a global allocation registry (including assignment limits and VO-formation consistency), capacity pre-reservation, partner discovery with coalition validation, and duration and success rules based on BO size, organizational efficiency, and deadline feasibility ($t_{complete} \leq D$).

Transition-level run logs record token and BO identifiers, organization type, lifecycle stage, guard variables ($\rho_{skill}, \rho_{res}, slack$), delays, coalition state, and termination causes. KPIs including acceptance, collaboration, success, coalition size, and failure mode distributions are aggregated per archetype, with steady-state analysis over the final 100 time units.

6 Results and Discussion

This section presents experimental findings organized around the three research questions. Results demonstrate that metric-parameterized semantic execution produces clearly differentiated organizational behaviors despite identical HLPN topology, and that explicit failure mode tracking enables precise bottleneck diagnosis.

6.1 Aggregate Performance Across Archetypes (RQ2)

Table 1 presents steady-state performance metrics across all five archetypes. Adhocracy dominates across all metrics, reflecting its overall capability profile, which supports fast evaluation, flexible execution, and large coalition coordination. Machine Bureaucracy underperforms due to lower agility and cohesiveness, producing evaluation friction and stricter feasibility thresholds. Professional Bureaucracy and Divisionalized Form show moderate balanced profiles. Simple Structure exhibits high collaboration propensity despite low acceptance, indicating a stronger tendency toward partnership under capacity constraints.

RQ2 confirmation: Archetypes exhibit clearly differentiated behaviors under identical HLPN topology through metric-dependent guards, delays, and routing, validating that shared HLPN generates structural heterogeneity through parameterized execution semantics.

Table 1. Steady-state opportunity-handling performance by archetype.

Archetype	Accept Rate	Success Rate	Collaboration Rate	Coalition Size
Adhocracy	0.698	0.788	0.748	4.78
Machine Bureaucracy	0.319	0.346	0.573	3.21
Professional Bureaucracy	0.497	0.563	0.634	3.53
Divisionalized Form	0.478	0.543	0.607	3.61
Simple Structure	0.333	0.408	0.746	3.48

6.2 Failure Mode Analysis (RQ3)

Table 2 summarizes dominant failure modes by archetype. *Adhocracy*'s primary bottleneck is resource aggregation in collaboration (1,246 INSUFFICIENT_RES), reflecting aggressive opportunity-seeking that pushes opportunities into collaboration where combined resources become limiting. *Machine Bureaucracy* shows evaluation-stage filtering dominance (2,579 LOW_MARGIN), confirming strict thresholds as the primary constraint. *Simple Structure* exhibits dual bottlenecks (3,462 threshold failures +889 resource failures), reflecting collaboration-intensive strategy under tight capacity.

RQ3 addressed: Rule-based semantic execution externalizes decision gates, enabling mechanism-level bottleneck diagnosis with traceable reasons tied to guard evaluations and validation failures.

Table 2. Dominant failure modes by archetype.

Archetype	Primary Failure	Secondary
Adhocracy	INSUFFICIENT_RES (1,246)	LOW_MARGIN (470)
Machine Bureaucracy	LOW_MARGIN (2,579)	NO_PARTNER (199)
Professional Bureaucracy	LOW_MARGIN (1,308)	INSUFFICIENT_RES (272)
Divisionalized Form	LOW_MARGIN (1,329)	INSUFFICIENT_RES (209)
Simple Structure	LOW_MARGIN (3,462)	INSUFFICIENT_RES (889)

6.3 Multi-Token Concurrency and Architectural Validation (RQ1)

The framework successfully managed 102,983 semantic firings across 14 organizations handling 9,879 opportunities over 9,878 time units. Multiple organizations simultaneously attempted claim acquisition while individual organizations processed concurrent threads, and coalition formation involved multi-party atomic validation with no deadlocks or inconsistent states. Success rates of 0.993–0.997 (completed/started) indicate accurate slack computation and effective pre-reservation preventing overcommitment.

RQ1 validation: Rule-based semantic execution of a multi-token high-level Petri net successfully embedded within ABM represents the complete BO lifecycle (selection, claiming, evaluation, solo/collaborative execution, termination). Evidence includes: (i) all six stages executed with traceable firings; (ii) domain semantics operationalized as transition-firing side effects; (iii) multi-token concurrency without inconsistency; (iv) time-dependent feasibility via slack checks; (v) resource contention via pre-reservation gates; (vi) coalition semantics with explicit failure reasons; (vii) 102,983 logged events enabling diagnostic analysis. The HLPN serves as an executable coordination layer bridging ecosystem ABM and organization process semantics, providing formal precision together with explicit rule-based expressiveness.

These results also have architectural significance. In this framework, the HLPN acts as a coordination layer between ecosystem-level ABM, which captures emergence and stochastic interaction among heterogeneous organizations [4, 5], and organization-level process semantics, where the shared HLPN provides formal precision, concurrency handling, and traceable guard evaluations. Because all organizations execute the same HLPN topology, observed differences in acceptance, collaboration, and failure patterns can be attributed more directly to capability metric vectors rather than to different process structures. The framework therefore shows that embedding a shared HLPN execution layer within ABM improves both analytical rigor and practical interpretability.

7 Conclusion and Future Work

This paper presented a hybrid simulation framework for opportunity-driven decision-making in collaborative business ecosystems by integrating ABM with the rule-based semantic execution of a multi-token high-level Petri net. The framework bridges ecosystem-level interaction and organization-level decision semantics, enabling concurrent handling of BOs while preserving traceability of claims, feasibility checks, collaboration routing, coalition formation, and execution outcomes. The results show that a shared Petri-net topology, parameterized by organizational capability metrics, generates clearly differentiated behaviors across Mintzberg-inspired archetypes without requiring type-specific branching logic.

A second contribution is the explicit parameterization of guards, thresholds, delays, and routing decisions, which makes it possible to diagnose not only what happened but why. The generated logs expose mechanism-level bottlenecks such as evaluation-stage filtering, insufficient resources, and partner unavailability, and support simulation-based design and stress-testing of coordination mechanisms before platform deployment. In practical settings, the model can be calibrated with organizational skill matrices, workload data, response-time assumptions, and collaboration-network data.

The present study remains a controlled baseline: it focuses on opportunity-only dynamics, assumes fixed capability metrics, considers a prototype-scale setting, and does not yet incorporate disruptions, learning, trust evolution, strategic behavior, or empirical calibration to a specific domain. Future work will extend the model toward disruption-aware dynamics, adaptive policies, longer-term capability evolution, strategic interaction, larger-scale validation, and domain-specific instantiations.

Acknowledgments. This work had partial support of the Portuguese Agency FCT, in the framework of the research unit CTS - Centro de Tecnologia e Sistemas/UNINOVA/FCT/NOVA, with reference UID/0066/2025.

References

1. Moore, J.F.: Predators and prey: a new ecology of competition. Harv. Bus. Rev. **71**(3), 75–86 (1993)
2. Camarinha-Matos, L.M., Afsarmanesh, H.: Collaborative networks: a new scientific discipline. J. Intell. Manuf. **16**, 439–452 (2005). https://doi.org/10.1007/s10845-005-1656-3
3. Mintzberg, H.: Structure in Fives: Designing Effective Organizations. Prentice Hall, Upper Saddle River (1992)
4. Gómez-Cruz, N.A., Loaiza Saa, I., Ortega Hurtado, F.F.: Agent-based simulation in management and organizational studies: a survey. Eur. J. Manag. Bus. Econ. **26**(3), 313–328 (2017). https://doi.org/10.1108/EJMBE-10-2017-018
5. de Amorim Silva, R., Braga, R.T.V.: Simulating systems-of-systems with agent-based modeling: a systematic literature review. IEEE Syst. J. **14**(3), 3609–3617 (2020)
6. Buchs, D., Klikovits, S., Linard, A.: Petri nets: a formal language to specify and verify concurrent non-deterministic event systems. In: Carreira, P., Amaral, V., Vangheluwe, H. (eds.) Foundations of Multi-Paradigm Modelling for Cyber-Physical Systems, pp. 177–208. Springer, Cham (2020). https://doi.org/10.1007/978-3-030-43946-0_7
7. Guerreiro, R., Barros, J.P., Gomes, L.: High-level petri nets for modeling cyber-physical multi-agent systems. In: Camarinha-Matos, L.M., Ferrada, F. (eds.) DoCEIS 2025. AICT, vol. 759, pp. 250–260. Springer, Cham (2025). https://doi.org/10.1007/978-3-031-97051-1_18
8. Ramezani, J., Camarinha-Matos, L.M.: A collaborative approach to resilient and Antifragile business ecosystems. Proc. Comput. Sci. **162**, 604–613 (2019). https://doi.org/10.1016/j.procs.2019.12.029
9. Ramezani, J., Gomes, L., Graça, P.: Crisis response modes in collaborative business ecosystems: a mathematical framework from plasticity to antifragility. Mathematics. **13**(15), 2421 (2025). https://doi.org/10.3390/math13152421
10. Graça, P., Camarinha-Matos, L.M.: Evolution of a collaborative business ecosystem in response to performance indicators. In: Camarinha-Matos, L.M., Afsarmanesh, H., Fornasiero, R. (eds.) PRO-VE 2017. AICT, vol. 506, pp. 629–640. Springer, Cham (2017). https://doi.org/10.1007/978-3-319-65151-4_55
11. Camarinha-Matos, L.M., Fornasiero, R., Ramezani, J., Ferrada, F.: Collaborative networks: a pillar of digital transformation. Appl. Sci. **9**(24), 5431 (2019). https://doi.org/10.3390/app9245431
12. Ramezani, J., Camarinha-Matos, L.M.: Approaches for resilience and antifragility in collaborative business ecosystems. Technol. Forecast. Soc. Change. **151**, 119846 (2020). https://doi.org/10.1016/j.techfore.2019.119846
13. Borshchev, A.: The Big Book of Simulation Modeling: Multimethod Modeling with AnyLogic 6. AnyLogic North America, Lisle (2013)
14. van der Aalst, W.M.P.: The application of petri nets to workflow management. J. Circuits Syst. Comput. **8**(1), 21–66 (1998). https://doi.org/10.1142/S0218126698000043
15. Jensen, K.: Coloured Petri Nets: Basic Concepts, Analysis Methods and Practical Use, vol. 1. Springer, Berlin, Heidelberg (1996). https://doi.org/10.1007/978-3-662-03241-1

Support IOPT-Tools Interoperability Through Import and Export PNML-Compliant Format

Diogo Nuno Natário[1,2(✉)], Anikó Costa[1,2,3], and Luis Gomes[1,2,3]

[1] School of Science and Technology, NOVA University Lisbon, Lisbon, Portugal
d.natario@campus.fct.unl.pt, {akc,lugo}@fct.unl.pt
[2] Center of Technology and Systems, UNINOVA, Caparica, Portugal
[3] Intelligent Systems Associate LAboratory (LASI), Porto, Portugal

Abstract. IOPT-Tools is a web-based development environment for designing discrete-event controllers as part of embedded and cyber-physical systems, based on the IOPT-Nets class of Petri nets. Currently, the tool relies on a proprietary format for storing and reading model files, which limits interoperability with other Petri net–based tools. To overcome this limitation, this paper presents import and export mechanisms that enable the conversion of models between the native IOPT format and the Petri Net Markup Language (PNML) standard. These mechanisms facilitate model sharing and reuse across heterogeneous tools while preserving structural and semantic properties, as well as tool-specific characteristics. By supporting PNML-based interoperability, the proposed approach promotes collaboration among diverse tools and contributes to a more integrated and efficient development ecosystem.

Keywords: Petri Nets · Place-Transition Nets · IOPT-Nets · IOPT-Tools · PNML · Discrete-event Systems · Controller Systems

1 Introduction

The increasing complexity and scale of modern digital systems have led to a growing demand for techniques that facilitate and accelerate their development [1]. In this context, graphical modeling languages play a crucial role in supporting system design and analysis [2]. Among these approaches, Petri nets have proven particularly effective for modeling digital systems.

Originally developed by Carl Adam Petri to describe chemical processes, Petri nets have since been widely adopted for the modeling and development of complex digital systems [3]. Their expressive power has motivated the creation of numerous tools that employ Petri nets as both modeling and execution languages, enabling the design, simulation, and analysis of system behavior in applications such as embedded systems and discrete controllers [4]. Innovation in these tools is essential for tackling societal challenges, as it supports the development of increasingly complex systems required for their resolution.

Published by Springer Nature Switzerland AG 2027
L. M. Camarinha-Matos and F. Ferrada (Eds.): DoCEIS 2026, IFIP AICT 790, pp. 386–397, 2027.
https://doi.org/10.1007/978-3-032-28939-1_27

To enable the exchange and sharing of models between tools that use Petri nets as modeling and execution languages, the Petri Net Markup Language (PNML) standard was created [5]. PNML defines an XML-based syntax for tools to use to store, interpret, and exchange Petri net models in a standardized and interoperable manner [6].

IOPT-Tools is a tool used in academic and research environments. It is a free, web-based platform that adopts the IOPT-Nets class of Petri nets as its modeling language and supports the complete digital system development process. This process includes modeling, simulation, property verification, state space generation, and the automatic generation of C and VHDL code for implementation on software and hardware platforms, respectively [7]. Consequently, IOPT-Tools enables rapid prototyping and efficient validation of models during the testing phase.

Over the years, IOPT-Tools and the IOPT-Nets class have been developed and extended through projects, MSc and PhD theses, and scientific publications. However, these contributions did not consider compatibility with the PNML standard. As a result, IOPT-Tools users encounter difficulties when exchanging models with other PNML-compliant tools, limiting interoperability and hindering collaboration with external entities.

Based on these challenges, the following Research Question was formulated: How can interoperability be achieved between the standard PNML format and the proprietary IOPT-Tools format to enable wider adoption and sharing of IOPT-Tools' developments, innovations, and unique features?

To address this question, the following Research Hypothesis was proposed: Developing robust import and export mechanisms that convert models from the standard PNML format to the IOPT-Tools format and vice versa will achieve interoperability between the two formats, enabling accurate preservation of model semantics, supporting IOPT-Tools' unique features, and facilitating broader adoption and sharing of its developments and innovations.

In this context, this paper presents the PNML import and export mechanisms developed in this work. These mechanisms enable seamless model exchange between IOPT-Tools and other PNML-compliant tools, supporting interoperability across heterogeneous modeling environments and fostering collaboration in the development of digital system modeling tools better suited to address societal challenges.

The remainder of this paper is organized as follows. Section 2 relates this work to contributions tackling societal challenges. Section 3 introduces the IOPT-Nets class of Petri nets and the associated IOPT-Tools development environment. Section 4 briefly introduces the PNML standard format. Section 5 describes the proprietary format used by IOPT-Tools and the import and export mechanisms developed in this work. Finally, Sect. 6 concludes the paper and outlines directions for future work.

2 Contribution to Technological Innovation to Tackle Societal Challenges

The increasing complexity of digital systems has become a significant societal challenge in recent decades. As these systems grow in scale, interconnectivity, and functionality, their design and validation demand more sophisticated modeling approaches.

Engineers and researchers often struggle to accurately represent system behavior, verify correctness, and ensure reliability, particularly in safety-critical or highly distributed environments. This difficulty in modeling complex digital systems not only slows down innovation but also increases the risk of design flaws, inefficiencies, and unforeseen failures.

To address this challenge, advanced modeling tools have been developed to support the design and analysis of digital systems. Among these is IOPT-Tools, a research-oriented framework under active development. It aims to simplify and accelerate the development process by providing formal modeling techniques, verification capabilities, and automated generation of execution code ready for implementation. IOPT-Tools enables developers to better understand system behavior, detect inconsistencies early, and improve overall design quality. In this way, the tool directly contributes to tackling the broader societal issue of managing complexity in digital system development.

Despite its potential and ongoing advancements, IOPT-Tools faces a significant limitation that hinders its wider adoption and impact: the lack of compatibility with the PNML (Petri Net Markup Language) format. PNML is a widely recognized standard for representing Petri nets, facilitating interoperability between tools and promoting collaboration across the research and engineering communities. Without support for this format, IOPT-Tools remains relatively isolated, making it difficult to share models, integrate with other platforms, or benefit from existing ecosystems of tools and resources. As a result, its innovative features and advantages are not as accessible to the broader community as they could be.

This work aims to address this limitation by exploring ways to make IOPT-Tools compatible with the PNML format. By enabling interoperability, the tool can extend its reach beyond its current boundaries, allowing users to exchange models seamlessly and leverage complementary technologies. More importantly, this compatibility would facilitate the dissemination of the tool's unique properties and ongoing developments, fostering collaboration and accelerating progress in the field.

Ultimately, achieving PNML compatibility represents a crucial step toward amplifying the impact of IOPT-Tools. By integrating it into a broader ecosystem, this effort contributes to reducing the barriers associated with modeling complex digital systems. In doing so, it supports the overarching societal goal of making system design more accessible, reliable, and efficient, thereby helping to mitigate one of the key challenges of modern digital engineering.

3 State of the Art

3.1 Place-Transition Class of Petri Nets

The most common class of Petri nets, known as Place–Transition (P/T) nets, is widely used across a variety of domains and applications due to its expressive power in modeling and specifying system behavior [8]. However, as all autonomous Petri net classes, this class supports abstract system's modeling but lacks modeling explicit dependencies of the external environment.

As a result, P/T nets are inadequate for the development of embedded systems, such as discrete-event controllers, that must interact with non-autonomous elements by processing external information (e.g., sensor inputs) and producing external outputs (e.g., actuator commands) [7]. Limitations like these motivated the development of several extensions to the original P/T formalism, including Synchronized Petri Nets [9], Signal Interpreted Petri Nets [10], and Input–Output Place–Transition Nets (IOPT-Nets), among others.

3.2 Input-Output Place-Transition Nets Class

The IOPT-Nets class extends the traditional P/T formalism with non-autonomous features that enable interaction with the external environment. Such interaction is supported through input signals, input events (which are used to analyze input signals and trigger upon the detection of specific conditions [11] [12]) and output signals and output events (which, when triggered, induce changes in output signal behavior).

In IOPT-Nets, a transition may fire only if it satisfies two distinct conditions. First, it must be Enabled from an autonomous perspective, meaning that all input places should contain the required number of tokens as specified by the connecting arcs. Second, it must be Ready from a non-autonomous perspective, which requires that external conditions, such as guards and input events, are satisfied. Furthermore, when transitions fire and tokens are produced, they may influence output signals and output events [13].

The IOPT-Nets formalism also enriches the core Petri net elements (places, transitions, and arcs) with additional attributes:

- Places may be assigned with a bound to inform code generators of the required size of auxiliary variables; time domain and channel type, which are useful for modeling globally asynchronous locally synchronous (GALS) systems; comments; and signal output actions to enforce specific behaviors on output signals.
- Transitions may be assigned priorities to ensure deterministic behavior in the presence of conflicts; Guards and input events to constrain their firing; and output events that are triggered upon firing. As with places, transitions may be associated with time domain, comments, and signal output actions.
- Arcs may be defined with a type (normal, test, or channel).

IOPT-Nets operate in discrete time steps, each associated with a tick that represents the temporal progression of the system. The formalism adopts maximal step semantics, whereby, at each tick, all transitions that are both Enabled and Ready fire simultaneously. This execution model ensures deterministic behavior, thereby providing the predictability required for reliable system development.

3.3 IOPT-Tools Development Environment

IOPT-Tools is a research and academic platform that is freely accessible through a web browser (http://gres.uninova.pt/IOPT-Tools) and does not require any software installation.

Developed with the IOPT-Nets class of Petri nets, IOPT-Tools supports the complete development cycle of digital systems, such as discrete-event controllers and embedded systems [14], by offering a comprehensive set of integrated tools. The model editor provides a graphical interface that allows users to create models by adding places, transitions, arcs, signals, and input and output events, which can be freely positioned on a Cartesian plane. The simulator enables the evaluation of model behavior through token-based simulation, also providing timing diagrams. The state space generator supports formal analysis by identifying key model properties, including reachability, deadlocks, and boundedness. Additionally, the query tool allows for the formal verification of user-defined properties.

IOPT-Tools also includes automatic code generators capable of producing executable C and VHDL code from the developed models, making them ready for deployment on software or hardware platforms.

The platform enables fully graphical model development, encompassing not only the addition and interconnection of Petri net elements but also the visual design and refinement of the model to enhance readability. This capability is supported by a graphical interface based on Scalable Vector Graphics (SVG) [15], which allows flexible and precise control over the visual representation of models.

4 Petri Net Markup Language Standard Format

The ISO/IEC JTC 1/SC 7 (International Organization for Standardization / International Electrotechnical Commission—Joint Technical Committee on Information Technology, Subcommittee on Software and Systems Engineering) developed the ISO/IEC 15909 standard, which defines the Petri Net Markup Language (PNML). This standard consists of three parts: Part 1: Concepts, definitions and graphical notation [16], Part 2: Transfer format [6], and Part 3: Extensions and structuring mechanisms [17].

Part 2, which is the focus of this work, specifies the XML-based syntax for storing and exchanging Petri net models. It defines the PNML Core Model, which establishes the fundamental XML structure that all conforming tools must follow, independently of the employed class of Petri nets, whether low-level or high-level. The Core Model defines the principal structural elements of PNML, including nets, pages, places, transitions, arcs, graphical nodes, identifiers, textual annotations, references, and related constructs.

In addition to the Core Model, the PNML Transfer Format defines the Place/Transition extension, intended for tools supporting the original Place/Transition Petri net class or classes derived from it, such as IOPT-Nets. This extension specifies additional constructs, including place initial markings and arc weights or inscriptions. The Transfer Format also provides extensions for high-level Petri net classes. In the context of this work, only the PNML Core Model and the Place/Transition extension were considered, enabling IOPT-Tools to import and export models conforming to the low-level Place/Transition Petri net class.

5 IOPT-Tools Internal Format and Import and Export Mechanics

5.1 Comparison Between the PNML and IOPT Formats

IOPT-Tools employs an internal representation for storing files commonly referred to as the IOPT format. This format was originally derived from the standard PNML format. However, as the development and extension of IOPT-Nets progressed, and as IOPT-Tools evolved to support these extensions, the internal format gradually diverged from

PNML. This work identifies the main differences between the PNML and IOPT formats. However, due to space limitations, not all differences are presented.

The identified differences are divided in three sections: the XML file initialization, the definition of the net element, and the representation of Petri net elements.

Regarding file initialization, the development of IOPT-Tools originally inherited from the Snoopy tool [18], which required local installation on the user's machine. This approach was later replaced by a web-based solution, removing this requirement and improving usability. Nevertheless, the file initialization still includes the Snoopy element, which is not part of the PNML specification.

In the PNML format, the *pnml* element must be the root element of the file and must include a namespace attribute indicating that the file conforms to the PNML Transfer Format. Since the IOPT format is not PNML-compliant, this namespace attribute is not included.

Regarding the definition of nets, the PNML specification requires all nets to be defined directly within the *pnml* element. Although this structure is used, IOPT-Tools currently supports only a single net per file, as the presence of more than one net causes the tool to fail. Figure 1 shows a comparison of an IOPT-Net in the original IOPT format and converted to the PNML format.

```
<net id="1" name="Petri_Net" type="IOPT">
  <input>...</input>
  <output>...</output>
  <variable>...</variable>
  <place id="2">...</place>
  <transition id="3">...</transition>
  <arc id="4" source="2" target="3">...</arc>
</net>
```

IOPT

```
<net id="n1" type="http://www.pnml.org/version-2009/grammar/ptnet">
  <name>
    <text>Petri_Net</text>
  </name>
  <page id="ioptPage">
    <toolspecific tool="iopt-tools" version="1.3">
      <input>...</input>
      <output>...</output>
      <variable>...</variable>
    </toolspecific>
    <place id="p2">...</place>
    <transition id="t6">...</transition>
    <arc id="a10" source="p2" target="t6">...</arc>
  </page>
</net>
```

PNML

Fig. 1. Comparison of the contents of the same net in IOPT format (left) and PNML format (right).

The PNML format also mandates the use of pages within each net to contain Petri net elements. IOPT-Tools does not support pages, and consequently all Petri net elements are placed directly within the *net* element. Furthermore, elements representing non-autonomous features specific to the IOPT-Nets class (such as signals, events, and variables) are also stored directly within the *net* element. These are represented using elements such as *input* and *output* for signals and events, and *variable* for variable declarations.

To achieve PNML compliance, these IOPT-specific elements should be encapsulated within a *toolspecific* element, with the tool attribute identifying IOPT-Tools and the version attribute indicating the current version, as shown in Fig. 1.

Additionally, the net name is stored as an attribute of the net element, which is not compliant with the PNML specification. An extra attribute specifying the net type as IOPT is also present, which has no equivalent in PNML.

Regarding Petri net elements (namely places, transitions, and arcs) their properties are represented as direct child elements. For instance, for a place, IOPT-Tools stores the properties *name*, *initialMarking*, *graphics*, *comment*, *bound*, *timedomain*, and *signalOutputActions* as children of the place element, as can be seen in Fig. 2.

```
<place id="2">
   <name>...</name>
   <initialMarking>...</initialMarking>
   <graphics>...</graphics>
   <comment>...</comment>
   <bound>...</bound>
   <timedomain>...</timedomain>
   <signalOutputActions>...</signalOutputActions>
</place>
```

IOPT

```
<place id="p2">
   <name>...</name>
   <initialMarking>...</initialMarking>
   <graphics>...</graphics>
   <toolspecific tool="iopt-tools" version="1.3">
      <comment>...</comment>
      <bound>...</bound>
      <timedomain>...</timedomain>
      <signalOutputActions>...</signalOutputActions>
   </toolspecific>
</place>
```

PNML

Fig. 2. Comparison of the contents of the same place in IOPT format (left) and PNML format (right).

However, the PNML specification for low-level Petri nets permits only *name*, *initialMarking*, and *graphics* to appear as direct children. To ensure compliance with the PNML Transfer Format, all additional properties specific to IOPT-Nets and IOPT-Tools should be encapsulated within a *toolspecific* element associated with IOPT-Tools and nested within the corresponding Petri net element, as shown on the right side of Fig. 2.

The same principle applies to transitions and arcs, for which PNML defines only *name* and *graphics* (and *inscription* for arcs), with all remaining features required to be stored within a tool-specific extension. An example of a transition is presented in Fig. 3, and an example of an arc is shown in Fig. 4. Important to mention that the graphics element of IOPT-Tools for arcs does not comply with the PNML format, so this element is stored inside the *toolspecific* element when converting to the PNML format.

```
<transition id="3">
  <name>...</name>
  <graphics>...</graphics>
  <comment>...</comment>
  <priority>...</priority>
  <signalInputGuards>...</signalInputGuards>
  <inputEvents>...</inputEvents>
  <outputEvents>...</outputEvents>
  <timedomain>...</timedomain>
  <signalOutputActions>...</signalOutputActions>
</transition>
```

IOPT

```
<transition id="t6">
  <name>...</name>
  <graphics>...</graphics>
  <toolspecific tool="iopt-tools" version="1.3">
    <comment>...</comment>
    <priority>...</priority>
    <signalInputGuards>...</signalInputGuards>
    <inputEvents>...</inputEvents>
    <outputEvents>...</outputEvents>
    <timedomain>...</timedomain>
    <signalOutputActions>...</signalOutputActions>
  </toolspecific>
</transition>
```

PNML

Fig. 3. Comparison of the contents of the same transition in IOPT format (left) and PNML format (right).

```
<arc id="4" source="2" target="3">
  <type>...</type>
  <graphics>...</graphics>
  <inscription>...</inscription>
</arc>
```

IOPT

```
<arc id="a10" source="p2" target="t6">
  <inscription>...</inscription>
  <toolspecific tool="iopt-tools" version="1.3">
    <type>...</type>
    <graphics>...</graphics>
  </toolspecific>
</arc>
```

PNML

Fig. 4. Comparison of the contents of the same arc in IOPT format (left) and PNML format (right).

5.2 Import and Export Mechanics

IOPT-Tools only supports files strictly in its native IOPT format. Uploaded files were loaded without any conversion, meaning that files in other formats would result in errors. Likewise, the only available download option was to export the model exactly as stored internally, exclusively in the IOPT format.

The objective of this work is to extend IOPT-Tools with support for the PNML Transfer Format, enabling interoperability with other Petri net–based modeling tools. To achieve this, import and export mechanisms were developed to allow IOPT-Tools to load, interpret, convert, and generate PNML files.

For file uploads, the import mechanism first identifies the format of the uploaded file. If the file is already in IOPT format, it is loaded directly without modification. If the file is in PNML format, it is first converted into the IOPT format and only then loaded into IOPT-Tools. This approach allows IOPT-Tools to manipulate models created in other Petri net tools, provided they use the PNML standard.

For downloads, a new export option was added that converts the current model into PNML format before downloading it to the user's device. The original download option remains available and continues to export the model exactly as stored in the IOPT format. Additionally, an export option was also added to convert the IOPT model into a

P/T model in the PNML format, without any tool-specific information. Figure 5 presents the approach used.

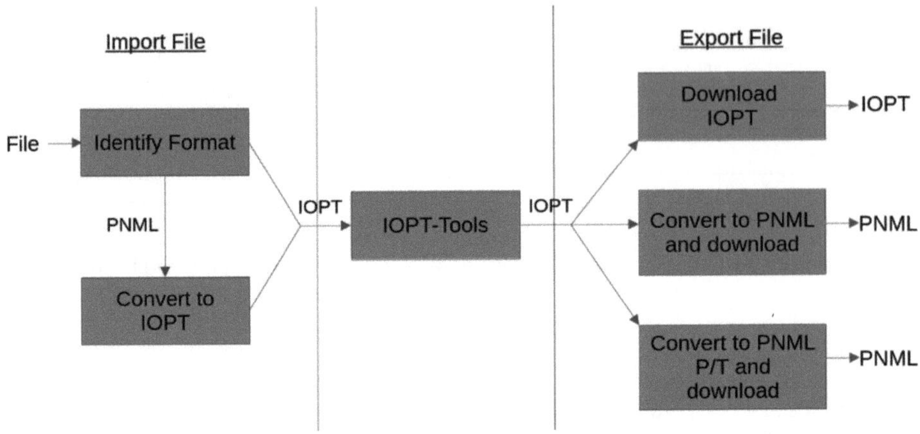

Fig. 5. Import and export file structure developed.

Both the import and export mechanisms were designed to preserve all information from the original model during conversion. During import, properties not directly used by IOPT-Tools (such as pages and elements specific to other tools) are retained. However, because IOPT-Tools does not (currently) support pages, Petri net elements (places, transitions, and arcs) are removed from their pages and placed directly within the net. To enable correct restoration during export, graphical elements are created with an attribute storing the identifier of their original page.

Additionally, because IOPT-Tools does not rely on its own <toolspecific> element to read tool-exclusive properties, the child elements of <toolspecific> nodes marked with the *iopt-tools* attribute are removed from those nodes and placed in their parent element, allowing them to be correctly interpreted by IOPT-Tools.

During export, the IOPT model is converted into PNML format. Petri net elements are restored to their original pages, and the page reference attributes added during import are removed. Any non-standard properties associated with the net, pages, or individual elements are treated as IOPT-Tools–specific and stored within a <toolspecific> element that explicitly references IOPT-Tools.

To validate the performance and correctness of the developed import and export mechanisms, models from the Model Checking Contest [19] were used. In particular, complex models based on the Place/Transition Petri net formalism are especially suitable for evaluating the performance of the developed mechanisms. These models were used to verify that the import mechanism functions as intended, converting models from the initial PNML format into the correct IOPT format with syntax fully compatible with IOPT-Tools.

To evaluate the export mechanisms, the imported models (as well as additional models created directly within IOPT-Tools) were modified to include IOPT-Tools specific properties. This allowed confirmation that the export mechanism accurately converts models from the IOPT format back into standard PNML syntax, ensuring full compliance with the specification. Due to space limitations, the listing of the files produced by the import and export mechanics was not included in this work.

With the introduction of PNML support, users can now upload models in either IOPT or PNML format and download them in both formats directly from the main menu, significantly broadening compatibility with external tools that rely on the PNML standard. These developments also enable the use of external models for systematic testing and stress evaluation, supporting further tool development and research. These mechanisms are currently available in a temporary version of IOPT-Tools and are expected to be integrated into the main version in the near future.

6 Conclusions and Future Work

Although IOPT-Tools uses a similar internal format, it is not currently fully compliant with the PNML Transfer Format. This limitation hinders the exchange of models with tools that adhere to the standard and may discourage collaboration among users of different tools, potentially obstructing innovation in the development of Petri net tools.

To address these limitations, and as a clear response to the initial Research Question, import and export mechanisms were developed as part of this work. These tools enable seamless model exchange by allowing PNML files (whether created manually or generated by other tools) to be imported into the IOPT-Tools internal format. Similarly, models created or modified in IOPT-Tools can be exported to the standard PNML format, ensuring compatibility with tools that support the standard. Through the validation process, it was verified that the proposed mechanics achieve the intended functionality, supporting the initial hypothesis.

Addressing the lack of interoperability between IOPT-Tools and the PNML standard represents a meaningful step toward enhancing the tool's relevance and impact within the broader research and engineering community. By enabling compatibility with a widely adopted format, this work not only facilitates model exchange and collaboration but also allows the advanced capabilities of IOPT-Tools to be more effectively leveraged beyond its original scope. This contribution supports the broader societal goal of reducing the complexity associated with modeling digital systems, promoting more accessible, efficient, and reliable design processes. Ultimately, bridging this gap strengthens the potential of IOPT-Tools as a valuable instrument in tackling the ongoing challenges posed by increasingly complex digital infrastructures.

To improve compatibility with the PNML standard, minimize potential issues arising from model import and export, and ensure greater compliance, future work should focus on adding native support for pages in IOPT-Tools. This enhancement would enable the generation of fully compliant PNML files, simplify import and export mechanisms, and allow users to create more organized and structured models by decomposing complex systems into pages.

Acknowledgements. This work was financed by the Portuguese Agency FCT - Fundação para a Ciência e Tecnologia, in the framework of the research unit CTS - Centro de Tecnologia e Sistemas/UNINOVA/FCT/NOVA, with reference UID/0066/2025, and through the PhD scholarship with the reference 2024.05386.BD.

References

1. Bazydło, G.: Designing reconfigurable cyber-physical systems using unified modeling language. Energies. **16**(3), 1273 (2023). https://doi.org/10.3390/en16031273
2. Elwert, M., Ramsaier, M., Eisenbart, B., Stetter, R., Till, M., Rudolph, S.: Digital function modeling in graph-based design languages. Appl. Sci. **12**(11), 5301 (2022). https://doi.org/10.3390/app12115301
3. Girault, C., Valk, R.: Petri Nets for System Engineering: a Guide to Modeling, Verification, and Applications. Springer, Berlin, Heidelberg (2003). https://doi.org/10.1007/978-3-662-05324-9
4. Kumbhar, V., Chavan, M.: A review of petri net tools and recommendations. In: Proceedings of the International Conference on Applications of Machine Intelligence and Data Analytics (ICAMIDA 2022), pp. 710–721. Atlantis Press, Dordrecht (2023). https://doi.org/10.2991/978-94-6463-136-4_61
5. Billington, J., et al.: The petri net markup language: concepts, technology, and tools. In: van der Aalst, W.M.P., Best, E. (eds.) Applications and Theory of Petri Nets 2003. LNCS, vol. 2679, pp. 483–505. Springer, Berlin, Heidelberg (2003). https://doi.org/10.1007/3-540-44919-1_31
6. ISO/IEC: Systems and software engineering—high-level Petri nets—part 2: transfer format. ISO/IEC 15909-2, Geneva (2011)
7. Pereira, F., Moutinho, F., Costa, A., Barros, J.-P., Campos-Rebelo, R., Gomes, L.: IOPT-tools – from executable models to automatic code generation for embedded controllers development. In: Bernardinello, L., Petrucci, L. (eds.) Application and Theory of Petri Nets and Concurrency. Lecture Notes in Computer Science, vol. 13288, pp. 127–138. Springer, Cham (2022). https://doi.org/10.1007/978-3-031-06653-5_7
8. Peterson, J.L.: Petri nets. ACM Comput. Surv. **9**(3), 223–252 (1977). https://doi.org/10.1145/356698.356702
9. Moalla, M., Pulou, J., Sifakis, J.: Synchronized petri nets: a model for the description of non-autonomous systems. In: Winkowski, J. (ed.) Mathematical Foundations of Computer Science 1978, Lecture Notes in Computer Science, vol. 64, pp. 374–384. Springer, Berlin, Heidelberg (1978). https://doi.org/10.1007/3-540-08921-7_85
10. Frey, G., Minas, M.: Editing, visualizing, and implementing signal interpreted Petri nets. In: Proceedings of AWPN, vol. 2000, pp. 57–62
11. Natário, D., Gomes, L.: Specification of complex events and their integration in the IOPT-tools development environment. In: 2024 8th International Young Engineers Forum on Electrical and Computer Engineering (YEF-ECE), pp. 70–75 (2024). https://doi.org/10.1109/YEF-ECE62614.2024.10625383
12. Gomes, L., Natário, D., Costa, A., Barros, J.-P., Campos-Rebelo, R.: Event-based modeling of input signal behaviors for discrete-event controllers. Appl. Sci. **14**(12), 5289 (2024). https://doi.org/10.3390/app14125289
13. Gomes, L., Barros, J.P.: Refining IOPT petri nets class for embedded system controller modeling. In: IECON 2018 – 44th Annual Conference of the IEEE Industrial Electronics Society, pp. 4720–4725 (2018). https://doi.org/10.1109/IECON.2018.8592921
14. Gomes, L., Barros, J.P., Costa, A., Nunes, R.: The input-output place-transition petri net class and associated tools. In: 2007 5th IEEE International Conference on Industrial Informatics, pp. 509–514 (2007). https://doi.org/10.1109/INDIN.2007.4384809
15. Mozilla Developer Network: SVG: Scalable vector graphics (2025). https://developer.mozilla.org/en-US/docs/Web/SVG. Accessed 10 Feb 2026
16. ISO/IEC: Systems and software engineering—high-level Petri nets—part 1: concepts, definitions and graphical notation. ISO/IEC 15909-1, Geneva (2004)

17. ISO/IEC: Systems and software engineering—high-level Petri nets—part 3: extensions and structuring mechanisms. ISO/IEC 15909-3, Geneva (2019)
18. Heiner, M., Herajy, M., Liu, F., Rohr, C., Schwarick, M.: Snoopy—a unifying petri net tool. In: Haddad, S., Pomello, L. (eds.) Application and Theory of Petri Nets 2012 Lecture Notes in Computer Science, vol. 7347, pp. 398–407. Springer, Berlin, Heidelberg (2012). https://doi.org/10.1007/978-3-642-31131-4_22
19. Model Checking Contest: Model Checking Contest (2026) https://mcc.lip6.fr/2026/. Accessed 10 Feb 2026

Transforming Isolated Data Lakes into Federated Dataspaces: A Sovereign Architecture for Precision Medicine

Nuno Nunes[1,2(✉)], Pedro A. Sousa[1,2], Gracinda R.Guerreiro[3], João P. Pimentão[1,2], and Maria Torrente[4]

[1] Department of Electrical Engineering, NOVA School of Science and Technology (NOVA FCT), Universidade Nova de Lisboa, Lisbon, Portugal
nm.nunes@campus.fct.unl.pt, {pas,pim}@fct.unl.pt
[2] Centre of Technology and Systems (UNINOVA-CTS), Lisbon, Portugal
[3] Department of Mathematics and Center of Mathematics and Applications (NOVA Math), Nova School of Science and Technology (NOVA FCT), Universidade Nova de Lisboa, Lisbon, Portugal
grg@fct.unl.pt
[4] Medical Oncology Department Puerta de Hierro-Majadahonda University Hospital, Madrid, Spain
maria.torrente@salud.madrid.org

Abstract. Precision medicine offers a pathway to personalized care, yet its progress is stalled by isolated applications, data silos and strict governance and privacy regulations. Centralized data lakes are frequently proposed solutions but often fail to solve these issues due to inherent data lock-in. To address these limitations, this study establishes a robust architectural pipeline to transform isolated data lakes into federated dataspaces. Using Eclipse Dataspace Components, this paper designs a decentralized ecosystem architected for compliance with IDSA RAM 4.0, Gaia-X and European Health Data Space standards, applied within the European project SHARE [1]. The technical implementation facilitates secure, policy-based contract negotiation, ensuring institutional sovereignty over data while enabling authorized external access. By improving discoverability and compliance, this methodology provides a scalable foundation for collaborative research. This work highlights an architectural shift to facilitate secure data exchange without compromising control, contributing to a more resilient infrastructure to accelerate clinical discoveries and research.

Keywords: Federated Dataspaces · Decentralized Ecosystem · Data Sovereignty · Secure Data Exchange · Precision Medicine

1 Introduction

The promise of precision medicine, tailoring clinical interventions to the unique genetic and phenotypic profile of individual patients, relies heavily on the availability of vast, high-quality, and longitudinal datasets [2]. However, the practical translation of this

Published by Springer Nature Switzerland AG 2027
L. M. Camarinha-Matos and F. Ferrada (Eds.): DoCEIS 2026, IFIP AICT 790, pp. 398–413, 2027.
https://doi.org/10.1007/978-3-032-28939-1_28

promise is frequently obstructed by fragmented data ecosystems. Research institutions and healthcare providers often operate as data islands where valuable information remains trapped in isolated data lakes and silos due to technical heterogeneity and stringent privacy regulations like the General Data Protection Regulation (GDPR) [3, 4].

To address these barriers, in February 2020, the European Commission published "A European Strategy for Data" [5], aiming to foster digital transformation by creating rules that facilitate cross-border data access and utilization. A central pillar of this strategy is the establishment of Common European Data Spaces, with a primary focus on the health sector. This momentum culminated in the 2022 proposal for the European Health Data Space (EHDS), which aims to unleash the potential of health data for both primary use (patient care) and secondary use (research and innovation) [3]. By 2025, the EHDS framework was further solidified through new regulations designed to ensure that data remains under the control of the originating producers while being accessible in a secure, policy-compliant manner [6].

Despite these policy advancements, a technical gap remains between centralized data storage models and the decentralized reality of modern healthcare. Traditional centralized data lakes often lead to data lock-in, failing to provide the sovereign control required by institutions [7]. In response, the International Data Spaces Association (IDSA) has defined the IDS Reference Architecture Model (RAM) 4.0 [8], which structures a trustworthy data ecosystem across five architectural layers: Business, Functional, Information, Process, and System, supported by horizontal aspects such as security and governance [4]. However, current implementations rarely bind identity, policy enforcement, and contract negotiation into a single operational pipeline suitable for regulated clinical environments. While this framework provides conceptual guidance, its concrete operationalization in highly regulated clinical environments remains an open challenge.

This paper addresses this challenge by detailing the design and development of an architectural pipeline engineered to transform static, isolated data lakes into dynamic, federated dataspaces. By leveraging Eclipse Dataspace Components (EDC) [9], the proposed approach implements a decentralized ecosystem aligned with IDSA RAM 4.0 and Gaia-X principles [8, 10]. The architecture is applied and demonstrated within the European project SHARE (SpanisH cAnceR data spacE) [1], facilitating the secure and sovereign sharing of clinical datasets from the EU-funded CLARIFY project [11, 12]. By replacing manual data-sharing agreements with automated, policy-based contract negotiations, the system enables authorized external access to clinical data while ensuring that providing institutions retain full sovereignty, thereby bridging the technical gap between local data storage and cross-border research collaboration, providing a resilient infrastructure to meet the pressing healthcare challenges of modern society [13]. While the SHARE project provides empirical requirements and initial validation, the proposed architectural pipeline is designed as a domain-agnostic reference model for any regulated health data ecosystem.

This work investigates how decentralized data-sharing architectures can support secure and compliant collaboration in precision medicine. The central research question guiding this study is: How can isolated clinical data lakes be transformed into federated, sovereign dataspaces that enable EHDS-compliant data sharing without centralizing data or compromising institutional control?

It is hypothesized that the technical binding of identity management, policy enforcement, and contract negotiation into a single, automated architectural pipeline, based on the IDS Reference Architecture Model, enables trustworthy data exchange while maintaining institutional sovereignty for precision medicine. This approach is expected to reduce administrative friction in clinical research without requiring the physical replication of sensitive datasets.

Addressing this question requires examining several interconnected challenges: (i) First, it is necessary to determine how identity management, policy enforcement, and contract negotiation mechanisms can be technically bound into a single end-to-end workflow that supports automated and trustworthy data exchange; (ii) Second, the research evaluates which architectural patterns are most effective in operationalizing the IDSA Reference Architecture Model (RAM) 4.0 within highly regulated healthcare environments, where legal accountability and auditability are essential; and (iii) Finally, the study critically analyzes the practical trade-offs introduced by decentralized governance and policy-based access control, including their implications for system complexity, negotiation latency, and usability in real-world clinical settings.

Together, these objectives shape the architectural design decisions, implementation strategies, and critical evaluation presented throughout the paper.

2 Creating Dataspaces to Tackle Societal Challenges

Modern healthcare systems face structurally complex challenges, including cross-border research coordination, aging populations, rising oncological incidence, and increasing regulatory scrutiny. Isolated institutional infrastructures and traditional centralized data aggregation models are insufficient to meet these challenges [14], the efficacy of any response is significantly diminished in such contexts compared to the potential of a shared dataspace. While the Big Data paradigm enabled large-scale biomedical analytics, its reliance on custodial data transfer conflicts with contemporary European governance frameworks that emphasize data minimization, accountability, and institutional sovereignty.

The architectural shift from centralized repositories to federated dataspaces represents not merely a technological evolution but a structural redesign of how trust, liability, and control are operationalized. In centralized infrastructures, responsibility for compliance is largely procedural and contract-based, often requiring extensive legal mediation before data exchange [4]. In contrast, the proposed dataspace architecture embeds governance into the runtime itself. Identity verification, credential validation, and policy enforcement are executed programmatically prior to data access, transforming regulatory compliance from an administrative burden into an enforceable technical property.

This transformation has direct societal implications. By automating contract negotiation and binding it to decentralized identity claims, institutions can participate in collaborative research without relinquishing custodial control over sensitive clinical assets. The ability to grant conditional, revocable, and purpose-bound access reduces perceived institutional risk, thereby lowering participation barriers for hospitals and research centers that would otherwise avoid cross-border data sharing due to legal uncertainty.

The SHARE [1] project serves as a real case-study of this technological response to a specific societal challenge: the burden of cancer across Europe. Cancer research depends on the linkage of diverse, multimodal data, ranging from genomic profiles to longitudinal electronic health records, that is currently scattered across hundreds of member-state institutions [1]. By establishing a federated cancer research data hub, the project leverages dataspace technology to homogenize scientific productivity across the EU, ensuring that breakthrough discoveries in prevention and therapy are not delayed by technical or legal fragmentation. This architecture is poised to support the UNCAN project [15, 16], which specifically aims to utilize such federated hubs to identify new research gaps and accelerate the roadmap for precision oncology across Europe.

Importantly, the societal value of this approach does not stem from increased data throughput alone. Instead, it arises from the formalization of sovereignty as an enforceable system capability. By binding governance rules to machine-executable policies and decentralized identity proofs, the architecture redefines trust as a verifiable interaction rather than an assumed relationship. This paradigm enables scalable, cross-institutional collaboration without central custodianship, strengthening Europe's capacity to address complex healthcare challenges through coordinated yet sovereign data ecosystems.

3 Literature Review

The challenge of multi-stakeholder data integration has been extensively explored in the context of the Internet of Things (IoT). Significant contributions from EU-funded initiatives, such as INTER-IoT and ASSIST-IoT, established the foundations for semantic interoperability through layered frameworks and mediators that homogenize heterogeneous platforms [19, 20]. These projects successfully demonstrated how semantic technologies could bridge data silos in industrial and maritime domains. However, while these IoT-centric architectures focus on the Interoperability Plane (ensuring systems can talk to each other), the highly regulated environment of precision medicine requires a primary focus on the Sovereignty Plane. This research builds upon the 'connector' paradigm established in earlier IoT research but shifts the technical burden from semantic mediation to policy-based contract enforcement and decentralized identity verification as mandated by the emerging EHDS framework.

Early biomedical data-sharing infrastructures focused on centralized repositories and national data hubs, enabling large-scale analytics but requiring data replication and long-term custody transfer [21]. These platforms demonstrated scientific value by enabling large-scale, statistically robust biomedical analyses but exposed governance limitations, particularly regarding consent management, accountability, and cross-border data reuse [22]. This collect-and-store approach increasingly conflicts with the stringent data minimization and purpose limitation principles mandated by the GDPR [3, 23]. Furthermore, centralization often results in institutional data silos, where the lack of transparency regarding subsequent data reuse leads to a reluctance among hospitals to contribute high-value clinical assets [24].

Federated data access models were introduced to mitigate these issues by allowing institutions to retain local control while responding to standardized queries

[21]. Although federated approaches reduce data movement, they often assume pre-established trust relationships and provide limited support for dynamic policy negotiation, usage enforcement, or auditability [4, 23]. As a result, compliance remains largely procedural rather than technical [21].

While the concept of Federated Database Systems has existed in academic literature since the mid-1980s [25], early architectures focused primarily on schema integration and distributed query processing. Subsequent evolution into Mediator-based architectures [26] addressed data heterogeneity but assumed a relatively static trust environment. This research extends these classical foundations by introducing a sovereign governance layer required for modern, highly-regulated clinical environments, where the challenge has shifted from simple technical connectivity to the automated enforcement of usage control policies.

From a governance perspective, the focus has shifted toward the concept of Data Sovereignty, defined as the capability of an entity to maintain self-determination over its digital assets [27, 28]. This is particularly relevant in the context of the European Data Governance Act (DGA) [27], which seeks to foster trust by introducing data altruism and neutral data intermediaries. Yet, the literature identifies a persistent implementation gap: while these policy models are conceptually robust, they are rarely integrated into the end-to-end technical pipelines required for the heterogeneous, multimodal data environments of precision medicine [23, 28, 29]. Consequently, the burden of compliance remains procedural and administrative, significantly delaying clinical research cycles [23].

Dataspaces have recently emerged as a decentralized architectural response to these challenges, emphasizing shared governance and sovereign control [4, 25, 26]. Complementary initiatives such as Gaia-X introduce compliance services and federated identity principles to establish trust across autonomous organizations [4]. Despite this conceptual maturity, empirical studies indicate that most dataspace implementations remain experimental, domain-agnostic, or insufficiently validated in regulated healthcare settings [23].

The emergence of Common European Data Spaces and the EHDS represents a decentralized architectural response to these gaps. Unlike previous centralized attempts, the EHDS framework emphasizes shared governance, cross-border interoperability, and sovereign control via Connectors [3, 4]. Complementary initiatives such as Gaia-X have introduced the technical requirements for federated identity and compliance services, using Verifiable Credentials (VCs) and Decentralized Identifiers (DIDs) to automate trust establishment between autonomous organizations [4, 30].

Despite this conceptual maturity, empirical validation remains scarce. Most dataspace implementations are currently domain-agnostic or experimental, failing to account for the specific technical and ethical work required in a highly regulated clinical setting [23]. The identified gap in the literature is not the absence of standards, but the lack of an operational architecture that binds identity, policy enforcement, and contract negotiation into a single, automated pipeline. This research addresses that gap by demonstrating how existing dataspace components can be orchestrated to support real-world cancer research under the EHDS-aligned constraints in projects such as SHARE [1].

4 Architectural Methodology for Transforming Data Lakes into Federated Dataspaces

The fundamental challenge in precision medicine is that most high-quality datasets reside in passive data lakes, centralized repositories designed for scalability that often inadvertently create a "data lock-in" effect [2, 7]. To address this, we implement an architectural wrapper that transforms these isolated lakes into nodes within a dataspace. Unlike a storage location, a dataspace is a decentralized infrastructure for trustworthy sharing where participants interact based on shared governance and technical standards [8]. This shifts the focus from simple data storage to sovereign data utility, ensuring that data remains persistently at its source while access is granted through standardized connectors that negotiate usage policies in real-time [31].

The transformation process requires a clear definition of Participants and their associated Profiles. In this architecture, participants are categorized into three primary roles: Data Providers (typically hospitals or clinics), Data Consumers (researchers or trial coordinators), and Intermediaries (clearing houses for compliance). Each participant is assigned a Profile that dictates their level of authority within the domain. For example, a hospital may expose its entire data lake to internal staff, but only a specific subset, such as a designated trial group, to external collaborators. This domain-specific mapping ensures that the wrapper understands the organizational context of the data it is protecting.

This transformation begins by creating a digital representation of the data lake's contents, turning raw files into Data Assets. Instead of moving or duplicating the original datasets, the architecture creates a set of metadata descriptors that point back to the local source. This is a critical distinction: the data never leaves the institutional boundary during this phase. Instead, a pointer is established within the connector that knows exactly where the data lives, whether in a cloud bucket or a local server, while keeping those coordinates hidden from any external party.

First, the data must be represented as an asset and the second stage of the transformation involves wrapping it in a Policy Layer. In a traditional data lake, security is often all or nothing, but a dataspace allows the institution to attach specific rules directly to the data itself. Using standardized protocols, described in detail in Sect. 5, a hospital can define exactly who is allowed to see a specific data instance, for what research purpose, and under what legal conditions. This policy layer supports multiple levels of Granularity, moving beyond binary access to include: (i) Raw Data Access for authorized clinical processing; (ii) Aggregate Statistics for population health monitoring; and (iii) Induced Models or insights where only the result of an algorithm is shared, rather than the data itself. This essentially turns a static file into a sovereign data asset that carries its own terms of use, allowing the system to automate the handshake between a researcher and the provider.

The final step in this transformation is the creation of a Trust Anchor. By linking the local infrastructure to a decentralized identity system, the data lake gains a verifiable decentralized identity within the network. The trust framework operates at various scales of identity, allowing for the verification of the institution as a whole, specific departments, or even individual patients who may provide sovereign consent for their data to be included in a specific research cohort. This allows other participants to recognize the institution as a trusted partner without needing a central authority to vouch for them. When a research request arrives, the framework acts as a policy enforcement mechanism: it verifies the researcher's identity, checks if they meet the specific requirements of the data's policy, and only then creates a temporary, secure pipe to stream the data directly from the local source to the authorized user's environment. This ensures that the data is accessed rather than replicated, allowing the institution to terminate the stream and revoke access at any moment. Through this pipeline, a previously isolated data lake is successfully unlocked, becoming a sovereign participant in a larger, collaborative ecosystem without ever sacrificing control over its sensitive assets.

5 Dataspace Architecture

The transition from isolated data storage to a federated ecosystem requires a clear architectural blueprint. This section defines the fundamental components of the proposed dataspace architecture and explores how these components are instantiated and orchestrated to enable sovereign, policy-driven data exchange in a federated environment.

The novel scientific contribution of the proposed architecture lies in the formalization of the Policy-Identity-Access binding. Unlike general-purpose federated systems, this architecture operationalizes a late-binding mechanism between metadata descriptors (Assets) and physical access points (DataAddresses), governed by machine-executable ODRL contracts. This represents a shift from procedural trust (legal agreements) to technical trust (enforced policy), providing a reproducible model for data sovereignty in precision medicine.

5.1 Modular Component Assembly

The architecture is inherently modular, using an extension-based system to assemble functional runtimes known as Connectors. In this framework, each participant operates a Connector, which serves as the primary gateway for sovereign data exchange. These connectors are assembled from three primary components: the Control Plane (signaling and policy), the Data Plane (data transmission), and the Identity Hub (credential management). The organization of these modules and their respective protocol layers is illustrated in Fig. 1.

To ensure traceability, the architecture employs a hierarchical identification scheme:

- **Participant ID**: Identifies the legal entity within the dataspace.
- **Component ID**: A persistent identifier for specific deployments, such as a localized Data Plane
- **Runtime ID**: An ephemeral identifier unique to an active instance, utilized for cluster synchronization and telemetry.

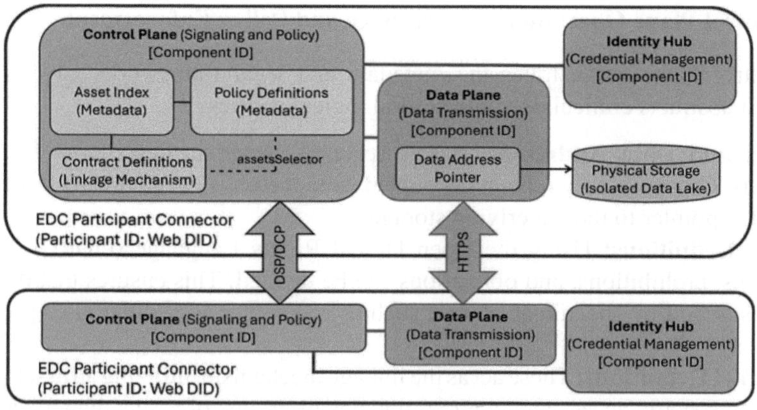

Fig. 1. Communication between two Modular EDC Participant Connectors, highlighting the separation of the Signaling Layer (DSP/DCP) and the Transfer Layer (HTTPS).

5.2 Protocol Standards

A dataspace is defined as a decentralized context wherein multiple participants, ranging from research institutions to autonomous clinical services, exchange data based on shared governance and technical standards. In this architecture, the EDC connector serves as the Participant Agent, orchestrating interactions through two primary protocols:

- **Dataspace Protocol (DSP)**: Acting as the common language of the ecosystem, the DSP [32] defines asynchronous messaging patterns for catalog retrieval, contract negotiation, and the initiation of data transfers.
- **Decentralized Claims Protocol (DCP)**: Layered upon the DSP, the DCP provides the trust framework. It facilitates the presentation and verification of decentralized identities and verifiable credentials, enabling providers to make policy-based access decisions.

5.3 Identity and Management Domains

Identity management is critical to maintaining institutional sovereignty. Each participant is assigned a unique URI (Uniform Resource Identifier), typically a Web DID (Decentralized Identifier). The EDC supports diverse deployment topologies to reflect complex organizational structures:

- **Federated Identifiers:** Organizations may deploy clustered control plane instances that share a single identity, ensuring high availability without compromising the participant's singular entry point.
- **Management Domains:** To accommodate large-scale medical centers, the architecture supports distinct management domains. This allows internal departments to manage EDC connectors independently while presenting a unified catalog and set of endpoints to the dataspace.
- **Autonomous Operating Units:** In scenarios where subdivisions operate with distinct legal or geographic requirements, the EDC can be configured with discrete identities, treating each unit as a unique dataspace participant.

5.4 Control Plane Operations: Governance and Policy Enforcement

The Control Plane orchestrates the metadata and legal frameworks governing data sharing. It abstracts clinical data into several logical entities:

- **Assets and Data Addresses:** Assets serve as metadata descriptors for clinical datasets. Crucially, they remain decoupled from the physical data via a DataAddress object, a pointer to the underlying storage.
- **Policy Definitions:** Using the Open Digital Rights Language (ODRL) [33], permissions, prohibitions, and obligations can be defined. This ensures that data usage is constrained by specific attributes, such as researcher accreditation or geographic location.
- **Contract Definitions:** These act as the linkage mechanism, utilizing an assetsSelector to apply specific access and contract policies to groups of assets dynamically. This late-binding approach allows security policies to be established prior to the existence of the assets themselves.

5.5 Asynchronous Negotiation and Transfer Logic

Data exchange within the architecture is strictly asynchronous, leveraging state-machine transitions to ensure transactional reliability. The interaction between a consumer and a provider is depicted in Fig. 2, which illustrates the control and data planes' orchestration consisting of the following stages:

1. **Catalog Discovery:** The process begins with the Consumer Control Plane requesting a catalog from the Provider Control Plane.
2. **Contract Negotiation:** Upon selecting a dataset, the consumer initiates a negotiation. The control planes exchange messages to evaluate claims against contract policies. Successful finalization results in a Contract Agreement, a persistent, legally binding artifact that serves as a token for subsequent access.
3. **Transfer Process Management:** Once an agreement is reached, the Consumer Control Plane initiates a Transfer Process. As shown in Fig. 2, the control planes manage the signaling and state transitions (e.g., REQUESTED, STARTED) to synchronize the upcoming data flow.
4. **Data Transfer:** In the final stage, the Data Planes handle the transmission of the payload. By separating the control from the data path, the architecture ensures that the Control Planes do not become bottlenecks, allowing for high-throughput, low-latency transfers between storage endpoints.

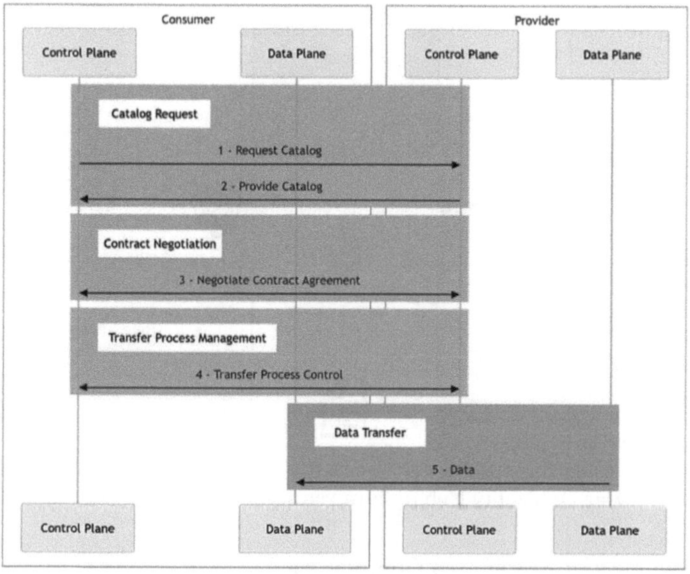

Fig. 2. State-machine transitions for negotiation.

5.6 Identity and Trust Infrastructure

In a federated dataspace, trust is established dynamically through verifiable cryptographic proofs rather than central imposition. The proposed architecture operationalizes this through a decentralized trust model, the workflow of which is depicted in Fig. 3. This process illustrates how a Research Centre (Connector A) and a Hospital (Connector B) utilize an Identity Hub and the Decentralized Claims Protocol (DCP) to verify credentials before any data exchange occurs.

The foundation of this trust layer rests on Decentralized Identifiers (DIDs) using the *did:tdw* method, providing globally resolvable, ledger-less identities suited for regulatory healthcare oversight [30]. Trust assertions, such as clinical certifications or ethical approvals, are presented as Verifiable Credentials (VCs) issued by recognized National Health Authorities. These VCs are managed by the EDC Identity Hub, which acts as a participant's digital wallet, selectively disclosing claims during contract negotiations to satisfy GDPR data minimization principles.

To bridge the gap between federated trust and institutional infrastructure, the system integrates Keycloak as an OpenID Connect (OIDC) provider, translating legacy internal logins (LDAP/AD) into the tokens required for dataspace authentication. Secure interoperability is further ensured by a Dynamic Attribute Provisioning Service (DAPS), which issues short-lived, DID-bound access tokens for both control-plane signaling and data-plane transfers. This multi-layered approach binds legal trust at the Business Layer to cryptographic enforcement at the System Layer, transforming compliance into an automated technical capability.

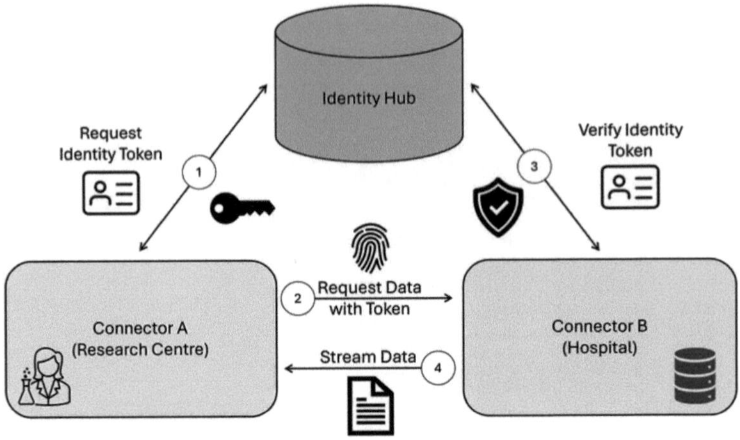

Fig. 3. Secure data exchange workflow between a Research Centre (Connector A) and a Hospital (Connector B) utilizing an Identity Hub for trust verification.

5.7 Governance and Automated Compliance

The scaling of federated research requires shifting from manual, legal-heavy data sharing agreements to automated, policy-based enforcement, namely:

- **Granular Policy Enforcement:** While ODRL handles high-level contract logic, the Open Policy Agent (OPA) provides a specialized engine for deep inspection of access requests. By utilizing the Rego policy language [34], the system can enforce complex constraints, such as ensuring a researcher's clinical accreditation was issued by a recognized national authority within a specific timeframe.
- **Digital Clearing House (DCH):** To ensure alignment with European standards, the architecture incorporates the Gaia-X Compliance Service. This decentralized notary automatically validates participant claims against the Gaia-X Trust Framework, issuing the necessary compliance credentials required to join the federated network.

5.8 Catalog Services

To ensure that clinical assets within the dataspace are discoverable across borders, the architecture implements a federated metadata layer centered on the Federated Catalog Service. This component allows nodes to broadcast their availability by asynchronously crawling participating connectors and aggregating their catalog metadata into a unified, searchable index. This approach enables a centralized discovery experience for researchers while strictly adhering to the principle of data sovereignty.

6 Implementation Environment

The transition from a conceptual framework to a functional precision medicine dataspace requires a robust, cloud-native infrastructure designed for high availability, security, and scalability. The architecture is fully containerized using Docker to ensure component isolation, with orchestration managed via Kubernetes (K8s). This provides the necessary self-healing resilience through automated health checks and horizontal elasticity for the Data Plane, which is critical for handling the high-throughput demands of genomic analysis without impacting Control Plane signaling.

Cryptographic security and secret management are facilitated by HashiCorp Vault [34], which serves as the primary engine for managing Participant DID private keys and OIDC client secrets. Vault utilizes dynamic, lease-based tokens to minimize vulnerability windows and employs a distributed unseal mechanism among multiple trusted administrators to ensure that no single entity maintains total control over the cryptographic root of trust. Relational state management, encompassing contract agreements, transfer processes, and catalog metadata, is handled by a high-availability PostgreSQL cluster (orchestrated by Patroni) to provide the durable audit trails essential for EHDS compliance. To prevent data leakage, the system enforces isolation through separate database schemas for the Control Plane and Identity Hub, adhering to the principle of least privilege. Finally, Keycloak is integrated as an Identity Provider (IdP) to bridge legacy institutional infrastructures (LDAP/AD) with the federated dataspace, mapping existing credentials to JSON Web Tokens (JWT) to reduce operational complexity for clinical staff.

7 Preliminary Results and Critical Discussion

The primary outcome of this research is the successful deployment of an operational architectural pipeline capable of transforming static, isolated clinical data lakes into sovereign participants within a federated dataspace. Within the context of the SHARE project [1], the architecture enables autonomous institutions to establish trusted connections, publish governed data assets, and negotiate access through automated, policy-based contracts grounded in decentralized identity claims.

Compared to traditional data-sharing workflows within the project, which relied on bilateral legal agreements and manual approval processes, the proposed and implemented approach substantially reduces administrative friction. Authorization processes that previously required extended human mediation were replaced by automated contract negotiations executed at runtime. While this work does not yet provide a quantitative performance benchmark, qualitative evaluation with participating institutions confirmed that governance enforcement and auditability were significantly improved, particularly in cross-institutional and cross-regional scenarios.

At this stage, the evaluation focuses on architectural feasibility, governance automation, and functional correctness rather than throughput optimization. While we acknowledge that empirical performance metrics are currently limited, this foundational phase is necessary to validate the security and policy enforcement mechanisms before moving to large-scale performance benchmarking. The results demonstrate that identity verification, policy evaluation, and contract enforcement can be technically bound into a single, end-to-end pipeline that aligns with EHDS principles while preserving institutional data sovereignty.

A critical analysis of the implementation reveals some limitations and trade-offs inherent to decentralized, policy-driven architectures:

- **Semantic Interoperability**: While the architecture effectively enables secure and governed access to distributed clinical data, it does not resolve semantic heterogeneity across institutions. Local data lakes continue to rely on diverse standards such as HL7 FHIR, OMOP CDM, or proprietary schemas. The architecture deliberately separates governance and access control from semantic harmonization, which must be addressed through complementary tooling or domain-specific transformation layers.
- **Identity Management Complexity**: Decentralized identity mechanisms are essential for enforcing sovereignty and trust, yet they introduce operational challenges. Managing institutional wallets, verifiable credentials, and trust anchors remains non-trivial for non-technical clinical and administrative personnel, highlighting the need for higher-level abstractions and user-oriented management interfaces.
- **Negotiation-Induced Latency**: Contract-based access control introduces an unavoidable delay prior to data access due to credential verification, policy evaluation, and agreement finalization. Although typically limited to seconds, this latency represents a conscious design trade-off that prioritizes accountability, legal certainty, and traceability over immediate access.

Overall, the findings indicate that the primary contribution of the proposed architecture lies not in maximizing data transfer performance, but in enabling trustworthy, scalable, and regulation-aware data sharing within highly sensitive clinical environments. Additionally, to address the operational barriers identified, specifically the complexity of managing a cloud-native stack (Kubernetes, HashiCorp Vault) in typical hospital environments, future iterations of this architecture aim to provide pre-configured connector-in-a-box deployment templates. These will abstract infrastructure management while maintaining the security required for clinical data.

8 Conclusions and Future Work

This paper presents a sovereign architectural approach to precision medicine that moves beyond the structural limitations of centralized data lakes. By leveraging open-source technologies such as Eclipse Dataspace Components, Open Policy Agent, and Keycloak, the proposed pipeline demonstrates how institutional control over clinical data can be preserved while enabling secure, policy-governed collaboration across organizational and national boundaries. The architecture operationalizes key principles of the European Health Data Space by ensuring that data remains under the authority of its originators while still being discoverable and accessible for authorized secondary use.

The framework was initially developed and applied within the SHARE project [1], where it serves as a reference architecture for secure and sovereign health data exchange in a real-world oncology research setting. Building on these foundations, the architecture is planned for further application within the UNCAN project [17, 18], where it will support a broader federated environment for European cancer research and facilitate the integration of multimodal oncological datasets across institutions.

While the proposed architecture focuses on the governance and connectivity plane, it establishes a modular and extensible foundation that allows for the future integration of domain-specific data contracts and harmonization tools.

Future work will focus on extending the architectural capabilities in the following directions:

- **Federated Learning Integration**: Exploring how the dataspace infrastructure can support the orchestration of algorithms alongside data, enabling federated learning workflows that further reduce data movement while preserving privacy and sovereignty.
- **Automated Regulatory Compliance**: Enhancing policy enforcement mechanisms to support automated verification of regulatory requirements, such as the presence of valid patient consent or ethical approvals, as part of the contract negotiation process.
- **Semantic Interoperability and Data Harmonization**: Investigating the integration of secondary transformation layers, such as mapping distributed clinical datasets to common data models like OMOP CDM or HL7 FHIR, to resolve semantic heterogeneity while maintaining the established sovereign governance protocols.
- **Simplified Deployment and Operational Accessibility**: Developing streamlined, connector-in-a-box deployment templates to reduce the operational complexity of the cloud-native stack, thereby lowering the barrier for hospital IT departments while preserving security.

These extensions aim to further strengthen the role of federated dataspaces as a foundational infrastructure for compliant, scalable, and collaborative precision medicine research in Europe, strengthening the capacity of technological innovation to tackle complex societal challenges.

Acknowledgments. This work was partially funded through FCT (the Fundação para a Ciência e a Tecnologia, I.P.) - for N.N., P.A.S. and J.P.P. - under the scope of projects CTS/00066 and UIDB/06107/2023-CREATE - and for G.R.G. - under the scope of projects UID/297/2025 and UID/PRR/297/2025 (Center for Mathematics and Applications-NOVA Math).

References

1. European Comission, SHARE (2025) SpanisH cAnceR data spacE (SHARE). EU Funded Project of Hospital Universitario Puerta de Hierro Majadahonda, Medical Oncology Service, Madrid, Spain. Funded by the European Union - NextGenerationEU - through the Spanish Ministry for Digital Transformation and Civil Service, under the investment program for the promotion of sectoral data spaces. https://healthdataspace.es/. Accessed April 2026
2. Baumgartner, M., et al.: Health data space nodes for privacy-preserving linkage of medical data to support collaborative secondary analyses. Front. Med. (2024). https://doi.org/10.3389/fmed.2024.1301660
3. Hussein, R., et al.: Getting ready for the European health data space (EHDS): IDERHA's plan to align with the latest EHDS requirements for the secondary use of health data. Open Res. Europe. **4**, 160 (2024). https://doi.org/10.12688/openreseurope.18179.1
4. Nagel, L., Lycklama, D.: How to build, run, and govern data spaces. In: Designing Data Spaces: the Ecosystem Approach to Competitive Advantage, pp. 17–28. Springer International Publishing, Cham (2022). https://doi.org/10.1007/978-3-030-93975-5_2
5. European Commission.: A European strategy for data. Communication COM(2020) 66 final, European Commission, Brussels. Accessed January 2026 (2020)

6. Hussein, R., et al.: Towards the European health data space (EHDS) ecosystem: a survey research on future health data scenarios. Int. J. Med. Inform. **170**, 104949 (2023). https://doi.org/10.1016/j.ijmedinf.2022.104949
7. Pingos, M., Mina, A., Andreou, A.: Transforming Data Lakes to data meshes using semantic data blueprints. In: Proceedings of the 19th International Conference on Evaluation of Novel Approaches to Software Engineering - ENASE, pp. 344–352. INSTICC, SciTePress (2024). https://doi.org/10.5220/0012620200003687
8. International Data Spaces Association.: IDS Reference Architecture Model (RAM) 4.0. Technical report, IDSA. https://internationaldataspaces.org/offers/reference-architecture/. Accessed January 2026 (2023)
9. Eclipse Foundation.: Eclipse Dataspace Components: Technical Documentation and Modular Architecture. Technical report, https://projects.eclipse.org/projects/technology.edc. Accessed January 2026 (2024)
10. Gaia-X European Association for Data and Cloud AISBL.: Gaia-X: A Federated and Secure Data Infrastructure. Technical report, Gaia-X European Association for Data and Cloud AISBL. https://gaia-x.eu/. Accessed January 2026 (2026)
11. European Commission and CLARIFY.: Cancer Long Survivors Artificial Intelligence Follow Up (CLARIFY). EU Funded Project. Grant Agreement ID: 875160, https://doi.org/10.3030/875160. Accessed April 2026 (2023)
12. Torrente, M., et al.: An artificial intelligence-based tool for data analysis and prognosis in cancer patients: results from the clarify study. Cancer. **14**(16), 4041 (2022). https://doi.org/10.3390/cancers14164041
13. Schurig, T., et al.: Updated remarks on the European health data space (EHDS). Regulation. **2025**(3) (2025). https://doi.org/10.17169/refubium-50116
14. Kim, S.Y., et al.: Dataspaces for collaborative. Research. (2025). https://doi.org/10.1109/BigData66926.2025.11402648
15. European Commission and UNCAN-CONNECT.: Decentralized Collaborative Network for Advancing Cancer Research and Innovation (UNCAN-CONNECT). EU Funded Project. Grant Agreement ID: 101215206, https://doi.org/10.3030/101215206. Accessed January 2026 (2024)
16. Boutros, M., et al.: Uncan.eu: toward a european federated cancer research data hub. Cancer Discovery. **14**(1), 30–35 (2024). https://doi.org/10.1158/2159-8290.CD-23-1111
17. Fortino, G., et al.: Towards multi-layer interoperability of heterogeneous iot platforms: the inter-iot approach. In: Integration, Interconnection, and Interoperability of IoT Systems, pp. 199–232. Springer (2017). https://doi.org/10.1007/978-3-319-61300-0_10
18. Szmeja, P., et al.: Assistiot: a modular implementation of a reference architecture for the next generation internet of things. Electronics. **12**(4), 854 (2023). https://doi.org/10.3390/electronics12040854
19. Li, R., et al.: Centralized and federated models for the analysis of clinical data. Ann Rev Biomed Data Sci. **7** (2024). https://doi.org/10.1146/annurev-biodatasci-122220-115746
20. Cunha-Oliveira, T., Ioannidis, J.P.A., Oliveira, P.J.: Best practices for data management and sharing in experimental biomedical research. Physiol. Rev. **104**(3), 1387–1408 (2024). https://doi.org/10.1152/physrev.00043.2023
21. Guggenberger, T.M., Langdon, C.S., Otto, B.: Data spaces as meta-organisations. Eur. J. Inf. Syst., 1–21 (2025). https://doi.org/10.1080/0960085X.2025.2451250
22. Hulsen, T.: Sharing is caring—data sharing initiatives in healthcare. Int. J. Environ. Res. Public Health. **17**(9), 3046 (2020). https://doi.org/10.3390/ijerph17093046
23. Heimbigner, D., McLeod, D.: A federated architecture for information management. ACM Trans. Inf. Syst. **3**(3), 253–278 (1985). https://doi.org/10.1145/4229.4233
24. Wiederhold, G.: Mediators in the architecture of future information systems. Computer. **25**(3), 38–49 (2002). https://doi.org/10.1007/s12599-019-00614-2

25. Jarke, M., Otto, B., Ram, S.: Data sovereignty and data space ecosystems. Bus. Inf. Syst. Eng. **61**(5), 549–550 (2019). https://doi.org/10.1109/2.121508
26. Otto, B.: The evolution of data spaces. In: Designing Data Spaces: the Ecosystem Approach to Competitive Advantage, pp. 3–15. Springer International Publishing, Cham (2022). https://doi.org/10.1007/978-3-030-93975-5_1
27. Shabani, M.: The data governance act and the EU's move towards facilitating data sharing. Mol. Syst. Biol. **17**(3), e10229 (2021). https://doi.org/10.15252/msb.202110229
28. Papp, A., et al.: Data mesh and data space: a comparative analysis with a focus on governance. In: International Conference on Innovations for Community Services, pp. 144–156. Springer (2025). https://doi.org/10.1007/978-3-031-94263-1_10
29. Brunner, C., et al.: Did and VC: untangling decentralized identifiers and verifiable credentials for the web of trust. In: Proceedings of the 2020 3rd International Conference on Blockchain Technology and Applications, pp. 61–66 (2020). https://doi.org/10.1145/3446983.3446992
30. Nagel, L., et al.: Design principles for data spaces: position paper. Technical report, E. ON Energy Research Center, https://doi.org/10.18154/RWTH-2022-09082 (2021)
31. International Data Spaces Association.: Dataspace Protocol Specification v1.0. Technical Standard, IDSA, https://docs.internationaldataspaces.org/ids-knowledgebase/dataspace-protocol. Accessed January 2026 (2024)
32. De Vos, M., et al.: Odrl policy modelling and compliance checking. In: International Joint Conference on Rules and Reasoning, pp. 36–51. Springer (2019). https://doi.org/10.1007/978-3-030-31095-0_3
33. Open Policy Agent.: Policy Language — Rego Documentation. Technical report, Open Policy Agent, https://www.openpolicyagent.org/docs. Accessed January 2026 (2026
34. HashiCorp, Inc.: HashiCorp Vault — Secrets Management and Data Protection. Technical report, HashiCorp, Inc., https://www.hashicorp.com/en/products/vault/use-cases/data-protection. Accessed January 2026 (2026)

Smart Cities and Sustainable Urban Systems

Analysis of Environmental Profiles of Logistics Companies in Estonia to Enhance Technology Choice

Rene Maas[1,2](✉), Eduard Shevtshenko[1,2], Hendrik Laanemets[1,2], Tatjana Karaulova[2], and Rõõt Laigu[2]

[1] University of Tartu, Ülikooli 18, 50090 Tartu, Estonia
rene.maas@ut.ee, {eduard.sevtsenko,hendrik.laanemets}@tktk.ee
[2] TTK UAS, Pärnu mnt 62A, 10135, Tallinn, Estonia
{tatjana.karaulova,root.laigu}@tktk.ee

Abstract. Growing environmental and regulatory requirements are driving logistics companies to implement solutions that enhance sustainability and improve resource efficiency. In practice, however, companies often lack clarity on which technological choices align with their strategic objectives and the priorities arising from environmental targets. This descriptive study applies thematic content analysis to environmental technological maturity among Estonian logistics companies to map key sustainability practices through the lens of Supply Chain Operational Reference performance metrics. In parallel, the technologies in use are identified and mapped. The resulting dataset is combined with company logistics domain information to conduct an exploratory cluster analysis and develop a typology of firms. The typologies reflect distinct environmental profiles and help to clarify associations between sustainability practices and technology adoption. In the final stage, sustainability best practices are classified within the identified typologies to support companies in selecting technologies that best enable sustainable transformation. The study contributes to the academic literature by using systematic thematic analysis to highlight the relationships between sustainable technology practices and the profiles of their use. The study proposes a maturity-technology alignment model that enables firms to select technologies consistent with their logistics domain and sustainable strategy. The study forms part of the TTK Logistics lab strategic compass, which enables companies to evaluate the alignment between their current strategy and actual direction to identify technological gaps required to achieve strategic outcomes.

Keywords: Sustainable Practices · Logistics · Sustainable Performance · Sustainable Technology · SCOR · Environmental Practices

L. M. Camarinha-Matos and F. Ferrada (Eds.): DoCEIS 2026, IFIP AICT 790, pp. 417–430, 2027.
https://doi.org/10.1007/978-3-032-28939-1_29

1 Introduction

Corporate strategies define organisational aims [1], but implementation requires translating aspirations into measurable targets [2]. In line with "you get what you measure," metrics direct managerial attention and decision-making [3] and should be selected to operationalise strategy and support decisions, not merely reporting [4].

The same logic applies to environmental stewardship [5]. Firms claiming sustainability should embed aligned environmental metrics to ensure strategic ambitions translate into operations [6], supported by process changes and enabling technologies [7, 8]. When metrics and processes are aligned, interventions should be visible as KPI changes, for example, adopting alternative fuels to reduce greenhouse gas emissions.

To assess environmental performance and the technologies enabling it, we use profile-based differentiation [9, 10]. We argue that firms with similar environmental profiles can transfer practices and technologies, and that some technologies influence profile outcomes more strongly than others. In this study, we operationalise this by using SCOR environmental performance metrics: SCOR links processes, metrics, and best practices in a standardised structure [11], enabling comparable assessment of firms' sustainability profile maturity. SCOR [11] already includes sustainability indicators (Environmental and Social). Therefore, this article does not require the development of a separate system of environmental metrics, but rather builds on the existing standardised architecture of processes and indicators.

Although typically used for operational process design and management, we posit that SCOR can also support environmental profiling; combined with information on firms' technological bases, it enables cross-firm technology comparisons and evaluation of technologies contributions to environmental objectives.

Current sustainability assessments are often high-level (e.g., ESG reporting) and rarely link specific technologies to process- and metric-level environmental outcomes. Many indicators emphasise governance and capture inputs rather than process outputs [12], while fragmented, non-standardised metrics limit comparability and constrain transfer learning [13]. Accordingly, a framework is needed that connects high-level sustainability objectives to process-level KPIs and links technology adoption to changes in SCOR environmental performance metrics, enabling consistent profile-based comparisons and identification of transferable best practices. This study focuses on supply chain processes and environmental metrics: *social* and *economic* dimensions are outside the scope. We pose three research questions:

RQ1: *What are the main sustainable maturity typologies of logistics companies in Estonia?*
RQ2: *What are the main technologies supporting the environmental maturity level?*
RQ3: *What companies are related to the highest or lowest sustainable maturity level?*

The paper is structured as follows: Sect. 3 reviews the existing literature; Sect. 4 describes the data collection from logistics companies and methods for data analysis; Sect. 5 analyses logistics companies' environmental typologies; and Sect. 6 presents conclusions and future work.

2 Relation to the Conference Topic

Technology has long been seen as a driver of efficiency, a supporter of human work, and an enabler of process automation. Automation typically delivers time savings that can be reallocated or used to increase volumes, and it reduces error rates, lowering rework and repetitive tasks and further improving efficiency.

Increasingly, technology-based automation also affects environmental outcomes: automated and digitised processes may become less environmentally burdensome, although the direction and magnitude depend on implementation choices and indirect impacts. Proper digitisation not only saves time but also reduces errors compared to manual work, while digital documentation can reduce paper use and conserve natural resources. By enabling resource conservation, technology can help address socio-environmental challenges such as climate change and sea-level rise and mitigate the growth of CO_2 emissions. Similarly, substituting fossil fuels with biofuels can reduce petroleum product consumption and preserve non-renewable resources [14]. Expanding firms' awareness of and access to environmentally oriented technologies may therefore support more positive global environmental outcomes.

3 Related Literature

The *freight and logistics* sector is highly carbon-intensive, and mounting regulatory and stakeholder pressure has made environmental performance a strategic priority for logistics [15]. Post-2015 research examines whether digital logistics technologies, when coupled with enabling managerial practices, improve green KPIs such as *CO_2 emissions* and *fuel consumption* [15]. Despite heterogeneous methods and contexts, findings generally indicate net reductions associated with stronger logistics performance and targeted technology adoption.

Field and case studies report measurable operational gains: *automated port monitoring reduced* container journey carbon by 6% (imports) and 23% (exports) [16], and *GIS route optimisation* in municipal waste collection reduced weekly distance by 81.27 km (4%) and fuel use by 145.86 l (10%) [17]. Cross-country analyses suggest *ICT diffusion* and *green managerial* practices jointly predict better environmental outcomes, indicating that technology must be embedded in management systems to realise benefits [15, 18].

Optimisation and *circular supply-chain* models often project larger reduction potentials, typically, 20–30% and up to 47% under combined strategies. But these represent upper bounds on scenarios rather than consistently observed field effects [17]. Methodologically, studies span panel econometrics, *GIS modelling* with paired tests, *RFID deployment measurement*, *telematics-based observational* analyses, and *multi-objective optimisation.* However, attribution remains challenging because single-tool effects are rarely isolated, longitudinal and SME-focused evidence is limited, and green-KPI measurement is uneven [18].

Overall, technologies that improve visibility, planning, and real-time execution tend to reduce fuel use and carbon KPIs, with *eco-driving feedback* and *fleet electrification* repeatedly highlighted as strong near-term levers.

The Supply Chain Operations Reference (SCOR) model integrates process descriptions, performance measurement, and best practices within a unified model, thereby enabling consistent and comparable analysis across organisations [19]. The framework is commonly applied to describe supply chain activities, performance, and managerial practices in a standardised manner [20].

Structurally, the SCOR model is organised around five core process six categories: Plan, Source, Transform, Fulfil, Order, and Return, which together capture the end-to-end logic of supply chain operations and support systematic performance evaluation and benchmarking [20, 21].

More recent research extends the application of the SCOR model towards digitalisation and data-driven supply chain management, highlighting its role in structuring data, performance metrics, and customer-oriented analysis within modern supply chain systems [21].

4 Research Contribution and Innovation

4.1 Methods and Data Collection

This study is descriptive and uses a mixed-methods approach in which qualitative and quantitative analyses complement each other. The qualitative approach is used to develop the data structure and to interpret the substantive content disclosed on companies' websites, whereas the quantitative approach is applied to the statistical processing of the coded data and cluster analysis.

The study assumes that companies that define and position themselves as environmentally responsible also communicate relevant activities, technologies, and goals through their online channels [22, 23]. In addition, it is assumed that environmental initiatives may be linked to firms' strategic positioning and the pursuit of competitive advantage [24–26].

Online Company Sustainability Responsibility, which involves using digital platforms, corporate websites, social media, and reports to transparently share sustainability and ethical efforts with stakeholders, is a well-known practice.

Data were collected from the official websites of Estonian logistics companies identified in the Estonian Commercial Register [27]. Estonia is a digital country with high transparency standards and stringent environmental performance requirements, enabling the reliable use of website data from a wide range of companies. Companies were selected based on the following industry classifications: *land transport and transport via pipelines, water transport, air transport, warehousing,* and *postal and courier activities.* Only firms with functional websites containing sufficient relevant content were included in the analysis ($n = 35$).

In the first stage of the study, environmental indicators were extracted from the SCOR framework and used as the basis for the coding scheme. The selection of indicators was primarily guided by their suitability for analysing website-disclosed information and by the potential to assess links between a given indicator and the activities/technologies communicated.

From SCOR levels 1–3, the analysis included indicators that are unambiguously distinguishable and whose substantive meaning is clearly interpretable. For example, the indicator "*water disposal*" was excluded due to limited applicability, whereas "*water consumed*" was included. The final set of environmental indicators comprised: (EV. 2.1) *use of renewable materials;* (EV. 2.3) *consumption of renewable energy,* (EV. 1.3) *water consumption;* (EV. 1.4) *greenhouse gas emissions;* and (EV. 1.5) *waste generation.*

Data structure development began with a systematic content analysis of company websites. The qualitative information was then converted into a machine-readable format, and the indicators were checked for conceptual overlap and distinctiveness.

Coding was conducted based on information presented on companies' websites, linking each identified activity or goal to the corresponding SCOR environmental indicator. Each indicator was coded on an intensity scale from 0 to 3, where higher values reflect more specific and measurable disclosure- *maturity level*:

0 – no description or reference to an activity affecting the indicator;
1 – general or superficial description of an activity;
2 – a specific activity accompanied by the technology or method used to achieve it;
3 – inclusion of measurable values, targets, and/or performance metrics.

In addition, supplementary attributes were collected on technologies that companies described as sustainable solutions for influencing the respective indicators.

Based on data collected from company websites, six technology classes were defined to capture solutions that firms use or plan to implement: (1) *vehicle fleet* and *alternative fuels*, (2) *routing and digitalisation*, (3) *warehouse automation* and *digital solutions*, (4) *energy and buildings*, (5) *packaging, waste, and circularity*, and (6) *measurement and standards*. Each technology class was coded as binary (*present/absent*).

Companies were also assigned to five main functional classes based on their logistical activity: (1) *road-*, (2) *sea-*,(3) *air-*,(4) *rail transport,* and (5) *warehousing.*

To further differentiate company profiles, background variables were added based on prior literature and data availability [28–30]. The variables included *company age, number of employees, and revenue.* These data were obtained from a publicly available business database and used to describe companies.

The initial analysis indicated that the variability of the indicators *EV.1.3 Water Consumed* and *EV.3.6 Water Recycled and Reused* across firms was nearly identical. Therefore, *EV.1.3* was retained for subsequent analysis, and the information from EV.3.6 was integrated.

The coded dataset was transferred to the *RStudio* software for further analysis. To assess inter-firm differences, *Gower* distance was used, as it is suitable for variables measured on different scales, including ordinal variables [31]. An advantage of this method is that it does not assume linearity of differences between scale levels.

Ward's hierarchical cluster analysis was applied to the resulting distance matrix to group companies based on similar environmental website-based profiles and to identify naturally occurring clusters in the data [32]. The number of clusters was evaluated using the Silhouette score, which indicated an optimal $K = 2$. However, to enhance the practical value of the analysis and to achieve more meaningful differentiation between profiles, a solution with $K = 4$ clusters was ultimately selected. Several clustering variants were tested, with the four-cluster variant yielding the best results. Cluster solutions should be useful and interpretable, not just statistically optimal [33].

In the final stage, the technology classes collected during the early phase of data structure development were incorporated into the analysis. This enabled linking each firm's membership in a given environmental profile to the set of technological solutions it uses. These associations allow assessment of which technologies are characteristic of different profiles and provide input for the development of best practices.

5 Discussion of Results

Some companies adopt technology without closing the loop between goals, KPIs, and outcomes. Although the measured maturity level primarily reflects a company's external communication, it nonetheless encompasses the organisation's activities, technologies, and objectives. Therefore, the information on the company's website could be interpreted as an indicator of its sustainability.

5.1 Identification of Typologies

Ward's hierarchical clustering yielded *four* clusters (Fig. 1). These clusters reflect four distinct environmental profiles among logistics companies operating in Estonia.

Id	Cluster nr	EV ID	0	1	2	3	Id	Cluster nr	EV ID	0	1	2	3
1	1	EV.1.3	33	58	9	0	11	3	EV.1.3	38	62	0	0
2	1	EV.1.4	0	0	0	100	12	3	EV.1.4	0	0	100	0
3	1	EV.1.5	0	42	50	8	13	3	EV.1.5	0	50	50	0
4	1	EV.2.1	0	25	42	33	14	3	EV.2.1	24	38	38	0
5	1	EV.2.3	0	17	16	67	15	3	EV.2.3	0	12	88	0
6	2	EV.1.3	60	40	0	0	16	4	EV.1.3	0	0	20	80
7	2	EV.1.4	0	70	20	10	17	4	EV.1.4	0	0	0	100
8	2	EV.1.5	30	60	10	0	18	4	EV.1.5	0	0	0	100
9	2	EV.2.1	50	40	10	0	19	4	EV.2.1	0	40	0	60
10	2	EV.2.3	30	60	0	10	20	4	EV.2.3	0	0	0	100

Fig. 1. Assessed environmental maturity level across the clusters. Each cell represents a portion of the variable (EV ID).

5.1.1 Cluster 1

Companies in this cluster generally demonstrate a high level of measurement and quantitative target-setting, although coverage is uneven across environmental dimensions. The climate domain is the strongest: technologies and targets related to greenhouse gas emissions are most frequently both specified and reported in measurable terms. This is followed by the energy dimension, for which more than two-thirds of companies report measurable indicators (67%). For renewable materials, practices vary: some companies limit themselves to describing the technology, while others also report measurable outcomes.

The main shortcomings of this profile relate to the water and waste dimensions. In the water domain, companies often mention actions but often lack clear descriptions of technological solutions or metrics. In the waste dimension, companies tend to present technologies and activities aimed at influencing performance, yet measurable values and quantitative targets are generally not reported. Based on the maturity level of environmental dimensions, we label this cluster typologically as "*GHG and renewable energy leaders.*"

5.1.2 Cluster 2

Companies in the second cluster do not position themselves as environmentally responsible organisations, which is reflected in a low overall level of environmental maturity. Although the GHG dimension is mentioned relatively often (70%), concrete measures are reported much less frequently (20%), indicating general awareness rather than systematic action. The water dimension is practically absent in this cluster.

In the waste domain, the pattern is largely declarative: mention is high (60%), but it is not supported by described technologies, measurable indicators, or clearly articulated implementation measures. Based on the maturity level of the environmental dimensions, we label this cluster typologically as "*early-stage environmental maturity.*"

5.1.3 Cluster 3

Companies in the third cluster describe their environmental activities and the technologies they use, but lack measurable indicators to assess the current state or to manage progress toward targets. This is particularly evident in the GHG dimension: activities and/or technologies are reported by all companies (100%), yet they lack quantitative indicators or explicit targets. A similar pattern is observed for renewable energy (88%), whereas the representation of activities/technologies in the waste dimension is more moderate (50%).

Thus, the practical implementation side is largely in place, but target-based management and the translation of actions into measurable performance are missing. The renewable/recyclable materials dimension is fragmented: companies are evenly distributed across the lower maturity levels (0–2), indicating heterogeneous practices and a lack of standardisation. Based on the maturity levels of the environmental dimensions, we label this cluster typologically as "*technology adopters.*"

5.1.4 Cluster 4

Companies in the fourth cluster position themselves clearly as environmentally responsible organisations on their websites and communicate their activities in this area consistently and visibly. The GHG dimension stands out most strongly: companies describe both the technologies implemented and quantitative targets for emissions reduction, indicating maturity in strategic management as well as in measurement and reporting.

At the same time, the renewable/recyclable materials dimension is unevenly represented within the cluster. This suggests that some companies address the topic at an overly general level, while others move directly from broad statements to measurable figures without sufficiently articulating intermediate steps (e.g., specific measures, implementation logic, or monitoring systems). Based on the maturity level of the environmental dimensions, we label this cluster typologically as the "*best-practice leaders.*"

5.2 Logistical Domain Analysis

The distribution of firms' business activities reveals clear differences across clusters (Fig. 2). It is important to note that the activity categories are not mutually exclusive: a single company may operate in multiple segments simultaneously and therefore fall into more than one activity category.

cluster	n	class_1	class_2	class_3	class_4	class_5
1	12	83%	33%	42%	17%	83%
2	10	70%	20%	20%	20%	30%
3	8	75%	38%	12%	38%	38%
4	5	60%	100%	40%	20%	20%

Fig. 2. Cluster shares are categorised according to their logistical business activities.

In terms of activity diversity, *Cluster 2* has the narrowest profile, whereas the broadest range of activities is observed in *Clusters 1 and 4.*

In *Cluster 1*, warehousing and road transport dominate. Companies in this cluster are primarily integrated logistics service providers, including 3PL firms, whose service portfolios cover multiple supply-chain functions. At the same time, the cluster also includes companies engaged in air transport, suggesting in some cases a broader or more international service model.

Cluster 2 consists mainly of road haulage companies and is the most specialised cluster. The shares of warehousing and multimodal operations are lower, indicating a narrower service profile and more limited capabilities across different stages of the supply chain. Based on company profiles, these are predominantly traditional carriers.

Cluster 3 comprises multimodal companies, with business activities distributed relatively evenly. A stronger signal emerges for rail transport, while maritime transport and warehousing are also substantially represented. This structure points to firms that play a more coordinative role in the supply chain or organise intermodal transport operations.

Cluster 4 is composed predominantly of firms associated with maritime transport. Although some road and air transport activities are also present, this is likely driven by group structures and multiple business units. The cluster is characterised by larger companies with greater international reach.

5.3 Technological Choices

Companies' technological choices were classified into classes: tech_1–6. Technologies and activities described by firms were mapped to these classes (Table 1), providing a structured overview of which solutions and practices were currently communicated within each class. Mapping also supports best-practice identification by showing which technologies and activities other companies could realistically adopt to raise environmental maturity. In total, 189 technologies or initiatives were identified during data collection from websites. Technologies could be used for the TTK Compass solution or studied further in the future.

Table 1. Technology classes suitable for logistics, with frequent examples from websites.

Id	Technology class	Frequent examples
tech_1	Fleet & alternative fuels	Electric vehicles, LNG/CNG, HVO
tech_2	Routing/telematics/optimisation	TMS, route optimisation
tech_3	Warehouse automation & digitalisation	WMS, sorting lines, robots
tech_4	Energy & buildings	Solar Power, LED, energy efficiency
tech_5	Packaging/waste/circulation	Packaging management systems, reverse logistics systems, waste circulation
tech_6	Measurement/standards	ISO 14001/50001, audits, ESG reports

5.4 Technological Distribution

Clear differences emerge between the clusters in terms of their technological distribution (Fig. 3). A single company could utilise multiple technologies.

EV_cluster	n	tech_1	tech_2	tech_3	tech_4	tech_5	tech_6
1	12	83%	75%	42%	67%	83%	50%
2	10	30%	10%	20%	10%	20%	50%
3	8	63%	50%	13%	38%	50%	50%
4	5	100%	60%	40%	60%	60%	0%

Fig. 3. Cluster shares according to the technology classes

Companies in *Cluster 1* employ the most diverse technological portfolio to implement their environmental strategy. This may be explained by the fact that these same companies also most frequently defined strategic goals, which, in turn, presuppose a broader set of solutions. Technologically, the cluster is dominated by *Class 1* (vehicle fleet, alternative fuels), *Class 2* (route optimisation, process digitalisation), and *Class 5* (packaging, circular economy, reuse/recycling).

In *Cluster 2*, the technological selection concentrates mainly on *Class 1* (vehicle fleet, alternative fuels) and *Class 6* (measurement and standards). However, the overall presence of technologies in this cluster remains limited, consistent with its generally low level of technological articulation. This cluster also represents the lowest level of environmental maturity.

In *Cluster 3*, technologies are, in broad terms, more evenly distributed, yet a clear difference compared to *Cluster 1* emerges in *Class 3* (warehouse automation and digitalisation), where representation is weaker. This suggests that the cluster includes relatively fewer companies that provide warehousing-related functions or invest in their automation. *Class 1* (vehicle fleet and alternative fuels) remains the most strongly represented.

The technological profile of *Cluster 4* is clearer and more narrowly focused than in the previous clusters. The primary emphasis is on *Class 1* (vehicle fleet and alternative fuels). Given that these companies predominantly provide maritime and air transport, such specialisation towards alternative fuels is expected. The remaining technologies are mainly distributed across *Classes 2, 4, and 5*. A distinctive feature of this cluster is the near absence of *Class 6* (measurement and standards). Nevertheless, interpretation should take into account that this is the smallest cluster ($n = 5$).

6 Practical and Theoretical Contributions

This study's *practical contribution* is a diagnostic framework that helps companies (1) assess environmental maturity via cluster membership and (2) identify and adopt best practices from more advanced peers. Cluster-based positioning offers a benchmark for evaluating current capabilities, mapping development needs, and clarifying constraints that impede progression to higher maturity levels.

The empirical results indicate several actionable improvement paths. In maritime transport, maturity could be raised with relatively low effort by clearly and systematically communicating ISO standards and related management practices on company websites. Cluster assessment also enables practice transfer across transport modes and business domains. For example, in road transport, substantial heterogeneity was observed in specific areas.

In warehousing, the water-consumption dimension appeared underdeveloped, signalling a need to define actions, implement suitable metrics, and set explicit targets. In road transport, the weakest profile is aligned with the traditional carrier, yet the wide variation across firms suggests clear scope for targeted adoption of GHG-reduction practices. Beyond technical measures, these practices should be made visible: communicating with partners and the broader public about GHG-reduction mechanisms.

Overall, the maturity diagnostic supports a positive development cycle in which firms prioritise dimensions, define target levels, and progress stepwise toward higher maturity. By grounding improvement in peer benchmarks, the framework enables evidence-based adoption of leading activities and technologies from advanced firms and supports systematic, guided improvement.

From a *theoretical perspective*, the study advances sustainable supply chain management by demonstrating that technology adoption is neither random nor directly proportional to maturity; it depends on the environmental maturity profile and the logistics domain in which the company operates. Based on these insights, the study proposes a maturity-technology alignment model that enables firms to select technologies consistent with their logistics domain and sustainable strategy.

7 Conclusions and Future Work

The aim of the study was to analyse the environmental sustainability profiles of companies in Estonia's logistics sector and to derive the main typologies from these profiles. By incorporating technological classes, we assessed how they are distributed across different profiles. A cluster analysis of the data collected during the company mapping revealed distinct levels of environmental maturity. Subsequently, the internal structure of each cluster was examined with respect to both technological choices and business activity areas. The results are consistent with previous research on firms' environmental technology adoption maturity levels [34–36].

We answer research questions as follows:

RQ1: *What are the main sustainable maturity typologies of logistics companies in Estonia?*

Based on the analysis, four segments were identified: *GHG and renewable energy leaders; early-stage environmental maturity; technology adopters; and best-practice leaders.*

RQ2: *What are the main technologies supporting the sustainable maturity level?*

We identified 189 technologies and initiatives during the data collection phase. It means companies are willing to state the technologies they use on their websites, and it could be used to assess a company's environmental maturity level. Findings also demonstrate an opportunity for collective learning. Companies that state technologies on their website could be analysed and over taken. It still has to align with the company's environmental strategy, domain and resources for successful implementation.

RQ3: *What companies are related to the highest or lowest sustainable maturity level?*

Considering business activities and technologies together, a higher share of warehousing activities was concentrated in *Cluster 1*, which was also characterised by a greater prevalence of energy- and facility-related solutions, as well as circular-economy and waste-management technologies. In the most mature cluster (*Cluster 4*), maritime transport predominated, accompanied primarily by the deployment of fleet and alternative-fuel technologies and by a clearer definition of measurable indicators and target levels.

In the least mature cluster (*Cluster 2*), road transport was dominant. However, the visibility of telematics/optimisation solutions and energy-related solutions was low. This suggests that differences in maturity are driven not only by the business activity domain, but also by firms' capabilities and willingness to communicate implemented solutions and their outcomes online in an evidence-based and systematic manner.

Finally, the study contributes to the development of the *TTK logistics laboratory* by identifying typologies of Estonian logistics sector companies and technological choices to achieve a higher level of environmental technology adoption maturity. Results of the work could be used to develop the logistics compass, supporting companies in their technological choices by comparing their actual practices with desired strategies.

7.1 Future Work

The analysis indicates that a more fine-grained analysis of maturity levels would enable moving toward smaller, more meaningful units of direction that better capture firms' strategic choices in environmental sustainability.

We acknowledge the study's weaknesses. Cluster analysis was performed on a small population ($n = 35$) and may affect the conclusions, especially for the cluster (*cluster 4*). Subjective assessments were made at several points in the work: during the environmental metrics influencing, during the cluster interpretation, and during the selection of the number of clusters.

References

1. Yang, H., Morgan, S.L.: Business strategy and corporate governance: theoretical and empirical perspectives. In: Business Strategy and Corporate Governance in the Chinese Consumer Electronics Sector, pp. 23–46. Elsevier eBooks (2011). https://doi.org/10.1016/b978-1-84334-656-2.50002-8
2. Burney, L.L., Henle, C.A., Widener, S.K.: A path model examining the relations among strategic performance measurement system characteristics, organizational justice, and extra- and in-role performance. Account. Organizations Soc. **34**(3–4), 305–321 (2009). https://doi.org/10.1016/j.aos.2008.11.002
3. The Balanced Scorecard—Measures that Drive Performance. Harvard Business Review. https://hbr.org/1992/01/the-balanced-scorecard-measures-that-drive-performance-2 (1992, January 1)
4. Neely, A., Gregory, M., Platts, K.: Performance measurement system design. Int. J. Oper. Prod. Manag. **15**(4), 80–116 (1995). https://doi.org/10.1108/01443579510083622
5. Searcy, C.: Corporate sustainability performance measurement systems: a review and research agenda. J. Bus. Ethics. **107**(3), 239–253 (2011). https://doi.org/10.1007/s10551-011-1038-z
6. Figge, F., Hahn, T., Schaltegger, S., Wagner, M.: The sustainability balanced scorecard – linking sustainability management to business strategy. Bus. Strateg. Environ. **11**(5), 269–284 (2002). https://doi.org/10.1002/bse.339
7. Attaran, M.: Information technology and business-process redesign. Bus. Process. Manag. J. **9**(4), 440–458 (2003). https://doi.org/10.1108/14637150310484508
8. Kubrak, K., Milani, F., Nava, J.: Digital technology-driven business process redesign: a classification framework. In: Lecture Notes in Business Information Processing, pp. 205–221 (2023). https://doi.org/10.1007/978-3-031-33080-3_13
9. Merello, P., Barberá, A., De La Poza, E.: Is the sustainability profile of FinTech companies a key driver of their value? Technol. Forecast. Soc. Chang. **174**, 121290 (2021). https://doi.org/10.1016/j.techfore.2021.121290
10. Yavuz, O., Uner, M.M., Okumus, F., Karatepe, O.M.: Industry 4.0 technologies, sustainable operations practices and their impacts on sustainable performance. J. Clean. Prod. **387**, 135951 (2023). https://doi.org/10.1016/j.jclepro.2023.135951
11. SCOR Model. https://scor.ascm.org/performance/introduction (n.d.).
12. OECD. Behind ESG Ratings: Unpacking Sustainability Metrics (2025)
13. Saeed, M.A., Kersten, W.: Supply chain sustainability performance indicators – a systematic literature review. Logist. Res. **13**(6) (2020)
14. Huo, H., Wang, M., Bloyd, C., Putsche, V.: Life-cycle assessment of energy use and greenhouse gas emissions of soybean-derived biodiesel and renewable fuels. Environ. Sci. Technol. **43**(3), 750–756 (2008). https://doi.org/10.1021/es8011436
15. Centobelli, P., Cerchione, R., Esposito, E.: Pursuing supply chain sustainable development goals through the adoption of green practices and enabling technologies: a cross-country analysis of LSPs. Technol. Forecast. Soc. Chang. **153**, 119920 (2020a). https://doi.org/10.1016/j.techfore.2020.119920
16. Efimova, A., Saini, M.: Assessing carbon emissions reduction by incorporating automated monitoring system during transit: a case study. Acta Logistica. **10**(1), 79–88 (2023). https://doi.org/10.22306/al.v10i1.357
17. Sulemana, A., Donkor, E.A., Forkuo, E.K., Oduro-Kwarteng, S.: Effect of optimal routing on travel distance, travel time and fuel consumption of waste collection trucks. Manag. Environ. Qual. Int. J. **30**(4), 803–832 (2019a). https://doi.org/10.1108/meq-07-2018-0134
18. Li, J., Anser, M.K., Tabash, M.I., Nassani, A.A., Haffar, M., Zaman, K.: Technology- and logistics-induced carbon emissions obstructing the green supply chain management agenda:

evidence from 101 countries. Int J Log Res Appl. **26**(7), 788–812 (2021a). https://doi.org/10.1080/13675567.2021.1985094
19. Shevtshenko, E., Maas, R., Murumaa, L., Karaulova, T., Raji, I.O., Popell, J.: Digitalisation of supply chain management system for customer quality service improvement. J. Mach. Eng. (2022). https://doi.org/10.36897/jme/147803
20. Ntabe, E., LeBel, L., Munson, A., Santa-Eulalia, L.: A systematic literature review of the supply chain operations reference (SCOR) model application with special attention to environmental issues. Int. J. Prod. Econ. **169**, 310–332 (2015). https://doi.org/10.1016/j.ijpe.2015.08.008
21. Maas, R., Karaulova, T., Shevtshenko, E., Popell, J., Raji, I.O.: Development of SCOR database for digitalisation of supply chain customer feedback analysis. Eng. Econ. **34**(4), 439–455 (2023). https://doi.org/10.5755/j01.ee.34.4.31618
22. Biloslavo, R., Trnavčevič, A.: Web sites as tools of communication of a "green" company. Manag. Decis. **47**(7), 1158–1173 (2009). https://doi.org/10.1108/00251740910978359
23. Capriotti, P., Moreno, A.: Communicating corporate responsibility through corporate web sites in Spain. Corporate Commun. Int. J. **12**(3), 221–237 (2007). https://doi.org/10.1108/13563280710776833
24. Endrikat, J., Guenther, E., Hoppe, H.: Making sense of conflicting empirical findings: a meta-analytic review of the relationship between corporate environmental and financial performance. Eur. Manag. J. **32**(5), 735–751 (2014). https://doi.org/10.1016/j.emj.2013.12.004
25. Sun, X., Askary, A.E., Meo, M.S., Zafar, N.U.A., Hussain, B.: Green transformational leadership and environmental performance in small and medium enterprises. Econ. Res. Ekonomska Istraživanja. **35**(1), 5273–5291 (2022). https://doi.org/10.1080/1331677x.2021.2025127
26. Bresciani, S., Puertas, R., Ferraris, A., Santoro, G.: Innovation, environmental sustainability and economic development: DEA-bootstrap and multilevel analysis to compare two regions. Technol. Forecast. Soc. Chang. **172**, 121040 (2021). https://doi.org/10.1016/j.techfore.2021.121040
27. Ettevõtteregister | Registrite ja Infosüsteemide Keskus. https://www.rik.ee/et/e-ariregister/ettevotteregister (n.d.)
28. Ali, W., Frynas, J.G., Mahmood, Z.: Determinants of corporate social responsibility (CSR) disclosure in developed and developing countries: a literature review. Corp. Soc. Responsib. Environ. Manag. **24**(4), 273–294 (2017). https://doi.org/10.1002/csr.1410
29. Fifka, M.S.. Corporate Responsibility Reporting and its Determinants in Comparative Perspective – a Review of the Empirical Literature and a Meta-analysis. ideas.repec.org. https://ideas.repec.org/a/bla/bstrat/v22y2013i1p1-35.html (2013)
30. Hahn, R., Kühnen, M.: Determinants of sustainability reporting: a review of results, trends, theory, and opportunities in an expanding field of research. J. Clean. Prod. **59**, 5–21 (2013). https://doi.org/10.1016/j.jclepro.2013.07.005
31. Szepannek, G., Aschenbruck, R., Wilhelm, A.: Clustering large mixed-type data with ordinal variables. ADAC. **19**(3), 749–767 (2024). https://doi.org/10.1007/s11634-024-00595-5
32. Jain, A.K.: Data clustering: 50 years beyond K-means. Pattern Recogn. Lett. **31**(8), 651–666 (2009). https://doi.org/10.1016/j.patrec.2009.09.011
33. Everitt, B.S., Landau, S., Leese, M., Stahl, D.: Cluster Analysis. Wiley (2011)
34. Ageron, B., Gunasekaran, A., Spalanzani, A.: Sustainable supply management: an empirical study. Int. J. Prod. Econ. **140**(1), 168–182 (2011). https://doi.org/10.1016/j.ijpe.2011.04.007
35. Batz, A., Oleśków-Szłapka, J., Stachowiak, A., Pawłowski, G., Maruszewska, K.: Identification of logistics 4.0 maturity levels in polish companies—framework of the model and preliminary research. In: Ecoproduction, pp. 161–175 (2019). https://doi.org/10.1007/978-3-030-33369-0_10

36. Lin, T., Wang, K.J., Sheng, M.L.: To assess smart manufacturing readiness by maturity model: a case study on Taiwan enterprises. Int. J. Comput. Integr. Manuf. **33**(1), 102–115 (2019). https://doi.org/10.1080/0951192x.2019.1699255

Smart Governance for Better Living: Empirical Analysis of Public Services and Digital Transformation Impact on Urban Quality of Live

Sara Rupacz(✉), Izabela Jonek-Kowalska, and Aneta Michalak

Faculty of Organization and Management, Department of Economics and Computer Science, Silesian University of Technology, Gliwice, Poland
{sara.rupacz,izabela.jonek-kowalska}@polsl.pl

Abstract. The primary objective of this article is to assess the relationship between urban quality of life and Smart Governance in 19 major Polish cities aspiring to become Smart Cities. The Smart Governance analysis encompasses five dimensions: overall assessment of municipal service quality, availability of e-services, transparency of administrative procedures, transparency of decision-making processes, and anti-corruption measures undertaken by municipal authorities. The research employed a diagnostic survey method administered to a representative sample of 1,863 residents. Data analysis was conducted using descriptive statistics and multiple linear regression to determine the relationships between public service quality and its determinants. The findings indicate that e-service availability and corruption prevention constitute the most significant factors influencing public service quality. While transparency and public accessibility of information regarding municipal decisions exert a more moderate influence on residents' satisfaction, they nonetheless demonstrate a strong association with respondents' perceptions of municipal services. These findings offer valuable insights for developing economies seeking to enhance Smart Governance mechanisms and improve residents' quality of life.

Keywords: Smart Governance · Public Services · Urban Quality of Life · Digital

1 Introduction

Smart Cities (SC) constitute an urban planning concept oriented toward optimizing residents' quality of life [1–3]. The coordination of activities in this area rests primarily with municipal authorities [4]. The level of satisfaction of the local community, as well as the degree of operationalization of Smart City concept assumptions, will depend on the effectiveness of their policies [5].

Over the past decade, Smart Governance has undergone significant transformation. In the initial phase, the bureaucratic model dominated, characterized by a hierarchical management structure and the primacy of municipal authority competencies. Subsequently,

Published by Springer Nature Switzerland AG 2027
L. M. Camarinha-Matos and F. Ferrada (Eds.): DoCEIS 2026, IFIP AICT 790, pp. 431–450, 2027.
https://doi.org/10.1007/978-3-032-28939-1_30

evolution occurred toward a consumer model, within which local governments adopted the role of provider of the highest quality public services for the local community. The next phase was the participatory model, in which residents acquired the status of co-creators of intelligent urban solutions and co-decision-makers in governance processes. Currently, both in academic discourse and management practice, the implementation of a platform model is postulated, in which local administration creates conditions for co-creation of public value by residents through integrated socio-technical systems that combine data, services, technologies, and social actors [6]. This evolution has imposed requirements on cities. They must combine their existing operational principles with digital transformation and enhanced social participation.

In the area of digitization, one of the key challenges is the digitalization of public services, enabling residents to handle administrative matters online via the Internet [7]. Numerous studies to date [8–12] indicate that public e-services contribute to reducing city operating costs, improve the effectiveness of resident service delivery, and foster their engagement in city life. Thus, they have a positive impact on creating truly sustainable and smart cities.

Digitization and social participation in the Smart City concept find a common dimension in urban information and communication platforms. These serve both to increase the transparency of municipal decisions and to facilitate interactive knowledge exchange among urban stakeholders. Previous analyses of these platforms' functioning indicate their significant contribution to planning intelligent urban solutions and sustainable urban development [13, 14].

The research presented in this article refers to cities operating in one of Europe's emerging economies. The socio-economic difficulties faced by these economies further complicate the Smart City creation process. One of the key problems in this regard is the technocratic approach to decision-making rooted in local administration [15–17]. This significantly limits the transparency of decision-making processes, thereby impeding social participation. It also does not foster local community engagement in the decision-making process, as residents are not treated as equal partners. Under such conditions, it is difficult to create an atmosphere of mutual trust.

Corruption at the local, regional, and national levels remains an ongoing problem in emerging economies [18–22]. This negative phenomenon strongly affects residents' emotions and attitudes, seriously limiting their belief in social justice and proper, procedurally compliant handling of their affairs.

Considering the above observations, this article evaluates the quality of public services from the perspective of residents of 19 Polish cities in the context of overall urban quality of life. The study references contemporary trends and the Smart City development model encompassing the digitization of public services and the city's communication channels with the local community. Classic determinants of residents' satisfaction with municipal government operations were also considered, relating to such aspects of Smart Governance as transparency of decision-making processes and anti-corruption efforts. As emphasized above, these elements may still significantly impact the quality of life in cities of emerging economies.

The research presented in this article constitutes a component of a doctoral dissertation devoted to organisational innovativeness in emerging and developing economies. It represents a direct response to the persistently low rankings of these economies in international and European innovation indices. This is a matter of considerable importance from the perspective of reducing socio-economic disparities and advancing sustainable development.

Situating the research within an urban context enriches the existing body of knowledge on the socio-technological dimensions of Smart City development in regions confronted with economic challenges. Bridging the gap between developing and developed economies constitutes a formidable social challenge that demands in-depth analysis. Such analysis should be conducted not only through the lens of hard quantitative data on the advancement of contemporary technologies, but also from the perspective of the ordinary resident, as it is they who experience the quality of urban life and who alone are capable of meaningfully evaluating it.

The findings of the conducted analyses make the following contributions to the body of research on the impact of urban technological innovation on addressing societal challenges:

- they enable an assessment of the level of advancement of selected technological innovations in the cities of a developing economy aspiring to Smart City status;
- they incorporate a social perspective on the evaluation of technological innovations, highlighting the necessity of integrating residents' experiences and opinions into the assessment process;
- they diagnose the social challenges accompanying the development of urban technologies and Smart Governance in developing economies;
- they contribute to the goal of reducing socio-economic inequalities by advocating for the responsible and inclusive implementation of technological innovations in the urban sphere.

2 Societal Challenges in Smart Governance Literature Review

The fundamental objective of the Smart City concept is to improve the quality of urban life, achieved in practice primarily through the implementation of cutting-edge information and communication technologies [23]. Solutions of this kind are generally readily visible to city residents [24]. However, as evidenced by the findings of Szczepańska et al. (2023) [25], they are not always utilized. This is most attributed to their limited attractiveness or perceived utility, as well as to the presence of digital barriers. Considering the above, increasing emphasis is being placed on the necessity of designing smart cities with the active participation of residents and in accordance with their actual needs and expectations [26].

Existing research on quality of life demonstrates that it is shaped by a broad range of determinants [27, 28]. Studies conducted among urban residents consistently indicate that Smart Living is the domain of greatest interest to them [29]. This is largely because Smart Living solutions directly address everyday living conditions. These conditions, in turn, exert a significant influence on residents' satisfaction with urban life.

It should be noted, however, that Smart Living outcomes are substantially dependent on effective and efficient city governance. Smart Governance thus functions as a mediating domain in shaping urban quality of life. Prior research on the relationship between quality of life and Smart Governance identifies two particularly salient dimensions. The first concerns the accessibility and ease of use of e-services [30]. In this regard, the prevention of digital exclusion plays a critical role [31, 32].

The second key dimension is identified by De Guimarães et al. (2020) [33] and Dhenge and Nimbarte (2024) [34]. Their findings highlight the importance of trust, transparency, and accountability of local authorities. These factors foster an environment conducive to cooperation and civic engagement in urban decision-making [35, 36]. Such engagement is widely regarded as a defining characteristic of modern, fully sustainable cities.

Research by Hartley (2023) [37] demonstrates that residents' expectations of local authorities vary according to age, income level, and gender. Higher levels of education are associated with greater demands regarding fairness and transparency in urban governance. Nevertheless, residents remain primarily concerned with the tangible outcomes of governance decisions. Administrative improvements are perceived as secondary and are expected to serve as a means of enhancing quality of life.

Contemporary Smart Governance scholars also draw attention to the barriers that constrain the effectiveness of this domain [38]. The most frequently identified include low levels of civic participation and insufficient resident awareness of available solutions. On the part of municipal authorities, limited institutional capacity represents a significant impediment [39]. As a result, Smart Governance remains one of the least developed dimensions of the Smart City concept [40].

It should be emphasised, however, that despite residents' limited direct interest in Smart Governance, this domain exerts a discernible influence on their urban quality of life. The findings of Hong and Lee (2023) [41] and Gil et al. (2021) [42] provide compelling evidence that effective and efficient city governance contributes to improvements in quality of life. Conversely, inconsistent and ineffective governance undermines these improvements, even in cities equipped with advanced technological solutions [43].

In developing economies, effective Smart Governance encounters additional impediments, stemming primarily from technological deficiencies, including limited access to modern IT and ICT solutions — a condition largely attributable to insufficient financial resources [44, 45]. The implementation of smart urban solutions is further hindered by competency gaps within local public administration structures [46]. Local authorities also face considerable difficulties in the effective enforcement of regulations, which are frequently characterised by low transparency and, in some instances, susceptibility to corruption [47].

The infrastructural deficiencies, low levels of network connectivity, and digital illiteracy substantially constrain the adoption of new technologies among residents [48]. A further factor impeding the implementation of smart solutions is the pervasive resistance to change observed within local communities [49].

In summary, improving quality of life constitutes a significant social challenge for contemporary cities. This challenge is of relevance in developing and emerging economies, which strive to close the socioeconomic gap separating them from more advanced countries. Effective Smart Governance may play an important role in addressing this challenge. For these reasons, the present article focuses on the analysis of this domain across 19 Polish cities, examined within the context of a developing economy.

3 Methodology

Given the importance of public services in shaping quality of life in Smart Cities, this article poses the following research problem: How are quality of life and quality of public services evaluated in Polish cities from the residents' perspective, and what factors determine them?

To answer this research problem, a survey was conducted in 19 cities with county rights located in the Silesian Voivodeship. A total of 1,863 respondents participated. This was a representative research sample, also at the level of each individual city, selected with a fraction of 0.5, confidence level of 95%, and standard error of 8%. In the survey questionnaire, respondents evaluated 6 aspects of urban life. The evaluation was conducted using a scale from 0 to 10. This provided respondents with a broad opportunity to express their own opinion on an intuitive and recognizable scale based on the decimal system. The evaluated aspects of urban life concerned:

- quality of life in the city – overall assessment;
- quality of public services in the city – overall assessment;
- accessibility of e-services;
- accessibility of information about municipal decisions on online platforms;
- transparency of municipal decisions;
- anti-corruption efforts.

Accordingly, the first two questions in the questionnaire were exploratory in nature. The next two referred to the digitization of municipal services. And the last two addressed issues directly related to Smart Governance.

The selection of variables was guided by two key aspects of Smart Governance. The first is a direct derivative of the Smart City concept, which — as noted in the introduction — is intrinsically linked to the digitalisation of urban life. Its foundations lie in the development of information and telecommunication technologies. Within the domain of Smart Governance, this digitalisation manifests in digital services offered to residents and online information and discussion platforms that foster civic participation. For these reasons, two survey questions addressed the evaluation of these aspects of urban quality of life.

The second aspect of Smart Governance derives from the fundamental challenges faced by many emerging and developing economies. These challenges constitute a significant barrier to Smart City development. The aspect in question is the transparency of public authorities. These variable shapes trust in urban decision-makers and influences the level of residents' engagement in local democracy. Accordingly, two survey questions addressed the transparency of municipal decision-making and anti-corruption efforts in local government, respectively.

In addition to these four questions, the questionnaire included two general questions. The first concerned the overall assessment of quality of life in the city. This allowed for a comparison between Smart Governance evaluations and general residential satisfaction. The second addressed the overall quality of public services. This variable served as the dependent variable in the study, assumed to be influenced by the four independent variables related to digitalisation and decision-making transparency.

The questionnaire ultimately comprised six substantive questions, formulated as follows: *How do you rate the following aspects of life in your city on a scale from 0 to 10, where 0 means very poor and 10 means excellent?* The questionnaire also included demographic questions concerning age, gender, household size, and place of residence.

The study was conducted using the CAWI method (Computer-Assisted Web Interviewing). Its technical execution was commissioned to a social research agency. The questionnaire was distributed directly to respondents from the surveyed cities, ensuring sample representativeness, randomness, and a one-hundred-percent response rate. The choice of research method — namely, a survey conducted among residents — was informed by several considerations that are also reflected in the Smart City literature. First, the overarching goal of Smart City implementation is the improvement of quality of life [50, 51]. Yet, as the literature review reveals, relatively little attention has been devoted to assessing this quality from the residents' perspective. Most existing studies assume a priori that proposed solutions will inherently enhance local community satisfaction. It therefore seems warranted to verify empirically whether this is indeed the case.

Second, the social dimensions of development are frequently marginalised within the Smart City concept in favour of technology and innovation [52–54]. The social reception of these advancements, along with the accompanying challenges, tends to be overlooked. This poses a direct threat to the sustainable development of smart cities and generates a risk of social exclusion. Social research — that is, surveying the local community — enables the diagnosis of these challenges. It also shifts attention from the technological aspects of Smart City to humanistic considerations, thereby balancing contemporary approaches to the implementation of smart urban solutions.

Considering the above considerations, which are extensively documented in the literature, the present study adopts a survey-based approach as its primary analytical method. It should be noted that, by its very nature, this type of study is subject to the subjective assessments of the respondents. Nevertheless, the authors of the present article contend that this approach is entirely justified in the context of measuring quality of life — a category that is, by definition, inherently subjective. Furthermore, residents are the primary recipients of smart urban solutions and are therefore fully entitled to evaluate them. Finally, it is their subjective assessments that will ultimately shape the perception of Smart Governance, as well as inform decisions regarding the choice of place of residence.

The results of the reliability assessment of the questionnaire constructed in this manner are presented in Table 1. The data contained therein indicate that the developed research instrument exhibits excellent internal consistency (Cronbach's alpha coefficient > 0.90). The narrow confidence interval demonstrates the high reliability of the measurement scale.

In processing the survey results, descriptive statistics were used first, including:

- measures of central tendency – mean, median, mode to aggregate and compare responses to individual questions;
- measures of variability – standard deviation, coefficient of variation to assess the differentiation of the local communities studied;

Table 1. Assessment of survey questionnaire reliability.

Specification	Value
Sample size	1 863
Number of items	6
Scale mean	35.3113
Scale standard deviation	12.2699
Cronbach's alpha of the scale	0.9337
−95% CI for Cronbach's alpha of the scale	0.9289
+95% CI for Cronbach's alpha of the scale	0.9382
Standard error of measurement	0.0315
Mean inter-item correlation	0.6936
Standardized Cronbach's alpha	0.9314

- asymmetry and skewness – to compare the distribution of respondents' answers to the normal distribution and determine the range of extreme assessments of the phenomena studied.

In the second stage of analysis, multiple linear regression was employed, which allows examination of the relationship between one dependent variable and multiple independent variables. The function describing it has the following form (1):

$$Y = \beta_0 + \beta_1 X_1 + \beta_2 X_2 + \beta_3 X_3 + \ldots + \beta_n X_n + \varepsilon \quad (1)$$

where:

Y - dependent variable,
$X_1, X_2, X_3 \ldots$ - independent variables (predictors),
β_0 - intercept,
$\beta_1, \beta_2, \beta_3 \ldots$ - regression coefficients,
ε - random error.

During the research, it was assumed that the dependent variable is the quality of public services. The independent variables are: accessibility of e-services, accessibility of information about municipal decisions on online platforms, transparency of municipal decisions, and anti-corruption efforts.

Before developing the multiple linear regression model, residual analysis was performed to verify its key assumptions, including: linearity of relationship, homoscedasticity, normality of residual distribution, and independence of residuals.

The following parameters were used to assess model reliability:

- R - multiple correlation coefficient measuring the strength of the linear relationship between the dependent variable and the set of independent variables, taking values from 0 to 1;

- R^2 - coefficient of determination specifying the proportion of variance in the dependent variable explained by the regression model, expressed as the ratio of the explained sum of squares to the total sum of squares;
- Adjusted R^2 - adjusted coefficient of determination accounting for the number of predictors in the model and penalizing for excessive increase in the number of independent variables;
- Standard error of the estimate - measuring the average deviation of observed values of the dependent variable from values predicted by the regression model;
- Residual sum of squares (RSS) - sum of squared residuals representing the total variability unexplained by the model, calculated as the sum of squared differences between observed and predicted values;
- Total sum of squares (TSS) - total sum of squares representing the total variability of the dependent variable, calculated as the sum of squared deviations from the mean;
- Explained sum of squares (ESS) - sum of squares explained by the model, representing the portion of variability in the dependent variable explained by the independent variables;
- F - F-statistic (Snedecor's F) used to test the significance of the entire regression model by comparing explained variance to unexplained variance;
- p-value - test probability value determining the level of statistical significance at which the null hypothesis of no relationship between variables is rejected;
- AIC - Akaike Information Criterion - information criterion used for comparing the quality of statistical models by balancing model fit and complexity;
- AICc - Corrected Akaike Information Criterion - corrected Akaike information criterion containing a correction for small samples, preventing excessive favoritism toward complex models;
- BIC - Bayesian Information Criterion (Schwarz Criterion) - Bayesian information criterion used for model selection by penalizing complexity more strongly than AIC, particularly with large samples;
- MAE (Mean Absolute Error) - mean absolute error representing the average absolute value of differences between observed and predicted values, serving as a measure of model prediction accuracy.

In the final stage of the research, the results were discussed and summarized.

4 Results

The description of the research results is presented in two parts. The first addresses the obtained assessment of urban life and quality of public services. The second analyzes the factors shaping the quality of public services in the cities studied.

4.1 Quality of Life and Quality of Public Services

Figure 1 presents the mean values of residents' assessments concerning quality of life and public services and their individual components. Tables 3, 4, and 5 contain descriptive statistics for individual questions, dividing them into three groups:

- overall assessment of urban quality of life and quality of public services (Table 3),
- assessment of public service digitization (Table 4),
- assessment of smart urban governance – smart governance (Table 5).

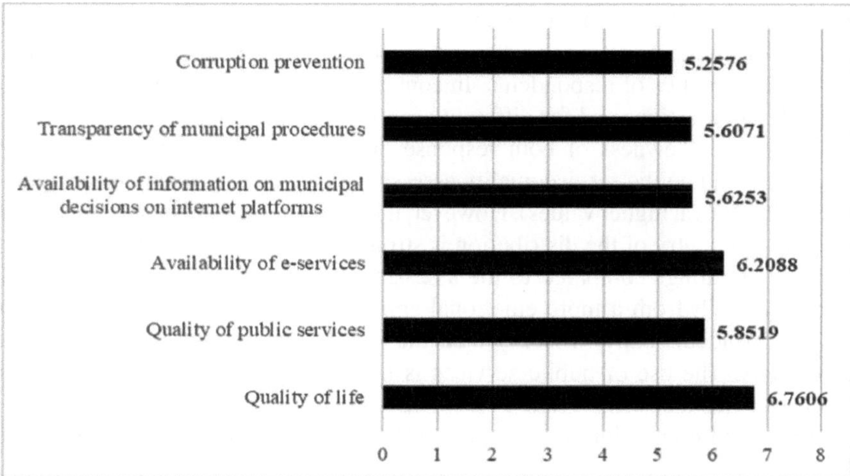

Fig. 1. Arithmetic mean of responses to survey questions

Table 2. Descriptive statistics for questions on quality of life and quality of public services in the city.

Specification	Quality of life	Quality of public services
Mean	6.7606	5.8519
Median	7	6
Mode	7	7
Mode frequency	485	335
Standard deviation	1.9302	2.4020
Coefficient of variation	28.55%	41.05%
Lower quartile	6	5
Upper quartile	8	8
Skewness	−0.9015	−0.5227
Kurtosis	1.2605	−0.1048

According to Fig. 1, the quality of urban life in general terms is assessed significantly higher than the quality of public services. On an eleven-point scale, quality of life is evaluated as good (mean above 6.7, median and mode at 7). In contrast, the quality of public services receives rather average ratings (mean above 5.6, median 6 and mode 7, however with significantly lower frequency than in the case of quality of life). This indicates that residents are not satisfied with the support offered by municipal offices.

Assessments of urban quality of life are also decidedly less varied than assessments of public service quality (lower standard deviation and lower coefficient of variation) – Table 2. The local community therefore perceives the conditions of their place of residence in a similar manner, regardless of its location in the region and the sociodemographic characteristics of respondents. In contrast, the quality of public services varies across different locations and for different groups of respondents.

The negative skewness of both response distributions indicates that most of the quality of life and public service quality assessments are concentrated on the right side of the distribution (at higher values). However, it is worth noting that in the case of quality of life, the asymmetry of the distribution is stronger, which means a greater number of extremely low ratings compared to the assessment of municipal service quality. This pattern may result from a more emotional approach to general living conditions that accompany residents daily, whereby their unfavorable nature may be felt longer and more strongly. The use of public services is incidental in nature; therefore, negative experiences associated with it fade over time.

The above differentiation is also confirmed by the high and positive kurtosis occurring in the assessment of quality of life. In this case, extreme ratings – both low and high – occur more frequently than in relation to the assessment of public service quality.

In the further part of the analysis, the level of digitization of public services in the cities studied is presented (Table 3).

Table 3. Descriptive statistics for questions on availability of e-services and availability of information on municipal decisions on internet platforms.

Specification	Availability of e-services	Availability of information on municipal decisions on internet platforms
Mean	6.2088	5.6253
Median	6	6
Mode	7	5
Mode frequency	322	325
Standard deviation	2.3462	2.4886
Coefficient of variation	37.78%	44.24%
Lower quartile	5	4
Upper quartile	8	7
Skewness	−0.4840	−0.3996
Kurtosis	−0.1174	−0.3328

According to the data contained in Table 3, the accessibility of e-services is assessed higher than the accessibility of information about municipal decisions on online platforms (higher arithmetic mean and mode, higher lower and upper quartiles). Greater agreement among respondents also occurs in the case of this element of digitization (lower standard deviation and lower coefficient of variation). While this indicates a moderate level of digitization of municipal services, it is uniformly felt and noticed, and therefore genuinely present in the cities studied.

In turn, the average assessment of the accessibility of information about municipal decisions on the Internet demonstrates municipal authorities' reluctance to publicize both the decisions themselves and the circumstances of their adoption. Such an approach contradicts key assumptions of public finance concerning the transparency of public information. It also does not correspond with the Smart City idea, according to which residents not only know what decisions city authorities are making but also participate in the process of making them. It is difficult to assume that information deficiencies result solely from the low level of digitization of municipal offices, since they offer higher accessibility of more complex e-services.

The shape of response distributions for both survey questions is similar and does not deviate significantly from the normal distribution. Negative skewness indicates a slightly greater number of extremely negative assessments of digital solution accessibility. Meanwhile, negative kurtosis indicates a fairly uniform distribution of ratings around the arithmetic mean.

In the study, respondents also evaluated the transparency of municipal decisions and anti-corruption efforts (Table 4).

Table 4. Descriptive statistics for questions on transparency of municipal procedures and corruption prevention.

Specification	Transparency of municipal procedures	Corruption prevention
Mean	5.6071	5.2576
Median	6	5
Mode	5	5
Mode frequency	334	460
Standard deviation	2.4484	2.4940
Coefficient of variation	43.67%	47.43%
Lower quartile	4	4
Upper quartile	7	7
Skewness	−0.3767	−0.3001
Kurtosis	−0.2667	−0.2918

According to the data contained in Table 4, the transparency of municipal decisions was assessed at a level like the accessibility of public information on the Internet. These issues are interrelated, and the digitization of public information constitutes a tool supporting its transparency. These are assessments expressing moderate satisfaction, characterized by high variation (high standard deviation and coefficient of variation). Among respondents there are also residents extremely dissatisfied with the transparency of municipal decisions (negative skewness). This may result from their personal experiences or be related to high expectations and ethical standards.

Of all the studied aspects of quality of life and smart governance, residents assess municipal authorities' activity in anti-corruption efforts decidedly most poorly (lowest mean, median, mode, and lower quartile). Such an assessment may result from two circumstances. First, it may stem from a lack of information about decisions made and their substantive justification. Second, it may be the consequence of irregularities in the decision-making process that city authorities wish to conceal from the local community. This second explanation is undoubtedly supported by the reluctance of city authorities to share information concerning city operations.

Such assessments and the attitude of municipal authorities do not foster building social trust or civic engagement of residents. In this context, it is difficult to speak of full implementation of the Smart City concept if it is limited solely to the implementation of modern technologies, including ensuring the accessibility of e-services, while lacking a foundation in the form of cooperation between municipal administration and the local community. The essence of implementing the Smart City concept lies in treating residents as subjects. A manifestation of this approach includes, among others, ensuring transparency of activities financed from public funds, which also originate from the budgets of local community households.

4.2 Determinants of Public Service Quality

In the next stage of the research, the dependence of public service quality on individual components included in the survey, relating respectively to public service digitization and Smart Governance, was identified. Multiple linear regression was used for this purpose.

Table 5 presents the results of residual analysis for the developed model. According to these results, the model is correctly constructed. The mean of residuals equals 0. The Durbin-Watson statistic is $d \approx 2$, which indicates the absence of residual autocorrelation and confirms the validity of applying multiple linear regression. Although normality tests indicate deviation from normal distribution ($p < 0.001$), with a sample of $N = 1{,}863$ and no autocorrelation ($DW = 1.97$), the ordinary least squares estimators remain consistent and asymptotically efficient. It is therefore possible to model public service quality using multiple linear regression.

The parameters of the obtained multiple regression model are presented in Table 6. The data presented indicate that all variables are statistically significant, i.e., they demonstrate a relationship with the quality of public services in the cities studied. The confidence intervals do not contain zero values and are positive, which confirms the strength and direction of the relationship. The standard error values for individual coefficients are relatively low compared to the estimated parameters for the independent variables, which indicates the precision of the model estimates.

The obtained model shows that the strongest positive impact on public service quality is exerted by the accessibility of public e-services. Residents therefore expect digitization of public life, which generates their satisfaction with the actions of city authorities.

Table 5. Parameters of residuals in the multiple linear regression model.

Specification	Value
Mean	0
Standard deviation	1.2124
Durbin-Watson d	1.9701
Residual normality: d statistic	0.0698
Degrees of freedom	14
p-value	<0.000001

Solutions characteristic of the Smart City concept are appreciated and noticed by them, which demonstrates acceptance of the direction of digital transformation in Silesian cities.

The second factor significantly influencing the local community's assessment of public service quality is corruption prevention. Residents therefore expect the elimination of administrative and political pathologies. The greater the emphasis placed on such activities, the higher the social satisfaction. Considering that anti-corruption efforts were rated lowest, the identified relationship implies an urgent need for their intensification.

Slightly less significant in shaping satisfaction with public service quality are the transparency of municipal decisions and public accessibility of information about how they are made. This most likely results from the fact that residents primarily expect efficient handling of matters that directly concern them. This efficiency is most strongly influenced by an effective e-service system and the absence of corruption. The multiplicity and diversity of municipal decisions mean that residents are not interested in each one, which in turn weakens the impact of these variables on the assessment of service quality.

The reliability assessment of the obtained multiple linear regression model is presented in Table 7. The value of the multiple correlation coefficient indicates a very strong relationship between public service quality and the independent variables. The model explains over 74% of the variability in the dependent variable, while the remaining factors shaping public service quality, not included in the study, account for only approximately 26% of this variability. This demonstrates that in the survey, respondents addressed the most significant determinants of public service quality.

The statistical significance of the model is confirmed by low p-values and a high F-statistic value. The prediction quality of the model is also confirmed by the mean absolute error (MAE) value of 0.8622. This means that the average deviation of the model's predicted values from actual values does not exceed 1 point on the measurement scale of 0 to 10 used. Considering the above results, it can be concluded that the presented multiple linear regression model is characterized by high reliability.

Table 6. Multiple linear regression model parameters.

Specification	Coefficient b	Standard error of b	Lower 95% confidence interval	Upper 95% confidence interval	t statistic	p-value	Standardized coefficient b
Intercept	0.5304	0.0808	0.3719	0.6888	6.5641	<0.000001	–
Availability of e-services	0.2723	0.0203	0.2324	0.3121	13.3947	<0.000001	0.2660
Availability of information on municipal decisions on internet platforms	0.2265	0.0251	0.1773	0.2757	9.0330	<0.000001	0.230885
Transparency of municipal procedures	0.2035	0.0244	0.1556	0.2513	8.3421	<0.000001	0.2108
Corruption prevention	0.2313	0.0211	0.1899	0.2727	10.9506	<0.000001	0.2402

Table 7. Assessment of multiple linear regression model reliability.

Specification	Value
Number of variables in the model	4
R	0.8633
R^2	0.7452
Adjusted R^2	0.7447
Standard error of the estimate	1.2137
Residual sum of squares (RSS)	2 737.0861
Total sum of squares (TSS)	10 743.1111
Explained sum of squares (ESS)	8 006.0249
F	1 358.6706
p-value	<0.000001
AIC - Akaike Information Criterion	726.7069
AICc - Corrected Akaike Information Criterion	726.7672
BIC - Bayesian Information Criterion (Schwarz Criterion)	769.4165
MAE (Mean Absolute Error)	0.8622

5 Discussion

The findings of the present study indicate that the quality of life of residents across 19 Silesian cities — located in one of the largest developing economies in Europe — is at an average level. This suggests that considerable effort remains to be made to improve living conditions for local communities. Drawing on the results of prior research, a range of improvement measures within the Smart Living domain may be postulated in this regard, as this dimension of the Smart City concept appears to exert a direct influence on urban quality of life.

Among the analyzed dimensions of Smart Governance, the accessibility of e-services emerges as the strongest determinant of its overall assessment, a finding consistent with earlier research. The ability to handle administrative matters electronically allows residents to save time and fulfil their administrative needs at a convenient time and place. The relatively high rating assigned to e-service accessibility suggests that this is an area in which municipal authorities operate with a degree of effectiveness. Nevertheless, the considerable gap between this rating and the maximum possible value indicates room for further improvement and simultaneously points to the risk of digital exclusion among certain segments of the local community. This situation calls for targeted interventions and remedial measures, such as the organization of digital literacy training and the creation of public spaces equipped with devices facilitating access to e-services.

The second most influential factor shaping the level of Smart Governance in the studied cities is anti-corruption activity. As evidenced by the literature, corruption constitutes a characteristic weakness of developing economies. Yet this particular sphere of local authority activity received the lowest ratings among all analyzed dimensions, reflecting a lack of trust among local communities towards public decision-makers. This conclusion is further corroborated by the low ratings assigned to the transparency of municipal decision-making processes.

The circumstances described above may substantially impede the implementation of the Smart City concept and, consequently, limit the potential for improving residents' quality of life. As prior analyses suggest, opacity in urban policy and ineffective Smart Governance can undermine the benefits derived from all other smart urban solutions.

The findings of the conducted research allow for the formulation of the following recommendations addressed to the concept of Smart Governance:

- prioritizing the transparency and accountability of municipal authorities, implemented through the maintenance of open databases concerning public expenditure and municipal decision-making;
- making public consultations mandatory regarding key decisions in the area of urban governance;
- developing and publishing registers of contracts concluded with external contractors and the remuneration of municipal administration employees;
- systematic publication of the results of independent external audits;
- periodic reporting on the degree of implementation of the programmatic commitments of municipal authorities;
- introducing transparent and timely procedures for processing requests for access to public information;

- gradual expansion of the availability of public e-services and open digital platforms;
- conducting information campaigns and organizing training aimed at counteracting digital exclusion among residents.

6 Conclusions

The research presented shows that the quality of life in the cities studied is assessed by most residents as satisfactory or good. However, the quality of public services offered by municipal administration is evaluated much more poorly. It cannot therefore be concluded that it exerts a favorable impact on the image of cities and the living conditions of local communities. Smart Governance does not directly contribute to improving the quality of life in Silesian cities.

Of the four analyzed elements of public services, respondents rated municipal authorities' anti-corruption efforts lowest. The transparency of municipal decisions, including the accessibility of information about the principles of their adoption, was also assessed as average. The accessibility of e-services was rated highest, which demonstrates effective digitization of resident services by the cities studied.

The quality of public services in the cities studied is most strongly influenced by the accessibility of e-services and anti-corruption efforts. These are issues directly related to the life of the average resident. The transparency and accessibility of information about decisions made in the city are of lesser importance for local community satisfaction. Nevertheless, in the multiple regression model they remain in a strong and statistically significant relationship with the quality of public services.

The obtained results confirm the accuracy and effectiveness of the chosen direction of city digitization, which constitutes one of the conditions for building a Smart City. Nevertheless, the low level of transparency of municipal decisions and weak corruption prevention negatively affect the quality of urban life. They do not foster building an atmosphere of social trust nor create foundations for resident participation in city governance.

Under such circumstances, technological progress and increasing levels of digitization are unable to guarantee solid foundations for creating a fully sustainable Smart City. The cities studied must therefore strengthen the traditional foundations of Smart Governance to truly become smart and work effectively toward improving the quality of life of urban communities.

The research presented in the article has several significant limitations. First, it focuses on one region, which affects its cognitive value and the scope of possibilities for generalizing the results. Nevertheless, it is based on a large and representative sample of residents from the Central and Eastern European region, which increases its objectivity and the reach of conclusions in relation to other emerging economies.

Second, the research method employed was a diagnostic survey, which is associated with the subjectivity of respondents' assessments. These are conditioned by both the history of their own experiences and individual expectations and views. However, this is a method characteristic of social research and appropriate for identifying quality of life, which also constitutes a derivative of subjective, individual feelings and needs. Furthermore, quality of life is an inherently subjective category, perceived and experienced by urban residents in a distinctly individual and personal manner. The role of municipal authorities, in turn, is to manage and organize public services in such a way as to effectively meet the needs of the local community.

Third, the analysis focused exclusively on Smart Governance and its role in shaping residents' quality of life. Other areas related to a greater or lesser degree to the level of satisfaction with urban life were not analyzed.

Consequently, one of the key directions for further research should be the assessment of remaining determinants of urban life and their impact on residents' perception. It is also worthwhile to confront subjective assessments of the local community with objective data concerning Smart Governance and other determinants of quality of life. An interesting and valuable research avenue would also be to conduct a comparative analysis of Smart Governance in other Central and Eastern European countries.

References

1. Han, M.J.N., Kim, M.J.: A critical review of the smart city in relation to citizen adoption towards sustainable smart living. Habitat Int. **108**, 102312 (2021). https://doi.org/10.1016/j.habitatint.2021.102312
2. Jonek-Kowalska, I., Wolniak, R.: Smart Cities in Poland: Towards Sustainability and a Better Quality of Life? 1st edn. Routledge, London and New York (2024). https://doi.org/10.4324/9781003358190
3. Jonek-Kowalska, I., Wolniak, R.: Exclusion in Smart Cities: Assessment and Strategy for Strengthening Resilience, 1st edn. Routledge, London and New York (2025). https://doi.org/10.4324/9781003499992
4. Clement, J., Manjon, M., Crutzen, N.: Factors for collaboration amongst smart city stakeholders: a local government perspective. Gov. Inf. Q. **39**(4), 101746 (2022). https://doi.org/10.1016/j.giq.2022.101746
5. Nam, T., Pardo, T.A.: The changing face of a city government: a case study of Philly311. Gov. Inf. Q. **31**, S1–S9 (2014). https://doi.org/10.1016/j.giq.2014.01.002
6. Janowski, T., Estevez, E., Baguma, R.: Platform governance for sustainable development: reshaping citizen-administration relationships in the digital age. Gov. Inf. Q. **35**(4), 1–16 (2018). https://doi.org/10.1016/j.giq.2018.09.002
7. Aditya, T., Ningrum, S., Nurasa, H., Irawati, I.: Community needs for the digital divide on the smart city policy. Heliyon. **9**(8), e18932 (2023). https://doi.org/10.1016/j.heliyon.2023.e18932
8. Díaz-Díaz, R., Muñoz, L., Pérez-González, D.: Business model analysis of public services operating in the smart city ecosystem: the case of SmartSantander. Futur. Gener. Comput. Syst. **76**, 198–214 (2017). https://doi.org/10.1016/j.future.2017.01.032
9. Zhaoyuan, F., Xiaofeng, L.: Retention of the highly educated migrants: from the perspective of urban e-service capability. Cost Effectiveness and Resource Allocation. **22**(1), 7 (2024). https://doi.org/10.1186/s12962-024-00509-4
10. Khodabakhsh, P., Fathi, H., Mashayekhi, S.: Planning for future Urban Services in the Smart City era: integrating E-services in urban planning process. Armanshahr Arch. Urban Dev. **9**(16) (2016)
11. Pérez del Hoyo, R., Visvizi, A., Mora, H.: Inclusiveness, safety, resilience, and sustainability in the smart city context. In: Visvizi, A., Pérez del Hoyo, R. (eds.) Smart Cities and the UN SDGs, pp. 15–28. Elsevier, Amsterdam (2021). https://doi.org/10.1016/B978-0-323-85151-0.00002-6

12. Lu, H.P., Chen, C.S., Yu, H.: Technology roadmap for building a smart city: an exploring study on methodology. Futur. Gener. Comput. Syst. **97**, 727–742 (2019). https://doi.org/10.1016/j.future.2019.03.014
13. Wang, D., Liang, Y.F., Dou, W.: How does urban industrial structure upgrading affect green productivity? The moderating role of smart city development. Struct. Chang. Econ. Dyn. **72**, 133–149 (2025). https://doi.org/10.1016/j.strueco.2024.09.017
14. Islam, M.K., Ya, C., Sultana, S.: E-government impact on sustainable development goals (SDGs): a bibliometric insight. Soc. Sci. Humanities Open. **12**, 101743 (2025). https://doi.org/10.1016/j.ssaho.2025.101743
15. Niedziałkowski, K., Chmielewski, P.: Challenging the dominant path of forest policy? Bottom-up, citizen forest management initiatives in a top-down governance context in Poland. Forest Policy Econ. **154**, 103009 (2023). https://doi.org/10.1016/j.forpol.2023.103009
16. Maziashvili, M., Kowalik, I., Pleśniak, A.: The antecedents of participation in city branding: a comparison between Poznan (Poland) and Kutaisi (Georgia). Cities. **141**, 104473 (2023). https://doi.org/10.1016/j.cities.2023.104473
17. Sienkiewicz-Małyjurek, K., Zyzak, B.: Overcoming social and ethical challenges of AI through organizational resilience. A PLS-SEM approach. Telematics Inform. **96**, 102210 (2025). https://doi.org/10.1016/j.tele.2024.102210
18. Wagner, M.: Evading spatial planning law—case study of Poland. Land Use Policy. **57**, 396–404 (2016). https://doi.org/10.1016/j.landusepol.2016.06.005
19. Uryga, D., Geirbo, H.C., Romanowska, M., Duda, E.: Two crises. Constructing the meaning of the "climate crisis" by the residents of Gdańsk. Polit. Geogr. **123**, 103422 (2025). https://doi.org/10.1016/j.polgeo.2025.103422
20. Havel, M.B.: Neoliberalization of urban policy-making and planning in post-socialist Poland–a distinctive path from the perspective of varieties of capitalism. Cities. **127**, 103766 (2022). https://doi.org/10.1016/j.cities.2022.103766
21. Przybyła, K., Kachniarz, M., Hełdak, M., Ramsey, D.M.: The functional structures of polish cities with particular emphasis on changes in their financial function. Cities. **168**, 106379 (2026). https://doi.org/10.1016/j.cities.2025.106379
22. Gonzalez-Aquines, A., Cordero-Perez, A.C., Kowalska-Bobko, I.: Differences of corruption types in selected Western and central-eastern health systems during the COVID-19 pandemic: a rapid review. Front. Public Health. **11**, 1269189 (2023). https://doi.org/10.3389/fpubh.2023.1269189
23. Chang, S., Smith, M.K.: Residents' quality of life in smart cities: a systematic literature review. Land. **12**(4), 876 (2023). https://doi.org/10.3390/land12040876
24. Smith, M.K., Chang, S.: Quality of life and overtourism in Budapest: resident experiences and smart solutions. Worldwide Hospital. Tourism Themes. **17**(4), 452–464 (2025). https://doi.org/10.1108/whatt-03-2025-0086
25. Szczepańska, A., Kaźmierczak, R., Myszkowska, M.: Smart city solutions from a societal perspective—a case study. Int. J. Environ. Res. Public Health. **20**(6), 5136 (2023). https://doi.org/10.3390/ijerph20065136
26. Viale Pereira, G., Cunha, M.A., Lampoltshammer, T.J., Parycek, P., Testa, M.G.: Increasing collaboration and participation in smart city governance: a cross-case analysis of smart city initiatives. Inf. Technol. Dev. **23**(3), 526–553 (2017). https://doi.org/10.1080/02681102.2017.1353946
27. Shami, M.R., Rad, V.B., Moinifar, M.: The structural model of indicators for evaluating the quality of urban smart living. Technol. Forecast. Soc. Chang. **176**, 121427 (2022). https://doi.org/10.1016/j.techfore.2021.121427
28. Dash, A.: Modeling the moderating effect of technology anxiety on the relationship between smart city–built environment and the quality of life of citizens. J. Facil. Manag. **22**(5), 811–827 (2024). https://doi.org/10.1108/jfm-06-2022-0061

29. Smith, M.K., Chang, S., Michalkó, G.: Smart living and quality of life: domains and indicators. J. Urban Regional Anal. **16**(2), 181–210 (2024). https://doi.org/10.37043/jura.2024.16.2.1
30. Gc, S.B., et al.: E-governance, citizen satisfaction and net benefits: the moderating effect of digital divide. Cogent Bus. Manag. **11**(1), 2402512 (2024)
31. Li, J., Dong, Y., Siemers, O.: Digital exclusion and citizen engagement with e-government services in China. Int. J. Public Sect. Manag., 1–22 (2025). https://doi.org/10.1108/ijpsm-03-2025-0135
32. Wiig, A.: The empty rhetoric of the smart city: from digital inclusion to economic promotion in Philadelphia. Urban Geogr. **37**(4), 535–553 (2016). https://doi.org/10.1080/02723638.2015.1065686
33. De Guimarães, J.C.F., Severo, E.A., Júnior, L.A.F., Da Costa, W.P.L.B., Salmoria, F.T.: Governance and quality of life in smart cities: towards sustainable development goals. J. Clean. Prod. **253**, 119926 (2020). https://doi.org/10.1016/j.jclepro.2019.119926
34. Dhenge, V., Nimbarte, G.: Governance, ease of living, and citizens' perception: components for quality-of-life assessment in mid-sized smart cities. Int. J. Human Capital Urban Manag. **9**(2), 100–189 (2024). https://doi.org/10.1007/978-981-99-8811-2_55
35. Worrakittimalee, T., Pienwisetkaew, T., Naruetharadhol, P.: The role of smart governance in ensuring the success of smart cities: a case of Thailand. Cogent Soc. Sci. **10**(1), 2388827 (2024). https://doi.org/10.1080/23311886.2024.2388827
36. Przeybilovicz, E., et al.: Citizen participation in the smart city: findings from an international comparative study. Local Gov. Stud. **48**(1), 23–47 (2022). https://doi.org/10.1080/03003930.2020.1851204
37. Hartley, K.: Public perceptions about smart cities: governance and quality-of-life in Hong Kong. Soc. Indic. Res. **166**, 731–753 (2023). https://doi.org/10.1007/s11205-023-03087-9
38. Egba, V.N., et al.: Digital governance and citizen trust in Nigeria's public sector: urban and semi-urban residents' perceptions of socio-technical dynamics of inclusivity and institutional transformation. SN Social Sciences. **6**(3), 101 (2026). https://doi.org/10.1007/s43545-026-01372-1
39. Oliveira, T.A., Oliver, M., Ramalhinho, H.: Challenges for connecting citizens and smart cities: ICT, e-governance and blockchain. Sustainability. **12**(7), 2926 (2020). https://doi.org/10.3390/su12072926
40. Aldegheishem, A.: Assessing progress towards smart governance in Saudi Arabia. Humanit. Soc. Sci. Commun. **11**(1), 1–9 (2024). https://doi.org/10.1057/s41599-024-03235-7
41. Hong, S.G., Lee, D.: Development of a citizen participation public service innovation model based on smart governance. Serv. Bus. **17**(3), 669–694 (2023)
42. Gil, O., Cortés-Cediel, M.E., Cantador, I.: Citizen participation and the rise of digital media platforms in smart governance and smart cities. Int. J. E-Planning Res. **8**(1), 19–34 (2019)
43. Wijayasinghe, S., Sachitra, V.: Smart city development and improvement of quality of life in urban cities of Sri Lanka: citizen-centric approach. J. Global Responsibil. **16**(3), 431–450 (2025)
44. Alshamaila, Y., Papagiannidis, S., Alsawalqah, H.: Smart cities in Jordan: challenges and barriers. Cities. **154**, 105327 (2024)
45. Maghsoudi, M., Mohammadi, N., Bakhtiari, M.: Artificial intelligence and sustainable development: public concerns and governance in developed and developing nations. Cleaner Environ. Syst., 100340 (2025). https://doi.org/10.1007/s11628-023-00536-w
46. Somak, O., Dmytrenko, I., Ninyuk, I., Suray, I., Nakonechnyi, O.: Innovative practices of public administration: approaches to public sector management in the era of digitalization and open government. J. Theor. Appl. Inf. Technol. **104**(2) (2026). https://doi.org/10.5281/zenodo.18454478

47. Hellowell, M., et al.: Private provision of health services in Ukraine: a qualitative exploration of current policy challenges, and considerations for reform. Health Policy. **158**, 105349 (2025). https://doi.org/10.1016/j.healthpol.2025.105349
48. Bozkurt, Y., Rossmann, A., Pervez, Z., Ramzan, N.: Assessing data governance models for smart cities: benchmarking data governance models on the basis of European urban requirements. Sustain. Cities Soc. **130**, 106528 (2025). https://doi.org/10.1016/j.scs.2025.106528
49. Gao, N., Lin, Z., Yang, B.: The effect of digitalization on disaster response in local government: quasi-experimental evidence from smart city infrastructure in China. Int. J. Disaster Risk Reduc. **135**, 106043 (2026). https://doi.org/10.1016/j.ijdrr.2026.106043
50. Chen, Z., Chan, I.C.C.: Smart cities and quality of life: a quantitative analysis of citizens' support for smart city development. Inf. Technol. People. **36**(1), 263–285 (2023). https://doi.org/10.1108/ITP-07-2021-0577
51. Lin, C., Zhao, G., Yu, C., Wu, Y.: Smart city development and residents' well-being. Sustainability. **11**(3), 676 (2019). https://doi.org/10.3390/su11030676
52. Hollands, R.G.: Will the real smart city please stand up? Intelligent, progressive or entrepreneurial? City. **12**(3), 303–320 (2008). https://doi.org/10.1080/13604810802479126
53. Kitchin, R.: Making sense of smart cities: addressing present shortcomings. Camb. J. Reg. Econ. Soc. **8**(1), 131–136 (2015). https://doi.org/10.1093/cjres/rsu027
54. Kitchin, R.: The real-time city? Big data and smart urbanism. GeoJournal. **79**(1), 1–14 (2014). https://doi.org/10.1007/s10708-013-9516-8

Using Digital Participatory Platforms for Deliberation Aimed at Achieving Sustainable Development Goals

Kamila Rożnowska(✉) and Katarzyna Sienkiewicz-Małyjurek

Faculty of Organization and Management, Department of Management, Silesian University of Technology, Gliwice, Poland
{kamila.roznowska,katarzyna.sienkiewicz-malyjurek}@polsl.pl

Abstract. Public administrations increasingly use digital participatory platforms (DPPs) to enhance citizen engagement, support informed dialogue, and improve decision-making aligned with the Sustainable Development Goals (SDGs). This paper examines the role of DPPs in deliberative processes by conceptualizing them as socio-technical systems that combine technological affordances with institutional and procedural conditions. It aims to answer three research questions: 1. How can DPPs support effective deliberation? 2. What is the current level of implementation of DPPs in deliberation worldwide? 3. How do DPPs engage citizens in achieving the SDGs? Drawing on a conceptual-analytic approach and international comparative evidence, the study identifies how DPPs influence representativeness, access to information, deliberative quality, and the co-creation of public value. It highlights the uneven adoption of DPPs worldwide, the risks associated with digital divides, algorithmic opacity, and the potential of emerging AI tools to reshape digital deliberation practices.

Keywords: Digital Participatory Platforms · Deliberation · Sustainable Development Goals · Public Governance · Citizen Engagement · Socio-Technical Systems · Digital Transformation

1 Introduction

Governments around the world face a convergence of climate, social, and economic challenges, making the achievement of the Sustainable Development Goals (SDGs) increasingly urgent. SDG11 emphasizes the need for inclusive, safe, resilient, and sustainable public spaces. A significant development in this area is the emergence of digital participatory platforms (DPPs). These platforms are software environments designed to facilitate the co-creation of public services, including agenda-setting, co-design, decision-making, and monitoring [1, 2]. DPPs offer scalability, traceability, and more equitable civic engagement compared to traditional offline methods. They incorporate tools for deliberative consultation, such as argumentation spaces, structured feedback loops, and participatory budgeting workflows [3, 4].

Published by Springer Nature Switzerland AG 2027
L. M. Camarinha-Matos and F. Ferrada (Eds.): DoCEIS 2026, IFIP AICT 790, pp. 451–467, 2027.
https://doi.org/10.1007/978-3-032-28939-1_31

However, as this field has developed, widespread criticism has emerged. Much of the early literature and many implementations in local governments have focused primarily on technical or interface-level issues, such as platform functionality. At the same time, insufficient consideration has been given to outcomes that truly matter for public value, including consultation quality, policy effectiveness, inclusiveness, and progress on SDGs [3, 4, 5]. This gap highlights the need to view DPPs not merely as IT artifacts, but as socio-technical systems embedded in institutional procedures and approaches to public decision-making [6]. In particular, the application of deliberative consultations in the digital public sphere positions DPPs as infrastructures that could improve the quality of argumentation, counteract polarization, and enhance legitimacy if thoughtfully designed and managed [7, 8].

While digital participatory platforms are often presented as tools capable of enhancing inclusiveness and deliberative quality, their actual capacity to increase citizen participation in decision-making remains contingent on broader socio-political conditions. In highly polarized societies, participation does not automatically translate into deliberation, and deliberation does not necessarily result in meaningful influence on decisions. Therefore, DPPs should be understood not as participation-enhancing technologies per se, but as conditional infrastructures, whose effectiveness depends on institutional openness, moderation regimes, informational integrity, and citizens' trust in governance processes. This paper offers an integrated conceptual framework that links stages of deliberation, specific DPP functions, and SDG-oriented public value creation. Its originality lies in systematically mapping how DPPs operate across deliberative stages and in identifying their conditional effectiveness as socio-technical systems rather than stand-alone technological solutions. This paper operationalizes the socio-technical perspective by analytically linking deliberation stages, specific platform functions, and institutional conditions of implementation.

1.1 Motivations and Research Questions

Scholarly literature and practice often focus on the technical aspects of e-participation platforms, such as interfaces [3, 4]. At the same time, they underemphasize consultation management, including key elements such as integrating citizen input into formal decision-making processes and budget allocations [9, 10]. There is limited comparative evidence linking consultation design choices to the quality of deliberation and to policy outcomes aligned with the SDGs across different governance contexts and levels of digital government maturity [2, 11]. Additionally, systemic barriers such as digital divides, trust issues, and privacy concerns are often addressed superficially, even though they significantly influence participation and deliberation outcomes [12].

The preliminary part of the PhD thesis aims to address these gaps by framing DPPs as socio-technical systems, and this manuscript aims to identify the nature of deliberation and, based on this, seeks answers to the following research questions:

1. How can DPPs support effective deliberation?
2. What is the current level of implementation of DPPs in deliberation worldwide?
3. How do DPPs engage citizens in achieving the SDGs?

The main hypothesis of this article is that DPPs catalyze sustainable development not only through technology but primarily through the co-production of their functionality, transforming citizen input into outcomes aligned with the SDGs.

The SDGs are not treated in this paper as a substantive policy domain but as a governance framework that enables comparison, accountability, and public value orientation. Their use allows deliberative processes to be analyzed not only as participatory exercises but as instruments embedded in policy implementation cycles.

1.2 Relation to the Technological Evolution to Tackle Societal Challenges

Digitally mediated public deliberative consultations are a cornerstone of participatory governance and democratic innovation [7], aiming to drive technological evolution to tackle societal challenges. They enable governments to co-create public value by integrating citizen perspectives into policy design, service delivery, and strategic planning [13]. This topic directly addresses the design, management, and optimization of consultation processes, which are increasingly digital and data-driven.

Public consultations have evolved from traditional on-site meetings to digital platforms that leverage AI, big data, and collaborative tools. These platforms embody socio-technical complexity: they combine technical architectures with social processes [14, 15]. Technological evolution to tackle societal challenges promotes research on smart systems and cyber-physical integration, and managing deliberative consultations in a digital context requires similar principles, including system interoperability, user-centered design, and secure data governance.

Additionally, technological evolution is not limited to hardware or software engineering; it encompasses digital ecosystems that transform society. Public consultations, when digitized, become complex engineered systems that require interoperability, security, and user-centric design [16, 17]. Moreover, the topic advances co-creation paradigms that bridge technical innovation and social impact.

1.3 Methodology

The study employed a conceptual-analytic approach, encompassing a literature review and an analysis of EU and OECD strategic documents [18]. This approach allowed for the organization of knowledge, the reconstruction of the process, and the identification of the role of DPPs in deliberation. The conceptual analytic approach is frequently used in public policy research, governance, and institutional studies [19, 20].

The literature review focused on peer-reviewed journal articles and policy reports addressing digital participation, deliberative democracy, and DPPs, published primarily between 2018 and 2025. The literature was selected using thematic relevance criteria, focusing on deliberative democracy, digital participation, and socio-technical governance perspectives. The comparative analysis draws on publicly available records from the OECD Deliberative Democracy Database, which were systematically examined to identify patterns in DPP adoption, formats, and geographical distribution.

1.4 Theoretical and Practical Value

While deliberative processes in Europe and worldwide have been recorded by the OECD since 1979, with over 700 conducted to date, in Central and Eastern European countries, this participatory format is in its early stages of development due to the transition from autocratic socialism to civic democracy. It should be noted that the OECD's Deliberative Democracy Database is based on submissions, so individual differences may exist between the database's content and the actual number of deliberations conducted. For example, in Poland, 13 local deliberations have been conducted so far, with nine reported in the database. Therefore, in discussing the contribution of research on deliberative procedures, the practical implementation of these procedures in future public participation processes is emphasized, thereby improving the quality of outcomes in co-creating public value [21].

Furthermore, the use of DPPs in deliberative processes is becoming particularly important in an era of intensified dissemination of artificial intelligence (AI) and digital tools, which are influencing the transition of DPP functionality from supporting tools [22] to tools that automate the process [23].

This study deliberately adopts a conceptual-analytic approach. Given the fragmented and context-dependent nature of deliberative practices using digital platforms, the primary objective is not to measure impact, but to structure the analytical dimensions through which such impacts could be meaningfully assessed in future empirical research. By clarifying functions, stages, and conditions of DPP-supported deliberation, the paper seeks to contribute to theory-building rather than outcome evaluation.

2 The State of the Art

In recent years, DPPs have become one of the most important mechanisms for connecting residents with the government. Extensive research into their functionality has led to numerous definitions. This paper adapts the definition of DPPs, according to which they constitute "a specific type of civic technology explicitly built for participatory, engagement and collaboration purposes that allow for user generated content and include a range of functionalities (e.g. analytics, map-based and geo-located input, importing and exporting of data, ranking of ideas) which transcend and considerably differ from social media such as Social Networking Sites and Microblogging (Facebook, Twitter and Instagram). DPPs thus allow for different levels and intensities of citizen engagement and participation" [24], p. 54. Figure 1 illustrates the architecture of the DPP conceptualized as a socio-technical system composed of interrelated institutional, social, functional, and technical layers, embedded within a shared normative environment.

Figure 1 highlights that the effectiveness of DPPs depends on the interaction between governance arrangements, social actors, platform functions supporting deliberative stages, and technical infrastructure. These layers operate within a normative environment shaped by trust, inclusiveness, and fairness, which conditions both citizen engagement and the legitimacy of deliberative outcomes.

DPPs offer scalable ways to propose ideas, deliberate, co-create policies, and monitor their implementation. They enable greater scale and inclusiveness of citizen engagement,

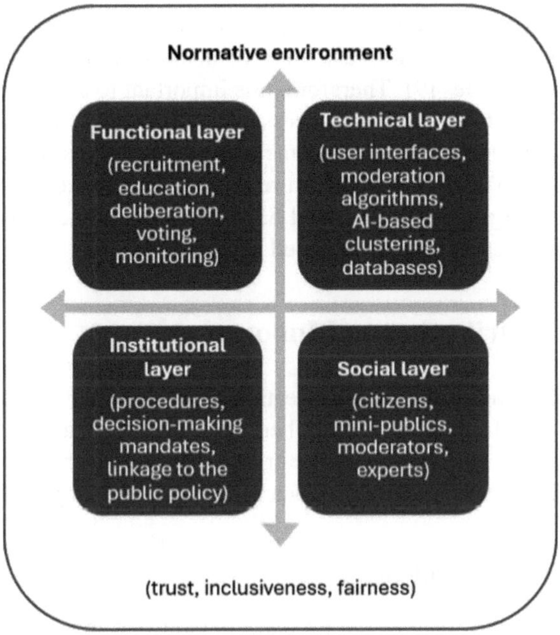

Fig. 1. The typical architecture of DPPs. Source: own elaboration

while improving the quality and impact of public decision-making on sustainable development outcomes [24]. This impact stems from increased transparency and accountability and translates into building trust through citizen participation in real political decisions and providing transparent criteria and justifications for decision-making [3, 7]. Furthermore, DPPs facilitate the alignment of decision-making processes with local context and objectives, and citizen-generated data supports monitoring the implementation of the SDGs [4, 9, 25].

However, research points to a persistent gap between technology itself and its impact on deliberative quality and measurable progress towards the SDGs, underscoring the crucial role of socio-institutional configurations. International comparative studies show that similar technologies yield different outcomes across governance cultures, administrative competencies, and levels of digital government maturity [2, 9]. Furthermore, numerous risks are associated with the implementation of DPPs, including: digital inequalities such as access and competence, as well as selection bias, which reduce the representativeness of the decision-making process [2, 26], polarization and inequality of citizen participation with weak deliberative facilitation [7, 8], regulatory constraints [27], opaque platform algorithms [28], and privacy and data protection risks [29] that undermine trust in platforms.

Moreover, international research shows that the same type of DPPs yields divergent outcomes depending on governance culture, administrative capacity, and policymaking approaches. Analyses conducted in Brazil, the United Kingdom, and the Netherlands have identified evolving citizen roles—contestation, acceptance, and collaboration—shaped by governance and institutional receptivity [2]. Findings from Madrid and

Barcelona, in turn, demonstrate that open, commons-based processes combined with iterative adaptation are crucial for sustaining democratic values and embedding DPPs into decision-making cycles [9]. Therefore, it is important to examine the determinants and impacts of DPPs on deliberative processes in public decision-making, the level of citizen digital engagement in SDG implementation, and to identify the most effective ways to utilize DPPs. The reviewed literature reveals gaps concerning the alignment of deliberative design, digital platforms, and SDG-oriented public value creation, which directly inform the research questions posed in this study.

3 Research Contribution and Innovation

Building on the reviewed literature, this section moves beyond synthesis by proposing an original analytical framework for deliberation into four stages and systematically assigning the functions of digital participatory platforms to each stage. This framework enables comparative analysis and provides a basis for future empirical validation.

3.1 The Nature of Deliberation

Deliberation is a specific form of public participation that involves engaging a representative group of citizens in the policy-making process by providing conditions for impartial discussion – including access to reliable data – on issues important to the local community, while respecting differences of opinion to achieve consensus and develop implementable recommendations [30]. In the literature, the creators of deliberative techniques define them most simply as opinion-forming processes ("what people would think if they had time to think"), rather than as static opinion aggregation ("what people think") [31]. Therefore, for the procedures to be considered deliberative, they must meet specific criteria that distinguish them from conventional public consultation formats. The analyses conducted allowed us to identify four key characteristics of deliberation.

First, the representativeness of mini-publics [32]. This is one of the key stages in designing deliberative processes, involving selecting a method for recruiting participants. Typically, this involves a two-stage drawing based on specified demographic characteristics, intended to ensure the representativeness of views and the creation of mini-publics. Two-stage sampling involves: drawing a representative research sample from the total number of residents in the community; inviting the selected research sample to register; and conducting a second drawing from among the registered group to select participants for the deliberation. For this reason, mini-publics are referred to as "the city in a nutshell," as the aim of the drawing is to maximize the representativeness of opinions. Unlike traditional consultations, deliberation – unlike "everyone off the street" – will not involve "anyone randomly selected off the street."

Second, the educational component meets the requirements of fairness and impartiality [33]. This is the stage in which randomly selected deliberative participants acquire knowledge about the issues being discussed. The educational component equips participants with the competencies to participate in deliberation. At this stage, opinions begin to form.

Third, the deliberative process itself involves discussion among participants, supported by independent experts and facilitators [34]. This results in the development of a set of recommendations that should be implementable and implemented by the public authorities once the required level of support (e.g., 80% compliance) is achieved among the mini-publics' participants.

However, contemporary deliberation increasingly takes place in contexts marked by affective polarization, declining epistemic trust, and competition between factual evidence and ideological narratives. Under such conditions, access to information alone is insufficient to ensure informed judgment. Deliberative processes supported by DPPs must therefore incorporate mechanisms that actively counteract confirmation bias and disinformation.

Fourth, there's the implementation of the developed recommendations. This is the process of verifying and monitoring the implementation of the expectations articulated during the deliberative process. Already at this stage of this discussion, we can observe that the potential for DPPs is high at every stage of the deliberative process, particularly during participant recruitment through the selection of software for designing research groups based on the existing demographic data of the given community, as well as during the deliberative stage itself through the use of platforms that support reflection and voting on proposals, which will then be included in the list of developed recommendations. Secondly, DPPs can be used in the educational stage as distance learning platforms and in the implementation monitoring stage, which usually involves publication on websites whose implementation progress is updated at agreed time intervals.

3.2 Functions of DPPs in Deliberation Focused on SDGs

The analysis of deliberation characteristics provided the basis for identifying the functions that DPPs can perform in deliberative processes supporting SDGs implementation. Their importance can be assessed as:

- key, meaning they have a higher impact on achieving the objectives of a given stage than if implemented without DPPs;
- supporting, meaning they affect the achievement of the objectives of individual deliberation stages, but in the absence of DPPs, they may have limited or no impact on the deliberation process itself, as the objectives of a stage can be achieved independently;
- supporting-key, meaning they can have a positive impact using DPPs, but the stage's objectives can still be achieved independently.

The socio-technical perspective is operationalized through the analytical mapping presented in Table 1, which links technical platform functions with social and institutional dimensions of deliberative processes. Table 1 presents an authorial analytical synthesis based on the literature reviewed in Sect. 2, mapping deliberation stages to DPP functions relevant for SDG-oriented governance.

Ensuring the representativeness of mini-publics is one of the most important requirements for conducting public participation. As indicated above, unlike general consultations, which allow all interested parties to participate, deliberation introduces an element of verifiable representativeness and fair participation through random sampling. Other stages of deliberation may, but do not necessarily, be supported by DPPs, as local or

Table 1. Deliberation functions and the importance of using DPPs at individual stages in the SDG implementation process.

Deliberation Function	Deliberation Stage	Importance of Using DPPs
Representativeness	1 - Randomization	Key
Education and Developing Informed Judgments	2 - Education	Supportive
Accessibility/Inclusiveness	2 - Education 3 - Proper Deliberation	Supportive Supportive/Key
Co-creation of Public Value	3 - Proper Deliberation 4 - Monitoring	Supportive/Key Supportive/Key
Representativeness		

regional deliberations involve several dozen participants, enabling "analog" deliberation. However, in deliberations involving a larger number of participants (supraregional, national, international), DPPs can prove crucial in streamlining the process, for example, by enabling remote participation, which can increase turnout and, thus, indirectly enhance process representativeness.

3.3 The Current Level of Implementation of DPPs in Deliberation Aiming at the SDGs

Analysing existing data on deliberative processes worldwide, recorded by the OECD since 1979, we can observe that the implementation of DPPs has so far accounted for a small percentage (14,48%). Table 2 provides detailed results.

The analysis of the collected data shows that the dominant method of conducting deliberation focused on the implementation of the SDGs worldwide is direct, face-to-face meetings – they constitute over 85% of all deliberations recorded. A growing number of deliberations using DPPs has been observed since 2020, due to the coronavirus pandemic, which significantly limited the possibility of face-to-face meetings. However, it is worth noting that the first deliberation on DPPs in Australia took place in 2019. The types of DPPs recorded in the database are noteworthy – in most cases, these included the Zoom conferencing platform and similar tools enabling remote communication. DPPs were used in isolated cases – the Interactio and Decidim platforms – and the use of project websites was recognized as a DPP application.

It is important to emphasize that while the OECD database is a valuable source of information on deliberative processes worldwide, it has certain limitations. The source data is reported individually by deliberative practitioners or deliberative organizers in the form of project fiches, so not all deliberative processes can be reported, even if they were conducted before 2023. Furthermore, project fiches do not always fully present all data, which had to be noted in the table as "no data" or "–" if a given piece of information was not mentioned.

While the OECD Deliberative Democracy Database provides the most comprehensive global overview of deliberative practices, it remains based on self-reported project

Table 2. Recorded deliberative processes, including the use of DPPs.

Country	No. of deliberations conducted from 1979 to 2023	No. of deliberations with DPPs (T – total; O – online; H – hybrid)	DPPs used
Australia	75	T: 11; O: 3; H: 8	Zoom – 7; Ausgrid 'YourSay' website powered by EngagementHub - 1
New Zealand	1	T: 1; H: 1	no data
Canada	45	T: 4; O: 4	Zoom
South Korea	5	–	–
USA	21	T: 3; O: 2; H: 1	Zoom - 2
China	3	–	–
Argentina	1	–	–
Mongolia	2	–	–
Brazil	5	–	–
Japan	167	–	–
Mexico	1	T: 1; O: 1	Zoom
Colombia	1	T: 1; H: 1	Zoom; Whatsapp
Netherlands	22	T: 4; O: 1; H: 3	Zoom – 4; Project website - 1
Austria	46	–	–
Belgium	20	T: 2; H: 2	no data
Estonia	4	T: 1; O - 1	Zoom, Google Slides, Google Forms
Denmark	41	T: 9; O -2; H - 7	Zoom - 4
France	43	T: 16; O: 5; H: 11	Zoom: 5; Website: 2
Germany	81	T: 9; O: 4; H: 5	Zoom: 3; Webex Meetings: 2; Teams: 1; Secure room online: 1
Spain	15	T: 1; O: 1	Zoom: 1
Ireland	6	T: 1; H: 1	Zoom; Mi-Voice
Italy	12	T: 1; O: 1	Zoom; Decidim
Poland	9	T: 3; O: 3	Zoom: 2
Finland	4	T: 3; O: 3	Zoom: 3
Portugal	4	–	–
Hungary	4	–	–

(continued)

Table 2. (*continued*)

Country	No. of deliberations conducted from 1979 to 2023	No. of deliberations with DPPs (T – total; O – online; H – hybrid)	DPPs used
Luxembourg	5	T: 1; H: 1	Basecamp
Norway	1	–	–
United Kingdom	56	T: 26; O: 19; H: 7	Zoom: 17; Teams: 1; Your Priorities:1; Miro: 1; Other textual collaborative tools: 1
Switzerland	9	–	–
Bosnia and Herzegovina	1	–	–
Montenegro	1	–	–
Georgia	1	–	–

Source: own elaboration based on [35]

fiches. As such, it captures the occurrence and format of deliberations rather than their societal or policy impact. In particular, the presence of a digital platform does not indicate whether deliberative outcomes informed actual policy decisions or contributed to measurable SDG progress. This limitation reinforces the need to treat database findings as indicative rather than evaluative.

3.4 Engaging Citizens on DPPs to Achieve SDGs

The analysis continued with a focus on identifying ways for citizens to engage digitally in implementing the SDGs. This analysis examined five types of platforms and evaluated their potential effects and opportunities for achieving the SDG goals and indicators. Table 3 presents the findings.

As shown in Table 3, digital forms of citizen engagement enable more inclusive, transparent, and responsive decision-making processes in the public sector. Platforms such as public consultation portals (e.g., Decidim, CONSUL), open data portals, crowdsourcing mechanisms, complaint and whistleblowing systems, and thematic deliberative platforms create an ecosystem of tools that support collaboration among public administration, civil society, and the private sector.

Public consultation portals such as Decidim and CONSUL are used in European cities, such as Barcelona and Helsinki, to co-create mobility and spatial planning strategies [40, 50]. Open data portals, for example, in Estonia and Denmark, enable citizens to analyze infrastructure investments, reducing information asymmetry and strengthening trust in public institutions [53, 54]. Crowdsourcing data and citizen science initiatives (e.g., monitoring air quality in cities) fill data gaps in monitoring SDG indicators and build climate awareness. Thematic platforms for thematic deliberation, such as the European Conference on the Future of Europe or local climate assemblies in the Netherlands,

Table 3. Methods of engaging citizens in achieving the SDGs through DPPs.

Type of DPPs	Effect	SDG Goals	Sample Sources
Public consultation portals (e.g., Decidim, CONSUL, participatory budgeting)	Increasing the representativeness and quality of dialogue, policy responsiveness, and institutional accountability	SDG 11: Mechanisms for public participation in urban planning SDG 16: Percentage of people who consider decision-making to be inclusive and responsive, satisfaction with public services	[36–41]
Open data portals	Reducing information asymmetry, facilitating public control, and strengthening trust in public institutions	SDG 9: Infrastructure development, increasing technology availability, strengthening innovation capacity SDG 16: Satisfaction with public services, access to information SDG 17: Creating public-private and social partnerships	[42–44]
Crowdsourcing data for SDGs (e.g., environmental monitoring)	Filling SDG data gaps (especially environmental), increasing the frequency and quality of measurements	SDG 11, 14, 15: environmental indicators, e.g., urban air quality, marine pollution, endangered species SDG 13: Building climate awareness	[25, 45, 46]
Complaint portals, reporting, and whistleblowing	Detecting abuse, shortening response times, and increasing accountability	SDG 16: Increasing satisfaction with public services and access to information SDG 17: Increasing partnerships between public administration and society	[47–50]
Platforms for thematic deliberation, e.g., climate, transport, housing	Improving the quality of debates and the legitimacy of decisions, supporting the implementation of sectoral policies	SDG 11: Access to safe and sustainable urban infrastructure and services, participatory city planning SDG 13: Integration of climate actions into policies, awareness-raising, and climate education SDG 16: Satisfaction with public services, inclusive public decisions	[7, 51, 52]

improve the quality of debates and support the implementation of climate policies [7, 52]. It can therefore be concluded that digital deliberation tools not only facilitate access to information and decision-making processes but enable the co-creation of public policies, which is a prerequisite for the effective implementation of many sustainable development goals. It is worth noticing that while SDG 11 provides a frequent application context for local deliberative processes, SDG 16 constitutes the core governance framework underpinning public participation, transparency, and institutional accountability.

4 Discussion of Results and a Critical View

DPPs are not just technological artifacts, but – if responsibly designed and implemented – can be crucial for achieving the SDGs by meeting the demands for greater inclusiveness, accessibility, representativeness, universality, and reliability in participatory processes. This aligns with the basic assumptions of deliberation, which, as a specific form of public participation, aims, on the one hand, to activate residents in the co-creation of public value. On the other hand, in times of high disinformation risk [55], it can serve a protective function by fostering informed civic attitudes resistant to factual manipulation. This therefore confirms the adopted main hypothesis that the use and development of DPPs influence sustainable development by supporting the transformation of citizen input into results aligned with the SDGs.

However, despite the perceived importance of DPPs for deliberation in achieving the SDGs, based on the over 700 deliberations recorded by the OECD, we see that the use of digital platforms has so far accounted for a small share of all recorded processes, with a significant increase observed after 2020, which was related to the coronavirus pandemic and limited opportunities for face-to-face meetings. This may indicate that face-to-face meetings remain the primary form of participatory processes, and it should be remembered that the recruitment process for citizens' assemblies is often still conducted by traditional mail. However, research shows that both in-person deliberations and those using DPPs achieve their intended goals, according to participants [56]. Therefore, it should be recognized that the decision on whether and to what extent to use DPPs should remain a choice of the community affected by the deliberation. This will preserve the supportive, rather than exclusive, functions of DPPs [30].

The findings suggest the need to critically reflect on how to maintain deliberative quality in hybrid or fully digital environments. While online discussions can enhance participation, they present challenges such as fragmented attention, reduced emotional connection, and fewer opportunities to build interpersonal trust. Digital environments can facilitate structured and equitable discussions but also pose risks, such as decreased empathy and increased cognitive overload. This result highlights the importance of designing DPPs that include embedded facilitation, tools for reflective thinking, and mechanisms to manage cognitive strain.

However, the growing integration of artificial intelligence into digital participatory platforms introduces some ambivalence. On the one hand, AI-based tools can support moderation, argument clustering, and inclusion at scale. On the other hand, the same technologies enable large-scale opinion steering, synthetic content generation, micro-targeted persuasion, and the amplification of polarizing frames. In such environments, deliberative platforms risk becoming arenas not of reasoned exchange, but of competing narrative engineering. This issue significantly limits the assumption that digital participation necessarily reinforces democratic decision-making.

Overall, the successful use of DPPs in deliberative processes aimed at supporting the implementation of SDGs requires more than just access to technology. It necessitates institutional readiness, strong governance frameworks, inclusive outreach strategies, and thoughtful design choices that uphold core deliberative principles. Therefore, any future expansion of DPP-based deliberation should be approached as a socio-technical challenge, necessitating coordinated progress in policy, organizational culture, platform design, and civic digital competencies.

The analysis suggests that digital participatory platforms do not inherently increase citizens' influence on decision-making. Their effectiveness depends on the extent to which deliberative outputs are institutionally coupled with formal decision-making procedures. Without explicit feedback loops, and accountability mechanisms, participation risks remaining symbolic rather than consequential.

5 Conclusion and Further Work

The main contribution of this paper lies in conceptual clarification rather than empirical validation. By systematically mapping the functions of digital participatory platforms across the stages of deliberation and linking them to SDG-oriented public value creation, the study provides an analytical scaffold for future empirical and comparative research on digital deliberation.

However, this study has several limitations that should be acknowledged. First, the research adopts a conceptual-analytic approach and does not include primary empirical data; therefore, it does not allow for causal claims regarding the societal impact of digital participatory platforms on deliberative outcomes or SDG implementation. Second, the comparative analysis relies on secondary, self-reported data from the OECD Deliberative Democracy Database, which captures the occurrence and formal characteristics of deliberative processes rather than their quality, effectiveness, or policy impact. As a result, the presence of digital platforms in recorded deliberations should be interpreted as indicative rather than evaluative. Third, the analytical framework proposed in this paper is interpretative and based on literature synthesis, which may not fully capture context-specific institutional, cultural, or political factors shaping deliberative practices. These limitations notwithstanding, the study aims to provide a structured conceptual foundation that can inform and guide future empirical, comparative, and experimental research on digital deliberation and socio-technical governance. The paper points to several concrete directions for future research, particularly in the context of the growing integration of artificial intelligence into digital participatory platforms.

First, there is a need for systematic empirical studies examining AI-supported facilitation tools in digital deliberation, including platforms such as the Stanford Online Deliberation Platform. In particular, future work should assess how AI-assisted moderation and clustering of arguments influence deliberative quality, equality of participation, and the scalability of deliberative processes.

Second, the growing use of generative AI in DPPs raises critical questions about the detection and mitigation of manipulative, violent, or strategically misleading communication. This creates opportunities for interdisciplinary research combining deliberative democracy, computational linguistics, and AI ethics.

Third, future studies should investigate the effects of real-time visualizations of opinion distributions in AI-based DPPs. While such tools may enhance transparency and group awareness, they may also bias opinion formation by reinforcing early majorities or discouraging minority viewpoints.

Finally, comparative research is needed to examine under what institutional, epistemic, and governance conditions AI-enhanced digital deliberation contributes positively to public decision-making and the achievement of the SDGs.

References

1. König, P.D.: Citizen-centered data governance in the smart city: from ethics to accountability. Sustain. Cities Soc. **75**, 103308 (2021). https://doi.org/10.1016/j.scs.2021.103308
2. Przeybilovicz, E., et al.: Citizen participation in the smart city: findings from an international comparative study. Local Gov. Stud. **48**(1), 23–47 (2022). https://doi.org/10.1080/03003930.2020.1851204
3. Menendez-Blanco, M., Bjørn, P.: Designing digital participatory budgeting platforms: urban biking activism in Madrid. Comput. Support. Coop. Work. **31**(4), 567–601 (2022). https://doi.org/10.1007/s10606-022-09443-6
4. Palacin, V., McDonald, S., Aragón, P., Nelimarkka, M.: Configurations of digital participatory budgeting. ACM Trans. Comput.-Hum. Interact. **31**(2), 1–28 (2024). https://doi.org/10.1145/3635144
5. Bouzguenda, I., Alalouch, C., Fava, N.: Towards smart sustainable cities: the role digital citizen participation could play in advancing social sustainability. Sustain. Cities Soc. **50**, 101627 (2022). https://doi.org/10.1016/j.scs.2019.101627
6. Hovik, S., Giannoumis, G.A.: Linkages between citizen participation, digital technology, and urban development. In: Hovik, S., et al. (eds.) Citizen Participation in the Information Society: Comparing Participatory Channels in Urban Development, pp. 1–23. Springer International Publishing, Cham (2022). https://doi.org/10.1007/978-3-030-99940-7_1
7. Mikhaylovskaya, A.: Enhancing deliberation with digital democratic innovations. Philos. Technol. **37**(1), 3 (2024). https://doi.org/10.1007/s13347-023-00692-x
8. Davies, J., Procter, R.: Online platforms of public participation: a deliberative democracy or a delusion? In: Proceedings of the 13th International Conference on Theory and Practice of Electronic Governance, ICEGOV'20, pp. 746–753, Athens (2020). https://doi.org/10.1145/3428502.3428614
9. Smith, A., Prieto Martín, P.: Going beyond the smart city? Implementing technopolitical platforms for urban democracy in Madrid and Barcelona. J. Urban Technol. **28**, 311–330 (2021). https://doi.org/10.1080/10630732.2020.1786337
10. Rożnowska, K., Jasniok, M., Sienkiewicz-Małyjurek, K.: Public consultations in public governance–past and future research directions. Organ. Manag. Sci. Q. **3**(59), 77–96 (2022)
11. Shin, B., Rask, M., Tuominen, P.: Learning through online participation: a longitudinal analysis of participatory budgeting using big data indicators. Inf. Polity. **27**, 517–538 (2022). https://doi.org/10.3233/IP-211551
12. Vassilakopoulou, P., Hustad, E.: Bridging digital divides: a literature review and research agenda for information systems research. Inform. Syst. Front. **25**(3), 955–969 (2023). https://doi.org/10.1007/s10796-020-10096-3
13. Khan, A., Krishnan, S.: Citizen engagement in co-creation of e-government services: a process theory view from a meta-synthesis approach. Internet Res. **31**, 1318–1375 (2021). https://doi.org/10.1108/INTR-03-2020-0116
14. Herterich, M.M., Dremel, C., Wulf, J., von Brocke, J.: The emergence of smart service ecosystems—the role of socio-technical antecedents and affordances. Inf. Syst. J. **33**(3), 524–566 (2023). https://doi.org/10.1111/isj.12412
15. Thomas, A.: Digitally transforming the organization through knowledge management: a socio-technical system (STS) perspective. Eur. J. Innov. Manag. **27**(9), 437–460 (2024). https://doi.org/10.1108/EJIM-02-2024-0114

16. Papadopoulos, T., Alexopoulos, C., Charalabidis, Y.: Evaluating chatbot architectures for public service delivery: balancing functionality, safety, ethics, and adaptability. Front. Polit. Sci. **7**, 1601440 (2025). https://doi.org/10.3389/fpos.2025.1601440
17. Kożuch, B., Sienkiewicz-Małyjurek, K.: Trust and Digital Transformation in the Public Sector. Taylor & Francis, New York (2024). https://doi.org/10.4324/9781032678849
18. Jaakkola, E.: Designing conceptual articles: four approaches. AMS Rev. **10**, 18–26 (2020)
19. Barreteau, O., Bots, P.W., Daniell, K.A.: A framework for clarifying "participation" in participatory research to prevent its rejection for the wrong reasons. Ecol. Soc. **15**(2), 1 (2010)
20. Galego, D., Lotta, G., Baker, K.: Exploring the nexus of common good and the neo-Weberian state: a comparative analysis of Brazil and Mexico. Public Adm. Dev. **45**(3), 185–322 (2025). https://doi.org/10.1002/pad.2105
21. Ufel, W.: I Wrocławski Panel Obywatelski jako przykład zastosowania praktyki deliberacyjnej [The 1st Wrocław Citizens' Panel as an example of the application of deliberative practice]. Studia z Polityki Publicznej. **9**(4), 95–114 (2022). https://doi.org/10.33119/kszpp/2022.4.5
22. García, D.L., Calleja-López, A., Linares-Lanzman, J.: Collective intelligence and digital participatory platforms: Learnings from Barcelona's Decidim. In: Boucher, S., Hallin, C.A., Paulson, L. (eds.) The Routledge Handbook of Collective Intelligence for Democracy and Governance, pp. 326–338. Routledge, London (2023). https://doi.org/10.4324/9781003215929-29
23. Vagnoni, S., Palirani, M.: Fostering deliberative democracy in the digital age: an AI-powered platform for enhanced citizen engagement in legislative processes. In: 2025 Eleventh International Conference on eDemocracy & eGovernment (ICEDEG), pp. 339–341 (2025). https://doi.org/10.1109/ICEDEG65568.2025.11081638
24. Falco, E., Kleinhans, R.: Digital participatory platforms for co-production in urban development: a systematic review. Int. J. E-Planning Res. **7**(3), 52–79 (2019). https://doi.org/10.4018/IJEPR.201807010
25. Borghys, K., Vandercruysse, L., Veeckman, C., Temmerman, L., Heyman, R.: Localizing the sustainable development goals in smart and sustainable cities: how can citizen-generated data support the local monitoring of SDGs? A case study of the Brussels capital region. Front. Environ. Sci. **12**, 1369001 (2024). https://doi.org/10.3389/fenvs.2024.1369001
26. Kirklies, P.C., Neumann, O., Hohensinn, L.: Promoting digital equality in co-production: the role of platform design. Gov. Inf. Q. **41**(1), 101903 (2024). https://doi.org/10.1016/j.giq.2023.101903
27. Townley, C., Koop, C.: Exploring the potential and limits of digital tools for inclusive regulatory engagement with citizens. Gov. Inf. Q. **41**(1), 101901 (2024). https://doi.org/10.1016/j.giq.2023.101901
28. Selten, F., Klievink, B.: Organizing public sector AI adoption: navigating between separation and integration. Gov. Inf. Q. **41**(1), 101885 (2024). https://doi.org/10.1016/j.giq.2023.101885
29. Kong, I., Janssen, M., Bharosa, N.: Realizing quantum-safe information sharing: implementation and adoption challenges and policy recommendations for quantum-safe transitions. Gov. Inf. Q. **41**(1), 101884 (2024). https://doi.org/10.1016/j.giq.2023.101884
30. Paulis, E., Kies, R., Östling, A.: Public deliberation in the digital age. Platforms, Participation, and Legitimacy. Routledge, London (2025). https://doi.org/10.4324/9781003435204
31. Fishkin, J.: Democracy and Deliberation. A New Direction for Democratic Reforms. Yale University Press (1991)
32. Carson, L., Hart, P.: What randomness and deliberation can do for community engagement. In: International Conference on Engaging Communities, pp. 14–17, Brisbane (2005)
33. Fishkin, J.: When the People Speak. Deliberative Democracy and Public Consultation. Oxford University Press (2011)

34. Gastil, J.: By Popular Demand: Revitalizing Representative Democracy through Deliberative Elections. University of California Press (2000). https://doi.org/10.1017/S0003055402510364
35. OECD Deliberative Democracy Database.: https://www.peoplepowered.org/resources-content/oecd-deliberative-democracy-database
36. Decidim.: https://decidim.org/
37. Consul Project.: https://oecd-opsi.org/innovations/consul-project/
38. Open Source Observatory (OSOR).: https://interoperable-europe.ec.europa.eu/collection/open-source-observatory-osor/document/case-study-consul-democracy#ftnt
39. Nolan-Flecha, N.: Next generation diversity and inclusion policies in the public service: Ensuring public services reflect the societies they serve. OECD Working Papers on Public Governance, No. 34, OECD Publishing, Paris (2019). https://doi.org/10.1787/51691451-en
40. Borge, R., Balcells, J., Padró-Solanet, A.: Democratic disruption or continuity? Analysis of the Decidim platform in Catalan municipalities. Am. Behav. Sci. **67**(7), 926–939 (2023). https://doi.org/10.1177/00027642221092798
41. Gastil, J.: A theoretical model of how digital platforms for public consultation can leverage deliberation to boost democratic legitimacy. J. Deliberative Democr. **17**(1), 78–89 (2021). https://doi.org/10.16997/10.16997/jdd.963
42. Ponti, M., Craglia, M.: Citizen-generated data for public policy. European Commission Joint Research Centre, Ispra, JRC120231 (2020). chrome-extension://efaidnbmnnnibpcajpcglclefindmkaj https://marisaponti.org/wp-content/uploads/2020/03/ponti_jrc-report-final.pdf
43. Saner, R., Yiu, L., Nguyen, M.: Monitoring the SDGs: digital and social technologies to ensure citizen participation, inclusiveness and transparency. Dev. Policy Rev. **38**(4), 483–500 (2020). https://doi.org/10.1111/dpr.12433
44. Aziz, A., Herrera-Murillo, D.J., Nogueras-Iso, J., Lacasta, J., Lopez-Pellicer, F.J.: Identifying the evolution of open government data initiatives and their user engagement. IEEE Access. **12**, 84556–84566 (2024). https://doi.org/10.1109/ACCESS.2024.3414282
45. Exploring New Frontiers in Citizen Participation in the Policy Cycle, OECD Public Governance Reviews, OECD Publishing, Paris (2025). https://doi.org/10.1787/77f5098c-en
46. OECD Guidelines for Citizen Participation Processes, OECD Public Governance Reviews, OECD Publishing, Paris (2022). https://doi.org/10.1787/f765caf6-en
47. OECD Online Dispute Resolution Framework, OECD Public Governance Policy Papers, No. 59, OECD Publishing, Paris. https://doi.org/10.1787/325e6edc-en
48. Baljija, S.K., Min, K.S.: Evaluating the effectiveness of whistleblower protection: a new index. D&P. **5**, e28 (2023). https://doi.org/10.1017/dap.2023.20
49. Walle, Y.M.: Breaking digital silence: AI, structural bias, and the uneven landscape of whistleblowing. AI Soc., 1–10 (2025). https://doi.org/10.1007/s00146-025-02758-0
50. Tackling civic participation challenges with emerging technologies: Beyond the hype, OECD Public Governance Policy Papers, 72, OECD Publishing, Paris (2025). https://doi.org/10.1787/ec2ca9a2-en
51. Community of Practice of the Competence Centre on Participatory and Deliberative Democracy, https://cop-demos.jrc.ec.europa.eu/resources/report
52. Rosa, P., Guimaraes Pereira, Â.: Harnessing innovation on online deliberation, Publications Office of the European Union, Luxembourg (2025). https://data.europa.eu/doi/10.2760/1524483
53. Espinosa, V.I., Pino, A.: E-government as a development strategy: the case of Estonia. Int. J. Public Adm. **48**(2), 86–99 (2025). https://doi.org/10.1080/01900692.2024.2316128
54. Gonzálvez Gallego, N., Nieto Torrejón, L.: Government data openness and coverage. How do they affect trust in European countries? J. Data Info. Sci. **6**(1), 139–153 (2021). https://doi.org/10.2478/jdis-2021-0010

55. Gsenger, R.: Platform governance under the digital services act: a perspective on disinformation. Inf. Commun. Soc., 1–19 (2025). https://doi.org/10.1080/1369118X.2025.2590561
56. Abukmail, H., Dennison, R.A., Usher-Smith, J.A., Taylor, L.C.: Assessing the quality of community jury deliberations in online and in-person community juries using a deductive coding framework. Health Expect. **28**(6), e70486 (2025). https://doi.org/10.1111/hex.70486

Smart Infrastructures

Multi-agent Framework with Blockchain-Based Audit Trails for Securing Industrial Greenhouse Gas Monitoring Infrastructure

Timileyin Abiodun[1(✉)], Nnamdi Nwulu[1,2], and Peter Olukanmi[3]

[1] South Africa-Switzerland Bilateral Research Chair in Blockchain Technology, University of Johannesburg, Johannesburg, South Africa
abioduntimileyin19@gmail.com, nnwulu@uj.ac.za
[2] Centre for Cyber Physical Energy and Water Systems, University of Johannesburg, Johannesburg, South Africa
[3] School of Electrical and Electronics Engineering, University of Johannesburg, Johannesburg, South Africa
polukanmi@uj.ac.za

Abstract. Accurate and trustworthy Greenhouse Gas (GHG) monitoring systems are essential for emission accountability mechanisms, which support the accomplishment of global net-zero emission goals. Recent studies reveal urban inventories underreport emissions by 18.3%, and methane emissions in the energy sector are 70% higher than official figures. This study proposes iGuard, a novel framework combining multi-agent autonomous Artificial Intelligence (AI) with distributed ledger technology to create a vulnerability-resistant, real-time emission monitoring infrastructure. The agents employ a Long Short-Term Memory (LSTM)-based autoencoder for temporal anomaly detection, a random forest model for identifying network intrusions in Internet of Things (IoT) communication channels, and cryptographic hashing for verification. All agents operate under a consensus mechanism to provide unified threat assessments, with security events immutably recorded on the blockchain for forensic audit trails. Evaluation on the EPA CEMS and NF-ToN-IoT datasets achieved 100% tampering detection, 95.61% network intrusion accuracy, and consensus-driven precision improvements of up to 5.78 percentage points, while maintaining sub-500 ms latency.

Keywords: Industrial IoT Security · Greenhouse Gas Monitoring · Multi-Agent System · Blockchain · Cyber-physical Systems

1 Introduction

Climate change and its devastating consequences, such as intensifying natural disasters and accelerating global warming, have compelled nations worldwide to commit, through the Kyoto Protocol and the Paris Agreement, to achieving net-zero emissions

Published by Springer Nature Switzerland AG 2027
L. M. Camarinha-Matos and F. Ferrada (Eds.): DoCEIS 2026, IFIP AICT 790, pp. 471–491, 2027.
https://doi.org/10.1007/978-3-032-28939-1_32

and mitigating these effects [1]. Central to the success of this goal is the reliable monitoring of Greenhouse Gas (GHG) emissions, particularly from industrial sources, due to their large volume of emissions [2]. Currently, monitoring largely depends on manual reporting, where companies submit spreadsheets detailing their emissions annually [3, 4]. However, this approach has significant limitations, which include susceptibility to human error and data manipulation. Evidence supports this, showing that 18.3% of urban inventories underreport their emissions [5], and methane emissions in the energy sector are estimated to be 70% higher than officially reported figures [6].

These limitations have led to the proposal of Internet of Things (IoT)-powered sensors that can automatically collect emissions data and transmit it directly to regulators with minimal human intervention [7]. While this technological shift addresses many of the shortcomings of manual reporting, it also introduces new vulnerabilities. Malicious actors could tamper with sensor data to underreport emissions and avoid carbon penalties, compromise the networks connecting the sensors, or replay outdated data to hide periods of high emissions [8]. Beyond these targeted attacks, IoT systems are inherently vulnerable to broader cyber threats, including unauthorised access, data breaches, and identity spoofing [9]. The consequences of such exploits can be severe, potentially leading to operational shutdowns, safety violations, and a fundamentally compromised emissions reporting system.

To counter these threats, many security solutions have been proposed. However, most GHG monitoring systems still rely on single-method approaches, such as ML-based techniques that focus only on anomaly detection or zero-trust architectures [10]. While these methods are valuable in their own right, they have notable limitations, including high False Positive Rates (FPR), difficulty detecting complex multi-vector attacks, and challenges in adapting to the diverse constraints of industrial environments [11].

Recent literature increasingly advocates for integrated multi-agent security frameworks that combine the strengths of various Machine Learning (ML)-based models across multiple domains [12], cryptographic integrity verification, and blockchain-based audit trails to ensure robust industrial GHG monitoring [13]. Despite this growing consensus, no comprehensive operational framework currently exists that seamlessly integrates these components into a unified system. To address this gap, this study proposes iGuard, a framework that leverages multi-agent Artificial Intelligence (AI) and blockchain technology to detect and prevent anomalies in emission records captured in real-time using IoT sensors, as illustrated in Fig. 1. Specifically, iGuard aims to: (i) detect and mitigate anomalies in real-time emissions data, (ii) defend against cyberattack vulnerabilities within IoT networks, and (iii) provide an immutable audit trail via blockchain for forensic analysis. In doing so, the framework offers a robust, real-time, and scalable security solution for industrial GHG monitoring infrastructure, enhancing accurate threat detection while ensuring regulatory-grade data integrity and auditability.

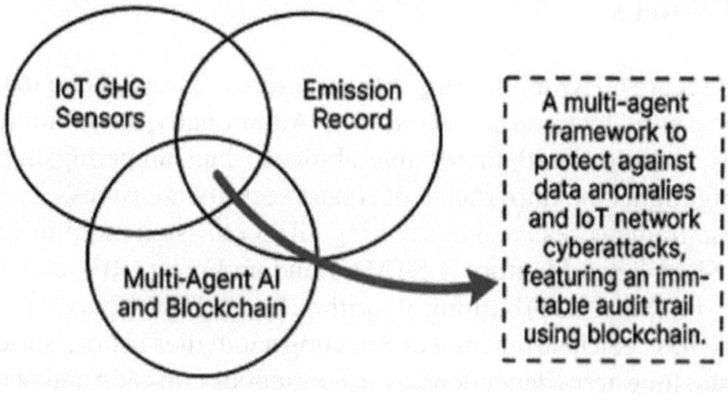

Fig. 1. Multi-agents framework and Blockchain audit trail for Emission Record Integrity and Network Security.

2 Relation to Technological Innovation to Tackle Societal Challenges

Climate change is one of the most pressing societal challenges of our time. Its harmful effects, ranging from global warming and extreme temperatures to natural disasters like flooding and wildfires, pose a direct threat to human livelihoods and habitats [14]. If GHG emissions continue to rise, these consequences will only worsen. Therefore, accurately monitoring these emissions is essential for designing and implementing effective mitigation strategies.

The integrity of emissions data has far-reaching societal implications. It directly influences carbon pricing mechanisms, regulatory compliance verification, corporate accountability, and the credibility of international climate agreements, such as the Paris Agreement [15, 16]. Any compromise in these areas not only undermines environmental policy but also erodes public trust in the institutions responsible for climate governance. The iGuard framework addresses this critical societal challenge through technological innovation, ensuring the reliability, security, and trustworthiness of industrial GHG monitoring infrastructure.

More broadly, the societal benefits and impacts of the framework span several dimensions. By safeguarding the accuracy of emissions data, iGuard helps protect the environment by enabling informed and timely policy interventions. It enhances the integrity and trust of carbon markets by ensuring that the data supporting emissions trading schemes is verifiable and tamper-proof. Its blockchain-based audit trail improves corporate environmental accountability by providing transparent, immutable records of emissions reporting. Additionally, the modular and scalable design of iGuard makes it accessible to various industries, ensuring that robust monitoring isn't limited to large-scale enterprises alone. Most importantly, by promoting the reduction and accurate reporting of GHG emissions, the framework supports a broader public health agenda, since cleaner air and a more stable climate are vital to the well-being of communities worldwide.

3 Related Works

The need for a secure GHG monitoring infrastructure is essential due to the accelerating climate change caused by these emissions [14]. Additionally, the saturation of IoT-based sensor systems, combined with their vulnerability to data tampering and cyber-physical threats [17], highlights the importance of robust security measures.

Some of the frameworks used in securing GHG emission monitoring infrastructure include Long Short-Term Memory (LSTM), Random Forest (RF), and the Secure Hash Algorithm 256-bit (SHA-256) hashing algorithm. The LSTM network, a type of recurrent neural network, has been instrumental in detecting anomalies in time-series data due to its ability to capture long-term dependencies in continuous emission and network data [18]. The RF network has also proven capable of identifying complex attack patterns in real-time by combining spatial and temporal feature extraction [19]. Additionally, SHA-256, a cryptographic hash function used alongside blockchain's immutability features, ensures transparent and trustworthy audit trails for vulnerability and threat logs, facilitating forensic audits of the system [13].

Each component of the Multi-Agent System (MAS) provides targeted detection capabilities, but existing literature highlights their complementary limitations. LSTM autoencoders rely on a reconstruction error threshold calibrated during training. This threshold-based approach is sensitive to noise and can yield inconsistent detection results near the decision boundary, leading to higher false alarm rates [20]. More critically, [21] shows that ML models deployed on streaming IoT sensor data, such as GHG, are susceptible to concept drift. This can lead to model divergence and a decline in detection accuracy. Random forest classifiers achieve high multiclass accuracy; however, they are more sensitive to changes in feature distribution and require a large labelled training set to generalise effectively across heterogeneous network environments [19]. Hash-based integrity verification offers deterministic tamper detection without relying on probabilistic reasoning. Ref. [10] demonstrated that classical hash functions remain vulnerable to quantum computing attacks via Grover's algorithm. These complementary limitations form the rationale for the multi-agent architecture used in this study, which allows each technique to compensate for the blind spots of the others.

Recent studies have explored the integration of blockchain with AI-based intrusion detection [22], multi-agent Distributed Denial-of-Service (DDoS) defence [23], and carbon emission data sharing [24] within the IoT domain. Table 1 provides a comparison of these and other related approaches across five security dimensions relevant to industrial GHG monitoring infrastructure.

Table 1. Comparative Analysis of Related Studies.

Study	Emission Anomaly Detection	Network Intrusion Detection	Data Integrity Verification	Blockchain Audit Trail	Multi-Agent Coordination
[7]	Partial	No	No	No	No
[11]	Partial	No	Partial	No	No

(continued)

Table 1. (*continued*)

Study	Emission Anomaly Detection	Network Intrusion Detection	Data Integrity Verification	Blockchain Audit Trail	Multi-Agent Coordination
[19]	No	Yes	No	No	No
[22]	No	Yes	Partial	Yes	No
[24]	No	No	Partial	Yes	No
[23]	No	Yes	Partial	Yes	Yes
[25]	No	No	Partial	Yes	Yes
iGuard (proposed framework)	Yes	Yes	Yes	Yes	Yes

As shown in Table 1, no existing framework addresses all five security dimensions simultaneously. Studies that combine blockchain with multi-agent coordination [23, 25] do not focus on emission-specific monitoring, while emission-focused approaches [7, 11] lack blockchain audit trails and multi-agent architectures.

MAS and consensus protocols powered by distributed AI offer a pathway for decentralised, autonomous decision-making in dynamic, adversarial environments [26]. However, the fragmentation of GHG monitoring infrastructure security across the literature means that each framework focuses only on a subset of security requirements, lacking interoperability across various sources of vulnerabilities [27]. To address this gap, this study proposes the iGuard framework, which integrates emission anomaly detection, network intrusion detection, data integrity verification, blockchain auditing, and multi-agent coordination within a unified architecture.

4 Study Framework

4.1 System Architecture

The autonomous actions of the IoT system require collaborative decision-making, which is facilitated by a MAS. In a MAS, decisions are decentralised across multiple agents, making the system less vulnerable to the threat of a single point of failure and promoting a more collaborative approach to IoT system security [9].

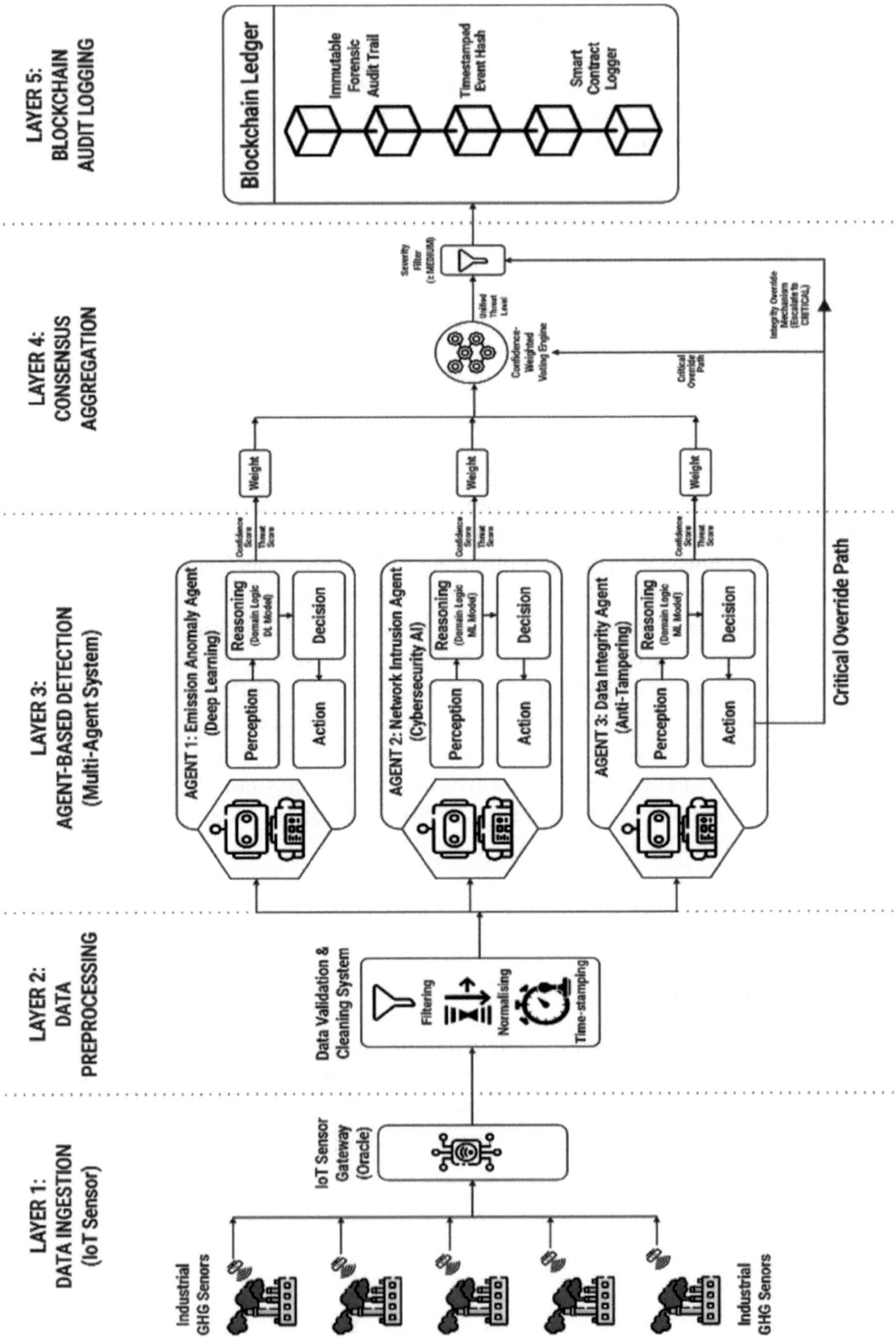

Fig. 2. System Architectural Diagram.

This study proposes iGuard, a framework that employs a multi-agent autonomous security system to protect against anomalies and network vulnerabilities within the GHG monitoring infrastructure in an industrial setting. As shown in Fig. 2, the architecture consists of five interconnected layers: data ingestion, data processing, agent-based detection, consensus aggregation, and blockchain audit logging. A detailed description of each layer is provided below:

1. **Data Ingestion**: This layer uses IoT-powered sensors to capture GHG emissions from industrial emitting entities. The collected data is then passed to the second layer as an oracle, serving as the conduit for transmitting emission records for further processing.
2. **Data Preprocessing**: This is the second layer, where the sensed records are validated and properly cleaned through filtering, normalisation, and timestamping before being passed to the agent for autonomous decision-making.
3. **Agent-Based Detection Layer**: This layer enables decentralised decision-making across three different agents: the Emission Anomaly Agent, the Network Intrusion Agent, and the Data Integrity Agent. Each agent operates through four modules, starting with the perception module, which ensures incoming data is properly validated. The second module handles reasoning by applying domain-specific detection logic. The third module is the decision module, where detected threats (if any) are classified, and confidence scores are calculated. The final module is the action module, which generates a standardised assessment for the consensus layer.
4. **Consensus Aggregation Layer**: This component consolidates the threat classifications from each agent to produce a unified threat level. A key design feature allows it to override other agents' assessments when data manipulation is detected. In such cases, the threat classification from other agents is bypassed, and the event is escalated to a critical threat level.
5. **Blockchain audit logging**: Implemented when the threat level is classified as medium severity or higher, by saving the details on the blockchain ledger to ensure an immutable forensic audit trail.

4.2 Datasets

4.2.1 EPA CEMS Dataset

The United States Environmental Protection Agency (EPA) Clean Air Markets Program Data (CAMPD) [28] was used as the time series dataset to train the deep learning model, which serves as the reasoning module for Agent 1. The dataset consists of hourly records of carbon emissions and power generation from power plants across the United States, generated through the Continuous Emission Monitoring System (CEMS). The version used for this study, downloaded via an API key, comprises 1,103,592 hourly readings collected between January 2022 and December 2023. It covers 18 power generation facilities across 5 states, encompassing 47 different operational units.

The main variables considered include CO_2 mass (tonnes), SO_2 mass (tonnes), NO_x mass (tonnes), gross electrical load (MW), and heat input (MMBtu). Data preprocessing revealed 546,225 rows (49.5%) with null emission records, which were verified to correspond to non-operating hours by cross-referencing with the operational time field. These non-operational periods were removed, resulting in a total of 556,817 valid hourly records for model training and evaluation.

4.2.2 NF-ToN-IoT-v3

The NF-ToN-IoT-v3 dataset [29], a network flow dataset, was used in this study to train the ML model, which acts as the reasoning module for Agent 2. Created by the University of Queensland, the dataset includes various network attack scenarios used for training and testing ML-based network intrusion detection models. It comprises a total of 27,520,620 network flows, ranging from normal benign traffic to nine different attack categories, such as backdoor, injection, cross-site scripting (XSS), and more.

Due to computational constraints, the dataset was reduced to 2,000,000 network flows using stratified random sampling. This process was carried out in a way that ensured the original class distribution was maintained within a 0.01% deviation. After preprocessing (removing four non-predictive columns such as timestamps and nine highly correlated features with $|r| > 0.9$), the final dataset consisted of 40 network flow characteristics.

4.3 Agent Design

4.3.1 Agent 1: Emission Anomaly Detection

The emission anomaly detection agent used a Long Short-Term Memory (LSTM) autoencoder architecture [30], trained exclusively on normal operational data. The model learns to reconstruct typical emission patterns. Anomalies are identified when the reconstruction error exceeds the calibrated threshold. The use of LSTM enhances the agent's ability to detect temporal dependencies in continuous emission monitoring data [31]. The architecture consists of an encoder with two stacked LSTM layers, containing 64 and 32 hidden units, respectively. These layers compress input sequences into a 32-dimensional latent representation, which is then reconstructed by a symmetric decoder. The input sequences comprise 24 consecutive hourly readings, representing a single operational day. Each day includes 19 engineered features, divided into five categories as shown in Table 2.

Table 2. Feature Engineering Categories and Purposes

Category	Features	Purpose
Emission Values	CO_2, SO_2, NO_x, Load, Heat (normalised)	Core sensor measurements
Temporal Encoding	Cyclical hour, day-of-week, month (sin/cos pairs)	Cyclical time representation
Emission Ratios	CO_2 per load, heat per load, NO_x per load	Operational intensity metrics
Rate of Change	Load differential, CO_2 differential, heat differential	Temporal derivatives
Rolling Statistics	6-h rolling mean, 6-h rolling std. (load)	Short-term trend indicators

The decision threshold was calibrated using the reconstruction error distribution from the validation set, estimated with eq. 1.

$$\text{threshold} = \mu + k\sigma \quad (1)$$

Where μ is the mean and σ is the standard deviation of the validation set reconstruction error distribution. After several trials to achieve a FPR below 2%, a multiplier of 2.5 was chosen because it keeps the FPR under 2% while also demonstrating high detection sensitivity. Therefore, the threshold used was 0.003587, as calculated using eq. 2.

$$\text{threshold} = 0.000565 + 2.5(0.001329) = 0.003587 \tag{2}$$

4.3.2 Agent 2: Network Intrusion Detection

The RF classifier algorithm [32] was configured with 100 decision trees and balanced class weights in the study to model the reasoning module of the network intrusion detection agent. This RF algorithm is a versatile technique used for classification and regression tasks. It works by constructing decision trees and further improving the overall performance of the model through the predictions of other trees [33]. The model configuration ensures it effectively handles class imbalance in the dataset.

The network intrusion detection agent, powered by the RF modelling process, analyses 40 NetFlow features, including packet counts, byte volumes, and more. Feature importance analysis identified inbound bytes, destination port, longest flow packet, Layer 7 protocol, and outbound bytes as the most discriminative attributes.

The threat score generated by the agent is calculated using Eq. 3.

$$\text{Threat Score} = 1 - \text{P(benign)} \tag{3}$$

Where P(benign) is the probability of a benign class as predicted by the RF model. The confidence level of the threat score is estimated using Eq. 4.

$$\text{Confidence} = \max_{c \in C} \text{P(c)} \tag{4}$$

Where $C = \{\text{benign, malicious}\}$ is the set of classes and $P(c)$ is the predicted probability for class c.

4.3.3 Agent 3: Data Integrity Verification

The agent that ensures data integrity was implemented using cryptographic hash chain verification with the SHA-256 algorithm, providing a tamper detection mechanism that does not rely on the uncertainty of ML algorithms. Secure Hash Algorithm 256-bit (SHA-256) is a cryptographic hash function standardised by the National Institute of Standards and Technology (NIST) as part of the SHA-2 family. It is an iterative, one-way hash function that provides 128 bits of collision resistance, making it difficult for an attacker to find two distinct inputs that produce the same hash output [34].

Each emission reading is recorded by computing a chain hash that includes the current data (d_t), timestamp (ts_t), sensor identifier (id_s), and the previous chain hash (H_{t-1}), as shown in Eq. 5.

$$\text{H}_\text{t} = \text{SHA256}(\text{d}_\text{t} \mid \text{ts}_\text{t} \mid \text{id}_\text{s} \mid \text{H}_{\text{t}-1}) \tag{5}$$

This chaining mechanism ensures that any change in the historical record invalidates subsequent hashes, making selective tampering of data easily detectable. The agent provides three possible classifications: VERIFIED (hash match), INTEGRITY VIOLATION (hash mismatch), and UNVERIFIED (no stored hash available for comparison). Compared to the ML agents, the tampering detection agent operates with a binary threat score, which is either 0.0 or 1.0, and a deterministic confidence of 1.0. This demonstrates the mathematical certainty of cryptographic verification.

The agents in the iGuard framework are implemented in an autonomous manner, allowing each agent to independently execute its detection logic and produce an assessment score in real time without human intervention. The internal reasoning modules are fixed at deployment, prioritising determinism and reliability in safety-critical industrial monitoring environments. The adaptive agent architecture, in which agents update their models in response to new threat patterns, will be explored in future work.

4.4 Consensus Mechanism

The consensus engine aggregates individual agent assessments using confidence-weighted voting. The three agents operate independently without directly communicating with each other. Coordination is achieved through a process where each agent processes its designated input, assesses the domain, and submits a standardised report that includes a threat score, confidence level, and threat level to the consensus engine. This engine then synthesises the assessments from each agent into a unified threat decision. This indirect coordination model reduces inter-agent coupling, ensuring that the failure or compromise of one agent does not disrupt the operation of the others. The unified score is calculated using Eq. 6.

$$\text{weighted score} = \frac{\sum_{\mathrm{i}=1}^{\mathrm{n}} \mathrm{w_i} \cdot \mathrm{c_i} \cdot \mathrm{s_i}}{\sum_{\mathrm{i}=1}^{\mathrm{n}} \mathrm{w_i} \cdot \mathrm{c_i}} \tag{6}$$

Where w_i is the weight of agent i, set to 1/3 each; c_i represents the agent's confidence score for the current assessment; s_i is the agent's threat score; and n is the number of active agents. This formula ensures that high-confidence assessments have a greater influence on the final decision when the agents' decisions are combined, while uncertain predictions are disregarded.

The choice of confidence-weighted voting was motivated by a comparison with alternative aggregation methods. Examples of this alternative include simple majority voting and uniform score averaging, both of which treat all agent outputs as equally reliable, without accounting for the varying confidence levels that arise from agents working in different domains and using different methods. Additionally, while Dempster-Shafer Theory (DST) supports more expressive uncertainty reasoning, it requires explicit belief-function modelling, particularly the construction of basic probability assignment functions over a shared frame of discernment. This remains an open research challenge, especially when combining heterogeneous probabilistic and deterministic outputs [35]. Bayesian inference also requires well-calibrated prior probabilities for each detector. When aggregating decisions from heterogeneous detectors under Bayesian frameworks, ensemble performance can degrade due to distributional heterogeneity [36].

The confidence-weighted voting techniques used in this study are computationally efficient, interpretable, and domain-agnostic, allowing the agent to influence scales naturally based on per-assessment certainty. This allows both probabilistic and deterministic agent outputs to be accommodated without modification.

The weighted scores are mapped to five distinct threat levels, which are categorised as shown in Table 3.

Table 3. Threat level classification and corresponding system responses.

Threat Level	Score Range	Response
NONE	[0.0, 0.3)	Continue monitoring
LOW	[0.3, 0.5)	Increase monitoring frequency
MEDIUM	[0.5, 0.7)	Alert operator; log to blockchain
HIGH	[0.7, 0.9)	Isolate affected sensors
CRITICAL	[0.9, 1.0]	Immediate response; full isolation

The critical threat design feature of the consensus engine ensures that integrity takes precedence over other mechanisms. This means that once Agent 3 reports an INTEGRITY VIOLATION, the threat level is immediately escalated to CRITICAL, regardless of the assessments from other agents. This principle makes cryptographic verification serve as the ground truth, as any tampered data will render the ML assessment unreliable.

4.5 Blockchain Audit Trail

Blockchain is preferred as the audit trail mechanism over alternatives such as centralised append-only databases and distributed file systems. This is due to the drawbacks of other audit trail mechanisms, which include: the centralised storage system being vulnerable to a single point of failure, making it possible for audit records to be deleted without traceability. While distributed databases improve availability, they lack cryptographic chaining, which prevents guaranteeing immutability. Blockchain's append-only ledger and cryptographic hash chaining features ensure that once a security event is recorded, it cannot be altered or removed [9]. This property is essential for regulatory-grade audit trails in the industrial greenhouse gas monitoring environment.

An Ethereum-compatible architecture was chosen due to Ethereum's mature smart contract platform (Solidity), along with well-documented security features and extensive tooling support [37]. To evaluate the smart contract, Ganache was used. Ganache is a local Ethereum blockchain simulator that replicates the Ethereum Virtual Machine (EVM) environment without requiring network access or transaction fees [38], making it ideal for controlled experimental evaluation.

The blockchain audit trail was implemented as a Solidity [37] smart contract named AuditTrail.sol, consisting of 337 lines of code. It was deployed on Ganache [38], a local Ethereum-compatible blockchain network preloaded with testnet Ethers for simulation purposes. The developed smart contract stores two types of records, which include:

1. **SecurityEvent**: This captures the consensus outcomes, which comprise the timestamp, threat level, weighted score, agent agreement metric, and a SHA-256 hash of the full consensus result to ensure off-chain evidence verification.
2. **HashCommitment**: This serves as the anchor for Agent 3's on-chain hash storage for each registered record. This on-chain storage prevents attackers from retroactively tampering with the hash authentication baseline, even if the iGuard host system is compromised.

The threat logging threshold is set at MEDIUM severity and above to ensure that severe threat events are immutably stored without overloading the blockchain with routine monitoring data.

4.6 Experimental Setup

4.6.1 Attack Injection

To assess the agents' capability to identify anomalies and network intrusions, synthetic attacks were introduced into the test datasets across three domains: real-time emission attacks, network attacks, and data tampering attacks.

- Real-time emission attacks were categorised into six types: (i) Replay: substitution of historical records; (ii) False Injection: reducing values by 30–50% to demonstrate underreporting of emission records; (iii) Gradual Drift: a linear reduction of data by 50% over a 24-h period; (iv) Sensor Freeze: constant values over a sequence of time; (v) Noise Injection: injection of Gaussian noise [39] with a standard deviation of 0.15–0.25; and (vi) Spike Injection: extreme values occurring at random intervals of 3–5 h.
- Network Attacks: Nine types of network intrusion attacks from the NF-ToN-IoT-v3 dataset [29] were used, targeting the network intrusion detection agent. These attacks include DDoS, DoS, scanning, backdoor, injection, XSS, password attacks, Man-in-the-Middle (MitM), and ransomware.
- Data Tampering Attacks: Three types of attacks were synthesised under this category to target data tampering detection Agent 3. These include modifying GHG emission values by 20–50%, altering timestamps, and changing sensor IDs.

4.6.2 Evaluation Configuration

To evaluate the effectiveness of each agent, seven different agent configurations were used, as shown in Table 4.

Table 4. Agent configuration settings.

Configuration	Agent 1	Agent 2	Agent 3	Purpose
All Agents	Enabled	Enabled	Enabled	Full system baseline
Emission Only	Enabled	Disabled	Disabled	Single-agent baseline
Network Only	Disabled	Enabled	Disabled	Single-agent baseline

(*continued*)

Table 4. (*continued*)

Configuration	Agent 1	Agent 2	Agent 3	Purpose
Integrity Only	Disabled	Disabled	Enabled	Single-agent baseline
No Integrity	Enabled	Enabled	Disabled	ML-only configuration
No Network	Enabled	Disabled	Enabled	Agent 1 + 3 combination
No Emission	Disabled	Enabled	Enabled	Agent 2 + 3 combination

Each configuration processed emission sequences with three-domain attack injections, for a total of 61 attacks. These included 23 emission attacks, 23 network attacks, and 15 data tampering attacks. This setup allows for a direct comparison of each agent's detection capabilities across the different configurations.

5 Results and Discussion

5.1 Individual Agent Performance

Table 5 summarises the performance of all three agents evaluated on their respective datasets. Agent 1, the LSTM-based emission detection agent, was tested on 555,368 sequences, comprising 444,295 normal and 111,073 attacked cases. The model achieved an accuracy of 90.67%, with a high precision of 97.46%. However, its recall of 60.78% is considered moderate. Additionally, the model has an F1-score of 74.87%. The FPR of 1.98% meets the operational target of less than 2%. Detection rates varied significantly depending on the attack type; sudden anomalies such as spike injection (99.97%) and noise injection (98.96%) were detected accurately, while more subtle attacks that mimic normal operational patterns, like gradual drift (5.19%) and sensor freeze (29.47%), proved more challenging to reliably identify.

Table 5. Individual agent performance metrics and detection capabilities.

Metric	Agent 1 (LSTM)	Agent 2 (RF)	Agent 3 (Hash)
Accuracy	90.67%	95.61%	100%
Precision	97.46%	92.22%	100%
Recall	60.78%	98.61%	100%
F1 Score	74.87%	95.31%	100%
False Positive Rate	1.98%	5.31%	0%
Inference Latency (ms)	10.41	61.42	0.175
No Emission	Disabled	Enabled	Enabled
Agent 1 Detection Rate by Attack Type:			
Spike / Noise Injection		99.97% / 98.96%	
False Injection / Replay		86.50% / 44.57%	

(*continued*)

Table 5. *(continued)*

Metric	Agent 1 (LSTM)	Agent 2 (RF)	Agent 3 (Hash)
Sensor Freeze / Gradual Drift		29.47% / 5.19%	
Agent 2 F1 Score by Attack Class:			
DDoS / Backdoor / Ransomware		99.02% / 99.94% / 100%	
DoS / XSS / Injection		96.77% / 97.78% / 93.71%	
Scanning / MitM / Password		69.43% / 68.15% / 92.56%	

Agent 2, the RF-based network intrusion detection system, was evaluated on 299,912 network flows, achieving an accuracy of 95.61% and a ROC-AUC of 0.9966. Binary attack detection resulted in a recall of 98.61% and a precision of 92.22% (F1 score of 95.31%). Per-class analysis showed excellent performance on high-frequency attack types such as DDoS (F1 = 99.02%), Backdoor (F1 = 99.94%), and Ransomware (F1 = 100%). However, lower precision was observed for attacks that are harder to distinguish from legitimate network activity, such as scanning (57.82%) and Man-in-the-Middle (MitM) (68.15%).

The third agent, SHA-256 hash chain verification, operates in a deterministic manner, achieving a 100% detection rate, 0% false positives, and a latency of 0.175 ms. Any tampering with the stored record will immediately result in a hash mismatch, demonstrating that the cryptographic technique provides an output that complements the probabilistic detection capabilities of the ML-based agents.

5.2 Multi-configuration Ablation Study

The ablation study presented below evaluates each agent configuration across 23 sequences with 61 pre-created attack injections (including 23 emission anomalies, 23 network intrusions, and 15 data tampering incidents). These attacks were derived from predefined categories within each agent's detection domain, focusing on controlled evaluation of configuration-level coverage rather than overall detection performance. The full-scale detection performance metrics, along with recall rates for unseen and subtle attack variants, are reported in Sect. 5.1.

Table 6 presents the detection rates (DR), average latency, and threat level distribution across the different configurations.

Table 6. Detection performance and threat level distribution across agent configurations (23 sequences, 61 attacks).

Configuration	Emission DR	Network DR	Tampering DR	Mean Latency	CRITICAL Count
All Agents	100%	100%	100%	514.61	15
Emission Only	100%	–	–	254.42	16
Network Only	–	100%	–	397.36	21

(continued)

Table 6. (*continued*)

Configuration	Emission DR	Network DR	Tampering DR	Mean Latency	CRITICAL Count
Integrity Only	–	–	100%	126.97	15
No Integrity	100%	100%	–	342.76	17
No Network	100%	–	100%	181.27	15
No Emission	–	100%	100%	240.97	15

All configurations achieved 100% detection within their respective operational domains, with zero false positives. The configurations involving all agents successfully detected all attacks across all three domains. The single-agent configurations (Emission only, Network only, and Integrity only) demonstrated expected blind spots in attack domains they did not cover. This validates the need for multi-agent coverage to ensure comprehensive threat detection across the various domains of real-time industrial GHG emission monitoring infrastructure.

When the tampering detection agent (Agent 3) is enabled, the system correctly identifies exactly 15 threats as CRITICAL, matching the 15 tampering attacks in the test data. This confirms that the integrity override mechanism functions as intended. However, without Agent 3, the system overreports the number of CRITICAL threats, counting 17 instead of 15. This occurs because the ML agents alone cannot precisely distinguish between data tampering and other highly severe attacks.

These results are interpreted within the context of the evaluation design. The 100% detection rates reflect performance on pre-crafted attack injections drawn from known categories, which is a controlled setup that assesses configuration-level coverage rather than overall detection capability. In real-world scenarios, attacks may exhibit subtler patterns or adversarial adaptations that are not represented in the injected test cases. This is evidenced by Agent 1's full-scale evaluation results shown in Table 5, where recall drops to 60.78% across the entire test set, with only a 5.19% gradual drift detected. The ablation study confirms that multi-agent coverage eliminates the blind spots of individual agents, but this does not guarantee immunity to all possible attack variants once deployed.

5.3 Consensus System Evaluation

A comparison between single-agent detection and the full multi-agent consensus system demonstrates performance improvements resulting from the agents' collaboration. Table 7 illustrates these improvements, while Fig. 3 visualises the enhancement in precision alongside the reduction in false positive rates. Precision and false positive rates stand out because the former measures the accuracy of positive predictions, while the latter indicates how well incorrect predictions are minimised.

Table 7. Performance comparison: single-agent detection versus multi-agent consensus.

Domain	Metric	Single-Agent	Consensus	Improvement
Emission	Precision	89.13%	94.68%	+5.55 pp
Emission	FPR	1.85%	0.60%	−1.25 pp
Network	Precision	92.22%	98.00%	+5.78 pp
Network	FPR	5.31%	1.19%	−4.12 pp
Integrity	Detection	0%[a]	100%	+100 pp

[a]Without Agent 3, tampering attacks are undetectable by ML agents alone.

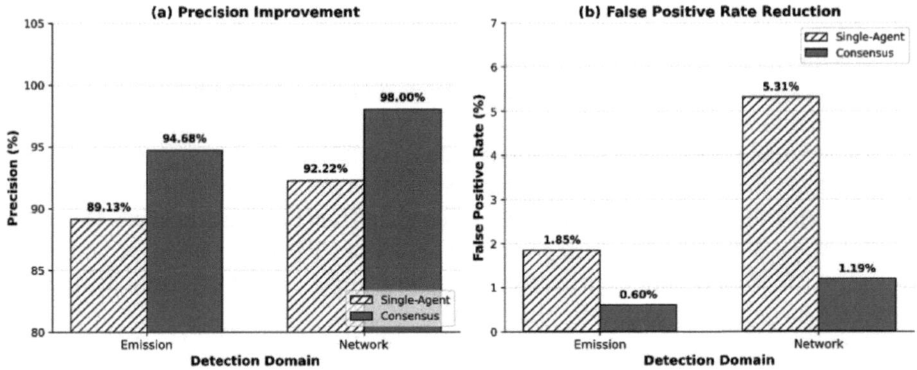

Fig. 3. Single-agent versus consensus system performance comparison.

The combination of the three agents to form the consensus mechanism improved emission detection accuracy by 5.55 percentage points (pp) (89.13% to 94.68%) while reducing the FPR by 1.25 points (1.85% to 0.60%). Network detection showed even greater improvements, with precision increasing by 5.78 pp. (92.22% to 98.00%) and the FPR decreasing by 4.12 points (5.31% to 1.19%). Most notably, the integrity detection (impossible outside of Agent 3) achieved 100% coverage through the cryptographic verification mechanism. When integrity violations are detected, the threat level is escalated to CRITICAL, regardless of the ML agent outputs.

5.4 Blockchain Immutability Verification

The integrity of the blockchain audit trail was validated through six automated unit tests, which assessed contract design, event persistence, hash integrity, sequential ordering, tamper detection, and retrieval consistency. As shown in Table 8, all six tests passed, confirming the append-only architecture of the smart contract, which includes 2 write functions and 12 read functions, with no possibility of deleting or modifying data.

Table 8. Blockchain immutability verification test results.

Test	Property Assessed	Evidence	Result
Contract Design	Append-only architecture	2 write functions, 12 read functions; no delete or modify operations	Pass
Event Persistence	Immutability of logged records	Events retrieved from the ledger match original submissions	Pass
Hash Integrity	Cryptographic record uniqueness	Each logged event assigned a unique 64-character transaction hash	Pass
Sequential Ordering	Temporal block ordering	Block numbers increase monotonically (453, 454, 455)	Pass
Tamper Detection	Detectability of record modification	Any post-submission modification produces a detectable hash mismatch	Pass
Retrieval Consistency	Query reliability	All events retrieved consistently and completely across repeated queries	Pass

The six tests shown in Table 8 confirm the three essential properties of a regulatory-grade audit trail. First, the append-only architecture ensures that no contract functions can modify or delete records. Second, cryptographic integrity is maintained through a unique 64-character transaction hash that detects any post-submission alterations. Third, temporal ordering is preserved by a monotonic increase in block numbers, as demonstrated by the sequence 453, 454, and 455. Blockchain logging accounts for the dominant latency component, averaging 250 ms (range: 194–379 ms), which constitutes the majority of the overall latency. This was addressed by ensuring that only medium-severity events are logged to the blockchain. In a production deployment on a permissioned Ethereum network such as Hyperledger Besu, consensus parameters can be optimised for lower confirmation latency, suggesting that real-world deployment times would likely fall within or below the values reported here.

The current evaluation has several limitations. First, Agent 1 demonstrates reduced sensitivity to subtle emission attack patterns: gradual drift and sensor freeze achieve detection rates of only 5.19% and 29.47% respectively, as these patterns closely resemble normal operational behaviour within the LSTM autoencoder's training distribution. Second, the ablation study evaluates 23 sequences with 61 pre-crafted attacks drawn from known categories. Instances involving a broader range of diverse attacks have yet to be assessed. Third, the blockchain evaluation was conducted on the Ganache network, a local Ethereum simulator. Latency and throughput may differ on a production permissioned blockchain. Fourth, the consensus mechanism assigns equal base weights of one-third to each agent; in deployment scenarios where certain domains pose systematically higher threat levels, adaptive weighting could be more effective. Beyond these evaluation constraints, real-world deployment may face additional engineering challenges, such as integrating with existing Supervisory Control and Data Acquisition (SCADA) and industrial control system architectures and managing model drift as emission patterns and network traffic characteristics evolve over time.

6 Conclusion and Future Work

This study presented iGuard, an autonomous multi-agent framework designed to secure industrial GHG monitoring infrastructure. The framework integrates three specialised agent models, each addressing a distinct security aspect. The first agent, an LSTM encoder, detects anomalies in emissions data, achieving an accuracy of 90.67% with a FPR of 1.98%. The second agent, a RF-based classifier, handles network intrusion detection, attaining an accuracy of 95.61% and an ROC-AUC of 0.9966. The third agent employs a SHA-256 hash chain mechanism for data integrity verification, achieving a 100% detection rate. Rather than operating independently, these three agents collaborate through a confidence-weighted consensus mechanism, resulting in measurable improvements over single-agent detection. Specifically, precision increased by 5.55 pp. and 5.78 pp. in the emissions and network domains, respectively, while FPR decreased by 1.25 and 4.12 pp. in the corresponding domains.

The ablation study further confirmed that each agent provides essential capabilities within its respective domain, with the combined system achieving a 100% detection rate across all threat categories. Notably, the integrity override mechanism accurately escalated all 15 tampering attacks to CRITICAL status, highlighting the importance of combining probabilistic ML models with deterministic cryptographic verification. The blockchain audit trail also passed all six immutability tests, ensuring the system offers tamper-proof forensic logging suitable for post-incident investigations. Beyond detection effectiveness, the study evaluated system latency to assess its feasibility for real-world deployment. Results showed that six out of seven configurations met the 500 ms real-time processing target, with the full configuration averaging a latency of 514.61 ms. Although this slightly exceeds the threshold, it remains operationally viable due to the conditional blockchain logging strategy, which limits record storage to threats assessed as medium severity or higher.

While the results presented in this study demonstrate the viability of iGuard as a unified security framework for industrial GHG monitoring, there are still opportunities for further improvement. Future work will focus on enhancing the emissions anomaly and network intrusion detection agents by incorporating attention-based or transformer architectures to better identify subtle and less common attack patterns. Additionally, there will be an exploration of an adaptive consensus mechanism in which agent weights are updated dynamically based on per-domain detection accuracy, allowing the system to progressively give more weight to the most reliable agents.

References

1. Köhnke, F., et al.: On the path to net-zero: establishing a multi-level system to support the complex endeavor of reaching national carbon neutrality. Front. Clim. **5**, 1056023 (2023). https://doi.org/10.3389/fclim.2023.1056023

2. Abiodun, T.P., Nwulu, N., Olukanmi, P.: Pioneering emission trading in Africa: an architectural design of a blockchain-powered carbon trading system. J. Br. Blockchain Assoc. **7**, 1–10 (2024)
3. Beck, J., et al.: Addressing data gaps in sustainability reporting: a benchmark dataset for greenhouse gas emission extraction. Sci. Data. **12**, 1497 (2025). https://doi.org/10.1038/s41597-025-05664-8
4. Terzini, F., Hayes, E.: Greenhouse gas emissions tracking: making it count. APPEA J. **63**, S455–S459 (2023). https://doi.org/10.1071/AJ22207
5. Gurney, K.R., Liang, J., Roest, G., Song, Y., Mueller, K., Lauvaux, T.: Under-reporting of greenhouse gas emissions in U.S. cities. Nat. Commun. **12**, 553 (2021). https://doi.org/10.1038/s41467-020-20871-0
6. IEA: Methane emissions from the energy sector are 70% higher than official figures, https://www.iea.org/news/methane-emissions-from-the-energy-sector-are-70-higher-than-official-figures. Last Accessed 10 Jan 2026
7. Hamidu, I., Afotey, B., Ayatul-Lahi, Z.: Design and development of a low-cost sensor IoT computing device for greenhouse gas Momitor from selected industry locations. Scalable Comput. Pract. Exp. **23**, 363–376 (2022)
8. Bengtsson, J.: The ghost in the building: non-invasive spoofing and covert attacks on automated buildings. Forensic Sci. Int. Digit. Investig. **52**, 301880 (2025). https://doi.org/10.1016/j.fsidi.2025.301880
9. Kaushik, D., Gulia, P., Gill, N.S., Yahya, M., Shukla, P.K., Shreyas, J.: Synergizing blockchain and AI to fortify IoT security: a comprehensive review. Artif. Intell. Rev. **59**, 41 (2026). https://doi.org/10.1007/s10462-025-11434-0
10. Chawla, D., Kumari, S., Rathore, R.S., Mehra, P.S., Das, A.K., Kumar, N.: Quantum blockchain for internet of things: a systematic review, proposed solutions and challenges. Comput. Electr. Eng. **126**, 110524 (2025). https://doi.org/10.1016/j.compeleceng.2025.110524
11. Liu, B., Zhang, Z., Hu, S., Sun, S., Liu, D., Qiu, Z.: A security trade-off scheme of anomaly detection system in IoT to defend against data-tampering attacks. Comput. Mater. Contin. **78**, 4049–4069 (2024)
12. Huang, M.-T., Zhai, P.-M.: Achieving Paris agreement temperature goals requires carbon neutrality by middle century with far-reaching transitions in the whole society. Adv. Clim. Chang. Res. **12**, 281–286 (2021). https://doi.org/10.1016/j.accre.2021.03.004
13. Abiodun, T.P., Nwulu, N.I., Olukanmi, P.O.: Application of blockchain technology in carbon trading market: a systematic review. IEEE Access. **13**, 5446–5470 (2025). https://doi.org/10.1109/ACCESS.2024.3523672
14. Jha, M.K., Dev, M.: Impacts of climate change. In: Azrour, M., Mabrouki, J., Alabdulatif, A., Guezzaz, A., Amounas, F. (eds.) Smart Internet of Things for Environment and Healthcare, pp. 139–159. Springer Nature, Cham (2024). https://doi.org/10.1007/978-3-031-70102-3_10
15. Wang, X., Zhu, L., Liao, H.: Toward efficient mitigation solutions: source-based carbon pricing and economic implications in China. J. Ind. Ecol. **29**, 794–812 (2025). https://doi.org/10.1111/jiec.70011
16. Xie, Y., Faure, M.: The regulation of third-party verification entities in greenhouse gas emissions trading schemes: lessons from China. Regul. Gov. **20**, 273–288 (2026). https://doi.org/10.1111/rego.70085
17. Maraveas, C., Piromalis, D., Arvanitis, K.G., Bartzanas, T., Loukatos, D.: Applications of IoT for optimized greenhouse environment and resources management. Comput. Electron. Agric. **198**, 106993 (2022). https://doi.org/10.1016/j.compag.2022.106993
18. Bandaru, L., Irigireddy, B.C., Pvnr, K., Davis, B.: DeepQC: a deep learning system for automatic quality control of in-situ soil moisture sensor time series data. Smart Agric. Technol. **8**, 100514 (2024). https://doi.org/10.1016/j.atech.2024.100514

19. Majidian, S.Z., TaghipourEivazi, S., Arasteh, B., Ghaffari, A.: Optimizing random forests to detect intrusion in the internet of things. Comput. Electr. Eng. **120**, 109860 (2024). https://doi.org/10.1016/j.compeleceng.2024.109860
20. Park, J., Seo, Y., Cho, J.: Unsupervised outlier detection for time-series data of indoor air quality using LSTM autoencoder with ensemble method. J. Big Data. **10**, 66 (2023). https://doi.org/10.1186/s40537-023-00746-z
21. Mehmood, H., Khalid, A., Kostakos, P., Gilman, E., Pirttikangas, S.: A novel edge architecture and solution for detecting concept drift in smart environments. Futur. Gener. Comput. Syst. **150**, 127–143 (2024). https://doi.org/10.1016/j.future.2023.08.023
22. Mansour, R.F.: Blockchain assisted clustering with intrusion detection system for industrial internet of things environment. Expert Syst. Appl. **207**, 117995 (2022). https://doi.org/10.1016/j.eswa.2022.117995
23. Aydin, H., Aydin, M.A.: A multi-agent-based DDoS detection and defense system design with federated learning and blockchain in public cloud network environment. Clust. Comput. **28**, 1018 (2025). https://doi.org/10.1007/s10586-025-05700-7
24. Zhang, X., Liu, H., Yang, F.: Enhanced traffic carbon emissions data sharing and modeling via blockchain and personalized federated learning in IIoT ecosystem. IEEE Internet Things J. **12**, 31064–31077 (2025). https://doi.org/10.1109/JIOT.2025.3571952
25. Abegaz, M.S., Abishu, H.N., Yacob, Y.H., Ayall, T.A., Erbad, A., Guizani, M.: Blockchain-based resource trading in multi-UAV-assisted industrial IoT networks: a multi-agent DRL approach. IEEE Trans. Netw. Serv. Manag. **20**, 166–181 (2023). https://doi.org/10.1109/TNSM.2022.3197309
26. Kang, M., Yin, D.: Agent coordination and cooperation based on the cognitive models: observe-orient-decide-act loop. Multiagent Grid Syst. **21**, 38–55 (2025). https://doi.org/10.1177/15741702251334757
27. Javadi, A., Sadeghi, S., Pahlevani, P., Bagheri, N., Rostampour, S., Bendavid, Y.: Secure and efficient lightweight authentication protocol (SELAP) for multi-sector IoT applications. Internet Things. **30**, 101499 (2025). https://doi.org/10.1016/j.iot.2025.101499
28. U.S. Environmental Protection Agency: Clean Air Markets Program Data (CAMPD): Continuous Emission Monitoring System (CEMS) Hourly Emissions Data, https://campd.epa.gov/ (2024).
29. Luay, M., Layeghy, S., Hosseininoorbin, S., Sarhan, M., Moustafa, N., Portmann, M.: Temporal Analysis of NetFlow Datasets for Network Intrusion Detection Systems, http://arxiv.org/abs/2503.04404 (2025). https://doi.org/10.48550/arXiv.2503.04404.
30. Hochreiter, S., Schmidhuber, J.: Long short-term memory. Neural Comput. **9**, 1735–1780 (1997). https://doi.org/10.1162/neco.1997.9.8.1735
31. Zhang, Z., Yang, X., Liu, Y., Song, Y.: Network-level control of intermittent bus lanes using multi-agent deep reinforcement learning with multi-feature state prediction. IEEE Trans. Autom. Sci. Eng. **22**, 18360–18369 (2025). https://doi.org/10.1109/TASE.2025.3586674
32. Breiman, L.: Random forests. Mach. Learn. **45**, 5–32 (2001). https://doi.org/10.1023/A:1010933404324
33. Xu, Z., Xiong, S., Wang, K., Zhang, Y.: Real-time stress prediction of robotic arms based on random Forest agent model. In: 2025 International Conference on Electrical Drives, Power Electronics & Engineering (EDPEE), pp. 999–1003. IEEE, Athens (2025). https://doi.org/10.1109/EDPEE65754.2025.00181
34. National Institute of Standards and Technology (US): Secure hash standard. National Institute of Standards and Technology (U.S.), Washington, D.C. (2015). https://doi.org/10.6028/NIST.FIPS.180-4.
35. Beechey, M., Lambotharan, S., Kyriakopoulos, K.G.: Evidential classification for defending against adversarial attacks on network traffic. Inf. Fusion. **92**, 115–126 (2023). https://doi.org/10.1016/j.inffus.2022.11.024

36. Guarino, S., Vitale, F., Prete, E.D., Faramondi, L., Mazzocca, N., Setola, R.: d -TV-DBN: a hierarchical and distributed architecture for scalable cyber-physical anomaly detection with Bayesian networks. IEEE Trans. Emerg. Top. Comput., 1–12 (2025). https://doi.org/10.1109/TETC.2025.3573051
37. Wood, G.: Ethereum: A Secure Decentralised Generalised Transaction Ledger, https://ethereum.github.io/yellowpaper/paper.pdf, (2014).
38. Truffle Suite: Ganache: Personal Blockchain for Ethereum Development, https://archive.trufflesuite.com/ganache/ (2023).
39. Dai, Y., Ding, H., Zhao, S., Liu, Z.: Robust provenance classification of curcumae radix (Yujin) using nir-hsi: preprocessing, nested CV and morphology effects. Microchem. J. **222**, 117170 (2026). https://doi.org/10.1016/j.microc.2026.117170

Graph Based Generation of Navigable 3D Environments from Deformable Map Pieces

Diogo de Andrade[1(✉)] and Nuno Fachada[2,3]

[1] HEI-Lab, Lusófona University, Lisbon, Portugal
diogo.andrade@ulusofona.pt
[2] Lusófona University, Lisbon, Portugal
nuno.fachada@ulusofona.pt
[3] INESC INOV-Lab, Lisbon, Portugal

Abstract. This work presents a graph-driven pipeline for controllable generation and structural analysis of navigable 3D environments. The approach integrates automatic connector extraction from arbitrary meshes, surface-based structural representation using Steiner tree optimization, navigation-aware deformation of modular elements, and graph-based constraint solving for global layout synthesis. Unlike grid-based or volumetric skeletonization methods, the framework operates directly on surface-derived graphs, enabling designer-guided generation while preserving navigability and structural coherence. High-level spatial intent is encoded as authored graphs and resolved through constraint-based assembly, supporting mixed-initiative content creation workflows. Beyond game development, the methodology establishes a geometry-aware abstraction layer applicable to simulation, training systems, digital twins, and spatial prototyping. Two stages, 1) connection point detection and 2) structural extraction, have been fully implemented and validated, while deformation and graph-based assembly remain under active development within the doctoral research trajectory.

Keywords: Structural Representation · Structure Extraction · Navigation Mesh · Steiner Tree · Geometry Processing · Procedural Content Generation · Game Level Analysis

1 Introduction

Procedural content generation (PCG) has long played an important role in game development, offering solutions for compression, replayability, and scalability [1]. While commonly employed to automate the production of large volumes of content, PCG techniques are also used to augment human creativity by facilitating exploration and extending a designer's expressive capacity. In particular, Mixed-Initiative Content Creation (MICC) frameworks integrate computational assistance into the design workflow, supporting designers through collaborative, feedback-driven processes [2]. Within this context, early level prototyping plays a crucial role, as designers can work with simplified geometry to examine spatial layout and player flow while deferring visual detail. This

Published by Springer Nature Switzerland AG 2027
L. M. Camarinha-Matos and F. Ferrada (Eds.): DoCEIS 2026, IFIP AICT 790, pp. 492–503, 2027.
https://doi.org/10.1007/978-3-032-28939-1_33

practice commonly referred to as whiteboxing or greyboxing, enables rapid iteration and broad spatial experimentation, establishing a structural foundation that later artistic and polishing stages can refine [3].

This paper proposes a pipeline that enables designers to prototype 3D environments from a high-level navigation graph and a collection of modular map pieces. These pieces, derived from arbitrary 3D models, are automatically annotated with connection points and their structure is extracted to support both deformation and graph-based placement. A designer-defined graph encodes the intended spatial logic—such as rooms, paths, or gameplay constraints—and the system selects, places, and deforms suitable pieces to fit this layout. A graph-based constraint solver, inspired by the Wave Function Collapse (WFC) algorithm [4, 5], is proposed to promote global coherence while enforcing semantic and structural constraints. This process aims to balance automation with designer control, promoting iterative workflows and expressive greyboxing capabilities.

Unlike most earlier systems, which require extensive handcrafted annotations and exhibit limited awareness of global structure, this approach aims to minimize manual effort across the pipeline. All stages from piece extraction to structure analysis and placement are automated, with the designer providing two inputs: a library of geometric elements that the system converts into deformable map pieces, and a high-level spatial intent encoded as a navigation graph. This paper presents the pipeline in its current form, documenting the stages already implemented and validated, and outlining the remaining components under development.

Beyond its potential for production workflows, the proposed pipeline also supports research-oriented applications. By generating controllable 3D environments from explicit structural graphs, it enables systematic variation of spatial parameters such as connectivity, flow, or navigational complexity, facilitating experimental studies in level design, player behavior, and procedural evaluation. This doctoral research addresses:

1. RQ1: Can arbitrary 3D geometry be automatically converted into reusable elements with reliable entry/exit connection annotations suitable for assembly?
2. RQ2: To which extent can navigable structure be abstracted directly from surface-derived representations in a way that is sufficiently compact for downstream reasoning, while remaining faithful to traversability?
3. RQ3: Is it possible to adapt an existing deformation method to reshape map pieces to satisfy target connection configurations while preserving navigability and structural semantics?
4. RQ4: Can a designer-authored navigation graph be used as a backbone for the generation of 3D environment geometry, accounting for both combinatorial compatibility and deformation feasibility?

This article is organized as follows: Sect. 3 reviews some work related to the pipeline; Sect. 4 describes the proposed pipeline, current implementation status and some considerations for future developments; Sect. 5 presents some of the preliminary results obtained; Sect. 6 discusses the work, and finally Sect. 7 offers some conclusions.

2 Technological Innovation to Tackle Societal Challenges

The proposed pipeline models spatial design as a graph-driven, geometry-aware engineering process that combines algorithmic generation with explicit human control. Operating within a mixed-initiative paradigm, AI-based structural reasoning assists design decisions without removing human oversight.

This human-in-the-loop approach promotes responsible use of generative technologies by ensuring transparency, controllability, and traceability in how spatial configurations are produced. By enabling systematic exploration of constrained navigable layouts, the framework can support simulation, training, and digital twin applications where accessibility, safety, and structural feasibility are critical.

The research therefore advances technological innovation that balances automation with accountability, contributing toward resilient and human-centered spatial systems.

3 Related Work

Procedural content generation (PCG) has traditionally been dominated by grid-based approaches, particularly in roguelike and platformer games. Systems such as *Rogue Legacy* [6] and *The Binding of Isaac* [7] rely on tile-based layouts populated with pre-authored rooms that satisfy handcrafted adjacency rules. The WFC algorithm has become a popular constraint-based alternative, assembling valid configurations of visual or spatial tiles from a small set of examples [4]. Although effective, these systems remain bound to discrete lattice representations, limiting their applicability to continuous and gridless 3D environments.

Extensions of WFC beyond regular grids have been explored in several forms. While the standard WFC algorithm derives adjacency rules from example patterns, Kim et al. [5, 8] instead specified these rules manually, adapting the approach to non-grid topologies through constraint propagation on navigation mesh samples. Their method generates graphs that classify regions by gameplay semantics (e.g., "weak monster", "strong monster", or "reward") rather than producing spatial layouts. Cooper [9] further extended this idea to operate entirely on graphs, introducing *Sturgeon-GRAPH*, a grammar induction framework that learns connectivity rules from example data and produces new graphs consistent with those structures. The former thus represents an authored rule formulation of graph-based WFC, while the latter exemplifies an example-driven approach to graph synthesis. The proposed pipeline instead builds upon designer-authored navigation graphs. Rather than requiring the designer to define abstract rules or rely on example datasets, it directly follows designer intent through constraint-based placement of deformable 3D geometry.

Beyond tile- and graph-based methods, several systems have explored gridless spatial assembly. Snappable Meshes [10] supports piece-based composition of 3D environments for greyboxing but relies on manual annotation of connection points and uses a stochastic, Markovian-style assembly process driven by local adjacency probabilities, without explicit designer control over structure. The proposed pipeline extends this idea by replacing manual annotation with automated connection point detection and structural extraction [11, 12], and by substituting stochastic assembly with a designer-authored navigation graph that encodes high-level spatial intent. Furthermore, the introduction of deformation enables each map piece to be reshaped to fit new contexts, effectively expanding the expressive range of the original piece library.

Several works have also approached environment generation from path- or sketch-based specifications. *path2level* [13] generates levels from designer-authored player paths using constraint solving, framing playability as the existence of valid traversal routes. Similarly, Snodgrass [14] proposed an example-driven binary space partition method that translates 2D sketches into playable layouts. Both highlight the value of abstract spatial guides for generation—a principle shared by this work—but remain limited to 2D and explicitly grid-based representations, in contrast with the gridless 3D formulation pursued here.

Mixed-initiative frameworks have likewise incorporated path-based reasoning, establishing a lineage of tools that integrate procedural generation with designer input. Hoyt et al. [15] combined automated play analysis with a co-creative Mario-level editor, while Guzdial et al. [16] visualized "design gradients" to show how edits affect level solvability. These examples illustrate the longstanding use of path representations in mixed-initiative design and provide a foundation for more expressive co-creative workflows. Systems such as *Tanagra* [17] and *Sentient Sketchbook* [3] further exemplify this philosophy, guiding automated generation through designer-provided abstractions. The proposed pipeline extends this paradigm to 3D spatial design, focusing on geometry-aware greyboxing rather than 2D level layout.

Beyond algorithmic generation, several learning-based approaches have represented or synthesized structures through statistical or reinforcement models. Rupp and Eckert [18] introduced G-PCGRL, a reinforcement learning framework for procedural graph generation, while Kalogerakis et al. [19] applied machine learning techniques to 3D mesh segmentation and labeling. Although effective in controlled settings, such approaches rely on extensive annotated datasets for training, which are rarely available and costly to produce during the early stages of game development. Guzdial and Riedl [20] further demonstrated unsupervised extraction of level structures from gameplay video. These works highlight complementary directions focused on data-driven generation, whereas the proposed pipeline adopts a deterministic, geometry-aware approach designed for rapid iteration during greyboxing, where generalization from large datasets is neither feasible nor necessary.

4 Proposed Pipeline and Current Status

The proposed pipeline, summarized in Table 1, consists of four stages, each yielding outputs for the downstream components. Two of these stages are fully implemented [11, 12], the third is under development, while the fourth and final stage is still in a planning phase. The following subsections describe each of these stages in detail.

4.1 Map Piece Creation

The first stage of the pipeline transforms arbitrary 3D geometry (Fig. 1a) into map pieces. A map piece is defined as a bounded, navigable region with annotated entry and exit

Table 1. The four stages of the proposed pipeline for enabling designers to quickly prototype 3D environments with expressive greyboxing capabilities.

Stage	Input	Output	Status
1. Map piece creation	3D geometry	Map piece (= 3D geometry + entry/exit points + bounding volume)	Fully implemented [11]
2. Structure extraction	Map piece	Directed connectivity tree	Fully implemented [12]
3. Deformable piece generation	Map piece + directed connectivity tree	Deformable map piece	Under development
4. Graph-based generation	Designer-authored graph + deformable piece set	Greybox environment geometry	Under design

points (Fig. 1b) and a bounding volume, making it suitable for constraint-based assembly during generation.

The method builds a navigation mesh, extracts boundary candidates, and detects connector segments through local visibility tests on the boundary; the corresponding geometric segments are then matched back to the original mesh. This process is fully implemented and completely automated [11].

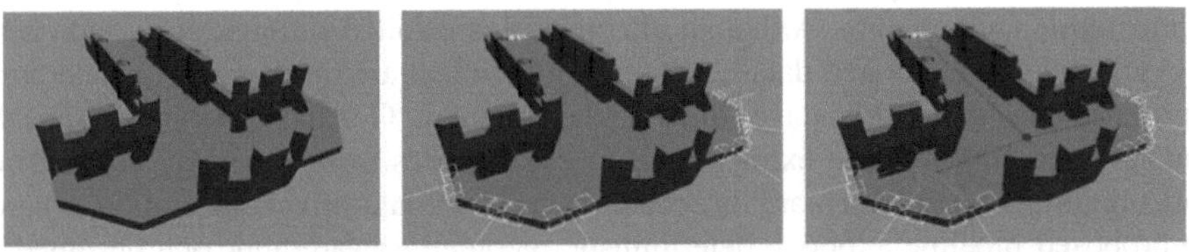

(a) (b) (c)

Fig. 1. Example of steps 1 and 2 of the proposed pipeline applied to a 3D geometry: a) an initial 3D geometry block; b) map piece, obtained after step 1 of the pipeline, with the entry/exit points highlighted in white lines facing outwards (cubes indicate connection constraints); and, c) map piece with the directed connectivity tree (extracted in step 2 of the pipeline) connecting the entry/exit points.

4.2 Structure Extraction

To enable intelligent deformation and semantic matching, each map piece must have an internal representation of its navigable structure. This is achieved through a surface-based graph abstraction computed over the navigation mesh.

The structure extraction algorithm [12] produces a rooted Steiner tree capturing the internal connectivity of the mesh (Fig. 1c). The method 1) discretizes the navigation mesh into a weighted adjacency graph; 2) selects terminals from connectors (optionally adding a central node); 3) computes an approximate Steiner tree [21]; 4) roots the tree using betweenness centrality [22]; and 5) simplifies the result using line-of-sight pruning and angular continuity constraints.

The resulting structure operates directly on the surface, without assuming any volumetric interpretation of the geometry. By capturing the essential connectivity of the navigable space, the tree serves as a reliable scaffold for subsequent stages in the pipeline, including deformation and node-to-piece matching during graph-based generation.

4.3 Deformable Piece Generation

Deformable piece generation is a work-in-progress and constitutes a key research contribution of this pipeline. The objective is to reshape map pieces to satisfy target connection configurations while preserving navigability and the structural semantics captured by the extracted representation. This improves reuse and integration during graph fitting without requiring bespoke assets per layout element. Without deformation, connector placement conventions (e.g., predominantly cardinal orientations) can reintroduce grid-like biases even under gridless assembly, limiting expressive range.

Other strategies for increasing variation, such as mesh segmentation and statistical recombination, have been considered. However, these approaches typically depend on annotated data, domain-specific parameterizations, or visual priors, and they do not directly target navigability preservation in early-stage greyboxing workflows. The proposed approach therefore focuses on deterministic, data-independent geometric adaptation guided by navigation-derived structure. An illustrative example of the deformation goal is shown in Fig. 2.

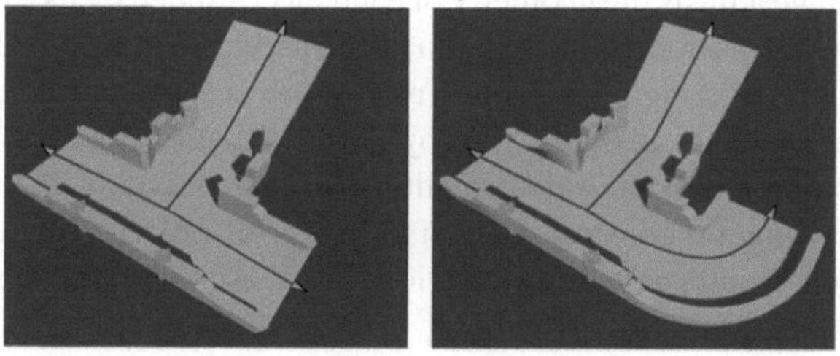

(a) (b)

Fig. 2. Conceptual overview of the deformation process. (a) original map piece with extracted control skeleton (Steiner tree); and, (b) deformed geometry shaped by repositioned control points, illustrating flexible alignment with a target layout.

Deformation research focuses on identifying a transformation model that preserves navigability while allowing substantial geometric adaptation. The extracted Steiner tree acts as a control skeleton, and vertex displacements are computed through weighted combinations of node transformations.

Several deformation paradigms are under evaluation, including Linear Blend Skinning (LBS) [23], Dual Quaternion Skinning (DQ) [24], As-Rigid-As-Possible (ARAP)

[25] surface deformation, and Embedded Deformation [26]. The objective is not visual fidelity but preservation of traversal continuity, clearance, and structural semantics.

For the cage-based methods, influence computation strategies (Euclidean, geodesic, segmentation-aware) and corrective post-processing mechanisms are being investigated to mitigate self-intersections and structural collapse. Comparative evaluation will determine the most suitable model for geometry-aware greyboxing.

4.4 Graph-Based Map Generation

The final stage of the pipeline involves assembling a complete game environment from a set of prepared map pieces and a high-level graph specified by the designer. This component is intended to support early-stage level prototyping (greyboxing), where designers define the spatial logic of a level without committing to final visual or mechanical details.

The input to this stage consists of two components: 1) a deformable map piece library, where each piece is annotated with connection points, a structural Steiner tree, and the support structures for the deformation; and 2) a designer-authored graph, which encodes intended spatial structure. Nodes represent rooms or sections, and edges represent traversable connections.

The goal of the generation system is to select, place, and deform map pieces such that the final configuration realizes the designer's intended structure. To achieve this, we propose the use of a constraint satisfaction algorithm, with the current candidate being the WFC algorithm, extended to operate on arbitrary designer-authored graphs rather than uniform grids. Each node in the graph is assigned a map piece, while each edge represents a required connection between two pieces. These connections are implemented by pairing compatible connection points on the corresponding pieces. During assembly, the deformation stage adjusts the geometry of each piece guided by its extracted structure so that the chosen connection points align in space and realize the adjacency prescribed by the graph, without altering the semantic role of the pieces themselves.

Key challenges include defining entropy and selection heuristics that incorporate deformation feasibility, encoding deformation parameters within the state space, and enforcing global semantic constraints such as traversal ordering or tagged gameplay roles. These aspects require extending traditional WFC-style propagation to continuous, geometry-aware domains.

While work on this module has not yet begun, its development is central to realizing the full potential of the pipeline. The integration of deformation aware piece fitting with constraint propagation holds promise for expressive and controllable greyboxing workflows. Future work will explore the adaptation of WFC to this hybrid setting, potentially incorporating optimization or learning based techniques to improve performance and flexibility.

5 Preliminary Results

To assess the viability of the proposed pipeline, we evaluated its two implemented components: the automated creation of map pieces, with detection and annotation of their entry/exit points, and the extraction of structural connectivity through surface-based graphs. These evaluations aim to verify that the methods produce outputs compatible with downstream deformation and generation tasks, while maintaining navigability and interpretability. A more extensive evaluation of each component is presented in our prior work [11, 12]. Here, we summarize key qualitative outcomes relevant to the pipeline's goals.

5.1 Map Piece Creation

Map pieces are generated from arbitrary 3D geometry through automatic detection of entry/exit points and construction of a bounding volume. The method was evaluated using the map piece sets released with Snappable Meshes [10]. For the current pipeline, the bounding volume is not yet required downstream.

Evaluation was performed through visual comparison against the original handcrafted connectors. A detection was considered correct when it aligned with the manual annotation within a small positional tolerance and preserved traversal direction. All handcrafted connectors were successfully recovered. In addition, the method frequently identified additional geometrically valid connector locations.

Figure 3 illustrates a representative example, comparing automated detection (left) with handcrafted annotations (right). The additional connectors are geometrically feasible but may not always align with conventional design heuristics, motivating optional validation or filtering in future workflows.

The approach requires initial tuning of geometric thresholds; however, these parameters remain stable across assets of similar characteristics. For medium and large libraries, the reduction in manual annotation effort outweighs the tuning overhead.

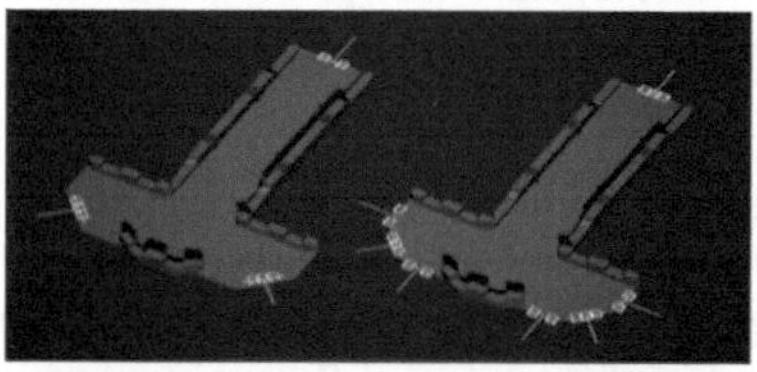

Fig. 3. Comparison between handcrafted (left) and automated (right) entry/exit point placement.

5.2 Structure Extraction

The structure extraction algorithm was used to generate simplified representations of navigable paths within individual map pieces.

Figure 4 shows several examples in both simple and more complex geometry. In most cases, the structure follows expected navigation routes, including curved and sloped regions. Some outputs, such as the one depicted in Fig. 4b, are valid but may diverge from designer intuition. Others, as in the case of Fig. 4c, illustrate the algorithm's sensitivity to minor navigation mesh inconsistencies.

The resulting skeletons consistently connect entry/exit points while reducing geometric complexity into path-relevant structures. These results suggest that the extracted structures reflect the overall geometry and traversability of each piece, covering the full navigable area and capturing its intended spatial logic. They are also consistent with designer expectations and the navigational semantics of the original geometry.

6 Discussion

The proposed pipeline bridges procedural generation and designer intent by treating navigable environments as structurally annotated, deformable 3D components organized through explicit navigation graphs. Rather than generating geometry directly from stochastic or example-based models, the approach decouples spatial logic from geometric realization. High-level structure is authored as a graph, while geometry adapts to satisfy that structure under navigability constraints. This separation promotes interpretability, as spatial decisions remain explicit and traceable throughout the generation process.

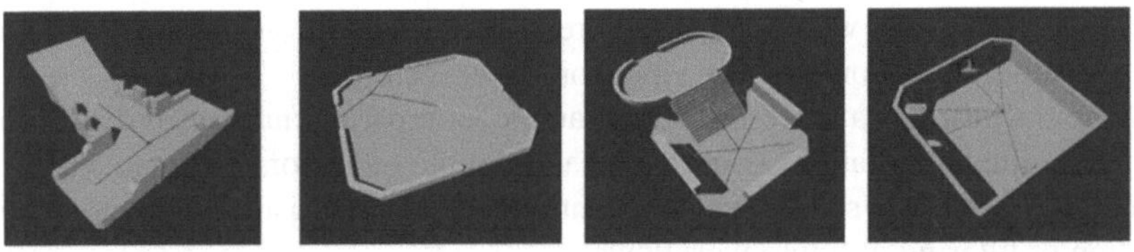

(a) (b) (c) (d)

Fig. 4. Structure extraction results for several example map pieces, with the different colors representing the depth of the tree (red is depth 1, yellow is depth 2, cyan is depth 3, etc), and the red sphere represents the root of the tree: (a) corridor 5 map piece, with a ramp; (b) hub 2 map piece, correct but counter-intuitive; (c) hub 5 map piece, incongruities in the navigation mesh lead to small inconsistencies in the output; and, (d) hub 6 map piece.

The implemented stages demonstrate that arbitrary geometry can be transformed into reusable elements and abstracted into compact structural representations suitable for downstream reasoning. In contrast to volumetric skeletonization or purely geometric segmentation, the use of surface-derived Steiner trees yields a navigation-centered abstraction aligned with traversal semantics. This representation acts as a structural intermediary between raw mesh data and constraint-based assembly, enabling geometric processing to directly support combinatorial reasoning.

Conceptually, the pipeline suggests a hybrid generation paradigm in which continuous geometric adaptation and discrete graph reasoning operate in a coupled manner. Traditional PCG methods often prioritize either combinatorial layout synthesis (e.g., tile- or grammar-based systems) or geometric modeling in isolation. By integrating deformation-aware geometry with graph-driven constraint solving, the approach advances a unified framework capable of addressing both structural expressiveness and spatial feasibility.

The main limitations arise from parameter sensitivity in connector detection and dependency on navigation mesh fidelity, which can propagate inconsistencies into the extracted structures. Current results are primarily qualitative and depend on the fidelity of the generated navigation meshes. Parameter sensitivity in connector detection and boundary sampling can require dataset-specific tuning, which can affect robustness across heterogeneous asset libraries. Structural extraction can inherit artifacts from navigation mesh discretization and can be sensitive to minor inconsistencies, as illustrated by occasional counter-intuitive skeletons and localized irregularities.

Although qualitative validation indicates reliable recovery of traversal points and connectivity, systematic quantitative evaluation remains necessary. Future work will formalize metrics for connector detection accuracy, structural stability under mesh perturbation, deformation-induced distortion, navigability preservation, and constraint satisfaction success rates across controlled benchmark sets. Since the deformation and constraint-solving stages remain incomplete, end-to end performance, scalability, and failure modes for full graph fitting have not yet been empirically characterized; completing these stages is required for a full pipeline-level evaluation.

Ongoing research focuses on selecting deformation models that preserve path continuity and clearance under substantial geometric adaptation, and on extending graph-based constraint propagation to incorporate deformation feasibility and semantic compatibility. Completing these stages will enable end-to-end evaluation of scalability and robustness, transforming the pipeline from a modular proof-of-concept into a comprehensive framework for graph-driven spatial generation.

7 Conclusion

This paper proposes a modular pipeline aimed at designer-driven procedural generation of 3D environments from high-level spatial logic. By treating level structure as a graph authored by the designer and map pieces as deformable, semantically enriched units, the system enables automated generation of navigable geometry while preserving human control over flow, pacing, and design intent.

Two components have been implemented and validated: automatic connector detection for extracting entry/exit points from arbitrary geometry, and surface-based structural abstraction through rooted Steiner trees over navigation-mesh derived graphs. The results indicate that connector extraction can recover traversal locations consistent with handcrafted annotations while often identifying additional viable connectors, and that the extracted trees capture piece connectivity in an interpretable and compact form. Current limitations include parameter sensitivity and dependence on navigation mesh fidelity, which can produce occasional counter-intuitive structures. Ongoing doctoral research focuses on completing the remaining two stages: deformation and graph-based generation aims to realize designer-authored graphs through constraint satisfaction.

Beyond game production, the framework can support controlled experimentation in level design and procedural evaluation. The long-term goal is to deliver a complete framework for graph-driven, constraint-aware level generation that supports rapid iteration, procedural authoring, and designer-centered control in 3D game environments.

Acknowledgments. This research was partially funded by the Fundação para a Ciência e a Tecnologia under grants/projects: UID/05380/2025, UID/PRR/05380/2025, UID/PRR2/05380/2025, UID/6486/2025, UID/PRR/6486/2025, UID/PRR2/06486/2025, and CEECINST/00002/2021/CP2788/CT0001, as well as by the Instituto Lusófono de Investigação e Desenvolvimento under Project COFAC/ILIND/COPELABS/1/2024. The authors would like to thank Eduardo Rocha for creating the visualization used in Fig. 2, illustrating the effect of navigation-aware deformation.

References

1. Hendrikx, M., Meijer, S., Van Der Velden, J., Iosup, A.: Procedural content generation for games: a survey. ACM Trans. Multimedia Comput. Commun. Appl. **9**(1) (2013). https://dl.acm.org/doi/10.1145/2422956.2422957
2. Liapis, A., Smith, G., Shaker, N.: Mixed-initiative content creation. In: Shaker, N., Togelius, J., Nelson, M.J. (eds.) Procedural Content Generation in Games: a Textbook and an Overview of Current Research, pp. 195–214. Springer, Cham (2016). https://doi.org/10.1007/978-3-319-42716-4_11
3. Liapis, A., Yannakakis, G.N., Togelius, J.: Sentient sketchbook: computer-assisted game level authoring. In: 8th International Conference on the Foundations of Digital Games, New York (2013)
4. Gumin, M.: WaveFunctionCollapse: bitmap & tilemap generation from a single example with the help of ideas from quantum mechanics. GitHub (2016). https://github.com/mxgmn/WaveFunctionCollapse
5. Kim, H., Lee, S., Lee, H., Hahn, T., Kang, S.: Automatic generation of game content using a graph-based wave function collapse algorithm. In: 2019 IEEE Conference on Games (CoG), pp. 1–4, London (2019). https://doi.org/10.1109/CIG.2019.8848019
6. Cellar Door Games: Rogue Legacy (2013)
7. McMillen, E.: The Binding of Isaac: Rebirth. Nicalis, Inc. (2014)
8. Kim, H., Hahn, T., Kim, S., Kang, S.: Graph based wave function collapse algorithm for procedural content generation in games. IEICE Trans. Inf. **E103-D**(8), 1901–1910 (2020). https://doi.org/10.1587/transinf.2019EDP7295
9. Cooper, S.: Sturgeon-graph: constrained graph generation from examples. In: Proceedings of the 18th International Conference on the Foundations of Digital Games, FDG '23, New York (2023). https://doi.org/10.1145/3582437.3582465
10. Silva, R.C.E., Fachada, N., de Andrade, D., Códices, N.: Procedural generation of 3D maps with snappable meshes. IEEE Access. **10**, 43093–43111 (2022). https://doi.org/10.1109/ACCESS.2022.3168832
11. de Andrade, D., Fachada, N.: Automated generation of map pieces for Snappable meshes. In: Proceedings of the 18th International Conference on the Foundations of Digital Games, FDG '23, New York (2023). https://doi.org/10.1145/3582437.3582483
12. de Andrade, D., Fachada, N.: Structural tree extraction from 3d surfaces. Preprint https://arxiv.org/abs/2510.15886 (2026). https://doi.org/10.48550/arXiv.2510.15886
13. Cooper, S., Guzdial, M.: path2level: Constraint-based level generation from paths. In: 2023 IEEE Conference on Games (CoG), pp. 1–4, Boston (2023). https://doi.org/10.1109/CoG57401.2023.10333205
14. Snodgrass, S.: Levels from sketches with example-driven binary space partition. In: Proceedings of the AAAI Conference on Artificial Intelligence and Interactive Digital Entertainment, pp. 73–79 (2019). https://doi.org/10.1609/aiide.v15i1.5227
15. Hoyt, A., Guzdial, M., Kumar, Y., Smith, G., Riedl, M.O.: Integrating automated play in level co-creation. Preprint https://arxiv.org/abs/1911.09219 (2019). https://doi.org/10.48550/arXiv.1911.09219
16. Guzdial, M., Sturtevant, N., Yang, C.: The impact of visualizing design gradients for human designers. In: Proceedings of the AAAI Conference on Artificial Intelligence and Interactive Digital Entertainment, pp. 18–25 (2021). https://doi.org/10.1609/aiide.v17i1.18886

17. Smith, G., Whitehead, J., Mateas, M.: Tanagra: a mixed-initiative level design tool. In: Proceedings of the Fifth International Conference on the Foundations of Digital Games, FDG'10, pp. 209–216, New York (2010). https://doi.org/10.1145/1822348.1822376
18. Rupp, F., Eckert, K.: G-PCGRL: procedural graph data generation via reinforcement learning. In: 2024 IEEE Conference on Games (CoG), pp. 1–8, London (2024). https://doi.org/10.1109/CoG60054.2024.10645633
19. Kalogerakis, E., Hertzmann, A., Singh, K.: Learning 3d mesh segmentation and labeling. In: ACM SIGGRAPH 2010 Papers, SIGGRAPH'10, New York (2010). https://doi.org/10.1145/1833349.1778839
20. Guzdial, M., Riedl, M.: Game level generation from gameplay videos. In: Proceedings of the AAAI Conference on Artificial Intelligence and Interactive Digital Entertainment, pp. 44–50 (2016). https://doi.org/10.1609/aiide.v12i1.12861
21. Kou, L., Markowsky, G., Berman, L.: A fast algorithm for steiner trees. Acta Informatica. **15**, 141–145 (1981). https://doi.org/10.1007/BF00288961
22. Freeman, L.C.: A set of measures of centrality based on betweenness. Sociometry. **40**(1), 35–41 (1977). https://doi.org/10.2307/3033543
23. Magnenat-Thalmann, N., Laperriére, R., Thalmann, D.: Joint-dependent local deformations for hand animation and object grasping. In: Proceedings on Graphics Interface'88, pp. 26–33. CAN (1989). https://doi.org/10.20380/gi1988.04
24. Kavan, L., Collins, S., Zára, J., O'Sullivan, C.: Geometric skinning with approximate dual quaternion blending. ACM Trans. Graphics (TOG). **27**(4), 1–23 (2008). https://dl.acm.org/doi/10.1145/1409625.1409627
25. Sorkine, O., Alexa, M.: As-rigid-as-possible surface modeling. In: Proceedings of the Fifth Eurographics Symposium on Geometry Processing, SGP'07, pp. 109–116. DEU, Goslar (2007). https://doi.org/10.2312/SGP/SGP07/109-116
26. Sumner, R.W., Schmid, J., Pauly, M.: Embedded deformation for shape manipulation. In: ACM SIGGRAPH 2007 Papers, SIGGRAPH'07, p. 80. Association for Computing Machinery, New York (2007). https://doi.org/10.1145/1275808.1276478

Urban Traffic Control Enabled by Optical IoT and Deep Reinforcement Learning

Gonçalo Galvão[1(✉)], Manuela Vieira[1,2], Manuel Augusto Vieira[1,2], Mário Véstias[3], and Paula Louro[1,2]

[1] Instituto Superior de Engenharia de Lisboa (ISEL), Instituto Politécnico de Lisboa (IPL), Lisbon, Portugal
goncalo.galvao@isel.pt

[2] UNINOVA-CTS and LASI, Quinta da Torre, Monte da Caparica, 2829-516 Caparica, Portugal

[3] INESC INOV, Lisbon, Portugal

Abstract. This work presents an Optical Internet of Things (O-IoT) framework for smart urban mobility, integrating Visible Light Communication (VLC) and Deep Reinforcement Learning (DRL) to optimize traffic signal control in real time. Each intersection operates as an autonomous DRL agent, forming a decentralized optical IoT network where VLC enables low-latency, high-bandwidth communication among intersections. Two different deep reinforcement learning (DRL) models were employed, namely the Proximal Policy Optimization (PPO) algorithm and the Deep Q-Learning (DQL) algorithm, within the Simulation of Urban Mobility (SUMO) simulator, with Visible Light Communication (VLC) used to capture dynamic traffic and pedestrian data. Simulation results demonstrate that VLC-enhanced Multi-Agent Reinforcement Learning (MARL) approaches can effectively manage critical urban intersections, showing that both models are capable of learning the dynamics of a traffic environment composed of nine homogeneous intersections. The model based on a Deep Q-Network (DQN) exhibits superior performance compared to MAPPO, highlighting the differences between value-based and policy-based algorithms in MARL scenarios. The proposed framework demonstrates how optical wireless communication can enable scalable, adaptive, and resilient traffic systems, supporting the development of intelligent and sustainable smart cities.

Keywords: Visible Light Communication (VLC) · Deep Reinforcement Learning (DRL) · Traffic Signal Optimization · Connected Vehicles (CV) · Multi-Agent Systems · Urban Traffic Management · Traffic Flow Simulation

1 Introduction

Urban mobility is increasingly constrained by persistent traffic congestion, driven by rapid urban population growth and the rising number of vehicles in metropolitan areas. This results in longer travel times, higher fuel consumption, increased emissions, and reduced productivity.

Published by Springer Nature Switzerland AG 2027
L. M. Camarinha-Matos and F. Ferrada (Eds.): DoCEIS 2026, IFIP AICT 790, pp. 504–515, 2027.
https://doi.org/10.1007/978-3-032-28939-1_34

Despite these challenges, traffic management systems have not evolved at the same pace. Many cities, including Lisbon, still rely on rigid, pre-timed signal plans that fail to adapt to real-time traffic conditions or unexpected events such as congestion peaks and accidents. Additionally, traditional monitoring systems depend on fixed sensors with limited coverage, restricting the availability of timely and detailed traffic data.

As a result, traffic control remains largely reactive rather than adaptive. Given that urban intersections are key points of congestion and traffic propagation, there is a clear need for intelligent, data-driven systems capable of dynamically adjusting signal control based on real-time conditions.

1.1 Motivation

The motivation for this work lies in the limitations of current traffic management systems and the growing demand for intelligent and sustainable mobility. Traditional approaches fail to fully utilize data from connected vehicles, while advances in AI and communication technologies enable more adaptive, data-driven solutions [1].

To address these challenges, the following research question is proposed:

How can the integration of Visible Light Communication (VLC) and Reinforcement Learning (RL) technologies be explored to develop an adaptive traffic signal control system that optimizes traffic flow, reduces congestion, and enhances the safety of both vehicles and pedestrians in urban environments?

VLC can use existing lighting infrastructure to enable fast, low-latency communication between vehicles and traffic signals [2]. Combined with DRL, it supports adaptive control strategies that improve intersection efficiency and reduce congestion.

The novelty of this work lies in leveraging VLC to extract real-time traffic information from the environment and integrating it with intelligent decision-making mechanisms. The proposed framework evaluates different DRL algorithms (DDQN and PPO) and introduces a Strategic Anti-Blocking Phase Adjustment (SAPA) mechanism, which dynamically extends green signal durations based on space–time traffic perception, considering both local queue lengths and the occupancy of neighboring intersections. This enables more coordinated and efficient traffic control compared to conventional approaches.

2 Technological Innovation to Tackle Societal Challenges

Urbanization and population growth have intensified several societal challenges in modern cities, particularly those related to mobility, transportation, and public safety. Among the most pressing issues are traffic congestion, road safety risks, environmental pollution, and reduced accessibility for pedestrians and other vulnerable road users. Traffic congestion leads to longer travel times, higher fuel consumption, increased greenhouse gas emissions, and higher levels of air pollution, directly affecting economic productivity and public health [3]. Road safety is also compromised, as dense traffic conditions, poorly coordinated intersections, and unpredictable pedestrian flows increase the likelihood of accidents, particularly involving pedestrians and cyclists. Additionally, inefficient traffic management can exacerbate social inequities, as certain communities may face longer commute times, reduced access to services, or exposure to higher levels of environmental pollutants, further highlighting the societal dimension of urban mobility challenges.

Traditional traffic management strategies, such as fixed-time or pre-programmed signal plans, have limited capacity to respond to dynamic and unpredictable traffic patterns. While these approaches may provide adequate performance under stable conditions, they are often unable to adapt to fluctuations in vehicle volumes, pedestrian activity, or unexpected events such as accidents and road closures. Consequently, inefficiencies arise in the form of vehicle queuing, unnecessary stops, increased delays, and higher emissions, all of which contribute to broader societal problems, including decreased urban livability, reduced economic efficiency, and heightened public stress levels. Moreover, conventional systems often prioritize vehicular traffic at the expense of pedestrian safety and comfort, creating further risks for vulnerable road users.

Addressing these societal challenges requires innovative technological solutions capable of adapting to real-time conditions and managing the complex interactions within urban traffic networks. Advances in connected vehicle technologies, such as VLC, enable the collection of precise and timely information from vehicles and pedestrians, providing traffic management systems with a detailed understanding of current road conditions. When combined with artificial intelligence methods, particularly deep reinforcement learning, this data allows the development of intelligent traffic signal control systems that can dynamically optimize the allocation of green time at intersections, reduce vehicle queues and delays, and improve pedestrian safety [4]. These adaptive systems consider both local conditions and the broader traffic network, ensuring that actions benefiting a single intersection do not create negative consequences elsewhere.

Intelligent, data-driven traffic management systems not only improve operational efficiency but also address multiple societal concerns simultaneously. By reducing congestion, they decrease travel time and fuel consumption, mitigating environmental impacts such as greenhouse gas emissions and air pollution. By incorporating pedestrian behavior into decision-making, these systems enhance the safety and accessibility of vulnerable users, promoting equity in urban mobility [5]. Furthermore, by optimizing traffic flow, cities can experience improved economic efficiency, higher productivity, and better quality of life for residents.

3 Literature Review

3.1 Recent Advances and Challenges in Vehicular Visible Light Communication

For ITS to be effective, a large-scale deployment of intelligent vehicles and infrastructures is required to ensure comprehensive data acquisition and dissemination. Although Radio Frequency (RF) communication has traditionally supported these systems, the rapid growth of mobile data traffic has exposed the limitations of the RF spectrum [6]. In contrast, the visible light spectrum offers vast, unlicensed bandwidth capable of supporting high-capacity communication networks.

VLC, enabled by the advancement of LED technology, utilizes light intensity modulation for data transmission and photodetectors or camera sensors for signal reception. When integrated with V2V (Vehicle-to-Vehicle) and V2I/I2V (Vehicle-to-Infrastructure

/ Infrastructure-to-Vehicle) frameworks, VLC has the potential to substantially enhance vehicular communication performance, particularly in dense traffic environments.

Despite its advantages, VLC faces notable challenges in outdoor environments, where factors such as strong sunlight, fog, rain, and snow can attenuate or saturate optical signals, leading to performance degradation. Therefore, VLC is best positioned as a complementary rather than a substitutive technology to RF communication. The hybrid use of VLC and RF can provide a more resilient communication framework, VLC offering high-capacity line-of-sight links, while RF maintains connectivity under non-line-of-sight or adverse weather conditions.

Recent studies have examined the impact of outdoor environmental conditions on VLC performance [7], particularly in terms of bit error rate (BER), as well as the influence of inter-vehicle distance. In [8], a VLC system for tunnels is studied, focusing on I2V communication and considering not only the typical LoS channel from infrastructure transmitters but also NLoS components, including reflections from tunnel walls. Similarly, [9] provides a detailed investigation of V2V communications, analyzing diverse environmental conditions, varying lateral distances between vehicles, and the influence of ambient light during both daytime and nighttime scenarios. The results are promising, demonstrating the robustness and capacity of VLC even under challenging conditions. Nonetheless, performance degradation is observed under dense fog, high ambient light intensity, or large inter-vehicle distances, highlighting the limitations of the technology in extreme outdoor scenarios.

While prior studies focus primarily on the physical-layer performance of vehicular VLC systems, their integration with data-driven control strategies remains largely unexplored. In contrast, this research investigates a framework that combines VLC-based traffic sensing with reinforcement learning to enable intelligent and adaptive traffic signal control.

3.2 Intelligent Urban Traffic Management Through Deep Reinforcement Learning

Deep Reinforcement Learning has emerged as a promising paradigm for optimizing vehicular communication and traffic flow. Research efforts in this domain range from relatively simple cases, such as single intersections controlled by an individual RL agent, to large-scale multi-intersection networks governed by MARL agents.

Broadly, MARL algorithms can be divided into two main families: value-based and policy-based approaches. Value-based techniques, such as DQL, estimate a value function representing the expected return of each possible action and select the one with the highest predicted value. These methods are computationally efficient and particularly suitable for independent or parameter-sharing settings.

Several studies investigate the use of deep Q-learning for adaptive traffic signal control. In [10] a DQN-based traffic signal control approach is developed for partially observable intersections with connected vehicles. The research introduces a novel state representation and reward design for low detection scenarios, and simulation results demonstrate that the model improves efficiency and robustness compared to traditional actuated controllers, remaining effective for connected vehicle penetration rates above

20%. In [11], a Deep Q-learning model is proposed for real-time adaptive traffic signal control, leveraging both local and adjacent intersection data. The study shows that short, multi-step actions outperform longer ones in reducing delay, increasing speed, and improving intersection capacity, demonstrating the effectiveness of DQN for real-time traffic optimization.

While these value-based approaches learn the expected return to select actions, policy-based methods directly learn a mapping from states to actions, often using an actor–critic framework. PPO has been widely applied to adaptive traffic signal control. Single-intersection PPO methods using LSTM-based state encoding have shown significant improvements in vehicle speed, queue length, and halting duration [12]. Extending this, federated PPO enables distributed training across multiple intersections, improving model generalization, convergence speed, and collaboration between agents, while reducing waiting time and communication overhead [13].

Although previous studies have explored various reinforcement learning approaches for traffic signal optimization, the present work distinguishes itself by leveraging vehicular connectivity through VLC to gather high-resolution traffic data in real time. Beyond simply controlling intersections, this study emphasizes arterial traffic patterns, making a clear distinction between radial and circular roads and incorporating a wide range of traffic scenarios that reflect realistic urban conditions, including both vehicular and pedestrian flows. By doing so, it allows the training of DQN and PPO-based neural networks capable of learning complex spatial and temporal traffic patterns across the city. Both models are designed not only to optimize overall traffic flow and reduce congestion but also to ensure pedestrian safety and prioritize the protection of critical urban zones, providing a more resilient and adaptive city-wide traffic management framework compared to existing approaches.

4 Research Contributions and Results

4.1 Vehicular Connectivity Through VLC

Building upon current technological advancements, this paper introduces a novel framework that establishes the synergistic integration of VLC-based localization services with a learning-driven traffic signal control paradigm. The core focus is on optimizing both vehicle and pedestrian mobility across multi-intersection networks. The proposed V-VLC architecture, depicted in Fig. 1, capitalizes on this principle by incorporating both vehicles and infrastructure components within a unified V2X framework. These communication protocols are embedded within MARL framework, enabling the system to dynamically manage both vehicular and pedestrian flows during signal control. This framework defines request and response/message zones, where vehicles approaching an intersection communicate with the intersection manager, acting as the controlling agent, once they are at a sufficient distance. Vehicles request permission to pass the intersection while providing traffic information about the remaining vehicles in their lane.

To enable real-time monitoring and control, a laboratory-scale VLC system was developed to emulate a V2X (Vehicle-to-Everything) communication environment, including V2V and V2I/I2V links. Traffic scenarios are generated using the SUMO simulator, providing essential parameters such as vehicle positions, speeds, queue lengths,

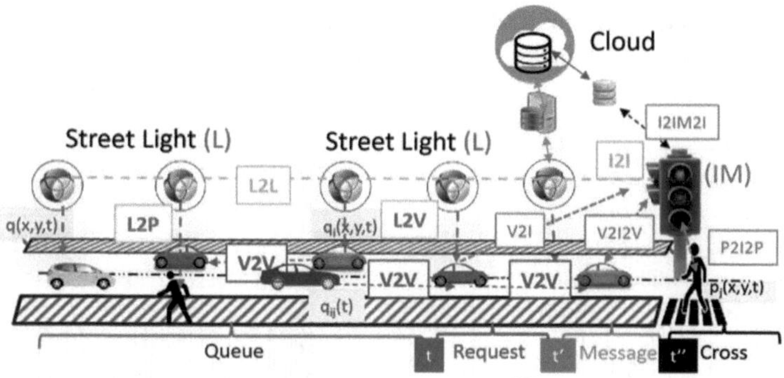

Fig. 1. A 2D representation of the V-VLC architecture. At each intersection, a queue–request–response protocol is applied: approaching vehicles and pedestrians issue crossing requests (V/P2I), and traffic signals, functioning as intelligent agents, acknowledge these requests (I2V/P).

and waiting times. Communication messages are encoded according to a dedicated protocol (Table 1) and transmitted via VLC through an interface with the LED controller in the laboratory setup, simulating optical data transmission through vehicle lighting systems, streetlamps, and traffic signals. The transmitted signals are captured by photodetectors representing receivers embedded in vehicles and roadside infrastructure, allowing the intelligent agent to recover traffic information and optimize intersection control to improve traffic flow efficiency.

Table 1. Message protocol defined for each of the V-VLC communications.

		COM	Position												
L2V	Sync	1	x	y	END	Hour	Min	Sec	Payload (32 bits)						EOF
V2V	Sync	2	x	y	Lane (0–7)	Nº Veic.	END	Hour	Min	Sec	Car IDx	Car IDy	nº behind		EOF
V2I	Sync	3	x	y	TL (0–15)	Nº Veic.	END	Hour	Min	Sec	Car IDx	Car IDy	nº behind		EOF
I2V	Sync	4	x	y	TL (0–15)	ID veic	END	Hour	Min	Sec	Car IDx	Car IDy	nº behind	Phase	EOF
P2I	Sync	5	x	y	TL (0–15)	Direct.	END	Hour	Min	Sec	payload				EOF
I2P	Sync	6	x	y	TL (0–15)	Phase	END	Hour	Min	Sec	Payload				EOF

The communication protocol structures information exchange in a frame with synchronization, identification, and payload fields. Each frame starts with a 5-bit synchronization block [10101] marking the Start of Frame (SOF), followed by a 12-bit time block encoding hours, minutes, and seconds. ID blocks indicate the type of communication (L, V, P, I) and include transmitter location, lane, requested traffic lights, number of following vehicles, assigned ID, cardinal direction, and active phase, depending on whether the message is a request or response. Traffic-related messages may include vehicle identifiers, road conditions, waiting times, and weather information. The frame ends with a 4-bit End of Frame [0000]. Fig. 2 a) and b) illustrate the multiplexed signal and decoded messages exchanged between vehicles/pedestrians and traffic lights.

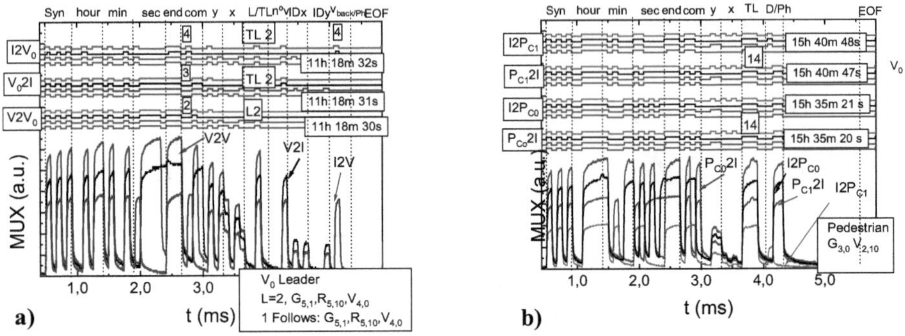

Fig. 2. MUX signal exchange visualization and decoded message flow between a) Vehicles-Traffic Lights (V2I, I2V) and b) Pedestrians-Traffic Lights (P2I, I2P).

4.2 Marl Traffic Control System Based on Traffic Strategies

The traffic scenario under study is illustrated in Fig. 3 and consists of nine homogeneous intersections, each with four approaches. Each approach includes one lane for through and right-turn movements and a dedicated lane exclusively for left turns. A total of nine traffic signal phases is considered: eight phases allocated to vehicular movements and one exclusive phase for pedestrian crossings, ensuring their safety while using the crosswalks at the intersections.

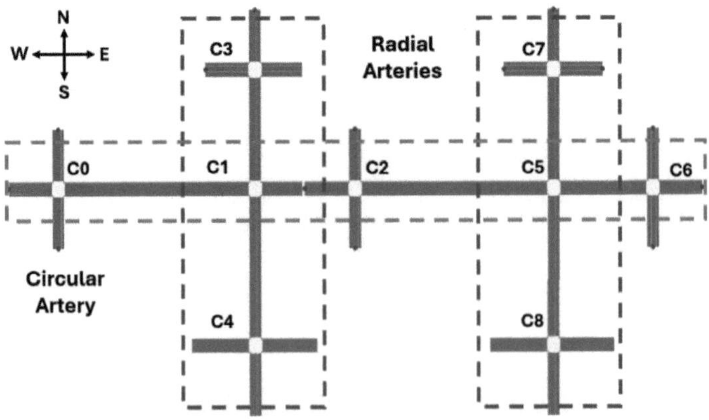

Fig. 3. Traffic scenario consisting of nine homogeneous four-arm intersections, including two radial arteries (C3–C4 and C7–C8) and one main circular artery (C0–C6). Intersections C1 and C5 belong to both radial and circular arteries, making them the most critical intersections in the network.

Distinct traffic control strategies were designed and implemented, each represented by a dedicated neural network. As summarized in Table 2, these strategies provide complementary approaches to managing the variability and complexity of urban traffic dynamics. For this study, two main strategies were selected. Both are radial-priority strategies simulating peak-hour conditions: the afternoon peak focuses on predominantly outbound traffic (C4/C8 to C3/C7), while the morning peak emphasizes inbound traffic (C3/C7 to C4/C8). These scenarios allow the system to replicate realistic urban flow patterns and assess how adaptive control responds to directional traffic imbalances.

Table 2. Summary of traffic control strategies applied simulating real city traffic patterns.

Network	Strategy	Priority Artery	Direction Focus	Description
1	Radial Out	Radial C3/C1/C4	Northbound (S → N)	Prioritizes radial artery with outbound radial flow.
2	Radial In	Radial C3/C1/C4	Southbound (N → S)	Prioritizes radial artery with inbound radial flow.

For each strategy, two neural networks are trained using both DDQN and MAPPO algorithms, and the performance of the resulting models is compared. Specifically, key traffic efficiency metrics are evaluated, including vehicle queue lengths, waiting times, pedestrians halting and travel times. Both the training and testing of the networks were conducted in SUMO simulator [14], under traffic conditions comprising 2600 vehicles and 1000 pedestrians circulating within the environment.

4.3 SAPA and Neural Networks Architectures

One of the key contributions of this research is the Strategic Anti-Blocking Phase Adjustment (SAPA) module, which refines the duration of green phases after they are selected by the learning agent. While the RL model decides which phase to activate, SAPA determines how long it should remain active using real-time data obtained through VLC-based sensing.

SAPA operates by analyzing both upstream queue lengths and downstream occupancy levels. If downstream traffic conditions are favorable (low occupancy), the system extends the green phase to clear queues efficiently. Conversely, when downstream occupancy approaches critical levels, SAPA limits the green duration to prevent spillback and network congestion. Green times are constrained within predefined bounds to ensure stability. Additionally, SAPA incorporates spatial awareness by considering neighboring intersections and applying adaptive priority weights to different traffic flows, allowing better coordination across the network. This mechanism reduces blocking, improves traffic flow, and enhances the effectiveness of the learning process by enabling more informed and adaptive control decisions.

Both neural networks encode the traffic environment by combining vehicle position, normalized speed, and pedestrian presence in waiting zones; the parameters of both models are summarized in Table 3.

Table 3. Main parameters used in the DDQN and PPO models.

DDQN Model		PPO Model	
Parameter	**Value**	**Parameter**	**Value**
Input Layer	164	*Optimizer*	Adam
Hidden Layers	2	*Actor Learning Rate*	0.0001
Width Hidden Layers	400	*Critic Learning Rate*	0.0003
Batch Size	128	*Discount Factor*	0.99
Discount Factor	0.75	*GAE*	0.95
Output Layer	9	*Rollout Horizon*	2048
Training Epochs	100	*PPO Epochs*	10
Learning Rate	0.0001	*Minibatch Size*	512
Optimizer	Adam	*PPO Clipping*	0.2

For both models, the reward function is defined by two components: vehicular waiting time and pedestrian waiting time. These components are equally weighted (50/50), ensuring a balanced optimization of traffic efficiency and pedestrian mobility.

4.4 Simulation Results Discussion

To analyze the results obtained from the simulation, several average-based performance metrics were considered, namely Average Queue Length (AQL), Average Pedestrian Halting (APH), Average Vehicle Speed (AVS), Average Waiting Time (AWT), and Travel Time (TT). The evaluated models include DDQN and MAPPO, both with and without the SAPA block, allowing for an assessment of the impact of this component. Tables 4 and 5 present the results for the Radial Out and Radial In strategies, respectively.

When comparing the DDQN-SAPA and DDQN models across both strategies, the former demonstrates a 42% reduction in the number of vehicles in queues, a 15% increase in average vehicle speed, and reductions of 18% and 42% in waiting time and travel time, respectively.

Similarly, when comparing the MAPPO-SAPA and MAPPO models, the former achieves an approximate 32% reduction in queue length, a 16% increase in average speed, and reductions of 23% and 29% in waiting time and travel time, respectively.

A comparison between both SAPA-enhanced models indicates that DDQN-SAPA outperforms MAPPO-SAPA, showing an approximate 25% reduction in average queue length, an increase of 3% in average speed and 13% in waiting time, and a 21% reduction in travel time, thus emerging as the best-performing model.

These results suggest that effective traffic management requires not only intelligent phase activation but also adaptive control of green phase durations. Such adaptability allows the system to respond to real-time traffic conditions and to the capacity of downstream intersections to accommodate incoming vehicles after phase activation.

Table 4. Main parameters used in the DDQN and PPO models for strategy Radial Out.

	AQL (vehicles)	APH (pedestrians)	AVS (Km/h)	AWT (seconds)	TT (minutes)
DDQN-SAPA	6,77	0,99	36,9	8,44	3,58
DDQN	10,83	0,99	32,25	10,15	6
MAPPO-SAPA	9,55	1,29	35,24	7,2	4,87
MAPPO	11,28	0,85	31,76	7,74	5,76

Table 5. Main parameters used in the DDQN and PPO models for strategy Radial In.

	AQL (vehicles)	APH (pedestrians)	AVS (Km/h)	AWT (seconds)	TT (minutes)
DDQN-SAPA	5,85	1,55	37,51	7,6	3,2
DDQN	10,8	1,94	32,22	9,42	5,88
MAPPO-SAPA	7,39	1,34	36,79	6,99	3,74
MAPPO	14,19	1,59	30,37	11,58	6,45

5 Conclusions

Conventional fixed-time traffic control systems are limited by their inability to adapt to real-time traffic conditions, leading to inefficiencies and increased delays. To address this issue, this study proposes an intelligent traffic control framework that optimizes signal phases to improve traffic flow and reduce congestion.

The solution assumes a fully connected environment enabled by VLC, where vehicles communicate with each other and with the infrastructure. The collected traffic data feeds a MARL system that dynamically adjusts signal phases according to current demand. Additionally, two traffic generation strategies were designed to represent realistic urban mobility patterns, capturing both inbound and outbound peak traffic flows.

To obtain the experimental results, both DDQN (value-based) and MAPPO (policy-based) models were evaluated with and without the integration of the SAPA block. From a statistical perspective, the comparison between the SAPA-enhanced models indicates that DDQN-SAPA outperforms MAPPO-SAPA, showing an approximate 25% reduction in average queue length, an increase of 3% in average speed and 13% in waiting time, and a 21% reduction in travel time, thus emerging as the best-performing model.

These differences can be attributed to the learning characteristics of each method. DDQN focuses primarily on local action–reward relationships without explicitly considering the global impact of individual agents' decisions. In contrast, MAPPO employs a centralized critic to account for overall system performance, penalizing locally beneficial actions if they negatively affect global traffic conditions, which may introduce certain limitations in this scenario.

These findings highlight the potential of the proposed intelligent control system as a scalable and adaptive solution for urban traffic management. However, the current study assumes ideal VLC communication and full vehicle equipment, which may not reflect real-world conditions.

Future work will focus on the development of a laboratory-scale VLC prototype to evaluate system performance under less controlled and more realistic conditions, as well as on analyzing the potential impact of communication delays, noise, and packet loss on overall system performance. Additionally, further research will aim to enhance the control framework by optimizing the neural networks and exploring more advanced algorithms to enable not only phase selection but also phase timing optimization and traffic prediction.

References

1. de Souza, A.M., et al.: Traffic management systems: a classification, review, challenges, and Fu-ture perspectives. Int. J. Distrib. Sens. Netw. **13**(4) (2017). https://doi.org/10.1177/1550147716683612
2. Pathak, P.H., Feng, X., Hu, P., Mohapatra, P.: Visible light communication, networking, and sensing: a survey, potential and challenges. IEEE Commun Surv Tutor. (2015). https://doi.org/10.1109/COMST.2015.2476474
3. Hounsell, N.B., Shrestha, B.P., Piao, J., McDonald, M.: Review of urban traffic management and the impacts of new vehicle technologies. IET Intell. Transp. Syst. **3**(4), 419–428 (2009). https://doi.org/10.1049/iet-its.2009.0046
4. Musa, A.A., Malami, S.I., Alanazi, F., Ounaies, W., Alshammari, M., Haruna, S.I.: Sustainable traffic management for smart cities using IoT-oriented intelligent transportation systems: challenges and recommendations. Sustainability. **15**(13) (2023). https://doi.org/10.3390/su15139859
5. Galvão, G., Vieira, M., Vieira, M.A., Véstias, M., Louro, P.: Intelligent traffic control strategies for VLC-connected vehicles and pedestrian flow management. Sensors. **25**, 6843 (2025). https://doi.org/10.3390/s25226843
6. Memedi, A., Dressler, F.: Vehicular visible light communications: a survey. IEEE Commun Surv Tutor. **23**(1), 161–181 (2021). https://doi.org/10.1109/COMST.2020.3034224
7. Yang, W., Liu, H., Cheng, G.: Modeling and performance study of vehicle-to-infrastructure visible light communication system for mountain roads. Sensors. **24**(17) (2024). https://doi.org/10.3390/s24175541
8. Ramzi, S.R., Hameed, S.M., Sabri, A.A.: VLC tunnels. Optics Continuum. **3**(10), 1990–2005 (2024). https://doi.org/10.1364/OPTCON.533167
9. Al Hasnawi, R., Marghescu, I., Rusu-Casandra, A.: Reliability and capacity evaluation for vehicle-to-vehicle VLC. In: Proceedings of the 2024 International Conference on Communications (COMM), pp. 1–6. IEEE (2024). https://doi.org/10.1109/COMM62355.2024.10741390

10. Ducrocq, R., Farhi, N.: Deep reinforcement Q-learning for intelligent traffic signal control with partial detection. Int. J. ITS Res. **21**, 192–206 (2023). https://doi.org/10.1007/s13177-023-00346-4
11. Celtek, S.A., Durdu, A., Ali, M.E.M.: Evaluating action durations for adaptive traffic signal control based on deep Q-learning. Int. J. ITS Res. **19**, 557–571 (2021). https://doi.org/10.1007/s13177-021-00262-5
12. Huang, L., Qu, X.: Improving traffic signal control operations using proximal policy optimization. IET Intell. Transp. Syst. **17**, 592–605 (2023). https://doi.org/10.1049/itr2.12286
13. Li, M., et al.: Federated deep reinforcement learning-based urban traffic signal optimal control. Sci. Rep. **15**, 11724 (2025). https://doi.org/10.1038/s41598-025-91966-1
14. Lopez, P.A., et al.: Microscopic traffic simulation using SUMO. In: 2018 21st International Conference on Intelligent Transportation Systems (ITSC), pp. 2575–2582, Maui (2018). https://doi.org/10.1109/ITSC.2018.8569938

Using Artificial Intelligence to Predict Gunfire Deaths

Eurico Clemente[1,2,3(✉)], Luis M. Camarinha-Matos[1], and Filipa Ferrada[1]

[1] NOVA School of Science and Technology, UNINOVA-CTS and LASI, NOVA University, Lisbon, Portugal
e.clemente@campus.fct.unl.pt, {cam,faf}@uninova.pt
[2] Instituto Superior de Engenharia de Lisboa, Lisbon, Portugal
[3] Polícia Judiciária, Lisbon, Portugal

Abstract. Predicting the number of shooting-related deaths can help police and governments prevent future outbreaks of social unrest, but for this to be effective, the prediction must have a high degree of accuracy. Although these predictions are complex to create due to various factors, such as the need for comprehensive data collection, verification of all that data, financial investment, development of statistical models, and more, this can be facilitated by dividing tasks among multi-organizations (creating a collaborative network). This collaboration between agencies is not limited to humans alone but also extends to humans and AI. In this context, a machine learning model was developed using the "Python" programming language, based on the Homicide Reports database, which contains 317,474 recorded events (actual firearm incidents), and achieves an accuracy of nearly 90%. The application of this model demonstrates that AI can play an essential role in predicting future firearm incidents. However, this depends on the success of the collaborative network.

Keywords: Firearms · Crime Fighting · Artificial Intelligence · Machine Learning · Collaborative Ecosystem · Federated Learning · Human-AI Collaboration

1 Introduction

With the recent progress of Artificial Intelligence (AI), it has become possible to process large amounts of information and enabling rapid statistical reasoning, namely, to make statistical predictions. In the near future, this reasoning may become an asset for public security by enabling early identification of potential criminal events and their motivations. This may help police and governments implement interventions and resource allocation strategies aimed at preventing and reducing incidents that could result in injuries or death.

Currently, public security AI applications focus on supporting investigation, through collecting information of crimes suspects, over large-scale processing of digital traces and unstructured information (e.g., online content and open-source intelligence) [1].

Published by Springer Nature Switzerland AG 2027
L. M. Camarinha-Matos and F. Ferrada (Eds.): DoCEIS 2026, IFIP AICT 790, pp. 516–533, 2027.
https://doi.org/10.1007/978-3-032-28939-1_35

This includes searching for evidence of crimes that have already been committed or planned to be committed for the near future. A significant portion of this data is obtained directly from users through forums and social networks. Compared with more traditional approaches, AI enables the collection and processing large amounts of heterogeneous information, such as impartially (without personal interest, skepticism, or value judgments), continuously (operating 24 h a day, 365 days a year), and from diverse sources (including websites, forums, software systems, and databases). Nevertheless, investigation last decision continues to be carried out by human agents.

However, AI can go beyond its current usage by predicting the expected number of deaths in future events[1] [2]. The benefits of this are quite significant, since accurate predictive models can inform evidence-based public policies, support the study of evolving criminal behavior, and, most importantly, enable prevention/oriented actions aimed at reducing future deaths.

The role of AI becomes even more evident as cities evolve into smart cities (SC), where large-scale sensing infrastructures and connectivity (IoT) expand the volume and diversity of data streams. These developments may improve the accuracy of death predictions while simultaneously reducing the need for human resources within criminal investigation agencies[2] . However, they also amplify practical challenges, as it is hard to compare data sets if they are not properly standardized.

Relevant signals are typically fragmented across multiple stakeholders beyond criminal investigation agencies (e.g., emergency services, hospitals, municipal services, community organizations) and represented in heterogeneous formats (e.g., tabular records, textual narratives, geo-temporal traces). In addition, the centralization of this data is often constrained (particularly in Europe) by data privacy concerns and organizational barriers, which can be addressed through federated learning.

To address these challenges, a collaborative ecosystem supported by "federated data space" principles is proposed, in which participants preserve data sovereignty while enabling controlled data sharing through common semantics, metadata, and usage policies. This combination of a collaborative ecosystem and federated data management provides a promising way to leverage prevention-oriented modelling for firearm fatality reduction while mitigating data centralization risks.

In line with this context, the general research question guiding this PhD work is: *To what extent a security-oriented collaborative ecosystem, combined with federated learning, could enable accurate and privacy-preserving prediction of gunfire-related fatalities using heterogeneous, multi-stakeholder data sources?*

While considering this broader question, this paper focuses only on a preliminary step related to the core predictive component: the development and evaluation of a machine learning model that estimates the expected number of deaths per gunfire-related event. As an initial step, it provides a necessary baseline for subsequent extensions

[1] An "event" is defined as the act of firing one or more shots by a perpetrator, occurring at a specific date and location. When the perpetrator is found guilty under the law, the event is considered a crime (in accordance with the presumption of innocence).

[2] In Portugal, the work methodology of the Judicial Police (PJ) follows the best practices outlined in the manual (BPM) of the European Network of Forensic Science Institutes (ENFSI), ensuring that each agent undergoes training over a significant period of time.

toward cross-stakeholders, privacy-preserving learning within a collaborative smart-city data ecosystem. As such, a machine learning (ML) model was developed using the Python programming language [3, 4]. The model's output (prediction) is numerical and can take any integer value, based on ensemble methods. For the algorithm, we used extreme gradient boosting (XGBoost) and sequential tree construction, where each new tree corrects the errors made by the previous one, in order to improve the predictions incrementally (tree by tree). Subsequently, the output of the developed model is compared with the actual results to verify its (effective) accuracy through the model checking phase.

The contribution of this study to the field of security is both significant and innovative, with the potential for future applications of an AI model to predict deaths at the public safety answering point, ultimately saving lives that would otherwise be lost.

The remaining of this paper is organized into the following sections: Sect. 2 discusses the contribution to address societal challenges; Sect. 3 briefly reviews the related literature; Sect. 4 presents a case study; Sect. 5 examines the main challenges; and Sect. 6 presents some conclusions.

2 Contribution to Tackling Societal Challenges

Firearm-related violence is a public health and safety issue of significant global importance, requiring coordinated, multi-level approaches at both the national and international levels. Mitigating the violence phenomenon requires the implementation of evidence-based public policies capable of inducing a structural paradigm shift in systems for the prevention and control of violent crime.

Quantitative analysis of the relationship between the occurrence of firearm-related incidents and the number of resulting deaths reveals an average fatality rate of approximately 12% [5], as shown in Fig. 1. This indicator reflects the intrinsic severity of this type of violence and underscores the need for targeted and sustained interventions.

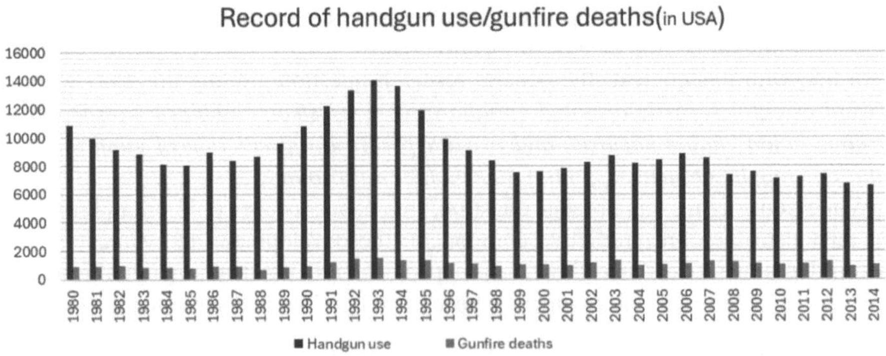

Fig. 1. Number of firearms-related events and deaths – DB Homicide Reports.

Firearm-related deaths constitute a pressing global social challenge, accounting for approximately 200,000 homicides annually [5]. This issue transcends national boundaries and generates substantial economic burdens, with estimated costs reaching $1.5 trillion per year across healthcare systems, public safety, lost productivity, and related sectors. Addressing this complex problem requires integrated and multidisciplinary approaches that encompass public health, policy development, and international cooperation.

The United Nations advocates for tackling violence through comprehensive, multisectoral strategies grounded in human rights principles, in alignment with the Sustainable Development Goals (SDGs), particularly SDG 16, which promotes peace, justice, and strong institutions.

While the "whole-of-society" approach, encompassing victim consultation, protection of vulnerable populations (including women, children, and youth), and the establishment of secure reporting mechanisms, remains essential, technological advancement should be considered a central and enabling factor in enhancing the effectiveness of these interventions.

According to the Small Arms Survey [6], firearms were used in approximately 46% of all violent deaths globally between 2010 and 2015, resulting in 214,000 deaths per year in the US context. This highlights the significant impact of firearm-related deaths on society.

With the application of AI, it is expected to be possible to predict the outcome of such events. In turn, this prediction allows police forces to focus on specific incidents; while also enabling policymakers to assess the true impact their policies may have on all citizens.

In this work, we defined as target applying AI to predict the number of deaths from gunfire. It includes:

- the problem: improving public security;
- the objective: to predict the exact number of deaths caused by each event;
- the advantages: defining concrete public policies to improve security;
- the application: AI uses information from previous events to predict the number of deaths in future events; measuring the performance of the model, where the predicted number of deaths must be as accurate as possible to allow the allocation of preventive measures such as police and medical support; and, finally, a comparison with the previous system, where predictions are made manually using available statistical evaluations (e.g., identifying more problematic neighborhoods).

3 Related Work

Collaborative ecosystems in the field of security studies bring together governments, academia, industry, and civil society to share information on threats and evidence-based policies. These systems aim to reduce data fragmentation through inclusive forums, knowledge exchanges, and interoperable platforms. In turn, collaboration between humans and AI is expected to improve security operations by combining human ethical judgment with AI predictive analysis, enhancing threat detection and reducing "operational blind spots" in public safety contexts [7].

Previous studies in this area were conducted using data from events in several countries; however, this data often suffers from significant delays due to GDPR regulations and media pressure (e.g., the publication of security levels). Some of these studies focus on general crime [8], while others address the specific topic of this study, i.e., deaths related to the use of firearms [9].

We can also find studies on the use of machine learning (ML) algorithms (both supervised and unsupervised learning) [10]; however, most of these studies focus on suicide prediction [11]. These studies are limited to identifying predictions through testing models. In contrast, we went a step further by comparing the predicted values with the actual values (checking model).

It should be noted that the most commonly used data in the identified studies come from the Homicide Report, covering the period between 1980 and 2014. In fact, the majority of these studies were conducted by the scientific community on the Kaggle platform [12], with a focus on filtering variables to detect potential crime patterns. Examples of such studies include those carried out by Kheirallah Samaha [13] and Kathakali Seth [14].

As for the predicted number of deaths caused by the use of firearms, we identified studies that use mathematical formulas [15]. However, these formulas are not applicable to all countries due to differences in social, cultural, and religious contexts, among other factors. In this regard, AI/ML makes a significant contribution by automatically adjusting to these differences (i.e., by entering data from these countries and calculating the formula). Nonetheless, each country or region should have its own dedicated collaborative ecosystem.

There are also non-academic studies on the potential added value of applying AI to predict the number of deaths, generally conducted by private companies such as Deloitte (a consulting firm) and Ping Na (an insurance company, which ranked second in AI generative patents in 2024) [16]. In our study we focus on developing a ML model designed to predict the exact number of deaths that will occur in the future, broken down by event. Unlike static formulas, our model applies a dynamic approach, making it potentially applicable in different regions.

More recently, literature has increasingly recognized that real-world public-safety analytics is not only a modelling challenge but also a data ecosystem challenge: relevant signals are typically distributed across multiple stakeholders (e.g., emergency services, hospitals, municipal services, community organizations) and stored in heterogeneous formats (tabular records, textual narratives, etc.). Instead of centralizing all data, *data spaces* have been proposed as a governed, interoperable approach in which participants keep control of their data (preserve data sovereignty) while enabling controlled sharing through common semantics, metadata, and usage policies [17, 18]. Developments in *data spaces* and *federated data spaces* [19] are becoming highly relevant in this context, as they address one of the main bottlenecks for AI in security and public safety: access to high-quality, distributed, and sensitive data.

In the security domain, EU-level initiatives have started to articulate and operationalize this direction, emphasizing controlled access, interoperability, and responsible AI development for law-enforcement and public-safety contexts. For smart-city settings, data-space thinking aligns with emerging discussions on federated urban data and digital-twin ecosystems, where multiple organizations contribute complementary data assets without relinquishing control, enabling cross-domain analytics while respecting governance constraints [20].

Data spaces and federated data spaces can be directly related to the concept of *Collaborative Business Ecosystems (CBEs)* [21, 22], as they provide the digital and governance infrastructure that enables large-scale, multi-actor collaboration.

Within a CBE, multiple independent organizations jointly create value by sharing resources, capabilities, and knowledge while maintaining their autonomy. However, effective collaboration at ecosystem scale requires a trusted mechanism for data exchange, coordination, and value co-creation. This is precisely where *data spaces* play a foundational role. Instead of centralizing information, each actor retains ownership of its data while exposing it under agreed policies. This aligns naturally with CBE principles of decentralization, autonomy, and distributed value creation. ***Federated data spaces*** extend this concept by adding stronger interoperability, governance, and trust frameworks across multiple ecosystems. They allow different data spaces (or sub-ecosystems) to interconnect, enabling cross-domain collaboration while preserving data sovereignty. This is particularly relevant in large-scale CBEs where value chains span multiple sectors and jurisdictions.

In parallel, federated learning (FL) (also referred to as federated machine learning [23]) has emerged as a promising technical enabler for collaborative model training when raw data cannot be pooled. In smart-city contexts, FL is often positioned as a practical cross-silo approach, allowing multiple organizations to jointly train models by exchanging model updates rather than data [24]. However, surveys and policy-oriented guidance highlight that FL does not eliminate all risks: model updates may still leak information, and FL deployments must account for statistical heterogeneity (non-independent and identically distributed data – non-IID data), system heterogeneity, and privacy–utility trade-offs, motivating careful governance and privacy-by-design mechanisms.

Taken together, these approaches support the idea for combining a collaborative, data-space-aligned ecosystem (to address interoperability, access control, and accountability) with FL-based learning (to reduce raw-data sharing) when applying prevention-oriented analytics to support public-safety in smart cites, even when data is distributed across different organizations and stored in different formats.

In this paper, it is developed and evaluated an ML model to estimate the expected number of deaths per gunfire-related event from incident descriptors. This provides a baseline for future work using multi-stakeholder, privacy-preserving learning (e.g., FL), supported by data-space governance and semantic alignment.

4 A Case Study

The Murder Accountability Project (MAP) is a collaborative ecosystem in which various stakeholders work continuously, sharing data, methods, and objectives within the same ecosystem [25]. The data contained in the Homicide Reports comes from both governmental and non-governmental sources, as shown in Fig. 2.

Thus, MAP considers a diverse group of stakeholders who interact primarily through data sharing, public advocacy, and technical support for investigations, creating a cycle in which better information leads to more solved cases and, in turn, to more data and cooperation. The Stakeholders performed are listed in Table 1.

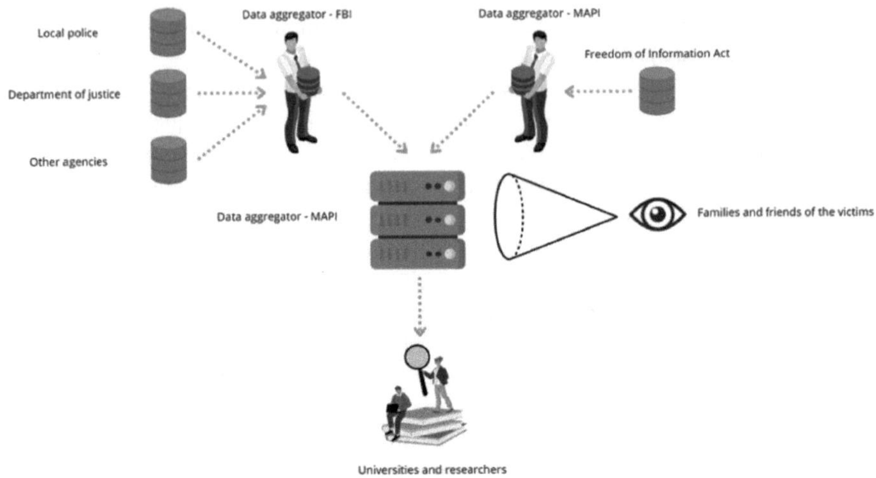

Fig. 2. MAP stakeholders - DB Homicide Reports (source: the author).

Table 1. Stakeholders of MAP.

Stakeholders	Role within the project
Group MAP board / volunteers	Management, curation, and operation of the project
Law enforcement	Data source, and use of data for investigation and response to criticism
Academics / criminologists	Analysis and validation of patterns to create AI
Victims / families	Data confirmation and indirect beneficiaries.
Donors	Funding of the operation.
Media / public	Data consumption, scrutiny, and dissemination.

4.1 General Method

Based on this scenario, a ML model was developed using the "Python" programming language [3, 4]. The model produces numerical (integer) predictions using an ensemble approach. Specifically, the XGBoost algorithm [26] was adopted, employing sequential tree construction in which each new tree iteratively corrects the errors of the previous ones, thereby improving prediction accuracy. Subsequently, the output of the developed model will be compared with the actual results to verify its (effective) accuracy through the checking model. The contribution of this study to the field of security is both significant and innovative, with the potential for future applications at the public safety answering point (PSAP), ultimately saving lives that would otherwise be lost. To enhance model robustness, ridge regularization (L2) should be used, and the mean absolute error (MAE) should be examined.

As a general approach, the typical steps of the machine learning application were followed:

- **Selecting a training data source:** Identify and collect relevant, reliable, and representative data aligned with the problem domain, ensuring sufficient coverage and quality for learning.
- **Data preparation to fit the ML algorithm:** Clean and preprocess the data (e.g., handling missing values, normalization, encoding categorical variables, feature selection/engineering) to make it suitable for the chosen algorithm.
- **Training phase:** Fit the model to the training dataset, allowing it to learn patterns and relationships between input features and target variables.
- **Validation phase:** Evaluate the model's performance using a separate dataset (or cross-validation), tuning parameters and assessing generalization before final testing or deployment.

4.2 Data Source

After reviewing the various databases (DB) available, we chose to use the Homicide Reports database from the Murder Accountability Project [25] for this experiment due to its open-access high quantity and quality of data. This non-profit association, established in 2015, is dedicated to educating the American public about the importance of accurately counting homicides in the United States (US), using data from the FBI's (Federal Bureau of Investigation) Event Report.

Thus, we can classify this ML as follows: it is a supervised learning task, as the learning process is based on real data from previous years (1980 to 2014); a regression task, as it predicts the exact number of deaths for each event; a multiple regression problem, since the system uses several variables (e.g., "victim sex" and "event type") to make the prediction; and a univariate regression, as we are trying to estimate a single variable.

As previously mentioned, training AI is limited by the available information, as its predictions of values (numerical and non-numerical), behaviors (actions), and reasoning depend on the statistical analysis (mathematical processing) of the data provided, both in terms of quantity and quality. Unfortunately, criminal investigation has an Achilles' heel, which is the identification of the perpetrator. This identification is almost always associated with the resolution of the event. However, as shown in Fig. 3, this is not always possible.

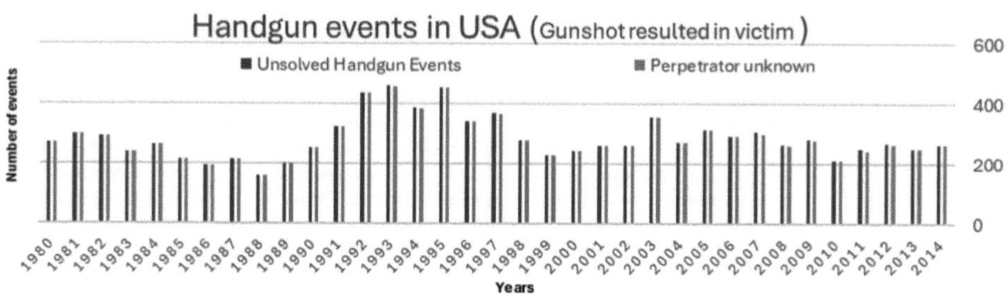

Fig. 3. Unsolved Handgun Events – DB Homicide Reports.

Perpetrators identification is crucial information for AI; its absence represents a data limitation that affects the accuracy of predictions.

The percentage of unidentified perpetrators varies from year to year, as shown in Fig. 4. Fortunately, the emergence of new information technologies over the years, along with the knowledge accumulated by forensic agencies (such as the police), has contributed to a gradual decrease in this percentage.

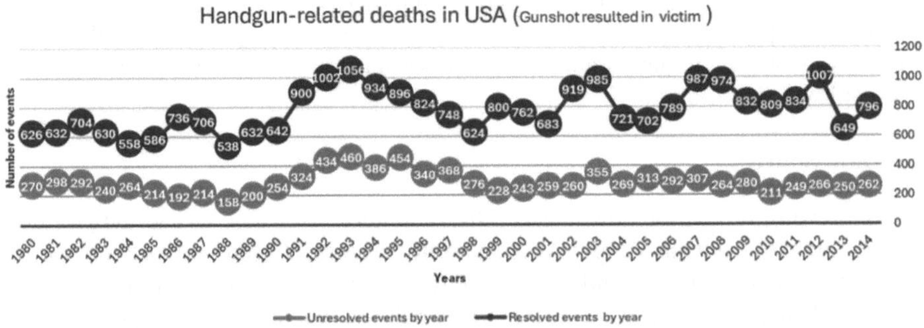

Fig. 4. Number of resolved and unresolved events – DB Homicide Reports.

4.3 Data Preparation Steps

The information collected between 1980 and 2014 was used to create the prediction model (training data set). In total, we have 638,454 recorded events, of which 317,474 involved handguns. To compare the predictions made by the ML with actual data, we used information from 2015 to 2023, covering 74,998 recorded firearm-related events (validation data set).

The tasks performed are listed in Table 2.

Table 2. Description of the tasks carried out for ML development.

	No	Task Description
Data Analysis	Task 1	Data loading – The (original) data from DB Homicide Reports were loaded through the Murder Accountability Project website [15].
	Task 2	Data rectification – Since the original data contained errors, these were manually corrected or removed one by one to rectify the database (e.g., a shooting victim's age recorded as 998 years was corrected to 98 years).
	Task 3	Filtering the data – The original database contains 15,322,896 data points (distributed across 638,454 rows × 24 columns). The ML for events involving "handgun" type firearms, the data is reduced to 7,619,376 data points (317,474 rows × 24 columns). A filtering process was then applied to the significant columns, as reducing the database size improves processing speed. This filtering, based on the minimum dataset (MdS), reduced the data to 5,079,584 data points (317,474 rows × 16 columns), a reduction of more than ten million data points.

(*continued*)

Table 2. *(continued)*

	No	Task Description
	Task 4	Definition of achievable values for each variable – To optimize computer processing, the achievable values for each variable must be defined. For example, in the column representing the relationship between the perpetrator and the victim, the values "boyfriend" and "girlfriend" were merged into a single category: "boyfriend/girlfriend." The above-mentioned variables had the following possible values: Year – "1980", "1981", "1982", "1983", "1984", "1985", "1986", "1987", "1988", "1989", "1990", "1991", "1992", "1993", "1994", "1995", "1996", "1997", "1998", "1999", "2000", "2001", "2002", "2003", "2004", "2005", "2006", "2007", "2008", "2009", "2010", "2011", "2012", "2013", "2014"; Month – "January", "February", "March", "April", "May", "June", "July", "August", "September", "October", "November", "December"; Incident – "0", "1", "2", "3", "4", "5", "6", "7", "8", "9", "10", "11", "12", "13", "14", "15", "16", "17", "18", "19", "20", "21", "22", "23", "24", "25", "26", "27", "28", "29", "30", "31", "32", …"999"; Event Type – "manslaughter by negligence", "murder or manslaughter"; Event Solved – "yes", "no"; Victim Sex – "female", "male", "unknown"; Victim Age – "0", "1", "2", "3", "4", "5", "6", "7", "8", "9", "10", "11", "12", "13", "14", "15", "16", "17", "18", "19", "20", "21", "22", "23", "24", "25", "26", "27", "28", "29", "30", "31", "32", …"99"; Victim Race – "Asian/Pacific Islander", "Black", "Native American/Alaska Native", "unknown", "White"; Victim Ethnicity – "Hispanic", "not Hispanic", "unknown"; Perpetrator Sex – "female", "male", "unknown"; Perpetrator Age – "0", "1", "2", "3", "4", "5", "6", "7", "8", "9", "10", "11", "12", "13", "14", "15", "16", "17", "18", "19", "20", "21", "22", "23", "24", "25", "26", "27", "28", "29", "30", "31", "32", …"99"; Perpetrator Race – "Asian/Pacific Islander", "Black", "Native American/Alaska Native", "unknown", "White"; Perpetrator Ethnicity – Hispanic", "not Hispanic", "unknown"; Relationship – Possible values: "acquaintance", "boyfriend/girlfriend", "brother", "common-law husband", "common-law wife", "daughter", "employee", "employer", "ex-husband", "ex-wife", "family", "father", "friend", "husband", "in-law", "mother", "neighbor", "sister", "son", "stepdaughter", "stepfather", "stepson", "stranger", "unknown", "wife"; Victim Count – "*0*", "*1*", "2", "*3*", "*4*", "5", "*6*", "*7*", "8", "*9*", "*10*".
ML	Task 5	Splitting the dataset – The dataset (1980 to 2014) was divided into two subsets: one for training the model and the other for testing. In this split, 85% of the data (± 4,317,647 data points) was used for training, while 15% was allocated for testing (±761,937 data points).
	Task 6	Computer programming (language) – The ML model was developed using the Python programming language in the Jupyter Notebook environment.
	Task 7	Running the model (algorithm) – The model was executed using XGBoost to predict the number of deaths in each future event.
Findings	Task 8	Verification of results (model check) – The values obtained from the model were compared with the actual data from 2015 to 2023.
	Task 9	Analysis on the application of AI – A thorough analysis was held on the real utility of AI applications and their added value to society (specifically in the context of public security).

4.4 Learning Steps

In this context, Table 3 presents the sub-tasks of Task 6, while Table 4 presents the sub-tasks of Task 7.

Table 3. Description of the sub-tasks of Task 6.

No.	Task Description
Task 6.1	Definition of the programming language – selecting a machine language that meets the required characteristics of efficiency, speed, and precision. We chose Python.
Task 6.2	Conversion of values for mathematical processing – Since ML interprets reasoning mathematically, non-numeric values (e.g., "object") had to be converted into equivalent numerical values (e.g., "int64").
Task 6.3	Correlation matrix verification – We assessed the importance of each variable to understand its impact on the prediction. Based on this analysis, we obtained the correlation matrix shown in Fig. 5.

The correlation matrix is essential for analyzing the relationships between variables, identifying: strong correlations (+1 in dark blue and −1 in dark red), removing redundant features (0 in white), and avoiding overfitting, among other things. Thus, it is useful for summarizing patterns, guiding feature selection, and validating statistical assumptions.

An inverted heatmap was used to better highlight the negative correlations in the matrix by inverting the standard color scheme (Fig. 5).

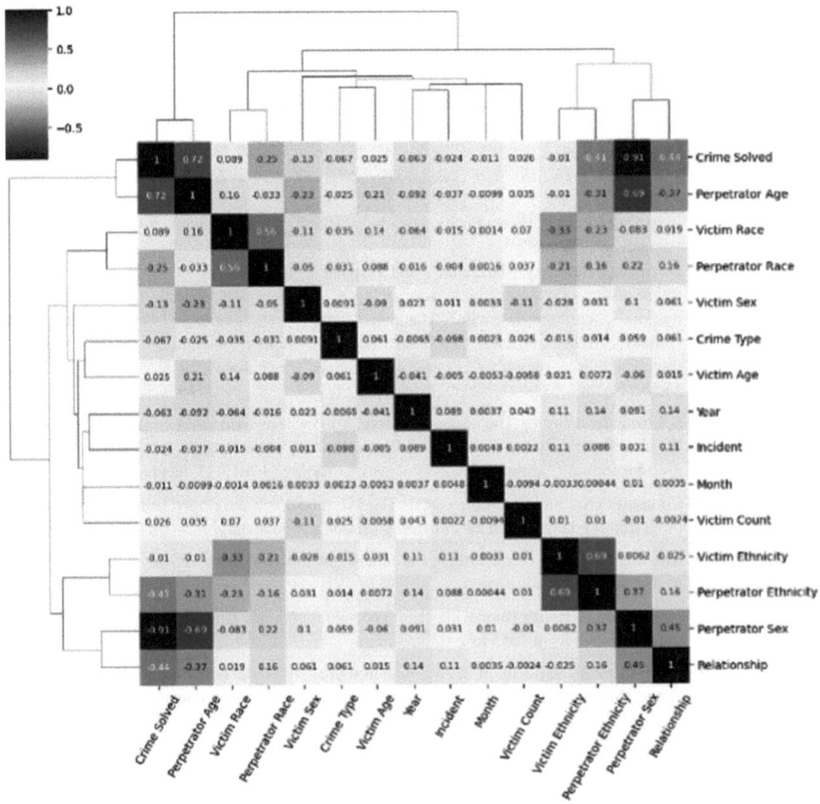

Fig. 5. Correlation matrix – inverted heatmap (screenshot from Jupyter Notebook).

The prediction will be made using the mentioned algorithm (XGBoost) (different algorithms result in different outcomes).

Table 4. Description of the sub-tasks of Task 7.

No	Task Description
Task 7.1	Definition of the learning algorithm – selecting an algorithm with the necessary characteristics. We chose XGBoost because it meets our needs and includes several configurations to help prevent overfitting, such as integrated regularization (L2). XGBoost builds decision trees sequentially, where each tree attempts to correct the mistakes made by the previous one.
Task 7.2	Basic learning – the first decision tree in the model is trained. In regression tasks, this initial model simply predicts the average of the target variable.
Task 7.3	Error calculation – After training the first tree, the errors between the predicted and actual values are calculated.
Task 7.4	Training trees – The next tree is trained to correct the errors of the previous one.
Task 7.5	Repetition of the process – This process continues with each new tree, gradually correcting the errors of the previous trees until training is complete.
Task 7.6	Combination of variations – The final prediction is obtained by summing all the variations from each tree.

Thus, as mentioned in Task 7.1, the mathematical reasoning [16] initially presents a generic prediction (base-zero), which then becomes an iterative process Task 7.5, with each new tree reducing the previous errors. Mathematically, the model is represented as follows:

$$\hat{y}_i = \sum\nolimits_{k=1}^{K} f_k(x_i) \tag{1}$$

where $\hat{y}_i$ is the prediction, and K is the number of trees.

The two most important components are the loss function and the regularization term. The loss function measures how well the model fits the data and is mathematically defined by the following formula:

$$obj(\theta) = \sum\nolimits_{i}^{n} l(y_i, \hat{y}_i) + \sum\nolimits_{k=1}^{K} \Omega(f_k) \tag{2}$$

where $l(y_i, \hat{y}_i)$ is the loss function, which computes the difference between the true value and the predicted value, and $\Omega(f_k)$ is the regularization term which discourages overly complex trees.

The regularization term simplifies complex trees by penalizing their leaves, specifically the number of leaves and their size, as defined by the following formula:

$$\Omega(f_t) = \gamma T + \frac{1}{2}\lambda \sum\nolimits_{j=1}^{T} w_j^2 \tag{3}$$

where γ is a regularization parameter that controls the complexity of the tree, and λ is a parameter that penalizes the weight of the leaves.

Finally, to determine how to divide the nodes in the tree, we calculate the information gain for each division (branch). The information gain for a division is calculated using the following formula:

$$Gain = \frac{1}{2}\left[\frac{G_L^2}{H_L + \lambda} + \frac{G_R^2}{H_R + \lambda} - \frac{(G_L + G_R)^2}{H_L + H_R + \lambda}\right] - \gamma \quad (4)$$

where G_L, G_R are the sums of gradients in the left and right child nodes, and H_L, H_R are the sums of Hessians in the left and right child nodes

When calculating information gain for each division, XGBoost selects the branch that yields the highest gain. This helps reduce errors and improve the model's performance, which is why we chose this algorithm.

The developed ML model demonstrated high predictive accuracy, achieving an accuracy rate of 91.75%, as shown in Fig. 6.

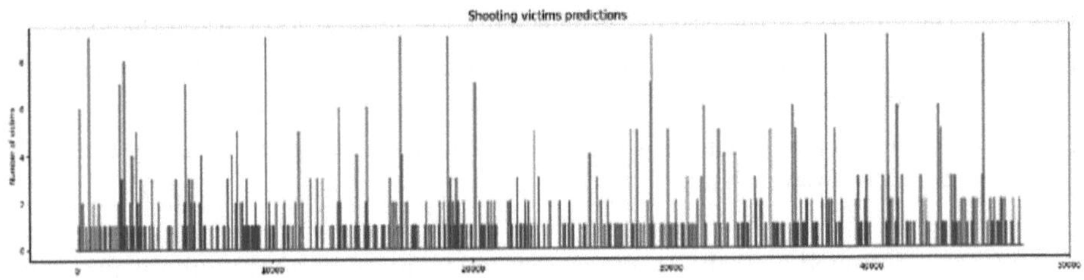

Fig. 6. Precision and output (screenshot from Jupyter Notebook).

4.5 Model Validation

As mentioned above, we use a supervised ML model with data spanning from 1980 to 2014, divided into training and validation data sets to evaluate the model (Task 5). Afterwards, the model's output is verified using the DB from 2015 to 2023.

In summary, supervised ML uses data to learn patterns and relationships between variables (training model), which are then tested to evaluate their accuracy (testing model). This test (logical test) resulted in an accuracy value greater than 90% (precision), as shown in Fig. 6. However, the contribution of AI can only be measured by comparing the predictions for 47,620 future events with the actual event records from 2015 to 2023. From this comparison, we found that the predictions were correct (compared to the actual data) 89.21% of the time. Figure 7 shows the difference between the prediction and the actual records. The differences were cataloged based on the variation in the number of deaths:

$$|\hat{y}_i - y_i| \quad (5)$$

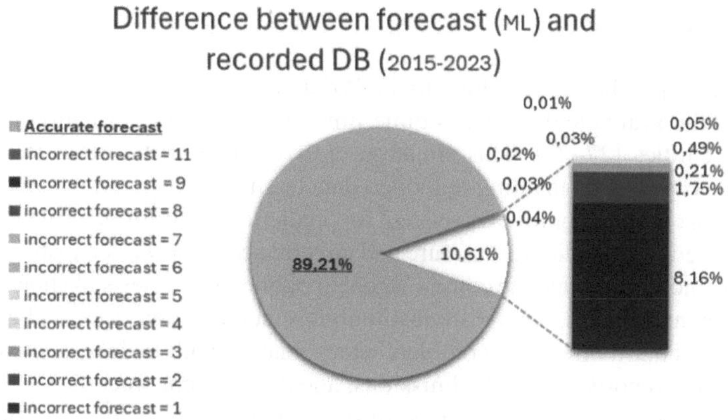

Fig. 7. Differences between $\hat{y}_i$ and y_i.

4.6 Analysis of Results

A relevant aspect is the limitation of available data, specifically incomplete information. As mentioned above, not all events can be resolved, and the inability to identify the event perpetrator is the primary factor contributing to non-resolution. To verify the impact of this issue, a hypothetical new database has been created by filling in missing data with hypothetical values. For example, missing data in the "victim sex" column (219 entries) was replaced, with 84.50% marked as "male" (178 entries) and 15.43% as "female" (31 entries). After completing the missing data, the model achieved an effective result of over 90% (previous 89.21%). Thus, it is evident that the ML model requires complete data to improve its accuracy. In turn, improving accuracy allows for better management of human resources (such as police officers, doctors, and others), materials (vehicles and fuel), and finances (public funds), as well as fostering a greater sense of citizen safety.

In addition to the considerations outlined above, highly reliable statistical modeling should be used, first and foremost, as a tool for proactive governance, with the aim of enabling the preventive mobilization of specialized intervention units, including social support services, mental health care, and conflict mediation mechanisms. Such an approach should take precedence over increased surveillance and longer prison sentences. It is essential to impose strict regulatory and procedural restrictions on the creation of individualized records of "potential suspects," in accordance with the European legal framework of the presumption of innocence (Article 48 of the Charter of Fundamental Rights of the European Union), and these must be accompanied by robust safeguards regarding data protection, procedural guarantees, and social rights.

This study demonstrates that the integration of detailed records of firearm incidents allows for a high level of statistical accuracy and predictive reliability. These datasets can support evidence-based policymaking by public authorities, particularly in the design and calibration of public safety interventions, as well as assist law enforcement agencies in the probabilistic identification of risk patterns associated with criminal behavior or even terrorism, while remaining subject to strict legal and ethical constraints.

5 Challenges

An attempt to apply the same method to the Portuguese case did not produce satisfiable elements, as the available database is quite limited and much information is dispersed in different entities [27–29]. This situation clearly points to the need to establish a collaborative ecosystem, enabling federated data learning.

The design of a collaborative ecosystem for predicting firearm-related deaths requires a clearly defined organizational structure and governance framework capable of aligning multiple stakeholders around the common goal of public safety. Key stakeholders include law enforcement agencies, healthcare institutions, emergency services, and government agencies, each contributing in a complementary manner with their respective datasets, such as criminal reports, hospital admissions, and demographic records.

The development of collaborative ecosystems requires close cooperation regarding both data and the underlying data infrastructure, including procedures for data collection and verification of data accuracy, as well as securing the necessary financial resources and conducting subsequent technical studies.

In addition to the above, it should be noted that data protection policies are becoming increasingly restrictive (namely in Europe); to prevent data misuse, federated learning can be used (the model is trained locally with its own data and sends only model updates, such as weights or gradients, to the others stakeholders).

Furthermore, the transition to a hybrid model of collaboration between humans and AI brings both benefits and challenges: while humans remain the final decision-makers, AI serves as a decision-making aid. AI used as a tool or teammate for rapid and accurate statistical forecasting represents an important step in the right direction. In this context, AI contributes computational power and pattern recognition capabilities, while humans provide ethical judgment and continuous feedback.

A major constraint within this ecosystem arises from limitations in data access. Information related to firearm violence is inherently sensitive and often includes personal and identifiable data. As a result, data sharing among stakeholders is frequently restricted, leading to incomplete datasets and potential bias in predictive models. In addition, heterogeneity in data formats and collection practices further complicates integration efforts.

6 Conclusions

Crime and security are often viewed as opposing and structurally irreconcilable dimensions: while crime must be combated, security must be preserved and strengthened. In this context, the scientific community has increasingly explored the use of new technologies, particularly artificial intelligence, to support crime prevention, due to its ability to predictively model complex phenomena. Consequently, this study evaluates the feasibility of using AI to predict mortality associated with incidents involving firearms.

To this end, a ML model was developed and trained on a dataset of 317,474 real-world incidents recorded between 1980 and 2014, obtained from the DB Homicide Report database in the United States. The data set was divided into training (85%, approximately 269,853 events, corresponding to about 4,317,647 records) and testing

(15%, approximately 47,621 events, corresponding to about 761,937 records). In this experiment, the XGBoost algorithm was used, which demonstrated high performance, achieving an accuracy rate of over 90% (91.76%). Subsequently, the predictions generated by the model (47,624 events) were compared with actual records from the database covering the period from 2015 to 2023. This comparison revealed a predictive accuracy of approximately 89.21%, as illustrated in Fig. 6. This temporal segmentation into two distinct periods (1980–2014 and 2015–2023) was designed to assess the model's ability to generalize to future scenarios.

Despite the inherent complexity of processing large volumes of data and the underlying mathematical calculations, the results indicate that AI can support accurate prediction of patterns related to gun violence. However, prediction quality is highly dependent on the availability of reliable and comprehensive data, which typically requires a collaborative ecosystem involving multiple entities. Such an ecosystem, potentially supported by federated data spaces, would enable more advanced analyses, including the identification of emerging risks, behavioral patterns across population segments, and the evaluation of public policy impacts.

Future work will focus on improving model accuracy by incorporating additional variables, such as detailed criminal histories and behavioral indicators. In parallel, efforts will be directed toward establishing a multi-stakeholder collaborative framework to support more effective human–AI collaboration in crime prediction and prevention.

Acknowledgements. This work was supported by the Portuguese Foundation for Science and Technology (FCT) through the grant UID/00066/2025, CTS – Center of Technology and Systems.

References

1. European Union Agency for Law Enforcement Cooperation.: "AI and policing The benefits and challenges of artificial intelligence for law enforcement", Europol Innovation Lab, https://doi.org/2813/0321023.
2. Heller, S.B., Jakubowski, B., Jelveh, Z., Kapustin, M.: Machine learning can predict shooting victimization well enough to help prevent it. Rev. Econ. Stat. (2024)
3. VanderPlas, J.: Python Data Science Handbook: Essential Tools for Working with Data. O'Reilly Media, Inc (2016)
4. Géron, A.: Hands on Machine Learning with scikit-learn, keras, and tensorflow, 2nd edn, pp. 66–130. O'Reilly (2019)
5. United Nations Office on Drugs and Crime: Global study on homicide 2023. https://www.unodc.org/documents/data-and-analysis/gsh/2023/Global_study_on_homicide_2023_web.pdf150.
6. Briefing paper - Survey about Small Arms.: Firearms and Violent Deaths.: https://www.smallarmssurvey.org/sites/default/files/resources/SAS-Research-Note-60.pdf (2018)
7. Raji, I., Sholademi, D.B.: Predictive policing: the role of AI in crime prevention. Int. J. Comput. Appl. Technol. Res. **13**(10), 66–78 (2024). https://doi.org/10.7753/IJCATR1310.1006
8. Dakalbab, F., Abu Talib, M., Abu Waraga, O., Bou Nassif, A., Abbas, S., Nasir, Q.: Artificial intelligence & crime prediction: a systematic literature review. J. Soc. Sci. Humanit. **6**(1), 100342. https://doi.org/10.1016/j.ssaho.2022.100342

9. Mohamed, R., Mfowabo, M.: Exploring global gun violence prediction through machine learning models. Int. Conf. Artif. Intell. Appl., 205–211 (2023)
10. Panchumarthi, L.Y., Lavanya, P., Sumalatha, S.: Insights into gun-related deaths: a comprehensive machine learning analysis. In: 15th International Conference on Computing Communication and Networking Technologies (ICCCNT), pp. 1–7 (2024)
11. Laqueur, S., Smirniotis, C., McCort, C., Wintemute, J.: Machine learning analysis of handgun transactions to predict firearm suicide risk. J. JAMA Network. **5**(7), e2221041
12. Kaggle (data science): website available: https://www.kaggle.com. Accessed in 15 Nov 2024
13. Kheirallah S. (Kaggle notebook): Who Killed Who? Homicide Reports 1980–2014. https://www.kaggle.com/code/khsamaha/who-killed-who-homicidereports-1980-2014. Accessed in 15 Nov 2024
14. Kathakali S. (Kaggle notebook).: Exploratory Analysis - Homicide Report. https://www.kaggle.com/code/kathakaliseth/exploratory-analysis-homicide-report. Accessed in 15 Nov 2024
15. Alves, L.G., Ribeiro, H.V., Rodrigues, F.A.: Crime prediction through urban metrics and statistical learning. Phys. Statist. Mech. Appl. **505**, 435–443 (2018)
16. Deloitte, Surveillance and Predictive Policing Through AI. https://www.deloitte.com/global/en/industries/government-public/perspectives/urban-future-with-a-purpose/surveillance-and-predictive-policing-through-ai.html. Accessed 26 Apr 2026
17. Bacco, M., Kocian, A., Chessa, S., Crivello, A., Barsocchi, P.: What are data spaces? Systematic survey and future outlook. Data Brief. **57**, 110969
18. Singh, A.K., et al.: A security analysis of European data space architectures. Data Sci. Eng. (2025). https://doi.org/10.1007/s41019-025-00311-z
19. Jarke, M., Otto, B., Ram, S.: Data sovereignty and data space ecosystems. Bus. Inf. Syst. Eng. **61**, 549–550 (2019). https://doi.org/10.1007/s12599-019-00614-2
20. Gil, J., Petrova-Antonova, D., Kemp, G.J.: Redefining urban digital twins for the federated data spaces ecosystem: a perspective. Environ. Plann. B: Urban Anal. City Sci. https://doi.org/10.1177/23998083241302578
21. Graça, P., Camarinha-Matos, L.M.: Performance indicators for collaborative business ecosystems – literature review and trends. Technol. Forecast. Soc. Change. **116**, 237–255 (2017). https://doi.org/10.1016/j.techfore.2016.10.012
22. Camarinha-Matos, L.M.: Sustainable collaborative business ecosystems. In: Proceedings of 24th International Conference on Informatics in Economy. Smart Innovation, Systems and Technologies, vol. 471. Springer, Singapore (2026). https://doi.org/10.1007/978-981-95-6136-0_1
23. Yang, Q., Liu, Y., Chen, T., Tong, Y.: Federated machine learning: concept and applications. ACM Trans. Intell. Syst. Technol. **10**(2), 1–19 (2019). https://doi.org/10.1145/32989
24. Zheng, Z., Zhou, Y., Sun, Y., Wang, Z., Liu, B., Li, K.: Applications of federated learning in smart cities: recent advances, taxonomy, and open challenges. Connect. Sci. **34**(1), 1–28. https://doi.org/10.1080/09540091.2021.1936455
25. Murder Accountability Project (Tracking America's unsolved homicides).: website available: https://www.murderdata.org. Accessed in 18 Nov 2024
26. Chen, T., Guestrin, C..: GBoost: A scalable tree boosting system. https://arxiv.org/pdf/1603.02754. Accessed 10 June 2016
27. Instituto Nacional de Estatística.: (Portuguese mortality statistics portal, cause-of-death database).: website available: https://www.ine.pt/xportal/xmain?xpid=INE&xpgid=ine_base_dados

28. Secretaria-Geral do Ministério da Administração Interna.: Relatórios Anuais de Segurança Interna (RASI 2025). https://www.ssi.gov.pt/publicacoes/rasi/RASI2025.pdf. Accessed in 18 Apr 2026
29. Polícia Judiciária.: Análises de Criminalidade. https://www.policiajudiciaria.pt/wp-content/uploads/2025/07/Anexo2AnaliseCriminInvestestigadaPJ2024aguardahomologacao.pdf Accessed in 18 Apr 2026

Stability of Electrophysiological Signals: Findings from Preliminary Measurements in Different Clinical Environments

Ana Isabel Ferreira[1,2,3](✉), Cláudia Quaresma[1,2], and Carla Quintão[1,2]

[1] Laboratory of Instrumentation, Biomedical Engineering and Radiation Physics, Physics Department, Nova School of Science and Technology, NOVA University of Lisbon, Caparica, Portugal
aix.ferreira@campus.fct.unl.pt

[2] Associated Laboratory in Translation and Innovation Towards Global Health (REAL), NOVA School of Science and Technology, NOVA University of Lisbon, Caparica, Portugal

[3] Health Department, School of Health Sciences, Polytechnic Institute of Beja, Beja, Portugal

Abstract. Electrophysiological signals reflect the electrical activity of cells and tissues. Visual evoked potentials (VEPs) provide insight into the functional integrity of the visual system and are generally stable across laboratory conditions. In contrast, electrodermal activity (EDA), an index of sympathetic nervous system activity, remains comparatively underexplored. This preliminary study assessed the temporal stability of VEP and EDA measures across two clinical settings. VEP latencies at the Oz, PO7 and PO8 electrodes were consistent across settings. For EDA, latency and phasic driver parameters remained stable over a three-month period. However, the number of skin conductance responses and the area only varied as a function of time of day, with the tonic component additionally influenced by recording location and day. Overall, these findings indicate differential stability across electrophysiological measures and recording conditions. Larger-scale studies are required to support robust statistical inferences and enhance generalizability. Notwithstanding, the present study confirms the stability of VEPs while highlighting the need for caution in the longitudinal interpretation of EDA measures, particularly the mean tonic component. Notably, time of day emerged as the factor influencing the greatest number of EDA parameters; therefore, standardization of the recording period is recommended in future studies.

Keywords: Electrophysiological Signals · Stability · Visual Evoked Potential · Electrodermal Activity · Repetitive Measures

This chapter relates to the topical section 'AI in Biomedical Systems'

Published by Springer Nature Switzerland AG 2027
L. M. Camarinha-Matos and F. Ferrada (Eds.): DoCEIS 2026, IFIP AICT 790, pp. 534–547, 2027.
https://doi.org/10.1007/978-3-032-28939-1_36

1 Introduction

Electrophysiological signals are electrical measurements produced by biological cells and tissues that reflect ionic fluxes and membrane polarization in nervous cells [1]. Electrophysiology techniques listen to these signals by measuring electrical activity, allowing for the decoding of intercellular and intracellular messages [2].

Visual evoked potentials (VEPs) are one of the techniques used to measure electrophysiological activity. In this specific case, they assess the functional integrity of the visual pathway, from the retina to the primary visual cortex [3]. Different brain structures, (e.g., the visual cortex, thalamus, lateral geniculated body), receive, process and respond to visual stimuli generating electrical activity. VEPs are extracted from the electroencephalographic activity in the visual cortex recorded from the overlying scalp and provide important diagnostic information [4]. As both stimulus and acquisition system characteristics have substantial effects on the waveform, peak time and amplitude of responses, meaningful interpretation requires stimulators and acquisition systems to be accurate [5]. Different kinds of standardized stimuli could be used to assess the visual cortex function and pattern reversal checkerboard is one used in children [6]. The reverse stimuli pattern is the preferred stimuli in clinical situations because of its low variability in waveform and timing [7, 8]. The electrophysiological pattern develops during the first years of life, and the parameters most assessed in adults include latency and amplitude of N75 / P100 / N135 [6, 8].

Electrodermal activity (EDA) refers to the continuous yet variable electrical phenomena occurring at the level of the skin, which result from the action of the autonomic nervous system, specifically its sympathetic branch acting on the sweat glands [9]. The EDA signal originates from the eccrine sweat glands, which are located in the hypodermis and open through pores in the epidermis, and are likewise innervated by the sympathetic nervous system [10]. The assessment of EDA is a non-invasive and low-cost procedure. Its use is well established in the fields of psychology, physiology and neurology [11–13]. This electrophysiological signal could be influenced by a variety of internal and external variables that can affect its measurement and interpretation. Arousal level, stress, fatigue, and hydration status are the internal variables most frequently described in the literature as influencing the EDA signal [14, 15]. As external variables can influence the EDA parameters, the ambient temperature, physical activity and kind of stimuli used are recognized influencing variables [14–17].

Given that electrophysiological signals, particularly EDA, can be affected by external and contextual factors, it is crucial to investigate how the parameters under study evolve over time in healthy adults. In this context, the aim of the present study is to investigate the stability of VEPs and EDA signals obtained across time from healthy adults when a pattern-reversal checkerboard stimulus is used. In addition, the study seeks to determine whether electrophysiological performance is comparable between the two assessment settings.

2 Tackling Societal Challenges

Contemporary society requires personalized, specific, and accurate assessment in order to enable early diagnosis and, when necessary, multidisciplinary intervention [18, 19]. Within this context, the integration of electrophysiological measures into clinical approaches has become increasingly relevant, particularly when such assessment is combined with traditional follow-up procedures implemented in clinical settings.

It is within this societal challenge that the broader research project entitled "Development of Visual and Motor Skills in Preterm and Full-Term Infants" emerges, within which the present study on the stability of electrophysiological signals is situated. This study is essential to determine the parameters to be included in the data analysis of the main research project.

3 Material and Methods

3.1 Research Line and Ethical Approval

The present study forms part of a broader longitudinal research project entitled "Development of Visual and Motor Skills Development in Preterm and Full-Term Infants." This research is conducted with infants during the first year of life and involves data collection in different clinical settings, as outlined in the published protocol [20]. In this context the investigation reported here examines the stability of electrophysiological signals recorded in two different clinical settings across multiple time points and follows the specific workflow presented in Fig. 1.

This research was conducted in accordance with the ethical principles outlined in the Declaration of Helsinki for studies involving human participants and received approval from the ethics committees of both institutions involved in data collection: Maternidade Drº Alfredo da Costa (MAC) and Unidade Saúde Familiar da Baixa (USF- Baixa).

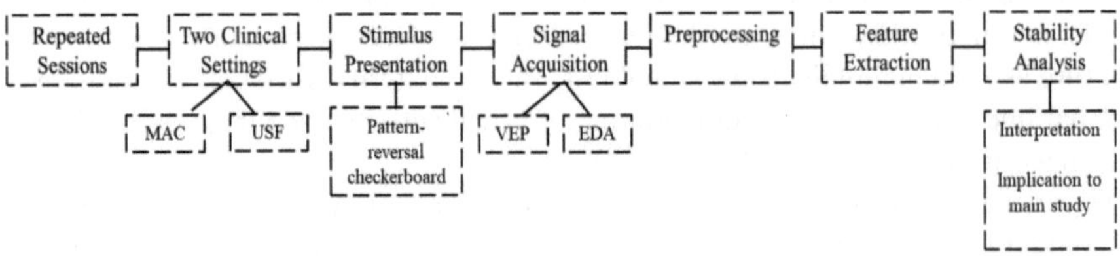

Fig. 1. Workflow used in the study

3.2 Stimuli, Tools and Space Used in Data Collection

The methodological procedures for VEPs and EDA data collection used in the present study were consistent with those employed in the main research project and have been described previously [20].

In summary, a black-and-white reversing checkerboard pattern was presented for 120 s at a reversal rate of one per second. Stimulus presentation was performed by E-Prime® software, which was integrated with gRecorder® (for VEP acquisition) and

OpenSignals® (for EDA recording). All software and equipment operated on a Dell computer (Intel® Core™ 2 Duo, 4.00 GB RAM) that projected the image onto an LG Flatron W1934S 19-inch monitor.

For VEP data collection, electrodes were positioned at Oz, PO7, and PO8, with Fz serving as the ground and an earlobe electrode as the reference. These gel-based electrodes were mounted using an adult cap (medium size) belonging to the g.Nautilus® system. For EDA data collection, pre-gelled Ag/AgCI electrodes were placed on the foot, following the procedure described in a previous study [21].

All equipment, software, and visual stimuli were synchronized, allowing for the insertion of time stamps corresponding to the instances that each visual stimulus was presented.

In this research, data collection was conducted in the same locations and under the same environmental conditions as those used in the main study "Development of Visual and Motor Skills Development in Preterm and Full-Term Infants".

3.2.1 Facility at Maternidade Dr. Alfredo da Costa

At MAC, the assessment office is located on the first floor, in an area accessible exclusively to staff and distant from the ambulatory facilities. This setting ensures a quiet environment, providing optimal acoustic conditions for data collection. The room is equipped with a window that allows the entry of natural light and includes artificial lighting. During the data collection period, the room was used exclusively for research purposes. Artificial lighting was not employed, and only minimal natural light entered, ensuring that the assessments were conducted under stable ambient lighting in all sessions [4]. The computer screen was positioned on the desk, in front of the participant and approximately 70cm away, as can be seen in Appendix - Fig. 7. The room maintained a moderate temperature, ranging from 21.0 °C to 23.9 °C across the three days of measurements (in the Appendix a table displaying the range of temperatures across measures is presented). Outside the research period, this room, with an approximate area of 10m2, is used for small meetings or as a study space.

3.2.2 Facility at Unidade Saúde Familiar da Baixa

In USF-Baixa, all research assessments were conducted in a room located on the first floor, with an approximate area of 15m2. This room is separate from the ambulatory facilities and is not typically used by patients. It is usually reserved for staff meetings, small group work, and other internal professional activities. The room is equipped with artificial lighting and a window that provides indirect natural light, allowing for assessments to be carried out under scotopic conditions. During the research period, the room was used exclusively for research assessments, with the temperature maintained between 20.2 °C and 24.9 °C (see Table 5 in Appendix).

3.3 Participants

To examine the stability of VEP and EDA measures across time in two different clinical settings, the previously described paradigm was applied to a healthy 22-year-old adult female. This participant was selected due to her willingness to participate, and her availability for repeated assessments throughout the longitudinal data collection period. As previously described, the present study is part of a larger research project; therefore, all sessions were conducted in the same rooms used for the assessments of preterm and full-term infants (the participants from the main research).

3.4 Repetitive Measures Implementation

The data collection with the young adult occurred during three consecutive months, as can be seen in the Appendix. The rationale for the repetitive measure is to account for the change of temporal conditions (month, day, period of day, take) and the clinical data collection place. Temperature was monitored using a digital application called "Termómetro Preciso", developed by Simple Design LLC®. This tool estimates both indoor and outdoor temperature by integrating data from the smartphone's battery and CPU sensors, as well as artificial intelligence algorithms.

On each day of assessment, five measures are collected to verify if repetition influences the electrophysiological results.

3.5 Data Processing

The signal processing of VEPs and EDA data was performed using personalized algorithms developed in MATLAB and customized for each type of electrophysiological signal, although the triggers were interconnected to ensure synchronization between the presentation of the visual stimulus and the corresponding timestamp, as described in the study protocol article [18]. In summary, the algorithm designed for the analysis of VEPs included the use of fourth-order Butterworth filters, the selection of the optimal segment for standard deviation calculation, artifact removal, and the identification of triggers in the data file for the computation of evoked potentials. This allows the extraction of latency and amplitude, from the deflections that characterize the VEPs (N75, P100 and N135) in each electrode used (Oz, PO7 and PO8). In the literature, the most frequently analyzed parameters are the P100 latency and amplitude measured at the Oz electrode [3, 4]. However, a multichannel approach, incorporating electrodes such as O1, O2, PO7, and/or PO8 is also acceptable as it provides complementary spatial information [3]. In the present analysis, the research team opted to evaluate latency and amplitude based on the deflection observed across all active electrodes used (Oz, PO7 and PO8), as this constitutes a preliminary step in preparing the data analysis for the main study.

The EDA data processing includes a downsample from 500 to 100 Hz, followed by the raw data conversion to microsiemes. Then a 50-point moving average filter was used, followed by the use of Ledalab as required to separate the phasic from the tonic component. A specific skin conductance response (SCR) window of 1 to 4s with a 0.01 μS SCR amplitude was utilized. In EDA, the data analysis was inspire in previous literature [12, 22], however an in-depth analysis was performed with the inclusion of the number of skin conductance responses, latency (in s), amplitude (in μS), phasic driver (in μS), area (in (μS)2) and average of tonic component (in μS).

3.6 Statistical Analysis

In the repeated measures analysis, the statistical procedure included the assessment of data stability (latency and amplitude of each deflection at Oz, PO7, and PO8), as well as the number of skin conductance responses, latency, amplitude, area, phasic driver, and mean tonic component. The analysis considered the following variables: recording location, day, take, and period of day. For this reason, a linear mixed model was employed, as it allows the distinction between fixed effects (location, day, take, and period) and random effects (differences across repeated conditions) [23]. In the output, the significance (p-value) of each fixed effect was examined to determine whether statistically significant differences occurred.

4 Results

The stability of the electrophysiological signals across the different recording sessions was examined across time (day, take and day period) in two different clinical settings (local).

Regarding the VEPs, latency and amplitude of the three main deflections (N75, P100, and N135) were analysed at the active electrodes Oz, PO7, and PO8. From an overall perspective, latency did not show any statistically significant variation across deflections or electrodes over repeated measurements (Table 1, 2 and 3). In contrast, amplitude exhibited a slightly different pattern, showing significant differences as a function of the recording day for most electrodes and deflections. However, the other variables under study related to time (take, and day period) and location, did not produce statistically significant effects. All results related to the VEPs are presented in Table 1, 2 and 3. The level of significance is specified and indicated whenever statistically significant differences are observed.

The repeated measures of EDA highlight the stability of the outcomes across recordings, with respect to the latency (p values > 0.05 in all variables), the average of phasic driver (p values > 0.05 in all variables) and the area (p values > 0.05 in location, day and take), as can be seen in Table 4.

Table 1. Values obtained for repeated measurements (n = 30) of electrode OZ

	Location (F/p)	Day (F/p)	Take (F/p)	Period (F/p)
Latency OZ N75	F = 0.000, p = 1.000	F = 0.232, p = 0.795	F = 0.653, p = 0.631	F = 0.239, p = 0.630
Latency OZ P100	F = 0.079, p = 0.782	F = 0.681, p = 0.517	F = 0.201, p = 0.935	F = 0.079, p = 0.782
Latency OZ N135	F = 0.570, p = 0.459	F = 0.400, p = 0.675	F = 0.742, p = 0.574	F = 1.847, p = 0.189
Amplitude OZ N75	F = 1.066, p = 0.314	F = 12.121, p < 0.001***	F = 1.370, p = 0.278	F = 0.459, p = 0.505

(continued)

Table 1. (*continued*)

	Location (F/p)	Day (F/p)	Take (F/p)	Period (F/p)
Amplitude OZ P100	F = 1.862, p = 0.187	F = 19.023, p < 0.001***	F = 0.882, p = 0.491	F = 0.247, p = 0.625
Amplitude OZ N135	F = 1.315, p = 0.264	F = 3.700, p = 0.042*	F = 0.978, p = 0.440	F = 0.382, p = 0.543

* Significant; ** Very Significant; *** Extremely Significant

Table 2. Values obtained for repeated measurements (n = 30) of electrode PO7

	Location (F/p)	Day (F/p)	Take (F/p)	Period (F/p)
Latency PO7 N75	F = 1.582, p = 0.222	F = 0.096, p = 0.909	F = 2.207, p = 0.103	F = 0.063, p = 0.804
Latency PO7 P100	F = 2.540, p = 0.126	F = 2.268, p = 0.128	F = 1.800, p = 0.166	F = 1.175, p = 0.291
Latency PO7 N135	F = 2.895, p = 0.104	F = 0.162, p = 0.851	F = 1.258, p = 0.317	F = 0.018, p = 0.894
Amplitude PO7 N75	F = 0.001, p = 0.973	F = 6.974, p = 0.005**	F = 2.990, p = 0.042	F = 0.038, p = 0.848
Amplitude PO7 P100	F = 1.017, p = 0.325	F = 24.029, p = < 0.001 ***	F = 0.324, p = 0.859	F = 0.110, p = 0.744
Amplitude PO7 N135	F = 2.452, p = 0.132	F = 5.116, p = 0.015**	F = 1.096, p = 0.384	F = 0.084, p = 0.775

* Significant; ** Very Significant; *** Extremely Significant

Table 3. Values obtained for repeated measurements (n = 28) of electrode PO8

-	Location (F/p)	Day (F/p)	Take (F/p)	Period (F/p)
Latency PO8 N75	F = 2.638, p = 0.121	F = 0.213, p = 0.810	F = 1.446, p = 0.258	F = 0.001, p = 0.975
Latency PO8 P100	F = 2.148, p = 0.159	F = 1.890, p = 0.178	F = 1.043, p = 0.411	F = 0.006, p = 0.937
Latency PO8 N135	F = 2.432, p = 0.134	F = 0.395, p = 0.678	F = 2.037, p = 0.126	F = 0.777, p = 0.388
Amplitude PO8 N75	F = 1.227, p = 0.282	F = 6.827, p = 0.006 **	F = 2.849, p = 0.053	F = 0.240, p = 0.630
Amplitude PO8 P100	F = 0.105, p = 0.749	F = 15.129, p = < 0.001 ***	F = 0.369, p = 0.828	F = 1.172, p = 0.291
Amp. PO8 N135	F = 0.145, p = 0.707	F = 2.755, p = 0.087	F = 2.128, p = 0.113	F = 0.023, p = 0.881

* Significant; ** Very Significant; *** Extremely Significant

Table 4. EDA results

	Location (F/p)	Day (F/p)	Take (F/p)	Period (F/p)
SCRs	F = 1.874 p = 0.185	F = 0.785 p = 0.469	F = 2.411 p = 0.081	F = 18.026 p < .001***
Latency	F = 0.000 p = 0.987	F = 0.107 p = 0.899	F = 1.137 p = 0.366	F = 0.018 p = 0.895

(*continued*)

Table 4. (*continued*)

	Location (F/p)	Day (F/p)	Take (F/p)	Period (F/p)
Amplitude	F = 3.674 p = 0.069	F = 4.544 p = 0.023*	F = 0.975 p = 0.442	F = 2.612 p = 0.121
Phasic driver ($\bar{x}$)	F = 0.129 p = 0.723	F = 1.777 p = 0.194	F = 0.662 p = 0.626	F = 2.958 p = 0.100
Area	F = 2.806 p = 0.109	F = 1.640 p = 0.218	F = 0.850 p = 0.509	F = 8.378 p = 0.009**
Tonic component ($\bar{x}$)	F = 12.104 p = 0.002 *	F = 27.533 p < .001***	F = 1.499 p = 0.238	F = 10.529 p = 0.004*

* Significant; ** Very Significant; ***Extremely Significant; SCRs- skin conductance responses.

However, significant differences (albeit with varying magnitudes) were found in the following parameters:

- the number of skin conductance responses as a function of the day period at which the recording was taken ($F = 18.026$, $p < 0.001$) as presented in Figure 2;
- the amplitude as a function of the day ($F = 4.544$, $p = 0.023$), as presented in Figure 3;
- the mean tonic component as a function of location ($F = 12.104$, $p = 0.002$), day ($F = 27.533$, $p < 0.001$), and time of day ($F = 10.529$, $p = 0.004$), as presented in Figure 4, 5 and 6.

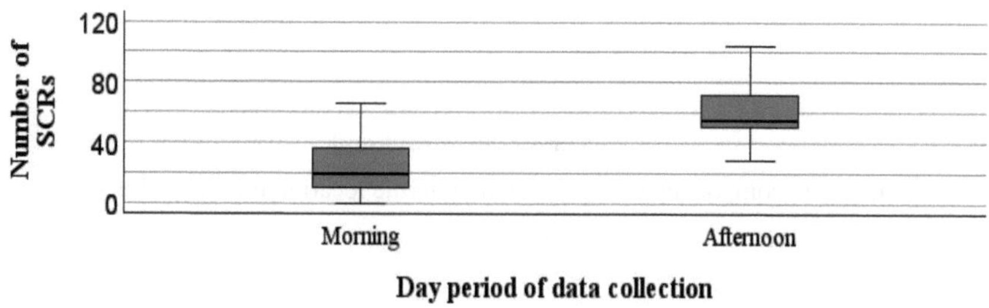

Fig. 2. Number of SCRS according the day period for data collection

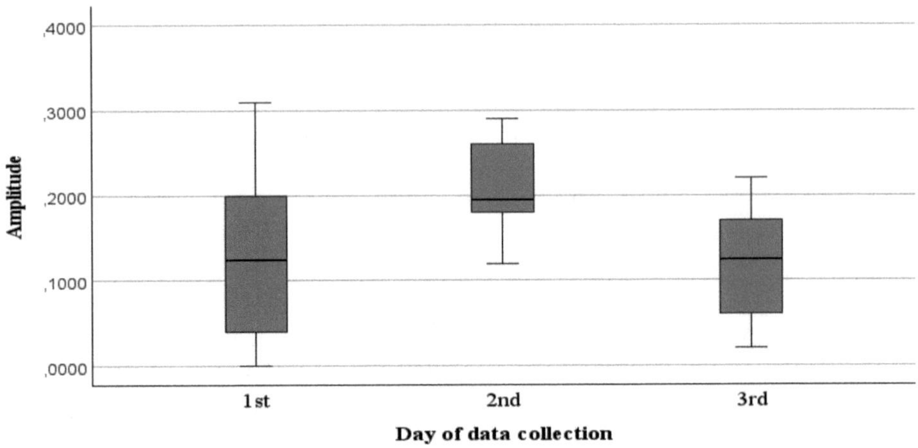

Fig. 3. Amplitude level according to the day for data collection

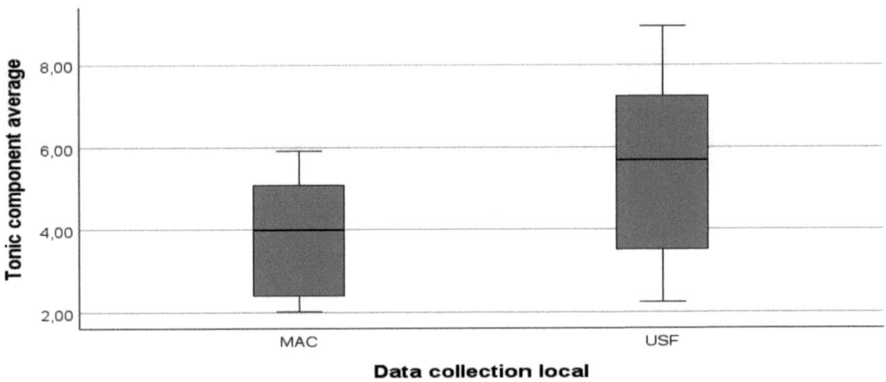

Fig. 4. Tonic component average according to the location for data collection

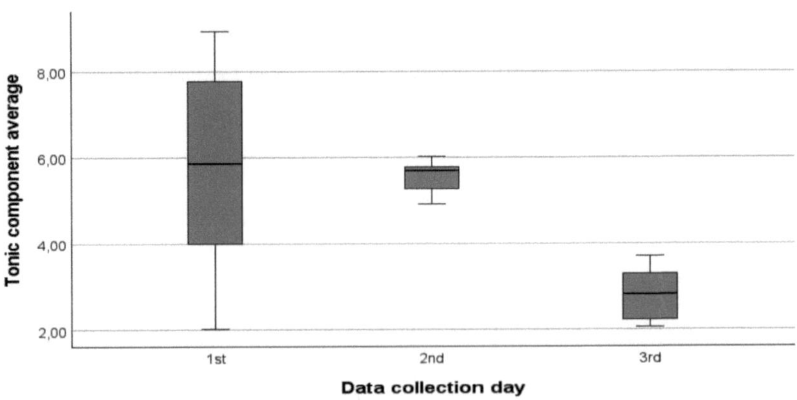

Fig. 5. Tonic component average according to the day for data collection

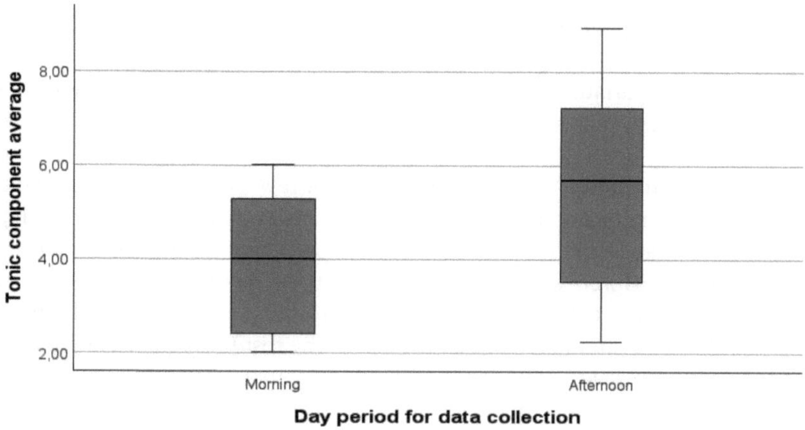

Fig. 6. Tonic component average according to the day period of data collection

5 Discussion

The present findings reinforce the stability of VEPs latency across time, which is consistent with previous literature [4, 8, 24]. With respect to location, in clinical ambulatory settings, it is also evident that this does not influence the latency results. Amplitude, by contrast, has been less extensively investigated, and the differences observed across days may be attributable to several hypotheses. As is well known, amplitude partly depends on the quality of the connection between the electrode and the scalp. Therefore, factors such as the amount of conductive gel applied to each electrode or the presence of scalp oil may influence amplitude values [25, 26]. It is also important to note that in most pediatric and adult VEPs studies, only latency measures are typically reported and analyzed. In addition, the use of lateral electrodes for data collection in VEPs was supported by the International Society for Clinical Electrophysiology of Vision guidelines [8]. In the present study no differences between the stability of the three electrodes are found. So, in this preliminary study the VEPs latency of all electrodes collected reveals a stable electrophysiological signal.

EDA is a signal with specificities, and in literature some variables that could influence the results as well as some evidence for use robustness both in laboratory and ecological settings are identified [27, 28].

In the present preliminary study, the EDA latency and phasic driver are the parameters more stable across all variables. The number of skin conductance responses and the area only vary according to the period of the day for data collection, with an increased number of responses in the afternoon. From those results obtained in a healthy adult, the recommendation is to have caution in comparing EDA results collected across time and in different places, more specifically the ones obtained in the main research study "Development of visual and motor skills in Pre-term and Full-term infants". Additionally, the time of day during which the EDA signal was collected may have influenced the EDA parameters; therefore, it is advisable to standardize the time of day for EDA data collection. Based on the results obtained in healthy adults, caution is recommended when comparing EDA results across time and between different locations, particularly within the average tonic component, considering that in the present study, it is the less stable variable.

The temperature variation, with a difference of approximately 3 to 4 degrees Celsius between days, suggests that such modest differences are unlikely to account for the EDA results.

Regarding the limitations of the present study, a few aspects warrant acknowledgment. Firstly, the small sample size constrains the generalizability of the findings. To overcome this limitation the increased number of participants could allow a test-retest statistical analyses. Moreover, the number of trials of this preliminary study should ideally have been consistent across both contexts, morning and afternoon. Future investigations could further strengthen the robustness of the results by increasing the number of days and / or participants.

6 Conclusion

The present study highlights the stability of VEPs latency from a longitudinal perspective, demonstrating robustness when exposed to variations such as the clinical setting of data collection, the take (or repetition number), and the time of day. However, amplitude shows differences between data collection days.

Regarding EDA, the results are less promising, as the number of skin conductance responses, their amplitude, and mainly the average tonic component show statistically significant differences across variables. Nonetheless, some EDA components, such as latency and average phasic driver, remain stable over time. Taken together, these findings indicate that EDA analyses over time should be conducted with caution and that standardized procedures should be implemented whenever possible.

Acknowledgments. This work was supported by Fundação para a Ciência e Tecnologia (FCT, Portugal) through national funds [UI/BD/151321/2021] and [LA/P/0117/2020]. The dissemination of the results is also supported by the Scientific Support Grant from the Portuguese Society of Neurodevelopment (2025).

The authors wish to express their sincere appreciation to the participant for their invaluable contribution, and to the administration of both health institutions for authorizing the use of their facilities and providing logistical support. Their cooperation was instrumental to the successful implementation and continuity of the present repeated measures.

Appendix

Fig. 7. Data collection in MAC

Table 5. Flux for data collection in repetitive measurements.

	* Morning * MAC	* Afternoon * USF
1st month Day 1	1° take - 21.00°C	1° take - 20.20°C
	2° take - 21.00°C	2° take - 20.20°C
	3° take - 21.00°C	3° take - 20.30°C
	4° take - 22.10°C	4° take - 20.30°C
	5° take - 22.10°C	5° take -20.30°C
	Morning USF	Afternoon MAC
2nd month Day 2	1° take - 23.70°C	1° take - 22.80°C
	2° take - 23.20°C	2° take - 22.80°C
	3° take - 23.20°C	3° take - 22.80°C
	4° take - 23.10°C	4° take - 22.80°C
	5° take - 23.10°C	5° take - 22.80°C

(continued)

Table 5. (*continued*)

	* Morning * MAC	* Afternoon * USF
	Morning MAC	Afternoon USF
3rd month Day 3	1° take - 23.10°C	1° take- 24.00°C
	2° take - 23.10°C	2° take - 24.00°C
	3° take - 23.10°C	3° take - 24.00°C
	4° take - 23.90°C	4° take - 24.90°C
	5° take - 23.90°C	5° take - 24.90°C

MAC - Dr. Alfredo da Costa Maternity; USF – Baixa Family Health Unit.

References

1. Kandel, E., Koester, J., Hack, S., Siegelbaum, S.: Principles of Neural Science. McGrawHill (2021)
2. Carter, M., Shieh, J. C.: Electrophysiology. In: Guide to Research Techniques in Neuroscience, pp.91–118. Elsevier (2010)
3. Šuštar, H.M., et al.: ISCEV standard for clinical visual evoked potentials (2025 update). Doc. Ophthalmol. **151**, 97–112 (2025). https://doi.org/10.1007/s10633-025-10042-1
4. Odom, J.V., et al.: ISCEV standard for clinical visual evoked potentials: (2016 update). Doc. Ophthalmol. **133**, 1–9 (2016). https://doi.org/10.1007/s10633-016-9553-y
5. McCulloch, D.L., et al.: ISCEV guidelines for calibration and verification of stimuli and recording instruments (2023 update). Doc. Ophthalmol. **146**, 199–210 (2023). https://doi.org/10.1007/s10633-023-09932-z
6. Birch, E.E., Subramanian, V.: Visual evoked potentials in infants and children. In: Aminoff's Electrodiagnosis in Clinical Neurology, pp. 505–518. Elsevier (2012)
7. Daneshvarfard, F., Maarefi, N., Abrishami, M.H., Wallois, F.: A survey on stimuli for visual cortical function assessment in infants. Brain Dev. **40**, 2–15 (2018). https://doi.org/10.1016/j.braindev.2017.07.010
8. Odom, J.V., et al.: Visual evoked potentials standard (2004)*. Doc. Ophthalmol. **108**(2), 115–123 (2004). https://doi.org/10.1023/b:doop.0000036790.67234.22
9. Masi, G., Amprimo, G., Rechichi, I., Ferraris, C., Priano, L..: Electrodermal activity in the evaluation of engagement for telemedicine applications. In: 2023 IEEE International Conference on Pervasive Computing and Communications Workshops and other Affiliated Events, PerCom Workshops 2023. Institute of Electrical and Electronics Engineers Inc., pp. 130–135 (2023). https://doi.org/10.1109/PerComWorkshops56833.2023.10150380
10. Shaffer, F., Combatalade, D., Peper, E., Meehan, Z.M.: A Guide to Cleaner Electrodermal Activity Measurements. **44**, 90–100 (2016). https://doi.org/10.5298/1081-5937-44.2.01
11. Banganho, A., Santos, M., Da Silva, H.P.: Electrodermal activity: fundamental principles, measurement, and application. IEEE Potentials **41**, 35–43 (2022). https://doi.org/10.1109/MPOT.2020.2983381
12. Boucsein, W.: Electrodermal Activity -, 2nd edn. Springer, Wuppertal (2012)

13. Tronstad, C., Amini, M., Bach, D.R., Martinsen, Ø.G.: Current trends and opportunities in the methodology of electrodermal activity measurement. Physiol. Meas. **43** (2022). https://doi.org/10.1088/1361-6579/ac5007
14. Turpin, G., Shine, P., Lader, M.: Ambulatory electrodermal monitoring: effects of ambient temperature, general activity, electrolyte media, and length of recording. Psychophysiology **2**, 219–224 (1983). https://doi.org/10.1111/j.1469-8986.1983.tb03291.x
15. Hossain, M.B., Kong, Y., Posada-Quintero, H.F., Chon, K.H.: Electrodermal activity: applications and challenges. In: The Cambridge Handbook of Research Methods and Statistics for the Social and Behavioral Sciences, pp. 475--496. Cambridge University Press (2024)
16. Greco, A., Lanata, A., Citi, L., Vanello, N., Valenza, G., Scilingo, E.P.: Skin admittance measurement for emotion recognition: a study over frequency sweep. Electronics (Switzerland) **5** (2016). https://doi.org/10.3390/electronics5030046
17. Qasim, M.S., Bari, D.S., Martinsen, Ø.G.: Influence of ambient temperature on tonic and phasic electrodermal activity components. Physiol. Meas. **43**, 065001 (2022). https://doi.org/10.1088/1361-6579/ac72f4
18. Collins, F.S., Varmus, H.: A new initiative on precision medicine. N. Engl. J. Med. **26**, 372(9), 793–795 (2015). https://doi.org/10.1056/nejmp1500523
19. Liang, Z., Montgomery, J., Dingelstad, C., Koschel, A., Redford, M.: Making multidisciplinary team-based care (MTBC) a success in primary care: a scoping review care. J. Healthc. Leadersh. 681–695 (2025). https://doi.org/10.2147/jhl.s560629
20. Ferreira, A.I., Nunes, A., Silva, C., Tomé, T., Quaresma, C., Quintão, C.: Visual and motor skills development in preterm and full-term infants: a protocol for longitudinal data collection. MethodsX, **15** (2025). https://doi.org/10.1016/j.mex.2025.103546
21. Ham, J., Tronick, E.: A procedure for the measurement of infant skin conductance and its initial validation using clap induced startle. Dev. Psychobiol. **50**, 626–631 (2008). https://doi.org/10.1002/dev.20317
22. Fowles, D.C.: The measurement of electrodermal activity in children. In: Developmental Psychophysiology: theory, Systems, and Methods, pp.286–316. Cambridge University Press (2007)
23. Singer, J.D., Willett, J.B.: Applied Longitudinal Data Analysis: Modeling Change and Event Occurrence. Oxford University Press (2003)
24. Thompson, D.A., Mikó-Baráth, E., Hardy, S.E., Jandó, G., Shaw, M., Hamilton, R.: ISCEV standard pattern reversal VEP development: paediatric reference limits from 649 healthy subjects. Doc. Ophthalmol. **147**, 147–164 (2023). https://doi.org/10.1007/s10633-023-09952-9
25. Maus, D., Epstein, C., Herman, S.: Digital EEG. In: Schomer, D., Lopes da Silva F., (eds.). Electroencephalography - Basic Principles, Clinical Applications, and Related Fields, pp. 119–141. Lippincott Williams & Wilkins (2011)
26. Epstein, C.: Analog signal recording principles. In: Schomer D, Lopes da Silva, F., (eds.). Electroencephalography - Basic Principles, Clinical Applications, and Related Fields, pp.111–118. Lippincott Williams & Wilkins (2011)
27. Korkmaz, D., Knauth, K., Brands, A., Schmeck, M., Büning, P., Peters, J.: Ambulatory physiological measures obtained under naturalistic urban mobility conditions have acceptable reliability. Sci. Rep. **15** (2025). https://doi.org/10.1038/s41598-025-13216-8
28. Posada-Quintero, H.F., Dimitrov, T., Moutran, A., Park, S., Chon, K.H.: Analysis of reproducibility of noninvasive measures of sympathetic autonomic control based on electrodermal activity and heart rate variability. IEEE Access **7**, 22523–22531 (2019). https://doi.org/10.1109/access.2019.2899485

Author Index

A
Abiodun, Timileyin 471
Agulheiro, Paula 125
Almeida, João Rafael 32
Araújo, Rui Esteves 71
Arrieta, O. 199

B
Babaei, Zahra 313
Balamurugan, S. 341
Barata, Jose 313
Beckers, Miguel Afonso 329
Bochicchio, Andrea 240
Bosslau, Mario 20, 42

C
Camarinha-Matos, Luis M. 3, 516
Canilang, Henar Mike O. 226
Cheon, Yurim 226
Chiş, Radu 83
Clemente, Eurico 516
Coelho, Francisco 99
Colucci, Simona 358
Comas, Pau 173
Correia, Pedro 125
Costa, Anikó 386
Costa, Tiago 113

D
de Andrade, Diogo 492
de Paula Filho, Pedro Luiz 329
de Vasconcelos, José Braga 57
Diankatu, Mavambu 57
Dias, Diogo 113
Dias, Joana 125
Dicoiu, Alina 83
Donini, Francesco Maria 358
Dufo López, Rodolfo 186
Duque, Jorge 57

E
Esan, Oluwadamilola 274
Estêvão, Miguel 292

F
Fachada, Nuno 492
Ferrada, Filipa 516
Ferreira, Ana Isabel 534
Ferreira, Ana 125
Filipe, Vítor 57
Florea, Adrian 83
Fruggiero, Fabio 240

G
Galvão, Gonçalo 504
Goes, João 113
Gomes, Luis 373, 386
Gomes, Maria Isabel 292
Gomes, Nuno Teixeira 32
Graça, Paula 373
Guerreiro, Gracinda R. 292

H
Helerea, Elena 186
Hemalatha, J. 341

J
Januário-Silva, Francisco 157
Jonek-Kowalska, Izabela 431

K
Kalateh, Sepideh 313
Karaulova, Tatjana 417

L
Laanemets, Hendrik 417
Laigu, Rõõt 417
Lapão, Luís Velez 138
Leitão, Paulo 329
Leitão, Paulo 313

Published by Springer Nature Switzerland AG 2027
L. M. Camarinha-Matos and F. Ferrada (Eds.): DoCEIS 2026, IFIP AICT 790, pp. 549–550, 2027.
https://doi.org/10.1007/978-3-032-28939-1

Leite, Renato 71
Lim, Wansu 226
Londral, Ana Rita 125
Londral, Ana 138
Lopes, Rui Amaral 157
Louro, Paula 504
Luís, José Francisco 213

M
Maas, Rene 417
Madrigal, S. 199
Mancusi, Francesco 240
Martins, Ana 138
Menezes-Barros, Rafael 157
Michalak, Aneta 431
Morais, Alexandra 125
Morell, Antoni 173, 199
Mustaţă, Laurenţiu-Alex 186
Muşuroi, Cristian-Leonard 186

N
Natário, Diogo Nuno 386
Neghină, Mihai 83
Nikghadam-Hojjati, Sanaz 313
Nunes, Isabel L. 138
Nunes, Nuno 398
Nwulu, Nnamdi 259, 274, 471

O
Oliveira, José Luís 32
Olukanmi, Peter 259, 471
Oyedeji, Ajibola 259
Oyindamola, Adepoju Omoseni 274

P
Pătrăuşanu, Andrei 83
Parameswaran, S. 341
Patrício, João Tabanêz 157
Paulino, Nuno 213
Pegado, Antonio Monte 3
Pimentão, João P. 292, 398
Pires, Mafalda 125

Q
Quaresma, Cláudia 125, 534
Quintão, Carla 125
Quintão, Carla 534

R
R.Guerreiro, Gracinda 398
Rajathi, S. 341
Rajeswari, S. 341
Ramezani, Javaneh 373
Ramya, D. 341
Rocha, Andre Dionisio 3
Rodrigues, Pedro João 329
Rożnowska, Kamila 451
Rupacz, Sara 431

S
Sagarribay, Amets 125
Santos, Catarina 125
Santos, Patrícia 125
Schena, Verdiana 358
Schneider, Andreas 20, 42
Schuster, Thomas 20, 42
Scioscia, Floriano 358
Shevtshenko, Eduard 417
Sienkiewicz-Małyjurek, Katarzyna 451
Sousa, Pedro A. 292, 398

T
Tacla, Cesar Augusto 329
Torrente, Maria 398

V
Véstias, Mário 504
Vicario, Jose Lopez 173, 199
Vieira, Filipe 99
Vieira, Manuel Augusto 504
Vieira, Manuela 504
Vilanova, Ramon 173, 199

W
Waidelich, Lukas 20, 42

Y
Yoon, Youjeong 226

MIX
Papier aus verantwortungsvollen Quellen
Paper from responsible sources
FSC® C105338
FSC
www.fsc.org

If you have any concerns about our products,
you can contact us on
ProductSafety@springernature.com

In case Publisher is established outside the EU,
the EU authorized representative is:
Springer Nature Customer Service Center GmbH
Europaplatz 3, 69115 Heidelberg, Germany

Printed by Libri Plureos GmbH
in Hamburg, Germany